33

THE CHURCH RETROSPECTIVE

Theodolinda grants 'treasure' to the church of the Baptist with her son Adaloald. The *chioccia* is immediately recognisable, but note also the 'sapphire' cup on the left [reproduced by permission of the Museo del Duomo di Monza].

THE CHURCH RETROSPECTIVE

PAPERS READ AT
THE 1995 SUMMER MEETING AND
THE 1996 WINTER MEETING OF
THE ECCLESIASTICAL HISTORY SOCIETY

EDITED BY

R. N. SWANSON

PUBLISHED FOR
THE ECCLESIASTICAL HISTORY SOCIETY
BY
THE BOYDELL PRESS
1997

First published 1997

A publication of the Ecclesiastical History Society
in association with The Boydell Press
an imprint of Boydell & Brewer Ltd
PO Box 9, Woodbridge, Suffolk IP12 3DF, UK
and of Boydell & Brewer Inc.
PO Box 41026, Rochester, NY 14604-4126, USA

ISBN 0 9529733 0 8

ISSN 0424-2084

A catalogue record for this book is available
from the British Library

Library of Congress Cataloging Card Number: 97-8292

Details of previous volumes available from Boydell & Brewer Ltd

This book is printed on acid-free paper

Printed by Great Britain by
St Edmundsbury Press Ltd, Bury St Edmunds, Suffolk

IN MEMORY OF
ANDREW MARTINDALE

CONTENTS

Preface   xi

List of Contributors   xv

List of Abbreviations   xix

Introduction   xxi

Andrew Martindale   1
  T. A. HESLOP

'The faith of our fathers': the making of the early
Christian past   5
  RACHEL MORIARTY

Past creeds and present formula at the Council
of Chalcedon   19
  STUART G. HALL

Bringing the Holy Sepulchre to the west:
S. Stefano, Bologna, from the fifth to the
twentieth century   31
  COLIN MORRIS

Perceptions of the Anglo-Saxon past in the
tenth-century monastic reform movement   61
  SIMON COATES

St Symeon the New Theologian (949–1022):
Byzantine spiritual renewal in search of a precedent   75
  JOHN ANTHONY McGUCKIN

The past and monastic debate in the time of
Bernard of Clairvaux   91
  CHRISTOPHER HOLDSWORTH

A twelfth-century view of the historical church:
Orderic Vitalis   115
  MARJORIE CHIBNALL

A thirteenth-century genealogy of heresy 135
LUCY BOSWORTH

'Principium et origo ordinis': the Humiliati and
their origins 149
FRANCES ANDREWS

Ockham's vision of the primitive Church 163
TAKASHI SHOGIMEN

Wyclif and the wheel of time 177
MICHAEL WILKS

Theodolinda: the fifteenth-century recollection of
a Lombard Queen 195
†ANDREW MARTINDALE

European Calvinism: history, providence,
and martyrdom 227
ANDREW PETTEGREE

'By this mark you shall know him': clerical
celibacy and Antichrist in English Reformation
polemic 253
HELEN L. PARISH

The importance of dying earnestly: the metamorphosis
of the account of James Bainham in 'Foxe's *Book
of Martyrs*' 267
THOMAS S. FREEMAN

Conciliar authority in Reformation Scotland: the
example of the Kennedy/Davidson debate, 1558–63 289
MARTIN DOTTERWEICH

Impolitic pictures: providence, history, and the
iconography of Protestant nationhood in early
Stuart England 307
ALEXANDRA WALSHAM

Laudian Foxe-hunting? William Laud and the status
of John Foxe in the 1630s 329
DAMIAN NUSSBAUM

Text before trowel: Antonio Bosio's *Roma sotterranea*
revisited   343
SIMON DITCHFIELD

Fontevrault looks back to her founder: reform
and the attempts to canonize Robert of Arbrissel   361
J. M. B. PORTER

'To let the memory of these men dye is injurious
to posterity': Edmund Calamy's *Account* of the
ejected ministers   379
DAVID L. WYKES

Dutch Protestantism and its pasts   393
PETER van ROODEN

'Standing in the old ways': historical legitimation
of Church reform in the Church of England,
*c.*1825–65   407
R. ARTHUR BURNS

Benjamin Webb (1819–85) and Victorian Ecclesiology   423
J. MORDAUNT CROOK

Victorian Nonconformity and the memory of the
ejected ministers: the impact of the bicentennial
commemorations of 1862   459
TIMOTHY LARSEN

Christian civilization and Italic civilization: Italian
Catholic theses from Gioberti to Pius XII   475
OLIVER LOGAN

Reconstructing the Reformation: F. D. Maurice,
Luther, and Justification   487
JEREMY MORRIS

The Oxford Movement in late-nineteenth-
century retrospect: R. W. Church, J. H. Rigg,
and Walter Walsh   501
MARTIN WELLINGS

The study of the catholic tradition of the Kirk:
Scoto-Catholics and the worship of the reformers   517
DOUGLAS M. MURRAY

A pre-modern interpretation of the modern: the
English Catholic church and the 'social question' in
the early twentieth century   529
  BARBARA WRAITH

St Clare of Assisi and the Poor Clares: a new spring 547
  PAUL M. GERRARD

Index   563

'The Church Retrospective: Depictions and Representations' was chosen by Professor Andrew Martindale as the theme for the year of his presidency of the Ecclesiastical History Society, which was to be inaugurated in July 1995. Given the wide range of potential material, the theme attracted considerable interest, with over sixty communications being proposed for delivery at the summer conference. The result was a demanding programme for the meeting, held at the University of East Anglia at Norwich during what felt like the hottest days of an exceptionally hot July.

To everyone's regret and sorrow, Andrew Martindale did not share in the conference which he had inspired. Shortly after Easter he was diagnosed as suffering from a brain tumour, and died on 29 May 1995. His death was a grievous blow, to his family, to his University, and to the Society; all the more painful for being so totally unexpected. He had already done considerable work on his presidential address; although it was not delivered at Norwich, it was ready at the January meeting, and is printed here.

These unforeseen circumstances have affected the compilation of the present volume. Rather than offer an Introduction which might misrepresent the hopes and intentions of the theme's begetter, it seemed more appropriate simply to reprint Andrew Martindale's Call for Communications. How far the final selection of essays measures up to the aspirations there expressed is for the reader to judge: an immediate difference is the shortening of the title, as 'depictions and representations' in the end did not seem appropriate as a cover for the selected papers. That selection process necessarily occurred without Andrew Martindale's guidance; the contents might have been slightly different if his advice had been available.

The papers printed here comprise all but one of the main papers offered at the Norwich Conference and the Winter

Meeting, with a selection of the communications offered at Norwich. As usual, the decisions about which papers to include were hard to make, and harsh to implement: one group of communications could almost have resulted in a mini-volume in itself, on John Foxe. The aim has been to bring together papers which reflect the chronological and thematic range evident at the conference; in the process of trying to achieve an overall balance, several high-quality pieces could not be included. Hopefully, those not printed here will soon find a location elsewhere.

As usual, the Society has incurred many debts *en route* to this volume. The University of East Anglia's accommodation, both academic and domestic, was of an unprecedented standard – and with temperatures in the nineties, the novelty of en suite facilities was particularly appreciated. Especial thanks are due to Diana Wood who provided the main local contact at Norwich, taking on the heavy burden of ensuring that all went as Andrew Martindale would have wished. In addition to liaising with the University authorities, she also arranged a series of impressive and appreciated outings, and the Memorial Evensong held on the Wednesday of the conference. King's College London was again the venue for the Winter Meeting: as usual our thanks are due to all involved in ensuring that the day went smoothly.

Particular thanks must be expressed this year to Dr David Thompson, who agreed to serve as President for a second year, and at short notice oversaw a conference on a theme which he had not chosen. We are also grateful to Professor Colin Morris who – at equally short notice – agreed to deliver the first main paper at Norwich in place of the Presidential Address.

★   ★   ★

This is the first volume of the Society's publications to appear under the imprint of Boydell and Brewer, following the termination of the arrangements with Blackwell's. After so many years the break is something of a jolt; but companies and societies evolve, and our respective evolutions have reached a point where a mutually agreed separation seemed appropriate. The Society has greatly valued and appreciated the support and encouragement supplied by Blackwell's staff over the years, most recently from John Davey and Tessa Harvey. We look forward to an equally long and mutually beneficial relationship with Boydell: we are determined that the Society's publications will continue, and that the high production standards which have been one of their hallmarks will be maintained. As Editor, I am particularly grateful to Dr Richard Barber for making the transition a smooth one.

Robert Swanson

LIST OF CONTRIBUTORS

†ANDREW MARTINDALE
  Professor of Visual Arts, University of East Anglia
FRANCES ANDREWS
  Lecturer in Mediaeval History, University of St Andrews
LUCY BOSWORTH
  Research Student, University of Edinburgh
R. A. BURNS
  Lecturer in Modern British History, King's College London
MARJORIE CHIBNALL
  Fellow, Clare Hall, Cambridge
SIMON COATES
  Tutor in History, University of Edinburgh
SIMON DITCHFIELD
  Lecturer in Early Modern History, University of York
MARTIN DOTTERWEICH
  Research Student, University of Edinburgh
THOMAS S. FREEMAN
  Postdoctoral Fellow, Department of History, Rutgers University
PAUL M. GERRARD
  Research Student, King's College, University of London
STUART G. HALL
  Honorary Associate Research Professor, University of St Andrews
T. A. HESLOP
  Dean, School of World Art Studies, University of East Anglia
CHRISTOPHER HOLDSWORTH
  Professor of Medieval History, University of Exeter

TIMOTHY LARSEN
Lecturer in Church History, Covenant College, Coventry

OLIVER LOGAN
Lecturer in Italian and European History, University of East Anglia

JOHN A. McGUCKIN
Reader in Patristic and Byzantine Theology, University of Leeds

J. MORDAUNT CROOK
Professor of Architectural History, Royal Holloway and Bedford New College, University of London

RACHEL MORIARTY
Research Fellow in Theology, La Sainte Union College, Southampton

COLIN MORRIS
Emeritus Professor of Medieval History, University of Southampton

JEREMY MORRIS
Director of Studies and Tutor in Systematic Theology, Westcott House, Cambridge

DOUGLAS M. MURRAY
Lecturer in Ecclesiastical History, University of Glasgow

DAMIAN NUSSBAUM
Research Student, Queens' College, Cambridge

HELEN L. PARISH
Research Student, Jesus College, Oxford

ANDREW PETTEGREE
Reader in Modern History, University of St Andrews, and Director of the St Andrews Reformation Studies Institute

J. M. B. PORTER
Research Student, University of Nottingham

PETER van ROODEN
Research Centre Religion and Society, University of Amsterdam

TAKASHI SHOGIMEN
> Research Student, University of Sheffield

ALEXANDRA WALSHAM
> Lecturer in History, University of Exeter

MARTIN WELLINGS

MICHAEL WILKS
> Emeritus Professor of Medieval History, Birkbeck College, University of London

BARBARA WRAITH
> Research Student, De Montfort University, Bedford

DAVID L. WYKES
> Research Lecturer in History, University of Leicester

ABBREVIATIONS

Abbreviated titles are adopted within each paper after the first full citation. In addition, the following abbreviations are used throughout the volume.

ActaSS	*Acta sanctorum*, ed. J. Bolland and G. Henschen (Antwerp, etc., 1643–)
AHR	*American Historical Review* (New York, 1895–)
AnBoll	*Analecta Bollandiana* (Brussels, 1882–)
ARG	*Archiv für Reformationsgeschichte* (Berlin/Leipzig/ Gütersloh, 1903–)
BL	London, British Library
BN	Paris, Bibliothèque Nationale
CChr	*Corpus Christianorum* (Turnhout, 1953–)
CChr.CM	*Corpus Christianorum, continuatio medievalis* (1966–)
CUL	Cambridge, University Library
DNB	*Dictionary of National Biography* (London, 1885–)
Eccl.	*Ecclesiologist* (Cambridge, etc., 1841–68)
HistJ	*Historical Journal* (Cambridge, 1958–)
HMC	*Historical Manuscripts Commission*
HThR	*Harvard Theological Review* (New York/ Cambridge, Mass., 1908–)
JBS	*Journal of British Studies* (Hartford, Conn., 1961–)
JEH	*Journal of Ecclesiastical History* (Cambridge, 1950–)
JHI	*Journal of the History of Ideas* (London, 1940–)
JMRS	*Journal of Medieval and Renaissance Studies* (Durham, N.C., 1971–)
JThS	*Journal of Theological Studies* (London, 1899–)
LCL	Loeb Classical Library
MGH	*Monumenta Germaniae Historica inde ab a. 500 usque ad a. 1500*, ed. G. H. Pertz *et al.* (Hanover, Berlin, etc., 1826–)
MGH.Dip	*Diplomata in folio*
MGH.Schriften	*Schriften der Monumenta Germaniae Historica*
MGH.SRM	*Scriptores rerum merovingicarum*
MGH.SS	*Scriptores (in folio)*
nd	no date
ns	new series
OMT	*Oxford Medieval Texts* (Oxford, 1971–)

P&P	*Past and Present: A Journal of Scientific History* (London, 1952–)
PG	*Patrologia Graeca*, ed. J. P. Migne, 161 vols (Paris, 1857–66)
PL	*Patrologia Latina*, ed. J. P. Migne, 217 vols + 4 index vols (Paris, 1841–61)
PS	*Parker Society* (Cambridge, 1841–55)
RHE	*Revue d'histoire ecclésiastique* (Louvain, 1900–)
RS	*Rerum Brittanicarum medii aevi scriptores*, 99 vols (London, 1858–1911) = *Rolls Series*
sa	*sub anno*
SatR	*Saturday Review of Politics, Literature, Science, and Art* (London, 1856–1938)
SCH	*Studies in Church History* (London/Oxford, 1964–)
ScHR	*Scottish Historical Review* (Edinburgh/ Glasgow, 1904–)
SCH.S	*Studies in Church History: Subsidia* (Oxford, 1978–)
Traditio	*Traditio: Studies in Ancient and Medieval History, Thought, and Religion* (New York, etc., 1943–)
TRHS	*Transactions of the Royal Historical Society* (London, 1871–)

INTRODUCTION[1]

The Church is schizophrenic in relation to Time. For the Christian, life is a prologue to a life to follow. Present events and tribulations are but a preparation for a life to come. But Christianity is a historical religion. Both the significance of the present and the hope for the future lie in the promise of the past. The past, however, goes back not merely to the life of Christ, but to the beginnings of Time ('Before Abraham was, I am'); and whatever view is taken of the story of the Fall, the Church's history has been concerned with people and events. Doctrine, dogma, and revelation are all pinned to time and place, 'When Jesus was born in Bethlehem of Judaea in the days of Herod the King . . .'.

So how has the Church interpreted, re-interpreted, and used its past? In my own subject – the art of the Middle Ages and early Renaissance – there are many instances of decorative schemes which impose on the viewer some aspect or interpretation of the history of the Church. Many of these are anodyne in their impact and routine in their implications. Thus a sequence of types and antitypes offers a sort of historical perspective; and images of people and bishops may be an assertion of the apostolic succession. But there are many more historically challenging examples of retrospection. The late-thirteenth-century interpretation of the life of St Francis is an obvious example, while the nineteenth century is full of competing visual interpretations of the past.

But what about the 'real world'? It is a matter of common knowledge that reformers always appeal to the past – but so do traditionalists. How far has history provided the justification for action – or inaction? What weight has been attached to the recent as opposed to the distant past? Has the past ever seemed a millstone to be discarded at the earliest opportunity?

---

[1] Apart from one minor change to make it more appropriate for its present introductory function, this is the text distributed in November 1994 as the Statement of the Theme to accompany the call for communications for the Norwich conference.

Why should the past matter? How far have ecclesiastics and theologians sought the 'truth' about the past? What is Truth in Church history?

There are many possible points of entry into the topic. Many of these are likely to be concerned in some sense with challenging (or stabilizing) the present by appeal to the past. They will, nevertheless, vary vastly in time, place, and scale. An example at a very local level would be the presentation, interpretation, or re-interpretation of the life of a (long-dead?) patronal saint or founder. But there might in a very literal sense be a global angle. For if it is permissible to say that the history of the Church starts with the first verse of Genesis, the theological responses to the various forms of Darwinism become relevant. In any case any form of *aggiornamento* is likely to be accompanied by the realization that some part of the baggage of the past is being selectively dumped. In fact there are so many ways in which the institution and its members have been forced or felt impelled to defend, activate, interpret, or deny some aspect of the Church's history that it seems desirable to indicate a major constraint which should probably be observed with regard to this volume's theme. The topic is *not* 'the Church and History' but 'the Church and *its* past'. Saints and sinners, patrons and persecutors, popes and pastors – it is about the Church looking (selectively) back at itself.

Andrew Martindale

ANDREW MARTINDALE

On 16 October 1994, in what was to be the last research seminar he presented in the School of World Art Studies at the University of East Anglia, Andrew Martindale addressed assembled colleagues and graduate students on one of the aspects of medieval palace decoration which had recently being occupying his thoughts, the choice of heroes (and sometimes heroines too) represented in sculpture, painting, or tapestry in the great halls and chambers of the fourteenth and early fifteenth centuries. His title was 'Let us now praise famous men' (Ecclesiasticus 44.1), though by one of those quirks of mistranscription it appeared on the schedule that was sent out to advertise the event as 'Let us now praise funny men'.

Andrew himself could be wonderfully witty, but his own claim to a place in the hall of fame rests largely upon the quality of his scholarship. By that I do not mean simply that he could be trusted to get things right, but that at the root of his life as an academic was a series of perceptions and beliefs which help to justify (and, sadly, it seems increasingly to need justifying) the expression 'the humanities' to encompass the study of art, music, literature, and history. There are many passages from his published writings which proclaim these values, but as these are generally available and because his voice is perhaps more clearly to be heard in a semi-formal context, I would like to quote from his inaugural lecture, on Andrea Mantegna, given in 1974.

> I am a firm believer in the central importance of the human imagination – both as the subject of study of the art historian and as the most significant single virtue in the writing of history. Of course, all the historical techniques which one learns are indispensable; and the duties of the historian include all the chores of checking, transcribing, setting out in order and a hundred and one other things. But in the end . . . the choice between the

1

work as a whole receiving the breath of life or the kiss of death will depend upon imagination.

He continued: 'If I had given you a sermon tonight it would have been just this – history and imagination.'

There are a number of ideas in this short extract which speak volumes about Andrew as an academic and as a person. The words 'believer', 'virtue', 'duties', 'life', 'death', and 'sermon' all have strong religious and, in his case, Christian overtones. But the central concept is that of making the past live through a combination of carefully checked data and the historian's imaginative process. The past lives through the people who inhabited it. Their thoughts can be accessed through what they wrote or what is otherwise recorded about them, but for the art historian they are primarily accessible through imagery.

In his writings and through his teaching Andrew brought the past before the eyes of the present as an invigorating and stimulating set of exempla, generally singling out things which were case studies but were also paradigmatic. As a colleague too he worked by example. For much of the day he was to be seen at the further end of his glass-fronted office sitting at his desk like some fifteenth-century image of Jerome in his study, or talking to students or staff, singly or in groups. He was least happy in committees or responding to reports or memoranda – and there too he had a significant influence on those around him. The School of World Art Studies over which he presided for over two decades is still pervaded by a tendency to avoid bureaucracy.

His own inclinations helped to make us 'able ministers not of the letter but of the spirit' ('for the letter killeth but the spirit giveth life'). But despite his preferences for dealing with things on a personal level and trusting individuals to make wise decisions and act accordingly, Andrew's own sense of duty led him to devote a good deal of his time to serving on UGC and UFC committees, on the Council for the Care of Churches, and latterly as the Chairman of the Norwich Cathedral Fabric Advisory Committee. That sense of duty and his caring – about things, people, and the past – inevitably triumphed over reluctance to take on yet more work. In the end it was this *caritas* that underlay his actions both public and private: his humour and hospitality as much as his research and administration. We shall all miss him, whether as colleague, friend, scholar, or wise counsellor. But he will live in our memories and through his teaching and writing, and I am sure that these are the halls of fame which are the most appropriate monument to a lovely man.

T. A. Heslop
Dean of the School of World Art Studies
University of East Anglia

'THE FAITH OF OUR FATHERS':
THE MAKING OF THE EARLY CHRISTIAN PAST

by RACHEL MORIARTY

A hundred years ago, in 1895, London theatre audiences were treated to an interesting exchange on what we would now call the reception of early Church history. The play was Oscar Wilde's *The Importance of Being Earnest*, and in it the Reverend Dr Chasuble and Miss Prism are discussing marriage, not entirely hypothetically. Dr Chasuble '(with a scholar's shudder)' observes, 'The precept as well as the practice of the Primitive Church was distinctly against matrimony', and Miss Prism replies '(sententiously), That is obviously the reason why the Primitive Church has not lasted up to the present day'.[1]

In a volume devoted to 'the Church Retrospective', these disputants are significant players, for the early Church certainly has lasted up to the present day, at least in the minds of people looking for the sources of ecclesiastical Tradition and History. Dr Chasuble, for Tradition, sees the 'Primitive Church' as the self-validating reference point for its successor; Miss Prism, a good Anglican, takes a more pragmatic historical view. They are engaged in a polite version of a long-standing and still lively Christian dispute over finding models for today from the time of the Church's youth.

The Church has always based its future on its past, and the very earliest Church has had a special status as a touchstone for original faith and practice, the fresh dawn of the age of salvation. The period to which this status applies varies, but at its longest it covers the first four or five centuries, the so-called 'Undivided Church', from Pentecost to Chalcedon. Regularly in the history of churches ever since there have been moves to return again to parts of this pristine source – at the Renaissance and the Reformation, among early Nonconformists and nineteenth-century Anglo-Catholics, and in

---

[1] *The Importance of Being Earnest*, in Oscar Wilde, *Plays* (London, 1970), p. 279.

monastic movements, to give some examples; and arguments from 'the Fathers' have been used to defend change (for example in Cranmer's wish, which survives in the 1662 Book of Common Prayer, to restore 'the godly and decent order of the ancient Fathers'),[2] and to resist it (as in current argument against the ordination of women). Interpretations have conflicted as opponents appeal to what they call 'the New Testament Church', 'the patristic tradition', and other titles representing views of the Christian inheritance; but the notion of resort to an ancient line of tradition remains constant. Christianity demands a retrospective Church, in which perceived origins have a special authority.

This paper examines a paradox about this early Church tradition. The earliest Christians, both Jews and 'pagans', came from religious backgrounds which relied on ancient and ancestral practice (in Latin the *mores maiorum*), yet they were themselves in the opposite situation: they had no traditional past for their own practices, and had collectively rejected the past and the ancestors they were born with. The tradition we have inherited from them, however, again depends on our continuity with their past. So it seems reasonable to ask what the sources show about the way they turned their lack of history into a 'tradition' which has survived to the present day.

Can it even be suggested that early Christian historical tradition, as it has reached us from the first centuries, was at least partly composed, selected, and transmitted to help provide Christians with the past they lacked? This paper explores some aspects of that suggestion, considering some examples of how Christians presented their story, to see how they shaped a coherent inherited tradition, a kind of 'Christian Heritage Source-Pack', to match those of others and to act as a resource and a memory for later generations. These examples come from a fairly small field, mostly from apology and accounts of martyrdom, two literary forms of the first three centuries which dealt particularly with issues of

[2] See the Prefaces to the Prayer Books of 1549 and 1552, reprinted in, for example, *The First and Second Prayer Books of Edward VI*, Everyman Library (London and New York, 1910), pp. 3, 321; and 'Concerning the Services of the Church', section 2 in *The Book of Common Prayer, 1662*.

Christian identity, together with a few later examples; all but one are from Christian sources. The important question of the Jewish past of Christianity is not tackled in this study, but it will appear briefly later, in the course of discussion.[3]

The case begins in the relative calm of the fourth century when Eusebius, arranging his pre-Constantinian material in a new kind of retrospective edition, sets out the selection criteria for his plan for a History of the Church and reveals something of what he understands by tradition. His Christian predecessors have left records

> to admonish us on the path along which we ought to walk. We have gathered, therefore, from these whatsoever we have deemed profitable for the project in hand, and having plucked, as it were, from meadows of literature suitable passages, we shall attempt to embody them as an historical narrative: happy if we may preserve the successions from the Apostles of our Saviour. I trust that they will prove of benefit to those who are eager for the useful learning afforded by history.[4]

Two things are at once clear: Eusebius is committed to continuity with the past ('the successions'), but he expects to shape and use it for a precise purpose, to be 'useful'. He famously preserved invaluable sources, but already selection has been at work and some flowers dropped to make the structured posy of the Christian past. It is necessary to go further back to see what the surviving predecessors say, first about their own use of tradition, then about charges against Christians for rejecting their past, and finally in making a new tradition in response.

Right from the start, there is an assumption that ancestral tradition is important to credibility as a religious group.

---

[3] For comprehensive discussion of this subject, see E. P. Sanders, ed., *Jewish and Christian Self-Definition*, 3 vols (London, 1981–3) [hereafter Sanders].

[4] Eusebius, *Ecclesiastical History*, I, i [hereafter HE] in Eusebius, Bishop of Caesarea, *The Ecclesiastical History and the Martyrs of Palestine*, ed. H. J. Lawlor and J. E. L. Oulton, 2 vols (London, 1954) [hereafter Lawlor and Oulton], 1, p. 4. For Eusebius' contribution to Church history, see also Frances M. Young, *From Nicaea to Chalcedon* (London, 1983), pp. 1–21.

Christian reliance on it started, we are told, on the first day of the Church's life, when Peter, as soon as he could make himself heard over the babel of Pentecost, offered its credentials from Jewish tradition, in an address linking Christ to scriptural proof-texts about the Messiah.[5] In the second century, when personal links with Peter's time were almost gone, Irenaeus identified apostolic tradition as one of the markers of 'truth', that is, true Christianity. For him, 'The tradition of the Apostles is manifested in the entire world, and all who wish to see the truth can contemplate it readily in every church.'[6] Moreover, 'By knowledge of the truth we mean the teaching of the Apostles, and the order of the Church as established from the earliest times throughout the world.'[7]

The same stress on continuity is evident in martyrology, in this case the introduction to the story of Perpetua, a Roman matron who died at Carthage in about 202: 'The deeds recounted about the faith in ancient times were a proof of God's favour ... and they were set forth in writing precisely that honour might be rendered to God and comfort to men by the recollection of the past through the written word. Should not then more recent examples be set down?'[8]

Much later, in the fifth century, Vincent of Lérins could claim to define Catholic teaching (rather against the odds, historically) by saying, 'In the Catholic church we take care that we hold that which has been believed everywhere, always, by everyone. . . . And we shall observe this rule if we

---

[5]   Acts 2.14–26.

[6]   Irenaeus, *Against the Heresies*, III, iii, 4, in J. Stevenson, ed., *A New Eusebius*, new edn, revised W. H. C. Frend (London, 1989) [hereafter *NE*], p. 114.

[7]   Irenaeus, *Against the Heresies*, IV, viii, 8, in Henry Bettenson, ed., *The Early Christian Fathers* (Oxford, 1969), p. 89.

[8]   *The Martyrdom of Perpetua and Felicitas*, 1, in H. Musurillo, ed., *Acts of the Christian Martyrs* (Oxford, 1972) [hereafter Musurillo], p. 107, and introduction, pp. xxv–vi; see Stuart G. Hall, 'Women among the early martyrs', *SCH*, 30 (1993), pp. 1–21 and W. H. C. Frend, *Martyrdom and Persecution in the Early Church* (Oxford, 1965) [hereafter Frend], pp. 376–7. It seems possible that the presentation of this account, and perhaps others, was shaped to some extent by discussion on the whole question of the status of recent events in relation to the 'ancestral' past: see Rachel Moriarty, 'The claims of the past', to be published in a forthcoming vol. of Elizabeth A. Livingstone, ed., *Studia Patristica* (Papers presented at the Twelfth International Conference on Patristic Studies held in Oxford, 1995). See also n. 33 below.

follow universality, antiquity, consent.'[9] By this time, the historical virtues of universality, antiquity, consent have become the marks of 'tradition'.

It is clear that Christians were concerned to defend themselves against charges of having no past, and that they regarded those charges as crucial to their differences from their pagan neighbours. But before looking at the defence they offered we should see how they set out the charges themselves, usually in words attributed to opponents, for this shapes our present concern for the way they presented their own case.

Clement of Alexandria, who died in about 214, and wrote, it is thought, for a general educated audience interested in Christianity, addresses an objector thus (we shall see later how he replies to him): 'But, you say, it is not reasonable to overthrow a way of life handed down to us by our forefathers.'[10] Similarly, Minucius Felix, in a dialogue from 197 again aimed at an educated pagan public, makes the point more fully, in the words he gives his non-Christian character Caecilius:

> How much better it is to receive the teaching of our ancestors as the high priest of truth, to reverence the traditional religion, to worship the gods whom your parents taught you to fear before you knew them intimately, and not to pronounce judgement upon the divinities, but to believe our forefathers who, in a still uncivilized age, when the world was only just born, were thought worthy of having the gods as kindly or as kings! Thus it is that in every empire, province and city each nationality observes the ritual of its own family and worships its local divinities.[11]

Other second-century apologists tell the same tale. Origen's *agent provocateur* Celsus maintains that not to accept the

---

[9] Vincent of Lérins, *Commonitorium*, II, 6, quoted in J. Stevenson, ed., *Creeds, Councils and Controversies*, new edn, rev. W. H. C. Frend (London, 1989), p. 322.

[10] Clement of Alexandria, *Protrepticus*, x, 89, in *NE*, p. 180. For Clement's view of history, see Raoul Mortley, 'The past in Clement of Alexandria', in Sanders, 1, pp. 186–200.

[11] Minucius Felix, *Octavius*, vi, 1, in *NE*, p. 177.

Emperor as divinely appointed (that is, for him, with the authority of Jupiter) is to invite personal punishment and disaster from Rome's enemies.[12] Elsewhere he makes the telling point that Christian teachers persuade children not to obey their fathers and schoolteachers, and 'urge the children on to rebel' – a point echoed by critics of cults today.[13] The attack on Christians as presented here had two prongs: they were suspect on the public issue of civic loyalty and allegiance to the Emperor (seen as empowered by God and endorsed by ancestral practice), and on the more domestic issue of family and parental discipline.

The charge of rejecting ancestral gods, which amounted to 'atheism', was especially associated with persecution. Tertullian quotes the cry, 'The Christians to the lion!', as an example of the response of the urban Roman mob to any disaster;[14] and later Eusebius recalls the usual imperial case for persecution: 'How can men fail to be in every way impious and godless who have apostasized from their ancestral gods?'[15] The end of persecution came with the collapse of this case.

Eusebius and Lactantius, another defender of Christianity, both recorded the text of Galerius' Edict of Toleration of 311: 'It has been our special care that the Christians too who had left the persuasion of their forefathers should come to a better mind. ... Instead of following those constitutions of the ancients which peradventure their own ancestors had first established, they were making themselves laws ...' – but persecution failed to bring about a return to 'the institutions of the ancients', and it now seems that any prayer is better than none to avert national calamity. 'We therefore have thought it right to offer our speediest indulgence, that Christians may exist again .... It shall be their duty to pray

[12] Origen, *Contra Celsum*, viii, 67–9, in *NE*, pp. 135-6. For discussion of Celsus' attitudes see Robert L. Wilken, *The Christians as the Romans Saw Them* (New Haven, 1984) [hereafter Wilken], pp. 94–125, and Robert M. Grant, *Greek Apologists of the Second Century* (London, 1988), pp. 133–9; this book also covers other apologists cited in this paper.

[13] Origen, *Contra Celsum*, iii, 55, in *NE*, p. 116.

[14] Tertullian, *Apology*, xl, 2, in *NE*, p. 158; for Tertullian see T. D. Barnes, *Tertullian: A Historical and Literary Study* (Oxford, 1971).

[15] Eusebius, *Praeparatio Evangelica*, i, 2, in *NE*, p. 181 (note).

their god for our good estate, and that of the state.'[16] After more than 250 years, Christians can record that the positive value of prayer has prevailed over the negative pagan view that Christians are to be punished for rejection of the past, in its ritual and ancestral sense.

What is behind all this? The background to these Christians' accounts of the charges against them lies in an ideological base common in antiquity, where ancestral tradition was perceived as the key to securing personal, family, and political survival.[17] There is abundant evidence for this attitude in classical sources, especially among Romans, but it was common to most of the peoples over whom they ruled. Romans had always been taught that the safety of the Roman state depended on ancient customs, loyalty, and devotion to the gods, and since the time of Augustus, who died in AD 14, the view of a traditionally-based Rome marked out for a divine destiny was built into its public image and the educational system of the influential young, through writers like Virgil, Livy, and Horace, and supported by the cautious but significant introduction of a cult of the Emperor. Clearly there are elements here too of a constructed tradition, and of a mythical past based on an agenda of political expediency; but the picture depended on attitudes accepted by most of the Empire's subjects. The shared view of ancestral tradition gave it credence through-out the Empire, and a variety of ancestors, new religions, and philosophical positions did not ordinarily compromise ances-tral identity, since they were not seen as alternatives to one standard practice. As the author of the book of Acts noted, the Athenians were constantly looking for novelty, but in the speech put into Paul's mouth on the Areopagus he is careful to make the links backward from Christianity to traditional patterns of various kinds.[18]

---

[16] Lactantius, *On the Deaths of the Persecutors*, 34, in *NE*, p. 280; and see Eusebius, *HE*, viii, 17, 6–7, in Lawlor and Oulton, 1, p. 276, and discussion, 2, pp. 285–6.

[17] For discussion of these classical issues, see R. M. Ogilvie, *The Romans and their Gods* (London, 1979), especially pp. 112–25; A. H. M. Jones, *Augustus* (London, 1977), pp. 144–52; and especially Robin Lane Fox, *Pagans and Christians* (London, 1986). Lane Fox argues that ancestral tradition was not static, and that there was interest in change and development; see pp. 29, 258–60.

[18] Acts 17.21.

The earliest non-Jewish Christians were born into this setting, and many later ones educated into it and into its assumption that religious credibility, civic loyalty, and historical continuity went hand in hand. But if their refusal to sacrifice cut them off from the past of their neighbours, they still felt the need for a past of their own, for the sake of the development of their own religious community. There were other strands to this need: they wanted at first to establish themselves as a group who came from a variety of ancestral traditions; as they gained a history, they sought to package and circulate the record of Christian experience among their scattered communities, and eventually to lay down a shared foundation of Christian memory for later generations. Most important, they needed a past because it was their only guarantee of credible identity. As Christians present the case, their opponents did not understand their refusal to rely on the customs of their ancestors, nor their adoption of a religious culture which had no retrospective dimension. Collectively they were suspect citizens, individually they breached the sacred ties of family and the past; and under challenge and persecution they often repudiated everything that the weight of ancestral morality was supposed to sustain.

In spite of the limits of this discussion, it must be noted that Christians were challenged on their rejection of Judaism, and apologists discuss it.[19] Judaism had the edge over Christianity in the matter of ancestors, and was tolerated on this ground as a *religio licita*, a religion officially counted as acceptable. The Emperor Marcus Aurelius justified this (in our only non-Christian source) on the grounds that as a traditional Roman he 'always stood by the old places and the old ways'.[20] But after Christians and Jews separated, neither welcomed the other's immediate past, and the Christians were more struck by their differences than their similarities. In terms of scripture, spirituality, and theology the Christian Church saw itself as inseparably linked with the Old Testament past of the Jews and the early sources, notably the letter known as I Clement, work this out in detail. But this did not mean that

[19] See, for instance, Wilken, pp. 112–17, on Celsus, and Robert Markus, *Christianity in the Roman World* (London, 1974), pp. 1–26, on Tertullian and others.
[20] Marcus Aurelius, *Meditations*, i, 13; see Frend, p. 237.

Christians claimed the Jews' history as their own, nor that they mounted an ancestral case from a Jewish past. At the turn of the first century Ignatius had no time for identification with Jews, and said so decisively: 'It is outrageous to utter the name of Jesus Christ and live in Judaism',[21] though he was ready enough to claim the prophets as suitable persecuted forerunners.

Once Christians had set out their opponents' case, they gave themselves the chance to reply. They took up one of two general positions: either they assimilated the surrounding culture and drew out links to show that Christians shared the ordinary assumptions of the inhabitants of the Empire, and even accommodated these into a shared tradition; or they sharply repudiated any compromise with pagan attitudes and defied Roman authority, but redefined Christian ancestry and tradition in opposition to them. Either way, they contribute to a Christian past.

For the first strand, second-century apologetic insists that Christians regularly protested their civic decency. 'We . . . are of all people most piously and righteously disposed towards the Deity and towards your government', wrote Athenagoras to Marcus Aurelius;[22] while the anonymous author of the *Letter to Diognetus* complained of the mistreatment of Christians in spite of their exemplary conformity: 'They dwell in Greek or barbarian cities according as each one's lot has been cast, and follow the customs of the land in clothing and food, and other matters of daily life. . . . They obey the established laws, and in their own lives they surpass the laws.'[23]

This was taken further into the field of political loyalty; Christians were loyal to the Emperor and prayed for him. Tertullian claimed that 'We, on behalf of the safety of Emperors, invoke the eternal God', since the end of the world, and the suffering that will accompany it, is postponed by the peace which Rome has brought.[24] Others developed this into a more sophisticated pattern. God gives earthly

---

21 Ignatius, *To the Magnesians*, x, 3, in *NE*, p. 14.
22 Athenagoras, *Legatio pro Christianis*, 1, in *NE*, pp. 66–7.
23 *Letter to Diognetus*, v, 6, in *NE*, p. 55.
24 Tertullian, *Apology*, xxxii, 1; in *NE*, p. 162; and see Frend, pp. 365–80.

emperors power and glory, said Clement of Rome,[25] and the apology of Melito of Sardis presents the argument that the Church and the Empire, especially the *pax Romana*, work together for God's purposes. For him the success of the Empire is 'proof of the fact that it was for the good that our doctrine flourished alongside the Empire in its happy inception'.[26]

These passages show a presentation of history which joins Christians to the historical destiny and past of Rome, through its God-given rulers. In one sense this history divorces the Emperor from the exclusive support of the Roman state religion, but in another it unites Roman Christians again to their actual ancestors.

Some were more radical in embracing the pre-Christian past. Justin began a long tradition of claiming figures from earlier history as 'Christians before Christ', in his case the Greeks Socrates and Heraclitus, as well as non-Greeks or 'barbarians', among whom he includes Abraham; for 'those who lived with reason are Christians, even though they were thought atheists'. He was among the first to embrace as Christian the ideas and theory of Greek philosophers, who shared to some extent in the 'generative word', the *logos*: 'Whatever things were rightly said among all teachers, are the property of us Christians.'[27]

The argument Clement of Alexandria gives his opponent has already been considered (p. 9): he continues by claiming to develop and enhance ancestral tradition:

> Why do we not continue to use our first food, milk? . . . Why do we increase or diminish our family property, and not keep it at the same value as when we first received it? . . . Shall we not, even at the risk of displeasing our fathers, bend our course towards the truth and seek after him who is our real father, thrusting away custom as some deadly drug?[28]

---

[25] Clement of Rome, *Letter of the Romans to the Corinthians*, lxi, in J. B. Lightfoot, *The Apostolic Fathers*, ed. J. R. Harmer (London, 1926), p. 83.

[26] Eusebius, *HE*, iv, 26,8; in *NE*, pp. 65–6, and note.

[27] Justin, *Apology*, i, 46 and ii, 13, and *NE*, pp. 61–2.

[28] Clement of Alexandria, *Protrepticus*, x, 89, in *NE*, p. 181 (see n. 10 above).

For some Christians, the learned past was inescapable. Later, Augustine reflected movingly on the power of classical culture to inspire love and practical loyalty, and it must always have been hard to abandon the cherished past.[29] The wish to include the heroes of classical learning in a Christian framework sprang not only from reason but, surely, from a real admiration for them. Regulus, for example, a Roman hero who kept his word to the enemy at the cost of his life, is quoted with praise by Tertullian and Cyprian, and Augustine sees him as the noblest Roman of them all.[30] Elsewhere, Hermas naturally mistook the elderly woman who appears to him in a vision, really the Church, for the pagan Sibyl.[31] Classical language and thought, and literary and mythological models, permeate Christian writing, bringing with them, suitably adapted, the ancestry which many Christians had grown up with and learned to love, and offering a model of a united tradition for a world now saved from divisions. As ideas on classical tradition and allegorical exegesis developed, the treasures of classical scholarship came to be identified, by Origen, Gregory of Nyssa, and Augustine (for example), with the spoils taken from the Egyptians by the fleeing Hebrews at the Exodus.[32] Thus an alien past was, as it were, hallowed by association and an Old Testament model, and could be acknowledged as respectably as any similarly appropriated material.

On the other hand, there is a different set of models of repudiation of this heritage. Not surprisingly this is to be found mainly in accounts of martyrdom. Perpetua, for instance, a wealthy Roman matron, will not give in to her father's pleading nor the demand of the governor, but replied in a way that upsets every decent convention: 'Hilarianus said

---

[29] This theme appears especially in *City of God*: see Peter Brown, *Augustine of Hippo* (London, 1967), pp. 299–312.

[30] Augustine, *City of God*, i, 24, translated in St Augustine, *City of God*, trans. Henry Bettenson (London, 1972), p. 35.

[31] Hermas, *The Shepherd*, Vis. II, 1–4, in *NE*, pp. 51–2.

[32] Exod. 12.35–6. See discussion in Jaroslav Pelikan, *Christianity and Classical Culture* (New York, 1993), pp. 171, 187–8; and Gregory of Nyssa, *The Life of Moses*, trans. Abraham J. Malberbe and Everett Ferguson (New York, 1978), 2, 112–16, pp. 80–1, and 170–1, nn. 128–9; they also cite Origen, *Ep. ad Greg. Thaum.* (*PG* 11.88–9) and Augustine, *De Doct. Christ.* 2.40.61.

to me, "Have pity on your father's grey head – have pity on your infant son. Offer the sacrifice for the welfare of the emperors." "I will not", I retorted.'[33] Other accounts have the same kind of story, but claim a Christian pedigree with different rulers and different parents. Polycarp, the saintly Bishop of Smyrna, is invited to 'swear by the genius of Caesar, change your mind; say "away with the atheists!" ' He obeys the second (who are atheists, to a Christian?), but will not curse Christ: 'Eighty-six years have I served him, and he has done me no wrong: how then can I blaspheme my King and my God?'[34]

Others follow his example; they have their own family loyalty. Invited to name their parents, they name Christ; they are described as showing 'maternal love' to their 'brothers', 'before the Father'. One of the martyrs of Lyons, Sanctus, refuses to admit to any other identity: 'To all their questions he answered in Latin: "I am a Christian!" He kept repeating this again and again instead of giving his name, birthplace, nationality, or anything else.'[35] An apologist, Aristeides, explicitly gave Christians their ancestry: 'As for the Christians, they trace their line from the Lord Jesus Christ.'[36] In behaving scornfully to the ancestral traditions embodied in the Emperor and his religious trappings, they are all the same claiming and consolidating a shared Christian heritage, to replace the one they reject.

To conclude: these sources can be seen not simply as a set of documents revealing Christian history, but as material presented, and later selected, to make clear to later Christians the basis for relying on tradition; and to this selection was added, in explanation, the case made against Christians for not having an ancestral tradition, and their double response, to claim a tradition of their own by both accommodating and

---

[33] *The Martyrdom of Perpetua and Felicitas*, in Musurillo, pp. xvi and 115. Perpetua's story illustrates the painful need for all Christians sometimes to renounce ordinary family ties, but it may have a special significance for a female martyr, perhaps different from that of a male one. See Brent D. Shaw, 'The passion of Perpetua', in *P&P*, 139 (May, 1993), pp. 1–45, and Gillian Cloke, *This Female Man of God* (London, 1995), p. 35; and see n. 8 above.

[34] *The Martyrdom of Polycarp*, ix, 3, in *NE*, pp. 25–30.

[35] *The Martyrs of Lyons and Vienne*, in Musurillo, p. 69, and in *NE*, pp. 34–44.

[36] Aristeides, *Apology*, xv,1, in *NE*, p. 52.

renouncing the culture around them. Of the two types of source quoted, apology sets out its own case and answers it, and accounts of martyrdom fit history together with interpretation; but both convey firmly the traditions on which Christians would come to rely. They have Fathers and ancestral practices, they can define and defend them, and they expect their adherents to know what they are. This, it can be argued, did not happen by accident, but emerged as part of an exercise in teaching, recording, and packaging which went on into later centuries, even when defence was no longer necessary, and which both set Christians apart from their neighbours and united them with the best of their own past. The details and the process formed the tradition of the earliest Christianity, a tradition which still influences and shapes Churches today.

La Sainte Union College, Southampton

PAST CREEDS AND PRESENT FORMULA AT THE COUNCIL OF CHALCEDON

by STUART G. HALL

The Formula by which the Council of Chalcedon in 451 defined the Person of Christ is a classic case of the deliberate adjustment and interpretation of the past to suit a present need.[1] The assembled bishops at their fifth session gave their assent to a document which not merely prescribed a theological position in the face of the doctrines of Eutyches and Nestorius, but justified doing so in the face of historically-based objections to the enterprise.

First, after respectful remarks about the Emperors, the city and the church in which they met, the council fathers declare that Christ gave peace to his disciples 'to the intent that no one should vary from his neighbour in the doctrines of religion, but that the teaching of the truth should be uniformly set forth by all'.[2] In this they follow the patristic principle, normal since Tertullian and Irenaeus in the second century, that the truth was given in its entirety by Jesus to his followers, and that any addition or change was wrong: heresy was defined as innovation.[3] The Chalcedonian fathers next proceed to blame the 'evil one' for constantly devising new errors, and congratulate the Emperor Marcian for

---

[1] The text is accessible in English in J. Stevenson, *Creeds, Councils and Controversies*, new edn revised by W. H. C. Frend (London, 1989), no. 246, itself based on *The Oecumenical Documents of the Faith*, ed. with introduction and notes by T. Herbert Bindley, 4th edn rev. by F. W. Green (London, 1950), pp. 191–3, 232–5. For most purposes this is satisfactory, but Bindley and Green use a text of the Greek, based on Joannes Dominicus Mansi, *Sacrorum conciliorum nova et amplissima collectio*, 53 vols (Florence, 1759–1827), 7, cols 108–17 which disagrees at crucial points with the critical text in Eduard Schwartz, *Acta conciliorum oecumenicorum* (Berlin and Leipzig, 1933) [hereafter *ACO*], II.1.2, pp. 126–30 = Actio 5.30–34.
[2] *ACO*, II.1.2, p. 126 ll. 12–15 (= Actio 5.31).
[3] The subject was momentously and controversially set out by Walter Bauer in *Rechtgläubigkeit und Ketzerei im ältesten Christentum*, Beiträge zur historischen Theologie, 10 (Tübingen, 1934; 2nd edn rev. by Georg Strecker, 1964), and full documentation, critique, and updating in the English version ed. by Robert A. Kraft, *Orthodoxy and Heresy in Earliest Christianity* (London, 1972), where other views are discussed.

summoning them together to purge the flock of falsehood and feed it with truth. They have done this, they say, by a common sentence (referring chiefly to the deposing of Dioscorus and his supporters), and by renewing the faith of the Fathers through the Creeds of the 318 who had assembled at Nicaea in 325 and of the 150 who met in Constantinople in 381 (hereafter N and C respectively). On this more needs to be said.

To understand this part of the Formula we must look back at the Council's second session. Then, the imperial officials asked for a statement of pure faith, so that unanimity could be made apparent; for the Emperor and Senate wanted the Council to know that 'we keep the orthodox faith which was handed down by the 318 and by the 150 and by the rest of the holy and glorious Fathers and we make it our standard of faith'.[4] In response the bishops objected to setting out any other statement than what the Fathers had taught and left on record.[5] The need for Leo's dogmatic *Tome to Flavian* to deal with Eutyches was stated by leading bishops, then mention was made of Cyril, Celestine, and the Council of Ephesus, and finally a longer list of worthies including Athanasius, Hilary, Basil, and Gregory.[6]

After this N was read out in correct historic form, and met by thirteen acclamations, beginning, 'This is the faith of the orthodox,' but ending, 'Cyril so believed,' and, 'Pope Leo so expounded.'[7] C had not been mentioned since the imperial commissioners first spoke of it. It was now read out at their behest, presumably in the form in which it was found in the Constantinople archives. Its reception was comparatively muted; only three acclamations are recorded: 'This is the faith of all. This is the faith of the orthodox. So we believe.'[8] The Council then discussed other documents, which were later to

---

[4]   *ACO*, II.1.2, p. 78 ll. 10–15 = Actio 3.2. Schwartz is almost alone in reporting this as the third session (Actio). Most writers (including Bindley and Green) call this the second session, following the order set out in Charles Joseph Hefele and Henri Leclerq, *Histoire des conciles*, 2/ii (Paris, 1908), pp. 655–6. R. V. Sellers, *The Council of Chalcedon* (London, 1953), pp. 208–9 n. 1, seems to follow Schwartz.
[5]   Actio 3.3.
[6]   Actio 3.4–9.
[7]   Actio 3.11–12.
[8]   Actio 3.13–15.

be annexed to the Formula, and set up a committee under Anatolius of Constantinople to devise the desired Formula.

It was at this second session of Chalcedon that C first comes to our notice, no earlier record of it being verifiable.[9] It is not surprising if the bishops were unenthusiastic about so obscure a text. The Trinitarian crisis of the fourth century had been resolved by establishing N as the sole criterion of orthodoxy. This had happened in the 360s, when Athanasius and his Western allies urged the abandoning of all other formulae in its favour. Its singularity was reasserted at Constantinople in 381, whatever may be the origin there of C. More strongly still at Ephesus in 431 the Cyrilline majority enforced the exclusive use of N in its Canon 7 against the use of a Nestorian creed, and the Antiochene minority deployed it against Cyril's *Twelve Anathemas*.[10] This explains why at Chalcedon the bishops did not readily agree to formulate a new doctrinal statement as desired by the Emperors, nor did they respond very warmly to the reading of C. A Council which was to assert the primacy of the see of Constantinople not only in relation to the doctrinal issues, but also in various ways in relation to the other great sees of Rome, Alexandria, and Antioch, would certainly have found it convenient to elevate a document of that Council of Constantinople of 381, which had asserted, perhaps for the first time, that city's co-primacy as New Rome.[11] What has not been said, but might be true, is that C was already current as a baptismal creed in Constantinople, and that the confirmation of its use by a general council would remove a potential source of embarrassment.

When the Formula was presented and promulgated at the fifth and sixth sessions, both N and C were deliberately adopted and ratified. But there is a subtle argument deeply involved. The Formula says of N that as a 'statement of right and faultless faith' it 'shines above (προλάμπειν)'; of C it says

---

[9] For the origins of C see J. N. D. Kelly, *Early Christian Creeds*, 3rd edn (London, 1972), pp. 296–321; Wolf-Dieter Hauschild, 'Nicäno-Konstantinopolitanisches Glaubensbekenntnis', *Theologische Realenzyklopädie*, 24 (Berlin, 1994), pp. 444–56.

[10] Both texts accessible in Stevenson, *Creeds, Councils and Controversies*, pp. 309–10.

[11] Canon 3 of Constantinople; Canons 9, 17, 28 of Chalcedon. See Stevenson, *Creeds, Councils and Controversies*, pp. 117, 361–2.

that it 'is valid (κρατεῖν)', having been 'decreed for the destruction of the heresies then growing and for the confirmation of the same our catholic and apostolic faith'.[12] This notion, that creeds change but doctrine does not, is more fully developed in the text which follows N and C in the Formula of Chalcedon. This N-C Creed ('this wise and saving *symbolon* of the divine grace') was full and complete. But now that new heresies have arisen, denying *theotokos* or confusing the natures in Christ, in order to shut out evil machinations the Council has made a decree to the following effect:[13] N remains unchanged and pre-eminent,

> and because of those who resist the Holy Spirit it ratifies the teaching on the substance of the Spirit subsequently passed down by the 150 Fathers assembled in the Imperial City, which they made known to all, not as though making good some deficiency in their predecessors, but by scriptural testimonies elucidating their thinking about the Holy Spirit in opposition to those who were attempting to deny his sovereignty.[14]

On this basis the Council 'has accepted (ἐδέξατο)' two of Cyril's synodical letters in order to refute Nestorianism and 'to advise those who with devout zeal desire the meaning of the saving Creed'; and it subjoins also Leo's *Tome*, which conforms with Peter's scriptural confession and is a general defence against error.[15] It then proceeds, on lines which we cannot investigate now, to the cursing of specific errors and the elaborating of a creedal formula about the two natures of the one Jesus Christ.

In this way the present act of generating a Creed is justified. The Council of Constantinople had not implied that N was wanting: it had merely elucidated the meaning of N by clarifying its teaching on the Spirit. Similarly Cyril had written against Nestorius, and Leo against Eutyches: their views were not against the one faith of N and C, but

---

[12] Actio 5.31; *ACO*, II.1.2, p. 127 ll. 4–8.
[13] Actio 5.34; *ACO*, II.1.2, p. 128 ll. 15–25.
[14] Ibid., pp. 128 l. 25–129 l. 6.
[15] Ibid., p. 129 ll. 6–16.

expounded it. One could of course investigate the veracity of these claims, but the choice of documents has some plausibility. Cyril expounds N directly in his synodical letter to Nestorius, and quotes in full and approves a compromise formula with the Antiochenes in the other, the so-called 'Formula of Union'; while Leo cites the Creed (even if it appears to be the Roman rather than the Nicene) early in his *Tome*.[16] All these documents annexed to the Formula can therefore in some ways be seen as supplementary expositions of the existing Creed. Not only do they provide a correct exegesis, so the Council Fathers believe, of the existing immutable doctrine; they provide a precedent which will enable them to satisfy the imperial desire for a new Formula without abandoning the one and only Creed they have received.

There is one further problem, however, which we can only describe and not resolve. When Schwartz edited the conciliar documents he reconstructed the texts of the Creeds in a surprising way. Having been read at the second session in a pure form, they were produced in the Formula at the fifth session, and apparently promulgated at the sixth, in a form which assimilates them to each other. In an important article anticipating his edition, Schwartz explained that this was due to pressure by the Empress Pulcheria on the drafting committee: the facts had to fit the theory, and you could not have N differing so much from C in clauses which had nothing to do with the Holy Spirit, whose status was the whole justification for the existence of C. In English the Creeds of Schwartz's text read as shown in the table on pages 24–5.

Those who use Stevenson's *Creeds, Councils and Controversies*[17] or Bindley and Green's *Oecumenical Documents of the Faith*[18] will perceive that a totally different set of assimilative variants to N is there displayed. These can also be found in

---

[16] Cyril's *2nd Letter to Nestorius*, 2–3, and *Letter to John of Antioch*, 3–5, and Leo's *Tome to Flavian*, 2; all accessible in Stevenson, *Creeds, Councils and Controversies*, pp. 295–6 (22e–23a), 314–15 (105e–106c), 337.

[17] Stevenson, *Creeds, Councils and Controversies*, pp. 350–1.

[18] Bindley, *Oecumenical Documents*, pp. 191–2 with note on p. 194; translation p. 233.

Nicaea, pure form	Constantinople, pure form
We believe in one God the Father Almighty, of all visibles and invisibles the Maker; and in one Lord Jesus Christ the Son of God, begotten from his Father as onlybegotten, that is from the being of the Father, God from God, light from light, true God from true God, begotten not made, consubstantial with the Father, by whom all things came to be both those in heaven and those on earth, who for us men and for our salvation came down and was enfleshed and was made man, suffered and rose the third day, went up to the heavens, and is coming to judge living and dead and in the Holy Spirit. Those who say, 'There was when he was not,' and, 'Before he was begotten, he was not,' and allege that he came to be from the non-existent or from another substance or being, or that God's Son is mutable or variable,	We believe in one God the Father Almighty, the Maker of heaven and earth, of all visibles and invisibles; and in one Lord Jesus Christ the Son of God, the onlybegotten, who was begotten from his Father before all the ages, light from light, true God from true God, begotten not made, consubstantial with the Father by whom all things came to be, who for us men and for our salvation came down from the heavens and was enfleshed from Holy Spirit and Mary the Virgin, and was made man, was crucified under Pontius Pilate, and suffered and was buried and rose the third day according to the scriptures, and went up to the heavens and sits at the Father's right, and is coming again with glory to judge living and dead whose reign will have no end; and in the Spirit, the holy,
	the sovereign and lifegiving, which proceeds from the Father, which with Father and Son is together worshipped and together glorified, which spoke through the prophets; in one holy, catholic and apostolic Church.
(them) the catholic and apostolic Church curses.	We confess one Baptism for forgiveness of sins, we expect resurrection of the dead, and life of the coming age. Amen.[19]

[19] *ACO*, II.1.2, p. 79 ll. 16–26; p. 80 ll. 3–16 [my translations].

24

Creeds and Formula at Chalcedon

Nicaea, altered form	**Constantinople, altered form**
We believe in one God	We believe in one God
the Father Almighty,	the Father Almighty,
the Maker of heaven and earth,	the Maker of heaven and earth,
of all visibles	of all visibles
and invisibles _____;	and invisibles;
and in one Lord Jesus Christ	and in one Lord Jesus Christ
the Son of God,	the Son of God,
the onlybegotten,	the onlybegotten,
who was begotten from his	who was begotten from his
Father before all the ages,	Father before all the ages,
_____	_____
true God from true God,	true God from true God,
begotten not made,	begotten not made,
consubstantial with the Father,	consubstantial with the Father,
by whom all things came to be	by whom all things came to be,
_____	
who for us men and for our	who for us men and for our
salvation came down	salvation came down
	_____
and was enfleshed	and was enfleshed
	from Holy Spirit
	and Mary the Virgin,
and was made man,	and was made man,
	and was crucified
	under Pontius Pilate,
and suffered	_____
	and was buried,
and rose the third day,	and rose the third day
	_____
and went up to the heavens,	and went up to the heavens
	and sits at the Father's right,
and is coming	and is coming again with glory
to judge living and dead;	to judge living and dead
	whose reign will have no end;
and in the Holy Spirit.	and in the Spirit, the holy,
Those who say, 'There was when	
he was not,' and 'Before he	
was begotten, he was not,' and	
allege that he came to be from	
the non-existent or from another	
substance or being, or that	
God's Son is mutable or variable,	
	the sovereign and lifegiving
	which proceeds from the
	Father, which with Father and
	Son is _____ worshipped
	and together glorified, which
	spoke through the prophets;
them the catholic and	in one _____ catholic and
apostolic Church curses.	apostolic Church.
	We confess one Baptism for
	forgiveness of sins, we expect
	resurrection of the dead, and
	life of the coming age. Amen.[20]

[20] Ibid., II.1.2, p. 127 ll. 10–19; p. 128 ll. 2–14. Italics indicate changes to the pure text; lines indicate omissions.

Schwartz's *apparatus criticus*. They are chiefly additions to N: 'from heaven' after 'came down'; 'from Holy Spirit and Mary the Virgin' after 'incarnate'; 'crucified for us under Pontius Pilate'; 'and was buried'; 'according to the scriptures' after 'the third day' (also attested in C as altered); 'and sits at the Father's right'; 'again with glory' after 'is coming'; 'whose reign will have no end'. In dealing with either version, one is faced with places where apparently two powerful forces are at work: one assimilates the two creeds to each other, the other corrects them to the original pure form.

We cannot begin to resolve the questions these differences raise. But the following observations are in order. First Schwartz took the view that the changes his text reveals were deliberately made by Anatolius' committee, at the behest of the Emperors and especially of Pulcheria.[21] The manuscripts in which the pure forms appear are all later than the Council of Constantinople of 553, and in all the earlier documents, papal, imperial, or Monophysite, the texts are more or less assimilated. Some later texts have therefore been altered to give an apparently more correct version. If Schwartz is right, we have a fine case of historical adjustment by the Council of Chalcedon and its committee. C was introduced in order to justify a new formula, purporting to be N with adjustments to deal with heretics who denied the deity of the Spirit. On close scrutiny, as every creedal student knows, C appears as a different baptismal Creed, and is not merely N adjusted. So to minimize the obvious problem, the two texts were both adjusted to make them appear more alike. Thereafter other forces impinged, both official and scribal. Texts were adjusted back to the pure form by official pressure. At the same time further assimilations occurred, especially as C came into eucharistic use at Antioch and Constantinople during the century after Chalcedon.[22] Schwartz's theory has been challenged, and with it the correctness of his text of the

[21] E. Schwartz, 'Das Nicaenum und das Constantinopolitanum auf der Synode von Chalkedon', *Zeitschrift für die neutestamentliche Wissenschaft*, 25 (1926), pp. 38–88, esp. 76–8 idem, *ACO*, II.1.2, p. VI.
[22] Kelly, *Creeds*, pp. 348–51; Hauschild, 'Nicäno-Konstantinopolitanisches Glaubensbekenntnis', p. 454.

Chalcedonian Formula, chiefly by J. Lebon.[23] It is unthinkable, Lebon argued, that the bishops at Chalcedon, suspicious as they were about the new formula, would have allowed anything but the authentic text, especially of N, to be produced for ratification. What Schwartz thought unthinkable is, however, for Lebon true: the altered texts did come into the manuscript collections of the first hundred years after the Council, precisely because there were already in use many developed versions of 'the Nicene Creed': Eutyches at his trial was actually attacked for quoting N without the added phrase, 'from Holy Spirit and Mary the Virgin'.[24] Whether or not Diogenes of Cyzicus on that occasion had a form closely resembling C in mind, we cannot know; but that C was itself a baptismal Creed with elements of N, and was in use at Constantinople in that capacity, seems probable. Since the 318 Fathers of Nicaea were much better known in their liturgical variations than in their historic purity, it can be no surprise if variant texts came in when copyists worked on the Chalcedonian Formula. Furthermore, if there had been official textual cheating at Chalcedon, it is not credible that their Monophysite critics would have failed to charge them with it. Lebon weakens his case by resisting altogether the possibility that C already had official standing before Chalcedon, but in other respects seems to prevail.

To this rarefied and difficult discussion I can add only one observation. Schwartz's argument that the two Creeds were deliberately and officially assimilated at Chalcedon works best if the Formula is held to say, as I have myself believed it to say, that C is N with a few clauses added about the Holy Spirit.[25] It does not in fact say this. It says that C was 'decreed for the destruction of the heresies then growing and for the confirmation of the same our catholic and apostolic faith,' and ratifies it as 'the teaching on the

---

[23] Joseph Lebon, 'Les anciens symboles dans la définition de Chalcédoine', *RHE*, 22 (1936), pp. 809-76. Kelly, *Creeds*, p. 298, agrees, citing also G. L. Dossetti, *Il simbolo di Nicea e di Constantinopoli* (Rome and Freiburg, 1967), pp. 296ff.

[24] Diogenes of Cyzikos' words are in *ACO*, II.1.1, p. 91, ll. 21-30.

[25] Stuart G. Hall, *Doctrine and Practice in the Early Church* (London, 1991), pp. 232-3.

substance of the Spirit subsequently passed down by the 150 Fathers.' No more precise textual connection with N is assumed or asserted, any more than Cyril and Leo are seen as verbally bound to N.

Thus the Council of Chalcedon claims that it is right to develop the one true and original doctrinal statement of Nicaea, both in the simple confession of Constantinople and in longer discussions like Cyril's and Leo's, and that this in no way infringed the unique authority and sufficiency of N. Having done so, it can proceed to its own Definition with a good conscience. In fact the Council's own Definition failed to unite the Churches as the Emperors intended, though it did establish the Constantinople Creed as 'the Nicene Creed' for all the Church. We still live with the consequences of both the failure and the success. Historical reassessment of those ancient events is enabling the various Eastern Churches to overcome their longstanding divisions in ecumenical dialogue.[26] But the events of Chalcedon also have a wider theological interest. We now recognize that it took three decades for N to be adopted in the fourth century as the only possible Creed, and we have seen that the very people who valued it most used and developed it, rather than treated it as verbally infallible and invariable. That should be a warning about the nature of religious certainty and especially of Christian confession. Even at its most authoritative, the certainty exists in the realm of human contingency, and no text, however sacred, is ever permanently sufficient. The idea that doctrine had never changed was clung to down the centuries. It certainly used to govern High Anglicans, like the 'Apostolicals' of John Henry Newman's earlier years. Newman's departure from it in favour of a theory of doctrinal development enabled his conversion to Rome and at the same time brought him near contemporary post-Hegelian Protestantism; it eventually set modern Roman

---

[26] Summary of developments and bibliography in K. M. George, 'Oriental Orthodox-Orthodox Dialogue', and Ronald G. Roberson, 'Oriental Orthodox-Roman Catholic Dialogue', in *Dictionary of the Ecumenical Movement*, ed. Nicholas Lossky and others (Geneva, 1991), pp. 757–61; Fairy von Lilienfeld, 'Orthodoxe Kirchen', *Theologische Realenzyklopädie*, 25 (Berlin, 1995), pp. 423–64.

Catholics free to view ancient history and formulae with new eyes. Other Western Churches have shifted in comparable ways. The questions of dogmatic continuity faced at Chalcedon are therefore still with us: our view of the past shapes our doctrinal beliefs for the present and the future.

University of St Andrews

BRINGING THE HOLY SEPULCHRE TO THE WEST: S. STEFANO, BOLOGNA, FROM THE FIFTH TO THE TWENTIETH CENTURY[1]

by COLIN MORRIS

B y virtue of its basic pattern of belief, the Church is committed to looking back as well as forward. In his introductory letter for the Conference which has produced this volume, Andrew Martindale reminded us that 'doctrine, dogma, and revelation are all pinned to time and place'. Most of all are they rooted in Golgotha and the Holy Sepulchre, the site of the death and Resurrection of the Lord. It is true that, in particular since the Reformation, the theology of the Passion and Resurrection have often been discussed without reference to their historical location. Other Christians in other times, confident that the Holy Sepulchre discovered under Constantine was indeed the authentic place of Christ's Resurrection, desired to reach out to and to grasp its historical and geographical reality, for these embody the very time and place of their redemption.

They had many ways of doing so: pilgrimage, liturgy, drama, relics (above all, relics of the Cross), and artistic representation all performed this function. These things helped to generate a further desire: to bring the Holy Sepulchre to the West. As far as I know it was only once suggested that this should be done literally, in one of the more unrealistic policy discussions in the court of the Medici grand dukes of Tuscany.[2] There was, however, a strong and widespread interest in the creation of representations of the Holy Sepulchre, some purely symbolic, others designed as literal copies. The most famous of all the Jerusalems in the

[1] I am glad to express my thanks to the Leverhulme Trust for the award of an Emeritus Fellowship, which funded research on the continent, including visits to Bologna and other 'copies' of the Holy Sepulchre in Italy, Switzerland, and Germany.
[2] See D. Neri, 'La leggenda di trasferire il S. Sepolcro a Firenze', *La Terra Santa*, 65 (1989), pp. 73–6; see also his book, *Il S. Sepolcro riprodotto in Occidente* (Jerusalem, 1971), pp. 88–93.

West, perhaps, has been the complex of churches dedicated to S. Stefano at Bologna. It has been described as 'unique in the world' and as 'the only complete architectural complex built by faithful memory in imitation of the Holy Places at Jerusalem'.[3] This fascinating set of buildings has inevitably influenced our understanding of the purpose and the chronology of copies of the Sepulchre, but at the same time it presents many difficulties and has often been misinterpreted.[4]

S. Stefano lies on the road leading eastward from the old city nucleus of Bologna, and it is not one church, but a complex of buildings. Locally, it is generally called the *sette chiese*, although it is quite hard to identify the seven, and they only began to be counted as seven in the sixteenth century. The most distinctive part of the whole is the octagon known as S. Sepolcro. It is framed, to each side, by the larger churches of Crocefisso and SS. Agricola e Vitale. Continuing eastward from the octagon, there is a court, and beyond that another church, Trinità. In addition, there are the domestic buildings of the monastery, including a further cloister (Pl. 1). The whole has been dedicated, probably since the very beginning, to St Stephen, but the names of the component parts have changed disconcertingly over the

[3] G. Fasoli, 'Storiografia Stefaniana tra XII e XVII secolo', in G. Fasoli, ed., *Stefaniana: contributi per la storia del complesso di S. Stefano in Bologna* (Bologna, 1985) [hereafter *Stefaniana*], p. 27; C. Valenziano, 'Mimesis Anamnesis: spazio-temporale per il triduo pasquale', in I. Scicolone, ed., *La celebrazione del triduo pasquale, anamnesis e mimesis*, Studia Anselmiana, 102 (Rome, 1990), p. 33.

[4] There has been some outstanding work in recent years on the complex of churches. In this article, I am especially indebted to the studies by William Montorsi, *S. Stefano in Bologna*, 2 vols (Modena, 1980) [hereafter Montorsi], and L. Serchia, ed., *Nel Segno del San Sepolcro* (Vigevano, 1987) [hereafter Serchia]. For a full bibliography, see Serchia pp. 457–61. The section on Bologna in S. Stocchi, *L'Emilia-Romagna*, Italia Romanica, 6 (Milan, 1984) [hereafter Stocchi], pp. 301–37, is an excellent survey, primarily founded on the views of Montorsi. Important studies on copies of the Sepulchre in Western Europe include G. Dalman, *Das Grab Christi in Deutschland* (Leipzig, 1922); R. Krautheimer, 'Introduction to an iconography of medieval architecture', *Journal of the Warburg and Courtauld Institutes*, 5 (1942), pp. 1–33; C. Heitz, *Recherches sur les rapports entre architecture et liturgie à l'époque carolingienne* (Paris, 1963); Neri, *Il S. Sepolcro riprodotto in Occidente* (but the work is older than its date of 1971 suggests); G. Bresc-Bautier, 'Les imitations du S. Sépulcre de Jérusalem (IXe–XVe siècles). Archéologie d'une dévotion', *Revue d'histoire de la spiritualité*, 50 (1974), pp. 319–42; M. Untermann, *Der Zentralbau im Mittelalter: Form, Funktion, Verbreitung* (Darmstadt, 1989); and R. Ousterhout, 'Loca Sancta and the architectural response to pilgrimage', in R. Ousterhout, ed., *The Blessings of Pilgrimage* (Chicago, 1990), pp. 108–24.

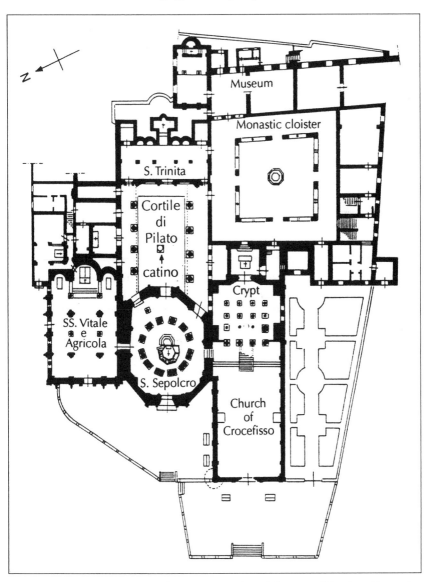

Plate 1   Plan of S. Stefano, Bologna, 1976 (adapted from guidebook, *Abbazia di S. Stefano* [Bologna, 1987]).

centuries. For the sake of simplicity, I will refer to them by their modern dedications.

The modern visitor will certainly not fail to notice the rich overlay of reminiscences of Jerusalem. The most dramatic is a large copy of the Holy Sepulchre (Pl. 2, 6). It is an odd and multi-purpose version. The tomb cavity itself contains the burial-place of St Petronius, the supposed founder of the complex. The structure is fitted with a pulpit or ambo and with a staircase which leads to a high-level platform on which stand an altar and a cross, clearly a reference to the place of the Crucifixion, or Calvary. The ambo is decorated with symbols of the evangelists typical of Italian Romanesque churches, and on the outside of the tomb there are fourteenth-century stucco illustrations of the events of Easter morning. This remarkable monument is located inside a nearly symmetrical building, the church of S. Sepolcro, which is in effect a lop-sided octagon. Whatever its original intention (and more of this shortly), it can now be seen as an approximate version of the shrine at Jerusalem, which had the Holy Sepulchre itself contained within the great rotunda or Anastasis, as it is technically known. This building is the heart of the matter, but the S. Stefano complex as a whole is densely scattered with reminiscences of the Passion Narratives.

The courtyard to the east has been known for centuries as the *cortile di Pilato*, and taken as a recollection of the place where Jesus was judged. At its centre there is a huge basin, apparently of classical origin, with a Lombard inscription datable to the 740s. The basin was provided with a stand in 1506 by Cardinal Giovanni de' Medici, the later Pope Leo X. Since the late Middle Ages this has been called the *catino di Pilato*, and taken to be the basin in which he washed his hands (Matthew 27.24) – in defiance of its immense dimensions, which render the imitation quite unrealistic (Pl. 3, 4). The courtyard also contains a wooden image of the cockerel which presided over Peter's denials, carved in about 1400. In the eastern range of buildings, there was from an early date a chapel of the Cross, in commemoration of Golgotha.

Unfortunately, there is little early historical material about the development of S. Stefano. The crucial passage is in the

Plate 2 The edicule of the Holy Sepulchre, Bologna, in its present form (from *Abbazia di S. Stefano* [Bologna, 1987]).

Plate 3   Exterior of the Sepulchre church, east side, from the Cortile di Pilato (from *Abbazia di S. Stefano* [Bologna, 1987]).

Life of Petronius, who was Bishop of Bologna from about 432 to 450. He is said to have been a relative and adviser of the Emperor Theodosius II at Constantinople, and when he was appointed bishop he found the city largely in ruins. In the course of the restoration of the city, his biographer tells us, 'he with much labour symbolically created a work, marvelously constructed, like the Sepulchre of the Lord in the form which he had seen, and carefully measured with a rod, when he was at Jerusalem'. The *Life* goes on to describe the buildings, including a cloister which

Plate 4   The *catino di Pilato* (from *Abbazia di S. Stefano* [Bologna, 1987]).

extended to the place which is figuratively called Golgotha, that is Calvary, where the Cross on which Christ was nailed for the salvation of the world was placed. . . . In this same place, which is called Golgotha, he set a Cross of wood, which in length and width was in all respects made like the Cross of Christ.[5]

The author adds that Petronius built an artificial mound some distance away to symbolize the Mount of Olives, and that the intervening valley was known as Jehoshaphat. The underlying purpose of producing at Bologna a precise imitation of Jerusalem would thus go back to the very beginning of S. Stefano, and to the first half of the fifth century. In the style of the modern theme park, it would reflect the layout of the Holy Places, including their precise measurements: a fifth-century attempt at virtual reality.

The trouble is that the earliest manuscript evidence for the *Life* is in a lectionary written for use at S. Stefano and completed in 1180. From the fact that the text breathes the spirit of the struggle of the communes against Frederick Barbarossa, the composition must be dated between 1164 and 1180. There had been a major discovery of relics in 1141, and this apparently led to a renewal of the cult of St Petronius, to the composition of a *sermo* about the relics, and to the *Life of Petronius*. The author was almost completely ignorant of the history of Petronius' own times, about which he makes a series of howlers. The narrative of events in the fifth century has rightly been called 'in many respects gratuitously absurd'.[6] On the face of it, its account of the foundation of S. Stefano must merely be dismissed. We are left only with a little information derived from other patristic sources.

---

[5] F. Lanzoni, *San Petronio vescovo di Bologna nella storia e nella leggenda* (Rome, 1907) [hereafter Lanzoni], pp. 231–2. I have assumed in the text that the anonymous author was describing in turn the model of the Sepulchre, the octagon which encloses it, and the present *cortile di Pilato*, but his intentions are not really very clear.

[6] M. Corti, ed., *Vita di San Petronio* (Bologna, 1962), p. xiii. The introduction to this book provides strong reasons for thinking that the thirteenth-century vernacular *Life*, which she edits, was a translation of a Latin 'first edition', of which the surviving Latin text is an inferior version. This earlier text, which does not survive, must nevertheless be dated after the middle of the twelfth century.

It appears that the bodies of the Bolognese martyrs, Agricola and Vitalis, were discovered by St Ambrose of Milan and Bishop Eusebius in 393; and we do have confirmation that Petronius was bishop at Bologna for a considerable period before 450.[7] That is the sum total of our literary information. The very general outline of the building history can be recovered. There were certainly palaeo-Christian structures there, and a total excavation would reveal a series of developments over the succeeding centuries. These culminated in an extensive Romanesque rebuilding, which probably began after a major earthquake in 1117, and which was further encouraged by the discovery of the relics in 1141. Any attempt to fill in that outline must be highly speculative. There is considerable agreement (but not unanimity) among recent scholars that the original S. Stefano may have consisted of a shrine to the two martyrs, together with a baptistry, which would have been octagonal in design, like so many of those built under the influence of the church of Milan.[8] In this case, the present S. Sepolcro, of which the fabric is largely twelfth-century, would preserve the ground-plan of its predecessor. There was also some early building beyond the central cortile, and it is plausible to suggest that this included a chapel with a relic of the Cross. Even this goes beyond our certain knowledge. Above all, once the reliability of the *Life of Petronius* is denied, there is no reason to suppose that the fifth-century buildings were designed as an imitation of the Holy Sepulchre, and we must look elsewhere for the moment of the 'Jerusalem explosion' at Bologna.[9]

[7] The finding of the relics is well summarized in F. Homes Dudden, *The Life and Times of St Ambrose* (Oxford, 1935), pp. 316–18 (with references). Brief, and slightly divergent, accounts are given of Petronius by Eucherius of Lyon and by Gennadius, *De viris illustribus*, ch. 42: see P. Schaff and H. Ware, eds, *Select Library of Nicene and Post-Nicene Fathers*, 2nd ser., 3 (New York, 1892), p. 393.

[8] The likelihood that the present S. Sepolcro was originally a baptistry is greatly increased if S. Stefano was at first the cathedral of the city. Lanzoni denied that it was ever a cathedral: see his Appendix 5. The summary in Stocchi, p. 307, is judicious: 'One can suppose, but not prove, that this basilica [SS. Vitale e Agricola] was the first cathedral of Bologna, or one of the first, and that the octagonal rotunda, properly called S. Stefano, was later added as its baptistry.'

[9] The phrase is that of Montorsi, p. 18.

The unhistorical character of the *Vita Petronii* has been recognized for centuries. Nevertheless, twentieth-century Bologna has not taken kindly to the demolition of its traditions, and a remarkable attempt was made in 1907 by Francesco Lanzoni, who produced the definitive edition and analysis of the work, to re-assert the value of the tradition. He accepted that 'the legend of St Petronius deserves very little credence', but contended that it incorporated a nucleus of authentic recollection.[10] He interpreted the *Life* as attributing to Petronius three specific features: a copy of the Holy Sepulchre in the church of S. Sepolcro, a courtyard to the east of it, and beyond that a great church for the veneration of the Holy Cross. Lanzoni assumed that the author must have been describing the buildings as they existed in the later twelfth century, and for the moment we will accept that. He was however struck by what seemed to him a remarkable similarity with the main outline of the church of the Holy Sepulchre at Jerusalem. At both, there is a Holy Sepulchre enclosed in a circular (or, at Bologna, an octagonal) building, an open courtyard to the east, and a basilica of the Cross beyond that. At Jerusalem the location of the tomb, cut into the rock of an original quarry, meant that the whole complex had a peculiar orientation, with the main altar of the basilica at the west end. S. Stefano appears to share the same curious design, with the copy of the tomb similarly at the western end. If we are prepared to go so far with Lanzoni, we must reach the conclusion that the essential structure of S. Stefano, and not just its later furniture and decorations, were designed as a representation of the church of the Holy Sepulchre at Jerusalem (Pl. 5, 6).[11]

[10] Lanzoni, p. 71. So also p. 51: 'the value of the *Vita* as a whole is rather slight'.

[11] Lanzoni, p. 114: 'The three edifices at Bologna were oriented like the constructions at Jerusalem. The obvious conclusion is therefore that the architects of the edifices at Bologna intended to reproduce the Constantinian constructions at Jerusalem.' Recent work in the church of the Holy Sepulchre has inevitably generated an enormous amount of publication, among which there are important works by C. Coüasnon, *The Church of the Holy Sepulchre in Jerusalem* (Oxford, 1974); V. C. Corbo, *Il santo sepolcro di Gerusalemme*, 3 vols (Jerusalem, 1981–2); and S. Gibson and J. E. Taylor, *Beneath the Church of the Holy Sepulchre* (London, 1994). For an excellent summary, see G. S. P. Freeman-Grenville, *The Basilica of the Holy Sepulchre in Jerusalem* (Jerusalem, nd [1995]).

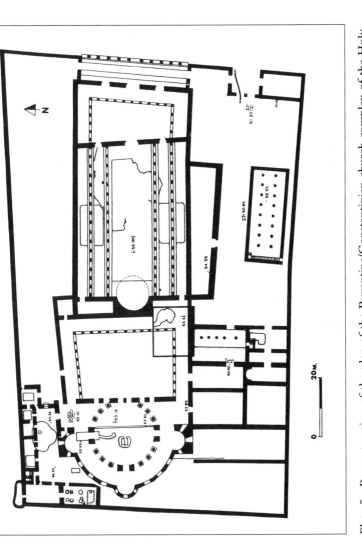

Plate 5   Reconstruction of the plan of the Byzantine/Constantinian church complex of the Holy Sepulchre, Jerusalem (from S. Gibson and J. E. Taylor, *Beneath the Church of the Holy Sepulchre* [London, 1994], reproduced by permission of Dr Shimon Gibson).

Plate 6   The shrine of the Holy Sepulchre, Jerusalem, 1838 (from David Roberts, *The Holy Land* [London, 1842–3]).

Of course, that does not determine the date of the plan, and some scholars have supposed that it was produced by the Romanesque rebuilding.[12] To Lanzoni, the crucial argument in dating was the extensive destruction at Jerusalem produced by the Persian conquest in 614. The rebuilding which followed at the hands of the Patriarch Modestus made significant changes in the original Constantinian plan, and it seemed to him that the outline of S. Stefano reproduced the first design, as it was before 614. If the complex was like that in 600, it is reasonable to accept the ascription of the plan to Bishop Petronius around 450.[13] Amid all the alterations and accretions of later centuries, S. Stefano (on this view) is a living proof of the way in which church builders, beginning in the years after 400, strove to bring Jerusalem to the West.[14]

We shall shortly have to examine the force of this argument, but first we must consider its practical consequences. Already during Lanzoni's lifetime large changes were being made to the fabric of the *sette chiese*. Church

---

[12] In particular, it has been argued by Robert Ousterhout that the Romanesque octagon was an imitation of the Anastasis as it was rebuilt about 1050, after the destruction of the original by Caliph al-Hakîm. See his article, 'The Church of S. Stefano: a "Jerusalem" in Bologna', *Gesta*, 20 (1981), pp. 311–21, which is essentially reproduced in Italian in *Stefaniana*, pp. 131–58; also his 'Osservazioni sulla galleria del S. Sepolcro a S. Stefano di Bologna', *Stefaniana*, pp. 159–67. The fact that Ousterhout is a major authority on the shrine at Jerusalem requires one to take his detailed analysis very seriously. For the contrary view, see Serchia, pp. 147–8, where he specifically rejects Ousterhout's argument, and asserts that in the rebuilding after 1141 'nothing was added which could in any way refer to the planometry of the sanctuaries on Golgotha, as they were restored by Constantine Monomachos', that is in the mid–eleventh century.

[13] Some confirmatory arguments from liturgy were presented by Giulio Belvederi, in his article, 'La liturgia della Passione a Gerusalemme e in Occidente al secolo IV e al secolo V', *Rivista di Archaeologia Cristiana*, 8 (1931) [hereafter Belvederi], pp. 315–46. Belvederi was right in supposing that the ceremonies which he was discussing originated in Jerusalem in the mid–fourth century, but he ignored the fact that they were widespread in the West in the Carolingian period. There are no grounds for thinking that Bologna was early and unique in its imitation of the Jerusalem liturgy.

[14] Giulio Belvederi was an even more enthusiastic advocate of continuity than Lanzoni: 'We may say that Bolognese tradition has every reason to claim and be considered to be true and worthy of belief. . . . It can be concluded that from a desire to represent to the mind and hearts of believers far away from the Holy Places of the Passion, . . . Petronius constructed in his episcopal see sacred edifices which from the earliest period until now have been recalled with the same of Jerusalem.' (Belvederi, pp. 324, 346)

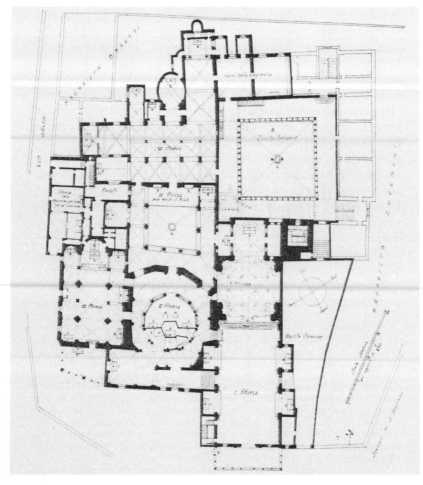

Plate 7   Plan of the basilica complex, 1870 (from *Abbazia di S. Stefano* [Bologna, 1987]).

restoration in nineteenth-century Italy was necessarily different from that occurring north of the Alps. It could not be a Gothic revival, because there was so little Gothic to revive; but the Risorgimento helped to create a new desire for the protection and renewal of ecclesiastical buildings. Restoration, so-called, often involved the re-design of buildings to replace Baroque or Renaissance additions and to make them conform to what architects saw as appropriate to the period in which they had been planned.[15] The founder of restoration at Bologna was Count Giovanni Gozzadini, a man of great wealth and national influence, and a fine scholar, especially as an archaeologist: he was, for example, the first discoverer of the Villanovan culture of pre-Roman Italy. Above all, he was a passionate lover of Bologna, and was President of the Deputazione di Storia Patria per le provincie della Romagna from its foundation in 1860. In 1869, he submitted to the Ministero della Pubblica Istruzione in Rome an application to assist the restoration of the complex. The official architect was Raffaele Faccioli, but Gozzadini was involved at the most detailed level, and his publications document the progress of the work fully (Pl. 7, 8).[16]

The argument for 'restoration' was clear. The *sette chiese* were of unique important in the history of architecture, and the Romanesque buildings were overlaid by later construction. The octagon, the most important of them, had been redecorated and refurnished in the eighteenth and early nineteenth centuries, and its original shape was concealed by a later medieval chapel and a corridor or *androne*. The difficulty was also clear: there was no way of determining the original form of the Romanesque buildings. Gozzadini's plans were based on the extension of the design of surviving portions and on large-scale borrowing from other North Italian buildings, all leavened by an exceedingly free use of the artistic imagination. In 1869, the Deputazione di Storia Patria resolved to proceed to the removal from the octagon of the painting and other works which had been introduced there around 1804. The Ministero della Pubblica Istruzione approved the project and provided a grant, but from the beginning there was tension between Gozzadini's ideal of total restoration and the more conservative spirit of the authorities in Rome, who were worried both by the philosophy and by the cost. During the 1870s and 1880s the Bologna initiative proved unstoppable, and huge alterations

---

[15] See the crucial article of Camillo Boito, 'I nostri vecchi monumenti: conservare o restaurare?', *Nuova Antologia di Scienze, Lettere e Arti*, ser. 3, 87 (1886), pp. 480–506.

[16] Serchia, ch. 1. Some of Gozzadini's major articles are listed in the bibliography there, pp. 457–8.

Plate 8   The edicule within the octagon, 1829 (from A. Basoli, *Vedute pittoresche della citta di Bologna* [Bologna, 1833], photo: Boston Athenaeum).

were made to the fabric. 'Not one of the buildings in the sanctuary was spared.'[17] The west front of one of the churches, SS. Vitale e Agricola, was provided with a complete replacement which appears to be totally inauthentic. Perhaps the oddest feature was the rebuilding of the copy of the Sepulchre itself: the pulpit was switched to the other side and the staircase totally redesigned. Since this strange structure was unique, it is hard to see what principles of political correctness required its transformation. Even when the restoration approached authenticity, the damage done was disastrous. The rebuilding of the exterior of the octagon was based on surviving patterns in the original brickwork, and probably the result is not unlike its appearance around 1200; but the special feature of Bologna was its long history of building and rebuilding under the formation of a Jerusalem ideal, and the surviving evidence was now destroyed in the interests of artistic uniformity. A unique historical palimpsest was destroyed, to be replaced by an (admittedly quite pleasant) Romanesque pastiche.[18]

With the twentieth century, the restoration reached the east end of the complex. The designers now were Mgr Giulio Belvederi and Edoardo Collamarini. Belvederi lacked the width of Gozzadini's scholarship, although he exceeded him in the specially Italian quality of local patriotism, *campanilismo*. The issue at the east end was not merely one of artistic taste: a crucial point of historical scholarship was involved. On the face of it, there was a very serious weakness in Lanzoni's argument about the design of the primitive church. He believed that the *Vita Petronii* gave evidence of the three elements of octagon, cortile, and church of the Cross. However, in his time, there was no church of the Cross. The area beyond the courtyard was occupied by a wing of the monastery, which was known as the church of Trinità, but which in reality was nothing more than a string of chapels, varied in date and incoherent in layout. Although one of these was indeed dedicated to the Cross, the structure was a pathetic substitute for Constantine's great church of the

17 Montorsi, pp. 172-3.
18 See the remarks of Montorsi, pp. 192-8.

Martyrium of which it was supposed to be a recreation. With one of the three elements missing, the whole theory rested on very insecure foundations. To explain this discrepancy, Lanzoni seized upon a number of clues: the *Life of Petronius* seemed to him to be describing a richly decorated church at the place of the Cross, and there was also a helpful account by an antiquary who described extensive ruins on the site about 1600. From these sources, he arrived at the conviction that 'the *ecclesia Sancte Crucis*, or the Golgotha of Bologna, has disappeared, but it certainly existed in the twelfth century'.[19]

Belvederi was determined to search for this third element. The excavations which he undertook were poorly recorded, but evidently failed to find the foundations of a great church. Nevertheless, amidst a polemic of remarkable savagery, he proceeded to provide what he was convinced had once been there, demolished the buildings which existed and based a new structure on a mixture of the palaeo-Christian and Romanesque foundations.[20] The result can be called truly extraordinary. It is a sort of corridor with side-chapels which cannot possibly reflect the original form of the basilica at the Holy Sepulchre, and indeed does not resemble any church familiar from any liturgical tradition. One can only echo William Montorsi's sad conclusion that 'in the former church of Golgotha the restoration reached the heights of pure destructive vandalism'.[21]

The modern visitor to the *sette chiese* may derive the impression that he or she is seeing a complex which has been wonderfully dedicated, from the fifth century to the twentieth, to the presentation in the West of the Holy Places of Palestine. The unhappy reality, however, is better expressed by Luciano Serchia: 'the apparent formal integrity of the S. Stefano complex. . . is the fruit of scholarly renewals designed *ab antiquo*, in a single moment, by the learned

---

[19]   Lanzoni, p. 112.

[20]   The whole Lanzoni-Belvederi position was powerfully criticized by A. Testi Rasponi, 'Note marginali al L. P. di Agnello: IV. Vita Sancti Petronii Episcopi et Confessoris', *Atti e Memorie della R. Deputazione di Storia Patria per le provincie di Romagna*, ser. 4, 2 (1912) [hereafter Testi Rasponi], pp. 120–262. Belvederi's own conclusions from the excavations can be found in his article, 'La S. Giuliana Bolognese', *Rivista di Archeologia Cristiana*, 4 (1927), pp. 141–50.

[21]   Montorsi, p. 236.

members of the Deputazione di Storia Patria Bolognese and by the Works Department of S. Stefano'.[22]

During the final part of this paper, let us avert our eyes from the sad spectacle of the devastation wrought by academic scholarship upon a unique architectural monument. The question remains, when and why did Jerusalem come to Bologna? Is the history of this site typical of Holy Sepulchre veneration in the West, or a special and unusual instance of it? Lanzoni's attempt to recreate the early history of the design is almost certainly erroneous. Curiously, given his outstanding knowledge of the material, his handling of the Bologna evidence is the worst feature. He takes from the *Life of Petronius* a description of a threefold architectural complex: octagon, courtyard, and basilica of the Cross. He ignores all the rest of the buildings, of which one church at least, SS. Vitale e Agricola, although it cannot be dated with confidence, is undoubtedly early. Its absence from the account in the *Life* creates serious doubts about the traditions which it preserved. Moreover, as we have seen, the great basilica of the Cross at the eastern end never existed, although there may well have been a chapel of the Cross there. Lanzoni's misconceptions about the Holy Sepulchre site at Jerusalem, while equally damaging, are easier to understand. As a result of the excavations during the past twenty years, we now have a much clearer picture of the buildings as they would have been seen by Petronius – assuming, that is, that he ever saw them: we have no evidence other than the *Life* that he went to Jerusalem, and its account of the reasons for his visit are implausible. Until the recent excavations, reconstructions had to be based on the literary evidence, which undoubtedly contained confusing features. It has always been a problem that Eusebius of Caesarea, who provides much the fullest account of Constantine's activities, omits the finding of the Cross and the location of Calvary. Because of the variations of the terminology among the early descriptions, Lanzoni seems to have been confused between Constantine's great basilica or

---

[22] Serchia, p. 35. Strictly, there were two 'moments', since the restorations of Gozzadini had a rather different motive from those perpetrated under the influence of Belvederi.

Martyrium, and the hill of Calvary, where a great cross had been placed; and he misunderstood the nature and scope of the reconstruction after the Persian destruction, which occupied a vital place in his dating.[23]

The fact is that there is no evidence, from literature or inscriptions, of any special Jerusalem devotion at Bologna before the ninth century.[24] Lanzoni was influenced in his attempt to find Jerusalem at Bologna in the fifth century by an important book published by Hartmann Grisar in 1899, which represented the early churches of Rome as deliberate recreations of the Holy Places of Palestine.[25] It is true that the Holy Sepulchre was of great importance to Latin Christians in the fourth and fifth centuries, and that they were eager to bring home the spiritual and redemptive power of the Holy Places. They did so, above all, by the import of relics, predominantly of the Holy Cross. Thus at Rome in the 460s (that is, shortly after Petronius' episcopate at Bologna) Pope Hilary added three chapels to the baptistry at the Lateran, dedicating one of them to the Holy Cross, and subsequently Pope Symmachus provided an oratory of the Cross at St Peter's at the Vatican.[26] There were mosaics of Jerusalem, too, notably the magnificent one which still survives in S. Pudenziana, Rome, and which was created in the early years of the fifth century. Nevertheless, we do not find architectural imitations of Jerusalem as described in the *Vita Petronii*. The one Western church which does seem to have been known as 'Jerusalem' in this early period was the Sessorian basilica at Rome. The palace had belonged to Helena, Constantine's mother, and the Emperor himself was said in the *Liber Pontificalis* (probably about 500) to have 'dedicated the name of the church, which is still to our own day called

23 Lanzoni, p. 112: 'The Holy Cross was the principal ornament of the ancient basilica of Calvary at Bologna, as it was of the basilica of Constantine.'

24 The Lombard inscription on the *catino di Pilato* of about 740 contains a mysterious abbreviation 'IHB', but the attempt to treat this as a reference to 'Jerusalem' seems far-fetched.

25 H. Grisar, *Antiche basiliche di Roma imitanti i sanctuari di Gerusalemme e Betlemme*, Analecta Romana, 1899.

26 L. Duchesne, ed., *Liber Pontificalis* [hereafter *LP*], i, 2nd edn (Paris, 1955), pp. 242, 261.

"Jerusalem" '[27] The title persisted for centuries, until it was extended to the present S. Croce in Gerusalemme. It probably received its original title from the presence there of an important fragment of the Holy Cross and of earth from the Holy Sepulchre, which determined its liturgical function as the location for the veneration of the Cross by the Roman church. It was certainly not in any sense a reproduction of the plan of the shrines at Jerusalem. Neither at Rome, nor at Bologna, nor anywhere else, is there any evidence of the production of architectural or planometric copies of the Holy Sepulchre in the late Roman period.

At Bologna overt references to Jerusalem begin in 887, when a diploma of Charles the Fat refers to 'St Stephen which is called holy Jerusalem'.[28] Papal confirmations in subsequent centuries confirm this usage.[29] The nature of the new situation is given a little more definition from a report that a certain S. Bononius learned in his youth 'to visit those Holy Places, which the blessed Petronius had created in his homeland in the image of Palestine'. The *Life of Bononius* must have been written before 1040, and he would have been a young man in the 970s.[30] It is also interesting to note that the neighbouring church of St John, which stands on a slight rise, appears in 959 and 1045 with the title *ecclesia Sancti Iohannis in monte Oliveto*. It sounds as if the church was being taken as a symbol of the Mount of Olives over against the 'Jerusalem' just down the road.[31] These bits of evidence are very patchy, but taken together they indicate that the church was being

[27] *LP* i, p. 179, where 'our own day' probably refers to the beginning of the sixth century. In the late Middle Ages, a mosaic inscription datable before 434 still survived in the church, and referred to it as 'the holy church Jerusalem'.

[28] The diploma of 887 only gives the name of the church, without any details, among a list of possessions: P. Kehr, ed., *Die Urkunden der deutschen Karolinger*, 2, *MGH Dip.* II (Berlin, 1937), no. 171, pp. 276-7. For a document of 1017 see Lanzoni, p. 104.

[29] So Gregory VII, 22 March 1074: 'the monastery of St Stephen, which is called Jerusalem, and which St Petronius built' (J. v. Pflugk-Harttung, ed., *Acta Pontificum Romanorum Inedita* [Tübingen, 1889, repr. Graz, 1958], no. 158, pp. 122-3). This was followed by documents of Paschal II in 1114, Lucius II in 1144, and Anastasius IV in 1153.

[30] On the relationship of the two *Lives* of Bononius, and some of the dating problems, see Lanzoni Appendix 3, and Testi Rasponi, pp. 166-7.

[31] For references, see Belvederi, pp. 340-1. The grant of 959 is damaged, but Belvederi argues convincingly that the reference is to S. Giovanni di Monte Oliveto.

called 'Jerusalem' before the end of the ninth century, and that in the tenth century there were monuments which recalled the Holy Land, and liturgical ceremonies connected with them. Moreover, by 1040 at the very latest the origin of these was being attributed to St Petronius around the middle of the fifth century.

These liturgical developments would fit within the pattern of contemporary devotion. Carol Heitz has claimed that, where Carolingian worship is concerned, Jerusalem was the basis of everything. The ceremonial instituted by Abbot Angilbert at his great monastery of Centula or St-Riquier was focused upon the celebration of Holy Week, and much of it recalls the customs of the church of Jerusalem. The ritual was processional, or 'stational' to adopt the technical term, and appears to derive many elements (such as the Palm Sunday procession and the veneration of the Cross) from Jerusalem practice. Regardless of whether these influences came directly to the Carolingian court from Palestine, or whether the system was evolved by borrowings from earlier practices in the West, the contemporary concern with Palestine is well established. It is doubtful whether pilgrimages to the Holy Land were frequent in the eighth century, but (apart from Charlemagne's diplomatic links with Palestine) a great deal was known about the Holy Places from Adamnan's *De Locis Sanctis* and from the work which Bede based upon it. Designers and architects favoured Jerusalem symbolism rather than any attempt to imitate the Holy Places literally. Depictions of the women on Easter morning are liable to show the Tomb, startlingly to our eyes, as a tower: the 'Westwork' of the great Carolingian abbeys which were the special centre of the Easter liturgy (Pl. 9). A more literal and precise approach to the Holy Sepulchre seems to be characteristic of the tenth century. That was the period when the *Quem queritis* ceremony, re-enacting the visit of the women to the Sepulchre, was very widely adopted, and when for the first time attempts were made to create fairly exact imitations of the Sepulchre itself. Although there are one or two earlier possible instances, the first case which can be cited with confidence is the Sepulchre created by Bishop Conrad, an enthusiastic pilgrim to Palestine and confidant of the Ottonian court, at Constance shortly after 950.

Plate 9   The Three Maries at the Tomb: Staatsbibliothek zu Berlin – Preussischer Kulturbesitz, MS Theol. Lat. Fol. 2, fo. 132v, reproduced by permission.

All of this establishes the context of developments at Bologna, but does not provide us with the details. Changes in the status of the church may help to explain what happened: S. Stefano was restored to the authority of the diocesan bishop in 973, and the first reference to a monastery on the site, under Abbot Martin, is in 983.[32] By this time, the title 'Jerusalem' was almost certainly being given to a number of major churches in Italy, presumably because (as Franco Cardini suggests) there were major Jerusalem relics there. The evidence from Bologna suggests something stronger than this, for at least from the 970s, based on the *Life of Bononius*, there are clear signs of a serious attempt to reproduce the Holy Places there, signs which cannot readily be matched elsewhere at that date.[33] The evidence, with all its limits, thus fits a scenario within which Bologna adopted in the ninth century a stational liturgy, with Jerusalem reminiscences and the nickname 'Jerusalem'. This was apparently followed by a deliberate representation of some of the buildings in the Holy Land. They could well have included the creation within the octagon of the first specific copy of the Jerusalem Sepulchre itself, which would then be roughly contemporary with Bishop Conrad's at Constance. All of this is highly speculative. It fits what we know about S. Stefano locally and it places it within the general evolution of the Jerusalem cult in the West. The decisive evidence for the dating, and the name of the genius who developed the *sette chiese* in this way, is missing.

With the *Vita Petronii* shortly before 1180, we at last arrive on solid ground. At least it tells us how a monk of Bologna imagined a reproduction of the Holy Places in the West. He

[32] The monastery, however, could be older: the change in 973, for all we know, may have been a response to pressure by a monastic community which was already established there. The *Life of Bononius* would suggest a flourishing religious life in the 970s, although it does not strictly compel one to believe in it.

[33] William Montorsi is inclined to discount any major change in this period, and suggests that 'Jerusalem' simply meant a place of pilgrimage, a 'Mecca for pilgrims': see Montorsi, p. 19. For references to literature on the use of the name 'Jerusalem', see F. Cardini, 'L'inizio del movimento crociato in Toscana', in E. Sestan, ed., *Studi di storia medievale e moderna*, 1 (Florence, 1980), pp. 138–9. The monastery of Tuscolo was said to have been called 'Jerusalem', and the same name was given to the district where it stood: diploma of Benedict VIII, 26 April 1017, in H. Zimmermann, ed., *Papsturkunden 896–1046*, 2 (Vienna, 1985), no. 516, pp. 981–3.

says that Petronius provided a copy of the Holy Sepulchre, built with the exact measures that he had taken himself when he was in Palestine. There was a place which symbolized Golgotha or Calvary, and which was marked with a Cross. Outside the complex, Petronius had raised a mound to represent the Mount of Olives, with a round church and, within it, 'in the midst of the courtyard is the place, from which in sight of the disciples Christ ascended into heaven. In the same place the Holy Spirit came upon them.'[34] There was now a demand in the West for representations of the Holy Places at Jerusalem, executed in a fairly literal way. We are well into the period in which people were building quite careful copies of the Sepulchre.[35] It is natural to assume, although the point is curiously difficult to prove, that the main reason for this development was liturgical: the ceremony of the visit to the Tomb on Easter morning demanded something to represent the Sepulchre, and in all probability encouraged churchmen to provide a structure which looked like it.

It is one thing to say that the *Vita Petronii* allows us an insight into the aspirations of the 1170s to bring Jerusalem to the West. It is quite another to suppose, as Lanzoni did, that the text is a witness to what was at S. Stefano at the time. We have to allow for the historical equivalent of the False Memory Syndrome. By this time, the sites at Jerusalem would be well known at Bologna, and Petronius' biographer might well have been describing what he knew of the Holy Places or telling us how splendid the buildings used to be, on the assumption that the founding father would have made a good job of it. The account is questionable at almost every point. The description of Golgotha or the place of the Cross,

---

[34] Lanzoni, p. 232.
[35] At Paderborn, Bishop Meinwerk had built a church 'in the likeness of the Holy church of Jerusalem'. In the foundation charter of 25 May 1036, one of the witnesses, Abbot Wino of Helmershausen, was said to have brought back from Jerusalem 'the measures of the church and Sepulchre'. See G. Mietke, *Die Bautätigkeit Bischof Meinwerik von Paderborn und die frühchristliche und byzantinische Architektur* (Paderborn, 1991). The chapel of St Michael at Fulda, built early in the ninth century, probably did not contain the copy of the Holy Sepulchre which has been wrongly ascribed to it: O. Ellger, *Die Michaelskirche zu Fulda als Zeugnis der Totensorge* (Fulda, 1988).

which was crucial in Lanzoni's reconstruction, certainly makes it sound splendid (although not necessarily large). The splendours may be purely imaginary. Even the most solid of the statements in the *Life of Petronius* raises problems. Undoubtedly, there was a copy of the Sepulchre within the octagon.[36] There is no means of knowing whether the one there now is a replacement of the Sepulchre of 1180, or partial rebuilding. As it stands now, it is a composite, which incorporates the Tomb in the base and then has a representation of Calvary on top. The liturgical aim of associating the Sepulchre and Calvary in the one site is clear: but this is a different architectural expression of it from the one given in the *Life*, where the two are separated by a courtyard.

When we turn outside the complex proper, there is evidence to show that the hill across the main road was by this time crowned by the church of St John the Evangelist, and it is likely that this acted as the starting point of the Palm Sunday procession. But the text seems to make it round, like the Imbomon at Jerusalem which celebrated the Ascension, and there is no reason to think that it was ever that shape, and it is doubtful whether the Ascension was commemorated there. Without doubt, the hill was natural, and not, as the text says, artificially raised by Petronius' command. It looks very much as if the author starts from a familiar identification (this represents liturgically the Mount of Olives) and adds a series of statements of recent devising or his own imagining. As a whole, the *Vita Petronii* expresses the desire, powerfully stimulated by the Crusades, to represent in the West the splendour of Jerusalem, and it is the most elaborate statement, in its period, of the wish to create a systematic layout of the Holy Places. It is more questionable whether this had really been done at S. Stefano, or whether there was any coherent plan behind the elements of Jerusalem representation there.

---

[36] The mention in the *Sermo* of the 'Sepulchre created by St Petronius' provides a clear confirmation of the existence of a version in 1141: see Lanzoni, p. 243. The design of the main part of the existing monument is most naturally seen as late twelfth-century (so that it may, or may not, have been there in 1180). The depictions of the events of Easter morning on the outside of the Tomb are clearly much later additions.

By the time we encounter the next substantial evidence about the Jerusalem at Bologna, in the sixteenth century, it is clear that the complex had been filled with an abundance of reminiscences of the Passion. Monks of the Celestinian Order had taken over at S. Stefano in 1493, and they produced a series of books to publicize the indulgences available for pilgrims and the spiritual exercises appropriate to the sacred sites. The richest of them is an attractive book by Francesco Patricelli, *The Chronicle of the Mysterious and Holy Church and Monastery of S. Stefano at Bologna, traditionally called Jerusalem,* which he published in 1575.[37] This book depended for its history very heavily on the *Vita Petronii,* but it also explored the many references to the Passion which were now incorporated in the buildings. We find once more that reminiscences are being duplicated: for example, one of the chapels 'represents the house in which our Lord Jesus Christ celebrated the Last Supper with his apostles. And it also represents the garden in which he was ... arrested.'[38] Patricelli provides the first enumeration of seven churches in the site, claiming that they were a representation of the seven ancient churches of Rome. S. Stefano had now become a major pilgrim centre, dense with recollections of the Passion, although it was only with the last of these Celestinian books, that of Antonio Casale in 1637, that it was specifically said that Bologna provided a substitute for the journey to Jerusalem which had now become very difficult.[39] These devotions reflect at S. Stefano a desire in the Church at large to commemorate in detail the places of Christ's Passion, which was particularly evidently in Lombardy and at Florence.

The development of the interest in copies of the Holy Sepulchre in the Florentine Renaissance is strikingly illustrated by the life-size model built by Alberti for the chapel of S. Pancrazio in the Rucellai palace in 1468. There is a still

[37] Francesco Patricelli, *Cronica della misteriosa et devota chiesa e Badia di S. Stefano in Bologna* (Bologna, 1575). For a survey of these publications as a group, see G. Fasoli, 'Storiografia Stefaniana tra XII e XVII secolo', in *Stefaniana,* pp. 27–49.

[38] Patricelli, *Cronica,* p. 43: 'rappresenta la Casa, nella quale il Nostro Sig. Giesù Christi, fece l'ultima cena con gli suoi Apostoli. Et rappresenta ancora, l'horto, nel qual'fu egli ... preso.'

[39] For details, see Fasoli, 'Storiografia Stefaniana', p. 40.

more remarkable recreation of the Holy Places of Jerusalem, clearly designed for pilgrimage and for the meditation of the Passion, at S. Vivaldo in Val d'Elsa.[40] It was planned by Tommaso da Firenze in connection with the Franciscan friary there, and the first clear sign of its development can be found in a letter of Leo X in 1516, much the same time as the beginning of Celestine writing at S. Stefano. This ambitious attempt to reproduce the layout of the pilgrimage sites in a series of chapels and pavilions expresses, much more systematically, the type of devotion which had developed around the complex at Bologna. Both sites fit into the general pattern of interest in the Stations of the Cross, which were also evolving in the same period.

S. Stefano at Bologna is a crucial site in the tradition of Western interest in Jerusalem. Its interpretation has been dominated by the passage in the *Life of Petronius*, which was understood as describing the form of the *sette chiese* when it was written in the twelfth century and as providing reliable evidence of its initial purpose in the fifth century, and was subsequently taken as normative in the extensive rebuilding during the period of so-called 'restoration'. In essence, this complex would thus be seen as always the same, *semper eadem*. Recent examination suggests a different conclusion. Further archaeological investigation will clarify many features which are at present in doubt, but the signs are that the evolution of Bologna reflected changing fashions in Jerusalem devotion. The first evidence of a realization of Jerusalem there emerges at the same time as the Carolingian interest in a liturgical reproduction of Jerusalem, and it may (this matter is still in doubt) have developed further with the Ottonian concern with reproductions of the Sepulchre. By the twelfth century, the matter was unambiguous: the *Life of Petronius*, whether it provides a description of the site or a fantasy about it, is undoubtedly a powerful expression of Christendom's desire, in the period of the Crusades, to bring the Holy Sepulchre to the West. During the later Middle Ages and the Counter-

---

[40]   See Neri, ch. 12, and F. Cardini and G. Vannini, 'San Vivaldo in Valdelsa: problemi topografici ed interpretazioni simboliche di una "Gerusalemme" cinquecentesca in Toscana', in *Religiosità e società in Valdelsa nel basso Medioevo*, Atti del Convegno di S. Vivaldo, 29 settembre 1979, Società Storica della Valdelsa, 1980.

Reformation, the site and its interpretation evolved further in line with the growth of the affective piety of the Passion, which provided sites such as San Vivaldo and above all the devotion to the Stations of the Cross. And finally, the desire in the modern period for authentic 'restoration', based as it was on dubious criteria, has left us with the fascinating but infuriating S. Stefano complex as we see it today.

University of Southampton

PERCEPTIONS OF THE ANGLO-SAXON PAST IN THE TENTH-CENTURY MONASTIC REFORM MOVEMENT*

by SIMON COATES

Retrospection is a recognized characteristic of reform movements. An appeal to the past legitimates ideological concerns which seek to replace a state of affairs considered decadent and decayed. Reforming rhetoric depends on the past as a means of proving its value and credibility. Such preservation of the past as a key organizing principle in transforming events is necessarily selective and often has a tendency towards schematization and simplification. Not only does the reforming agenda determine what aspects of the past are remembered, and hence what aspects are buried, but it also determines who is responsible for the act of remembering itself.[1] 'Different groups of people remember things in different ways.'[2] The purpose of this paper is to examine the manner in which the Anglo-Saxon past was perceived and utilized during the tenth-century monastic reform movement. It will be shown how, under an influence which was heavily Benedictine in inspiration, the collective memory of monks created a picture of the Anglo-Saxon past which was 'all of a piece and all monastic'.[3] The past was closely linked to the exercise of power. It will thus

* An earlier version of this paper was first presented in a somewhat different form in St Andrews in February 1995. I am very grateful to Robert Bartlett, Richard Sharpe, Alan Thacker, David Rollason, Catherine Cubitt, and Christopher Holdsworth for discussion and comment.

[1] There is a rapidly growing literature on the role of memory in medieval culture, among the studies see Janet Coleman, *Ancient and Medieval Memories. Studies in the Reconstruction of the Past* (Cambridge, 1992); James Fentress and Chris Wickham, *Social Memory* (Oxford, 1992); Mary Carruthers, *The Book of Memory. A Study of Memory in Medieval Culture* (Cambridge, 1990); Patrick Geary, *Phantoms of Remembrance. Memory and Oblivion at the end of the First Millenium* (Princeton, 1994).

[2] Chris Wickham, 'Lawyers' time: history and memory in tenth- and eleventh-century Italy', in H. Mayr-Harting and R. I. Moore, eds, *Studies in Medieval History Presented to R. H. C. Davis* (London, 1985), p. 54.

[3] A. T. Thacker, 'Æthelwold and Abingdon', in B. Yorke, ed., *Bishop Æthelwold: his Career and Influence* (Woodbridge, 1988) [hereafter, *Bishop Æthelwold*], p. 63.

be shown how this monastic view of the past competed with an alternative tenth-century view and was ultimately to triumph over its competitor.

The monks of the tenth century cultivated an historiographical tradition which exalted the age of Bede. They did so for a specific purpose: history acted as propaganda which justified their take-over of the religious system.[4] It legitimized the ideology which they sought to espouse, providing them with examples of monastic organization which they could follow. The replacement of clerical communities by communities of monks was presented as a return to the golden age of Northumbrian monasticism exemplified by Bede. The influence of literary models derived from Bede can be traced in their writings. The writings of Bede provided the monastic reformers with literary *topoi* which they could use to justify their own policies, methods, and concerns. The reign of Edgar was perceived to mark the recovery of a golden age in ecclesiastical life which had existed in the seventh and eighth centuries. The reformers therefore did not see their insistence on the imposition of the Rule of St Benedict as innovatory but rather as an act of restoration. Bede's *Historia Ecclesiastica* offered the reformers precedents and advice. The prologue to the *Regularis Concordia*, the code of observance of the monastic reform movement, shows that the author probably read the *Responsiones* of Gregory the Great found in Bede's *Historia Ecclesiastica*. It claimed that the reformers summoned monks from the reformed monasteries of Fleury and Ghent because they called to mind 'the letters in which our holy patron Gregory instructed the blessed Augustine that for the advancement of the rude English Church, he should establish therein the seemly customs of the Gallic Churches as well as those of Rome'.[5] Furthermore, the *Regularis Concordia* quoted from Bede's letter to Bishop Egbert of York when it

[4] Antonia Gransden, 'Traditionalism and continuity during the last century of Anglo-Saxon monasticism', *JEH*, 40 (1989), pp. 169–70.
[5] *Regularis Concordia*, ed. and trans. T. Symons (London 1953), p. 3; Bede, *Historia Ecclesiastica Gentis Anglorum*, ed. and trans. B. Colgrave and R. A. B. Mynors, *Bede's Ecclesiastical History of the English People* (Oxford, 1969) [hereafter Bede, *HE*], pp. 78–103.

authorized that monks of a cathedral monastery should elect a bishop from their own number in the same way as monks of an ordinary monastery elected their abbot. If no one suitable could be found they were authorized to choose a monk from another monastery.[6]

Further texts associated with the monastic reform movement utilized Bede's writings. Two more or less authentic texts concerning the monastic foundations at Ely and Peterborough refer explicitly to Bede; whilst the first section of the document known as *An Old English account of King Edgar's establishment of monasteries* quoted from the *Historia Ecclesiastica* when it recounted the establishment of Christianity in English through the impact of Gregory the Great's mission.[7] St Oswald's biographer Byrthferth, a monk from Ramsey, records how Oswald was motivated to re-establish a monastery at Ripon after having called to mind the original foundation made by St Wilfrid.[8] The reformers' invective against clerical communities was also influenced by Bede. Bede's *Letter to Egbert* had attacked the licentiousness of clerics, and its condemnation of secular owners of monasteries who gave land to their wives for the foundation of convents was strikingly similar to the allegations found in the *Life of St Oswald* that unreformed communities contained married clerks who squandered treasure on their wives.[9] Similarly, Bede's concern with the manner in which appropriation of monastic lands by the lay nobility led to the secularization of monasteries and a decline of the religious life influenced the prohibition of secular overlordship of

6   Symonds, *Regularis Concordia*, p. 6; Bede, *Epistola ad Ecgbertum*, ed. C. Plummer, *Venerabilis Baedae Opera Historica*, 2 vols (Oxford, 1896), 1, p. 413.

7   Peter H. Sawyer, *Anglo-Saxon Charters: an Annotated List and Bibliography*, Royal Historical Society Guides and Handbooks, 8 (London, 1968), nos. 779, 782; Patrick Wormald, 'Æthelwold and his continental counterparts: contact, comparison, contrast', in *Bishop Æthelwold*, p. 40; 'An Old English account of King Edgar's establishment of monasteries', in D. Whitelock, R. Brett, and C. N. L. Brooke, *Councils and Synods with other Documents relating to the English Church, I, 871–1204* (Oxford, 1981), pp. 142–54, at pp. 143–5. Its account is based on Bede, *HE*, pp. 68–79, 114–17, 122–35.

8   'Vita Oswaldi archiepiscopi Eboracensis', in J. Raine, ed., *The Historians of the Church of York and its Archbishops*, 3 vols, *RS* (London, 1879–94), 1, p. 462. For Byrthferth's authorship see M. Lapidge, 'The hermeneutic style in tenth-century Anglo-Latin literature', *Anglo-Saxon England*, 4 (1975), pp. 91–5.

9   Plummer, *Bedae Opera*, pp. 413–16; Raine, *Historians*, 1, p. 411.

monasteries outlined in the *Regularis Concordia*.[10] Furthermore, in the *Historia Ecclesiastica* the reformers found a
concern for the unity of the English Church. This influenced
their own concerns with unity found in the espousal of a
uniform Benedictinism which would govern English
ecclesiastical life.

In appealing to the pre-Viking past the Benedictine
reformers therefore created a picture of it as age of uniformity
marked by universal adherence to the Rule of St Benedict.
This perception of the past was, however, the invention of
the monastic reformers themselves. It injected bias into
Anglo-Saxon history by ignoring the fluidity and diversity
within early Anglo-Saxon monasticism and by suggesting
that the Rule of St Benedict was the standard rule by which
monks regulated their lives in the early Anglo-Saxon period
when in actuality it was merely one rule among many.[11]
Furthermore, it suggested that monks could be easily
separated from the secular clergy and that monasteries were
in need of reform because they had fallen away from strict
Benedictine standards.

The tenth-century reformers possessed a strong interest in
the cult of saints. Memory and retrospection are central to
such a phenomenon. Invocation, the act of remembering a
saint, bound together the past and present, linking the holy
dead to a living audience. Relics could trigger off memory. St
Oswald used the relics of the Northumbrian saints for his
attempted refoundation at Ripon, placing the bones of
Ripon's original founder, Wilfrid, in a shrine.[12] Æthelwold
exploited the cult of saints in his reformed monasteries,
including the feast of St Ætheldreda of Ely in his benedictional, promoting the cult of St Swithun at Winchester by

---

[10] Plummer, *Bedae Opera*, pp. 415–16; Symons, *Regularis Concordia*, p. 7.

[11] On the diversity evident in early Anglo-Saxon monastic life see Patrick Sims-
Williams, *Religion and Literature in Western England, 600–800* (Cambridge, 1990),
pp. 115–17; Patrick Wormald, 'Bede and Benedict Biscop', in Gerald Bonner, ed.,
*Famulus Christi: Essays in Commemoration of the Thirteenth Centenary of the Birth of the
Venerable Bede* (London, 1976), pp. 141–69; Sarah Foot, 'What was an early Anglo-
Saxon monastery?', in J. Loades, ed., *Monastic Studies* (Bangor, 1990), pp. 48–57;
idem, 'Anglo-Saxon minsters: a review of terminology', in John Blair and Richard
Sharpe, eds, *Pastoral Care before the Parish* (Leicester, 1992), pp. 212–26.

[12] Raine, *Historians*, 1, p. 462.

translating the body to a new shrine and lavishing relics on Thorney.[13] Late tenth- and early eleventh-century writers gave the monastic reformers, Dunstan, Æthelwold, and Oswald, literary recognition. In so doing they revived a well-established Anglo-Saxon hagiographical tradition where Bede again appears to have been the predominant influence. The *Life of St Oswald* borrowed a passage from Bede's prose *Life of St Cuthbert*, whilst its concern with the topography of the Ramsey area mirrors Bede's interest in topographical details.[14] Wulfstan of Winchester utilized Bede's writings in a number of instances in his *Life of St Æthelwold*. Its story of how Æthelwold broke up silver vessels from the church treasury to give them to the poor is similar to a story of King Oswald found in Bede's *Historia Ecclesiastica*.[15] Ælfric drew heavily on Bede's *Historia Ecclesiastica* for his *Lives of Saints* and Byrthferth was a Bedan scholar, his *Enchiridion* being a virtual commentary on Bede's books on time.[16]

The expulsion of worldly canons from cathedrals and their replacement with monks (which forms a central theme of *Lives* such as the *Life of St Æthelwold* and *Life of St Oswald*) is notably absent from the *Life of St Dunstan* by the anonymous author known only as 'B'. He was probably a canon himself, and hence not inclined to criticize the gourmandizing married clerks of English cathedrals.[17] B's *Life of St Dunstan* presented an ideal of sanctity which drew upon a model different from the writings of Bede employed by the monastic reformers. Its presentation of Dunstan's status as a

---

13   *The Benedictional of St Æthelwold*, facsimile ed. G. F. Warner and H. A. Wilson (Oxford, 1910), p. 37; *Liber Vitae: Register and Martyrology of New Minster and Hyde Abbey, Winchester*, ed. Walter de Gray Birch (London, 1892), p. 286; Thacker, 'Æthelwold and Abingdon', pp. 59–63; *Willelmi Malmesbiriensis monachi de gestis pontificum Anglorum libri quinque*, ed. N. E. S. A. Hamilton, RS (London, 1870), p. 327.

14   Raine, *Historians*, 1, pp. 448, 454.

15   Wulfstan of Winchester, *Vita S. Æthelwoldi*, in *Wulfstan of Winchester: The Life of St Æthelwold* [hereafter *Wulfstan*], ed. M. Lapidge and M. Winterbottom (Oxford, 1991), pp. 44–7; Bede, *HE*, pp. 230–1.

16   Gransden, 'Traditionalism and continuity', pp. 183–4; M. Lapidge, 'Byrthferth of Ramsey and the early sections of the *Historia Regum* attributed to Symeon of Durham', *Anglo-Saxon England*, 10 (1982), esp. pp. 120–1.

17   *Wulfstan*, pp. 30–1; Ælfric, *Vita sancti Æthelwoldi*, ed. M. Winterbottom in *Three Lives of English Saints* (Toronto, 1972), pp. 22–3; Raine, *Historians*, 1, p. 411; Gransden, 'Traditionalism and continuity', p. 170.

saint reveals a retrospective tradition which rivalled the monastic reformers' own. The remainder of this paper will examine B's conception of sanctity and the use which it made of the Anglo-Saxon past.

B found sanctity in secularity, interpreting such secularity as the natural function of the place of ecclesiastics in society.[18] B's Dunstan is a saint involved in the world rather than in ascetic withdrawal from it. Dunstan did not seek solitude. He moved among the secular aristocracy and was at home within their world. A theme which runs through B's work is that of the close association of ecclesiastics with kings. Dunstan served as counsellor to King Eadmund, and in his descriptions of such service B cited a series of scriptural texts to justify such action. Dunstan was reminded of the duty of obedient service to a prince by the fact that the powers that be are ordained of God and damnation was reserved for those who resisted them.[19] Under King Eadred, Dunstan achieved a greater position at court by serving as the King's chief adviser and was entrusted with many title-deeds and treasures.[20] B therefore presented close association with the King as one of the essential qualifications for sanctity.[21]

In examining 'the aristocratic environment of early English Christianity', Patrick Wormald has shown how, in the age of Bede, the conversion of the English aristocracy was marked by the persistence of a secular and Germanic tradition in Church and society.[22] B's *Life* testifies that this process

[18] *Vita Sancti Dunstani*, ed. W. Stubbs in *Memorials of Saint Dunstan*, RS (London, 1874) [hereafter *Memorials*]. The *Life* is discussed in ibid., pp. x–xxx; Michael Lapidge, 'B and the *Vita S. Dunstani*', in Nigel Ramsay, Margaret Sparks, and Tim Tatton-Brown, eds, *St Dunstan: his Life, Times and Cult* (Woodbridge, 1992) [hereafter *Dunstan*], pp. 247–59; idem, 'The hermeneutic style', pp. 81–3; Nicholas Brooks, *The Early History of the Church of Canterbury* (Leicester, 1984), p. 246; D. Pontifex, 'St Dunstan in his first biography', *Downside Review*, 51 (1933), pp. 20–40, 309–25; Antonia Gransden, *Historical Writing in England c. 550 to c. 1307* (London, 1974), pp. 78–83; J. Armitage Robinson, *The Times of St Dunstan* (Oxford, 1923), pp. 81–103.

[19] Stubbs, *Memorials*, pp. 21–3, citing Matt. 22.21, Rom. 13.1–2.

[20] Stubbs, *Memorials*, pp. 29–30.

[21] David Rollason, 'The concept of sanctity in the early Lives of St Dunstan', in *Dunstan*, pp. 270–1; idem, *Saints and Relics in Anglo-Saxon England* (Oxford, 1989), pp. 167–74.

[22] Patrick Wormald, 'Bede, Beowulf and the conversion of the Anglo-Saxon aristocracy', British Archaeological Reports, British Series 46 (Oxford, 1978), pp. 32–95. The quotation is at p. 57.

continued into the tenth century. For Dunstan, close association with the King meant the appropriation of the values which the clerical wing of the aristocracy had regarded as the identifying badges of secular life. The Council of Clofesho of 747 had decreed that nunneries should not be dens of feasting, drunkenness, and luxury but habitations of those 'who read and sing psalms' rather than those who wove 'vainglorious apparel'. *Monasteria*, likewise, were not to be 'receptacles of recreative arts, of poets, harpers, musicians and buffoons, but habitations of those who pray and read and praise God'.[23] In addition to cultivating the art of harp playing, Dunstan was skilled in other crafts: painting, writing, and weaving. He designed a stole for Æthelwyn adorned with gold and gems.[24] Before he studied sacred and religious volumes he had studied songs about the ancestral race and funeral songs of a historical and narrative nature.[25] He was also not inclined to follow the warnings of Bede's *Letter to Egbert*, Alcuin, the English synodal tradition, and the *Regularis Concordia*, concerning ecclesiastical attendance at feasts.[26] B's Dunstan engaged in wining and dining on several occasions. Donald Bullough has stressed the importance of drinking to early medieval societies in his study of the aristocratic *convivium*, emphasizing how the barriers between the secular and ecclesiastical worlds were in a sense obliterated in solemn feasts.[27] Dunstan attended the dedication of a church at Winchester which was marked by a great celebration and *caritatis convivia*.[28] When Eadred failed in his

---

23   Council of Clofesho, 747 ch. 20, in *Councils and Ecclesiastical Documents Relating to Great Britain and Ireland*, ed. A. W. Haddan and W. Stubbs, 3 vols (Oxford, 1869–74), 3, p. 369.

24   Stubbs, *Memorials*, pp. 20–1; James Campbell, 'England c. 991', in Janet Cooper, ed., *The Battle of Maldon. Fiction and Fact* (London, 1993), pp. 11–12.

25   Stubbs, *Memorials*, pp. 10–11.

26   Plummer, *Bedae Opera*, pp. 407–18; *Alcuini Epistolae*, in *MGH Epistolae Karolini Ævi II*, ed. E. Dümmler (Berlin, 1974), pp. 42–4, 56–8, 167–70, 181–4; Haddan and Stubbs, *Councils*, 3, p. 369; Symons, *Regularis Concordia*, p. 7.

27   Donald Bullough, *Carolingian Renewal* (Manchester, 1992), p. 281; idem, *Friends, Neighbours and Fellow-Drinkers: Aspects of community and conflict in the Early Medieval West*, H. M. Chadwick Memorial Lectures, 1 (Cambridge, 1991); Campbell, 'England c. 991', pp. 5–6; on the importance of banquets to the tenth-century aristocracy see Heinrich Fichtenau, *Living in the Tenth Century* (Chicago, 1991), pp. 56–64.

28   Stubbs, *Memorials*, p. 14. Compare Byrthferth's account of the great

attempts to make Dunstan Bishop of Crediton, he asked his mother to attempt to get Dunstan to accept over dinner.[29] The story of how Eadwig left his coronation feast to consort with women and how Dunstan forcibly led him away from the women, placing the crown on his head and leading him back to the royal court, illustrates not only Dunstan's authority but also his presence at a banquet.[30] Thus B's Dunstan did not distance himself at all from the secular nobles of his time in his unrestrained and often harsh style of regulating and ruling and his love of the harp and weaving. He was a saint who moved in a world of music, magnificence, and treasure whose claims to sanctity were related to this world.

B's commitment to the values of the secular aristocracy and attribution of sanctity to an aristocratic ecclesiastic may be explained by his own background, predilections, and concerns. Although it has been proved that B was an Englishman, he spent much of his life on the continent as a canon at Liège in the notable cathedral school of St Martin's.[31] B's continental connections in part explain the features of his *Life*. Continental saints' *Lives* offered him literary models upon which he could draw. Firstly, the presentation of Dunstan's sanctity in B's *Life* is similar to that found in Ruotger's *Life* of Bruno, the tenth-century archbishop of Cologne who had died in 965.[32] Bruno of Cologne was both

celebrations held at Ramsey in 991 and the *convivium* which took place after the service in Raine, *Historians*, 1, p. 465, and Eadred's visit to lay the foundations of the new church at Abingdon where the mead was constantly renewed, as recounted in *Wulfstan*, pp. 22–5; Winterbottom, *Three Lives*, p. 20; Thacker, 'Æthelwold and Abingdon', pp. 56–7. On the significance of *caritatis convivia* see D. A. Bullough, 'What has Ingeld to do with Lindisfarne?', *Anglo-Saxon England*, 22 (1993), pp. 102–8.

[29] Stubbs, *Memorials*, pp. 29–30.

[30] Ibid., pp. 32–3.

[31] Lapidge, 'B and the *Vita S. Dunstani*', pp. 251–6; Alan Thacker, 'Cults at Canterbury: relics and reform under Dunstan and his successors', in *Dunstan*, p. 223; Brooks, *Church of Canterbury*, pp. 245–6.

[32] Rollason, 'Concept of sanctity', pp. 261–72; Ruotger, *Vita domini Brunonis Coloniensis archiepiscopi*, ed. B. Krusch, *MGH. SS*, IV (Hanover, 1841), pp. 252–75; L. Zoepf, *Das Heiligenleben im 10 Jahrhundert* (Leipzig and Berlin, 1908); F. Prinz, *Klerus und Krieg im frühen Mittelalter* (Stuttgart, 1971), pp. 175–200. For a view which challenges the perception of the *Vita Brunonis* as the expression of a characteristic ideology of the Ottonian church see T. Reuter, 'The "Imperial Church System" of the Ottonian and Salian Rulers: a reconsideration', *JEH*, 33 (1982), pp. 347–74, esp.

bellator and *orator*, harmoniously combining political and religious roles in the exercise of his episcopal office.[33] Bruno moved in the highest circles. He was the son of King Henry I of Germany and was called to court by his brother, Otto I, who made him chancellor and archchaplain. He also served for a period as Archduke of Lotharingia. Like Dunstan, he was said to have lived virtuously in the midst of the royal court, refusing to laugh at the comedies of classical authors, sleeping and bathing infrequently and always wearing a rough tunic and skins even when amongst his richly clad fellows. He also exercised political authority by instructing Otto I's rebellious son Liudolf to obey the king.[34] Secondly, it is possible to compare B's *Life* to those early medieval saints' *Lives* concerned with the *Adelsheilige* or 'noble saint'.[35] The thought-world of such *Lives* is dominated by conceptions of nobility, church, and service to the king. Such saints dominate Merovingian hagiography of the seventh and eighth centuries, and although they observe ideals of asceticism they remain tied to their own class and its scale of values.[36] Thus Arnulf of Metz was praised for his prowess as a warrior, Eligius of Noyon was competent in all the requirements of court service, and Corbinian cultivated a love of pedigree horses.[37] In their stress upon the compatibility between the religious and political roles of the saint

371, and J. Nightingale, 'Bishop Gerard of Toul (963–94) and attitudes to episcopal office', in T. Reuter, ed., *Warriors and Churchmen in the High Middle Ages: Essays Presented to Karl Leyser* (London, 1992), pp. 41–62.

[33] For further bishops who combined these roles see O. Köhler, *Das Bild des geistlichen Fürsten in den Viten des 10. 11. 12 Jahrhunderts*, Abhandlungen zur mittleren und neueren Geschichte, 77 (Berlin, 1935), pp. 9–45.

[34] *MGH. SS.*, IV, pp. 260, 263, 265–6.

[35] K. Bosl, 'Der Adelsheilige. Idealtypus und Wirklichkeit, Gesellschaft und Kultur im Merowingerzeitlichen Beyern des 7. und 8. Jahrhunderts', in L. Boehm, et al., eds, *Speculum historiale. Festschrift für Johannes Spörl* (Freiburg and Munich, 1965), pp. 167–87; G. Scheibelreiter, 'Der frühfrankische Episkopat. Bild und Wirklichkeit', *Frühmittelalterliche Studien*, 17 (1983), pp. 131–47; M. Heinzelmann, 'Sanctitas und Tugendadel', *Francia*, 3 (1977), pp. 741–52; F. Prinz, *Frühes Mönchtum im Frankenreich* (Munich and Vienna, 1965), pp. 496–503.

[36] F. Irsigler, 'On the aristocratic character of early Frankish society', in T. Reuter, ed., *The Medieval Nobility* (Amsterdam, New York, and Oxford, 1979), p. 117.

[37] *Vita Arnulfi*, ed. B. Krusch in *MGH. SRM*, II (Hanover, 1888), p. 433; *Vita Eligii*, ed. B. Krusch in *MGH. SRM*, IV (Hanover, 1902), p. 680; *Vita Corbiniani*, ed. B. Krusch in *MGH. SRM*, VI (Hanover, 1913), pp. 205–6, 211–14, 221.

and the manner in which commitment to aristocratic values and the involvement of individuals in worldly affairs could serve to establish rather than to diminish sanctity, such *Lives* are clearly comparable to B's own *Life*.

B left England for Liège in 960. Twelve years before, in 948, Archbishop Odo of Canterbury had acquired the relics of St Wilfrid which had been brought to Canterbury after King Eadred had burned Ripon on an expedition to the north. The theft of these relics was accompanied by the acquisition of a copy of Stephanus' *Vita Wilfridi* which was used by a member of the archbishop's *familia*, Frithegod, to produce a metrical *Life* of the saint.[38] This renewed interest in the cult of Wilfrid and the establishment of the cult at Canterbury may not have been lost on B, whose *Vita* was composed in an attempt to secure the patronage of Archbishop Ælfric. Although sharing the tenth-century monastic reformers' concern with the Anglo-Saxon past, the literary model which appears to have influenced the composition of his *Vita* was not derived from Bede. It was rather the *Life of Wilfrid* by Stephanus.

Stephanus' *Vita Wilfridi* has been compared with the *Lives* of the *Adelsheilige*, and Wilfrid's possession of an armed retinue and concern with treasure show how his sanctity in part reflected the aristocratic nature of early English Christianity.[39] Stephanus espoused a concept of sanctity based upon the ability of saints to suffer and overcome persecution. Wilfrid's defence of his diocese and monastic empire aroused enmity among both clergy and laity, leading to his exile. Dunstan was similarly a saint who suffered persecution. His diligence in his studies led his kinsmen at court to regard him with envy. They accused him of seeking

---

[38] Thacker, 'Cults at Canterbury', pp. 235–6; Brooks, *Church of Canterbury*, pp. 227–31. On Frithegod see Michael Lapidge, 'A Frankish scholar in tenth-century England: Frithegod of Canterbury/Fredegaud of Brioude', *Anglo-Saxon England*, 17 (1988), pp. 45–65. On the importance of translations of saints' relics in the late Anglo-Saxon period see D. W. Rollason, 'The shrines of saints in later Anglo-Saxon England: distribution and significance', in Richard Morris, ed., *The Anglo-Saxon Church: Papers on History, Architecture and Archaeology in Honour of Dr H. M. Taylor*, Council for British Archaeology Research Report, 60 (London, 1986), pp. 32–43; idem, 'Relic-cults as an instrument of royal policy c.900–c.1050', *Anglo-Saxon England*, 15 (1986), pp. 95–6.

[39] Wormald, 'Bede, Beowulf', p. 56.

after occult knowledge, expelled him from court and threw him into a pond.[40] When Eadwig came to power, Dunstan lost the favourable position at court he had attained under Eadred. His property was seized, and he was driven into exile in Gaul whilst his followers were punished.[41] Both Dunstan and Wilfrid were victims of the threats of royal women. Dunstan's exile was precipitated by Æthelgifu, whilst Wilfrid's monastic wealth aroused the envy of Egfrith's Queen, Iurminburg, who persuaded her husband to drive the Bishop into exile.[42] In the passages describing these events both B and Stephanus utilized the same motif, describing the offending women as wicked Jezebels.[43]

Although Wilfrid and Dunstan aroused the hostility of royal women, they also moved in more favourable female circles. Egfrith triumphed over the Picts whilst he obeyed Wilfrid, and the saint encouraged that King's first wife, Æthelthryth, to pursue the religious life.[44] Dunstan similarly was closely associated with a female saint, waiting upon the lady Æthelfleda, who had built a house at Glastonbury, during her last illness.[45] Wilfrid's devotion to the apostles Peter and Andrew found expression in his dedication of the churches at Ripon, Hexham, and Oundle to those saints whilst his devotion to St Peter was expressed through his consistent allegiance to the papal see.[46] This pattern of associating a saint with the apostles is found in B's *Life* when Dunstan experiences a vision of Peter, Paul, and Andrew, the three saints closely linked to Wilfrid, and is chastized by the latter for refusing to accept the bishopric of Crediton.[47] Wilfrid, like Dunstan, was also no stranger to banquets. The dedication of his church at Ripon was followed by a feast

[40] Stubbs, *Memorials*, pp. 11–13.
[41] Ibid., pp. 33–5.
[42] Eddius Stephanus, *Vita Wilfridi*, ed. and trans. Bertram Colgrave, *The Life of Bishop Wilfrid by Eddius Stephanus* (Cambridge, 1927) [hereafter *VW*], pp. 48–51.
[43] Janet Nelson, 'Queens as Jezebels: the careers of Brunhild and Balthild in Merovingian History', in her *Politics and Ritual in Early Medieval Europe* (London, 1986), pp. 1–48, is a subtle analysis of the use of this motif.
[44] *VW*, pp. 40–3.
[45] Stubbs, *Memorials*, pp. 17–18.
[46] *VW*, pp. 34–7, 44–7, 140–3.
[47] Stubbs, *Memorials*, pp. 30–1.

which lasted three days.[48] The sanctity of Wilfrid and Dunstan was proven in part by the fates of their enemies. B assumed that Eadwig's loss of territories north of the Thames and his premature death were a result of his failure to listen to wise councillors. Eadwig's punishment proved that God supported Dunstan whenever his devotion to God led him into conflict with secular powers. The punishment of Eadwig was marked by the elevation of Dunstan, who was recalled from exile by Edgar and raised to the episcopate.[49] King Aldfrith's refusal to accept the vindication of Wilfrid's rights by the apostolic see led to his death; and even though the King reconciled himself to Wilfrid on his death bed, he still perished.[50]

The parallels between B's *Life* and Stephanus' *Vita* are clear. Whereas the tenth-century monastic reformers thought and felt very much like Bede, B's *Life* is closer to Stephanus in its willingness to discuss Dunstan's involvement in secular affairs and to show the effect these had on Dunstan's ecclesiastical career. The relative lack of Canterbury material in B's *Life* when compared with the accounts of Dunstan's early career at Glastonbury suggests that B was connected not with Canterbury but with Glastonbury where he had perhaps trained, and was not therefore directly a witness to the promotion of Wilfrid's cult in mid-tenth-century Canterbury.[51] Thus, although the parallels between B and Stephanus' *Life* may not prove direct borrowing, it is clear that B's conception of sanctity owed more to Stephanus than to Bede. Dunstan's authoritative exercise of his episcopal office as found, for example, in B's account of his work as a judge contrasts with saints such as Cuthbert, Aidan, Chad, Cedd, and John of Beverley, who moved uneasily in secular society and sought withdrawal from it.[52]

B's perception of the Anglo-Saxon past, however, reveals him to be a man out of his time. Disturbed by the less

[48] *VW*, pp. 34–7.
[49] Stubbs, *Memorials*, pp. 35–7.
[50] *VW*, pp. 124–9.
[51] Lapidge, 'B and the *Vita S. Dunstani*', p. 257.
[52] Stubbs, *Memorials*, p. 49; Bede, *HE*, pp. 218–21, 226–9, 254–67, 278–89, 294–310, 314–17, 332–47, 404–15, 430–49, 456–73.

congenial atmosphere at Liège brought about by the rule of Bishop Notger, he sought employment in England. He wrote to Æthelgar, sometime abbot of the New Minster, Winchester, seeking permission to study there.[53] Winchester cathedral had, however, been purged of canons by Æthelwold in 964 and the New Minster founded in 966 upon strict Benedictine lines.[54] B also attempted to return home by addressing the *Life of St Dunstan* to Archbishop Ælfric seven years after Dunstan's death. Ælfric, however, was a monastic reformer who may have been responsible for the installation of monks at Christ Church.[55] B thus sought to return to a world which had been heavily influenced by monastic reform and was thus perceived as an outsider. As a clerk he was worldly and his pleas for patronage were to be ignored.

The competition for power over the past reflected in these rival retrospections was thus won by the collective memory of the monastic reformers, for whom Bede rather than Stephanus framed the agenda. Their espousal of the view that a uniform concept of Benedictinism governed the organization of monastic houses and that there were monastic cathedrals in the eighth century passed into later works written by Benedictine historians. William of Malmesbury accepted the view that the early Anglo-Saxon cathedral at Canterbury was staffed by monks and not secular priests. He described Oda as the first archbishop of Canterbury not to be in monastic orders, and also stressed that at least since the time of Archbishop Laurence there had always been monks at Canterbury.[56] Gervase of Canterbury specified that the seventh- and eighth-century archbishops had been monks before their election.[57] This picture was also accepted by David Knowles, who believed that early Anglo-Saxon houses were Benedictine in spirit if not in fact.[58]

---

[53] Stubbs, *Memorials*, pp. 385–8.

[54] *Wulfstan*, pp. 30–7.

[55] Brooks, *Church of Canterbury*, pp. 257–9.

[56] Hamilton, *Willelmi Malmesbiriensis de gestis pontificum*, pp. 21, 32.

[57] *The Historical Works of Gervase of Canterbury*, ed. W. Stubbs, 2 vols, *RS* (London, 1879–80), 2, pp. 338, 344.

[58] David Knowles, *The Monastic Order in England: A History of its Development from the Times of St Dunstan to the Fourth Lateran Council 940–1216*, 2nd edn (Cambridge, 1963), p. 24.

By composing a *Life* which in its thought-world and preoccupations had more in common with Stephanus' *Life of Wilfrid* than with Bede's writings, B allows an alternative, individual memory to be recovered. With its juxtaposition of accounts of banquets and the patronage of harpists in clerical environments alongside the saint's personal devotion, asceticism, and contribution to the growth of the Church, the more conventional content of a saint's *Vita*, B's *Life of Dunstan* serves as a valuable window on the state of the English Church before the monastic reform movement began in earnest in the latter half of the tenth century. It stands apart from many of the written sources of tenth-century England and serves as a useful counterbalance to them since it was not composed from a monastic perspective but rather by a member of the despised class of secular clerks whom the reformers attacked. Whilst the reformers remembered the Anglo-Saxon past as the golden age of Bede, B remembered it as the age of Wilfrid where secularity could be harnessed to the needs of the Church. In so doing B reveals that the importance of the part played by traditionalism and the Anglo-Saxon past in shaping the tenth-century Church was wider than has hitherto been supposed.[59]

University of Edinburgh

---

[59] Gransden, 'Traditionalism and continuity'; pp. 159–207.

ST SYMEON THE NEW THEOLOGIAN (969-1022):
BYZANTINE SPIRITUAL RENEWAL
IN SEARCH OF A PRECEDENT

by JOHN ANTHONY MCGUCKIN

INTRODUCTORY REMARKS

St Symeon the New Theologian is, without question, one of the most original and intriguing writers of medieval Byzantium. Indeed, although still largely unknown in the West, he is surely one of the greatest of all Christian mystical writers;[1] not only for the remarkable autobiographical accounts he gives of several visions of the divine light, but also for the passionate quality of his exquisite *Hymns of Divine Love*, the remarkable intensity of his pneumatological doctrine,[2] and the corresponding fire he brings to his preaching of reform in the internal and external life of the Church. He was a highly controversial figure in his own day. His disciples venerated him as a saint who had returned to the roots of the Christian tradition and personified its repristinization. His opponents, who secured his deposition and exile, regarded him as a dangerously unbalanced incompetent who, by overstressing the value of personal religious fervour, had endangered the stability of that tradition. The *Vita* which we possess was composed in 1054, in an attempt to rehabilitate Symeon's memory and prepare for the return of his relics to the capital from which he had been expelled when alive. This paper will investigate how he himself understood and appropriated aspects of the earlier tradition (particularly monastic spirituality), hoping

[1] There are now several English versions of selected works: G. A. Maloney, *Hymns of Divine Love* (Denville, N.J., 1975); C. De Catanzaro, trans., *St Symeon the New Theologian: The Catechetical Discourses* (New York, 1980) [hereafter cited as *Cat.* for the textual reference, and Catanzaro for pagination and commentary]; P. McGuckin, *Symeon the New Theologian: The Practical and Theological Chapters and the Three Theological Discourses* (Kalamazoo, Mich., 1982).
[2] Considered here only from the ecclesiological viewpoint, that is, the notion of the reception and transmission of Tradition (*Paradosis*).

to elucidate why he felt himself inspired to reformist zeal, and why many of his contemporaries (not simply his 'worldly opponents' as his hagiographer would have us believe) regarded him as unbalanced. It will end by attempting some reflection on what the controversy reveals on the larger front about how the Church 'selectively looks back on itself', so to paraphrase our president's description of the conference theme, and whether the model of tradition and its reception exemplified in this Byzantine writer can offer anything to the dialogue between history and theology which the doctrine of Tradition (*Paradosis*) inevitably initiates.

DETAILS OF THE LIFE

Symeon was born around 949,[3] a member of a highly placed aristocratic family. At eleven years of age he was sent to Constantinople for his education. His biographer, Nicetas Stethatos, portrays him as 'agrammatos', but this is merely one of the many *topoi* of hagiography with which Nicetas obscures important historical details in his subject's *Vita*, in a constant attempt to reduce every element of conflict from a life that had more than its fair share of it. Symeon's own writings show that he is high in the company of the finest Byzantine poets, well capable of elegant Greek even though he normally prefers a simple direct style.

In 963, after the death of Romanos II, a palace revolution brought down Symeon's uncle and patron, and the child's education was briefly interrupted. It was possibly at this time

---

[3] The chronology was established by I. Hausherr in his monograph, *Un grand mystique byzantin: Vie de Syméon le Nouveau Théologien, 949–1022, par Nicétas Stethatos*, Orientalia Christiana, 45 (Rome, 1928) [hereafter *Vie*]. In a recent paper I have argued that further political and external correspondences to those Hausherr had first noted add extra support to his basic schema. The late Prof. Christou has argued an alternative scheme, locating events seven years later, but this seems to me unconvincing, and gives undue weight to the hagiographer Nicetas, who is generally much confused in his narrative. Cf. my 'Symeon the New Theologian and Byzantine monasticism', in A. Bryer, ed., *Mount Athos and Byzantine Monasticism* (London, 1966) [= Papers of the 28th Symposium of Byzantine Studies, University of Birmingham, 1995].

that he first came to a monastery for protection and met the monk who, in later years, was to become his spiritual father, Symeon Eulabes of the Studium monastery. We learn that in 969, when Symeon was again well placed in the society of the imperial court, he consulted the elder who gave him spiritual books to read, particularly the *Spiritual Law* of Mark the Hermit, and recommended a small rule of prayer. Symeon tells us that a decisive event happened shortly afterwards which made him realize that it was none other than Symeon Eulabes who was the 'living saint in the present generation' whom he had been anxiously and urgently seeking to effect his reconciliation. In 969, the year of another bloody palace revolution, Symeon experienced an extraordinary vision of a brilliant light, bursting in on him ecstatically as he was saying his prayers in his chamber. As the light accustomed his eyes to its radiance, he realized that behind and beyond it there stood a yet greater light. Twenty-seven years after the event, while interpreting it for the benefit of his own monks, Symeon explained that the first light was the presence of his spiritual father, and the second was the divine presence to whom his spiritual father had presented him, thus effecting, as it were, the reconciliation he was longing for.

At the time, however, the vision of 969 did not seem much to alter his actual behaviour. The political upheavals soon settled down, and the young Symeon continued at court, hinting that his behaviour even deteriorated into greater dissoluteness. It is, of course, something of a *topos* in Byzantine literature to lament one's former sins; but the point is here genuinely meant by Symeon – not necessarily that he was any more corrupt than most in that period or social condition, but at least that his inner consciousness was more acutely aware of his failings. This anguished need for reconciliation prepared him for the real conversion experience that occurred seven years later, in 976, on the occasion of yet another *coup d'état*. This was the time of Symeon's second vision of the light, and it marks his definitive abandonment of politics and entry to the monastic state. Shortly after joining his spiritual father at the Studium, he witnessed the light again. The remarkable accounts of these visions (more seem to have followed) are contained in several separate, and different, versions in Symeon's own writings.[4] From this time onwards, the assurance of inner experience becomes, for Symeon, the ultimate canon of Christian authenticity. The visions had the effect of elevating, almost as two supreme principles of his thought thereafter, firstly the doctrine of the primacy of the spiritual father and his all-encompassing role as mediator (paradoxically) of the direct experience of God to the disciple, and secondly the central importance of 'tears' in the spiritual life. In the latter, Symeon emerges as one of the great expositors of the Greek patristic doctrine of *Penthos*, and suffice for now to translate that as meaning that for him there could be no authentic Christianity without corresponding affectivity, or perceived sensibility of the divine grace. For Symeon, if one was not sure, as a Christian, whether one had experienced the divine presence, then the answer was simply that one had *not*, and therefore was not a Christian at all, despite appearances to the contrary. This uncompromising doctrine of the priority of experience was the main cause at issue in his conflict with the patriarchal theologian Stephen of Nicomedia in his arraignment of 1003, and Symeon sets out his belief most consistently in the letter he addressed to the Synkellos on that occasion.[5] Both doctrines protected and encapsulated, in the strongest form, his basic assurance of direct revealed experience as the primary and only sure way of the theologian, and thus the main gate to the interpretation and transmission of the tradition. This explains why both aspects of his doctrine involved him almost immediately in major controversies.

Within the year of his entrance to the Studium, he had left for the smaller monastery of St Mammas by the Xerokerkos gate, and within three years, in 979–80, he was appointed as Higumen there. This rapid elevation, and equally rapid refurbishment of the site that followed, not only testifies to his reformist zeal, but also to the fact that he was acting as the second founder of the site, an aristocrat capable of calling upon substantial resources for the renovation of his new

---

[4] Cf. *Cat.* 16; 22; 35 (Eucharistic Prayer 1); *Cat.* 36 (Eucharistic Prayer 2); *Ethical Discourse* 5.

[5] *Vie*, pp. lxiii–lxv.

'household'. As soon as he was established as Higumen, Symeon tried to form the monks, many of whom had many years' experience, in this pattern of spirituality based upon his inner sensibility. While he did form an inner circle of disciples, we are told that no fewer than thirty monks openly revolted against him, sometime between 995 and 998. The hagiographer suggests it was a small group of disaffected worldlings, but thirty was a sizeable number for the time, undoubtedly the majority of the community. Within a few years of this unsuccessful revolt, the patriarchal court instigated another process of investigation. In 995, Symeon's liturgical cult of his spiritual father was forbidden, as part of a campaign aimed at discrediting and impugning the honour of Symeon himself, and in 1003 a formal trial was initiated against him, inquiring into his trinitarian orthodoxy in a process designed to show up his lack of formal theological training. In 1005 he was deposed from office and placed under house arrest in his own monastery. In 1009 he was exiled from the capital to Chrysopolis (Paloukiton) where he regathered a small community, and where he died in 1022. So much for the bare history. What does it reveal for us about the issue of the appropriation of tradition, and the role the re-interpretation of the past plays in the process of ecclesial reform or renewal?

REFORM IN SEARCH OF A PRECEDENT

Here I would like to consider two representative issues from the narrative: firstly, Symeon's own manner of appropriating the tradition as he perceived it; and secondly what this model of envisaging the working of Christian tradition suggests in the light of our contemporary concerns about historical relativism. Symeon's prior history as a dilettante aristocrat explains easily enough why, when he became a monk, he had little experience of, or access to, the written Christian tradition; and yet, within a few years of his monastic profession he was engaged in the teaching office of Higumen, and continued in that office for many years, with consider-able vigour. It is easier to fall back on the primacy of experiential knowledge when one is not too encumbered with textuality. Symeon's writings betray very little direct textual influences at all.

The scriptures are Symeon's most significant external source. These he applies in a widely spread carpet of allusions, and it is clear that regular hearing of the texts in a liturgically atomistic way was responsible for this familiarity he has which can allow him such a scriptural style, without necessarily involving him in any real biblical study. He is able, for example, to confuse St Paul and St James, as Holl has noted.[6] The only common explicit citation of author Symeon makes is to Gregory the Theologian (Nazianzen), and Gregory was not only the ultimate authority of the day, but even the common text used in the grammatical schools of the capital. Everyone knew Gregory. But although Gregory is the most commonly cited source, one observes that he is only mentioned six times in over three hundred pages of the English text of the *Catechetical Discourses*. Of these six instances two are merely symbolic, non-textual, allusions,[7] and of the other four, three consist of sentences using Gregory to argue that experiential perception is the goal of theology,[8] while the fourth applies him in a most uncharacteristic manner to press home the point of the necessity for tears:[9] all in all a most idiosyncratic employment.[10]

The really important find of Symeon's ascetical knowledge, and the authority for much of what he teaches, is, needless to say, the works (both written and preached) of his father Symeon Eulabes.[11] All his sources, even his own accounts of the visions of light he himself enjoyed, are ultimately subsumed to make two great points: the primacy

[6] Cf. C. Holl, *Enthusiasmus und Bussgewalt beim griechischen Mönchtum* (Leipzig, 1898), pp. 37–8.

[7] *Cat.* 5.15 (Catanzaro, p. 107); *Cat.* 29.2 (Catanzaro, p. 310).

[8] *Cat.* 4.16 (Catanzaro, p. 88); *Cat.* 22.6 (Catanzaro, p. 248); *Cat.* 28.13 (Catanzaro, p. 306).

[9] *Cat.* 29.5 (Catanzaro, pp. 313–14).

[10] Particularly in the light of what Hausherr has to say about his reliance: 'Un des rares auteurs qu'il parait avoir lus, saint Grégoire de Nazianze', *Vie*, p. 3 n. 2.

[11] The extent of that indebtedness has been expounded most recently by H. Alfeyev, 'St Symeon the New Theologian and Orthodox Tradition' (Oxford University D.Phil. thesis, 1995).

of the experience of grace in the life of a Christian, and the critical importance of the spiritual father in its actual mediation in the daily life of the Church.[12] Even when he is making conscious reference to his own experience, he is implicitly offering that experience as proof of his right to stand as successor to the spiritual father. In other words, he is offering the self-same paradigm, except that now, as Higumen, he is claiming by virtue of the experience mediated to him to be spiritual father in his own turn to the monks of St Mamas. He is demanding from them the same extra-ordinary degree of discipleship that characterizes that particular relationship of obedience to the living saint – a demand that resulted in the revolt of many of his monks, who felt this was to go far beyond the normal traditions of monastic obedience to the Higumen. Symeon, in short, has internalized the tradition to an extraordinary degree, and rendered it 'personalist' in a particularly intense manner. The authentic tradition of Christianity, therefore, is suggested to be a common and shared inner experience rather than a body of agreed external data.

His use of Gregory Nazianzen and his other patristic authorities comes to the same point. Of all that he has read, the dictum of the Theologian which Symeon has taken most to heart is that resonant *Praescriptio Haeretoricorum* from the beginning of the *Five Theological Orations*.[13] This he appeals to in the time of his trial, in his *Letter to the Synkellos Stephen*,[14] to the end that it is not everyone to whom the gift and right of theologizing has been given, only to those who have *experienced* the purification of divine grace and can thereby advance in the divine initiation. This elevation of the affective perception of grace over the logical strictures of doctrine was, needless to say, propounded in the fourth century by Gregory in the course of a precise apolegetical argument with

---

[12]   Cf. H. J. M. Turner, *St Symeon the New Theologian and Spiritual Fatherhood* (Leiden, 1990).

[13]   Orations 27–31, esp. Oration 27.3: *PG*, 36, col. 13.

[14]   The text is given in *Vie*, pp. lxiii–lxv. The specific *quaestio* given to Symeon related to the orthodoxy of his Trinitarian thought. The reply, as Hausherr notes, amounts to 84 verses, with only 30 related to the subject in hand, and the remainder dedicated to the premise that only the initiate can be a theologian.

Neo-Arian logicians.[15] It also has to be contextualized by remembering that Gregory was one of the most learned men of his age, one who believed that literary and philosophical culture were fundamentally necessary preparations for that very 'purification of the mind' which alone admitted the vision of God. For Gregory, who was among other things a devotee of Sappho, to set up such a prescriptive canon was one thing; for Symeon it was something else again. In the latter case, with a far more limited base of operation, and a much less universalist outlook, the result could only be a radical sharpening of the contrast in the overall theological picture.

Symeon's treatment of the text of Mark the Hermit is another example of the same process at work. He singled out Mark as one of the texts he could cite by name, and indeed the influential book that had been given to him by his spiritual father. This work, the *Spiritual Law*, is a collection of traditional fifth-century monastic apophthegms: a no-nonsense advocacy of regular observance of the ascetical life. When Symeon, now an abbot, refers back to the impact this work had on him as a young man, he reduces the whole argument to a synonym of his leaders' doctrine of spiritual affectivity. While he mentions the *Spiritual Law*,[16] he goes on to offer three citations from it that are actually from its companion volume *On those who think they can be justified by works*.[17] (Admittedly the treatises were always closely paired, but Photius at least was able to cite them as distinct works.) The summative citation Symeon chooses is illuminating, for he says that of those few axioms of the book which he had 'fixed in his heart' the chief one was the doctrine that internal spiritual conscience was the primary guide to truth.[18] Now this is an extraordinary exegesis of the whole, for the work was originally designed as a repudiation of the basic principle

---

[15] It was precisely designed to attack the logical propositionalism of the extreme Arian school of Aetius and Eunomius.

[16] *PG*, 65, cols 905–30.

[17] Ibid., cols 929–66.

[18] 'While he derived profit from all its passages, there were only three that, if I may say so, he fixed in his heart. The first was the one that reads as follows: "When you seek healing, take heed to your conscience. Do what it says, and you will find profit".' *Cat.* 22.2 (Catanzaro, p. 244).

of the Messalians against whom Mark was writing, namely that one could most certainly *not* rely on internal mystical experience as a canon of grace.[19]

Our final example of his manner of thus 'sharpening the contrasts' is provided by the interesting section in the sixth *Catechetical Discourse*. Symeon, now an abbot of about seventeen years standing, here reviews and summarizes the meaning of the whole prior monastic tradition. The section deserves close study, for it is clearly an attack on his opponents within the community. As is evident from any reading, however cursory, of the lives of the early monks, almost from any source one might care to choose, the emphasis in this 'desert literature' is on asceticism and regularity of *praxis* as the witness of true sanctity. The literature remained, for centuries, the standard catechetical reading of Eastern monasteries. We may not be too far off the mark if we recognize behind Symeon's rebuke in the text to 'those who look on themselves as equals of the saints of old', an attack on the ascetics of his community who preferred the rhythm of this traditional asceticism to the charismatic nature of Symeon's appeal to inner light. Symeon begins by offering an intimate and essentialist interpretation of the monasticism of the ancients: 'Do you wish to hear what our holy fathers did when they stayed in their cells?'[20] But then, in another bold hermeneutic he dismisses the whole ascetical literature as merely a preliminary to something far greater, an external reality that hardly touches what is really going on within: 'Read their lives, then, and first learn of their outward activities, and then I will tell you about the spiritual activities in which they were engaged. Those who wrote the lives of the saints described their outward activities . . . but they barely touched on their spiritual activity except as reflected in such activities.'

Symeon's claim to be able to open up, as master, the secrets of this inner life is, of course, a fairly obvious implicit claim to be the very 'equal of the saints of old' himself, exactly the

---

[19] J. Quasten, *Patrology*, 3 vols (Utrecht, 1975), 3, p. 506: 'At all events the author here comes into the open against the Messalians by energetically repudiating their basic principle, the identification of grace with mystical experience.'

[20] *Cat.* 6.1 (Catanzaro, p. 119).

claim he is deconstructing in regard to his antagonists. He takes the examples of Antony and Arsenius, the greatest masters, and goes on to demonstrate how these two illustrate his thesis that asceticism is only meant to be a prelude to the experience of the vision of Christ, and that without the experiential vision there is no gain in the monastic life. His exegesis of Antony's labours describes how all his struggle fell into insignificance before the vision he enjoyed: 'And when Antony saw this, and had been set free from those sufferings, he was filled with joy and said, "Lord, where were you until now?".' The account of where and how Antony actually 'saw' the face of Christ needs, however, to be supplied by Symeon from a generic scriptural passage;[21] for there is certainly no literary tradition that gives such an occurrence any prominence. Similarly with Arsenius, all is reduced to the point of seeing and experiencing. But here even Symeon senses that his argument is textually weak:

> Why did Arsenius perform all this asceticism? – so that he could experience and see the very thing that Antony the Great was given to see and experience! Why then is it not recorded that he saw the Lord? Was he not found worthy to see the Lord on the basis of all these toils? Far from it! He too was granted the vision of God, even though the narrator did not make this clear. If you want to be sure of this, go over the *Chapters* Arsenius himself composed[22] and you will know from them that in truth he too saw God.

Needless to say there is no work of Arsenius that focuses on this. The latest editor of Symeon's text adds a kindly footnote at this point: 'The work in question seems to have been lost, since no extant writing by this father seems to mention this.'[23]

---

[21] 1 Pet. 2.9. Cf. *Cat.* 6.2 (Catanzaro, p. 120).

[22] Many of the sayings of Arsenius (a highly cultured and learned teacher at the court before he entered the desert at Scete) are found in the *Apophthegmata patrum*, and as such were standard elements of monastic lore. Symeon could mean the *Doctrina et exhortatio* (*PG*, 66, cols 1617–22), but it is more likely that he means the *Kephalaia*, or sayings, in the *Apophthegmata*.

[23] Catanzaro, p. 121 n.1.

The 'work in question' never existed! The point is that Symeon claims to know what Antony and Arsenius experienced in their innermost soul purely by reference to the same experience in his own soul. The ultimate paradigm of tradition becomes that inner experience that is passed on from heart to heart within monasticism as its secret inner life, distinct from all external observances. In Symeon's case his initiation into monasticism is reduced to the single channel of his spiritual father's teaching, but this, *de facto*, is synonymous with the greatest of the monastic founders, since that spiritual father proved by his experience that he was the equal of this generation of those great saints of old, and thus supersedes them in the order of things by his providential proximity.

And so, the whole tradition comes down to the two Symeons, and is focused to a fine point in their doctrine of spiritual affectivity. Seeing and experiencing is thus the measure of all. For this reason, as the structure of this sixth *Catechetical Discourse* makes clear, the very reference to Antony and Arsenius, Sabas, and Euthymius serves only to introduce the life of his real paradigm of monastic spirituality.[24] This is none other than Symeon Eulabes, to whom the rest of the *Discourse* is dedicated: 'That most blessed saint of our own generation, Symeon Eulabes, who shone like the sun in the midst of the famous monastery of Studium'. This is the theology of interiority taken to its highest pitch, and set as the final arbiter, the highest measure of the authentic tradition of the Church. One notices the startling originality of the premise, for the only canon of the authentic tradition must, for Symeon, exist in the present generation of the Church, not in the past. Tradition is, then, the current authentic experience of grace, and it is against this canon that he understands the past to be correctly interpreted (he means 'authoritatively claimed') and by means of this canon that the direction of the future is set. This primacy of the present moment in Symeon's theology harmonizes with much other Eastern Christian thought on the 'Tradition' (*Paradosis*) that regards it as a living and dynamic reality in ways quite

---

[24]   *Cat.* 6.2–4 (Catanzaro, pp. 120–2).

distinct from the terms of argument employed in Western (Catholic and Protestant) apologetics on the subject.[25]

It is easy to see why Symeon caused alarm to his own contemporaries. The trial for heterodoxy in 1003, however, was evidently staged more to expose Symeon's lack of formal theological learning than as a serious attempt to prosecute any real doctrinal error. His hagiographer reduces the trial to a matter of his defence of the holy icons, and thus makes him out to be an iconodule confessor; but this context is fanciful. The trial did not turn on the question of icons, but on the issue of painting an icon of Symeon Eulabes, that is the unofficial canonization of his master which was at the heart of most of Symeon's adherence to the principle of the primacy of a theology of inspiration. For the patriarchal synod to refuse permission for the cult was a calculated way of limiting the extent of a doctrine that was otherwise shared by official orthodoxy, and clearly taught in the *Theological Orations* of Gregory Nazianzen which were standards of Byzantine confession, and to which not only Symeon, but also his opponents, appealed. The point was not whether God's inspiration was primary or not; rather the manner in which that inspiration was communicated. Symeon took a rigorist experiential view on that, others widened the remit of their understanding of 'inspiration'. On this central issue, then, the patriarchal court wished to temper Symeon's doctrine, not denounce it; yet this was the case only because the conditions prevailing in the early eleventh century meant that all the protagonists accepted the basis of that doctrinal tradition already established (in the most precise of manners) as ecumenical orthodoxy, and held to it firmly within a total society. In later centuries, of course, particularly in the Western Church, such important divergence could not have been so readily atoned by an implicitly agreed ecumenicity.

---

[25] For a fuller elaboration of the argument, see G. Florovsky, *Bible, Church, and Tradition: an Eastern Orthodox View* (Belmont, Mass., 1975).

CONCLUSIONS

As a conclusion to this all too rapid review, I would like to consider some of the implications of Symeon's style of appropriating the prior tradition on the basis of inner self-authenticating experience; and then to go on to sketch out some general thoughts on what relevance this theological model of reception may continue to have.

Symeon's intense and remarkable experiences provided him with the unquestioned certainty of his rightness, and his role as teacher and leader; for claims of authenticity are never far removed from claims to authority. To doubt his analysis of Christianity would be tantamount, for him, to doubting the very validity of the experience itself, which was out of the question. His problem, of course, lay in his efforts to convince others, who had not shared that experience directly, that his hermeneutic was the sole correct one. He believed that if obedience was given to him as spiritual father, in the same way that he had given it to his mediator Symeon Eulabes, then the experience would indeed open up for his disciples in their own turn. This is why he offers such a doctrine in the context of catechizing his own monks. But even in this limited world of the small monastic community, the offer proved the source of immense disagreements, and ultimately revolt. Inner spiritual experience, always associated in Christian tradition with the deepest forms of authenticity, is not always enough to control the transmission of tradition which, by definition, has to be common in a way that affective experience cannot hope to be. Despite his certainty of his rightness, Symeon was still enough of a public theologian to be aware of this, and so his attempts to argue how such a canon of experience can become 'normative' have an abiding interest for those who wish to consider the nature of the reception and the transmission of Christian tradition across the ages: an issue which has come to trouble the contemporary Church acutely in an age where the very principle of such *Paradosis* has come to be doubted, and where the problems of historical relativism have only become more acute since Newman's day.

Newman famously wrestled with the problem in his image of the 'development' of tradition in terms of organic and homogeneous growth. But that analogy, if pushed, raises the issue of growth not simply being progress, but the most inevitable model of change there can be, and also invites scepticism as to Newman's presumption that growth led to maturity, for it can equally be seen to lead to senility and decay. Symeon, of course, claimed nothing like this. His model of the reception of the tradition presumed that elect elements of his generation had been allowed to appropriate the 'self-same' reality, that same 'vision' and 'experience' that had motivated the earlier generations of fathers: the *semper idem* of the Risen Christ. Although he did not argue the case textually, and indeed might have had great difficulty in attempting so to do, his model remains instructive, and far from being hopelessly 'personalist' as may at first appear.

To support his notion he evoked the image of the Church as a 'Golden Chain':[26] the number of living saints in each generation that connected the present reality of Church to its past. These elect few were the ones, for Symeon, who represented authentic Christianity and by virtue of that experience were compelled to initiate others into that experience. In the concrete instance, he was citing Symeon Eulabes and himself as the latest two links in the system, whose experience had to be paradigmatic precisely because such initiations into the authentic Christian experience could only be delivered, or passed on, by direct personal intervention. The transmission and reception, therefore, was not necessarily de-textualized, but it was capable of being effected by personal communion alone. His ecclesiology was thus mystical, and rooted in the notion of communion and initiation. There is much in this that is a salutary corrective to notions of the reception of tradition that take their beginning purely in the logical and demonstrable order of textuality or historiography. The weakness of Symeon's model is usually argued to be in its non-

---

[26] Cf. Third Theological Chapter (3.4): McGuckin, *Symeon the New Theologian*, pp. 72-3.

specific nature: its unwillingness or inability to cite historical chapter and verse. Indeed, one may rightly be more worried by the potential effects in the Church of the unquestioningly certain 'visionary' than the stable tedium of the 'safe pair of hands'. But even so, such a critique of Symeon's model qualifies rather than invalidates it; and this on two grounds. In the first place the essential character of inner experiences is not hopelessly personalist. These things can always be deduced, measured, and assessed from the external signs of the caused effects. This is a very old evangelical maxim to do with fruits.[27] To this extent a mystical ecclesiology or a visionary concept of tradition such as that exemplified by Symeon can indeed be grounded in praxis and measured by visible canons. This is after all what Symeon himself taught. His insistence on the total priority of the visionary goal, and the charismatic commitment to radical discipleship, was allied with a clear programme of monastic observance which, for all his revolutionary-sounding phrases, is to all intents and purposes the standard Studite observance of most monastic houses in Constantinople in his time.[28] Secondly, his model deserves consideration because, for all its obscurities, such a view of Christian tradition, its reception and transmission, celebrates the priority of the personal over the institutional: a fundamental ordering of verities which Christianity has ever neglected to its peril.

From antiquity to the present day, the Church has shown anxiety over the question of how it should understand and pass on its essential life from generation to generation in all the vicissitudes of history. Symeon's point, in this theology of tradition, was that this was not the primary issue – rather, the Church's problem was how vitally it celebrates that life in each and every present generation. For him it was only in the quality of life of the present that there could be given any true recognition of the Church's spiritual

---

[27] Matt. 7.15–20.
[28] In *Cat.* 26 (Catanzaro, pp. 274–83) Symeon sets out his Typikon of the daily observances of the St Mamas community. It is quintessentially 'Studite' in character, and completely unremarkable and unobjectionable as far as his community could have been concerned.

communion with its past. This is an interesting and fertile theology of tradition, one that does not so much look to the past to prove continuity with the present, but looks to the present to demonstrate its communion with the past.

University of Leeds

THE PAST AND MONASTIC DEBATE
IN THE TIME OF
BERNARD OF CLAIRVAUX

by CHRISTOPHER HOLDSWORTH

The period from the earlier decades of the eleventh century to the middle of the twelfth is characterized by a number of great debates on subjects which arose out of some of the most significant aspects of the institutions of the time.[1] There was *the* struggle, that between kingdoms and priesthood, or empire and papacy as it has sometimes misleadingly been called, reflected in the huge folio volumes simply entitled *Libelli de Lite*.[2] At a rather rarer, theological level, there was a great argument about the sacraments, particularly the Eucharist, which had implications both for the status of the clergy (in particular their links with their lay patrons), and for relations between those churches which looked to Rome for their guidance and those which, if they focused anywhere, looked to Constantinople. Somewhat between these two levels, people argued about the right relationship between secular and regular clergy, while within the monastic family there was dispute about the best way in which men, and to a much lesser degree women, could make their route heavenwards. A great deal no doubt was said about all these issues at the time which has now evaporated, but much was written down, the residue which survives making up a series of the most sustained discussions in the West on any kind of subject since the great theological controversies of the fourth and fifth centuries.

Why these arguments were pursued with such energy then can be attributed to the availability of people with opportunity,

---

[1] Colin Morris, *The Papal Monarchy. The Western Church from 1050 to 1250* (Oxford, 1989), pp. 28–33, 34–78 and C. H. Lawrence, *Medieval Monasticism. Forms of Religious Life in Western Europe in the Middle Ages* (London and New York, 1984), pp. 125–45, for the background to this paragraph.

[2] *Libelli de Lite Imperatorum et Pontificum saeculis XI et XII conscripti*, ed. E. Dümmler et al., *MGH*, 3 vols (1891–7).

skills, and time to do so. These they enjoyed thanks to the more peaceful situation which their age enjoyed, compared to that of earlier days. With peace came the growth of population, and with both, prosperity and the economic resources to enable institutions for religion and learning to multiply. More people had the leisure to think, talk, and write, rather than just struggle to keep alive. They remained, of course, a very small group in society at large, but one sufficiently numerous to create circles in which ideas could be clarified through argument and discussion. It would be wrong to suggest that all over Europe such circles came into existence: we know yet little of them within Scandinavia, or eastern Europe but everywhere else, from Scotland to Sicily, Lisbon to Magdeburg, they can be found.

The intention of this paper is to explore one side of the fourth debate, that about the best way to heaven among monastic communities, and as my title hints I shall concentrate upon the arguments around the Cistercian Order to which Bernard of Clairvaux belonged, though I shall extend the period about which I speak to the end of the twelfth century. This is not unexplored territory, but the side of it which I hope to emphasize, namely the use of the past in the argument, has not, I believe, formed the core of earlier discussion.[3] This emphasis developed when Andrew Martindale wrote in July 1994 inviting a contribution to the theme which he had proposed for the Society during the year of his presidency, for what he called 'a Bernardine view . . . or some more general reflection on the topic from your knowledge of the eleventh and twelfth centuries'.

The last time the monastic debate of that period was discussed in a public lecture given in Britain which went on to be printed occurred in 1955; it was given by that lucid and eirenic, but rather unusual, Benedictine, Dom David Knowles.[4] Knowles's lecture on *Cistercians and Cluniacs* was given at the Dr Williams's Library in 1955 but it had,

---

[3] See, for example, Piero Zerbi, ' "Vecchio" e "Nuovo" monachesimo alla metà del seculo XII', in *Istituzioni monastiche e istituzioni canonicali in occidente (1123-1215)*, Miscellanea del Centro di Studi Medioevali, 9 (1980), pp. 3-24.

[4] David Knowles, *Cistercians and Cluniacs. The Controversy between St. Bernard and Peter the Venerable*, Friends of Dr Williams's Library, Ninth Lecture (Oxford, 1955).

according to a note inserted when it was reprinted in his *liber gratulatorius, The Historian and Character*, been drafted twenty years earlier, in 1934.[5] Such long maturation may have given it some of its force and characteristic charm, but the gap between the early thirties and now certainly suggests that the subject may benefit from a new look.

David Knowles focused upon two great individuals, whom he took to represent two wings of the monastic family: Bernard abbot of Clairvaux, for the Cistercians, and Peter the Venerable, abbot of Cluny, champion for that part of the monastic family. Now, that way of putting the problem seems rather unsatisfactory for two different reasons. On the one hand we recognize, thanks to the work of scholars who have found and discussed their writings, that far more people were involved than the two giants. Even in the very year that Knowles wrote his first draft, 1934, Dom Wilmart printed for the first time an anonymous Benedictine reply to Bernard's *Apology*, which only merited the briefest footnote in the printed lecture.[6] Another reply surfaced in one of the myriad articles of Dom Jean Leclercq in 1957.[7] Although neither of these new pieces is as exciting as Bernard's fireworks, or as serene and wise as Peter's words, nonetheless they reveal a much more varied landscape than Knowles recognized. The other development is perhaps of equal, if not greater, importance. It is being realized that to typify the argument as one between Cîteaux and Cluny is to narrow it down too much.[8] The Cistercian critique was of traditional Benedictine ways, wherever they were followed, and not just within houses which were in some constitutional sense attached to the great Burgundian house of Cluny. Part of the confusion has stemmed from the fact that the only word

5 Idem, *The Historian and Character and Other Essays* (Cambridge, 1963), p. 50, n. 1.

6 André Wilmart, 'Une riposte de l'ancien monachisme au manifeste de Saint Bernard', *Revue Bénédictine*, 46 (1934), pp. 296–344; Knowles, *Cistercians and Cluniacs*, p. 31 n. 2. There he called it 'a late defence': the adjective disappears in 1963, Knowles, *Historian and Character*, p. 74 n. 1.

7 Jean Leclercq, 'Nouvelle réponse de l'ancien monachisme aux critiques des cisterciens', *Revue Bénédictine*, 67 (1957), pp. 77–93, reprinted in idem, *Recueil d'études sur saint Bernard et ses écrits*, 5 vols (Rome, 1962–92), 2, pp. 69–85.

8 Conrad Rudolph, *The 'Things of Greater Importance'. Bernard of Clairvaux's* Apologia *and the Medieval Attitude toward Art* (Philadelphia, 1990), pp. 159–71.

available to contemporaries to describe traditional Benedictines was *Cluniacenses*.[9] So now we need to broaden our sights to consider not only what was written by members of Cluny's family but what, for example, the German monk Rupert of Deutz wrote about the Rule, and what the French monk-errant Abelard expressed on it to Heloise.

A third result of the last sixty years' scholarship radically affects what can and can not be said. More blocks of evidence have indeed been discovered, but one of the central, crucial, problems remains still in a tantalizing state. Many of the documents cannot be securely dated, and so sometimes one has the sensation that as one presses on any one of them it begins to move its place in time, and to become adjacent to a rather different set of writings, or indeed events. It is rather as though one were trying to create a firm path from a series of frozen blocks of water which move about in a distressingly irregular fashion as one treads upon them.

Let me take as an example what is undoubtedly the best known and most influential text written in the whole debate (best known and influential both in its day and ever since), namely Bernard's *Apology*, and its relation to one of Peter the Venerable's letters, number 28. Knowles himself once described their relationship with typically sharp words as 'a neuralgic point in twelfth-century monastic history'.[10] In 1955 he believed that Peter's letter dated from very early in his abbacy, soon after 1122, whereas he placed the *Apology* two or three years later.[11] At that time he observed in a footnote that the greatest Bernardine scholar, Vacandard, had shifted his own opinions on the date of Bernard's work from between 1123 and 1125, to 1127.[12] Later, in 1968, when reviewing Constable's edition of Peter's letters, Knowles briefly revealed, without supporting argument, that he too had changed his mind. Now he was prepared to accept Constable's 1126 to 1127 for Peter's letter, and to shift the *Apology* to a little before the spring of 1127.[13] Knowles, one

9   Ibid., pp. 162–3, 171, esp. p. 162 n. 426.
10   David Knowles, 'Peter the Venerable: champion of Cluny', *JEH*, 19 (1968), p. 215.
11   Knowles, *Cistercians and Cluniacs*, pp. 14 (and n. 14), 18.
12   Ibid., p. 18 n. 1.
13   Knowles, 'Peter the Venerable', p. 215.

may note, always believed that Bernard wrote after Peter, not a view which has commended itself to all scholars.[14] Indeed the most widely held view now is that the *Apology* dates from between November 1124 and early 1125, whilst Constable's date for Peter's letter has gained wide support. Bernard, that is to say, is generally agreed to have written before the abbot of Cluny. In what follows, I shall, however, work on a slightly different chronology which I tried to establish in an article published in 1994. It too accepts 1126/7 for Peter's letter but places the *Apology* back in 1122.[15] This discussion of the chronology of two sources must serve as a warning that the dating of nearly all of the twenty or so upon which this paper rests is also debatable.[16]

Little evidence survives which reacts to the new experiment in following the Rule of St Benedict which began in 1098 at Cîteaux, to the south of Dijon, for the first twenty years of its history. The earliest is a short narrative account put together by some of the pioneers to pass on their experience, *The Little Beginning*, or *Exordium Parvum*, so-called by scholars to distinguish it from the much longer and later *Exordium Magnum*. An enormous amount of energy has been spent in the last fifty years to try and establish just when this short story and a small number of associated documents were written down. As yet no common mind has emerged, though there is greater agreement that the letters embedded in the account, forming nine of its eighteen short chapters, are genuine, which takes us back to the very first years of Cîteaux's life.[17] Many, among whom I am one, would go

---

[14] Giles Constable, *The Letters of Peter the Venerable*, 2 vols (Cambridge, Mass., 1967), 2, pp. 270-4 for a beautifully clear discussion. Rudolph, *The 'Things'*, pp. 209-11, believes Peter wrote first. I have discussed his view in 'The early writings of Bernard of Clairvaux', *Cîteaux*, 45 (1994), pp. 48-50.

[15] Ibid., pp. 22-7 for the generally accepted dating, pp. 27-61 for a new one.

[16] Some readers may recall the notice standing beside the beech tree in which Piglet lived with its portentous message, 'Trespassers W.': A. A. Milne, *Winnie-the-Pooh* (London, 1926), p. 32.

[17] Despite its narrow title C. Holdsworth, 'The chronology and character of early Cistercian legislation on art and architecture', in Christopher Norton and David Park, eds., *Cistercian Art and Architecture in the British Isles* (Cambridge, 1986), pp. 40-55, surveys the problem to 1985. For a rather different view see Jean Baptiste Auberger, *L'Unanimité cistercienne primitive: mythe ou réalité?* (Achel, 1986), pp. 42-52, esp. at p. 50 on the letters. The same views are in idem, 'La Législation cistercienne

further, and hold that the *Exordium* had reached something substantially like its present form by 1119: it comes first, therefore, in this discussion.

We do not have, in fact, to stay with it for long, since only three notes about the period before 1098 are sounded there. The first and clearest, since it emerges in both letters and surrounding narrative, is that the founders looked back to the Rule of St Benedict as their guide.[18] It was their desire to follow it more strenuously and perfectly, *artius et perfectius*, which lead them out from Molesme to the relatively wild site at Cîteaux.[19] Once there, they determined to reject everything in their practice hitherto which they could not find in that Rule, singling out a series of issues relating to clothing and food. But where the Rule gave no guidance over what seemed to them a significant issue, for example, where a monastery should be founded, or how it should support itself, they turned to the only source they (and we) have for the way that Benedict had lived, the account given by Pope Gregory the Great in the second book of his *Dialogues*.[20] What they read there struck them with enormous force:

> And since they could not find either in the Rule or in the life of Saint Benedict that this teacher had possessed churches or altars, offerings or burial dues, tithes of other people, or ovens or mills or manors or serfs, and that women had ever entered his monastery or been buried there, with the exception of his sister, they renounced all these things . . . .[21]

primitive et sa relecture claravallienne', in Colloque de Lyon-Cîteaux-Dijon, *Bernard de Clairvaux, Histoire, Mentalités, Spiritualité*, Sources Chrétiennes, 380 (Paris, 1992), pp. 181–208.

[18] *Exordium Parvum*, I.2, XII.5, ed. and trans. François de Place, Gabriel Ghislain, Jean-Christophe Christophe, *Cîteaux documents primitifs* (Cîteaux, 1988), pp. 26, 40 [hereafter *Ex Parv.*].

[19] *Ex Parv.*, II.3 (p. 28). The message of the much shorter so-called *Exordium Cistercii*, I.4 (*ed. cit.*, p. 113) is fundamentally similar.

[20] *Ex. Parv.*, XV.2–5 (pp. 44–6): the most accessible edition of Dialogues II is *PL.* 66, cols 125–204; that in *Grégoire le Grand: Dialogues*, ed. A. de Vogüé, trans. P. Aubin, 3 vols (Paris, 1978–80), is very much better.

[21] I use the translation by L. J. Lekai in his *The Cistercians: Ideals and Reality* (Kent, Ohio, 1977), p. 459.

The implications of this for their economy were extensive, as was the deduction that they drew from another part of Gregory's account, that if they were to follow Benedict they should live in places withdrawn from people, 'in locis a frequentia populis semotis', and that no monastery should have less than twelve monks in it.[22] The only other part of the past which they took into account, according to *The Little Beginning*, was how the 'Holy Fathers' (whom they called 'the organ of the Holy Spirit') had laid down that tithes were to be divided into four: one quarter each for the bishop; the local priest; for visitors, widows, orphans, and the poor; and the last for the upkeep of the local church.[23] Here they may have been drawing upon knowledge gained from collections of canon law, or even from copies of Carolingian letters which refer to such a division.[24] But the overwhelming impression the *Exordium Parvum* leaves is of a group who took into account a very minor part of the past, that around the great Rule and its author. This impression comes across as well in such 'legislation' of the Cistercian pioneers which has a reasonable claim to come from the years up to 1119.[25] This should, perhaps, not surprise us: reformers nearly always keep their eyes on limited bits of earlier experience, just because they want to break free from the changes which the years have brought around the early ideal to which they want to return. The Cistercians, although clearly unsettled by their experience, did not often write long narrative histories to explain their situation (unlike some other groups identified by Richard Southern, for example the 'English' monks in the generation or two after the Norman cataclysm).[26] Although they were keen to avoid the accusation that they were instituting novelties – on the whole thought to be a bad thing in the early twelfth century – they found most of the material upon which they wished to establish their claim to be faithful

---

[22] *Ex. Parv.*, XV, 13–14 (pp. 46–8).

[23] *Ex. Parv.*, XV, 7 (p. 46).

[24] Giles Constable, *Monastic Tithes from their Origins to the Twelfth Century* (Cambridge, 1964), pp. 43–4, esp. p. 43 n. 3.

[25] See Holdsworth, 'The chronology and character'. The phrase 'as the Rule prescribes' or its equivalent is often sounded.

[26] R. W. Southern, 'Aspects of the European tradition of historical writing: 4, the sense of the past', *TRHS*, 5th ser., 23 (1977), pp. 243–63.

to the best in the past in a small segment of earlier monastic experience.[27] They were forced to look rather further, as time went by, but it was among the traditionalists that a wider past was really drawn upon for their defence. We can also recognize that looking back was something which had been done by those who tried to reform the relationship between priesthood and kingdoms, or indeed the inner life of the Church itself, in the previous century.

With Bernard of Clairvaux we find a slightly wider view of the past, though expressed with brevity combined with enormous vigour and an extraordinary knowledge of the Bible. Among his extensive writings two, neither of them explicitly works of history, stand out for their relevance to the debate about monasticism: a letter addressed to his cousin Robert, written perhaps in 1121, and his coruscating *Apology* completed a year or so later.[28] Robert had become a monk at Clairvaux even though his parents had promised when he was a child that he would enter Cluny. After a few years he despaired of what he had undertaken and, taking advantage of Bernard's absence, journeyed to the great Burgundian monastery. Some years later Bernard wrote a long letter imploring him to return, almost certainly realizing that what on the surface appeared to be a private letter would in fact become public knowledge. In it he made a great deal of Robert's own experience, but only once brought an earlier past into his armory. This happened when he challenged Benedict himself to judge whether the promise of Robert's parents or his own vow should have greater weight.[29] The past played a much greater role in his *Apology*.

Here he tried to do two very different things, both requested of him by William, Abbot of the Benedictine monastery of Saint-Thierry, not far to the northeast of Reims, with whom he had formed a close friendship since

---

[27] Beryl Smalley, 'Ecclesiastical attitudes to novelty c. 1100–c.1250', *SCH*, 12 (1975), pp. 113–31.

[28] For the dates see Holdsworth, 'The early writings', Letter One, p. 40: the *Apology*, pp. 39–54.

[29] Ep. I.8: *Sancti Bernardi Opera* [hereafter *SB Op*], ed. J. Leclercq, H. M. Rochais, and C. H. Talbot, 8 vols (Rome, 1957-77), 7, p. 6; Bruno Scott James, *The Letters of St. Bernard of Clairvaux* (London, 1953), p. 8.

1119 or 1120.[30] The first was to take to task Cistercians who were condemning other monks in a pharisaical manner, and the second to discuss those aspects of traditional monastic life which seemed to him excessive.[31] Bernard himself was aware of the difficulty of combining the two objectives in one work, and it was perhaps this realization that led him to adopt a satirical tone, particularly in the second part, where he deployed it in a blisteringly brilliant way; a tone he was never again to attempt at such length. He drew the past into his argument much more fully than anyone had done hitherto. From the start he appealed to people and events in the Bible for precedents for behaviour in his own day, since sacred history for Bernard (and for almost every other Christian then) was the most relevant history because within it God revealed his purposes.[32] So, although like the anonymous writers of the *Exordium Parvum* he held up every kind of monastic practice to the light of the Rule, he made it clear that the Rule itself had to accord with both the Gospel and the teaching of the apostles.[33] Three other parts of the past came into the arena in the second part where his prose sparkled most: the earliest monks in the desert, the great abbots of Cluny, and the first apostles. Let us look at each of these in turn.

The monks and hermits of the desert, about whom he must have known through *The Lives of the Fathers* and the works of Cassian (both recommended by Benedict himself) appear twice.[34] The first occasion was when Bernard recalled how in the time when the monastic order began Anthony and his friends visited each other and were so moved that they forgot to eat.[35] The second was when he wanted to scorn the way that monks of his own day took to advertising their weakness

---

[30] Holdsworth, 'The early writings', p. 52

[31] Ep. 84 *bis: SB Op*, 7, p. 219. Bruno Scott James did not know this letter. There is a translation in *The Works of Bernard of Clairvaux, 1. Treatises I*, by Jean Leclercq, Cistercian Fathers, 1 (Shannon, 1970) [hereafter *Works*], pp. 5–6.

[32] See, for example, his references to Noah, Daniel and Job, Martha and Mary, and Joseph: *Apology*, III.5: *SB Op*, 3, pp. 84–6; *Works*, 1, pp. 38–9.

[33] *Apology*, V.11: *SB Op*, 3, pp. 90–1; *Works*, 1, pp. 45–6.

[34] *Regula Sancti Benedicti*, 73.5: *The Rule of St. Benedict in Latin and English with Notes*, ed. Timothy Fry (Collegeville, Minn., 1981), pp. 296–7.

[35] *Apology*, IX.19: *SB Op*, 3, pp. 96–7: *Works*, 1, pp. 54–5.

by using sticks: 'Is this the way that Macarius lived? Is it
Basil's teaching or Anthony's command?' Bernard asked,
then pressing on with another rhetorical question, 'Did the
Fathers in Egypt adopt such a manner of life?'[36] The trio,
Anthony, Basil, and Macarius here enter for the first time
into the monastic debate of the twelfth century (though they
had performed in a debate over the eremitic life in the
previous century):[37] they were to play a larger role as time
went by. Here their arrival is followed with four great abbots
of Cluny hard on their heels, lined up in another question:
'Finally, did those holy men whom they [that is to say most
other Benedictine monks] claim as the founders and teachers
of their Order, Odo, Majolus, Odilo, and Hugh, did they
hold with such things or value them?' Here Bernard carried
his attack right on to his opponents' ground, making the
abbots of Cluny his allies as saintly critics of outrageous
behaviour. 'All these men were saints', he averred, 'and
because of this they were in accord with what the Apostle
said, "So long as we have food and drink we are content
[1 Timothy 6.8]." ' This enrolling of Odo and his successors
on the Cistercian side was developed later. Similarly
Bernard's third appeal to the experience of the early Church
in Jerusalem as described in Acts 2 as a model for monks,
appears again and again in later writings.[38] It has, indeed, long
been common, since at least the time of Cassian, to look there
for the origins of monastic practice, particularly the renunciation of private property.[39] With the *Apology*, therefore we see
more of the past being drawn into the discussion, and even
though what Bernard writes is extremely brief, only a few
sentences, they leave their mark on the reader.

[36] Ibid., IX.23 (for both the early monks and abbots of Cluny): *SB Op*, 3, p. 100:
Works, 1, pp. 58–9.
[37] Benedicta Ward, 'The desert myth. Reflections on the desert ideal in early
Cistercian monasticism', in M. Basil Pennington, ed., *One Yet Two: Monastic Tradition
East and West*, Cistercian Studies, 29 (Kalamazoo, Mi., 1976), pp. 192–3. Peter Damian,
for example, was even reminded of Paul and Anthony when he visited Cluny: Derek
Baker, ' "The whole world a hermitage": ascetic renewal and the crisis of western
monasticism', in Marc A. Meyer, ed., *The Culture of Christendom. Essays in Medieval
History in Memory of Denis L. T. Bethell* (London and Rio Grande, 1993), p. 220.
[38] *Apology*, X.24: *SB Op*, 3, p. 101: *Works*, 1, pp. 59–61.
[39] Glenn Olsen, 'The idea of the *Ecclesia primitiva* in the writings of the twelfth-
century canonists', *Traditio*, 25 (1969), pp. 66–8.

The next four sources all come from the traditional, black monk side of the debate. The first in time is William of Malmesbury's account of Cistercian beginnings in his *Gesta Regum Anglorum*, which dates to around 1123-4.[40] He was not hostile to the new group, and indeed inserted this rather alien matter into an account centred upon Anglo-Norman affairs because he admired Stephen Harding, the third abbot of Cîteaux, and a fellow Englishman. He writes mostly in the form of a discussion between the two parties within the community at Molesme, in which he gives Stephen the role of spokesman of the party wanting change. The only part of the past to which Stephen refers is the Rule, and although we must regard this account as literally a myth, a result of the ancient practice of invention recommended by rhetoricians, the earlier sources we have looked at show that William had picked up a very real concern of the reformers. But the fact that he says that they wished to follow the crumb of the Rule, 'medullam regulae', and that they delegated two monks who were both lettered and holy ('in quibus scientia litterarum cum religione quadraret') to find out Benedict's intention in the Rule ('auctoris regulae voluntatem') may suggest something else: that already by the early 1120s the Cistercians were having to admit that not all they did – for example the establishment of the lay-brotherhood – could be justified in the letter of the Rule.[41] The contrast between crumb and crust, inner meaning and outer words, was well known in biblical exegesis, and it is eminently conceivable that the reformers should have made such a distinction.[42]

[40] William of Malmesbury, *Gesta Regum Anglorum*, IV.334-7 in W. Stubbs, ed. *Willelmi Malmesbiriensis monachi. De gestis regum anglorum, libri quinque; Historiae novellæ libri tres*, 2 vols, RS, (London, 1889), 2, pp. 380-5. French translation and commentary in de Place et al., *Cîteaux documents*, pp. 171-83.

[41] *Gesta Regum*, IV.334 and 335 (Stubbs, *Willelmi Malmesbiriensis*, 2, pp. 381-2; de Place et al., *Cîteaux documents*, pp. 174-7). For a fine discussion of the debate see Giles Constable, 'Renewal and reform in religious life: concepts and realities', in Robert L. Benson and Giles Constable with Carol D. Lanham, eds, *Renaissance and Renewal in the Twelfth Century* (Cambridge, Mass., 1982), pp. 61-2.

[42] E.g. Bernard of Clairvaux to Henry Murdac: 'Quam libenter suas crustas rodendas litteratoribus Iudaeis relinqueres! . . . O quam libens partirer tibi calidos panes quod utique adhuc fumigantes, et quasi modo de furno, ut aiunt, recens tractos, de caelesti largitate crebro Christus suis pauperibus frangit!' *SB Op*, 7, p. 266: Scott James, *Letters*, pp. 155-6.

A very different reaction to the Cistercian model for monasticism is the anonymous *Reply* to the *Apology*, preserved in a unique late twelfth-century manuscript from the Augustinian priory of Southwark. Dom Wilmart, its editor, drew from it a sketch of what kind of person its author might be, and suggested Hugh of Amiens, a French Cluniac, as the most likely candidate.[43] He spent part of his life in England, first as prior at Lewes, then as abbot at Reading, before Henry I promoted him to the archiepiscopal see of Rouen.[44] This suggestion has gained acceptance, though the scholar who knows Hugh's certain works best, Thomas Waldman, has pointed out that stylistically the *Reply* is quite unlike anything else which Hugh wrote.[45] If Hugh was the author we are probably faced with something written whilst he was at Reading, namely between 1123 and 1130. He responds only to the second half of Bernard's work, though he had clearly read all of it. He took Bernard's actual phrases and dealt with them *seriatim*. Like Bernard he often adopted a satirical tone, but he is much more obviously learned. He scatters his pages with quotations and allusions from classical authors, as well as from more typical monastic sources like the great Latin Fathers, Ambrose, Augustine, Jerome, Gregory, and Cassian. This reflects the fact that he had spent time in the schools at Laon, along with another contributor to the debate, the Cluniac cardinal, Matthew of Albano.[46] But how does he deploy the past in his argument, and what past?

We can catch him *in media res* by observing his reaction to Bernard's reference to the four abbots at Cluny as those holy men who created that way of life. 'Truly,' Hugh comments, 'they were called saints who showed us how we might live, and especially because they kept to the principle of discretion.' Unlike Pharisees – here we may note the use of a word

[43] Wilmart, 'Une riposte', pp. 306–9.

[44] David Knowles, C. N. L. Brooke, and Vera C. M. London, *The Heads of Religious Houses in England and Wales 940–1216* (Cambridge, 1972), p. 63, for a better chronology than Wilmart.

[45] Personal communication.

[46] Hugh of Rouen, *Dialogorum Libri VII*, pref., to Matthew: 'Nos enim et una generis consanguinitas et ejusdem professionis in Christo junxit societas . . . quos Laudunense solum educavit et docuit; *PL*, 192, col. 1141.

Bernard himself had applied to some Cistercians[47] – they did not pile up a hard law on their followers, whilst those who have taken up new ways (that is, the Cistercians) plague their followers with 'excessive cold and hunger and labour . . . . Those who do not wish to temper the rigor of the Rule with discretion, destroy it rather than build on it.'[48] The Rule itself, in which discretion is called 'the mother of virtues', is turned back on Bernard.[49] Again Bernard's scurrilous tone is beaten with another use of Benedict's own words: 'Tell me, I implore you good abbot, how with this joking way of speaking do you fulfil that place in the Rule where father Benedict condemns with a perpetual ban buffoonery and words which stir laughter?'[50] Similarly the examples of Christ feasting with his disciples at the marriage at Cana, or in the house of Levi, are summoned to undermine Bernard's criticisms of monastic fine food, typified in what we might call the Delia Smith way with eggs. Here one may note that Hugh explicitly says that in citing two biblical examples he is using the historical sense of the text, rather than spiritualizing a message from it.[51] But amusing and to the point as Hugh is, we have to admit that he does not really extend the range of parts of the past to which he appeals, nor does he provide any examples of 'discretion' in action, or of the processes by which monasticism had changed since Benedict's day. For that we have to turn to a Benedictine writing in the Empire, Rupert of Deutz.

Until recently Rupert was one of the great unread authors among Bernard's contemporaries. Perhaps the very scale of his works, mostly lying in the yellowing, fragile pages of the *Patrologia Latina*, deflected all but the bravest souls. Now some may still underestimate him because, so far as we yet

---

[47] *Apology*, V.10: *SB Op*, 3, p. 90: *Works*, 1, p. 45.

[48] *Apology*, IX.23 (see n. 36 above): Wilmart, 'Une Riposte', pp. 311–14.

[49] *Regula*, 64.19, cf. 64.18, 70.6 (Fry edn, pp. 283, 292).

[50] Wilmart, 'Une riposte', p. 327: 'Dic, obsecro, bone abbas, dic, sodes, quomodo, hec iocosa dicendo, illum regule locum adimples, ubi scur[r]ilitatem et uerba risum mouencia pater Benedictus eterna dampnat clausura?' Cf. *Regula*, VI.9, 'Scurrilitates vero vel verba otiosa et risum moventia aeterna clausura in omni locis damnamus'. I have followed the translation by Justin McCann, *The Rule of Saint Benedict* (London, 1952), p. 37.

[51] Wilmart, 'Une riposte', p. 317: 'Atque, secundum historialem intelligentiam de qua presenter agimus . . . .'

know, his works do not seem to have circulated much outside Germany.[52] Yet his *On certain chapters of the Rule of St Benedict*, which still lies unloved in Migne, seems to approach the past in a new and exciting way.[53]

Rupert turned to the Rule when his own way of life came under attack with the foundation of the first Cistercian monastery within the Empire at Camp, not far to the northwest, in 1122.[54] It had been established by the Archbishop of Cologne, Frederick, with whom Deutz, lying just across the river from Cologne, had very close links. Rupert himself had been appointed abbot by him.[55] What Frederick called 'some branches of the new plantation of Cîteaux' which he wished 'to insert spiritually into the garden of our Church',[56] and his installation the year before of some regular canons in the decayed nunnery at Steinfeld in the Eiffel south of the city[57] might prove cuckoos in the nest as far as traditional Benedictines were concerned. Indeed, it was the fact that some of the newcomers visited local houses accusing them of not following the rules which they had professed, and enticing some to leave for pastures new, which forced Rupert to write.[58] He had other fish to fry with which we need not worry, so it was not until the second and third books of his treatise that he turned to issues raised by those whom he stigmatized as 'rather learned searchers into the Rule of blessed Benedict' – 'valde studiosos scrutatores Regulae beati Benedicti'.[59] Let us consider four of the issues which he discussed.

The first may now seem rather insignificant, that of when Alleluia should be sung at the end of psalms and responsories

[52] John H. Van Engen, *Rupert of Deutz* (Berkeley, Los Angeles, and London, 1983), pp. 81, 322, 333.

[53] Rupert of Deutz, *Super quaedam capitula Regulae divi Benedicti abbatis*, PL, 170, cols 477–538.

[54] Van Engen, *Rupert*, p. 314: J.-M. Canivez, 'Camp', *Dictionnaire d'histoire et de géographie ecclésiastiques*, 11 (Paris, 1949), col. 618 gives 1123.

[55] Van Engen, *Rupert*, p. 12.

[56] Constable, 'Renewal and reform', p. 44.

[57] Van Engen, *Rupert*, p. 324.

[58] Ibid., pp. 314–23. He notes, very helpfully, places where Rupert and Peter the Venerable use similar arguments.

[59] Rupert, *Super quaedam capitula*, II. xiii: PL, 170, col. 509.

during the Office.[60] Then the matter was contentious since the Cistercians, basing themselves upon the Rule, chapter 15, did this for a shorter period of the year than other religious, who followed Roman usages.[61] This was not the first time in monastic history that the issue had arisen: it had been debated during the reign of Louis the Pious, though whether Rupert and others knew this is not yet certain.[62] As historians we can also recognize that it has often been upon such small matters that huge quantities of ill-feeling have been aroused. Rupert's response was to admit that Benedict had had a different view, but he appealed to history to justify what he and most Benedictines did; for as he put it, 'at the time when blessed Benedict wrote this Rule, the times, stations and holy offices of the whole year had not been settled'. That, he stated, had been done by Pope Gregory who he realized was of a younger generation than Benedict – 'beato Benedicto secundum tempus sine dubio junior'.[63] Rupert here shows an awareness of change which, while it may not strike us as unusual, was in fact so at that time.

The second issue relates to clothing, and has three aspects. Firstly he attacked the Cistercians, on the basis of chapter 55 of the Rule, for wearing what he called habits of a dubious and indistinct kind of white. This has, incidentally, some claim to be the earliest description of what Cistercian habits looked like, but it is to be observed that Rupert claimed that if the traditionalists had worn white the new monks would have chosen black, just to be different.[64] He also defended the

---

60   Ibid., II. xiii: *PL*. 170, cols 508–9.

61   *Regula*, 15 (Fry edn, pp. 210–11).

62   Rosamund McKitterick, *The Frankish Kingdoms under the Carolingians* (London and New York, 1983), pp. 113–16 for this and other issues debated in the twelfth century. I am grateful to Dr McKitterick for drawing my attention to these similarities: few historians of the Cistercians refer to them, but see Bede Lackner, *Eleventh-Century Background of Cîteaux*, Cistercian Studies, 8 (Washington, D.C., 1972), pp. 35–9. There is room for more study of the question. The only quotation from Carolingian legislation I noticed occurs in Idung of Prüfening (*c*.1155), *Dialogue*, II.42: *Cistercians and Cluniacs. The Case of Cîteaux. A Dialogue between Two Monks. An argument on Four Questions by Idung of Prüfening*, trans. Jeremiah O'Sullivan, Cistercian Fathers, 33 (Kalamazoo, Mi., 1977), p. 87.

63   *Super quaedam*, II. xiv: *PL*, 170, col. 509: 'quo tempore beatus Benedictus hanc Regulam scripsit, necdum sic ordinata fuerunt tempora in Ecclesia Romana, sive stationes, et sacra totius anni officia.'

64   Ibid., III. xiii: *PL*, 170 cols 520–1.

use of furs by citing Benedict's own words which recognized that monks would need more clothes in colder areas ('in frigidibus regionibus amplius indigetur') and cited as precedents Adam and Eve, the Fathers in the desert, Benedict's own behaviour as described by Gregory, and a story about Benedict's disciple Maur rescuing a young monk from drowning. The young man later acknowledged that Benedict had been involved too, for he had recognized him from his sheepskin ('melotem').[65] The geographic argument was used again when discussing monastic underwear. While the Cistercians had rejected drawers because Benedict said not a word of them, Rupert claimed that monks should follow local custom. Since he and those with whom he was arguing lived in a province where underpants were the norm, they should be used by monks. If one lived where they were not, as in Britain and Ireland, they could be dispensed with, although Rupert confessed that he had been shocked when he saw that this was the case in Italy.[66]

Rupert's most original use of the past arose during his discussion of whether manual work was an essential part of the life of a monk, as the Cistercians and other new groups claimed. Here he asked the question, perhaps for the first time in this debate, of whether manual work was required by the Rule as necessary for salvation, or allowed to those monks who had to do it: was it 'iussa', commanded, or 'permissa', allowed? For a precedent he mentioned the way that in the Old Testament God allowed the Jews to offer the sacrifices of the Law.[67] Benedict, he claimed, had merely allowed manual labour, citing a passage in chapter 41 on the hours of meals, where the possibility is mentioned that monks may have work to do in the fields: 'si opus in agris habuerint'.[68] Where monks did not have such tasks, then they were not imposed. Peter protesting in Acts 6.2 that it was not reasonable 'to serve the word of God and serve tables', and Paul telling the Corinthians that they who 'preach the Gospel should live of the Gospel' (I Corinthians 9.14) were drawn on here. Paul,

---

65 Ibid., III. xvi: *PL*, 170, cols 523–4.
66 Ibid., III. xvii; *PL*, 170, cols 524–6.
67 Ibid., III. iv–vi: *PL*, 170 cols 513–15.
68 *Regula*, 41.3 (Fry edn, p. 240).

indeed, on the strength of II Corinthians 8 was said never to have worked except at Corinth. So Benedict in this perspective had only decreed manual work as a way of dealing with poverty, 'paupertatis solatium'.[69] But it is at this very point that Rupert drew upon actual examples of how Gregory and many others had acted to strengthen his case; it is this that makes him shine out among the people we have been considering so far. The pope had given estates, 'praedia', to monasteries, whilst Maur, Benedict's loved disciple (whom Rupert and everyone else then believed had brought the Rule to Francia), had accepted gifts from kings and princes so that the 140 monks who lived with him had income enough without needing to work, 'as the book of his life testifies' ('sicut testatur Liber Vitae ejus').[70] Rupert does not merely justify deviations from the Rule by arguing about its wording, but does so by citing apostolic practice and that of the man who should have known Benedict's mind best. He was, of course, unaware that the *Life* upon which he trusted is now recognized as a much later invention.[71]

Similar methods are used when he turns to the question of whether monks should become priests or not, something which he says was denied by the new monks.[72] This is interesting since there is not, it seems, any evidence that this issue was raised by the Cistercians, but it may have been by some other innovators. Rupert admitted that many of the great monks of the desert had not been priests (he names Paul, Anthony, Julian, Hilarion, and Macarius) but explained that this was so because they had to take to the desert to avoid persecution – 'in solitudinibus et in agris habitabant' – whereas in his day the condition of the Church was totally different: 'At nunc alius Ecclesiae status est'.[73] For Rupert, huge changes had occurred in the Church since the desert time, since the great in the world had filled towns and villages

---

[69] *Super quaedam*, III. vii: *PL*, 170, col. 515.

[70] Ibid., III. vii: *PL*, 170, col. 515.

[71] Cf. David Hugh Farmer, *The Oxford Dictionary of Saints* (Oxford, 1978), p. 273.

[72] *Super quaedam*, III. xi: *PL*, 170, cols 519–20.

[73] Ibid., *PL*, 170, col. 520. The term 'status' was used over thirty years later by the German Premonstratensian, Anselm of Havelberg, in his extraordinary, and much discussed, brief history of the world; cf. Smalley, 'Novelty', pp. 124–5.

with monasteries which they have endowed with rents, and the many Christians living around them have given alms, commending themselves to the prayers of the priests to the point where there are scarcely enough priests in a monastery to carry out their requests. Again, here Rupert shows an awareness of the ways that change occurred through developments in wider society which is exceptional. It appears, however, to be all of a piece with the rest of his writing, where the past is searched for evidence of the working out of divine intentions. His great work on the Trinity, for example, gives the longest account of the history of salvation since Augustine's *De Civitate Dei*, and takes the account down to his own day.[74]

Peter, the great Abbot of Cluny, drew into his thinking just as wide a range of the past as Rupert, but presents a less coherent view about the interaction between monasticism and other parts of society. His most substantial contribution to the debate (it covers nearly fifty printed pages) is that *Letter 28* which has already been referred to.[75] It is framed as a reply to twenty accusations from the Cistercian side, many of them not to be found in any surviving document, certainly not in Bernard's *Apology*. This fact alone is sufficient to see that he did not react to something which Bernard had written, even though he cast his thoughts in the form of a letter addressed to Bernard. Examination of it here will be restricted to two issues which had already been dealt with by Rupert, and one which was not.

On black as the colour of habits, Peter urged a new precedent: that of St Martin, something he must have read about in the *Second Dialogue* of Sulpicius Severus.[76] On manual work Peter, like Rupert, appealed to the example of Maur, though he did not mention directly those gifts which had made manual work unnecessary; he merely said that Maur had created a monastery in such a way that his monks were

---

[74] Van Engen, *Rupert*, p. 94; cf. pp. 282–91 for events coming into his *De victoria Verbi Dei*.

[75] Constable, *Letters*, 1, pp. 52–101.

[76] *Letter 28*, p. 57: Constable's annotation refers to *Dialogues*, II.3 (C. Halm, ed., *Sulpicii Severi, Libri qui supersunt*, Corpus Scriptorum ecclesiasticorum latinorum, 1 [Vienna, 1866], p. 183).

supplied with all necessities.[77] That he knew more emerges much later in the course of his discussion of whether monks could own castles, towns, peasants, and male and female serfs (an analysis clearly in line with the passage cited from the *Exordium Parvum* earlier).[78] Here Peter presented two different sorts of evidence involving Pope Gregory: a letter allowing monks to hold such property, and a passage from the *Life* by John the Deacon describing the kind of property which the Pope gave to the monasteries founded by him in Sicily. Then follow two extracts from the *Life of Maur* showing him accepting gifts of royal estates. Columbanus is also mentioned as doing the same – as, Peter claimed, had many of the saints. So Peter knew everything on the issue which Rupert did, but deployed it in a rather less effective manner. On at least one other issue, the length of the novitiate (not discussed by Rupert), Peter appealed to Christ's practice: he had not tried those he called with a year's probation.[79] Here Peter also drew on decisions of councils and popes who had often changed earlier institutions, citing *inter alia* Gregory's allowing of marriage within the fifth degree. This, one may suppose, he knew about either through a collection of canon law, or through Bede's *Ecclesiastical History*.[80] The fundamental issue for him here was that things laid down by the Fathers could be altered on account of either necessity or utility, a point he supported with quotations from the Council of Nicaea and from two people he believed to be popes. The whole tenor of his long letter is that deviations from the Rule had occurred as they were forced on monks by others, or had occurred as monks opened their way of life to others. Much later in his life, in 1144, Peter wrote again to Bernard to defend all the changes on the ground that by them charity had been best served.[81]

The seven works written between about 1119 and 1127 considered here show that both sides of the debate used the past to justify their own way of life. The traditionalists,

---

[77] Ep. 28.viii, pp. 70-1.
[78] Ep. 28.xviii, pp. 81-7: cf. p. 96 above.
[79] Ep. 28.i, pp. 58-62.
[80] See Constable's notes, p. 61.
[81] Ep. 111, pp. 274-99.

wishing to hold on to the old, naturally turned to a wider past than did the Cistercians, who hammered away with their appeal to the Rule and its founder. Both sides looked beyond the sixth century to the desert, to the apostolic Church, and further to precedents in the life of the Jews. The greatest virtuoso in that particular practice (which cannot be discussed in length here) was the anonymous writer of a short, unfinished, book, the *Libellus de diversis ordinibus et professionibus qui sunt in æcclesia*, who attempted to find an Old Testament precedent for every kind of religious life.[82] Broadly speaking this pattern occurs in the other fourteen works on the debate written during Bernard's lifetime and to the end of the twelfth century.[83] Because of this continuity, and a need to keep this paper within bounds, the discussion of these will try to draw out some new parts of the past which now appear.

The first new element appears in a withering letter which Hugh of Amiens' friend, Matthew of Albano, wrote to a group of Benedictine abbots who had met at Reims in the autumn of 1131 and decided upon various measures of reform, most of them moving in a Cistercian direction.[84] One matter which Matthew defended was the adornment of churches with gold and silver. This was something which the *Exordium Parvum*, early Cistercian legislation, and most famously the *Apology* had all attacked.[85] Almost inevitably Moses and Solomon brightening the Tabernacle and Temple at God's command appear; but then come Christian emperors

[82]   Cf. the admirable edition by G. Constable and B. Smith, *Libellus de diversis ordinibus et professionibus qui sunt in æcclesia*, OMT (Oxford, 1972).

[83]   Works not discussed below are a reply of the Benedictine abbots to Matthew of Albano (see n. 84); a letter of Archbishop Thurstan of York to William of Corbeil, Archbishop of Canterbury; a letter of Theobald of Étampes to Thurstan, and an anonymous Benedictine reply; the 'Golden Letter' of William of Saint-Thierry; the second anonymous reply to St Bernard (see n. 7 above); the *Dialogues* of Anselm of Havelberg (see n. 73 above); the *Dialogue* of Idung of Prüfening (see n. 62 above).

[84]   The whole dossier has recently been re-edited by Stanislaus Ceglar, 'William of Saint Thierry and his leading role at the first chapters of the Benedictine Abbots (Reims 1131, Soissons 1132)' in *William of St. Thierry. A Colloquium at the Abbey of St. Thierry*, trans. Jerry Carfantan, Cistercian Studies, 94 (Kalamazoo, Mi., 1987), pp. 34–112. Matthew's letter is at pp. 65–86.

[85]   Ceglar, 'William', pp. 79–81: cf. *Ex Parv.*, xvii.6–8 (de Place et al., *Cîteaux documents*, pp. 50–1), *capitula*, xxv–xxvi (ibid., pp. 134–5), *Apology*, XII.28–9 (*SB Op*, 3, pp. 104–6: *Works*, 1, pp. 63–6).

and kings who give treasures to beautify churches, with popes, saints, and great abbots doing the same. The point that a wide range of people made the splendour possible seems terribly obvious now, but in the context of this debate it appears as an unusual insight.

In contrast the letters exchanged between Heloise and Abelard around 1132 and 1135, about the religious life of women (a subject entirely missing elsewhere), scarcely bring in a wider past than we have seen already.[86] Heloise provoked two letters from her old teacher and lover when she asked to be told how 'the order of nuns began' and then presented many difficulties which Benedict's Rule created for women. Abelard's long historical account goes back to Jerusalem, but refers to no one later than Gregory I. His actual Rule, on the other hand, cites something much nearer to his own day: Gregory's VII's blunt assertion, 'In the Gospel the Lord says "I am Truth". He did not say "I am custom".'[87]

A little later, around 1136, Orderic Vitalis in his account of Cistercian beginnings puts into the mouths of the reformers a desire to imitate the life of the desert – something which was not in the earliest Cistercian documents, although it plays, as we have seen, a small role for Bernard.[88] Some years ago it was on the basis of such evidence that Benedicta Ward claimed that it was only in the second and third generations of the new experiment that this 'myth' of the desert grew

[86]   Letters 5–7: the best edition for 5–6 is by J. T. Muckle, 'The letter of Heloise on religious life and Abelard's first reply', *Mediaeval Studies*, 17 (1955), pp. 240–81, and for 7 by T. P. McLaughlin, 'Abelard's rule for religious women', *Mediaeval Studies*, 18 (1956), pp. 241–92. There is a very useful translation in *The Letters of Abelard and Heloise*, trans. Betty Radice (Harmondsworth, 1974), pp. 159–269, although she only summarizes Letter 6.

[87]   Letter 7; Muckle, 'Letter of Heloise', p. 206. The same passage is in Idung, *Dialogue* (see n. 62 above), I, 51 (p. 52). Augustine, *De Baptismo*, III. vi (*PL*, 43, col. 143) probably was the source for medieval quotations, but the sentiment is in Tertullian, *Liber de Virginibus Velandis*, I: 'Sed Dominus noster Christus veritatem se, non consuetudinem cognominavit.' (*PL*, 2, col 937). I owe this suggestion to the Revd Prof. Stuart Hall.

[88]   *The Ecclesiastical History of Orderic Vitalis*, VIII, 26, ed. and trans. Marjorie Chibnall, 6 vols, *OMT* (Oxford, 1969–80), 4, pp. 311–27. For the date of Book VIII, p. xix. Orderic's mention of Domus Dei, i.e. Noirlac, founded 1136, means that Dr Chibnall's suggestion that this part 'was written in 1135 or possibly 1136' needs minor reformulation: cf. Holdsworth, 'Orderic, traditional monk and the new monasticism', in Diana Greenway, Christopher Holdsworth, and Jane Sayers, eds, *Tradition and Change. Essays in honour of Marjorie Chibnall* (Cambridge, 1985), p. 25.

up.[89] This may be too severe. Even though Orderic was writing nearly forty years after events he had some basis for his 'invention', just as William of Malmesbury had for his. His abbot had visited Clairvaux in 1130, and he himself went to Cluny in 1132.[90] Some of those who told him of the early days at Cîteaux may have been survivors from them: Stephen Harding lived on well into the 1130s, and we know that he had travelled in Italy as a young man before settling at Molesme. In Italy he could very well have visited some of the very hermit communities which certainly did aim to imitate the desert. One should not forget, either, that Bruno, the founder of La Grande Chartreuse, was for a time a monk at Molesme, and he was thought to have been inspired by the desert.[91] Perhaps this is giving Orderic too much credence, but there can be no doubt that from the mid-1130s onwards the desert was an inspiration for Cistercians. Like another Eadmer, William of Saint-Thierry, when writing between 1145 and 1148 the life of his still-living friend whom he believed to be a saint, said that when he first went to Clairvaux he had been reminded of the desert: 'Wherever I turned my eye in wonder, it was as if I saw a new heaven and a new earth, and the ancient tracks of the ancient monks of Egypt, our fathers.'[92] Here he was doing something new: using the Cistercians' own recent past as a defence of their way of life.

This appeal to recent history is, in fact, one of the most innovative uses of the past on both sides of the debate in this later period. Almost at the very time that William was writing, Peter, an Augustinian prior of the church of St John at Sens, wrote to a friend, Bishop Hatto of Troyes, who had retired to Cluny to die.[93] Like Hugh of Amiens and Peter the

---

[89] Benedicta Ward, 'The desert myth', pp. 183–99, esp. 190–1.

[90] Holdsworth, 'Orderic, traditional monk', pp. 26–7.

[91] Stephen's travels are summarized by Lekai, *The Cistercians*, p. 17. See also H. E. J. Cowdrey, '*Quidam frater Stephanus nomine, anglicus natione*: the English background of Stephen Harding', *Revue Bénédictine*, 101 (1991), pp. 322–40: for Bruno's inspiration, see Ward, 'The desert myth', p. 192.

[92] *Vita Prima*, I.vii: *PL*, 185, col. 247. For the date see A. H. Bredero, *Études sur la 'Vita Prima' de Saint Bernard* (Rome, 1960), pp. 100–1.

[93] Giles Constable, 'The letter of Peter of St John to Hatto of Troyes', in Giles Constable and James Kritzeck, eds, *Petrus Venerabilis, 1156–1956, Studia Anselmiana*, 40 (1956), pp. 38–52.

Venerable, this Peter commended the life of the great monastery because great abbots had lived there who had been recognized as saints. But he went on to appeal to a new piece of history to round off his story. The success which Urban II had in preaching the Crusade at the Council of Clermont was, according to Peter, a result of his time as prior at Cluny. It was there that he 'acquired the skill and eloquence which were able to enlighten all the faithful and give to the Churches the courage to crush the infidel. And this great good flowed from the same holy place, from whose fountainhead that apostolic man drew the flood of holy religion and powerful eloquence.'[94] He also appealed to much more recent appearances of Christ to the monks in choir and chapter house, which he asked Hatto to confirm.

This kind of appeal to holy wonders in the recent past is seen most extensively in the last Cistercian work, the *Exordium Magnum*, compiled between 1186 and 1221 by Conrad of Eberbach. Here the saintly lives of abbots of Cîteaux itself and of Clairvaux are portrayed by telling of some of the miracles which they had done. The holy history of the new institution itself is deployed to demonstrate just how much it has been approved by God – the very line of defence which traditional monks had used as soon as they began to respond to their new rivals. What is more surprising is that Conrad also incorporated into the first part of his book not merely, as one might expect, an account of the beginnings of monastic life in the apostolic Church, its development in the desert, and the contribution of Benedict, but also miracles done by Odo and Hugh of Cluny.[95] Plums from Cluny's own history are, as it were, taken over as a proper prelude to the Cistercian story.

Here there is a certain irony, since by the time this defence was being made in such a massive style, the Cistercian way of life had begun to look not so far away from Cluny in the spectrum of monastic customs. The Cistercians had waxed prosperous, on the one hand, whilst the Cluniacs *strictu sensu* (thanks to the work of Peter the Venerable) had altered many

[94] Ibid., Constable's trans. pp. 47–8, Latin, p. 51.
[95] *Exordium Magnum Cisterciense sive Narratio de initio Cisterciensis ordinis auctore Conrado*, ed. Bruno Griesser (Rome, 1961), I, i–ii, iii–v, vi–ix, pp. 48–60.

of those practices from which the Cistercians had dissented.[96] The debate by then was running out of steam: there was little controversy between different followers of St Benedict in the later Middle Ages (there was, of course, argument between monks and mendicants). One other cause of this development, of a very different kind, is typified by the fact that writings of many of the early Cistercians were now to be found on every Benedictine bookshelf. Bernard, above all, had become one of the crucial spiritual guides for monks and nuns, however great a hammer of some of their predecessors he might once have been.[97] So there was no need to call in the old world of the past to justify the new. That had been a crucial part of the twelfth-century debate; but by the early thirteenth century the need to call Anthony, Benedict, Maur, or Odo to the defence of either side had gone. There was no longer a struggle.

University of Exeter

---

[96] These matters are contentious: for a measured account see Morris, *Papal Monarchy*, pp. 250-7.

[97] For the English evidence see Christopher Holdsworth, 'The reception of St Bernard in England', in Kaspar Elm, ed., *Bernhard von Clairvaux. Rezeption und Wirkung im Mittelalter und in der Neuzeit* (Wiesbaden, 1994), pp. 169-77.

A TWELFTH-CENTURY VIEW OF
THE HISTORICAL CHURCH: ORDERIC VITALIS

by MARJORIE CHIBNALL

Wh-hen Eusebius set out to write an Ecclesiastical History he claimed to be 'the first to undertake this present project and to attempt, as it were, to travel along a lonely and untrodden path'.[1] The claim was justified: there had been little room for religious history, even the history of pagan religions, in the works of classical historians and their imitators. Following the rules laid down by Thucydides, they concentrated on the political life of the present and its military consequences; they preferred oral to written sources, provided the historian had either been present at the scene of action or had heard reports from eye-witnesses.[2] Both in method and in content Eusebius was an innovator. Since his starting point was 'the beginning of the dispensation of Jesus' he was entirely dependent on written sources for more than three hundred years; and, innovating still more, he introduced documents such as letters and imperial edicts into his narrative. Far from being political and military, his subject matter was primarily the history of the apostles, the succession of bishops, the persecutions of Christians, and the views of heretics.[3] He was widening the scope of historical writing and using the techniques previously employed in the biographies of philosophers. It is not surprising that, once his work had been translated into Latin and extended by Rufinus and Jerome, it became the starting point for writers on ecclesiastical history for generations to come.

The *Ecclesiastical History* of Orderic Vitalis,[4] though not as innovatory and influential, was nevertheless 'truly a universal

---

[1] Eusebius, *The Ecclesiastical History*, ed. and trans. H. J. Lawlor and J. E. L. Oulton (London, 1927), I, i, 3.
[2] See A. D. Momigliano, *Studies in Historiography* (London, 1969), pp. 214–18.
[3] Eusebius, I, i, 1–2.
[4] *The Ecclesiastical History of Orderic Vitalis*, ed. and trans. Marjorie Chibnall, 6 vols, OMT (Oxford, 1969–80) [hereafter OV].

history of a new and original kind'.[5] It grew gradually, out of the writer's own experience; and there can be little doubt that for more than forty years history, as he came to understand and cherish it, was his deepest interest after his monastic vocation, which to him was always paramount. Born in 1075 near to Shrewsbury, where he saw the harsher side of the Norman conquest and also the first steps in the founding of a great abbey, he was sent away at the age of ten to be a child oblate in the Norman abbey of St Evroult.[6] There he had the advantage of a monastic school with a learned master, John of Reims, an adult *conversus* who had come to St Evroult after several years of study in the schools of Reims. Orderic's introduction to Church history was both through the study of the Bible, starting most probably with the historical books, and through the daily round of monastic observance. The liturgical year took him annually in sermons and readings through the life and teaching of Christ. The feast days of saints were marked by the *historiae* recounting their lives and virtues. Since it was not customary at St Evroult to promote children of the cloister, who had no experience in the outside world, to executive office, he was spared (for better or worse) the burdens of administration. He worked in the school and in the library, himself copying as well as supervising the copying of manuscripts. As time went on, he added marginal notes to chronicles or biblical commentaries, and even inserted lengthy interpolations. His master, John of Reims, had a keen interest in history; it may even have been a jealous interest, for Orderic remained very much an apprentice historian until ill-health reduced John's activity and perhaps persuaded him voluntarily to stand aside. This left the field clear for his more brilliant pupil.

Orderic insists repeatedly in his writing on his monastic duty to avoid idleness and to practise obedience; what he wrote was, he claimed, written at the command of his abbot,

---

[5] Peter Classen, '*Res gestae*, universal history, apocalypse', in Robert L. Benson and Giles Constable, eds, *Renaissance and Renewal in the Twelfth Century* (Cambridge, Mass., 1982), p. 390.

[6] For Orderic's life and studies see OV, 1, pp. 1–6, 14–29; Marjorie Chibnall, *The World of Orderic Vitalis* (Oxford, 1984), pp. 1–16, 33–4, and ch. 5.

first of Roger du Sap and then of his contemporary and friend, Warin des Essarts.[7] He did not set out, like Eusebius, with an overall plan; instead his work grew slowly, 'in ever-widening circles',[8] as Peter Classen has expressed it. At first he interpolated new sections into the *Gesta Normannorum ducum* of William of Jumièges;[9] nearly all of them were concerned with the history of St Evroult, its monks and its patrons, in both Normandy and Italy. These interpolations were purely factual. Then (still under orders) he began an independent history of his own abbey of St Evroult, so that the young monks might be better informed of the lives of the holy abbots and the patrons for whom they prayed daily in the choir; it included details of the properties which were confirmed by King Henry I after he visited the abbey in 1113. Readers of the present Book III[10] (the first to be written) cannot fail to be aware that he was visibly straining at the leash; he was only waiting for the word that would allow him to plunge freely, not just into the history of the families connected with St Evroult, but into the whole history of the Normans and of the conquest of England that had brought the abbey its English properties. Possibly by this time he had already copied Bede's *Ecclesiastical History of the English People*; the manuscript, written in his own beautiful handwriting, still survives in the library of the Bibliothèque de la Ville at Rouen.[11] From there it was only a short step to see a similar history of the *gens Normannorum* as a legitimate – indeed as a desirable – undertaking.

He did not stop there; his experience widened. In 1119 he was a representative of his abbey at the Council of Reims, and from there he travelled by way of Cambrai to England,[12] to visit Crowland Abbey, where Geoffrey of Orleans, pre-viously prior of St Evroult, was abbot. This enabled him to make a more extensive tour of England, staying at Thorney

7   OV, 1, pp. 130–4; 3, 4–9.
8   Classen, '*Res gestae*', pp. 388–9.
9   *The 'Gesta Normannorum ducum' of William of Jumièges, Orderic Vitalis and Robert of Torigni*, ed. and trans. Elisabeth M. C. van Houts, 2 vols, OMT (Oxford, 1992–5), 1, pp. lxvi–lxxvii.
10   OV, 2, pp. 2–189, especially pp. 104–5.
11   Rouen, Bibliothèque de la Ville, MS 1343.
12   OV, 1, pp. 25–6.

and Worcester and other abbeys. At Cambrai and Worcester he saw the universal chronicles of Sigebert of Gembloux and Marianus Scotus,[13] and realized that there was a place in monastic studies for new universal chronicles. Without abandoning his more substantial work, which he was already beginning to call an ecclesiastical history,[14] he collected material for a chronicle of the Church up to his own time (as, after Eusebius, Bede had pointed the way in his studies of chronology). It was possibly only after he had decided to amalgamate the two works, with the chronological survey making up the first two of thirteen books, that he clearly showed what he understood by ecclesiastical history.

How did he see the Church; and what were his perceptions of the Church in past time? The metaphor that he used in the first chapters he wrote was that of the vine:[15] it was always central to his life and to his thought. The parable of the workers in the vineyard had a special meaning for him. When he discussed the parable in his comments on the life of Christ in Book I he cited the various interpretations offered by commentators. One of these likened the workers who came at different hours to those serving God at different ages: in the morning in boyhood, at the third hour in adolescence, at the sixth in youth, and at the ninth in old age. He drew a hand in the margin pointing to *Mane puericia est*.[16] As a child of the cloister, he had begun working early in the Lord's vineyard to tend the vine of God's Church; and he remembered this again in the epilogue to his *History*, in which he described his own life and how he had laboured from boyhood in the vineyard of the vine of Sorech, confident of receiving the promised reward.[17] The metaphor must have sustained him in the rougher and more arid passages of monastic life. It was common enough in other writers; he could have found it in the *Gesta Normannorum ducum* of William of Jumièges.[18] But for him it had the immediacy of a life-long personal

13   Ibid., 2, pp. 186–9.
14   Ibid., 2, p. 188.
15   Ibid., 2, pp. 4–5.
16   Ibid., 1, pp. 143–4.
17   Ibid., 6, pp. 554–7; Chibnall, *World*, p. 224.
18   *Gesta Normannorum ducum*, I, i (ed. van Houts, 1, pp. 10–11).

experience, as vividly spotlit as are many of the most striking scenes in the paintings of Nicholas Poussin.

Following Eusebius, he included the history of the apostles and their successors, the bishops. But the passing of time and the accumulation of sources, reliable and unreliable, brought new problems which Eusebius had never been obliged to face. The first was whether to go beyond the scriptures which, since the fifth century, had been widely recognized as canonical, and to include writings suspected of being apocryphal. In writing the life of Christ, Orderic kept closely to the four gospels, following the guidelines laid down by St Augustine in his *De consensu evangelistarum*.[19] Although he knew the apocryphal *Gospel of Nicodemus*, and indeed had helped to copy it for his monastic library,[20] he made no use of it. He did not allow himself to be tempted into its dramatic account of the trial of Christ.

All self-restraint was, however, abandoned when he came to the Acts of the Apostles. Some of the apocrypha must have seemed peculiarly appropriate to the problems of the Church in his own day. In particular, the attack on simony, regarded by many of his contemporaries as equivalent to heresy, invited the introduction of the many legends that had gathered round the name of Simon Magus. Simon, the magician who had practised in Samaria before being con- verted and baptized, played a very small part in the canonical Acts. There he appeared briefly as the mercenary figure who offered Peter money in the hope of receiving the gift of the Holy Spirit. Peter rebuked him with the words, 'Your money perish with you, because you thought that the gift of God may be purchased with money'; and Simon, duly chastened, asked Peter to pray for him, that none of the things he had spoken should come upon him.[21] The legends that quickly sprouted around him forgot his penitence and remembered only that he had been a magician, and had tried to purchase holy orders. He was confused with another Simon, Simon of Gitta, a magician considered to be a founder of the Gnostic

[19] OV, 1, pp. 134–50; Augustine, *De consensu evangelistarum libri quattuor*, ed. F. Weihreich, Corpus scriptorum ecclesiasticorum latinorum, 43 (Vienna, 1904).
[20] Rouen, Bibliothèque de la ville, MS 1343, pp. 23–33.
[21] Acts 8.13–24.

heresy and the father of all heretics. Eusebius refers to the second Simon, who came to Rome and spread heresy there.[22]

Orderic knew Eusebius, and also the legends in the *Clementine Recognitions* and the *Passio SS Petri et Pauli* of the Pseudo-Marcellus, which enlarged on the theme of St Peter's rivalry with Simon. Its climax came in a contest of words and wonders, said to have taken place before Nero in Rome and to have led to the martyrdom of Peter and Paul. The legends, and the confusion of the two Simons, had taken so strong a grip in art no less than in literature that Orderic's sober abbreviation of the Acts of the Apostles broke down when he reached the episode of Simon's repentance. For Simon's request for Peter's prayers, Orderic substituted, 'Simon, however, scorning the words of the apostle, departed and after apostatizing aroused God's anger by many acts of wickedness.'[23] This twist in the narrative opened the way for a full use of the legends when Orderic came to recount the lives and teaching of Peter and Paul. Much of Orderic's second book is made up of other apocryphal writings, particularly those attributed to Abdias, Bishop of Babylon.[24] Finally his eager search for apostolic bishops conditioned him to accept in its entirety the *Life* of St Martial (a Bishop of Limoges who probably lived in the third century) attributed to Aurelian. This pseudo-Aurelian *Life*, which originated in the eleventh century and was probably the work of Adhémar of Chabannes, made Martial a contemporary of Christ. Adhémar was an indefatigable forger in the interests of the abbey of St Martial of Limoges, where he had been educated.[25] Orderic was not alone in accepting the forgery as genuine; the legend of Martial's apostolicity, which made him the first apostle of Aquitaine, received papal approval in 1031. It was accepted at St Evroult, and its importance for

---

[22] Eusebius, II, xiii, xiv. For the growth of legends about Simon Magus see H. E. J. Cowdrey, 'Simon Magus in South Italy', *Anglo-Norman Studies*, 15 (1993), pp. 77–80; F. L. Cross and E. A. Livingstone, eds, *The Oxford Dictionary of the Christian Church*, 2nd edn (Oxford, 1983), p. 1277.

[23] OV, 1, p. 166, 'Simon autem apostoli dicta paruipendens recessit, et apostata factus innumeris sceleribus iram Domini diu exacerbauit.'

[24] Ibid., 1, pp. 174–5, 178–9 and *passim*.

[25] Ibid., 1, p. 190 and n.2; L. Duchesne, 'Saint Martial de Limoges', *Annales du Midi*, 4 (1892), pp. 289–330.

Orderic is shown vividly in a manuscript commentary on the Gospel of St Matthew, attributed to Anselm of Laon, which Orderic helped to copy.[26] Orderic, a historical interpolator, had a habit of slipping a little extra information into the manuscripts he was copying, and he may have added the identification of St Martial with one of the seventy disciples, or commented on the unnamed child whom Jesus set in the midst of his disciples to teach them humility, 'Many say that this child was St Martial of Limoges.'[27] Even if he did not write this, he certainly endorsed it.

The anonymity of the seventy disciples of Christ, and the fact that many early lists of bishops, even when authentic, gave no dates for their lives, made it easy to claim early bishops as apostles of Gaul in the first century. Orderic's eagerness to accept their apostolicity sometimes came into conflict with his more detached interest in chronology. The liturgical commemoration of the saints was more positive on the traditional day of the month connected with their death or translation than on calendar years. In the whole second book of the *Ecclesiastical History* the sources uppermost in Orderic's mind were the *Vitae* read aloud in chapter and refectory, and the *legenda* and hymns (many of which he copied) incorporated in the liturgy.[28] Details of these could be fitted into the chronology of Bede or various monastic annals by imagining an intermittent silence in the sources. The problem appears, for example, in the history of the church of Rouen and in the succession of bishops there.[29] Orderic used the *Acta episcoporum Rothomagensium* compiled in the time of Archbishop William Bonne-Âme (1079–1110), which included St Nicaise as the first Bishop of Rouen.[30] Nicaise was said to have been sent to Rouen by St Denis, and legends current from at least the eighth century had claimed St Denis as a bishop sent to Gaul by Clement I, the successor of St Peter.[31]

---

[26] Alençon, Bibliothèque de la ville, MS 26.
[27] Ibid., fo. 185.
[28] OV, 1, pp. 164–200.
[29] Ibid., 3, p. 46.
[30] Ibid., 3, p. 36 and n.4.
[31] *Dictionnaire d'histoire et de géographie ecclésiastiques*, 14 (Paris, 1960), pp. 263–5; L. Duchesne, *Fastes épiscopaux de l'ancienne Gaule*, 3 vols (Paris, 1894–1915), 2, pp. 464–5.

Orderic accepted both this dating and the claim that St Taurin of Évreux, who had actually lived in the late fourth century, was also a disciple of St Denis. This antedating of the legends of St Denis and the first conversion of Gaul left a puzzling gap, and Orderic could only say that for a hundred and sixty years the church in Gaul was brought almost to nothing by savage attacks, adding that, 'No book of history explicitly tells us the race of the people who brutally overthrew Christians and idolaters alike, or whence they came, or under what prince or tyrant they wrought havoc.'[32] In this way Orderic succeeded in at least papering over the cracks between chronology and apostolic history.

So, starting from Eusebius, he was led into a history of the Church that was in some places straightforward, in others encrusted by legends. One theme followed naturally, and to write about it was a welcome part of Orderic's duty. He claimed in introducing the subject of the new monastic orders that,

> When the apostles were taken up into Heaven, the apostolic teachers came in their place; they became glorious through their words and deeds . . . and offered God the fruits of their labours, which are still acceptable. Though evil abounds in the world, the devotion of the faithful in cloisters grows more abundant and bears fruit a hundredfold in the Lord's field. Monasteries are founded everywhere in mountain valleys and plains . . . the swarm of cowled monks spreads all over the world.[33]

Like the early apostles, the monks spread the Christian faith by their example and by their teaching, which brought many converts to the monastic life. Benedictine monasticism and Columbanian practices spread to Gaul; in his own day the preaching of Bernard of Tiron and Vitalis of Savigny attracted crowds of men and women to new, more austere forms of monasticism. His description of these new orders is

32 OV, 3, pp. 46–7.
33 Ibid., 4, pp. 310–11.

refreshingly free from polemic.[34] Varied in detail, it is nevertheless traditional history, derived from written sources. Some, which he accepted in good faith, were actually recent forgeries, such as Abbot Odo of Glanfeuil's *Vita Sancti Mauri*, which was designed to claim that St Maur had brought the Rule of St Benedict to Gaul.[35]

He used written sources of a different kind to justify the holding of property, including tithes and spiritualities, by monks, and to show that laymen might redeem their sins by giving a portion of their wealth as alms to churches.[36] In explaining the passage in Genesis that describes Abraham's distribution of the spoils of Sodom,[37] he clearly relied on Bede, whose commentary on the passage recognized that a lover of justice might give such a share to soldiers who fought with him.[38]

Less literary, and even less authentic, were the popular legends that had crept into many recent lives of the saints. When Orderic wrote his account of the life of St Evroul he used not the earliest *Vita*, written soon after the death of the saint, which was a simple and moving account of a holy hermit who had founded a religious community with mixed Columbanian and Benedictine customs, but a later, expanded *Vita*, dating probably from the eleventh century.[39] He may not have known the original *Vita*; he certainly relied on the second which, conforming to the pattern favoured at that time, presented the saint's life as a heroic struggle. Simple events in the first *Vita* were dramatized as miracles in the second. Interpolated names of rulers, which made Evroul die in the reign of Childebert II, not Childebert III, and so pushed his life back more than a hundred years, caused problems of chronology. And besides these changes in the

---

[34] Ibid., 4, pp. xl–xlii, 310–35.

[35] See L. Halphen, 'La vie de Saint Maur; exposé d'une théorie de M. Auguste Molinier', *Revue historique*, 88 (1905), pp. 287–95.

[36] OV, 3, pp. 260–4.

[37] Gen. 14. 21–4.

[38] Bede, *Libri quatuor in principium Genesis usque ad natiuitatem Isaac et eiectionem Ismahelis adnotationum*, ed. Ch. W. Jones, CChrSL (Turnhout, 1969), pp. 192–3. For tithes see ibid., pp. 189–91.

[39] Chibnall, *World*, pp. 101–5; OV, 1, App. II (pp. 204–11); 3, App. I (pp. 263–4).

written life, Orderic included a few popular legends, possibly from those told to the pilgrims who flocked to the saint's shrine after his relics were brought to the abbey in 1132.[40] So we have the tale of the demon who sowed discord among the monks and was roasted by the saint in the village bread oven at Échauffour, and that of the bull of Bocquencé, who led a herdsman to the ruins of the first abbey in the depths of the forest.[41] These stories may have been added to give young monks something with which to hold the interest of future simple pilgrims. Normally Orderic was more restrained in his use of legend, and he omitted from his *History* the legend of the Saxon dancers, which he knew and had copied.[42] And however conscious he may have been of the apocryphal lives of the apostolic bishops, they merely stimulated his interest and did not intrude into his more sober later account of reform in the Church of his own day.

This account was based partly on the acts of councils which, following the example first set by Eusebius, he copied into his book. The 1072 Council of Rouen and many other disciplinary regulations forbade the sale of parochial cures and church offices and the marriage of priests;[43] that of 1097 enforced the Truce of God and forbade priests to perform homage to laymen.[44] These reforms were actively preached in Normandy, and Orderic regarded them as important for church welfare. He had, too, a natural respect for papal authority and papal legates. But the more extreme theories of a hierocratic Church, which were gaining ground in Rome, passed him by. When he heard, or was told the substance of, papal sermons in councils, the theme that fired his imagination so much that he thought it worth recording was that of peace within the Church itself, and, added to it, the need to

---

[40] Ibid., 3, pp. 338–43.

[41] Ibid., 3, pp. 265–303.

[42] BN, MS lat. 6503, fos. 61–70; the legend of a group of Saxon dancers who had profaned Christmas night with their songs and dances in a churchyard, and were condemned to continue dancing day and night for a year without rest. A pilgrim who claimed to be one of the dancers had visited a number of Norman abbeys, including Mont-Saint-Michel, carrying letters authenticating the miracle (*litterae nimio sudore et uetustate corruptae*) (L. Delisle, Preface, in Jules Lair, ed., *Matériaux pour l'édition de Guillaume de Jumièges* [Paris, 1910], pp. 18–19 and Pl. 3).

[43] OV, 2, pp. 284–93.

[44] Ibid., 5, pp. 18–21.

resist and overcome the persecutors of the Church. From the information brought back to his abbey after the Council of Clermont in 1095, he noted that Pope Urban urged the nobles of the West and their men to make a lasting peace among themselves, take the sign of the cross on their shoulders, and prove their valour against the pagans who had violated the holy places of Jerusalem and were persecuting the Christians there.[45] His personal recollection of the discourse he had heard pronounced at Reims in 1119 by Pope Calixtus was of a moving plea to those present not to waste their breath in vain contentions, but to strive to find peace as true sons of God.[46] Orderic saw the Church of his own day as sadly torn by dissensions and wars, but with a duty to condemn heresy and to take up arms if necessary against its oppressors. These themes are Eusebian in origin, but were developed in different ways.

The eleventh-century Church was not troubled by such dangerous and divisive doctrines as gnosticism.[47] Eucharistic controversy, sparked by Berengar of Tours, was confined to theological debate. Anti-clerical outbreaks, more prevalent in north Italy, were local. Even when more heterodox preachers, such as Peter of Bruys, stirred up civil disturbances in the twelfth century, these scarcely impinged on Orderic's world.[48] To him heresy was rejection of Church law; so simony (as we have seen) was 'simoniacal heresy'. The immediate threat came from unbelievers and persecutors: the Saracens, who were accounted heretics by some, including his contemporary, Peter the Venerable, Abbot of Cluny.[49] So Orderic enlarged his ecclesiastical history by incorporating in it the pilgrimages to Jerusalem that grew into Crusades and brought new kingdoms into

45 Ibid., 5, pp. 14–17.
46 Ibid., 6, pp. 260–5.
47 R. I. Moore, *The Formation of a Persecuting Society* (Oxford, 1987), p. 24, comments on 'the contrast between the years up to 1140 or thereabouts, when the episcopal response to heretical preaching was piecemeal, *ad hoc* and often mild, and the increasing determination to deal severely with it which became evident after that time'.
48 Chibnall, *World*, pp. 163–4.
49 *The Letters of Peter the Venerable*, ed. Giles Constable, 2 vols, Harvard Historical Studies, 78 (Cambridge, Mass., 1967), 2, pp. 275–8.

the Christian Church. He found his inspiration in the *Historia Ierosolimitana* of Baudry of Bourgueil. 'Never before', he wrote,

> has a more glorious subject been given to the learned than the Lord offered in our own day to poets and writers when he triumphed over the pagans in the East through the efforts of a few Christians, whom he had stirred up to leave their homes through an ardent longing to be pilgrims.[50]

He professed reluctance and incapacity, but there is something of the newly-elected bishop's *nolo episcopare* in the speed with which he succumbed: 'I too aspire to include this Christian enterprise . . . in the little book I am writing on ecclesiastical matters. I . . . dare not promise to accomplish such an arduous undertaking; yet I know not how to pass over such a noble theme in silence.'

His account of the First Crusade from its origin to the capture of Jerusalem and the battle of Ascalon is partly an abbreviation of Baudry's *Historia Ierosolimitana*,[51] filled out with information he had received from crusaders. It occupies the whole of Book IX; and he returned to describe the fortunes of the kingdom at some length in later books. Oral recollections were apt to be embellished during the long journey to the East in the heroic stories that make up the crusading *chansons*. The tales told by returning crusaders were half history, half romance.[52] Yet in spite of the alien elements, they earned their place in Orderic's ecclesiastical history, representing as they did the reactions to non-Christian cultures of the men, whether laymen or clerics, who made up the Christian Church. Orderic's concept was all-embracing. His Church was never merely the structured, hierocratic Church of the more extreme reformers; it was the whole body of the faithful, men and women, lay no less than clerical.

---

[50] OV, 5, pp. 4–7.
[51] *Baldrici episcopi dolensis historia ierosolimitana*, in *Recueil des historiens des croisades*, 16 vols (Paris, 1841–1906), 4.
[52] OV, 5, pp. xvi–xviii.

He was prepared to use every kind of information. Although in one place he rejected the *chansons* sung about St William of Gellone as unreliable,[53] other songs crept unrecognized into his history, through the narratives of the men who had heard them. Returned crusaders, or knights who had fought in Spain, and other eye-witnesses of battles often enlivened their narratives with heroic deeds they had heard in songs, which they passed on as authentic.[54] In recording oral traditions Orderic was, he said, preserving a record of events, so that it should not be lost 'as hail and snow melt in the waters of a swift-flowing river, swept away by the current never to return'.[55]

Archaeological evidence too aroused his curiosity. The Carolingian sarcophagi, still visible at the church of Notre-Dame-du-Bois across the valley from his own abbey and in the church of its priory at Saint-Céneri-le-Gérei,[56] were vivid reminders of the earlier monastic life in those places, of which he read in the lives of the saints. Sculpture and illuminated manuscripts carried the stories of real and imaginary episodes in the lives of saints, such as St Peter's contests with Simon Magus. They added a new dimension to his vision of the Church, as suggestive to him as the borders of the Bayeux Tapestry are to us. In the Tapestry some borders are purely decorative or traditional, with stylized trees or the everyday labours of the months. They shade through familiar fables, chosen to underline the theme of Harold's deceit depicted in the main part of the Tapestry, to break through at the most dramatic moments into the narrative itself: the ghostly fleet that underlines Harold's impending doom, the archers who played a crucial part in the battle, the slaughter and pillaging of the battle itself.[57]

[53] Ibid., 3, p. 218 and n.3. The *Vita* seen by Orderic was probably composed *c.* 1122.

[54] Ibid., 6, pp. xxii–xxiii; Chibnall, *World*, pp. 203–7.

[55] OV, 3, pp. 284–5.

[56] Ibid., 3, pp. 286–7, 156–7. Some of the stones from the sarcophagi at Saint-Céneri still survive, built into the foundations of the Romanesque church.

[57] On the borders of the Bayeux Tapestry see H. E. J. Cowdrey, 'Towards an interpretation of the Bayeux Tapestry', *Anglo-Norman Studies*, 10 (1988), pp. 49–65, at pp. 54–6, 62; H. Chefneux, 'Les fables dans la tapisserie de Bayeux', *Romania*, 60 (1934), pp. 1–35, 153–94.

Similarly, dreams, visions, and folklore impinge on Orderic's account of church history. They show themselves casually in the portents, such as eclipses and comets, described with a measure of detachment, and in the popular stories that creep into the more sober narrative lives of the saints. Most dramatically of all, they break into the central theme in the vision that the priest Walchelin had of 'Hellequin's hunt', where they are related to the most recent penitential teaching and the purpose of 'purgatorial fire'.[58] In short, they colour and enlarge Orderic's awareness of a history of the Church which is wide and deep enough to bring in the Church triumphant, and to touch questions of time, creation, and eternity.

Orderic's training and outlook were in no sense philosophical. He explicitly stood aside from speculative discussion. When Durand, the pious and learned Abbot of Troarn, died one side of his body was discovered to be white, the other half the colour of lead. This strange phenomenon, as Orderic noted, 'provided ingenious investigators with an opportunity for demonstrating the subtlety of their intelligence'. Some thought the left and right sides represented the active and contemplative, or the present and future life; others tried to see a prognostic of future events. Orderic, however, preferred simply to record the visible facts; and by doing so made it possible for a pathologist to offer a convincing medical interpretation eight hundred years later.[59] He was equally diffident about the learned debates he heard in 1119 at the Council of Reims. He gave the gist of a number of speeches, particularly those that praised peace or upheld Cluniac privileges. But on the intervention of Oldegar, Bishop of Barcelona, described as 'a man who, though small and emaciated, was remarkable for his learning and eloquence', he was content to make the terse comment that the Bishop 'made a subtle and very profound speech on the royal and sacerdotal offices, to which all who were capable of understanding it listened most avidly'.[60]

58 See below, pp. 130–2.
59 OV, 4, pp. 162–5.
60 Ibid., 6, pp. 274–5.

So it is not surprising that his conception of the Church in history should be, in scope at least, purely derivative. He never openly attempted to expatiate on such topics as time and eternity. His reading of the more philosophical writings of Augustine[61] and the exegesis of Bede and Jerome, no less than his daily round of monastic prayer and worship, left him with certain underlying assumptions. These are just indicated in the last words of his general Prologue,[62] when he wrote, 'First of all I will tell of the Beginning that has no beginning, by whose aid I aspire to come to the End that has no ending, so that I may sing devout praises with those above through eternity, to Him who is alpha and omega.'

The language is in part that of Eusebius; and perhaps at the back of his mind was Bede's commentary on the opening words of Genesis, *In principio creauit Deus coelum et terram* – that scripture shows that God omnipotent created the world at the beginning of time, himself existing eternally before time.[63] Whatever the philosophical assumptions behind such statements, Orderic was content to take them at their face value. One comprehensive passage at the beginning of his first book surveys the Church; it recalls the Word by which God the Father founded all things, the vine of the Church which he planted and which, tilled by faithful workers, puts up shoots all over the world, and finally it comes to earth at the moment of the Incarnation, where Orderic chose to begin his ecclesiastical history.[64] He did not attempt to write an earlier chronology or explore previous recorded history, explaining that he could not investigate Macedonian or

[61] For the influence of Augustine, Origen, and Boethius on medieval ideas on time and creation see Richard Sorabji, *Time, Creation and the Continuum* (London, 1983), especially pp. 115-24. As Sorabji warns, however, 'Many of the authors cited, especially those from the Judaeo-Christian tradition, did not achieve consistency in their accounts of eternal being'.

[62] OV, 1, pp. 132-3.

[63] Bede, *Libri quatuor in principium Genesis*, p. 3, 'Creationem mundi insinuans scriptura diuina apte primo statim uerbo eternitatem atque omnipotentiam Dei creatoris ostendit, quem enim in principio temporum mundum creasse perhibit, ipsum profecto ante tempora eternaliter extitisse designat.'

[64] OV, 1, p. 134. This was in fact a date frequently chosen as a starting point by writers of universal chronicles; see Timothy Reuter, 'Past, present and no future in the *Regnum teutonicum*', in Paul Magdolino, ed., *The Perception of the Past in Twelfth-Century Europe* (London and Rio Grande, 1992), pp. 15-36, at p. 33.

Greek or Roman affairs 'and many other matters worth the telling', because as a cloister monk of his own free will he was compelled to unremitting observance of his monastic duty.[65] He then stated his intention and method,

> to explain truthfully and simply the things which I have seen in our own times, or know to have occurred in nearby provinces. I firmly believe . . . that in time someone will come with greater understanding than myself, and greater capacity for understanding the various events taking place on earth, who will perhaps derive something from my writings and those of others like me . . . for the information of future generations.

It is the profession of faith of one who was a historian rather than a theologian or philosopher; nevertheless in his choice of matters to be recorded, and behind his recording of the facts as he learned them, there is always an awareness of 'the Beginning that has no beginning and the End that has no ending', and of the continuing presence of the saints.

Nowhere is the reality of the supernatural behind the natural and historical clearer than in the vision of Walchelin, priest of Bonneval, at the time of the siege of Courcy in 1090. Orderic heard it from the priest himself, who survived his ordeal and lived in good health for some fifteen years afterwards. When Orderic wrote it down enough time had elapsed for the theological speculation and penitential teaching familiar to priest and educated monk alike to have blended with the descriptive detail, without diminishing the terror and sombre magnificence of the vision itself.[66] In its richness and – yes – verisimilitude it is unique in medieval vision literature.

Walchelin described to Orderic his experience when, returning from a necessary late-night visit to a parishioner in a remote part of his parish, he heard a great tumult and the sound of galloping horses. Fearing that the horsemen might

---

[65] OV, 1, pp. 132-3.
[66] Ibid., 4, pp. xxxviii-xl, 236-51.

be the household troops of Robert of Bellême riding to the siege of Courcy, he tried to reach the cover of four medlar trees in a field some distance away. But before he could reach them he was ordered to stand by a man of gigantic stature, holding a mace, followed by a rabble on foot and a crowd of bearers, who carried about five hundred tree trunks like biers. Men trussed on the biers were being tormented by huge-headed dwarfs and fearful demons: all lamented the sins for which they were suffering. Walchelin recognized one of the principal sufferers as the slayer of a priest named Stephen, evidently known to him.

Next came a cavalcade of horsemen and women, the women riding on side-saddles studded with red-hot nails and crying out, 'Woe, woe'. Among the men were churchmen, including bishops and abbots, some of whom he recognized as men accounted holy, including Hugh, Bishop of Lisieux, and Gerbert, Abbot of Saint-Wandrille. Those who recognized Walchelin asked for his prayers. Last came a great army of knights 'in which no colour was visible save blackness and flickering fire' (one might almost say, as in Milton's hell, that the light was darkness visible). Among the knights were some whom he recognized, who suffered appropriately for their sins. One was Landry, the recently deceased *vicomte* and advocate of Orbec, who had taken bribes and perverted justice, and was now called a liar and mocked by his fellow-sufferers. Another horseman was William of Glos, the son of William of Breteuil's steward, Barnon of Glos, who had been guilty of usury; he had lent money to a poor miller with his mill as security, and had retained the mill though the profits had easily paid for the loan. The wretch begged Walchelin to warn his wife and son to restore the mill; but he resisted, afraid that no one would believe him. The horseman seized him with his burning hand and threatened his life until he called on the Virgin Mary. Help then appeared in the unexpected form of a knight, his own brother, who had brought him up and paid for his education in the schools of France, before taking part in the conquest of England and dying there. He told how, when Walchelin had said his first Mass, their father Ralph had been released from his torments, and his own had been lightened.

He hoped, with the help of Walchelin's prayers, to be released in a year's time.

After his ordeal the priest was seriously ill for a week; he then went to Lisieux and told the whole story to his bishop, Gilbert Maminot. Gilbert, being a physician, was capable of providing medical no less than spiritual remedies. But the priest carried for life the scar that had been caused by the hand of the terrible knight.

It would be possible to provide a rational explanation of the accident that befell the priest, and of the images that passed through his mind during his serious illness. Of greater interest is the form in which the vision is narrated, after passing through the minds of the priest himself – an educated man – and the monk historian who recorded it. When the priest said to himself, 'This is Herlequin's rabble', he was linking his vision to popular folklore, of which we may catch glimpses in sources as far apart as the Peterborough Chronicle, Walter Map's *De nugis curialium*, and the letters of Peter of Blois.[67] But the sins committed by the named individuals are described so precisely that we seem at times to be present in the confessional. Although annual confession was not made obligatory until 1215, the practice of confession, both at the point of death and after committing any serious crime, was spreading in the late eleventh century.[68] Orderic had probably talked to priests about it; when he described a riot that had broken out in a reforming synod at Rouen in 1119, he mentioned that a number of mature and pious old priests were attacked. The priests had been sitting quietly, 'either discussing confession and other salutary topics, or reciting their daily hours'.[69] Some, whom he named, were known to him; he would hardly have specified confession among the salutary topics if it had never been discussed with the monks. Even though the 'seal of the confessional' had not yet been imposed, the way was being

[67] *Anglo-Saxon Chronicle*, sa 1127; Walter Map, *De nugis curialium*, ed. M. R. James, rev. C. N. L. Brooke and R. A. B. Mynors, *OMT* (Oxford, 1983), pp. xxxix, 26–31, 370–1; Peter of Blois, *Epistola* 14, in *PL*, 207, cols 42–51.

[68] Alexander Murray, 'Confession before 1215', *TRHS*, ser. 6, 3 (1993), pp. 51–81; Jacques Le Goff, *The Birth of Purgatory*, trans. Arthur Goldhammer (London, 1984), pp. 213–16.

[69] OV, 6, pp. 292–3.

prepared. Conceivably Walchelin's own memory was so burdened by knowledge of the terrible crimes that had been revealed secretly in confession that they become externalized (and so describable) in his vision. Such a reaction and the historian Orderic's own practice of describing precisely phenomena he did not understand, would explain the vivid and totally compelling historical core of the vision.

Orderic was not just a historian; he was also a monk, and his informant was an educated priest. So history and folklore are joined by doctrinal teaching in the story as he told it. The wretches in the vision were not eternally damned; they were undergoing purgation. As Orderic eloquently expressed it,

> all unseemliness of which base humanity is guilty is burned away in purgatorial fire and the soul is purified by every kind of purgation that the eternal judge decrees. Just as a vessel, cleansed from rust and well polished, is placed in the treasury, so the soul, purified from the stain of every sin, is led into paradise.[70]

Purgatory was not then conceived as a place, but the possibility of purgation was constantly in the minds of monks whose regular duties included prayers for the dead. The practice was particularly common at Cluny, and in abbeys which, like St Evroult, were strongly influenced by Cluniac customs. Visions of the kind that already existed in the *Vitae* of Abbot Odilo of Cluny,[71] and were to be multiplied in the *De miraculis* of Peter the Venerable,[72] emphasized to laymen as well as clergy the need to perform penance during life, and to endow masses and prayers for the dead. Though Orderic was essentially a historian, and neither a theologian nor a philosopher, his daily life ensured that his conception of the Church and its history was never wholly limited by time. He made the writing of the history of the

---

[70]   Ibid., 4, pp. 240-1.

[71]   Jotsaldus, *De vita et virtutibus Sancti Odonis*, PL, 142, cols 878-9, describes how Odilo instituted the commemoration of all the dead at Cluny as the result of a vision; see also Peter Damiani, *Vita Sancta Odilonis*, PL, 144, cols 935-6.

[72]   *Petri Cluniacensis abbatis De miraculis libri duo*, ed. D. Bouthillier, CChrCM (Turnhout, 1988).

Church as he knew it virtually his life's work; but however strong the influence of other ecclesiastical historians, his was a total vision. He was in the end most strongly influenced by the experiences of the men and women, knights and churchmen, saints and sinners whom he knew, and by his own extensive reading and daily life as a Benedictine monk.

Clare Hall, Cambridge

A THIRTEENTH-CENTURY GENEALOGY OF HERESY

by LUCY BOSWORTH

How did the medieval Church cope with the existence, both in its past and its present, of dissent and heresy within its own body? The churchmen who were engaged in writing anti-heretical treatises in the twelfth and thirteenth centuries did not view the Church's doctrinal history as a process of interplay between new, and possibly heterodox, ideas which defined and refined those 'orthodox' doctrines which became acceptable to the Church.[1] Still less did they conceive of it in terms of Bauer's 'competing orthodoxies', one of which eventually became dominant.[2] For these polemicists, the Pauline injunction – *Oportet et haereses esse* in its Vulgate form (I Corinthians 11.9)[3] – was interpreted as meaning that there must always be heresies among them. Heresy had existed as a separate entity from the inception of the Church; indeed, it was viewed almost as God-given, part of God's scheme and the natural life of the Church, one of the four temptations sent to test and mould her.[4] Moreover, although the heresies which had

---

[1] For a useful, although now incomplete, list of the anti-heretical sources see W. L. Wakefield and A. P. Evans, eds, *Heresies of the High Middle Ages* (New York, 1969) [hereafter Wakefield and Evans], pp. 633–8. The sources contained in this list are directed against the so-called 'popular' heretical movements rather than those aimed more specifically at 'intellectual' heretics such as Abelard, these latter falling outside the scope of this article. Those authors who were concerned with popular heresy came from a wide range of geographical locations and occupations. A few were scholastic academics, many were inquisitors, some were popular preachers, others were parish priests or monks, but all wrote primarily to provide their colleagues with information about the beliefs and practices of their opponents, and the arguments with which these could be countered; all of which was an essential weapon in the institutional Church's struggle against heresy.

[2] W. Bauer, *Orthodoxy and Heresy in Earliest Christianity* (London, 1972).

[3] On the exegetical history of this verse see H. Grundmann, 'Oportet et haereses esse: das Problem der Ketzerei im Spiegel der mittelalterlichen Bibelexegese', in *Herbert Grundmann: ausgewählte Aufsätze, MGH. Schriften*, 25, 3 vols (Stuttgart, 1978), 1, pp. 328–63.

[4] A view expressed, e.g., by Bernard of Clairvaux: the persecutions and great doctrinal controversies were the earliest 'temptations' to which the Church was subjected; in Bernard's own times the Church was faced with avarice and ambition

135

troubled the Church at various times sometimes seemed to be only distinctly related, polemicists held firmly to the conviction that all of these apparently distinct heresies were in fact offshoots of the one heresy. Their understanding of the Church's doctrinal history, therefore, was of the intermittent manifestation, in a variety of guises, of this 'heresy' and its subsequent detection and repulsion by the Church. In looking back on this long history, polemicists were able to use past heresies to identify contemporary sects as heretical. At this level retrospection offered a means of combating the appeal of the ascetic and evangelical groups which were springing up during this period, many of which displayed an alarming potential to evade the control of the institutional Church. The retrospective example of the great heresies – the Arians and the Manicheans, for instance – thus provided a simple but effective method of warning the laity away from groups which the clerical and episcopal hierarchies found suspicious or threatening.

Nowhere is this attitude more apparent than in a 'genealogy of error'[5] – in this case a genealogy of the Cathars' beliefs – which appears in a number of thirteenth-century polemical works. The relevant passage first appears in Durand of Huesca's *Liber antiheresis* (written shortly before 1207):

In the books of the pagans we read that a certain philosopher, who was called Pythagoras, had instituted certain errors; for he said that after death the souls of men enter into other bodies, either men or dumb animals or birds, and on that account the eating of flesh is abominated. The people of the present time have commended these errors to themselves; and behold the beginning of their sect. The Marcionites, the Cerinthians and the Ebionites, in the time in which we read

among the clergy and the re-emergence of heresy; the final temptation would be the coming of the Antichrist and the Last Judgement. See J. Leclercq, 'L'hérésie d'après S. Bernard de Clairvaux', in W. Lourdaux and D. Verhelst, eds, *The Concept of Heresy in the Middle Ages: Proceedings of the International Conference of Louvain, May 13–16, 1973* (Louvain, 1976), pp. 12–14.

[5]   The phrase is W. L. Wakefield's. Cf. his 'Notes on some antiheretical writings of the thirteenth century', *Franciscan Studies*, 27 (1967), pp. 308–9.

that John the apostle preached in Asia, preached against the holy apostle John, said that the Son was less than the Father, and that all transitory things are not preserved by God, but made by evil; for which reason they were called *antichrists* by the blessed John. And your advocates received those errors from them. There were others in Persia, namely Zarohen and Arfaxat, who amongst other blasphemies said that the giver of the Mosaic law was the god of darkness; whose error was cursed by the blessed Matthew and Judah and Simon; and behold other defenders. There were others, namely Hymenaeus and Philetus,[6] who in opposition to Paul hardly believed in the resurrection at all, who were deservedly called Sadducees; and you believe similarly to those advocates. There was another who was ordained by the apostles, Nicholas by name, who having taught with the apostles said that for men to live with their own wives was one and the same sin as living with prostitutes or any other women. Similarly that person asserted two principles; which error was cursed in the Apocalypse, when the Lord said to the angel of the Ephesians: 'In this respect you have good, since you have hated the deeds of the Nicolaitans, whom I hate.'[7] And him likewise you have as your father. And there were others who were called Gnostics, who amongst other accursed things asserted two gods, one good and the other evil; and these you similarly have as fathers. There was another, Mani by name, and he asserted that all visible things were made by the devil. And there was another, Tatian by name, who abominated the flesh. And these you similarly have as father, and too many others whom it would take too long to enumerate.[8]

---

6 Cf. II Tim. 2.17.

7 Cf. Rev. 2.6.

8 'In libris paganorum legimus quendam philosophum, qui piccagoras dicitur, quendam errorem instituisse; dicebat enim animas post mortem hominis alia corpora vel hominum vel pecorum vel avium ingredi, et ideo carnes abhominatus est. Huius errores moderni sibi vendicaverunt; et ecce inicium secte eorum. Marchionem, cherintum, et ebionem, in tempore, quo iohannes apostolus predicabat, in asia fuisse legimus, qui contra sanctum iohannem apostolum predicantes minorem filium patrem [sic] dicebant, omniaque transitoria non a deo salvatore, set [sic] a maligno facta; ob quam causam a beato iohanne *antichristi* dicuntur. Et istos errores vestri

This passage appears in a more concise form in a later work of Durand's, the *Contra Manichaeos* (*c.* 1222–3), with the addition to the list of the Donatists and the omission of Pythagoras, the Gnostics and Mani.[9]

Trying to pinpoint particular sources for this 'genealogy of error' is not easy. Some of the statements concerning the more familiar heretics such as Mani and the Gnostics are similar to those contained in the traditional patristic catalogue of heresies,[10] with which the majority of medieval polemicists were familiar; but the references to Zarohen and Arfaxat occur in only one other instance in the polemical literature. Durand was clearly familiar with Alan of Lille's *Contra haereticos* (or at least with Book i which deals with the Cathars), since the *Liber antiheresis* reproduces the chapter *Quod Christus vere comederit et biberit* (i, 22) of Alan's treatise[11]

patroni ab illis acceperunt. Fuerunt alii in persida, zeroen scilicet et arfaxat, qui inter reliquas blasphemias datorem mosaice legis deum tenebrarum dixerunt; quorum error a beato matheo et iuda et simone exsecratus est; et ecce alios patronos. Fuerunt alii, ymeneus scilicet et filetus, qui paulo resistentes resurrexionem minime credebant, qui saducei merito vocati sunt; et istos similiter habetis patronos. Fuit alius, qui ab apostolis ordinatus fuerat, nicholaus nomine, qui ab apostolis discedens unum et idem peccatum dixit hominem agere cum propria coniuge quam cum meretricibus vel quibuslibet feminis. Este similiter duo principia asseruit; cuius error in apocalipsi detestatur, domino dicente angelo ephesi: "hoc habes bonum, quia odisti facta nicholaitarum, que ego odi." Et istum similiter habetis patronum. Fuerunt et alii, qui gnostici sunt dicti, qui inter cetera execramenta duos, unum bonum et alterum malum, deos asserebant; et istos similiter abetis patronos. Fuit et alius, manicheus nomine, qui omnia visibilia a diabolo facta asseruit. Fuit et aluis, tacianus nomine, qui carnes abominatus est. Et istos similiter abetis patronos, et quamplures alios, quos enumerare longissimum est.' Durand of Huesca, *Liber antiheresis*, i, De statu ecclesie, ed. in K.-V. Selge, *Die ersten Waldenser, mit Edition des Liber Antiheresis des Durandus von Osca*, 2 vols (Berlin, 1967), 2, pp. 97–8.

[9]   Durand of Huesca, *Liber contra Manichaeos*, xiv, ed. Ch. Thouzellier, *Une somme anti-cathare. Le 'Liber Contra Manicheos' de Durand des Huesca* (Louvain, 1964), pp. 237–9.

[10]   The most useful collection of these is F. Oehler, ed., *Corpus haeresiologicum*, 3 vols (Berlin, 1856–61). For discussion of these and related texts see J. McClure, 'Handbooks against heresy in the west, from the late fourth to the late sixth centuries', *JThS*, 30 (1979), pp. 186–97.

[11]   Alan of Lille, *De fide catholica contra haereticos sui temporis liber quatuor*, i, 22, *PL* 210, col. 324. On the *Contra haereticos* see E. Broeckx, *Le Catharisme* (Hoogstraten, 1916), pp. 216–20; D. Roché, ' "Le Contra haereticos" d'Alain de Lille', *Cahiers d'études cathares*, 16 (1965–6), pp. 24–48; Ch. Thouzellier, *Catharisme et valdéisme en Languedoc à la fin du XIIe siècle* (Louvain, 1969), ch. 3; C. Vasoli, 'Il "Contra haereticos" di Alano di Lilla', *Bullettino dell'Istituto storico italiano per il medio evo e Archivio muratoriano*, 75 (1963), pp. 124–72; Wakefield, 'Notes on some antiheretical writings', pp. 285–90.

and incorporates parts of other chapters.[12] Durand's genealogy does not appear in Alan's *Contra haereticos*, and in only one place does there appear to be a direct link between that work and the *Liber antiheresis*. This occurs in the eleventh chapter of the first book of Alan's *Contra haereticos: Qua ratione dicunt haeretici, daemones in corporibus humanis puniri* (i, 11). This states that: 'those who assert this have fallen into a Pythagorean error, which asserts that after death the soul of a sinful man deservedly enters into the body of another man or of a brute animal'.[13] Although not identical to the statement about Pythagoras in the *Liber antiheresis*, it is certainly similar enough to suggest that Durand was using Alan's treatise in this instance. One other similar reference occurs in the catalogue of heresies contained in Ebrard of Béthune's *Liber antiheresis*, which mentions that the *Pythagoraei* taught the transmigration of souls;[14] but the (admittedly uncertain) dating of Ebrard's treatise means that it was probably written after Durand's *Liber antiheresis*, although before his *Contra Manicheos*.

Wakefield and Evans suggest that a statement in the *Summa contra haereticos* attributed to St Peter Martyr of Verona about the derivation of Predestinarian errors may be an embryonic form of Durand's genealogy:[15]

For there are certain of them who say that everything good is predestined by the good god, but that everything evil is predestined by the devil; which error they took from Simon Magus and from the Manicheans who are said to have disseminated this wickedness. But others rave that everything below is ruled according to the motion and course of the stars and other heavenly

[12] A. Dondaine, 'Durand de Huesca et la polémique anti-cathare', *Archivum fratrum praedicatorum* [hereafter *AFP*], 29 (1959), pp. 238–9.

[13] 'Praeterea, qui hoc asserunt in errorem Pythagoricum cadunt, qui asseruit animam hominis merito peccati post mortem intrare in corpus alterius hominis vel bruti animalis.' *Contra haereticos*, i, 1, col. 17.

[14] Ebrard of Béthune, *Liber antiheresis*, ed. M. de La Bigne, *Maxima bibliotheca veterum patrum, et antiquorum scriptorum ecclesiasticorum*, 24 (Lyons, 1677), col. 1575. See Broeckx, *Le Catharisme*, pp. 221–2; some mention in A. Borst, *Die Katharer* (Freiburg, 1991), p. 22.

[15] Wakefield and Evans, p. 732 n. 39.

bodies, even the soul itself when it is clothed with flesh. Also they add that the world is eternal and that Adam was not the first man. Which error they appear to have taken primarily from the words of Aristotle, as will be clear from their arguments below . . . . But the fourth group consists of those who blaspheme that neither any angels nor the souls of men exist at the end of this life. The Sadducees were the first author of this stupidity, which afterwards was adopted by a certain person called Arabs who with his accomplices propounded the doctrine that the soul comes to an end with the flesh. A certain other person called Zeno with his disciples added that the soul will be destroyed a short interval after the destruction of the flesh.[16]

The only figures, however, which this passage has in common with Durand's genealogy (and in later reworking by Moneta of Cremona) are the Sadducees. Furthermore, none of the specific doctrines mentioned here correspond with those listed in the genealogy. Most conclusively, the later date of Peter Martyr's treatise (*c.* 1235) means that it could not itself have been a source for Durand's work, although the possibility of a common source must remain.

A further clue may lie in the reference to Zarohen and Arfaxat, two magicians who are almost certainly fictitious characters.[17] These two heretics appear in all occurrences of

[16] 'Sunt autem predestinatorum genera IIII^or. Quidam enim sunt qui dicunt bona omnia preordinata esse a deo bono, mala vero a diabolo cuncta; quem errorem traxerunt a Simone mago et a manicheis qui hanc perfidiam disseminasse leguntur. Alii vero delirant omnia inferiora regi secundum motum et cursum syderum aliorumque corporum superiorum, etiam animam ipsam dum tegitur carne. Addunt etiam quod mundus sit eternus et quod Adam non fuerit primus homo. Quem errorem videntur traxisse et dictis Aristotelis maxime, prout inferius in suis allegationibus patebit . . . Quartum vero genus est illorum qui blasphemant non esse angelos aliquos neque animas hominum ista vita finita. Cuius auctores stultite Saducei primo fuerunt quam postea mutatus est quidam nomine Arabs qui domaticavit [sic] cum complicibus suis animam cum carne finiti. Adiecit et quidam alius nomine Zeno cum discipulis suis quod post modicum intervallum carne perempta perimatur et anima.' St Peter Martyr of Verona (?), *Summa contra haereticos*, 23, ed. T. Käppeli, 'Une Somme contre les hérétiques de S. Pierre Martyr?', *AFP*, 17 (1947), pp. 331-2.

[17] Cf. T. Ricchini, *Moneta de Cremone: Adversus Catharos et Valdenses* (Rome, 1743; facsimile reprint Ridgewood, N.J., 1964), p. 411, n. 78. See also Selge, *Die ersten Waldenser*, 2, p. 7, n. for line 24; Thouzellier, *Une somme*, p. 75, n. for line 14.

this genealogy, but there is only one other reference to them in the polemical literature, in Eckbert of Schönau's *Sermones contra Catharos* (c. 1160). In the discussion of the origins of the Cathars in Sermon 1, Eckbert notes that two people named Zaroc and Arfaxat taught various dualist errors in Persia prior to the emergence of Mani.[18] He does not, however, mention that they were opposed to the Mosaic Law, so Durand presumably obtained at least some of his information from elsewhere. Wakefield and Evans also suggest that the unidentifiable 'Zeno' mentioned by Peter Martyr, who taught that the soul does not live after the death of the body, may be a scribal error for 'Zarohen', thereby giving some support to the possibility of a link between the two works;[19] but this rather tentative suggestion remains unsubstantiated. It is more probable, however, that the figure of Zarohen relates in some way to Zoroaster, from whom Mani was supposed to have derived some of his teachings. One possibility is that Zarohen (in these Latin texts 'Zeroen', 'Zarden' and 'Zaroc') is a corruption of Zurvan, the mythical god of Zurvanism, itself a philosophical and religious offshoot of Zorastrianism.[20] The identity of Arfaxat is even more problematic. The biblical references to a person of that name shed no light on the problem;[21] although through a confused tradition he may be identified with Artapat, an orthodox Zoroastrian opponent of Zurvanism.[22]

What is certain is that these passages themselves became a source for future polemicists. In the early 1240s, Durand's

---

[18]   Eckbert of Schönau, *Tresdecim sermones contra Catharos*, 1, ed. R. J. Harrison, 'Eckbert of Schönau's "Sermones contra Kataris" ', 2 vols (Ohio State University Ph.D. thesis, 1990), 1, p. 22 (I am grateful to Dr Harrison for permission to cite his unpublished work). The standard study of the *Sermones* is R. Manselli, 'Ecberto di Schönau e l'eresia catara in Germania all metà de secolo XII', in *Arte di storia: studi in onore di Leonello Vincenti* (Turin, 1965), pp. 309–38. See Harrison, 'Eckbert', 1, ch. 1 for biography of Eckbert.

[19]   Wakefield and Evans, p. 732 n. 39.

[20]   The descriptions of the myth of Zurvan in fact come from Christian Armenian and Syriac authors; their common source may be Theodore of Mopsuestia; on this cf. G. Gnoli, 'Zurvanism', in M. Eliade, ed., *Encyclopedia of Religion* (New York, 1987), p. 59. The standard work on Zurvanism is R. C. Zaehner, *Zurvan: a Zoroastrian Dilemma* (Oxford, 1955). See also D. Obolensky, *The Bogomils: a Study in Balkan Neo-Manichaeism* (Cambridge, 1948), pp. 14–15.

[21]   Gen. 10.21; I Chr. 1.17; Judith 1.1; Luke 3.36.

[22]   Cf. Obolensky, *The Bogomils*, p. 14.

genealogy was reworked by Moneta of Cremona in his monumental work *Adversus Catharos et Valdenses*.[23] This was in turn copied in certain manuscript versions of Benedict of Alignan's *Tractatus fidei* (1261), which insert Moneta's genealogy, along with extracts from the *Brevis summula*,[24] into the prologue.[25] Apart from rearranging the order slightly, the passage there is identical to the one in the *Adversus Catharos et Valdenses*. Moneta's genealogy is offered as an explanation of the origins of the Cathars' errors:

> For it was a certain Pagan, Pythagoras by name, who said that the souls of men enter into other bodies, namely of men or dumb animals, with which error many Pagans agree, and they are called the *Pythagorici*, whom the Cathars, who posit two principles, imitate, even in their beginning. Certain other treacherous people were also in this error, namely Zarohen and Arfaxat, who said that the giver of the law of Moses was the Prince of darkness, from whom all the Cathars, as far as this error is concerned, are derived. There were also amongst the Jews the Sadducees, who denied the resurrection of the body, from whom all Cathars originate. There was a certain other person, Mani by name, who posited two principles, and two creations, and two natures, whence the Manicheans are so-called, and from those certain of the Cathars took up the principles. The same asserted that all visible and transitory things were made by the Devil, hence they denied

---

[23] For biography of Moneta, see Wakefield and Evans, pp. 307–8. Some discussion in Broeckx, *Le Catharisme*, pp. 228–32. On the sources of the *Adversos Catharos et Valdenses*, see Wakefield, 'Notes on some antiheretical writings', pp. 297–9, 305–15.

[24] A late-thirteenth-century compilation of scriptural texts intended for the use of preachers against heresy. See Wakefield and Evans, pp. 351–61.

[25] Benedict of Alignan, *Tractatus fidei contra diversos errores super titulum de summa trinitate et fide catholica decretalibus*. See M. Grabmann, 'Der Franziskanerbischof Benedictus de Alignano (†1268) und seine Summa zum caput Firmiter des vierten Lateran-Konzils', in P. Ignatius-Maria Freudenreich, ed., *Kirchengeschichteliche Studien P. Michael Bihl, O.F.M., als Ehrengabe dargeboten* (Colmar, 1941), pp. 50–64, for details of these MSS. I have used Munich, Bayerische Staatsbibliothek, MS Clm 7453, fols 82r–355v; the genealogy appears at fols 90v–91r. Very few biographical details are known for Benedict; see Grabmann, 'Der Franziskanerbischof', p. 50.

that Christ had assumed that flesh from the Virgin. But they rejected the Old Testament, whom for the most part the Cathars imitate. There was also a certain Tatian by name, from whom the *Tatiani* are so-called, who condemned the eating of flesh, whom the Cathars imitate. The same for the *Valentiniani* from Valentinus, who said that Christ assumed nothing from the Virgin.[26]

There are a few differences in Moneta's version of the genealogy from that offered by Durand. Hymenaeus and Philetus are replaced by the Sadducees themselves and references to the Marcionites, Cerinthians, Ebionites, Nicolaitans, and Donatists are omitted. Moneta gives more information about Manichean beliefs than does Durand; otherwise this section is substantially the same as Durand's.

All of the doctrines mentioned may be loosely described as 'dualist'. There is clearly a strong mythical element in both Durand's and Moneta's genealogy. Zarohen and Arfaxat are, as we have seen, at best a distant reference to a long-dead religion, at worst entirely fictitious characters. Biblical figures such as the Sadducees or Hymenaeus and Philetus and the Nicolaitans were probably shadowy, semi-mythical figures by the thirteenth century. The very early sects mentioned here – the Marcionites, Cerinthians, Ebionites, Gnostics, Valentinians, Tatianians – would have undergone a similar process, whilst the arch-heresiarch Mani and his sect had long since passed into the realm of medieval legend. This genealogy is a bowdlerized version of the more precise and

---

[26] 'Fuit enim quidam Paganus Pythagoras nomine, qui animas hominum in alia corpora, hominum, scilicet, vel pecudum intrare, dixit, cui errori plures Pagani consenserunt, et dicti sunt Pythagorici, quos velu exordium suum Cathari, qui duo ponunt principia, imitantur. In hoc errore fuerunt etiam quidam alii perfidi, scilicet Zarden, et Arphaxat, qui dixerunt datorem legis Moysi esse Principem tenebrarum, a quibus omnes Cathari, quod hunc errorem derivati sunt. Fuerunt etiam apud Judaeos Saducaei, qui horum corporum resurrectionem negabant, a quibus omnes Cathari duxerunt originem. Fuit quidam alius Manes nomine qui due principia posuit, et duas creationes, duasque naturas, unde Manichaei dicti sunt quidam, et ab istis quidam Catharorum sumpserunt principia. Item omnia visibilia, et transitoria asserebant a Diabolo fabricata, unde Christum negabant carnem istam sumpsisse de Virgine. Vetus autem testamentum respuunt, quos Cathari plurimum imitantur. Fuit etiam quidam Tatianus nomine, a quo Tatiani quidam dicti sunt, qui esum carnium reprobavit, quem Cathari imitantur. Item Valentiniani a Valentino, qui Christum dixit nihil de Virgine assumpsisse.' *Adversus Catharos et Valdenses*, V, ii, 2, p. 411.

scholarly catalogues of heresy, reduced to the vestiges retained by popular memory. Our primary question, however, must be to ask what was the polemical purpose of including this passage in an anti-heretical work? Why use the example of past heresies, rather than examine the doctrines of the Cathars themselves? The purpose of the genealogy was two-fold. First, it was part of the ongoing debate between the Cathars and their orthodox opponents about the nature and identity of the true Church. Second, the genealogy was also directed at a wider audience: those members of the laity who might be attracted to the Cathar sect.

In one sense Moneta and Durand are doing no more with the genealogy than rehearsing the well-worn belief that the Cathars were the direct spiritual and historical descendants of the Manicheans. It is significant, however, that in both their works the genealogy appears within sections devoted to the nature of the Church. Both polemicists are concerned not only to highlight the heretical nature of contemporary Cathar beliefs, but conclusively to demonstrate that the Cathars are not the true Church. Thus, for example, Moneta:

> Having seen that the Roman Church derived from Christ as the head, I shall now show whence the Cathar Church originates. For just as it has been shown through the entirety of things believed by the Roman Church that that Church is the Church of Christ, so is it also shown by the entirety of things believed by them that their congregation is not the Church of God, neither did it derive its origin from him as she had, but rather from the Pagans, or the Jews, or the Christian Apostates.[27]

The Roman Church is the true Church, because the purity of its doctrines has been protected by the apostolic succession.

---

[27] 'Viso, quod Ecclesia Romana a Christo velut capite sumpsit exordium, nunc unde Catharorum Ecclesia originem duxerit ostendamus. Sicut enim per universitatem creditorum ab Ecclesia Romana ostensum est, quod ipsa est Christi ecclesia, ita etiam per universitatem creditorum ab eis ostenditur, quod eorum congregatio non est Dei ecclesia, nec ab ipso velut capite sumpsit originem, sed potius a paganis, aut Judaeis, aut Apostatis Christianis.' *Adversus Catharos et Valdenses*, V, ii, 2, p. 411.

Its teaching can be traced back to the first apostles and so to Christ himself. The Cathars' beliefs, on the other hand, can be traced back to the first enemies of the Church. The contrast which is constantly brought into play is between the historical continuity of heretical error, as manifested in various sects past and present, and the historical continuity of apostolic truth and true doctrine, preserved by the Roman and only true Church.

The genealogy also had a wider application. From a purely practical point of view, it was much easier for polemicists to highlight the dangers of a particular sect by giving it a familiar label (in this case 'dualist') which instantly marked out the adherents of that sect as heretics, than it was to examine in detail the intricate teachings of Catharism. Such an approach had the added advantage of ensuring that the sect had in effect already been condemned, and so there could be no argument as to its heretical status.[28] It is also illustrative of the widespread conviction that contemporary medieval sects could be classified according to the categories of past heresies. The dualist sects which occur in the second half of the genealogy were familiar names in the thirteenth century, not only from Augustine's works, but also from the patristic catalogues of heresies which were copied so assiduously by medieval polemicists. It was for this reason, for example, that Eckbert of Schönau appended extracts from some of Augustine's anti-Manichean works to his *Sermones*,[29] 'so that those who read it may fully perceive the whole heresy [i.e. Catharism] from the beginning, and understand why this heresy is fouler than all the heresies'.[30] Underlying this tactic was the conviction that the medieval sects were nothing more or less than a recrudescence of the heresies that had attacked

---

[28]   Cf. Gratian's definition of a heretic, which was highly influential among the anti-heretical polemicists: 'Omnis enim hereticus aut iam dampnatam heresim sequitur, aut novam confingit', *Decretum Gratiani*, C.24 q.1 d.a.c.1: *Corpus iuris canonici*, ed. E. Friedberg and L. Richter, 2 vols (Leipzig, 1879; reprint Graz, 1959), 1, col. 966.

[29]   From the *Contra epistolam Manichaei*, the *De moribus Manichaeorum* and the *De haeresibus*. See Harrison, 'Eckbert', 1, pp. 352-73.

[30]   'ut qui legerint possint quasi a fundamento totam hanc heresim plenius agnoscere et intelligant quoniam hec heresis omnium heresum sentina est'. Harrison, 'Eckbert', 1, p. 24.

the early Church. Thus Durand could address the Cathars not only as neo–Manicheans, but also as *moderni Marchionite*;[31] whilst both Eckbert and the inquisitor Anselm of Alessandria saw the Cathars as the direct spiritual and historical successors of the Manicheans.[32]

This genealogy therefore represents an essentially homogenous view of the Church's doctrinal history. It also represents a view in which the Church's own history is sharply distinguished from diabolical or heretical history: and in which 'heresy' arises and develops autonomously from the 'truth'. The idea that heresy (in the sense of erroneous doctrine) was a phenomenon which arose from outside the Church, rather than within it, was widespread amongst medieval polemicists. Heresy was not merely a corruption of the truth, rather a parallel but separate event, and so could not originate from inside the Church which was the repository and mediator of the truth. This idea had arisen early on in the Church's history: Hegesippus had applied *haeresis*, in its pejorative sense, to Jewish sects, whilst Hippolytus had traced the Christian heresies back not to Jewish sects but to the Greek philosophical schools, and pre-Christian systems of pagan thought.[33] Heresy was therefore only a further degeneration in systems of thought which were already erroneous. This sense was articulated by Isidore of Seville who argued that heresy, in its primary sense of 'choice', could not originate from anything which contained the truth.[34] This belief, which was accepted wholeheartedly by medieval polemicists, distorted their view of the Church's past doctrinal history and the true nature of the contemporary heresies with which they were dealing.

How representative of polemical thinking is the view depicted in the genealogy of error? The genealogy is part of a wider strategy in which polemicists sought to combat the

---

[31]   *Contra Manicheos*, xiv, p. 239.

[32]   Harrison, 'Eckbert', 1, pp. 17–24; Anselm of Alessandria, *Tractatus de hereticis*, 1, ed. A. Dondaine, 'La hiérarchie cathare en Italie, II: Le "Tractatus de hereticis" d'Anselme d'Alexandrie, O.P.', *AFP*, 20 (1950), pp. 308–10.

[33]   M. Simon, 'From Greek hairesis to Christian heresy', in W. R. Schroedel and R. L. Wilken, eds, *Early Christian Literature and the Classical Intellectual Tradition* (Paris, 1979), pp. 102–3.

[34]   Simon, 'From Greek hairesis', p. 104.

popular appeal not just of the Cathars, but also of other successful sects such as the Waldensians. In the case of the Cathars, a retrospective view was not strictly necessary in order to condemn them as heretical, since their dualist beliefs were manifestly non-Christian and unscriptural. Nevertheless, to anyone familiar with Augustine's anti-Manichean writings, the retrospective approach clinched the argument once and for all: the Manicheans had been condemned as heretics, and the Cathars were the spiritual and, according to some polemicists, the direct historical successors of the Manicheans. The Cathars had therefore in effect already been condemned, albeit implicitly. In the case of new groups such as the Waldensians, the retrospective approach appeared at first sight of less utility to polemicists, since there was no obvious link to earlier heresies. Paradoxically, however, retrospection proved to be much more helpful to polemicists in their attempts to classify as heretical those sects which did not fall clearly within the traditional patristic definitions of heresy. It was difficult for polemicists to warn the laity away from the Waldensians, for example, whose beliefs and practices (initially at least) seemed to be so similar to the Franciscans, who had received formal approval from the papacy. If they could suggest a link, however tenuous, between the Waldensians and earlier heresies, the dangerously heretical nature of the sects would be highlighted in the most immediate and effective way possible. Polemicists' emphasis on the earlier, formally condemned, sects as the spiritual ancestors of the medieval sects ensured that the phenomenon of religious dissent was fitted into a conceptual framework in which the salvation history of the true Church, and the diabolical history of the Church's enemies, ran side by side. By linking the old and the new in this way, it was made clear that contemporary sects were not merely composed of basically orthodox religious enthusiasts who had taken their adherence to the *vita apostolica* to extremes, but were the latest in a long line of heretics, which, although sometimes hidden from the eyes of the Church, had been in continuous existence from its establishment by the Devil. In this respect polemicists' use of the example of past heresies made the medieval sects appear more coherent, powerful, and dangerous than in reality they were. As such, it was part of the Church hierarchy's continuing struggle to control the expression of lay spirituality during the twelfth and thirteenth centuries. The diabolical succession of heretics which the polemicists paraded in the genealogy provided a powerful warning to the laity of the dangers inherent in the single-minded pursuit of the *vita apostolica*.

University of Edinburgh

'PRINCIPIUM ET ORIGO ORDINIS': THE HUMILIATI AND THEIR ORIGINS

by FRANCES ANDREWS

The origins of the Humiliati have long been a subject of discussion amongst historians. In the twentieth century the first person to grapple with the problems was Antonino de Stefano, who was quickly followed by Luigi Zanoni, later by Herbert Grundmann and Ilarino da Milano, and more recently by Michele Maccarrone, Brenda Bolton, and Maria Pia Alberzoni.[1] The modern writers have accepted de Stefano's view that the Humiliati first emerged in northern Italy in the late twelfth century.[2] The earliest references, dating from the 1170s, describe both a small group of lay men and women devoted to the religious life (*humiliati per deum*),[3] and an association of clerics living in community at the church of San Pietro Viboldone.[4] Although they initially sought papal approval, those who 'falsely called themselves Humiliati' were condemned in 1184 by Lucius III, not because they were guilty of doctrinal error but because they refused to stop preaching without authority or holding private meetings, probably also because of their rejection of oath-taking.[5] In spite of this

---

[1] A. de Stefano, 'Le origini dell'ordine degli umiliati', *Rivista storico-critica delle scienze teologiche*, 2 (1906), pp. 851-71. He returned to the subject in 1927: idem, 'Delle origine e della natura del primitivo movimento degli umiliati', *Archivum Romanicum* (1927), pp. 31-75. Luigi Zanoni, *Gli Umiliati nei loro rapporti con l'eresia, l'industria della lana ed i comuni nei secoli xii e xiii sulla scorta di documenti inediti* (Milan, 1911), pp. 3-93. Herbert Grundmann, *Religiose Bewegungen im Mittelalter*, 2nd edn (Darmstadt, 1961). Ilarino da Milano summarized his view in 'Umiliati', *Enciclopedia Cattolica*, 12 (Rome, 1954), cols 754-6. Michele Maccarrone, *Studi su Innocenzo III, Italia Sacra*, 17 (Padua, 1972). Brenda Bolton, 'Innocent III's treatment of the Humiliati', *SCH*, 8 (1984), pp. 73-82. Maria Pia Alberzoni, 'Gli inizi degli Umiliati: una riconsiderazione' in *La conversione alla povertà nell'Italia dei secoli xii-xv, Convegni del Centro di studi sulla spiritualità medioevale*, 27 (Todi, 1991), pp. 187-237.

[2] De Stefano, 'Le origini', pp. 851-9.

[3] Girolamo Tiraboschi, *Vetera humiliatorum monumenta*, 3 vols (Milan, 1766-8) [hereafter *VHM*], 2, pp. 120-1.

[4] Mauro Tagliabue, 'Gli Umiliati a Viboldone', in *L'Abbazia di Viboldone* (Milan, 1990), p. 15.

[5] See the brief description by the Anonymous of Laon, *Chronicon Universale*

setback the Humiliati flourished, and by the end of the twelfth century three distinct elements were recognizable: married or single lay men and women living a religious life while remaining in their own homes, male and female monastics living in common under a rule, and clerics living in some sort of canonical communities. In June 1201 these groups were brought back into the Church under the auspices of Innocent III. He gave approval to the three groups or 'orders' which recent research has revealed were already distinct before curial intervention,[6] but which were now organized into one framework along Cistercian lines.[7] It was a fortunate decision. Although groups described as 'Humiliati' were expelled from Cerea in 1203 and Faenza in 1206,[8] the Order of the Humiliati went on to enjoy spectacular success, becoming a major presence in the religious, economic, and administrative life of northern Italy in the thirteenth century.[9]

To modern historians this transition from condemned heretic to faithful religious can be seen as the resolution of a fascinating conflict between lay religious enthusiasm and the dictates of ecclesiastical authority. Yet the sources leave much about the origins of the Humiliati obscure. Who exactly were these people? Where did they come from? What was their social background? Above all, who was their leader? The heretical movements of the early twelfth century had been led by well-documented heresiarchs, and the new religious

(excerpts), ed. G. Waitz, *MGH SS*, XXVI (Hanover, 1882) pp. 449–50. The bull of condemnation is in *Corpus iuris canonici*, ed. E. L. Richter and E. Friedberg, 2 vols (Leipzig, 1881), 2, cols 780–2.

[6] Alberzoni has re-examined the register copy of the papal letter *Licet multitudini credentium*, sent to the Humiliati in December 1200, before the intervention of the papal delegates. It was partially mistranscribed in *PL* and her revisions show that it is already addressed to the three separate groups, demonstrating that they were already defined and that the three-tiered structure was not, as was previously believed, imposed by Innocent III and the Curia. The new transcription also reveals specific reference to clerics amongst the Humiliati. Alberzoni, 'Gli inizi', pp. 201 n.40, 205 n.47.

[7] The bulls of approval are edited in *VHM*, 2, pp. 128–48. An English translation of the first is given by Robert M. Stewart, *'De illis qui faciunt penitentiam'. The Rule of the Franciscan Order: Origins, Development, Interpretation* (Rome, 1991), pp. 365–71.

[8] On Cerea see 'Statuti rurali veronesi', ed. Carlo Cipolla, *Archivio Veneto*, 37–8 (1889), p. 344. On Faenza, see *PL*, 215, cols 1042–3.

[9] The fullest modern account of the thirteenth-century history of the order remains Zanoni, *Gli Umiliati*.

orders had a variety of more-or-less charismatic founder figures who inspired and organized their followers. For the Humiliati, however, the surviving notarial records, papal letters, and contemporary narrative accounts provide very few details. The one individual mentioned by name in the papal letters concerning the Humiliati, Guy of Porta Orientale in Milan, played a role in obtaining recognition of the lay tertiaries and enjoyed a certain prominence in the early thirteenth century,[10] but hardly qualifies as a founder figure comparable to Saints Dominic or Francis. Their social origins remain equally obscure. After decades of debate, recent research has shown that recruitment was never homogeneous; the lower and middle ranks of society seem to have prevailed, but members of wealthy families are also mentioned quite frequently.[11] The surviving contemporary evidence available to the historian is thus largely inconclusive about many aspects of the new Order.

Nor are there early accounts of the Order written by the brethren, unlike the numerous histories produced by their near contemporaries the Franciscans and Dominicans.[12] Perhaps the tripartite division and the strength of local or regional identities amongst the first Humiliati obscured any sense of a wider Order, so that the compilation of a history of the whole movement was inconceivable. Yet this does not explain the lack of even local accounts.

Perhaps their work regime did not encourage writing. Contemporaries described the poverty of their lifestyle and the energy of their preaching against heresy;[13] but there was no apparent emphasis on study. Yet the thirteenth-century brethren were by no means illiterate. In 1201 Innocent III referred specifically to the tonsuring of *laici litterati* in the

---

[10] Bolton, 'Innocent III's treatment', p. 79; Tagliabue, 'Gli Umiliati a Viboldone', pp. 11–15.

[11] The state of research is summarized in Lorenzo Paolini, 'Le Umiliate al lavoro. Appunti fra storiografia e storia', *Bullettino dell'Istituto storico italiano per il medio evo e Archivio Muratoriano*, 97 (1991), p. 234 and n.12.

[12] See for example, Tommaso da Celano, *Vita Prima Sancti Francisci*, in *Legendae S. Francisci*, ed. Quaracchi Fathers, *Analecta Francescana*, 10 (1926–41), pp. 1–126, or Jordan of Saxony, *Libellus*, ed. H. C. Scheeben, *Monumenta Ordinis Praedicatorum Historica*, 16 (Rome, 1935), pp. 1–88.

[13] See for example, *The Historia Occidentalis of Jacques de Vitry. A Critical Edition*, ed. J. F. Hinnebusch, *Spicilegium Friburgense*, 17 (Freiburg, 1972), ch. 28, pp. 145–6.

houses of the First order,[14] while Jacques de Vitry's *Historia Occidentalis*, written *c*.1220, describes them as *fere omnes litterati*.[15] A Franciscan briefly transferred to the Order with his books in the 1250s,[16] and the evidence from local records shows that some of the brethren were notaries.[17] Yet the first references to study and to Humiliati brethren attending the universities date to the fourteenth century. Constitutions of the Order issued in Monza in 1321 include a clause concerning those absent for study,[18] and in 1356 the Master General, Tiberius of Parma, sent a letter to two brothers from the Brera house in Milan who were living and studying in Paris.[19] By contrast, the early Dominicans saw learning and study as the essential means to achieving their mission of preaching and saving souls,[20] and the Franciscans soon followed them into the universities.[21] This connection undoubtedly both attracted and generated a large number of well-educated persons, who had the skill and interest to polemicize their Order's history. For the Franciscans, the charismatic drama of their founder's life and the long disputes before and after his death also undoubtedly provided extra motivation to write.

Of course there is another possible reason for the silence of the Humiliati about their origins. As the now highly respectable Order was going from strength to strength, there was no interest in writing a history of their beginnings, especially since it might draw attention to the close encounter of the early members with heresy. Why raise awkward questions by dragging up a less than fortunate and increasingly distant episode? The past, in such conditions, was best left as a foreign country.

[14] *Non omni spiritui*, 16 June 1201, ed. Tiraboschi, *VHM*, 2, pp. 139–48.

[15] Hinnebusch, ed., *Historia Occidentalis*, p. 144.

[16] Rosalind B. Brooke, *Early Franciscan Government: Elias to Bonaventure* (Cambridge, 1959), p. 225.

[17] For example, five or six notaries are recorded in Veronese houses between 1210 and 1246. Verona, Archivio di Stato, Fondo di Sta Maria della Ghiara, nos 29, 35, 139, 151, and 206.

[18] *VHM*, 3, p. 154.

[19] *VHM*, 1, pp. 278–9.

[20] W. A. Hinnebusch, *The History of the Dominican Order, 2, Intellectual and Cultural Life to 1500* (New York, 1973).

[21] See J. R. H. Moorman, *A History of the Franciscan Order from its Origins to the Year 1517* (Oxford, 1968), pp. 123–39.

Whether or not there was a conscious desire to forget the past, no Humiliati set out to write a chronicle of the Order in the thirteenth or fourteenth centuries. As Alberzoni has recently re-emphasized, the first full account was not by a member of the Order at all, but was written in the early fourteenth century by a Milanese Dominican, Galvano Fiamma (1283–*c*.1344).[22] Fiamma included brief accounts of the origins of the Humiliati in three different histories: the *Chronicon maius*,[23] the *Manipulus florum sive historia Mediolanensis*,[24] and the *Galvagnana*.[25] The accounts vary slightly, but all associate the Rule of the Order and the foundation of the lay tertiaries either directly or indirectly with the visit of Bernard of Clairvaux to Milan in 1135. How better for the Humiliati to obliterate any suspicion of heresy than to associate themselves with St Bernard? Guy of Porta Orientale is also attributed a key role. The *Chronicon maius* gives the shortest account, and although the link with the Humiliati is not here made explicit, Guy's important is clear. It relates simply that in 1135 Bernard founded the monastery of Chiaravalle near Milan with the special help of Guy *ex Capitanei porte Orientalis*.[26]

The *Manipulus florum* and the *Galvagnana* provide more details concerning the hypothetical connection with the Humiliati. In the *Manipulus florum*, Fiamma relates that Bernard also established the 'Order of Saint Bernard', whose first house was the *domus* of Porta Orientale, built by Guy. This same man then allegedly went to Rome, where Innocent III confirmed the Order.[27] According to Fiamma, because the

[22] M. P. Alberzoni, 'San Bernardo e gli Umiliati', in P. Zerbi, ed., *San Bernardo e l'Italia* (Milan, 1992), pp. 102–3 and nn.21–3. There is also a brief and slightly inaccurate reference to the approval of the Humiliati by Innocent III in the early fourteenth-century Chronicle of Francesco Pipino, a Bolognese Dominican, ed. L. Muratori, *Rerum Italicarum Scriptores*, 9 (1726), col. 633.

[23] Galvano Fiamma, *Chronicon extravagans et chronicon maius (ad an. 1216)*, ed. A. Ceruti, *Miscellanea di storia italiana*, 7 (Turin, 1869), pp. 506–773.

[24] Galvano Fiamma, *Manipulus florum sive historia Mediolanensis ab origine urbis ad annum circiter 1336*, ed. L. A. Muratori, *Rerum italicarum scriptores*, 11 (Milan, 1723), col. 632.

[25] Alberzoni, 'San Bernardo e gli Umiliati', p. 103 n.22, gives the text of the Galvagnana passage, based on Milan, Biblioteca Nazionale di Brera, MS AE X 10, fol. 70v.

[26] Fiamma, *Chronicon maius*, p. 641.

[27] Ibid.

Pope was Innocent 'the third', the Order was called Third and he notes, with a hint of polemic, that the Tertiary brothers had actually founded the First and Second orders of the Humiliati and carried out visitations of them (whether or not this was true in the 1170s, and it seems unlikely, Innocent III's letters of 1201 gave this responsibility to the clerical First order, in a structure following the model of the Cistercians).

Fiamma's credibility has rightly been questioned. The eighteenth-century historian of the Humiliati, Girolamo Tiraboschi (1731–94) commented that he inserted *multae fabulae* in his work, but accepted that he mixed 'truth with the falsehood'.[28] Early this century, Luigi Zanoni was more negative, calling Fiamma a credulous compiler and describing his account of the Humiliati in the *Manipulus florum* as 'un piccolo pasticcio'.[29] Since then, modern commentators on Fiamma's work have been divided,[30] and the origins of the story are certainly unclear. There were later houses of the Order dedicated to Bernard; indeed a new study of the spread of the cult of St Bernard in northern Italy attributes this in the first instance to the presence of the Humiliati.[31] A painting of the Saint giving the rule to the Third order, by Simone de' Crocefissi (*fl.* 1355–99),[32] almost certainly from the Humiliati Hospital of St Bernard in Bologna,[33] and Bernard's inclusion in a fresco-cycle painted by Giusto de' Menabuoi at Viboldone in 1349,[34] also encourage the view that Fiamma was drawing on traditions alive in the Order. Indeed, Alberzoni has argued that there could in fact have been a link at one remove between the Humiliati and Bernard. An elder Guy of Porta Orientale (who died in or before 1172) may have acted as St Bernard's aide in 1135, whilst one of his sons

[28] *VHM*, 2, p. 36.

[29] Zanoni, *Gli Umiliati*, pp. 11, 14.

[30] See E. Cochrane, *Historians and Historiography in the Italian Renaissance* (Chicago and London, 1981), p. 109.

[31] G. Spinelli, 'La diffusione del culto di san Bernardo in alta Italia', in Zerbi, *San Bernardo e l'Italia*, pp. 193–215.

[32] On Simone, see P. G. Castagnoli, ed., *Pittura bolognese del '300. Scritti di Francesco Arcangeli* (Bologna, 1978), pp. 184–208.

[33] I am grateful to Dr Lorenzo Paolini of the University of Bologna for this information.

[34] M. L. Gatti Perer, 'Gli affreschi trecenteschi', in *L'abbazia di Viboldone*, p. 134, fig. 91.

was the man involved in assisting the Tertiaries to obtain approval from Innocent III in 1201.[35]

Whether or not we accept the association with Bernard, or the dual role of the Porta Orientale family, Fiamma's chronicles remained the only full account of the Order before the fifteenth century. But by then the circumstances of the Order had changed, and there was perhaps greater need to write a history. Already in the early 1300s, there had been a fall in the number of houses of the First and Second orders. Two catalogues of the houses, dated 1298 and 1344, reveal thàt in those years, despite the emergence of 38 new houses, 166 had disappeared.[36] Indeed the lay Third order seems to have disappeared altogether by the 1360s, at least in Milan.[37] The loss of numbers must have affected the morale of those who joined, and may have contributed to the decision taken in 1374 to reduce the frequency of General Chapters to once every three years.[38] Then in the middle of the fifteenth century the Order was to be shaken by a crisis which seems unlikely to have been an isolated episode. The *domus* of Gessate outside Milan was lost to the Benedictines through what Pope Eugenius IV (1431–47) described as the 'guilt and negligence'[39] of the provost Balzarinus, who had been living a life of luxury with just two brothers under him. In the 1430s Eugenius gave the house to the Congregation of Sta Giustina in Pavia,[40] but in the following decade the evicted Humiliati, ignoring their General Chapter's reluctant renunciation of its rights to the house, reoccupied the monastery by force, expelling the Benedictines. When finally obliged to surrender

---

[35] Alberzoni, 'San Bernardo e gli Umiliati', pp. 104–5. Tiraboschi had already thrown doubt on the role of Guy, pointing out that he would have been too old by 1201: *VHM*, 1, p. 45.

[36] John of Brera includes the catalogues in his chronicle: *Chronicon ordinis humiliatorum*, ed. Tiraboschi, *VHM*, 3, pp. 229–86. The calculation of the loss is made in ch. 37, p. 273.

[37] Zanoni, *Gli Umiliati*, pp. 138–41, 285–99.

[38] 'Humiliatorum constitutiones in generalibus comitis editae', ed. Tiraboschi, *VHM*, 3, p. 178.

[39] Eugenius IV, 1433, cited in P. Puccinelli, *Chronicon Insignis Abbatiae SS Petri et Pauli de Glaxiate Mediolani* (Milan, 1655), pp. 6–9.

[40] Affiliated to Sta Giustina in Padua; see G. Forzatti Golia, 'Gli ordini religiosi della diocesi di Pavia nel medioevo', *Bollettino della società pavese di storia patria*, ns 41 (1989), pp. 24–5.

they destroyed anything of value, presumably so that the new occupants should not gain by repossession.[41]

It was in this troubled context, of which the Gessate crisis was a later but surely not isolated symptom, that John, a brother living in the Brera house in Milan,[42] set out to write a history of his Order. The *Chronicon ordinis humiliatorum*, which is the first extant narrative history, was completed in 1419 and included catalogues of the houses and lists of superiors, saints, and privileges. It was followed two years later by a crudely illustrated and abridged *Excerptum*.[43]

Naturally enough John's chronicle begins with a brief description of the nature of the Order and an account of its origins. It makes explicit use of privileges and notarial documents, many of which had been preserved in his community and are now in the Brera library in Milan; but it manages to obscure almost entirely the suspicions of heresy which surrounded the first Humiliati. However, this was not done by giving prominence to the traditional connection with Bernard. As far as that was concerned, a single passage (which may be a later interpolation),[44] notes only that those noble Milanese citizens who asked St Bernard for a *forma religiose vivendi* were not thereby the principal founders of the Order of the Humiliati.[45] Perhaps John was not concerned

---

[41]   Nicholas V to the archbishop of Milan, 1447, cited in Puccinelli, *Chronicon . . . de Glaxiate*, pp. 71–4.

[42]   Almost nothing is known of John, although Mercati has suggested that he may be the John of Marliano who compiled a collection of papal privileges between 1408 and 1435. G. Mercati, 'Due ricerche per la storia degli umiliati', *Rivista di storia della chiesa in Italia*, 11 (1957), pp. 177–8.

[43]   The earliest surviving manuscripts of the 1419 chronicle, both of which include later interpolations, date from the sixteenth century (Milan, Biblioteca Ambrosiana, MS V 9 sup, dated 1536 and MS BS 1,19 A 27 (sussidio), dated 1567), but an illustrated, if crudely executed and incomplete, copy of the *Excerptum* survives in a fifteenth-century codex (Milan, Biblioteca Ambrosiana, MS G 301 inf SP 66). Zanoni used a seventeenth-century copy for his edition (Milan, Biblioteca Ambrosiana, MS G 302 inf), *Gli Umiliati*, pp. 336–44. Comparison with the manuscript revealed only minor inaccuracies in his transcription. The copy was made at the Ambrosiana on the orders of Cardinal Federico Borromeo before his library possessed G 302 inf, which was acquired in 1802. C. Castiglioni, 'L'Ordine degli umiliati in tre codici illustrati dell'Ambrosiana', *Memorie storiche della diocesi di Milano*, 7 (Milan, 1960), p. 8. For further details on these manuscripts and those of the 1419 chronicle, see Zanoni, *Gli Umiliati*, pp. 248–52.

[44]   *VHM*, 1, p. 39.

[45]   John of Brera, *Chronicon*, ch. 10, p. 236.

because the story emphasized the role of the now defunct Third order. Whatever his reasons, John presented two other accounts for the origins of the First and Third orders which, together with the 'Bernard story', were to be adopted by later historians and to enjoy great longevity, forming the backbone of narratives of the origins of the Humiliati until the early twentieth century.

John's first version associated the origins of the Order with a group of noble Lombards exiled by one of the eleventh-century emperors. It was well-suited to the chronicler's purpose since, although it accepted the suspicion of heresy, it proved that, far from having heretical beginnings among the 'middle ranks' or worse of late twelfth-century *Lombardia*, the Humiliati's origins lay amongst the nobility of the early eleventh century. A group of nobles, mostly from Milan and Como, had been banished to Germany by the Emperor Henry II (1002-24), lest they should conspire against the Empire: *ne contra imperium machinarentur*. Whilst in exile they were 'inspired by the Holy Spirit to lay aside all worldly pomp and to serve God with humility', symbolically donning the ash-coloured, undyed robes later associated with the Order. As a result they won imperial permission to return to northern Italy and, choosing to continue their new way of life with their families, formed the first group of the Humiliati.[46]

This story both gave the Humiliati a sufficiently respectable genealogy and provided an appealing explanation of their name as describing individuals who had humbled themselves, or had been humbled by none other than the Emperor himself. We can only guess at its genesis. John of Brera was almost certainly drawing on long-standing tradition, perhaps based on the belief that, as they had become involved in the wool industry, the early Humiliati must have learnt their skills north of the Alps.[47] From such a premise it was but a small and attractive leap to make the connection with the accounts of early chroniclers such as Arnolfo in Milan, which tell of the exile of a group of Lombards to

---

[46] Ibid., chs 1-3, p. 230.
[47] Zanoni, *Gli Umiliati*, p. 13.

Germany in the early eleventh century.[48] Moreover, this had the advantage of attributing to the Humiliati the prestige of introducing the all-important wool trade to Lombard soil. John could even support his account of the eleventh-century origins by reference to a document which he mistakenly dated to 1037 and which purported to show that his house of the Brera had been in existence at that date.[49] The venerable antiquity and economic significance of the Humiliati (and of his own community in particular) were thus established beyond dispute.

Having established the eleventh-century origins of the Humiliati, John of Brera went on to recount the foundation of the First order by a priest, John of Meda, in the first half of the twelfth century.[50] The chronicle does not give many details of the life of this John, who was venerated as a saint in the Order, but they are sufficient to place him in a long hagiographical tradition. The whole story is completed in four chapters, which are very close to the brief and anonymous *Vita* edited by Suyskens for the *Acta Sanctorum*.[51] The key event, told in chapter nine of the chronicle, is the early twelfth-century foundation of the oratory of Rondineto near Como for men and women – the women, as befitted fifteenth-century standards, being strictly enclosed and veiled. The rest of the story is constructed around miracles. On a preaching journey to Milan, St John stayed at the Brera. While he was seeking food, an angel appeared in the form of a young man and gave him so much money that the whole community was able to eat abundantly.[52] This miracle had

[48] Arnolfo, *Gesta Archiepiscoporum Mediolanensium usque ad a. 1077*, eds L. C. Bethmann and W. Wattenbach, *MGH. SS*, VIII (Hanover, 1848), p. 11, cited in Zanoni, *Gli Umiliati*, p. 13. On Arnolfo see C. Violante, 'Arnolfo', *Dizionario Biografico Italiano*, 4 (Rome, 1962), pp. 281–2.

[49] John of Brera, *Chronicon*, ch. 10, p. 236. The document in fact dated to the fourteenth century: G. Giulini, *Memorie spettanti alla storia di Milano*, 9 vols (Milan, 1760–5), 3, p. 282.

[50] John of Brera, *Chronicon*, ch. 9, p. 235.

[51] Anonymous, 'Vita de S. Joanne de Meda', ed. C. Suyskens, *ActaSS*, September VII (Antwerp, 1760), pp. 358–60.

[52] John of Brera, *Chronicon*, chs 10–11, pp. 236–7. His *Excerptum*, ch. 16, pp. 339–40, has the same story with slight variations (for example, the Brera is not mentioned) and both versions vary slightly from that of the anonymous 'Vita de S. Joanne', *ActaSS*, Sept. VII, p. 359, the tone of which is less certain: 'unde credimus ipsum angelum Dei fore'.

also had a more recent sequel: one of the coins had survived and in 1403, when a thief's wife had tried to have a hole made in it, the smith had been unable to pierce it.[53] Finally, the saint's death in the Brera in Milan in 1159 also yielded miracles. His body was carried back to Como *honorifice* and, as it passed through the city, blood from the mouth cured a young girl with an eye complaint.[54]

Early in this century de Stefano dismissed the *Vita* of John of Meda as an 'apologia' made up of *topoi* and devoid of historical detail, which had 'nulla a che fare con una storia' – 'nothing to do with history'.[55] It is true that no Humiliati saint is documented in the twelfth or thirteenth centuries. However, a statue of John of Meda was placed over the door of the new Church of San Pietro Viboldone in the façade completed in 1348,[56] over seventy years before John of Brera was writing. Once again, the chronicler was at least drawing on a tradition alive within the Order and providing a creditable founder and focus where none had been recorded.

The chronicler John was living in the community of the Brera and he had access to the early archives of his house. His text reveals that he was familiar with the papal letters approving the Order at the beginning of the thirteenth century, almost two centuries after the supposed exile of the first Humiliati; but this did not present him with chronological difficulties. In the preface to his work, he placed the story of the 'exile' neatly into a wider time scale, though he failed to insert St John of Meda here. He described the 'exile' story as the *principium et origo ordinis*, followed by the *secunda aetas*, marked by the approval of the Rule in 1201 and the issuing of privileges for the Order by Innocent III. Finally, and with obvious Joachite overtones, the *tertia aetas* now in course had begun with the confirmation of the first Master General in 1246, and the later exemption of the Order from diocesan

[53] John of Brera, *Chronicon*, ch. 12, p. 237. For earlier examples of this *topos* of relics resisting the action of thieves, see P. J. Geary, *Furta Sacra. Thefts of Relics in the Central Middle Ages* (Princeton, N.J., 1978), pp. 128, 184-6.

[54] John of Brera, *Chronicon*, ch. 12, p. 237.

[55] A. de Stefano, 'Le origini dell'ordine degli umiliati', *Rivista storico-critica della scienze teologiche*, 2 (1906), pp. 858-9.

[56] The inscription dating the façade is published in Gatti Perer, 'Gli affreschi trecenteschi', p. 126.

authority.[57] With this tripartite chronology, which neatly echoed the tripartite structure of the Order,[58] John was able to establish the venerable antiquity of the Humiliati whilst at the same time acknowledging the importance of documentary evidence. Heresy is also strikingly absent. In order to explain the appeal to Innocent III, John admitted that people had been beginning 'to mutter that the Humiliati erred in certain matters'.[59] He even lists the reasons for this concern, including their unwillingness to swear oaths. But the focus is placed on minor problems concerning the Rule and the cohabitation of male and female religious, which John is careful to show were overcome by papal approval. The real sticking point which had got the Humiliati into trouble – their insistence on preaching without authorization – has disappeared from view.

The chronicle thus constructs a retrospective view of the early Humiliati which makes extensive use of papal letters and can be confirmed at several points. It bears comparison with that of other Orders, emphasizing a venerable genealogy and a respectable founder. However, difficulties with authority are neatly disguised and John's aim, which was surely to use history to emphasize the glorious nature of the Humiliati, is fulfilled by associating the Order with nobility and Empire.

Finally, the reference to the first Master General, whose election initiated the third age of the Order, reveals a more pressing purpose for writing, since it gave John an opportunity to use history to contest the legitimacy of events in his own day. He recorded that in 1246 the Master General had been elected by the three orders of the Humiliati and that such elections had continued until the early fifteenth century. However, since that time they had been impeded. The cause of the problem was the intervention of Pope Boniface IX in both 1398 and 1401. In place of an election Boniface had chosen Andrea Visconti as both provost of San Pietro

---

[57] John of Brera, *Chronicon*, preface, pp. 229–30. The relevant papal letters are in *VHM*, 2, pp. 198–200, 329–32.

[58] John of Brera, *Chronicon*, preface, p. 229.

[59] Ibid., ch. 16, p. 241: 'quia contra humiliatos tunc murmurabatur, quoniam ipsi in aliquibus errabant; licet essent Religiosi sanctae vitae.'

Viboldone and Master General of the Order (1401–31).[60] John issues a warning to those responsible for this enormity which hints at the improper methods used to overthrow ancient custom: 'He who is responsible will be judged by the just Judge, who is not moved by words or gifts and for whom a pure heart and good conscience are worth more than astute words or a full purse.'[61] John's purpose in writing was thus two-fold, and stands in a long tradition of chroniclers before him. He set out to lend glory to the past of his Order which would reflect well on its present and future, recording traditions some of which had perhaps not previously been written down and constructing an account which omitted the stain of heresy. But he also appealed to that past as a means of protesting against what he considered to be undesirable change in his own day. Perhaps his plea was heard, for in 1435 Eugenius IV initiated a reform of the Order which recognized the need for a properly elected Master General.

John's noble version of Humiliati history was to enjoy long currency. It was widely adopted and adapted by later historians of Milan, and the story of the exile was even turned into a folklore 'tradition' in the early nineteenth century.[62] Only at the beginning of this century did Antonino de Stefano finally undertake a revision based on the evidence available, proving beyond reasonable doubt the late twelfth-century date for their emergence, questioning the role of John of Meda and beginning at last to get to grips with the details of their brief encounter with heresy. When fully examined, however, the lack of retrospection in the Order's early years, and the careful use of the past by John of Brera, provide valuable evidence of the problems associated with the Church's attitude to its past, and of the potential utility and dangers of such historical enquiry.

University of St Andrews

---

60 Ibid., ch. 27, pp. 251–3, ch. 33, p. 263.
61 Ibid., preface, p. 230.
62 Domenico Carutti, 'Erberto e Guido, ossia l'origine degli Umiliati', in A. Brofferio, ed., *Tradizioni Italiane*, 2 vols (Milan, 1847–8), pp. 609–38.

OCKHAM'S VISION OF THE PRIMITIVE CHURCH

by TAKASHI SHOGIMEN

G ordon Leff once suggested that a distinctive feature of late medieval ecclesiology was 'a new critical historical attitude to the church'.[1] He argued that the recognition of a disparity between the apostolic and the contemporary Church is discernible equally in the thought of various thinkers such as Dante, Marsilius, and Wyclif, and in the popular movements of the Franciscan Spirituals and the Waldensians.[2] One of the important characteristics in this new criticism was historical interpretation of the Bible.[3] Concomitant with this, biblical studies had been experiencing a shift: Holy Scripture was no longer perceived as a mystified unity of divine words but as a record of historical events written by human authors.[4] And yet, Holy Scripture had been considered by the most learned men in the medieval world to be 'the most difficult text to describe accurately and adequately'.[5] Among the historical critics of the Church, too, could perhaps arise a concern with biblical hermeneutics: what is the most appropriate way to recover the truly historical vision of the apostolic Church as found in Scripture?

William of Ockham was indeed one of the political thinkers who attempted to attack the Church of his time in the light of his vision of the primitive Church. He was not exceptional in that he used Scripture very frequently in his political discourse. Current scholarship, however, tends to suggest that Ockham's interest in the Bible was rather perverse. His exegetical method has been considered to 'fall

[1] Gordon Leff, 'The making of the myth of a True Church in the later Middle Ages', *JMRS*, 6 (1971), pp. 1–15. See also idem, 'The apostolic ideal in later medieval ecclesiology', *JThS*, 18 (1967), pp. 58–82.
[2] Leff, 'The making of the myth', p. 1.
[3] Ibid., p. 2.
[4] See A. J. Minnis, *Medieval Theory of Authorship*, 2nd edn (Philadelphia, 1988), pp. 72, 103–12.
[5] Ibid., p. 4.

into the tradition of assembling texts and quotations from Scripture in order to bolster an argument', and 'it would be misleading to call this exegesis'.[6] Ockham's reasonableness in biblical hermeneutics has also been rejected with the assertion that 'in Ockham's polemical works right reason meant simply his own reason'.[7]

This paper is intended to portray some thoughts with respect to the role of biblical hermeneutics in Ockham's appeal to a vision of the primitive Church. To be sure, that vision was not sketched as an end in itself but in the context of his arguments against the papal doctrine of *plenitudo potestatis* and Marsilius of Padua's rejection of Petrine primacy. Ockham's interest centred around the principles of apostolic government in the early Church, using retrospection to produce a renewed vision for the future. The following comments, therefore, will highlight three pillars of the principles of apostolic government: ministerial rulership for the common good, coercion in a case of necessity, and St Peter's headship. Tracing Ockham's discourse on the first two reveals that his use of Scripture was not merely a polemical means. Rather, he was conscious of the fact that the dispute over the principles of ecclesiastical government in which he was involved was essentially one of biblical hermeneutics. As regards the third, it can be shown that through the medium of biblical hermeneutics Ockham produced a distinctively 'historical' vision of the primitive Church.

When he refuted the papal doctrine of *plenitudo potestatis*, William of Ockham proposed a principle to limit papal

---

6 André Goddu, *The Physics of William of Ockham* (Leiden, 1984), pp. 9–10.

7 Brian Tierney, *Origins of Papal Infallibility, 1150–1350*, Studies in the History of Christian Thought 6, 2nd edn (Leiden, 1988), p. 230. Ockham's biblical hermeneutics have attracted less attention than they deserve. This topic received cursory treatment, for example, in Henri de Lubac, *Exégèse médiévale: les quatre sens de l'écriture*, 2nd part, 2 vols (Paris, 1961-4), 2, p. 382. Systematic analysis and positive assessment were given probably for the first time by Johannes Schlageter, 'Hermeneutik der Heiligen Schrift bei Wilhelm von Ockham', *Franziskanische Studien*, 57 (1975), pp. 230-83, but he did not discuss in detail how Ockham applied his exegetical method in political discourse. Since Schlageter's seminal article, we have only Hermann Schüssler's important *Der Primat der Heiligen Schrift als theologisches und kanonistisches Problem im Spätmittelalter* (Wiesbaden, 1977).

power: 'the Christian law is a law of liberty'.[8] With several scriptural testimonies[9] he illustrated this principle of liberation from servitude to papal power. But Ockham eventually noted that, in order to deduce the above proposition, the key supporting evidence, Acts 15.28,[10] had to be interpreted in a less specific manner than his own exegetical principle allowed.[11] This deviation needed justification; Ockham revealed, referring to II Corinthians 13.10,[12] that the idea 'Christian law is a law of liberty' was based on a view of the apostolic government in the primitive Church which asserted that:

> although the apostles determined various canons and gave many orders besides the items enumerated in Acts 15, they never commanded their subjects without request or consent except in matters which concerned divine law or natural right, and were demanded by necessity or public utility, and could not be omitted without a cost.[13]

Ockham restated this idea in a simpler form, on the basis of II Corinthians 13.8, 10: 'the apostles have no power from God

---

[8] III *Dialogus* I, i, 5–7, in *Monarchia sancti romani imperii*, ed. Melchior Goldast, 3 vols (Frankfurt, 1614) [hereafter *Monarchia*], 2, pp. 776–9. Cf. *Breviloquium de principatu tyrannico* [hereafter *Brev.*] ii, 3–4, in *Wilhelm von Ockham als politischer Denker und sein Breviloquium de principatu tyrannico*, ed. Richard Scholz (Stuttgart, 1944), pp. 56–9; *Octo quaestiones de potestate papae* [hereafter *OQ*], i, 6, in *Guillelmi de Ockham Opera politica*, ed. H. S. Offler, 3 vols (Manchester, 1940–) [hereafter *OP*], 1, p. 29; *De imperatorum et pontificum potestate* [hereafter *IPP*], 1–3. For *IPP*, I have used H. S. Offler's edition which is to be included in the forthcoming volume of *OP*. Prof. D. E. Luscombe, who is in charge of its publication, kindly gave me permission to use a set of the galley proofs.

[9] Acts 15.19–31; II Cor. 3.17; Gal. 2.3–5, 4.31, 5.12–13; and Jas. 1.25.

[10] 'It has seemed good to the Holy Spirit and to us not to impose on you any further burden than these necessary things.'

[11] III *Dialogus* I, i, 7, p. 778.

[12] 'So I write these things while I am absent, so that when I am there, I shall not act too severely according to the authority that the Lord has given me for building up and not for destruction.'

[13] III *Dialogus* I, i, 7, p. 778: 'Ad hoc respondetur, quod licet Apostoli plures canones condiderint, et praeceperint multa praeter illa, quae enumerantur *Actuum decimo quinto*, nihil tamen praeceperunt subditis minime requisitis et non consentientibus, nisi quae erant de lege divina et iure naturali: et necessitas vel utilitas publica postulabat: et quorum praeceptio absque dispendio non poterat praetermini.'

over believers unless it leads to the utility of the subjects or of the community.'[14]

In order to show the positive aim of papal government Ockham expanded this sketch of the early Church. He argued that papal power was established by Christ for the advantage of its subjects except in case of necessity.[15] Christ did not say to Peter, 'Take off wool from my sheep and make your own clothing from it', or 'Squeeze milk from my sheep and drink it', or 'Kill my sheep and eat the meat'; Christ said to Peter, 'Feed my sheep' (John 21.17).[16] Papal rulership, therefore, must serve the common good of believers, not the private good of the pope and, according to Scripture, it embraces reading, prayer, divine ceremonies, and everything necessary to help a Christian to inherit eternal life.[17] Ockham considered such papal rule to be for the advantage of subjects, to be 'ministerial (*ministrativus*)' rule in sharp contrast to 'despotic (*despoticus*)' rule which was rule for the ruler's sake.[18]

It could be perfunctory to surmise that Ockham was here reiterating a traditional Thomist doctrine of the common good.[19] St Thomas's conception of the common good could not have been shaped without the reception of Aristotelian political science; likewise, Ockham praised ministerial rule and rejected despotic rule in the light of Aristotle's *Politics*. Unlike St Thomas, however, Ockham did not use Aristotelian political science as a paradigm. As Roberto Lambertini perceptively elucidated, Ockham was not modelling his theory of ecclesiastical government on Aristotelian politics, but was using the *Politics* as a reservoir of

[14]   Ibid., p. 779: 'Ex quibus [II Cor. 13.8, 10] colligitur quod Apostoli nullam potestatem habuerunt a Deo super fidelibus, nisi quae ad utilitatem subiecti vel communitatis cuiuscunque inducit.'
[15]   See *Brev.* ii, 5, pp. 59–63; *OQ* i, 7, pp. 34–8; iii, 4, pp. 103–6; *IPP* 6.
[16]   *IPP* 7.
[17]   Ibid., 8.
[18]   Ibid., 6.
[19]   Ockham's indebtedness to Thomas Aquinas in political thought was emphasized by C. C. Bayley, 'Pivotal concepts in the political philosophy of William of Ockham', *JHI*, 10 (1949), pp. 199–218; J. B. Morrall, 'Some notes on a recent interpretation of William of Ockham's political philosophy', *Franciscan Studies*, 9 (1949), pp. 335–69; and Mario Grignaschi, 'L'interprétation de la *Politique* d'Aristote dans le *Dialogue* de Guillaume d'Ockham', in *Liber memorialis Georges de Lagarde* (Louvain and Paris, 1970), pp. 59–72.

political arguments.[20] Without any doubt, at the bottom of Ockham's argument lay a biblical concern. In his discourse on communities in III *Dialogus* I, Ockham explained the meanings of the terms that Aristotle used, such as *dominus*, *dominans*, and *dominator*, and pointed out the ambiguity in the common academic use of these terms, which caused interpretations contrary to Aristotle's own intention. Strikingly, Ockham did not examine the various meanings of these terms according to natural philosophy, moral philosophy law, or vulgar usage. He provided, instead, two kinds of usage: one is the *dominus* who rules free subjects; the other is the *dominus* who rules slaves. Evidently this usage reflects Ockham's opposition of ministerial to despotic rule. We must draw attention to the fact that according to Ockham this vital distinction was a biblical one, and he used *dominus* in such a biblical sense in the propositions under discussion.[21] Clearly the nature of political discourse with which he was engaged was essentially biblical, not Aristotelian. In fact, a number of scriptural citations described the pope as a steward or servant in order to show that papal government must serve the interest of the subjects.[22] Ockham's doctrine of ministerial rulership for the common good was thus intended to be a biblical principle.

His emphasis upon rulership for the advantage of subjects accompanied an idea that the apostles exercised no coercive power except in case of utility or necessity. The proviso 'except in case of necessity' introduced flexibility to Ockham's vision of the biblical world. For instance, Christ and the apostles maintained their perfect poverty although they had money in the purse which Judas Iscariot carried because, Ockham argues, it was only for use in case of necessity.[23] Appeal to necessity saved apostolic perfection in poverty from its rejection on the basis of the episode of Judas'

---

[20] Roberto Lambertini, 'Wilhelm von Ockham als Leser der *Politica*: Zur Rezeption der politischen Theorie des Aristoteles in der Ekklesiologie Ockhams', in Jürgen Miethke, ed., *Das Publikum politischer Theorie in 14. Jahrhundert* (Munich, 1992), pp. 207-24.

[21] III *Dialogus* I, ii, 3, p. 792.

[22] Matt. 20.25-8, 23.11; Mark 10.42-5; Luke 22.25-7; and I Pet. 5.3. See OQ i, 7, pp. 36-7; iii, 4, pp. 103-6; III *Dialogus* I, i, 9, p. 781; *IPP* 7.

[23] *Opus nonaginta dierum* 94, in *OP*, 2, pp. 714-15.

purse (John 12.6 and 13.29). Ockham audaciously said that Christ would have exercised temporal power in case of necessity,[24] thus hinting at the possibility of the pope's occasional intervention in secular politics. Similarly, Ockham also modified an Aristotelian argument that no one should rule anyone else unless he was superior to all others in respect of virtue and wisdom. It seems clear to Ockham that Aristotle's intention was that it is not just for a man to rule his equals in virtue and wisdom unless it is expedient to raise up a man to rule his equals on account of utility or necessity.[25]

All these arguments were modelled on the canonist maxim 'necessity has no law'. Ockham referred to the De regulis iuris in the Decretales and probably also to its gloss,[26] and from them deduced an idea that an act contrary to divine precept could be licit in case of necessity. His appeal to the canonistic tradition was, however, endorsed by a conviction that this principle was, as found in Scripture, actually taught by Christ and guided Christ's own deeds in general. Ockham's justification of an act contrary to divine precept in a case of necessity manifests his deep concern with its biblical foundation. In III Dialogus I, he produced seven counter-arguments.[27] Ockham's treatment of the six counter-arguments based on canonistic or Aristotelian authorities was short.[28] However, to the biblically grounded argument that no Christian may contradict Christ's ordinance on the basis of Matthew 10.24,[29] Ockham's response was fully developed, demonstrating several examples of contradiction between Christ's precept and his own deeds,[30] and being followed by an elaboration of the hermeneutics of Holy Scripture.[31] Thus Ockham's reference to canonistic sources also revolved

---

[24] OQ i, 8, p. 39.
[25] III Dialogus I, ii, 15, p. 800.
[26] Ibid., ii, 20, p. 808. Prof. Brian Tierney has kindly suggested to me in correspondence that Ockham's reference to Matt. 12.3-4 and Luke 6.3-4 which followed the citation of the De regulis iuris (X 5.41.4: Corpus iuris canonici, ed. E. L. Richter and E. Friedberg, 2 vols [Leipzig, 1879-81], 2, col. 927) was possibly based on its gloss.
[27] III Dialogus I, ii, 21, pp. 808-9.
[28] Ibid., ii, 25-6, pp. 812-15.
[29] 'A disciple is not above the teacher, nor a slave above the master.'
[30] III Dialogus I, ii, 22, pp. 809-10.
[31] Ibid., ii, 24, pp. 811-12.

around his concern with the biblical foundations of political discourse.

Ockham's reception of the canonistic idea 'necessity has no law' introduced the dynamism of Aristotelian politics which suggests the possibility of constitutional change from regal to aristocratic rulership (or vice versa) to his discourse on papal government; the monarchic rulership by only one pope may be replaced by aristocratic rulership by more than one pope in case of necessity. However, as far as Ockham was concerned, this did not result in the denial of Petrine primacy. In fact, he defended St Peter's supremacy from a possible Aristotelian objection. After stating that Peter was inferior to John in terms of merit and to Paul in terms of wisdom, Ockham pretended to raise an objection to Petrine primacy on the grounds of an Aristotelian principle that government by a single ruler is not expedient if there are others equal to him in wisdom and virtue. Ockham argued that this objection could not stand if the people wished to obey one ruler due to their humility or their love for *res publica* or common utility.[32] When he said this, Ockham had in mind a vision of the early Church: 'the apostles, who knew Christ's ordinance because of their humility and obedience, were very prompt in obeying Peter in his whole lifetime'.[33]

How did Ockham come to hold this view? What is its biblical foundation? Ockham remained silent on this. At least, however, Book 4 of III *Dialogus* I displays his defence of Petrine primacy against Marsilius of Padua's rejection. Perhaps Marsilius' denial of St Peter's supremacy appeared to Ockham too serious to be ignored, since it claimed to be grounded on the authority of the Bible. Despite its ostensible biblical style, the Marsilian argument was ultimately based on St Jerome's authority.[34] According to this, *presbyter* and *episcopus* were synonymous in the early Church, distinguished only by the traits that these terms signified: the former was used for an elder person, the latter for a supervisor of the

---

[32] Ibid., iv, 24, pp. 865–6.

[33] Ibid., iv, 24, p. 866: 'Apostoli autem scientes ordinationem Christi ex humilitate et obedientia, promptissimi erant obedire Petro pro toto tempore vitae suae.'

[34] St Jerome, Epist. 146, *Ad Evangelum* (PL 22, 1192–5).

Christians. Marsilius argued that as the number of *presbyteri* increased, supervisors were elected who monopolized the title of *episcopus*. He emphasized that such a human election did not confer any sacerdotal power but only what he called 'household power *(potestas iconomica)*' to control other ecclesiastics without coercion while every priest received the same authority directly and justly from Christ. Marsilius had, therefore, concluded that priests and bishops were equal in terms of sacramental and penitential power, what he called the 'essential authority *(auctoritas essentialis)*' bestowed by Christ.[35]

Marsilius' arguments for this claim were almost exclusively dependent on scriptural citations,[36] and Ockham attacked it on the same biblico-hermeneutic ground. His advocacy of St Peter's supremacy was distinctively different from that of the papalist theologians such as James of Viterbo and Peter de la Palud; the latter theologians argued that the whole gospel demonstrates Petrine primacy, whereas Ockham claimed that particular references such as 'Feed my sheep' (John 21.17) and 'You are Peter' (Matthew 16.18) are the key evidence of St Peter's primacy.[37] Yet Ockham also noted that the verse 'You are Peter' could not be used on its own to prove Petrine primacy.[38] His solution was to appeal to the so-called 'two-sources' theory of catholic truth.[39] Ockham turned down the 'single-source' theory *(sola scriptura)*, according to which what is asserted explicitly or implicitly in the Bible is the only catholic truth and must be believed as necessary for salvation. To Ockham, there are many other catholic truths which must be believed even if they are indicated neither explicitly nor implicitly in Scripture, nor deduced from its content.[40] Accordingly, 'You are Peter' must be understood, as evidence of Petrine primacy, in the light of the words of holy

---

[35] Marsilius of Padua, *Defensor pacis*, ed. C. W. Previté-Orton (Cambridge, 1928) [hereafter *DP*], II, xv, 5–8, pp. 267–70.

[36] Ibid., II, xvi, pp. 273–88.

[37] Georges de Lagarde, *La Naissance de l'esprit laïque au déclin du moyen-âge*, new edn, 5 vols (Louvain and Paris, 1956–70), 5, pp. 106–7.

[38] III *Dialogus* I, iv, 13, p. 859.

[39] On Ockham's 'two-sources' theory, see Heiko Augustinus Oberman, *The Harvest of Medieval Theology*, 3rd edn (Durham, N.C., 1983), pp. 378–82.

[40] I *Dialogus*, ii, 1–3, in *Monarchia*, 2, pp. 410–14; III *Dialogus* I, iii, pp. 819–45.

men in the early Church. The words of Saints Anacletus, Marcellus, and Cyprian testified sufficiently that 'You are Peter' meant St Peter's headship.[41]

In this argument Ockham did not rely merely on a tradition of biblical interpretation. He relied also on his theory of knowledge.[42] It must be noted that Ockham did not attempt to prove that Christ's words, 'You are Peter', signify today the primacy of St Peter. Instead, he proposed an historical question of whether or not Christ appointed Peter as head of the other apostles;[43] Ockham was concerned with the fact in the past. Thus, how could we know that Christ's words, 'You are Peter', were actually intended to signify St Peter's headship? In the light of Ockham's epistemology, we are today unable to have evident knowledge of scriptural events because intuitive cognition of these events, which are not present in front of us, is naturally (*naturaliter*) impossible.[44] In his speculative work Ockham drew a distinction between intuitive and abstractive cognition with reference to the possibility of having the evident knowledge of a contingent proposition about the present. Intuitive cognition is 'that by virtue of which one can have evident knowledge of whether or not a thing exists, or more broadly, of whether or not a contingent proposition about the present is true'.[45]

---

41 III *Dialogus* I, iv, 13–16, pp. 859–61.

42 Prof. Janet Coleman recently produced a penetrating analysis of the relation between Ockham's intuitive cognition theory and his political discourse. In it, emphasis was laid on Ockham's application of logical method to biblical hermeneutics. See her 'The relation between Ockham's intuitive knowledge and his political science', in Jean-Phillipe Genet and Yves Tiliette, eds, *Théologie et droit dans la science politique de l'état moderne* (Rome, 1991), pp. 71–88. See also her *Ancient and Medieval Memories* (Cambridge, 1992), pp. 500–37.

43 III *Dialogus* I, iv, 1, p. 846.

44 To be sure, Ockham also argued that an intuitive cognition of non-existence could be produced by an act of divine absolute power: see William of Ockham, *Scriptum in librum primum sententiarum (Ordinatio)* [hereafter Ordinatio] i, Prologue, q. 1, a. 1, in *Venerabilis inceptoris Guillelmi de Ockham Opera philosophica et theologica ad fidem codicum manuscriptorum edita*, eds Philotheus Boehner, Gedeon Gál et al., 17 vols (St Bonaventure, N.Y., 1967–88), *Opera theologica* [hereafter OTh], 1, pp. 31, 38–9. Similarly, Ockham suggested that the primary, true meaning of a scriptural testimony might possibly be known to someone by a new divine revelation: see especially III *Dialogus* I, iii, 16–18, pp. 832–6. However, he also commented that no such case could ever be found: see I *Dialogus* ii, 25, p. 429.

45 Marilyn McCord Adams, *William Ockham*, 2 vols (Notre Dame, Ind., 1987), 1, p. 502, which refers to *Ordinatio* i, Prologue, q. 1, a. 1, in *OTh*, 1, pp. 31–2;

Abstractive cognition is, on the other hand, 'a noncomplex apprehension of terms by virtue of which it is not possible to have evident knowledge of whether or not a thing exists, or whether or not a contingent proposition about the present is true'.[46] Intuitive, not abstractive, cognition sufficiently guarantees the certitude of knowledge of a contingent truth because intuitive cognition entails the judgement of whether a thing exists here and now, and existence of the thing is necessary to produce evident knowledge of a contingent truth. But it is naturally (*naturaliter*) impossible for us to have intuitive knowledge of a proposition about the past because the situation represented by the terms in the proposition is not present to us.[47] Accordingly, as we can no longer witness the moment that Christ said to Peter, 'You are Peter', we cannot have evident knowledge of what Christ intended by those words.

Nevertheless, Ockham's theory of truth conditions explains that in order to determine whether a proposition about the past stated now is true or false, what must be examined is whether its corresponding present-tense proposition as stated in the past was then true or false. To put it in a formula, 'N was P' is true if and only if 'N is P' was true at some past time.[48] Ockham's argument for Petrine primacy adopts this logic of tensed proposition. Ockham argued that those who were the disciples of the apostles, or those who were taught by them, must be believed to have possessed the true understanding of Christ's words.[49] In particular, St Anacletus, who was a disciple of the apostles and was taught Scripture by St Peter, was unlikely to have a false understanding of the sentence, 'You are Peter', because he was learned and holy, and actually conversed with St Peter.[50]

Quaestiones in librum secundum sententiarum (Reportatio) ii, q. 12–13, in OTh, 5, pp. 256–7; *Quodlibeta septem* [hereafter *Quodl.*] v, q. 5, in OTh, 9, p. 496.

[46] Adams, *William Ockham*, 1, pp. 502–3, which refers to *Ordinatio* i, Prologue, q. l, a. 1, in OTh, 1, p. 32; *Quodl.* v, q. 5, in OTh, 9, p. 496.

[47] See above, n.44.

[48] Alfred J. Freddoso, 'Ockham's theory of truth conditions', in Alfred J. Freddoso and Henry Schuurman, eds, *Ockham's Theory of Propositions: Part II of the Summa Logicae* (Notre Dame, Ind., 1980), pp. 1–76.

[49] III *Dialogus* I, iv, 13, p. 859.

[50] Ibid., iv, 15, p. 860.

Parallelism is obvious here; to verify today that Christ's words, 'You are Peter', were intended to signify the primacy of St Peter, Ockham argued that St Peter's saintly contemporaries themselves had understood the words, 'You are Peter', to signify Petrine primacy for them in their own time.

Furthermore, intuitive cognition theory is the epistemological foundation of this. Clearly Ockham presumes that St Peter's understanding of Christ's words demonstrates Christ's intention; that is, St Peter's understanding is the true understanding.[51] Ockham also stresses the certitude of St Anacletus' direct experience of St Peter's teaching on Christ's words. In short, St Peter's intuitive knowledge of the proposition, 'You are Peter', is considered to have been transmitted without distortion to a disciple who was actually taught by St Peter. Reference to the record of the direct experience of scriptural events was, in view of Ockham's intuitive cognition theory, the only possible measure to obtain certain knowledge of these events.

Ockham perceived scriptural events strictly as the distant past, for absolutely true knowledge of the principles of ecclesiastical government existed only in the days of Christ and the apostles. Hence, the constitution of the Church was, for Ockham, perfected in the past by the words and deeds of Christ and the apostles. This is apparent in Ockham's idea of the succession to ecclesiastical offices. He rejects the Marsilian understanding of Matthew 28.19[52] that all the apostles were equal because all of them received the same power of teaching directly from Christ, not from St Peter. Ockham maintained that the denial of St Peter's superiority to the other apostles cannot be deduced from the equality in the power of teaching because every successor receives his ecclesiastical office from his predecessor, not from his superior, as in the case of the succession to secular status.[53] The offices of Church government were indeed of divine origin but, according to Ockham, God does not interfere in

---

51 Ibid., iv, 15, p. 860.
52 'Going therefore teach all nations, baptizing them in the name of the Father and of the Son and of the Holy Spirit.'
53 III *Dialogus* I, iv, 6, p. 853.

their succession. The maintenance of the organization of the Church was entrusted to human beings alone.

This forms a striking contrast to the idea of Marsilius. Marsilius considered that office was a habit of the mind and its efficient cause was God. When he conferred office on the apostles, Marsilius argued, Christ as a man exemplified the ministry which was inherited by priests, while Christ as God imprinted the priestly habit of mind on to the apostles. In like manner, the office has been passed on by ministry performed by the apostles and their successors, and at the same time, when the apostles or other priests put their hands on others and say the appropriate words, Christ as God imprints the priestly habit of mind on to the man who is worthy and willing to receive it.[54]

In the Marsilian theory of the succession to ecclesiastical office, Christ's bestowal of priestly office in the past is repeated today through the work of Christ as God. Ockham, on the other hand, regarded succession to office as a purely human institution, for Christ's determination of the constitution of the Church by conferring office was viewed strictly as an event in the past. The works of Christ as God are also considered to possess historical character.

Obviously Marsilius of Padua had no acute consciousness of the historicity of biblical events or, if he had, it was entirely different from that of Ockham. In fact, when he wrote of the primitive Church, Marsilius did not intend to appeal to the past as something on which the contemporary Church ought to be modelled. For him the Church in the time of the apostles was an imperfect community because it was ruled by non-Christian secular rulers, whereas the Church of his day, whose secular rulers were Christianized, was perfect.[55]

By contrast, Ockham *did* intend to appeal to the past, and at the same time, was fully aware of an abyss between past and present. Ockham's application of the 'two-sources' theory to his biblical defence of Petrine primacy leaves a trace of his hermeneutic effort to reconstruct the true picture of the early

---

[54] *DP* II, xv, 2, p. 264.
[55] Jeannine Quillet, 'Politique et évangile dans l'oeuvre de Marsile de Padoue', *Bulletin de philosophie médiévale*, 31 (1991), pp. 155-61.

Church, by which he attempted to illuminate the crisis in the Church of his time. Ockham did not use Scripture merely for the justification of his political claims; far from it. His discourse on papal government was intended to be biblical. Ockham's vision of the apostolic government in the primitive Church, therefore, should not be considered as a by-product of his premeditated political programme. It was an outcome of his biblico-hermeneutic search for the true knowledge of the distant past.[56]

University of Sheffield

[56] I am grateful to Prof. D. E. Luscombe, Prof. A. S. McGrade, Dr Stephen E. Lahey, Mr Stephen M. Conway, and Mr James A. Sheppard for their comments on an earlier draft of this paper.

by MICHAEL WILKS

During the 1370s Wyclif wrote to defend a monarchy which made extensive use of bishops and other clergy in the royal administration and yet was faced with aristocratic factions encouraged by bishops like Wykeham and Courtenay who espoused papal supremacy, if not out of conviction, at least as a very convenient weapon to support their independence against royal absolutism. At first sight Wyclif's attempts to define the right relationship between royal and episcopal, temporal and spiritual, power seem as confused as the contemporary political situation. His works contain such a wide range of theories from orthodox two swords dualism to a radical rejection of ecclesiastical authority well beyond that of Marsilius and Ockham that it seems as if his only interest was in collecting every anti-hierocratic idea available for use against the papacy. The purpose of this paper is to suggest that a much more coherent view of episcopal power can be detected beneath his tirades if it is appreciated that his continual demand for a great reform, a *reformatio regni et ecclesiae*, is inseparably linked to his understanding of the history of the Christian Church, and that in this way Wyclif anticipates Montesquieu in requiring a time factor as a necessary ingredient in constitutional arrangements.

Wyclif saw himself as a prophet preaching a message of salvation to a people of God for whom the Bible, especially the Old Testament, had a direct significance. He had so much to say about the importance of Scripture, evangelical liberty, apostolic poverty and the natural innocence of the early Church that it is hardly surprising that some of his later opponents came to criticize him and his followers for ignoring anything the Church had achieved after the first millennium.[1] One has only to consider his use of authors like

---

[1] For examples (Barton, Netter), see Anne Hudson, *The Premature Reformation* (Oxford, 1988), p. 250.

Grosseteste and Fitzralph, let alone less well publicized ones like Aquinas and Ockham, to recognize this criticism as obvious nonsense. Wyclif's was intended to be a universal system, and no one was more eclectic: everything was to be grist for the mill. But it is true that this entailed a refusal to believe that history and historic practices were obsolete and out of date: early sources should still be of relevance to his own time. Was the law of Christ, he once asked, to be allowed to survive for only three centuries whilst the rule of Antichrist went on for ever?[2] Human time might be a linear progression from the Creation to the end of the world, and he followed this scheme in his own work: the *Summa theologiae* ran from the genesis of the divine mandates through an investigation of natural law and civil society to the apocalyptic obsession with Antichrist which characterizes the later books. But this progression led to a Second Coming, the great return of Christ to the world and a new Jerusalem. This idea of return implied a turning round again, a repetition, a revolution not just in the modern sense of a change of government and society but in the classical sense of a movement back to what had gone before. Religion meant for Wyclif, as it had done for the Romans, *religare*, to bind back to the origins, and he adopted the notion that time was a circular process which turned like a wheel. As Aristotle, following Hesiod and Pythagoras, had suggested in the *Physics*,[3] the Greeks accepted that human affairs moved round in a circle through a series of periods in the same way that the heavenly bodies revolved and so must eventually return to their original position, a point marked by a cataclysm and a new beginning. Time, in other words, formed a great year. This great year theory had then been accepted by Cicero and other Roman authors, becoming a staple feature of prophetic material: the Sibylline Oracle, for example, spoke of

[2] *Dialogus*, 7, p. 16. Earlier debates on Wyclif's attitude towards tradition are discussed by M. Hurley, 'Scriptura sola: Wyclif and his critics', *Traditio*, 16 (1960), pp. 275-352.

[3] *Physics*, 223b; cf. *De gen. et cor.*, 336b; *Problemata*, 916a; *Protrepticus*, frag. 19. Wyclif's commentary on the *Physics* remains unpublished: see W. R. Thomson, *The Latin Writings of John Wyclif* (Toronto 1983), pp. 12-14; otherwise all references are to the Wyclif Society editions (London, 1883-1921).

'the circling years of time'.[4] With Wyclif this great year applies to the whole history of the Church from the beginning to the end of time – 'facta est in magno anno mundi'[5] – but during the Middle Ages there were numerous variants with competing suggestions for different successions and alternations of good and bad periods, and the principle achieved immense popularity in the more common form of the wheel of Fortune.[6]

It is important however to make the point that this was speculation about the nature of human time. Divine time was a different matter entirely: as was often said, a thousand years was but a day in the sight of God – or, perhaps more accurately, that God lived in an eternal present. Past, present, and future were all one in the divine mind.[7] This, Wyclif said, was duration (*duratio*) and must be distinguished from *tempus*, human time,[8] measured in this

---

[4] The standard account is G. W. Trompf, *The Idea of Historical Recurrence in Western Thought from Antiquity to the Reformation* (Berkeley and Los Angeles, 1979), esp. pp. 11–12, 62–75, 177, 202.

[5] *De Ecclesia*, 17, pp. 389–90; also 9, p. 197 for the succession of the seasons of the year. Plato is credited with the view that the world year lasts 36,000 terrestrial years: *De actibus animae*, i.3, p. 51.

[6] This derives from Boethius, *Philosophiae consolatio*, ii. *prol.* 1–6, where Philosophy is emphasizing the difference between divine and human justice: 'Haec nostra vis est, hunc continuum ludum ludimus: totam volubili orbe versamus, infima summis, summa infimis mutare gaudemus. Ascende si placet, sed ea lege, ne uti cum ludicri mei ratio poscet descendere iniuriam putes.' For a good late fourteenth-century example see *Somer Soneday* (Oxford, Bodleian Library, MS Douce 332), 'A wifman wiþ a wonder whel weue with þe wynde ... And Fortune Y fond', ed. T. Turville-Petre, *Alliterative Poetry of the Later Middle Ages* (London, 1989), p. 143 and fig. 5.

[7] *De Ecclesia*, pp. 106–7, citing Eccles. 3.14–15, and Aristotle on motion in the *Physics*, vii.1. Previous efforts to combine Aristotle's view of time (taken largely from *Physics*, iv.10–14, 218–23; also v.3, 226–7 and vi.1-2, 231-2 on the analogy of time as a line) with an Augustinian conception of God as in an eternal present, notably by Wyclif's predecessor at Merton, Thomas Bradwardine, are well set out by E. W. Dolnikowski, *Thomas Bradwardine: A View of Time and a Vision of Eternity in Fourteenth-Century Thought* (Leiden, New York, and Cologne, 1995), who rightly indicates the contribution of Euclidean mathematics here. The relevance of the *Categories* as a source passed on through Boethius and Anselm has been shown by G. R. Evans, 'Time and eternity: Boethian and Augustinian sources of thought in the late eleventh and early twelfth centuries', *Classical folia*, 31 (1977), pp. 105–18, who cites (p. 112) the significant passage in Abelard's *Dialectica* that time is either an indivisible instant or a composite succession of instants forming past, present, and future. See Dolnikowski, *Thomas Bradwardine*, pp. 42–3.

[8] The term *duratio* was probably borrowed from Augustine. Cf. *De logica*, iii.10,

world by a succession of ages. Once again there was an appeal here to Aristotelian physics: a line was to be seen two ways, either as a single thing or as a succession of dots next to each other – just as in philosophy it was necessary at different times to consider both the universal and the individuals. It was the same with time: it was either, as God saw it, a single eternity; or it was a constant movement of instants (what Chaucer would call degrees)[9] following each other round and round as on the face of a clock, which was how humanity saw it. This was why predestination was such a simple matter. If the future is the same as the past, then God has no difficulty in knowing who is elect and who is damned. But mankind trapped in the wheel of time can have no such certainty and must endure – accept *duratio* – until the succession of ages reveals whether the signs of salvation or perdition to be detected in human life are a true indication of what must be. There can be no sure salvation until human time matches up to divine time, until the circle of periods has completed its course, and there is a return to the perpendicular.[10]

Like so many of his contemporaries Wyclif accepted the Augustinian notion of the seven ages of man, and applied the same idea to the ages of the world.[11] There was what might be described as a world week of seven phases, with the

iii.172, 'et illum mundum durare in transitione successiva est tempus'; and see ii.17, i.224; iii.9, iii.34-5, 80-3; iii.10, iii.181, 196, 211, where he acknowledges that it was reading the *Physics* (apparently in a commentary perhaps by Averroes but probably Aquinas) which led him to change his original view of time through the theory of the line as 'continuatio et contiguatio'. The problem of dating the *De logica* remains unsolved.

9   In the *Nun's Priest's Tale*, vii. 2854-8, the cock crows more strongly 'Than is a clokke or an abbey orlogge. / By nature he knew ech ascencioun / Of the equynoxial in thilke toun; / For when degrees fiftene weren ascended, / Thanne crew he that it myghte nat been amended.' For the *Tales* as political and anti-clerical analogies see now L. Scanlon, *Narrative, Authority and Power: The Medieval Exemplum and the Chaucerian Tradition* (Cambridge, 1994).

10   *De Ecclesia*, 9, p. 198, 'et iterum oportet ut fiat nova appropinquatio ad perpendiculare, quodquam fiat directo post diem iudicii solsticium sempiternum, ut patet *Apocalypsis* ultimo; tunc enim invariabiliter coincident radius incidens et reflexus.'

11   Trompf, *Historical Recurrence*, pp. 207f. The connection between these concepts has already been pointed out by B. Smalley, *Historians in the Middle Ages* (London, 1974); and in general see now J. A. Burrow, *The Ages of Man* (Oxford, 1986).

lifetime of Christ featuring as a halfway stage.[12] The three periods of the Old Testament represented the youth of the world; there had been three ages of decline into old age since; and this led to a seventh or last age of the world, an apocalyptic period of Armageddon, and a prelude to the eighth day of eternal bliss, the great return to another Sunday. Wyclif insisted that his own time was the nadir of the process, the point at which the downward movement had virtually reached its lowest level: the world had never been in a worse condition, and the tyrant priests had brought the Church into the condition of the Last Days.[13] Satan had been bound for a thousand years, and so the history of the Church after Christ had begun in a state of apostolic purity, an age of saints, martyrs, and patristics. The first real downward lurch had occurred with the Donation of Constantine – like an injection of poison into the body of Christ[14] – but it was the eleventh century and the emergence of the Gregorian Church which indicated that the decline was serious and would be fatal.[15] So as a rule of thumb the older a doctrine was, like that of the Eucharist, the more correct and useful it was likely to be: conversely the later the pope concerned, the worse he would probably be.[16] Indeed it was only from around 1200, from the time of

---

[12]   The general principle is in *De mandatis divinis*, 16, pp. 211-14, although this has four ages for the Old Testament period, apparently to relate to Daniel's four world monarchies, as indicated by *De civili dominio*, iii, 15, p. 196. For three Old Testament ages see, e.g., iii.7, p. 60; cf. *De veritate sacrae scripturae*, 15, i.383, 'Nam tempore Crisostomi [who referred to heretical priests] . . . coepit calumnia; tempore Machometi amplius dissipata est; et a tempore editionis *Decretalium* decrevit honor et pruderantia legis scripturae continue, quod videtur esse via praeparatoria Antichristo'; *De civili dominio*, iii.17, p. 247, 'distinguere circumstantias temporum . . .. Aliter enim debent vivere patres veteris testamenti et in iuvenile aetate mundi . . . et aliter provectiones filii mundi senescentis . . ..'

[13]   *De Ecclesia*, 3, p. 51; also *De mandatis divinis*, 28, p. 410; 30, p. 474; cf. *De civili dominio*, ii.17, p. 240, 'Unde videtur michi quod nunquam ab origine mundi . . . cum hodie quod et dolendum est . . .'. On this topic see further M. Wilks, 'Wyclif and the great persecution', in M. Wilks, ed., *Prophecy and eschatology*, SCH.S, 10 (Oxford, 1994), pp. 39-63.

[14]   E.g. *De officio regis*, 7, p. 171.

[15]   *De eucharistia*, 9, p. 286.

[16]   Ibid., 2, p. 32, 'Quare ergo non crederetur tantae vel plus suae sententiae sicut debiliori sententiae succedenti? Ecclesia enim deteriorando quoad fidem scripturae procedit. Et iterum prior sententia plus consonat sensui, rationi, sanctis doctoribus et scripturis . . .'; also 9, p. 278; *De civili dominio*, ii.11, pp. 124-5.

the first really awful pope, Innocent III, that the situation went out of control.[17]

But the period before the 1200 watershed still had much to recommend it,[18] and the work of twelfth-century writers and legislators could be salvaged and reused: Wyclif plundered its intellectual treasures lavishly and shamelessly, thereby giving himself, as he saw it, an irrefutable claim to orthodoxy against his contemporaries. He maintained that moderates like John of Salisbury in philosophy and theology, and the reciprocal dualism between the claims of clerical and lay government in canon law put forward by the Decretists, had achieved a workable compromise. It was only the Decretalists, corrupted by their work on the texts of Innocent III and his successors, who had destroyed the carefully balanced relationship which should exist between king and bishop. That relationship – the king as vicar of God the divine ruler juxtaposed to the human vicar of Christ, the bishop – Wyclif borrowed wholesale from the Christology of the Anglo-Norman Anonymous,[19] a more significant source for the character of medieval English kingship than modern historians like to think. But what this meant in practical terms of the corresponding duties of kings and bishops had been clearly spelt out, he argued, by St Anselm.

It may not have been an Anselm that Sir Richard Southern would recognize, but Wyclif had initially been trained as a papalist, an Augustinian hierocrat, and knew how to make use of his sources for his own purposes, even if it turned the originals on their heads. When, for example, he eventually admitted that his double substance eucharistic theory required that the bread and wine should remain after consecration and conversion into the body and blood of Christ, it was, remarkably, from Anselm (amongst others)

---

[17] See the lengthy condemnation of Innocent III in *De eucharistia*, 9, pp. 274f., although Honorius III was worse for confirming the Orders of friars and Gregory IX for issuing the *Decretals* (p. 278; also 5, p. 142), and the move to Avignon made matters worse still, 4, p. 106.

[18] *De civili dominio*, ii.14, pp. 178–9.

[19] *De officio regis*, 1, pp. 10, 14; 6, pp. 121–2, 131; although he credits Augustine with this idea. See further G. H. Williams, *The Norman Anonymous of 1100 A.D.* (Cambridge, Mass., 1951). Perhaps after all, he was the Anonymous of York!

that he claimed support.[20] When he insisted that the contemporary Church had become an *ecclesia* of malignants,[21] too corrupt to be a vehicle of salvation, and therefore another covenant with God was needed, a new social contract of good lordship to replace the Petrine Commission, it was from Anselm that he borrowed his term to describe it. It was a chirograph, a document which recognized rights on both sides, and accordingly was made by dividing it down the middle. This, incidentally, is why Piers Plowman tore the pardon in half whilst the contemporary priest could not even recognize it as a contract of salvation.[22] But where Anselm was particularly significant for Wyclif was that he had been responsible for engineering the agreement of London in August 1107, a compromise arrangement which would later provide a basis for the Concordat of Worms in 1122 and the alleged settlement of the Investiture Contest. These agreements had defined a tripartite distinction of episcopal power. The old simple division between a bishop's internal and external powers was coming by the twelfth century to be described as on one side his *potestas ordinis*, the sacramental power given to a bishop by consecration; and on the other side his *ecclesiastica* or *potestas iurisdictionis*, granted by investiture with a ring and staff, the powers and properties of the see which he administered by right of office. But in addition there was a third capacity, the bishop's position as a baron or royal officer, his holding of *saecularia* or *regalia* which granted him powers, duties, and rights which might otherwise have been given to a layman: the custody of cities and castles, official functions, the right to levy tolls and dues, and the feudal obligations of fealty, knight service, and so on which went with them. Faced with a papal insistence that kings should not invest bishops, Paschal II's desire to do

[20] *De eucharistia*, 5, p. 131.

[21] *De officio regis*, 11, p. 251, kings are to act like an aggregate emperor 'contra ecclesiam malignantium . . . quamdiu manet civilitas sublunaris et clerus sic aspirat ad terrenum dominium'; also *De potestate papae*, 7, p. 139.

[22] *De civili dominio*, ii.16, pp. 318–19, citing Anselm, *Cur deus homo*, i.7 (*PL*, 158, col. 368): this cancels the charter of damnation in Col. 2.13–14; cf. *De benedicta incarnatione*, 6, p. 90; G. A. Benrath, *Wyclifs Biblekommentar* (Berlin, 1966), pp. 72–3 (on Jer. 17.13). See also St Bernard, *De consideratione*, ii.6 (*PL*, 182, col. 750); *Piers Plowman*, B.vii.116.

away with the third capacity (episcopal *regalia*), and Henry I's equally strong determination that all jurisdiction should flow from the king, Anselm in 1107 had arranged a compromise by which the king gave up the right to confer the bishop's jurisdictional power by investiture, but retained the right to confer the *regalia*, the bishop's other offices, *per sceptrum*.[23]

Although the fourteenth century normally preferred a simple distinction between a bishop's 'spirituals', which included things like tithes and oblations, and his 'temporals', his estates and offices,[24] the old legal subdivision of jurisdiction was still recognized. Thus when Wykeham came to terms with John of Gaunt in 1377, the bishop agreed to fit out three war galleys with fifty archers and fifty men-at-arms in each, and in return had its temporalities restored to him. It was specified that these temporalities included both the *temporalia* themselves and the bishop's feudal rights (*cum feodis militum*), the custody of castles, manors, and knights' fees. It was in this same year that Wyclif argued that the king had a double basis for refusing to allow papal taxation of the English Church: because it infringed both the royal jurisdiction as patron in chief and the king's feudal rights over his clergy.[25] And to cut a long story short, let me simply make the point that with Wyclif careful analysis of his multitude of condemnations of bishops for having jurisdiction at all – the task of bishops was to preach the truth and leave coercion to the laity[26] – shows that beneath these outpourings

[23] Eadmer, *Historia novorum*, ed. M. Rule, *RS* (London, 1884), p. 186. See further M. J. Wilks, '*Ecclasiastica* and *regalia*: papal investiture policy from the Council of Guastalla to the First Lateran Council, 1106–23', *SCH*, 7 (Oxford, 1971), pp. 69–85.

[24] This dualistic position is well stated by M. E. Howell, *Regalian Right in Medieval England* (London, 1962).

[25] For Wykeham see T. Rymer, *Foedera*, vii.148–9; cf. G. Holmes, *The Good Parliament* (Oxford, 1975), p. 192. *De potestate papae*, 10, pp. 222f. on papal taxation; also *De Ecclesia*, 15, p. 340 on royal rights during episcopal vacancies which allow him to take both feudal and patronage possessions: '. . . in mortibus multorum sacerdotum qui de rege tenent in feudo temporalia cedant regi. Unde ex iure patronatus confert beneficia . . . Unde cum rex praeter istas regalias aufert saepe temporalia . . .'.

[26] *De civili dominio*, ii.8, p. 73; this distinction of functions follows from the dual nature of Christ. As priest he is 'propheta magnus atque magister', but as king exercises 'correptio coactiva' as defined by Justinian in *Novella*, 6, (p. 77). *De officio regis*, 7, p. 186, 'Dixi autem alias quomodo domini temporales habent potentiam datam eis a Deo ut ubi spirituale bracchium Ecclesiae non sufficit convertere antichristos ewangelica praedicatione, ecclesiastica correctione vel virtutum exemplatione, saeculare bracchium adiuvet matrem suam severa cohercione, et specialiter in pseudo-clericis.'

Wyclif still operated with the traditional (and originally papal) tripartite distinction. Under divine lordship the clergy had a God-given authority which was quite separate from any Caesarean gift,[27] but this magisterial function was essentially non-political, a lordship of love belonging to clergy whose first duty was contemplation of the divine mysteries,[28] and whose superiority rested on their humility, perfection, and ability to provide an example of true Christian living.[29] For this Christ provided them with sacramental power, the indelible character of *potestas ordinis*,[30] but that is all. If therefore the bishops have jurisdiction, as indeed they do (which Wyclif sometimes categorizes as a *potestas executionis*)[31] this can only be a matter of human lordship and so must derive from the king.[32] For instance it was the king who decided that there should be separate civil and ecclesiastical courts.[33] In this way there was a *dualitas* of spiritual and temporal matters, and cases which were a mixture of both.[34] But, more significantly, temporal

[27] *De potestate papae*, 10, p. 236, 'Sacerdotes itaque Christi habent potestatem ante istam iurisdictionem caesaream edificandi populum ubicumque terrarum quantum sufficiunt, praedicando sancte conversando vel instar sanctorum doctorum scriptis sententiam catholicam commendando; talem autem potestatem regiminis independentem ab invicem habuerunt apostoli plus et minus . . .'; p. 246, 'sicut ante dotationem tempore quo crevit Ecclesia quando pure regulabatur per legem Christi et regebatur per sacerdotes socios sine praeeminentia humanitus instituta'.

[28] *De dominio divino*, i.1, p. 8, 'Et dominium correspondens voluntario ministerio ad aedificationem corporis Christi mystici voco caritativum dominium sive vicarium, quod habent ecclesiastici, sicut et servitium eo magis quo sunt in ministerio plus perfecti. Aliud autem est dominium coactivum quod quantum ad primam fundationem attinet est ecclesiasticis interdictum . . .'; *De civili dominio*, ii.3, p. 25, 'ecclesiastici quidem ex vi religionis non possident iuste haec temporalia nisi ipsa meruerint cogitatione contempliva'; also ii.9, pp. 86f. where both St Paul and Aristotle's *Physics* are called in support. In iii.21, pp. 436, 438, quoting lavishly from the *Politics*, he suggests a return to the Aristotelian principle that the clergy, being only a *pars civitatis*, should be drawn from old men no longer capable of being active citizens, only of contemplation.

[29] *De officio regis*, 6, p. 142; 8, p. 196; 12, pp. 275f. In *De potestate papae*, 7, pp. 140-1, clergy have the key of divine knowledge, not the key of power.

[30] *De potestate papae*, 2, pp. 32-3.

[31] *De potestate papae*, 11, p. 307, following FitzRalph, 'omnes potestates ordinis sunt aequales, nec minuitur etiam potestatis iurisdictiionis executio nisi de quanto rationabiliter est restricta'; *sent. ad* 1, p. 398, 'potestas ordinis . . . sufficit sine potestate regiminis vel iurisdictionis superaddita'.

[32] E.g. *De civili dominio*, ii.3, pp. 22-3; *De officio regis*, 6, pp. 118-19.

[33] *De civili dominio*, ii.14, pp. 167f., 173f.

[34] *De civili dominio*, ii.8, pp. 70-1, 'domini temporales regant immediate et directe

jurisdiction is to be distinguished between what the clergy hold *ut clerici* and what is a matter of the general wealth of the kingdom.[35] Feudal functions are distinct from endowed possessions. Following FitzRalph, Wyclif allows that the bishops have held *regalia* or *saecularia*[36] in England since the Conquest,[37] which is to be classified separately from the patronage exercised already by Anglo-Saxon rulers,[38] and which priests may hold in a non-priestly capacity as civil servants, feudatories, and recipients of royal grants.[39] They may have custody of some towns or castles, even be marcher lords;[40] but if so, they do it as if they are laity rather than clergy.[41]

suos subditos quoad temporalia et quoad corpus; consequentur autem et accessorie quoad animam . . . . Econtra autem sacerdotes Christi debent principaliter et directe regere quoad spiritualia carismata ut virtutes; consequenter autem et accessorie quoad bona naturalia et fortunae; et sic oportet suas iurisdictiones esse commixtas et mutuo se iuvantes . . . . Necesse est ergo Ecclesiam fulciri bracchio saeculari ut corpore, et clero ut anima, ut iuvent se reciproce in suis officiis a Domino limitatis instar animae et corporis in eodem supposito'; 12, p. 133, 'iurisdictiones saeculares et ecclesiasticae sunt super clericis commixtae'; also 9, pp. 84–5; 14, p. 173.

[35] *De potestate papae*, 5, p. 89.

[36] *De civili dominio*, iii.13, p. 223, 'ut redditu et praediis, castris vel aliis adiacentibus et sic militaris foedus, baronia, comitatus, ducatus, regnum et imperium vocantur dominia, quae contingit clericum cum suo clericatus habere sine civilitate ex quod civiliter non dominetur', citing FitzRalph, *De pauperie Salvatoris*, vi.31. For Wyclif's use of FitzRalph see K. Walsh, *A Fourteenth-Century Scholar and Primate: Richard FitzRalph in Oxford, Avignon and Armagh* (Oxford, 1981), pp. 378f.

[37] In *De eucharistia*, 9, p. 320, he argues that William I had had to seize all the wealth of the *ecclesia Anglicana* because the Anglo-Saxon clergy were so delinquent.

[38] *De Ecclesia*, 15, p. 336, 'et scimus pro tempore antequam Britones et Saxones dotarunt ecclesiam vel enim fuit ecclesia nostra dotata, et interim tempore Saxonum ante adventum Augustini fuit fides Christi infideliter praetermissa, tunc isti principes primo dotantes ecclesiam nostram non erant moti nisi titulo misericordiae donare plus vel minus nostrae ecclesiae . . .'.

[39] *De Ecclesia*, 15, pp. 350–1, 'Sed servire civiliter potest esse sine peccato. Nec oportet quod sic homo servit civiliter quod sit servus civilis, cum omnis dominus Angliae sub rege servit sibi civiliter . . . et sic serviunt clerici regi libere qui tenent de illo in capite . . . licet regi eos civiliter cohercere non in quantum sacerdotes sed in quantum regis elemosinarii vel homines eius legii contempnentes'; *De civili dominio*, iii.20, p. 416, 'si enim talis religiosus sit civilis dominus super baronias et comitatus . . . tunc est baro vel comes'.

[40] See his apparent approval of the priests of the Old Testament who had 'paucis villis cum suis suburbiis et iliis decimis, oblationibus . . .', *De civili dominio*, ii.4, p. 34; 5, p. 40, 'rex capit temporalia in manibus tamquam eorum dominus'; cf. iii.21, pp. 451–2, arguing that *regalia* cannot be lost from royal control and attacking the pope for trying to intrude foreigners into 'castra episcoporum'.

[41] He was still capable of confusing the difference by demanding that the clergy should pay homage for all landholdings and have military obligations: *De civili dominio*, ii.5, p. 39; ii.8, p. 75; ii.18, p. 268.

The real significance of this triple distinction for Wyclif, however, was that it was determined by history. Bishops had three different kinds of power because the history of the Church was to be seen as divisible into three distinct phases, and sources as diverse as St Paul and Joachim of Fiore could be summoned to justify this contention.[42] In the same way that the Old Testament recorded a transmission from the Garden of Eden to an age of innocence in which God's people were priests and kings, a lay priesthood by natural law, followed by the rule of the Levitical priesthood, so since the time of Christ there had been three types of clergy. First, an apostolic priesthood without coercive power; then a shared arrangement with coercion divided between kings and priests, and a dual system of courts and law; and now the worst condition of a clergy claiming all jurisdiction and rendering kings unnecessary.[43]

This meant that there had been three types of Church. In the beginning there had been the Church as a Church pure and simple, living in a golden age[44] of apostolic poverty because kings and emperors owned all the land and wealth, and being pagan were not even part of the Church. In such a self-sufficient community (*per se sufficiens*), clergy only needed sacramental power. This idyllic condition lasted until the time of Constantine, when the conversion of the Roman emperor began the age of endowment with kings and lay lords becoming patrons of a proprietary Church, granting the clergy lands and jurisdiction, and making a Gelasian dualism inevitable. The Donation of Constantine, which initiated the process *ex ritu gentilium*, should be seen, Wyclif maintained, as an endowment – a *dotatio*, not a

[42] I Cor. 15.20f.; and for Joachim, Trompf, *Historical Recurrence*, pp. 216–19; E. R. Daniel, 'Joachim of Fiore: patterns of history in the Apocalypse', in R. K. Emmerson and B. McGinn, eds, *The Apocalypse in the Middle Ages* (Ithaca, N.Y., and London, 1992), pp. 72–88. This was a popular theme in the later fourteenth century: see for example 'The Parlement of the Thre Ages', in Turville-Petre, *Alliterative Poetry*, pp. 67–100.

[43] *De civili dominio*, i.27, pp. 194–5; iii.21, pp. 437–8; *De veritate sacrae scripturae*, 4, i.67–70; 15, i.393.

[44] *De Ecclesia*, 23, p. 572, 'saeculum aureum ut in statu innocentiae'. It was equivalent to the state of nature because there was no private property, but first the laity, and then the clergy, abandoned common ownership: *De civili dominio*, iii.6, pp. 77–80; iii.8, pp. 111–13.

donatio[45] – because now the Church was married to the State, and the bishops had jurisdiction in the *respublica*. But now there is the third phase, the worst condition, in which the Church thinks it has become the State and owns everything in its own right.[46] The bishops claim *regalia* as an entitlement: they think they can do anything a layman can do and can staff all the offices of government – whilst the pope imagines he has become the emperor. There is an essential correlation between the three categories of episcopal power and the descent through the three historical periods of ecclesiastical degeneration.

It was however a cardinal principle for Wyclif that what goes down must be capable of going up again. His philosophy had taught him that there were two sides to any circle: there were *ordines descendi et ascendi*, falling and rising motions.[47] The *deformatio*[48] of the downward sweep of time can, and indeed must, be matched by a future upward movement of reformation or restitution, a return out of old age into a glorious new rebirth.[49] But just as the descent had been a periodic decline, so the corresponding improvement would have to be one step at a time. It was to be a Reformation by stages, or, to quote Margaret Aston, 'a

---

[45] *De civili dominio*, ii.7, p. 60, 'sic potest contingere quod Ecclesia Christi sit per apostolos saeculi iudices, optime regulata; secundo per reges, sed male, qui post dotationem ecclesiae constituunt sibi praepositos in suis ecclesiis; sed tertio pessime per sacerdotes qui aspirantes ad principale mundi civile dominium . . . possent perplexius mundum sibi subicere'; cf. iii.2, pp. 445–7; *De potestate papae*, 12, p. 395, 'Constantinum magnum qui dotavit ecclesiam'; 6, pp. 120–1; *De Ecclesia*, 14, p. 300, 'ius plenum ad totum imperium'; and therefore is the *dominus mundi* of Roman law, 'ex lege imperiali post dotationem factam a Caesare', 13, p. 282.

[46] This is the blasphemy of the papal lawyers which drives the bishops mad: 'sunt nimis multi maniaci . . . Et in istam blasphemiam ex defectu intellectus scripturae incidunt multi iuristae, facientes suos praepositos insanire', *De Ecclesia*, 14, pp. 320–1. Wyclif prefers to follow the 'deeper-going doctor of scripture' (possibly himself?) who saw this as the rule of the bramble in the parable of the trees of *Jud.*, 9.8–15: *De veritate sacrae scripturae*, 4, i.67–72.

[47] *De ente in communi*, 1, pp. 13–14; cf. Trompf, *Historical Recurrence*, pp. 167, 192.

[48] *De Ecclesia*, 11, p. 242.

[49] *De civili dominio*, ii.12, p. 153, 'restitutio Ecclesiae ad statum quem Christus docuit'; *De Ecclesia*, 9, p. 189, 'Ecclesia apostolica restituta ad vera privilegia primitiva'; *De potestate papae*, 11, p. 305, 'perfectionem status quem Christus instituit renovandi'.

gradual reconquest of Antichrist';[50] and since the clergy were the superior part of the Church it was appropriate that the process should begin by reform of the clergy.[51] The king should encourage clerical poverty by removing the civil wealth of prelates in particular, by abolishing *regalia* for bishops. But this first stage would leave the bulk of temporals intact: the bishop could still enjoy his episcopal estates and rights of office. He was being reduced to a very Aristotelian concept of poverty, not possessing excess wealth, a moderate sustenance fully sufficient for the ordinary needs of human life.[52] Nor was it a total rejection of the use of bishops and clergy in the work of government. It was a practice which Wyclif increasingly disliked, but the crown had too many clerical allies to abandon them out of hand. What Wyclif, with a long career in royal service himself, really meant was that the monarch should not employ worldly-minded bishops like Wykeham,[53] who accepted *regalia* for all the rewards of civil lordship that went with them, and then bit the hand that fed them by supporting subversive movements like the Good Parliament. It should be relying on spiritually-minded people like himself whose only aim was to serve God and the king. The *regalia*, the castles and towns, of which the

[50] M. Aston, ' "Caim's castles": poverty, politics, and disendowment', in B. Dobson, ed., *The Church, Politics, and Patronage in the Fifteenth Century* (Gloucester and New York, 1984), pp. 45-81, reprinted in her *Faith and Fire: Popular and Unpopular Religion, 1350-1600* (London and Rio Grande, Ohio, 1993), pp. 95-131, quotation at p. 131.

[51] *De potestate papae*, 12, p. 377, 'Et ex istis primo patet quod rex Angliae primo et principaliter daret operam ad regulandum clerum suum et specialiter episcopos et vivant similius legi Christi; totum enum regnum est unum corpus . . .. Ideo oportet . . . incipere a clero, cum sit pars principalis et stomachus corporis per quem cibi digestio et sanitas sunt ad caetera membra corporis derivanda. Oportet enim regem ab illus incipere secundum leges ordinis naturalis.'

[52] *De civili dominio*, iii.7, p. 93; iii.8, p. 109.

[53] *De civili dominio*, 11.13, pp. 146f., 'et specialiter praelatos qui secundum Apostolum, *Rom.*, 12.8, praesunt in sollicitudine . . . Unde clerus sollicitans se circa mundum, quod foret in laico licitum, degenerat ut sic a nomine clericali.' The principle that the bishop should act for the good of the king and his kingdom is in *De officio regis*, 6, p. 119, 'Confirmatur ex hoc quod rex fecit quid ex eius auctoritate fecerit legius homo suus: sed episcopi . . . sunt enim tales legii homines regis . . . ad finem ut in exequendo suum officium proficiat regno suo . . . ergo sunt ministri regis', which relates here to *spiritualia*, but see 2, pp. 27-9 for the objection to clergy holding lay offices. Similarly in *De civili dominio*, iii.16, p. 313, trade should be reserved to the laity, and clergy should only engage in it for a modest sustenance, not for private profit.

clergy have proper custody, are those of the kingdom of heaven,[54] and they should be denied earthly ones. But it was enough that the Reformation should begin as a reform.

At one time, for example the twelfth century, such reform might have been enough in itself. But now a return to traditional dualism will not do.[55] The catastrophe of the Age of Antichrist could only be met by an equally cataclysmic[56] upwards shift to complete ecclesiastical disendowment. Bishops must be deprived of the lands, wealth, and powers of their sees: the religious orders must cease to be possessioners. The clergy, Wyclif wrote, were to be dispossessed of both temporal staff and material sword;[57] which can be translated to mean that they should lose not only the *regalia* but the *potestas iurisdictionis* as well. The second stage was to be a real revolution, a returning of the wheel, a great restitution of wealth to the king, who would then redistribute it to the heirs of the original patrons, the lay lords. The living hand of kingship, as Wyclif put it, should counteract the dead hand of mortmain.[58] The king would be acting here as the vicar of God, reverting to his casual absolute omnipotence[59] as an act of necessity, that necessity that knows no law and permits any normally illegal action for the defence of the realm.

---

[54] *De officio regis*, 4, p. 67, 'Cum igitur quilibet clericus curatus habet commissum ad eius custodiam castrum vel villam regni coelorum, quod est Ecclesia . . .'.

[55] Thus the Donation of Constantine was made with good intentions and would have remained permissible if, on account of 'human fragility', a Gelasian distinction of powers had operated, *De Ecclesia*, 9, pp. 186–8; and see the use of Hugh of St Victor to argue for dualism in *De potestate papae*, 1, p. 7. The time factor is clear in *De civili dominio*, ii.11, p. 124, 'Olim quidam Romana curia irroravit vineam Domini aqua sapientiae Salvatoris, id est lege evangelica quae est doctrina Christi; sed modo dicitur quod fodiunt sibi cisternas, quae continere aquas non valent, statuendo traditiones humanas . . .'

[56] *De Ecclesia*, 16, p. 374, 'catheclismum appropriationis'. The idea of a three-stage loss of temporals is in *De civili dominio*, ii.14, pp. 180–1, 'Pro quo notandum quod triplex est renuntiatio bonorum vitae.'

[57] *De civili dominio*, ii.3, pp. 21–2, 'subtrahendo ab eis baculum temporalium ne furentur sic in simplices christianos. Magna quidem foret elemosina gladium materialiem de manu furiosi eripere . . .'; cf. *De logica*, i.11, i.35, 'Sicut vixerunt apostoli in Ecclesia primitiva, sic etiam tenetur vivere episcopi circa finem mundi.'

[58] E.g. *De Ecclesia*, 15, pp. 331–2. For mortmain see S. Raban, *Mortmain Legislation and the English Church, 1279–1500* (Cambridge, 1982).

[59] The references are legion: see for instance *De civili dominio*, ii.2, p. 16; ii.4, p. 28. This would be equivalent to a miracle, as had been the dispossession of the Templars, ii.1, p. 4.

Wyclif, never one to leave a stone unturned, reinforced his argument by pointing out that both English common law and Roman law already recognized the principle that lay patrons had a right to reclaim their patronage.[60] All endowed possessions were held conditionally on good service.[61]

Yet even this drastic remedy must prove in course of time to be insufficient, and would come to be simply a prelude to the third stage of the Reformation. According to the biblical model this must be a return to a Church in which all Christians by right of baptism were priests and kings,[62] and where the laity could function as its own clergy. There would be a lay Church, an *ecclesia saecularis*.[63] Now the laity could activate its basic original ability to hear confessions, to give indulgences, to administer baptism, to dispense with marriage regulations, to consecrate the Eucharist, and to determine controversial points of Scripture.[64] Every saintly man would be his own pope.[65] Understandably Wyclif was

[60] The important provisions are in the Statutes of Westminster II (1285) and Carlisle (1307) for monastic property, but should be distinguished from the right of reclamation for failure of feudal service in the Statutes of Marlborough (1267), Gloucester (1278) and Mortmain (1279). For a fuller discussion of Wyclif's use of this legislation see W. Farr, *John Wyclif as a Legal Reformer* (Leiden, 1974), pp. 96–138.

[61] *De civili dominio*, ii.4, p. 26; iii.22, p. 484 (citing FitzRalph).

[62] For the residual spiritual power of the laity, *De civili dominio*, ii.17, p. 240, 'Unde videtur michi quod nunquam ab origine mundi foret plus necessarium quod theologi et ecclesiastici sint vigiles, renunctiantes temporalibus in personis propriis, et hortantes saeculares ne propter nimiam affectionem ad temporalia amittant aeterna, quam est tempus instans, cum hodie, quod dolendum est, dicitur quod ecclesia Romana pro civili dominio conturbat contumeliis pauculos oves Christi quos Spiritus sanctus ex fide residente in laycis providebat'; and see the long and involved argument in *De Ecclesia*, 20, pp. 500–10, that *potestas ordinis* pertains in a special sense to all Christians and is not just reserved to the clergy for sacramental duties. Cf. *De potestate papae*, 1, pp. 10–11, 'Potestas ordinis vocatur potestas spiritualis quam habet clericus ad ministrandum Ecclesiae sacramenta ut spiritualiter prosit sibi et laicis, ut est potestas conficiendi, absolvendi et sacramenta ministrandi . . .. Potestas autem spiritualis communis, quam habet quilibet christianus, in exercendo opera spiritualia misericordie in se et in aliis . . .'

[63] *De Ecclesia*, 7, p. 156; cf. *De civili dominio*, iii.21, pp. 451, 'ecclesiae laycali'.

[64] *De civili dominio*, ii.8, p. 82; *De Ecclesia*, 23, pp. 576–7; *De potestate papae*, 11, pp. 307–8; 12, pp. 381; *De eucharistia*, 4, pp. 89–99; *De veritate sacrae scripturae*, 6, i.137.

[65] *De potestate papae*, 12, p. 368, 'cum papa dicit principaliter praeeminentiam sanctitatis . . . iuxta hanc viam quilibet debet esse papam, ut debet esse sanctissimus viatorum. Debet enim esse papa et quocunque iam viante sanctior'; also 11, p. 315, 'Sicut enim omnis christianus, et specialiter bonus presbiter, est sacerdos, sic est spiritualiter hostiarius, ceroferarius, lector, exorcista, subdyaconus, dyaconus et sacerdos.'

never too precise about this future ideal state any more than St Paul could give a detailed description of the kingdom of heaven, or Marx spell out the full nature of a truly Communist society; and many of his supporters must have wondered exactly what implications this would have for lay lordship, for the hierarchical arrangement of secular society. But as regards the clergy Wyclif was clear enough: the logic of the wheel of history predicted a return to total apostolic poverty. Tithes might be withheld or granted by the laity according to performance;[66] but all the cleric really needed was his clerical status and the ability to seek alms for bare necessities – all clergy would become mendicants dependent on charity.[67] Even clothing was questionable. He had, he remarked, no real objection to nude clergy, but clerics in a state of nature might catch a cold, and how then could they preach?[68] The distinction of clergy from laity would apparently remain in a functional sense that there had to be a part of the Church which specialized in giving instruction and performing sacramental duties, but that was all. All clergy were equal in terms of *potestas ordinis* as they had been in the apostolic Church: to be a bishop was a matter of office, not order.[69] The third strand of episcopal

[66]   *De civili dominio*, i.40, pp. 310–14; i.42, pp. 335–40, 345, 354–5; *De potestate papae*, 12, p. 351, 'Ex istis videtur sequi quod a quocumque praeposito spirituali notorie deficiente in suo officio licet stipendia mundana subtrahere ut decimas, oblationes et alias elemozinas speciales'; p. 358, 'populus debet decimas et oblationes suas ab ei concorditer et constanter subtrahere et in alios pios usus expendere'.

[67]   *De civili dominio*, ii.3, p. 18, 'relinquitur igitur ex quolibet evidenciis quod tota dotacio ecclesiae sit ex elemosinis dominorum. Quod, ne tradatur in oblicionem cavetur in cartis regni nostri Angliae quomodo rex et alii fundatores in puram et perpetuam elemosinam donarunt talia dominia ecclesiae. Ex quod videtur sequi correllarie quod omnes clerici nedum ad Deum ut omnes homines, sed quoad homines sunt mendici.' The dissolution of monasteries might be inferred from this, but it is more akin to the Cluniac ideal of the whole Church as a great monastery.

[68]   Clothing had not been necessary in the state of nature, but clergy now needed it in the harsher climate occasioned by sin: *De statu innocentiae*, 5, pp. 501–2; 10, p. 523.

[69]   *De potestate papae*, 10, p. 246, 'sic in Europa stat esse perfectos christianos secundum fidem Christi, etsi non recognoscant praeeminentiam pontificis Constantini . . . ymo patet ex dictis quomodo corpus Christi militaret securius atque perfectius subducto tali ordine caesareo; nam vivendo omnino exproprietarie sicut ante tempore dotationem quo crevit Ecclesia quando pure regulabatur per legem Christi et regebatur per sacerdotes socios sine praeeminentia humanitus instituta, melius et perfectius vixit quam modo. Nec est ratio quin per idem hodie viaret sic perfctius quem nunc viat, igitur cum hoc sit possibile, patet conclusio'; also 9, p. 199, 'ante dotationem Ecclesiae non fuerunt nomina cleri taliter baptizata et per

power was to be disposed of by effectively abolishing bishops.

There was nothing more important to Wyclif than the need for a proper perspective of the past history of the Church. Like so many reformers, he saw the past as much more than a mere matter of record: indeed, it was a lifeline of hope for the future, because it contained the promise of what was to come and defined the shape of that future as a three-stage process. He believed that the changes of successive moments and periods of earthly time as delineated by history could only be matched up to the eternal present of divine time by completing the circle of human duration until there was an eventual return to the beginning. There was, however, no precise temporal symmetry to this idea of applying the wheel of fortune to the Reformation; no suggestion that the Church would need another 1400 years to climb back once more to pristine condition. Earthly time could always be telescoped for divine purposes. Nevertheless the principle of a Reformation in stages indicated that the Second Coming was not imminent. Hastening on the process was no justification for living in immediate expectation of a new Jerusalem. Eventually there would be another Golden Age, but the initial prospects were for more suffering as the price of greater efficiency in the contest with Antichrist. Indeed, as time went by in England, the prospect of a successful Reformation seemed to become steadily more remote: the torrents of both popular and official piety appeared to have been safely diverted into more Catholic channels during the fifteenth century.[70] For Lollardy the wheel of time must have given the impression of being permanently stuck at the half hour, or even to be running backwards. But the clock was ticking.

Birkbeck College,
University of London

---

consequens nec dignitatum officia. Idem enim fuit ante dotationem Ecclesiae presbiter, episcopus et sacerdos' (again claiming support from FitzRalph); p. 201, 'sed concludit presbiteros, sacerdotes et episcopos sub nomine apostoli'.

70   As convincingly shown now by E. Duffy, *The Stripping of the Altars: Traditional Religion in England c.1400–c.1580* (New Haven and London, 1992). It might almost be said that the Counter-Reformation preceded the Reformation.

THEODOLINDA: THE FIFTEENTH-CENTURY RECOLLECTION OF A LOMBARD QUEEN

by ANDREW MARTINDALE*

This paper arises out of an art historian's interest in the frescoes of 'Queen Theodolinda's chapel' in the cathedral of Monza, executed *c*.1444 by the brothers Zavattari. Although these paintings have aroused intense regional interest, outside Italy they are possibly less well-

* *Preliminary note by Jane Martindale*:

When the Ecclesiastical History Society did Andrew Martindale the honour of electing him as its President he realized that one of his chief responsibilities was to propose the theme for the Society's Conferences during his year of office. He was aware that, although for many years his interests and profession had been bound up with the history of the visual arts, his intellectual training had begun as a 'straight' historian. That prompted him to choose as the theme 'the Church Retrospective' – on its own history. He was convinced that this theme would be a good one, given the abundance of evidence and documentation available from the earliest times. The papers delivered at Norwich in July 1995 surely justified his confidence in the wide appeal of this topic.

Before his untimely death, Andrew had prepared the core of the presidential address which he should have delivered in July. He was working on this while teaching students in Venice during the winter of 1994–5, and in late March revisited Monza cathedral and the chapel which was to be the central focus of his paper; but from conversations it was clear that he hoped and intended to spend more thought and time on the historical and artistic context of Queen Theodolinda's chapel, and to draw on works which were not available to him during a busy teaching term in Italy. He was not allowed time to do that. The paper delivered at the Society's Winter Meeting and printed here is centred on the core of Andrew's paper, but it needed reorganization according to the plan which had already been sketched in, and some additions – notably on the Monza treasure. The work on the treasure together with the illustrations supporting the delivered paper were supplied by John Mitchell, Andrew's colleague at the University of East Anglia. The re-shaping of Andrew's text has been done by Jane Martindale: both of us hope that this paper preserves the content and quality of what Andrew was composing – even though it is of course in a sadly unfinished form (see 'Endnote' on p. 223). In particular, Andrew had not had the time to work out the conclusions of his paper in any detail, although he had discussed the implications of the many-layered treatment of Queen Theodolinda's legend at Monza. One theme which could not be developed was that of the interaction between sacred and secular in monuments like the chapel discussed in the paper. He had already talked about this at an earlier conference of the Ecclesiastical History Society, but I know that he felt this was an almost inexhaustible topic: see his 'Patrons and minders: the intrusion of the secular into sacred spaces in the late Middle Ages', *SCH*, 28 (1992), pp. 143–78. I hope that what follows will not distort his views, or develop his ideas in directions which he would not himself have taken.

known than they deserve to be. They call forth the questions of how and why Theodolinda – a 'barbarian' queen who lived in the late sixth and early seventh centuries – could have come to assume such a central role for the church of Monza. The interpretation and re-interpretation of her story – perhaps the projection of the present back into the past? – offers an appropriate topic for the theme of 'The Church Retrospective'.

Monza lies about ten miles north of the great city of Milan; but despite the claim occasionally advanced in the Middle Ages that Monza was the 'capital of Lombardy and seat of that Kingdom', *caput Lombardiae et sedes regni illius* [*B*, col. 1080 – alleging that this was laid down by the Emperor Otto III, and followed by other emperors, too], it seems best-known today as the 'seat' of a 'world-famous' motor-racing track built in the park of a Napoleonic palace. Monza cathedral was originally associated with a palace of a very different régime belonging to Theodolinda, wife of the Lombard kings Authari and Agilulf. According to Paul the Deacon, this had originally been built by Theodoric, 'King of the Goths' [*PD*, IV, 21–2]: Theodolinda's palace was elaborately decorated. Today it is a building of late Gothic construction with an extraordinary late fourteenth-century façade (constructed before 1396), although its interior was heavily 'done over' in the eighteenth century (Plate 1). Discussion in this paper will be principally concentrated on the eastern chapel which flanks the chancel on its northern side (Plate 2). That chapel was originally dedicated to SS Vincent and Vitus, although for no obvious reason Anastasius was substituted for Vitus by the mid-fifteenth

The circumstances in which the paper was composed have meant that referenced footnotes could not be included: a short secondary bibliography is provided at the end of the paper. Citations of the two main primary sources are incorporated within the text of the paper:

(1) Paul the Deacon, *Historia Langobardorum*. For discussion of this source and an extensive bibliography down to 1986, see D. Bullough, 'Ethnic history and the Carolingians: an alternative reading to Paul the Deacon's *Historia Langobardorum*', in C. Holdsworth and T. Wiseman, eds, *The Inheritance of Historiography*, Exeter Studies in History, 12 (Exeter, 1986), pp. 85–105. The text is cited as *PD*, by books and chapters, not pages.

(2) Bonincontro de Morrigia, edited in L. Muratori, ed., *Rerum Italiae scriptores*, 12 (Milan, 1728), cols 1061–1184. The text is cited as *B*, by columns of the edition.

Plate 1   Façade of Monza cathedral (reproduced by permission of the Museo del Duomo di Monza).

century. However, this chapel is now universally called 'Queen Theodolinda's Chapel': since the early fourteenth century her sarcophagus has been placed here above ground, while, by the mid-fifteenth century, the walls were entirely covered with painted scenes portraying episodes connected with her life. (Only in the nineteenth century, apparently, was this chapel also associated with the 'Iron Crown' of the Lombards – that crown will not figure again until the very end of this paper.)

197

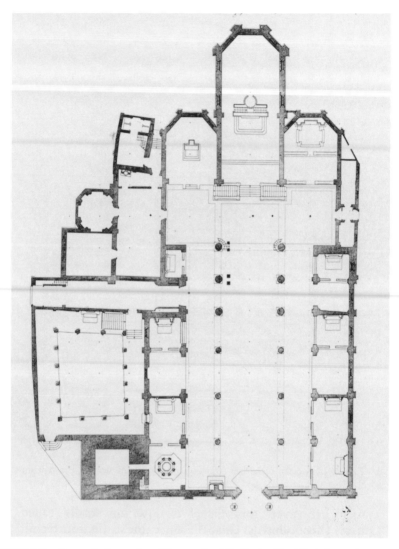

Plate 2   Ground plan today. The *capella della Regina Teodelinda* is to the north of the chancel; the central altar is a nineteenth-century arrangement (reproduced by permission of the Museo del Duomo di Monza).

Theodolinda (Queen *c.*590–*c.*627) was certainly a figure of great importance to the church in Monza even in her lifetime. Nevertheless, it is surprising to find that SS Vincent and Anastasius have been virtually ousted from the 'sacred space' of the chapel dedicated to them, where the walls are covered with scenes which are 'secular' in appearance – and to a considerable extent in content also. This phenomenon appears to be unique. The circumstances and manner in which it came about, however, can tell us much about how the Church viewed and re-interpreted its past. In this case we seem to be faced with nothing less than a re-creation in the later Middle Ages of the career of, and the legends surrounding, a Queen of the Lombards who lived in the sixth to early seventh centuries. There can be little doubt that this re-creation was largely brought about by the clergy of Monza cathedral, by means of both writings and visual representation. Why was the past re-shaped in this way? To address that question, this paper will first look at the Zavattari frescoes, and relate them to the sources used to build up Queen Theodolinda's story. Then it will investigate a number of problems associated with the emergence of the 'legend' in the fourteenth and fifteenth centuries.

Theodolinda's position as Queen of the Lombards is known chiefly through the information provided in the *Historia Langobardorum*, that mosaic of 'ethnic history' written by Paul the Deacon probably soon after the years 786/7 (according to Donald Bullough). Much of his information is reproduced in the Monza frescoes. She was, Paul tells us, the daughter of Garibald, King of the Bavarians. Authari, King of the Lombards, only sought her as his bride in the 580s, after he had failed to secure a Frankish alliance for himself. The reception by the Frankish King Childebert of Authari's messengers [*PD*, III, 28, 30] is shown in the frescoes. After Authari's death in 591 the Lombard dukes allowed her to choose her second husband – Agilulf, the dead king's brother; then after his death Theodolinda acted as recent for their son Adaloald, who was subsequently deposed. All this occurred *c.*616–26 [*PD*, IV, 5–6, 24, 41]. At that stage the Queen also disappeared from Paul the Deacon's pages, and neither her death nor her burial-place are mentioned by this historian of the Lombards. Paul's *Historia Langobardorum* does emphasize that Theodolinda was a Catholic who enjoyed good relations with Pope Gregory the Great (who sent her a copy of his *Dialogues* and whose letters are cited in the text), and he states that she dissuaded her second husband from attacking Rome. Paul records that she founded a church at Monza, which was very richly endowed and which was dedicated to St John the Baptist [*PD*, IV, 5, 6, 8–9, 21].

In view of the relative terseness of Paul's references to Theodolinda's career, it is perhaps startling to find that her story in *La cappella della regina Theodolinda* extends to forty-three scenes – considerably padded out, therefore. All Paul's anecdotes are included, but some new material of the greatest importance for the church of Monza is also added. A brief analysis of the arrangement of the programme is necessary (Plate 3). The first twelve scenes are all, so to speak, 'authentic Paul', but the painters dwell at considerable length on secular embassies and negotiations such as an incognito visit of Authari to the Bavarian court. Here Theodolinda is still unmarried and still north of the Alps. The following nine scenes (nos 13–21) on the same row show more scenes of similar secular content, culminating in Authari's victorious progress to Reggio Calabria where he strikes an antique column standing in the sea and declares that from henceforth this column will mark 'the frontiers of the Lombards' (Plates 4–6). The next eight scenes include the second marriage of the Queen and, importantly, Agilulf's conversion to Catholicism, and more marriage festivities [*PD*, III, 30, and see above].

At that point the painted scenes desert the *Historia Langobardorum* and, as we shall see, are based on a written source of far later date. The church of Monza becomes central to the painters' concerns, and Theodolinda's foundation and endowment are narrated in a way which bears many resemblances to other 'foundation legends'. Theodolinda has a dream and rides out in order to carry out its instructions (Plate 7): she has to find a place where the Holy Spirit hovers in the form of a dove. In due course a dove is found sitting in a great tree: in the legend, laboured play is made of the Latin term for Monza – *Modetia*. The heavenly voice says '*modo*' –

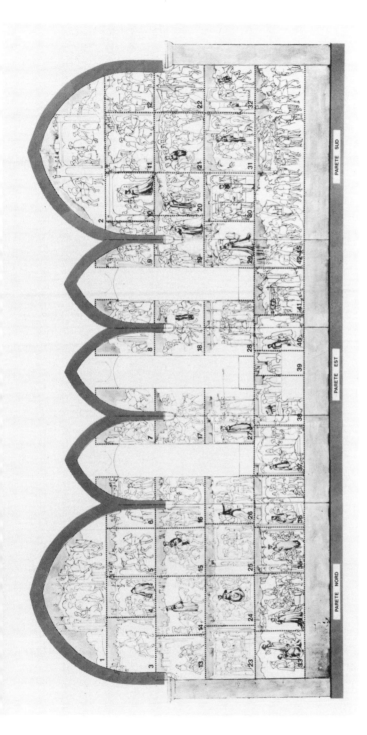

Plate 3   Scheme of the cycle of frescoes by the brothers Zavattari from Theodolinda's chapel (the damaged portions of the painting relating to Pope Gregory can be seen in nos 39–40 (reproduced by permission of the Museo del Duomo di Monza).

Plate 4 Theodolinda enters Italy to marry Authari (reproduced by permission of the Museo del Duomo di Monza).

Plate 5 Festivities at the marriage of Theodolinda and Authari at Verona
(reproduced by permission of the Museo del Duomo di Monza).

'now' or even 'here is the place': the Queen replies *'etiam'* –
'even so' or even 'all right'. After that, there follow different
phases of endowment: destruction of pagan idols, a presentation of treasure, 'records' (see Frontispiece). Pope Gregory
the Great is also involved.

The scene of Theodolinda's death and burial in her own
church bears the inscription: 'Queen Theodolinda who
created this serene temple lies here spread out beneath this
monument.' Although that might seem to bring the 'Monza
story' of Theodolinda to a natural conclusion, three further

Plate 6 Authari strikes the antique column to mark his victories and the frontiers of the Lombard territories (reproduced by permission of the Museo del Duomo di Monza).

scenes hark back to Paul the Deacon. These portray an episode in which, according to Paul, the Emperor Constans (in 660) was deterred from attacking the Lombards as a result of consulting a holy hermit about his campaigning prospects. The hermit reported after a night of prayer that Saints Peter and John the Baptist, together with the Archangel Michael, had told him that Constans had no chance of victory 'for' – to quote Paul's words – 'a certain Queen had come from another

Plate 7 The dove shows Theodolinda the place for the foundation of the church (reproduced by permission of the Museu del Duomo di Monza).

land and had built a church to St John the Baptist within the Lombards' territories. And because of that, the Saint interceded continuously on her behalf.' So Constans withdrew [*PD*, V, 6].

Some priorities were apparently established on the basis of this dense and complicated narrative. Since the chapel is very tall and narrow, it is easier to see the lower than the upper scenes: it is not therefore especially surprising to find that the foundation history of the church of Monza is placed in the lowest row, together with the founders' burials and especial emphasis on the Baptist. Pope Gregory the Great's involvement – unfortunately damaged – is at the very centre. All those scenes do have importance for the church of Monza, as well as a religious content and significance. Above that register, however, religious content or issues do not seem to have had much to do with the depiction of kings, queens, and embassies on the move in marvellously beautiful clothing, taking part in sumptuous cavalcades, engaged in public displays of wealth and power.

Why should Theodolinda have mattered to the clergy of this north Italian city at the time when these paintings were executed around the mid-fifteenth century? Before broadening out the investigation, it is worthwhile to enquire further into the sources for the episodes of Theodolinda's life which were portrayed by the brothers Zavattari. The central scenes relating to the foundation of the church of St John the Baptist at Monza are taken directly from a fourteenth-century history written by a chronicler called Bonincontro de Morigia. (It has been suggested that some parts of the frescoes are so close that they would serve as illustrations to Bonincontro's text.) In general Bonincontro wanted to record 'great and diverse novelties', especially as they related to Monza and Milan, but his aims were certainly more restricted than those of Paul the Deacon so many centuries earlier; for he wished also to provide accounts of the building and rebuilding of the church of Monza, the spoliation and restitution of its treasure, and incidents associated with John the Baptist – but also with a local *beatus* of the thirteenth century called Gerard. Where he needed to draw on Paul the Deacon, he was often selective (rejecting purely personal details of Theodolinda's life); elsewhere, as is shown by the details already quoted about Theodolinda's dream, the dove, and so on, he expanded very greatly on what is known from sources of the seventh to eighth centuries. But Bonincontro regarded Theodolinda above all as the Christian and orthodox foundress of the basilica of Monza [*B*, cols 1061, 1064, 1069–71]. In part this amplification of Paul's narrative helps to explain how Theodolinda came to occupy such an important place on the walls of a chapel initially dedicated to a group of saintly figures.

With the chronicle of Bonincontro de Morigia we are immediately brought into the disturbed world of fourteenth-century Italy, where it was almost impossible to disentangle the issues of secular and ecclesiastical politics, and where local communities often needed to take drastic action to avert danger to themselves or their possessions. (Four canons of Monza, for instance, buried, or hid, their church's treasure around the year 1323, while the city was sacked by a Guelf army in 1324 – on that occasion the Guelfs looted the plate still kept in the cathedral [*B*, cols 1130, 1139].) The chronicle itself – which possibly came from Monza cathedral – exists in a single manuscript and has been in the Biblioteca Ambrosiana, Milan, since 1606, when it was donated by Cardinal Borromeo. The text itself goes down to the year 1349, but was apparently intended to be continued. Its author lists his written and oral sources, but he was also, as we shall see, an eye-witness of some important episodes relating to Monza's history [*B*. col. 1089: *virorum venerabilium narratione*]. Bonincontro himself is a fairly mysterious figure, but a layman who in 1332 was joint commander of a body of 200 armed men who joined the service of Galeazzo Visconti of Milan, apparently on the orders of the commune of Monza, *per commune nostrum Modeotiae* [*B*, cols 1055, 1135]. Eleven years later (in 1343), when it was necessary to pursue the Monza treasure to the papal court at Avignon, Bonincontro himself [*ego scriptor*: *B*, col. 1178] was sent as one of Monza's ambassadors, with the assured backing of the Archbishop of Milan. Morigia was of knightly origins and Ghibelline in sympathy; but it has not been possible to determine whether when he wrote his chronicle he was still a layman, or had become a member of the clergy. His obvious attachment to the church of Monza, however, helps to explain how his chronicle came to be used as a basis for some of the most important scenes painted in *la cappella della regina Theodolinda* almost a century later.

Today Bonincontro's chronicle provides us with an insight into what was considered most valuable in the ecclesiastical traditions of Monza cathedral in the first half of the fourteenth century; and it probably also supplies a number of clues as to how the clergy of St John the Baptist's church – and other local inhabitants also – hoped to defend their material possessions and themselves at that time. It seems likely, too, that his writing enables us to perceive how, by the later Middle Ages, Theodolinda herself was being transformed from a 'barbarian' queen into a tutelary figure of power, hovering between the worlds of religion and secular politics. This impression is justified by an investigation of what is known about the rebuilding of Monza cathedral (from 1300, which is about the year of Bonincontro's birth). In this year, according to Bonincontro, a priest called Franzio de Gluxiamo had a vision: two women told him that in the church there were 'great things of God and of his saints to be venerated, and infinite indulgences which have remained hidden over a long time because of the ignorance of men. Seek and ye shall find.' Inspired by this celestial game of hide and seek, the canon went to an ancient Bible in the sacristy in which he allegedly found some writing concealed, saying 'these are the holy oils which John, unworthy and a sinner, brought from Rome to Monza [to] the lady Queen Theodolinda in the time of Pope Gregory'. That further clue is hardly explicit, but the cathedral chapter announced that the contents of a great *archa* which stood behind the high altar would be investigated. Apparently that investigation took place at night: the canons indeed discovered 'great things which cannot be told in a day or shown in a month'.

Bonincontro never explains precisely what was found in the *archa*, but his account seems to show how the authorities of the church of Monza came to draw on what material and spiritual resources were available to them in order to strengthen their local traditions and, perhaps, further their

Plate 8   *Ampulla* with representation of the Adoration of the Magi and Greek legend (reproduced by permission of the Museo del Duomo di Monza).

building programme. Morigia even asserts that 40,000 people from Lombardy (*terrarum Lombardiae*) were attracted to the cathedral by these rumours, proclamations, and dramatic turn of events [B, cols 1092–4]. In the first place, it is important to note that the two women of the priest's vision were St Elizabeth (significantly the mother of the Baptist) and Theodolinda herself (described here as *beata*). Secondly, this writing and the contents of the *archa* manifestly refer to two authentic pieces of evidence from Monza, which indubitably date from Theodolinda's own time – the sixth to early seventh centuries. One of these is the famous *notula* of John listing the tombs of the saints at Rome from which *oil* was brought in commemoration of the saints. But this holy oil has also survived, and adds another dimension to the fashion in which Theodolinda's medieval 'legend' was transformed around these years.

The artifacts which must have been the focus of this story are a group of sixteen lead and twenty-six glass *ampullae*. It is supposed that lead *ampullae* filled with oil were originally brought back from Jerusalem by pilgrims: these have attracted art historians' attention because their imagery, it has been argued, may well provide an impression of paintings and mosaics in the principal sanctuaries of the *loca sancta* at a very early – perhaps even Constantinian – date (Plate 8). (It is probably relevant that lead *ampullae* have also survived at Bobbio. That monastic foundation of 614 had associations with Theodolinda and the Lombard royal dynasty, too.) Thus John's *notula*, with its references to Rome, was presumably associated with the glass containers, and provided the basis for the fourteenth-century view that Pope Gregory had confided oil for presentation to a deacon called John. Between the seventh and fourteenth centuries, however, as far as we can see, little curiosity was shown about the holy oils in Monza – or about whether they came in lead or glass containers. When Bonincontro was writing, he stated that 'today the holy oils were described in writing and kept in a very beautiful marble chest near the high altar' – *olea sacra hodie in dicta ecclesia sunt ibi per ordinem scripta et in pulcherrima arca marmorea quae est post altare maius dicti templi reclusa* [B, col. 1071]. In the fifteenth-century frescoes, however, Pope Gregory's gift of oil is delivered in bulk – in a great golden jar.

At about the time that the church of Monza was being rebuilt, the canons of Monza seem to have hoped to revive interest in the sacred quality of the oils which they had long possessed. They very probably also wished to make more of the reputation and prestige of their patron saint, John the Baptist, although that may not have met with the responses which they required. As we have already seen in Paul the Deacon's narrative of the warning to the Emperor Constans, in the seventh century the Baptist was regarded as a powerful protector; centuries later Bonincontro calls him *patronus et defensor . . . terrae*, refers to him as a powerful *intercessor* for the Lombards in war, and also says that he kept Monza in his *custodia* [*B*, cols 1089, 1070, 1142]. The dedication of Theodolinda's church to St John the Baptist is moreover attributed to the fact that the Lombards and Romans had concluded peace on the Feast of St John's nativity [*B*, col. 1069]. According to Bonincontro it was another vision – of the Baptist this time – which deterred Galeazzo Visconti from attacking Monza and his plan to sack it so that 'not one stone' should stand 'upon another'. (On the other hand, that ruler did succeed in assuming power there by less drastic means [*B*, col. 1142].) But there was no major relic of the Baptist in Monza – and that appears to have been a disadvantage. One miracle is reported, linked to a relic described as *amputatio amputati capitis*. According to one of the canons, Count Ottolino de Curtenova mocked this relic, putting his hand into a crystal vessel in which it was exposed and jeering that this could be no more than billy goat's blood. A fearful shock, with death ensuring after a year's illness, followed a course which is familiar to readers of many books of miracles. Nevertheless, since there is only one further reference to the efficacy of this relic in protecting the church of Monza, it is probable that its credentials and provenance were less than first-class [*B*, cols 1092–4]. St John the Baptist does not seem to have had the power which, for instance, emanated from the body of St Cuthbert, who over the centuries had protected his own in northern England.

Almost inevitably this leads us back to Theodolinda. How did she come to attain that central position which she assumes in the chapel frescoes at Monza? It is scarcely surprising that her reputation was no longer the same as it had been in the pages of Paul the Deacon; but Bonincontro's treatment of Theodolinda draws attention to her religious qualities since, in addition to being described as *gloriosissima*, she is also called *devotissima, beatissima, sanctissima, christianissima*. Furthermore, in a remarkable chapter, he compares her foundation of Monza with that of Solomon's Temple, both being the outcome of divine inspiration; and also compares her with Jacob, because of his vow to mark the place where he dreamed of the ladder ascending to heaven [B, col. 1071]. In her visionary appearance to the canon of Monza, too, Theodolinda was fulfilling a role often reserved for the saints – indeed Elizabeth, with whom she made an appearance, was called *sancta*, whereas Theodolinda was attributed the title *beata*. It seems probable that Bonincontro was here giving currency to local attitudes to Theodolinda, as well as providing information drawn from local sources.

Before the time when Bonincontro wrote (probably in 1308), Theodolinda's remains were transferred to an above-ground sarcophagus – a translation accorded to saints as well as to the particularly illustrious. However, Agilulf's body was also transferred to this sarcophagus; and there does not seem to have been any suggestion that Theodolinda was then regarded as particularly holy. On the other hand, there may be a pointer to the way in which Bonincontro regarded this Queen buried in his own cathedral in his noting of the miracles associated with the joint burials of the German King Henry II and his wife Kunigunda at Bamberg [B, col. 1092: *Hic cum uxore sua in ecclesia Babinbergensi miraculis coruscando sepelitur*]. But – and quite apart from the merits of the different cases – official qualifications for sanctity were far more stringent in the fourteenth than in the early eleventh century; and it does not seem that Theodolinda even became an official candidate for canonization. Yet there still remains a possibility that in calling her *sanctissima* he may have been to some extent reflecting 'popular opinion'. It is worth speculating whether, if the canons of Monza had got going with their plans about two centuries earlier, Theodolinda might have been venerated as a saint – at least within the region over which the influence of the church of Monza extended.

Theodolinda left behind her in Monza mementos which ensured that she is still remembered today – and not just by art historians. For, whatever treasures she may have amassed in heaven, she certainly laid up treasures on earth; and overall this treasure seems continuously to have exercised a far greater hold on people's imaginations than the inscrutable pots of oil, or the Baptist's questionable relic. It also greatly contributed to the 'Theodolinda legend' which, by the later Middle Ages, had been created in Monza. This 'treasure' is the last element which needs discussion in this extended consideration of how the history of Theodolinda was re-shaped in the interest of the church of Monza. The fascination which it exercised, as well as its importance to the church, is apparent from its treatment both in written and visual sources. What survives is still, in the twentieth century, remarkable; but that anything at all now survives is perhaps almost miraculous, since it was at least twice abstracted *en masse* in the Middle Ages and then, in modern times, triumphantly looted by Napoleon.

The importance of the Monza treasure to Bonincontro is apparent throughout his narrative; he stresses that it had been stolen (*furatus*) and restored twice within living memory. In 1319, for instance, it was restored to the canons by Matteo Visconti, who had succeeded in forcing the Della Torre to disgorge what they had abstracted forty-six years previously: golden crowns, golden chalices, and other jewels adorned with pearls and precious stones [*B*, col. 1141]. The political and military disturbances in northern Italy led, as we have already seen, to the canons hiding their treasure in the early 1320s. When one of those responsible revealed the hiding-place, it was eventually delivered to *Hemerico Camerlengo Ecclesiae romanae* in Piacenza, and then immediately (in 1324) despatched to the pope in Avignon. The papal chamberlain had immediately recognized the scale of what he had got hold of – '*Res grandis est*', he is alleged to have exclaimed – but in this affair Bonincontro had no sympathies with the interest of the Roman Church, since he refers to those who handed over

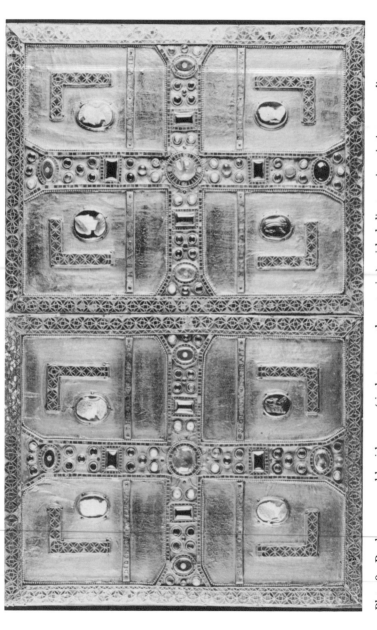

Plate 9   Book cover, gold with gems (sixth to seventh centuries) with dedicatory inscription recording Theodolinda's gift to the *basilica* of St John the Baptist, Monza (reproduced by permission of the Museo del

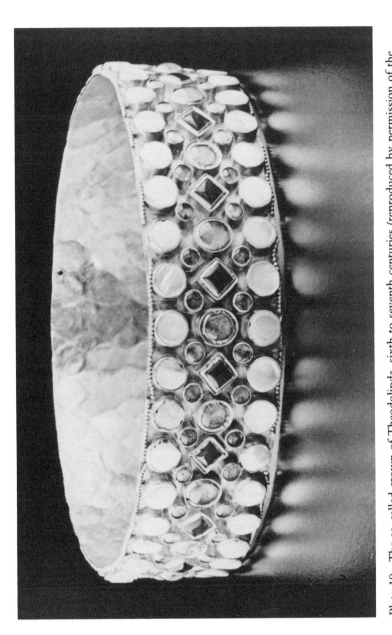

Plate 10   The so-called crown of Theodolinda, sixth to seventh centuries (reproduced by permission of the Museo del Duomo di Monza).

the treasure as plunderers of the *patria*: *plurimi viri iniqui, certi Mediolenses et Modoetienses preditores patriae* [*B*, col. 1141]. As recorded by Bonincontro, the stages by which this 'great thing' was returned to Monza is in itself a fascinating but protracted story. In particular, the chamberlain's gesture seems to have misfired, since Pope John XXII refused to accept the treasure, instead ordering an inventory to be made and promising to let the Monza canons (of whom a group was then present in Avignon) have it back 'at an opportune time'. Two pontificates later, during Clement VI's time, the moment was at last 'opportune', but (again as had already been suggested) it needed much pressure from the Archbishop of Milan and a fourteen-month embassy to Avignon. This was not an episode in which Bonincontro was involved but he notes – wonderingly perhaps? – that the treasure was eventually retrieved 'without any money passing hands': *absque ulla praestatione pecuniae* [*B*, cols 1179– 80; cf. cols 1141–2]. The role of the archbishop in the retrieval of the treasure is intriguing. In addition to con- summate skills of diplomacy and persuasion, on its return he added to the treasure and provided the canons with his own goldsmith to make necessary repairs to what had been damaged. The significance attached to the recovered treasure is best conveyed by the triumphant assertion that on 21 March 1344, when the archbishop celebrated High Mass in the cathedral, 'the whole treasure of this aforesaid church was placed above the said holy altar' [*B*, col. 1181]. The pressures which could be applied by the current archbishop would probably have helped – he was Giovanni Visconti (archbishop between 1342–54).

What was this treasure? Its early composition cannot be entirely reconstructed; but an ivory diptych of the poet and muse (early sixth-century) could have been given to the church by Theodolinda and the Lombard kings. By the fourteenth century a sapphire cup was certainly associated with the founders; while one of the two magnificent book covers bears an inscription noting that Theodolinda gave it to St John the Baptist 'in the basilica which she herself founded, in Monza near her palace' [*Il tesoro, Guida alla conoscenza del tesoro del Duomo di Monza*, no. 21: DE DONIS DI OFFERIT/

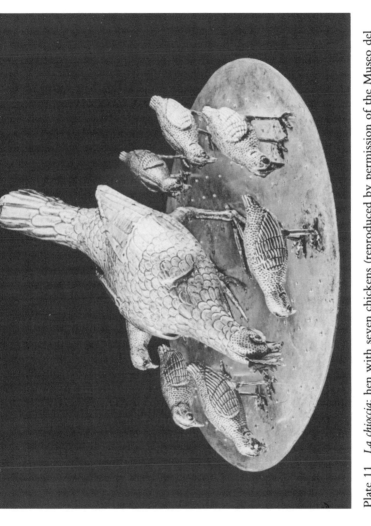

Plate 11 *La chioccia*: hen with seven chickens (reproduced by permission of the Museo del Duomo di Monza).

THEODELINDA REG/ GLORIOSISSIMA SCO IOHANNI BAPT//IN BASELECA/QUAM IPSA FVND/IN MODICIA/PROPE PAL.SVVM//. See Plate 9]. One of the surviving crowns has been associated with Theodolinda (plate 10), and a cross preserved in the Treasury is now thought to have been a pendant from it, as can be seen from an early nineteenth-century drawing of what was then surviving. Hanging votive crowns of this type were often presented by royal patrons to major churches in late Antiquity and the early Middle Ages. Of all Theodolinda's treasure, the best-loved and most inscrutable is the piece known as *la chioccia di Theodolinda* – 'the broody hen'. This silver and copper-gilt object is too big for a toy (the hen is virtually life-size): it has been interpreted as signifying both resurrection, and Christ's protection of his followers, in accordance with Matthew 23.37 and Luke 13.24 (Plate 11).

By the fourteenth and fifteenth centuries, certainly, Theodolinda and the treasure were inextricably linked, as can be seen from the portrayal of her gifts in the Zavattari frescoes (see Frontispiece). However, there is another, earlier, remarkable monument which also proves the closeness of this connection in the minds of contemporaries. It is the tympanum of the central west door of Monza cathedral, which would have confronted every visitor who approached the church from that direction (Plate 12). As befits a church dedicated to the Baptist, the lower register shows Christ's baptism, together with four saintly figures – Peter, Paul, and probably Elizabeth with Zacharias. Above, only one figure (the Baptist again) is portrayed as a saint, and he is presented with a crown by a female figure who is herself crowned. A kneeling man, spurred and crowned, who offers further gifts, and all the 'courtly' figures in this register have been plausibly identified as members of Theodolinda's family: her second husband, Agilulf, her son and her daughter. The treasure, too, may often have been linked with known objects, as the chapel frescoes show. The significance of Theodolinda's grant to Monza would have been accentuated by the representation of Theodolinda's portrayal with the *chioccia*, too.

Portrayal of these figures on the tympanum is remarkable by any standard. Benefactors were often represented with a

Plate 12 Tympanum of west door, Monza: general view. Note the crowns with crosses on the left side of the upper register and, on the right side, Queen Theodolinda's grants to the Baptist, and especially the *chioccia* (reproduced by permission of the Museo del Duomo di Monza).

diminutive church to signify their grants or foundation(s) of churches; but the association of identifiable benefactors with known objects, like the brooding hen, is unique. Inevitably, this raises problems of interpretation as well as queries about the aims which such an unusual monument was designed to fulfil. Initially it could be supposed that the dating of the tympanum would provide a solution to at least some of the problems associated with its interpretation; but, although this sculpture would normally be assigned to the first half of the fourteenth century, it cannot, on grounds of style, be dated much more narrowly than that. As the treasure was only intermittently kept safely in Monza during the years *c*.1300–50, the programme of the tympanum could have been designed for different purposes according to the time when it was planned and executed. During the years 1319–24, for instance, or after its return from Avignon in 1344, it could have proclaimed the cathedral's possession of the treasure together with Queen Theodolinda's generosity and the Baptist's defence of his own; whereas during the years when it was in the hands of the Della Torre family in Milan or at the papal *curia* in Avignon the design would surely have had rather different aims. In those circumstances it could have drawn attention to the lost 'rights' of the cathedral church of Monza. In either case Theodolinda's role, although central, seems ambiguous: she is not attributed any unambiguously 'sacred' symbol, but she and her family are allotted places which would normally have been reserved for saints or for episodes with a wide religious appeal, biblical scenes and ones with a didactic purpose, like the Last Judgement, or scenes from the life of the Virgin. Notwithstanding what has already been said, Theodolinda was surely a figure who would have been regarded first of all as a secular foundress and a woman who had bestowed great gifts on her religious foundation. Was it after all the treasure which mattered most in the later Middle Ages?

Whatever the answer to that question, by the mid-fifteenth century, when the Zavattari were engaged to decorate the chapel where Queen Theodolinda's sarcophagus had been placed in Monza cathedral, a version of her legend seems already to have been constructed from a curious amalgam of secular and religious elements, in which the Lombard Queen played a more prominent part than St John the Baptist, the cathedral's patron saint, or the venerated Pope St Gregory the Great. The chapel was in some sense a funerary one, but the paintings emphasize the part that Theodolinda played as foundress and benefactor, clothing her in the trappings of the highest fifteenth-century aristocratic fashion. Whereas there are hints in the written sources of the fourteenth century that Queen Theodolinda could be viewed as a figure who was, in some sense at least, holy, little of that is retained in the frescoes, apart from her dream and the vision of the dove. Nevertheless, her part in the conversion of Agilulf to Catholicism has an obvious religious significance compared to the activity of many saints in early *vitae*.

In the frescoes, the selection of themes and the emphasis on different episodes of Theodolinda's life and career show the way in which a regional church re-made its own past. The careful use of written historical sources is interesting even if, outside the regions of Monza and Milan, Paul the Deacon's 'ethnic' history has a significance which far outweighs the chronicle of the local patriot and antiquarian, Bonincontro de Morigia. The choice of themes and topics was selective, however, and should alert historians and art historians alike to the means by which such 'legends' evolved or were built up, and the symbols and substance of importance in an earlier era were transformed. It seems obvious, for instance, that the association of Queen Theodolinda with the treasure preserved at Monza in part accounts for the emphasis laid on her role as founder and chief benefactor of St John the Baptist's church at Monza; but exactly how the 'holy oils' and the *chioccia* came together with objects of more obviously liturgical use and material worth is now difficult to determine. That they were associated is proved by the tympanum and the frescoes. It should be noted, however, that the 'Iron Crown' of Monza, which has been deposited in Theodolinda's chapel since the nineteenth century, was not apparently accorded any prominence in Theodolinda's 'legend' in the later Middle Ages. In his edition of Bonincontro's Chronicle, Muratori noted that the author did not note the widely disseminated view that the 'Iron crown' was made from nails from Christ's Cross, or even state that it was preserved in Monza. However, Bonincontro was interested in this crown for its function in legitimizing royal rule in Lombardy; and he thought that the Archbishop of Milan, or failing him the Bishop of Monza, should be the *coronator* [*B*, cols 1055–6, 1077–8].

The evolution of Theodolinda's 'legend' in the later Middle Ages can surely only be understood if it is placed against the background of factional secular and ecclesiastical politics in Italy – perhaps also against the wider world of Christian Europe – during this era: the involvement of the Visconti, and the precise interplay of papal and north Italian ecclesiastical interests would certainly repay further investigation. There can be little doubt that Theodolinda's role as giver of treasure was emphasized in a period when that treasure was 'vulnerable'; but it would surely be an over-simplification to suppose that this was the chief or only purpose underlying this reworking of the church's past.

Undoubtedly, in the fourteenth and fifteenth centuries, the church (and I take that to include a layman like Bonincontro) had discarded the religious setting in which the 'true' Theodolinda of the sixth and seventh centuries had fulfilled her role as Queen – even if Bonincontro and the Zavattari brothers in their own ways did refer back to the eight-century history of Paul the Deacon. Although the Lombard kings possessed a fine secular palace at Monza in addition to the church founded by Theodolinda, in her own time the political and religious interests of the Lombard dynasty were far removed from those which would have been comprehensible 700 or more years later. The threats posed by renewed Byzantine interest in Italy in the seventh century, by the pressure of Franks from north of the Alps – indeed, by Lombard political expansion in general – had no direct relevance for the church of Monza when Lombards and Franks alike had disappeared from the Italian scene. In her own world and time, a woman like Theodolinda was probably only important in a time of 'instability' as the widow of a king 'without adult heirs'. That position also was transformed in subsequent centuries, in the legend(s) in which her husbands take second place. When Paul the

Deacon was writing the history of his own *gens* it has been asserted that he was already seeing the 'present in the past'. The development of Theodolinda's legend in subsequent centuries suggests that all those involved in the recollection of this Lombard Queen continued to do so.

University of East Anglia

ENDNOTE

Both Jane Martindale and John Mitchell realized that Andrew had left space in his own plan to discuss the dating of the Zavattari frescoes and their relationship to the paintings in the vault of Theodolinda's chapel. These include heraldic devices of the Visconti. But the paintings of this area, too, raise problems relating to the dates at which the Zavattari brothers were active in the chapel. Andrew had not had time to formulate his own conclusions. He considered that further work was needed on (i) a number of technical problems, for example the layers of paint and *intonaco* in the different parts of the chapel frescoes; (ii) the inscriptions, which are not easily visible in the vault without binoculars; (iii) the sequence of work undertaken in the chapel. He would almost certainly have devoted some discussion, too, both to the documentary sources, and to the verse in which the Zavattari recorded their activity. See, for the documents, R. Cassanelli and R. Conti, eds, *Monza: la capella di Teodelinda nel Duomo* (Milan, 1991), pp. 125–9; and for the verse which gives a date of 1444, ibid., p. 45.

SECONDARY BIBLIOGRAPHY

This is not intended to be comprehensive. The volumes edited by R. Conti (see below) have an extensive and specialized bibliography. What have been included here are references to other works and studies which Andrew Martindale consulted, or are of detailed significance for the specific topics which he followed up. It does not include more general works on the ecclesiastical or religious topics which would have been noted if he had finished his own address, or studies on painting and the decorative arts, since the comparative section of the address had not been written. [Jane Martindale].

G. Algeri, ed., *Storia di Monza e della Brianza. L'arte all'éta romana al Rinascimento*, 2 (Milan, 1984).

G. Anziani, 'Riflessioni su gli affreschi della cappella di Teodolinda', *Arte Lombarda*, 80-2 (1987).

X. Barbier de Montault, 'Le trésor de la basilique royale de Monza', *Bulletin monumental* (1884).

A. Bazzi, et al., 'Il restauro nella "Notula de olea sanctorum" di S. Gregorio Magna alla regina Teodolinda', *Studi Monzesi*, 8 (1992).

L. Beltrami and C. Fumagalli, *La cappella della regina Teodelinda in Monza e le sue pittore murali* (Milan, 1891).

C. Braddock, 'L'ascensione nella prima arte bizantina: le ampolle di Monza e Bobbio', *Studi Monzesi*, 6 (1990).

D. Bullough, 'Ethnic history and the Carolingians: an alternative reading to Paul the Deacon's *Historia Langobardorum*', in C. Holdsworth and T. Wiseman, eds, *The Inheritance of Historiography*, Exeter Studies in History, 12 (Exeter, 1986), pp. 85-105.

R. Cassanelli, ' "In quodam navello lapidis". Note in margine alla sepoltura e al sarcofago de Teodelinda nel Duomo di Monza', *Study Monzesi*, 5 (1989).

R. Cassanelli, 'Teodelinda regina o Santa? Appunti sulla politica viscontea delle imagini a Monza nel XIV e XV secolo', in R. Conti, ed., *La Messa di S. Michele* (Monza, 1990).

R. Cassanelli and R. Conti, eds, *Monza: la capella di Teodelinda nel Duomo* (Milan, 1991).

R. Conti, ed., *Il Duomo di Monza: i tesore* (Monza, 1990) [collected essays].

R. Conti, ed., *Il Duomo di Monza: la storia e l'arte* (Monza, 1991) [collected essays].

R. Conti, ed., *Il tesoro: guida alla conoscenza del tesoro Duomo di Monza* (Monza, 1993).

A.-F. Frisi, *Memorie storiche di Monza et sua corte*, 4 vols (Monza, 1794).

G. Giulini, *Memorie spettanti alla storia, al governo, e alle descrizione della città e della campagna di Milano nei secoli bassi*, 7 vols (Milan, 1760–1).

G. Haseloff, 'I reperti del sarcofago della Regina Teodelinda a Monza', *Studi Monzesi*, 5 (1989) [with reprint of article by Beltrami of 1889].

A. Herschel, 'Problems of patronage at Monza: the legend of Queen Theodelinda', *Arte Lombarda*, 80–2 (1987).

G. Langoni, 'Novità sul calice visconteo del tesoro del Duomo di Monza', *Studi Monzesi*, 9 (1994).

A. Martindale, 'Patrons and minders: the intrusion of the secular into sacred spaces in the late middle ages', *SCH*, 28 (1992), pp. 143–78.

Monza anno 1300. La basilica di S. Giovanni Battista e la sua facciata (Monza, 1988) [exhibition catalogue].

Monza. La basilica di S. Giovanni Battista in Monza, 3rd ed. (Monza, 1988) [guide].

F. Oppenheimer, *Il timpano del duomo di Monza* (Monza, 1958) [first published in English].

L. Vegas, 'Le pitture gotiche del duomo di Monza', *Studi Monzesi*, 4 (1989).

C. Wickham, *Early Medieval Italy: Central Power and Local Society, 400–1000* (London, 1981).

EUROPEAN CALVINISM: HISTORY, PROVIDENCE, AND MARTYRDOM

by ANDREW PETTEGREE

For students of the Reformation one of the main conceptual problems is undoubtedly the distance between the mind-set of our age and theirs. We look at the Reformation as a new beginning, the moment when the Church fragmented into competing Churches, and one of the fundamental developments of the Early Modern Age: a term which in itself presents a view of progress and change as one of the determining characteristics of the age.

Contemporaries, however, had a very different perception; they saw the movement for evangelical reform as one of renovation and renewal. They believed that they were attempting to recover what was best in the past of the Church, which had since become hopelessly corrupted. With others of their contemporaries they despised innovation. One can surely only understand Martin Luther if one recognizes the depth of his conservatism; that his personal crusade was to a large extent fuelled by a sense of moral outrage and indignation at what the papacy had done to his Church.

Our perception of the Reformation is in some respects much closer to that of the evangelical movement's contemporary opponents. They, as we do, perceived the Reformation as a movement of innovation, although to them this was of course a sinister development. They accused the reformers of having turned their back on the past, of rejecting the accumulated tradition of the historical Church. To Luther's denunciation of a corrupted papacy they returned simple but telling questions: Where is your history? Where are your saints? This was a shrewd thrust, particular in an age where the ideal vision of society was essentially changeless; where every innovation was validated in terms of some real or imagined historical precedent.

This paper will not be attempting a general treatment of how the Reformation dealt with this problem of its historical

227

past. It would be possible to explore this question in an interesting manner by describing the ways in which conservative criticism forced the reformers to address the problems of the historical roots of their movement; not least because the solutions they devised to these problems were in many respects bogus and implausible.[1] Instead, what follows will have a rather more particular focus, and one which tackles one of the central interpretative questions of my own work. It offers a presentation of a developing attempt to understand the mentality of European Calvinism; specifically of those who formed the pioneering generation of the international Calvinist movement in the middle years of the sixteenth century.

The attempt to penetrate the mind–set of a different age is a hazardous undertaking, fraught with many complexities. This is particularly so of Calvinism, a movement characterized by so many apparent contradictions: deeply disruptive, yet wedded to a political doctrine of loyalty to the established social hierarchy, and marked by both a strong sense of individual initiative and an almost stifling sense of community. But it is important that we make the attempt, because it is only if we understand the mentality of this movement that we can understand how the Reformation was rescued from its mid–century collapse by the rise of Calvinism. The extent of this mid–century collapse is not always recognized in the literature, but it is something at which I have hinted in the introduction to my edited collection on *The Early Reformation in Europe*, and which I think is largely borne out in the essays which follow.[2] For by the time of Luther's death in 1546 the Reformation movement was clearly in some difficulties. In Germany itself the military superiority of Charles V threatened during precisely these years to turn back the substantial institutional progress made by Lutheranism in the major princely states. Outside Germany the perspective was still more gloomy. By the end of the 1540s persecution had effectively stifled native reform

---

[1] See here the essays collected by Bruce Gordon, ed., *Protestant Identity and History in Reformation Europe*, St Andrews Studies in Reformation History, 3 (Aldershot, 1996), and particularly the excellent introduction by the editor.

[2] Andrew Pettegree, ed., *The Early Reformation in Europe* (Cambridge, 1992).

movements in both France and the Netherlands, countries where evangelicals had initially and realistically hoped for substantial progress. By the 1550s any vestige of the early Lutheran movements had been effectively shattered.[3] In England too the heady optimism of the reign of Edward VI would give way to the firm re-Catholicizing policies of Mary Tudor; in 1555 the best of English Protestantism was either in prison or in exile.[4] This left only Scandinavia, and portions of central and eastern Europe, where sympathetic local political structures had created space for the creation of a Lutheran-style Church.[5] For those committed to the preservation of the Old Church in Europe this mid-century hiatus must have been a time of hope and relative optimism.

The recognition of the extent of the mid-century crisis of the evangelical movement has concentrated attention on these crucial two decades, the 1540s and 1550s, when Protestantism was effectively, necessarily, re-created: what Heiko Oberman has called the 'Reformation of the refugees'.[6] This period has also formed the central core of my own work. For this was the time when the Reformation gained its vital second wind, before re-emerging in Western Europe in an astonishing burst of creative and destructive energy at the beginning of the 1560s. During this time the Reformation effectively regrouped in exile communities, in Geneva, Strasburg, and other German and Swiss towns, before breaking out in a surge of immensely violent activity which plunged France and the Netherlands into civil war, and carried England and Scotland into the Protestant camp. In the process, Calvinism reformed the religious map of Western Europe.

---

[3] Alastair Duke, *Reformation and Revolt in the Low Countries* (London, 1990); Andrew Pettegree, *Emden and the Dutch Revolt* (Oxford, 1992); Mark Greengrass, *The French Reformation* (Oxford, 1987); David J. Nicholls, 'The nature of popular heresy in France, 1520-1542', *HistJ*, 26 (1983), pp. 261-75.

[4] Andrew Pettegree, *Marian Protestantism: Six Studies*, St Andrews Studies in Reformation History, 4 (Aldershot, 1996).

[5] Ole Peter Grell, ed., *The Scandinavian Reformation* (Cambridge, 1995); Winfried Eberhard, 'Bohemia, Moravia and Austria', and David P. Daniel, 'Hungary', in Pettegree, ed., *Early Reformation in Europe*, pp. 23-69.

[6] Heiko Oberman, '*Europe afflicta*. The Reformation of the refugees', in *ARG*, 83 (1992), pp. 91-111.

Those who work on this period, however, are still some way from a total explanation of why Calvinism could and did have such an explosive and decisive effect at precisely this time. The appeal of Calvinism – and implicitly why Calvinism succeeded where Lutheranism had failed in an international context – is a question different generations of historians have naturally approached in different ways. In his *Geneva and the Coming of the Wars of Religion in France*, Robert Kingdon stressed the organizational genius of the movement. Calvin's Geneva was able to organize and form a French Church in its image, largely through sending out missionary ministers and the provision of clandestine literature.[7] It was a template and model I essentially followed in my *Emden and the Dutch Revolt*, where I attempted to show how Emden, the northern Geneva, played a largely parallel role in organizing and forming the young Dutch Calvinist church. Other historians have attempted to explain the appeal of Calvinism in terms of social geography. It is clear from the pioneering work of Natalie Davis, and from a sequence of local studies undertaken by Philip Benedict, David Rosenberg, and Henry Heller, that in France, for instance, certain groups in every community were more drawn to the new religion than others, often trades of high social prestige or those which involved new technology.[8]

All of these works have done a great deal to explain the character and impact of early Calvinism. But there is much about the phenomenon of mid-sixteenth-century Pro-testantism that they do not explain. One such element is the extraordinary aggressiveness and violence of the movement. This is a circumstance first identified in a seminal article of Natalie Davis, and brilliantly highlighted by the work of

---

[7] Robert M. Kingdon, *Geneva and the Coming of the Wars of Religion in France* (Geneva, 1956).

[8] Natalie Davis, 'Strikes and salvation at Lyons', in her *Society and Culture in Early Modern France* (London, 1975), pp. 1–16; Philip Benedict, *Rouen during the Wars of Religion* (Cambridge, 1981), pp. 71–94; Henry Heller, *The Conquest of Poverty. The Calvinist Revolt in Sixteenth Century France* (Leiden, 1986); David Rosenberg, 'Social experience and religious choice: a case study. The Protestant weavers and woolcombers of Amiens in the sixteenth century' (Yale University Ph.D. thesis, 1978).

Philip Benedict on Rouen.[9] Here it becomes clear that it was the sheer provocativeness of the Calvinists, breaching every convention of the local community in the quest not just for religious freedom, but for domination of the religious agenda, that destroyed the calm and peace of the city. And often these were actions led not by the movement's natural leaders, nobles, or ministers, but by ordinary lay members of the community. Exploring these events, as I have done particularly in attempting an explanation of the extraordinary violence of the Calvinist imagebreaking in the Netherlands in 1566,[10] brings home that in explaining what led ordinary men and women into such choices we need to look beyond their social location, and beyond the structures of the wider movement, towards what one might call the mind-set of Calvinist activism. What follows is an attempt to distil some of the essence of this new Calvinist culture.

It would be my contention that the essence of this mental culture was incubated and nurtured in the exile churches, and it is here that one should look if one is to distinguish a distinctive Calvinist mentality. The essence of this can perhaps be summed up in two words: providence and martyrdom. To talk of martyrdom may seem at first rather surprising: after all, by taking refuge abroad the exiles had manifestly avoided the prospect of a martyr's crown. But in the generally more complaisant climate of the 1540s the significance of this step must not be underestimated. There can be no doubt that for many exiles, the decision to abandon home and family was a martyrdom of sorts. John Calvin for one felt intensely the disorientation and distress of the exile's lot, and there is no doubt that his sense of suffering for Christ deeply informed his writings. 'To suffer persecution for righteousness' sake', as Calvin wrote in his *Institutes* in a section entitled, starkly, 'Bearing the cross in persecution and other calamities',

---

[9] Natalie Davis, 'The rites of violence', in *Society and Culture*, pp. 152–88; Benedict, *Rouen during the Wars of Religion*, pp. 49–70. See also now Denis Crouzet, *Les Guerriers de Dieu: la violence au temps des troubles de religion, vers 1525 – vers 1610*, 2 vols (Champ Vallon, 1990).

[10] Pettegree, *Emden and the Dutch Revolt*, ch. 5. Cf. Phyllis Mack Crew, *Calvinist Preaching and Iconoclasm in the Netherlands, 1544–1569* (Cambridge, 1978).

is a singular comfort . . . For it ought to occur to us how much honour God bestows upon us in thus furnishing us with the special badge of his soldiery . . .. Poverty, if judged in itself, is misery; likewise exile, contempt prison, disgrace; finally death itself is the ultimate of all calamities. But when the favour of our God breathes upon us, every one of these things turns into happiness for us.[11]

And the behaviour of those who, like himself, accepted this cross, was starkly contrasted with those who attempted to compromise with Catholicism. For these years when the exile churches first took shape were also, significantly, the years of Calvin's most concentrated polemical campaign against timid and half-hearted supporters of the Gospel who remained in Catholic countries, men and women whom Calvin characterized famously as Nicodemites.[12]

It was also Calvin's great theological gift to make all of this suffering seem part of a greater plan. Calvin clearly felt this was true for his own life. This comes across with particular force in his brief autobiographical writings, but the same spirit really infuses all of his writings, not least the systematic theology of the *Institutes*.[13] To those who responded to Calvin's strictures against Nicodemism that he could denounce such behaviour without risk from the comfort of Geneva, Calvin could quite honestly reply that his own life too had involved subordinating his own wishes to a strong sense of God's will. He had not intended to be a reformer or an active church leader, but on two separate occasions he had abandoned his own quietude as a result of a compelling and thoroughly unwelcome call to public office in Geneva; on the

---

[11] III, viii, 7: John Calvin, *Institutes of the Christian Religion*, ed. John T. McNeill, Library of the Christian Classics, 20–1, 2 vols (Philadelphia, 1960), p. 707.

[12] Particularly in his *Petit traicté monstrant que c'est que doit faire un homme fidele congnoissant la verité de l'evangile* (Geneva, 1543), and *Excuse a MM. les Nicodemites* (Geneva, 1544): Rodolphe Peter and Jean-François Gilmont, eds, *Bibliotheca Calviniana*, 2 vols (Geneva, 1991–4), nos. 43/6, 44/9. For a review of the literature on this subject see now my 'Nicodemism and the English Reformation', in *Marian Protestantism: Six Studies*.

[13] The author's preface to Calvin's Commentary on the Psalms is the most famous piece of autobiographical writing; John Calvin, *Commentary on the Book of Psalms*, Calvin Translation Society (Edinburgh, 1845), pp. xxxv–xlix.

second occasion giving up a life of study and service in the great cosmopolitan city of Strasburg, years that he would later look back on as the happiest of his life.[14] Only a strong sense of exterior calling would have dragged Calvin back to Geneva; and only a similar sense of God's constant presence and involvement in events would have sustained him through the turbulent and at times brutal power politics that preceded final victory over his Genevan opponents.

The effect of these personal experiences is readily evident in Calvin's writings. His letters place Genevan events in a strongly providential framework: an account which still has a powerful effect on the reader even when modern research has demonstrated that Calvin was extremely active in his own cause when it came to tipping the balance of Genevan power politics.[15] And in the *Institutes*, too, this strong sense of God's ceaseless intervention makes the sections on Providence seem some of the best and most powerful of the whole book. 'God's Providence governs all', as Calvin boldly asserts, 'for he is deemed omnipotent not because he can indeed act, yet sometimes ceases and sits in idleness, ... but because, governing heaven and earth by his providence, he so regulates all things that nothing takes place without his deliberation.'[16]

This sense of God's activity, this providential partisanship, was one which became fundamental to the whole Calvinist movement. Brilliantly captured in Calvin's writings, it was in fact basic to the whole culture of exile, since it was this which made sense of the otherwise bewildering experience of dispossession and hardship. The English exile writers resorted to much the same language to make sense of their own sense of dispossession at the end of the reign of Edward VI. The accession of Mary they explained as a beneficial judgement of God, not as his repudiation of the evangelical cause. God had sent Mary as a scourge of a sinful nation, which by greed and negligence had shown itself unworthy of

---

[14] Cornelis Augustijn, 'Calvin in Strasburg', in Wilhelm H. Neuser, ed., *Calvinus Sacrae Scripturae Professor* (Grand Rapids, Mi., 1994), pp. 166–77.

[15] William Naphy, *Calvin and the Consolidation of the Genevan Reformation* (Manchester, 1994).

[16] Calvin, *Institutes*, ed. McNeill, p. 200.

so good and Christian a king as Edward VI. But punishment was purgative, and the time of trial would surely pass, as it had for the children of Israel despite their many offences against God's law.[17]

That this time of recuperation and planning in exile could be turned to triumphant advantage was something which would be proved as the opportunity arose to plant the seeds of faith back in their native lands in the latter part of the 1550s. And when these brave early missionaries fell into the hands of the authorities, their suffering and sacrifice were faithfully recorded in their respective martyrologies. Now a genuine martyrdom reinforced the witness of the exile Churches abroad, recorded in the undecorated prose of Jean Crespin, and the more dramatically constructed narratives of the martyrologist of Dutch Calvinism, Adriaan van Haemstede.

These martyrbooks make a fascinating source, at least if one reads them together. Foxe, Crespin, and Haemstede all produced their collections at precisely this time: the martyrology is a phenomenon of precisely this phase of the growth of Calvinist Churches, when communities had begun to be planted, but where the successful establishment of official Churches was still some way away.[18] This is important to recognize when considering their purpose and function in the cultural life of the communities who would have read them. At one level this purpose is perfectly straightforward. The martyrbooks are a celebration of sacrifice, a sacrifice linked, explicitly in Haemstede, implicitly in Crespin and Foxe, with the sufferings of the true Church back to the time of the apostles. But the martyrbooks also have a much more explicitly pedagogic role, and one fundamental to any consideration of the Calvinist view of the historical past.

[17] Joy Shakespeare, 'Plague and punishment', in Peter Lake and Maria Dowling, eds, *Protestantism and the National Church in Sixteenth Century England* (Beckenham, 1987), pp. 103–23.

[18] On Crespin and Haemstede, see David Watson, 'Jean Crespin and the writing of history in the French Reformation', and Andrew Pettegree, 'Adriaan van Haemstede, the heretic as historian', in Gordon, *Protestant Identity*, 2, pp. 59–76; Jean-François Gilmot, *Jean Crespin. Un éditeur réformé du XVIe siècle* (Geneva, 1981); A. J. Jelsma, *Adriaan van Haemstede en zijn Martelaarsboek* (The Hague, 1970). On Foxe see now particularly David Loades, ed., *John Foxe and the English Reformation*, forthcoming in St Andrews Studies in Reformation History (Aldershot, 1997).

This is particularly strong in the work of the Dutch martyrologist, Adriaan van Haemstede, and this is the example on which I will concentrate for many of the remarks which follow; partly because Haemstede is the least well known of the major martyrologists, but partly also because in Haemstede the didactic purpose is particularly direct. Haemstede is a fundamental source for students of the Dutch Reformation, for he wrote his work while serving as minister to the small secret Calvinist church in Antwerp in the late 1550s. Alone of the major martyrologists, Haemstede was a witness and participant in some of the events he described. But because he wrote in Dutch, and his work has never been translated, knowledge of his text is largely confined to specialists in Dutch history. This is a shame, because Haemstede's martyrology is a great book, in some respects one of the unacknowledged masterpieces of Protestant history writing.

In the canon of Protestant Church history, Haemstede was certainly not the first in the field. Already some forty years previously, Luther had laid the foundations of a distinctive Protestant view of Church history in terms which to a large extent guided and formed those who came after.[19] Luther's view of the historic past encapsulated some of the leading themes of his theology. At the centre of Luther's interpretation of events stood a conviction that God and Satan were engaged in a continuous conflict.[20] The cornerstone of his historical perception was provided by the historical books of the Old Testament, which both Luther and Melanchthon interpreted as a continuing story of temptation to listen to the Devil's lies in various kinds of idolatry and apostasy. In this respect, as Peter Fraenkel puts it, 'the whole of sacred history appears as a series of ups and down of true doctrine'.[21] Such a framework provided a template equally applicable to the

[19] This paragraph follows substantially the excellent introduction to this subject in Robert Kolb, *For All the Saints. Changing Perceptions of Martyrdom and Sainthood in the Lutheran Reformation* (Macon, Georgia, 1987), pp. 19–27. John M. Headley, *Luther's View of Church History* (New Haven, 1963), is the standard work.

[20] Kolb, *For All the Saints*, p. 19. Heiko Oberman, *Luther. Man between God and the Devil* (London, 1989).

[21] Peter Fraenkel, *Testimonia Patrum. The Function of the Patristic Argument in the Theology of Philip Melanchthon* (Geneva, 1961), quoted Kolb, *For All the Saints*, p. 26.

history of the post-apostolic Church, where the papacy emerged as the agency of the Devil. Nevertheless, for Luther as for other Protestant writers, the true word of God was never truly submerged. Even the period of the papal tyranny was faintly illuminated by isolated individuals who continued to show obedience to the truth.

None of this was particularly unique to Luther. For all Protestant writers, the history of the Church took on a strongly providential tinge: in Luther's formulation, God had propelled the events of human life at all times. Evangelicals had no sense of a passive, inactive deity; rather God was constantly intervening to shape events.[22]

All of these themes found their echo when Foxe, Crespin, and Haemstede turned their hand to the new and distinctive form of Protestant martyrology. We can see all of the martyrologists weaving into their narrative a strong sense of historical vindication: an analogy, implicit or explicit, with the experience of the true Church of the apostles, and the suffering Church of subsequent centuries.

Haemstede is interesting not least because he is the first of the four major Reformed martyrologists to present the present persecutions as part of a complete scheme of Church history extending back to the beginnings of the Christian Church. Haemstede published his *Geschiedenis der vromer Martelaren* in 1559, when the works of neither Foxe nor Crespin, nor indeed the Lutheran chronicler Rabus, had reached their final, definitive form.[23] At this stage, therefore, only Haemstede offers a complete view of Christian persecutions, from the first biblical martyrs, Stephen, Paul, and Simon Peter, through the early Church to the victims of the medieval papacy. These sections of the work are comparatively short: the whole history of the Church up to Wyclif occupies less than forty-four pages, or ten per cent of the work, but they are integral to his whole scheme. And Haemstede's proved to be an influential vision. Jean Crespin would add to his folio edition of 1570 a new preface establishing the parallels between the sixteenth-century

[22] Compare Calvin in the *Institutes*, i, ch. 16: 'God's Providence governs all'; Calvin, *Institutes*, ed. McNeill, pp. 197–210.
[23] On Rabus see particularly Kolb, *For All the Saints*.

martyrs and those of the early Church (this was, significantly, the first edition of Crespin's work for which he had had access to Haemstede).[24] John Foxe's great work underwent a similar transformation at this stage of its development.[25]

Grafted into Crespin and Foxe at this late stage, this sense of the continuum of Church history was fundamental to Haemstede's agenda. And it had an immediate and pertinent contemporary application. One can see this if one considers how Haemstede applied the lessons of Church history to the particular circumstances of his own audience, the young persecuted Calvinist churches in the Netherlands.

When Dutch Calvinists met together in secret congregations they acted against the explicit prohibition of the royal authority. Conventicles, as these small evangelical gatherings had become known, had been banned in the Netherlands from the first *placards* against the new teaching in the 1520s, and from 1529 it became a capital crime to attend such a meeting.[26] In addition to the obvious dangers of church membership Dutch evangelicals had to defend themselves against a charge of wilful disobedience, and this was a matter of particular sensitivity in a land where Anabaptism, with its highly ambiguous attitude towards secular authority, had made a significant impact.[27] This issue, and the evangelical defence against such charges, was carefully ventilated in Haemstede's account of an exchange between the Antwerp martyr Gilles Verdickt and the official charged with his examination.

> The officer's most serious charge was that he had taken part in secret gatherings, which was against the King's

---

[24] *Histoire des vrays Tesmoins de la verite de l'evangile* (Geneva, 1570), sig. aiv^r-vii^r.

[25] It is interesting too to speculate whether Fox was aware of Haemstede's work when he devised his own more elaborate scheme for the definitive *Acts and Monuments* of 1563. For a first consideration of this question see now my 'Haemstede and Foxe' in Loades, *John Foxe.*

[26] For the placards, *Corpus documentorum inquisitionis haereticae pravatis Neerlandicae*, ed. P. Fredericq, 5 vols (Ghent and The Hague, 1889–1902), 4, pp. 43–5, 5, pp. 1–5. James Tracey, 'Heresy law and centralization under Mary of Hungary: conflict between the council of Holland and the central government over the enforcement of Charles V's Placards', *ARG*, 73 (1982), pp. 288–90.

[27] Cornelis Krahn, *Dutch Anabaptism* (The Hague, 1968); James Stayer, *Anabaptists and the Sword* (Lawrence, Kansas, 1976).

command. Gilles said, 'Sir, is it not commanded to speak God's word? To call the people to repentance?' The officer replied, 'Preaching should take place in the church, other sorts of meetings cause disorder.' To which Gilles replied that what was good in the church could not be evil out of doors, and he could not believe that it was the King's intention to forbid God's word, but above all there was no suggestion of disorder in the community.[28]

Here one sees the relevance of Haemstede's constant references to the fidelity of the martyrs' teaching to the pure word of Scripture, and of the historical context which Haemstede provides for his contemporary narratives. For if arrested evangelicals had taught nothing but the unadulterated word of Scripture, how could a legitimate authority place them under legal constraint? Similarly by placing the martyrs of Protestantism in a long context, Haemstede drives home the point that the true Church has always been a suffering, and often a persecuted, remnant, existing among a fallen people repeatedly seduced by the heathenish allure of false gods, pomp, and idolatry. This is the lesson of the Old Testament, the early Church, and of the medieval papacy, whose many corruptions Haemstede conveniently summarizes in tabular form.[29] But the point is that such a remnant has always survived: even in the worst days of the triumphant papal supremacy God left a few true Christians so that the world would not be entirely like Sodom or Gomorrah.[30] With the bracing examples of Arnold of Brescia, Adelbertus Gallus, and other brave enemies of Antichrist set before them, the Calvinists of Antwerp could congratulate themselves that they were the true inheritors of this tradition. In this context minority status becomes not the cause of despair but a vindication of righteousness.

---

[28] Adriaan van Haemstede, *De Geschiedenisse ende den dodt der vromer Martelaren* ([Emden], 1559), pp. 426-7. This and subsequent translated quotations from Haemstede are my own.

[29] 'D'artikelen der Papistiscer secten', ibid., pp. 41-2. The source of this pungent and telling list is not clear. Quite possibly it is, as Jelsma suggests, an original contribution of Haemstede's. Jelsma, *Adriaan van Haemstede*, pp. 276-8.

[30] Haemstede, *Geschiedenisse*, p. 36.

This is the true lesson to be drawn from Haemstede's pathbreaking decision to place the sixteenth-century martyrs in a complete historical context. And this is the context in which early Christian martyrs such as Ptolemy and Lucius, or Petrus, tortured for his refusal to worship images, spoke directly to the modern experience. Others offered the further encouragement of evidence of divine favour through miraculous manifestations at the place of execution. Despite their claims to be offering an authentic narrative, all the martyrologists make some use of such motifs. In Haemstede these are more likely to be instances of divine retribution visited on the persecuting magistrate, while Crespin makes greater play of martyrs who speak to the crowd even after their tongue has been cut out.[31] Such miraculous manifestations clearly drew on a martyr tradition dating back to the early Church, but in Foxe and Crespin such comparisons are necessarily implicit. By including his early historical sections Haemstede was in a position to include both modern miracles and these inspirational archetypes.[32]

The significance of these first introductory sections thus goes beyond the relatively small proportion of the volume's total length dedicated to the early Church centuries. In distilling from the available sources a short but eminently coherent history of the Christian persecutions, Haemstede presents a wholly plausible context for his own suffering community, now clearly identified with the righteous martyrs through all the ages. This is even more the case if one considers these early sections in the context of the

[31] Although frequently practised in France (to prevent the condemned stirring up the crowd gathered for their execution), this practice seems not to have been known in the Netherlands.

[32] Archetypes such as Romanus, the early Church martyr, whose end was marked by several miracles. The first attempt to put him to death was thwarted when a miraculous shower doused the flames; at the second, successful, attempt Romanus praised God despite the removal of his tongue. Haemstede, *Geschiedenisse*, pp. 25–6. For the early Church sources, H. Delehaye, 'S. Romain, martyr d'Antioche', *AnBoll*, 50 (1932), pp. 240–83. Cynthia Hahn, 'Speaking without tongues: the martyr Romanus and Augustine's theory of language in illustrations of Bern Burgerbibliothek Codex 264', in Renate Blumenfeld-Kosinski and Timea Szell, eds, *Images of Sainthood in Medieval Europe* (Ithaca, N.Y., and London, 1991), pp. 161–80.

important exhortatory epistle which Haemstede attaches to the beginning of his volume. Addressed to the Lords, Regents, and Stadholders of the Dutch provinces, this foreword permits Haemstede both to extend the historical context and to address one of his primary concerns in writing his book: calling the secular magistrate to a sense of his duty to protect the Christian community.[33] To this end Haemstede sets before the modern rulers of the Netherlands the godly examples of the Old Testament kings and patriarchs: Abraham, Moses, Joshua and David, Josias and Ezekiel, all of whom called their people to repentance and away from the worship of false gods. The present day magistrate should follow in their footsteps.[34]

But just as there are patriarchs and prophets, so the Old Testament is full of unjust rulers. 'So it has been from the beginning of the world and will be to the end, that the heedless world will persecute the children of light.'[35] A heedless people will fall into idolatry; the true preacher is left an isolated and persecuted figure. The Old Testament thus provides further obvious archetypes for the suffering Christians of Antwerp, not least in those righteous prophets and servants of God who refused to bow to unChristian commands. Haemstede here cites the significant examples of Micah and Amos, those rough-hewn prophets who preached an uncompromising doctrine of sin and repentance to a heedless people, or Daniel, whose fearless fidelity to the true God caused his precipitous fall from favour at the court of King Nebuchadnezzar.[36] But there are ominous lessons too for the magistrate in the fate of kings who strayed from the paths of righteousness, for whom the severest punishments are reserved. Haemstede here cites Saul, Jeroboam, and Ahab, all of whom suffered defeat and loss of their kingdoms for their wilful disobedience to God's law. To Haemstede it was manifestly clear, that 'those who follow the tyranny of Pharaoh, disobey God's word, and persecute God's people, will by

---

33 Haemstede, *Geschiedenisse*, sig. *ii^r–vii^r.
34 Ibid., sig. *ii^{r-v}.
35 Ibid., sig. *ii^v.
36 Ibid., sig. *iv^r.

God's hand be cast into the waters of corruption and be utterly destroyed.'[37]

In some senses this evocation of biblical prototypes is largely conventional; but it is clear that Haemstede is offering a deeper lesson for those who will go on to read the main text. This introduction, with its strong sense of dialectic rhythm woven into the narrative, extends the lessons of the early Church back into the beginnings of history. Haemstede takes comfort in the repeated waves of history. The people of Israel are repeatedly raised up and cast down; seen in this context the Christian centuries simply continue a timeless oscillation of sin and repentance.[38]

This discussion illustrates quite well the various levels on which the Protestant martyrology functioned as a pedagogic text. It was at one basic level comfort literature: it provided an explanation of current tribulation through reference to the sufferings of the people of Israel and the first Christian communities; an analogy which was also a vindication of their present conduct. It illustrates quite clearly the different ways in which Calvinists drew inspiration from Scripture: whereas the models for their organizational forms were largely drawn from the early Church and New Testament, their sense of historical continuity was in large measure based on an identification with the people of Israel in the Old Testament. It was a sense of history which allowed them to pass over the thousand years of Church history in between which they had to a large extent repudiated and discarded.

But having said this, I am not sure it is this historical sense which essentially defines the cultural essence of Calvinism. To a large extent this sense of historical heritage was common to all Protestant Churches; a necessary response to the rejection of the more recent developing tradition of the Catholic Church.[39] What essentially defines and marks out Calvinism is, I believe, the sense of providential activism to which I have already referred. We can see this too in the martyrologies.

[37] Ibid., sig. *v^r.
[38] Compare Luther: Kolb, *For All the Saints*, p. 26.
[39] Gordon, *Protestant Identity*.

On several occasions Haemstede includes with his martyr narratives fairly extensive Confessions of Faith or summaries of belief; the interrogations then offer a more lively and often appropriately simplified gloss on these fundamental doctrinal statements. It is worth quoting at length one such exchange, taken from the examination of Gilles Verdickt, a deacon of the Antwerp Church arrested on a proselytizing mission to Brussels, and subsequently executed. The extract gives a good indication of Haemstede's purpose in including what, while presented as reported or direct speech, is clearly a carefully structured piece of pedagogic writing. Verdickt is first questioned by a secular officer and interrogated on his sacramental beliefs:

> He questioned him first on the sacrament of the altar, to which Gilles replied that he recognised no such sacrament. 'So', said the officer, 'you are a profaner of the sacraments.' 'No, Sir', replied Gilles, 'it is your priests and monks who profane the sacraments, who have kept us and our forefathers in blindness and error, and led us to mute idols and damnation in Hell.'
>
> After this the minister of St Gaelen came to him, and later many other priests and monks with whom he conversed at length, especially over the sacrifice of the mass, through which they set at nought the unique sacrifice of Jesus Christ. He showed them that Christ cannot be offered up again for our sins or he must shed his blood again, for without the shedding of blood there is no forgiveness of sins. . .. He questioned them for two days, bringing them into great confusion. . ... His other question was, what scriptural foundation they had for withholding the cup from the people in the communion. Here they advanced many pretexts which were all without foundation, and could not stand against Christ's explicit command, 'Drink this, all of you.'[40]

There are several points that can be made here. Firstly one can note the theological sophistication of the largely self-

[40] Haemstede, *Geschiedenisse*, pp. 425-6.

educated men who, like Gilles Verdickt, made up the first generation of these Calvinist Churches under the cross. There is simply no comparison between the ordered, disciplined views expressed by men such as Gilles Verdickt, and the sincere but essentially unorganized individuals who made up the unformed evangelism of the 1540s.[41] Verdickt's witness, as he defended the beliefs of his Church against repeated attempts to break him down by expert clerical examiners, was a testimony to what had been achieved in fifteen years of exile.

That of course rather begs the question of whether these events occurred as Haemstede recorded them. I offer elsewhere some reflections on how far prison narratives of this sort may be regarded as truly 'authentic'.[42] Reading a number of these accounts inevitably raises suspicions: many of these stories are simply too perfect from a dramatic and pedagogic point of view, and the Gilles Verdickt narrative quoted above rather makes the point: how skilfully, and succinctly, the apparently uneducated Verdickt puts over the main doctrinal points Haemstede expects his audience to seize. One is also aware how the same motifs recur, not only in Haemstede, but in all the major martyrologists. But the question of authenticity, though interesting for another occasion, is rather beside the point when considering the effect of Haemstede's work on his intended audience. And here there is much more to be said. One can note, for instance, the underlying militancy even in this celebration of sacrifice. Several martyrs in Haemstede's narrative confront their judges with the paradox that death is to them a form of victory.

> After he had been in prison for about six or seven weeks, [Gilles Verdickt] was brought before the tribunal and condemned to be burned as a heretic. And

---

[41]   Alastair Duke, 'Dissident voices in a conformist town: the early Reformation at Gouda', in his *Reformation and Revolt*, pp. 60–70.

[42]   See my 'Heretic as historian', in Gordon, *Protestant Identity*, and 'Haemstede and Foxe', in Loades, *John Foxe*. The question of the authenticity of the martyrologists' accounts is now being investigated in a far more systematic and sceptical way. See Watson, 'Jean Crespin', and Tom Freeman's article in this volume.

because he was a quiet and composed man, endowed with great intelligence, he spoke up in a very courteous and skilful manner, thanking them for their judgement, and praying that God would forgive them what they did out of ignorance. Then he said, 'My lords, do you truly imagine that you will stamp out these faithful Christians, who you call heretics, with torture and executions? Oh how you deceive yourselves! Believe rather, that the ashes of my body shall be scattered through the town, and from it many Christians will spring up, for the blood of the martyrs is the seed of the faithful.'[43]

Events would do much to bear out Verdickt's defiant confidence. For within a few years executions in the Netherlands had become the focus of so much popular disquiet that they had virtually to be abandoned. The authorities' loss of control of this central act of justice was one of the first signs that the situation in the Netherlands was moving towards a fundamental political crisis.[44]

The other sense that comes through quite clearly in these martyr narratives is the sense of manifest destiny. It is a sense of providential inevitability quite detached from the cooler assessment of political strategy one may discern in the correspondence of some of the secular leaders of the movement. And it was, in my view, essential to understanding the nature and power of the Calvinist movement in these years. One can see the same sense of driving growth in the French movement at much the same time, a movement fuelled by a sense of inevitability and heedlessness of political consequences.

This is a point worth emphasizing, because it is not necessarily clear if one concentrates too exclusively on the actions and reactions of the leaders of the movement, particularly those like Calvin, established in the exile centres abroad. Nearer the scene of action the atmosphere was quite

[43] Haemstede, *Geschiedenisse*, p. 428.

[44] Pettegree, *Emden and the Dutch Revolt*, ch. 4. Alastair Duke, 'Salvation by coercion: the controversy surrounding the "inquisition" in the Low Countries on the eve of the Revolt', in his *Reformation and Revolt*, pp. 152–74.

different. What one senses, and this is equally true of either France or the Netherlands, is the sheer ungovernability of the Calvinist movement. The increasingly provocative behaviour of members of the small Dutch churches was by no means controlled and directed by the leaders of the movement. The ministers and lay leaders of the movement, particularly those like Calvin established in the exile churches abroad, on the whole had grave misgivings about open provocation of this nature. Calvin on several occasions advised the fledgling churches in France against acts of iconoclasm, or wanton provocation of the local Catholic authorities.[45] But nearer to the seat of action such advice was increasingly ignored, not least by ordinary lay members of the congregations acting on their own initiative. When a man like Carolus de Koninck returned from Emden and openly interrupted the celebration of Mass in his native Ghent, this was an entirely individual and largely spontaneous decision.[46] But it was from such acts, and the failure of the local authorities to preserve the social consensus for the execution of exemplary punishment on such miscreants, that the Dutch Revolt essentially emerged.

It was with this sense of individual initiative and responsibility that Calvinism succeeded in recovering some of the initial spirit of the Reformation. If Luther's preaching was in its inner core a call to Christians to remake their own individual relationship with a merciful God, by the church-building phase of the 1540s the movement had lost much of this vitality. Calvinism's stress on the responsibility of the individual within this providential framework restored much of its potency. For all that Calvinism was in one sense a collective experience, and the great surges of support depended to a large extent on the mentality of collective action, the first responses were always individual: the movements in France and the Netherlands ultimately grew out of individual decisions to defy and confront the established social norms. Early Calvinists had a clear intuitive sense of the importance of community, of how the solidarity

[45] See, for instance, his letters to the Brethren of Poitiers, 9 Sept. 1555 and to the church of Angers, 19 April 1556. *Letters of John Calvin*, trans. D. Constable, 4 vols (Edinburgh and Philadelphia, 1855-8), 3, pp. 223-5, 261-4.

[46] Haemstede, *Geschiedenisse*, pp. 417-19.

of the group could give strength to those making what was certainly in the first decades of church-building an aberrant cultural choice. But the protection of the group was generally available only when people had first taken a decisive step towards membership, abandoning the protection of normal social relations and often home, wealth, and safety into the bargain. In these situations the essential decision was truly an individual one, and often painful and hazardous.

This is a point brought home with great clarity when one turns to one of the great foundational texts of sixteenth-century Calvinism, the French *Histoire écclesiastique*. The *Histoire écclesiastique* was in effect the official history of the French Huguenot Church, compiled on the instruction of the French national synods during the 1560s and 1570s.[47] The account of the foundation of the first Calvinist church in Paris in this volume celebrates what was at one level obviously a collective act, but it still depended crucially on the initiative of two individuals, the Sieur de la Ferrière, whose need to have his child baptized precipitated the church-forming, and Jean de la Rivière, who accepted the call to ministry. In fact to a large extent the account of the church's foundation is presented in the context of de la Rivière's personal journey towards an understanding of true religion. As he came to his perception of the truth de la Rivière was forced to resist the blandishments of wealth, position, and family fealty, finally accepting a total breach with his father as the price of following his calling: 'But God used these means, wishing that La Rivière, who was twenty-two years old, should quit the earthly home of his carnal father, to build a spiritual home in Paris and build there a church which has been one of the greatest and most flourishing.'[48] Presented in the language of manifest destiny and calling, the account in this *Histoire* does not dissemble that this was a hugely painful individual choice.

[47] *Histoire écclesiastique des églises réformées au royaume de France*, G. Baum, E. Cunitz, and R. Reuss, eds, 3 vols (Paris, 1883–9). The first edition was published in 1580.

[48] Extract of the *Histoire écclesiastique* translated in Alastair Duke, Gillian Lewis, and Andrew Pettegree, eds, *Calvinism in Europe, 1540–1610. A Collection of Documents* (Manchester, 1992), pp. 66–7.

But it was with this sense of the possibilities of individual action that Calvinism was at its most disruptive and destructive. Liberating the individual to act according to the dictates of a providential destiny was to free potentially ungovernable forces, even in a movement with as strong a sense of central organization as Calvinism. This is certainly the feeling one has when considering the events leading to the outbreak of religious warfare in France. It is hard to say that by 1561 any member of the Calvinist hierarchy was in control of events; certainly not Calvin, who still stubbornly held to his strategy of political loyalism and conversion of the higher nobility. The work of scholars such as Philip Benedict, who have demonstrated the extent to which Calvinism had rendered major political centres such as Rouen virtually ungovernable by this time, explodes the older view of the French Wars as a product of Court faction effectively manipulating the religious movements for its own ends.[49] Rather, in both France and the Netherlands, one has a sense that the natural leaders of society on both sides were largely powerless in the face of a movement that had taken on a momentum of its own.[50] It was in precisely these years that the Calvinists' providential sense of destiny, nurtured through the long years of preparation in exile, was at its strongest: they thought they would win, and events seemed to be bearing them out. Even Calvin caught the tone in his own comments on events. Consider this as a reaction to the sudden death of Francis II in December 1560, an event which did in truth tip the scales decisively against the Catholic Guide faction at the French court:

> Did you ever read or hear of anything more opportune than the death of the King? The evils had reached an extremity for which there was no remedy, when all of a sudden God shows himself from heaven. He who

---

[49] Benedict, *Rouen during the Wars of Religion*, pp. 49–122.
[50] Willem Nijenhuis, 'The limits of civil disobedience in Calvin's last known sermons: development of his ideas on the right of civil resistance', in his *Ecclesia Reformata. Studies on the Reformation*, 2 (Leiden, 1994), pp. 73–94.

pierced the eye of the father [that is, Henry II], has now struck the ear of the son.[51]

It was an unanswerable analysis of events which did seem, after years of trial and tribulation, to be turning decisively in the Calvinists' direction. And one needs to understand how strong this triumphalist sense of manifest destiny was in order to make sense of events in this turbulent decade of Calvinist advance. Studying the Netherlands, I have been repeatedly struck by how unamenable the communities were to the process of normal political compromise; how little they were prepared, in 1566 for instance, to give in order to preserve the political alliance with the Confederate nobility.[52] This absence of a sense of *Realpolitik* was both a strength and a weakness, but it was only possible because of a mental culture which admitted of no half measures. They really thought they were going to win.

Of course this moment was fleeting; it hardly survived the end of the first war in France, and the massacre of St Bartholomew's Day dealt it a terrible blow. In the Netherlands the responsibilities of church building after 1572 brought Dutch Calvinists face to face with the realities of office and the compromises necessary in a pluralist society.[53] I would not for a moment claim that the culture of this mature Calvinism was to the same extent shaped by the same imperatives that I believe were crucial in the decade of expansion.

But something of the old spirit remained. This was true I think particularly of what I might call the minority imperative. The argument thus far may have led to the conclusion (and it is certainly something that I am increasingly convinced of in my own developing understanding of Calvinism as a religious movement) that there were factors in the psyche of Calvinism which made it particularly appropriate as the creed of an aggressive religious minority in

---

[51] Duke, Lewis, and Pettegree, *Calvinism in Europe: Documents*, p. 80.

[52] Pettegree, *Emden and the Dutch Revolt*, pp. 109–46.

[53] A. Th. van Deursen, *Bavianen en Slijkgeuzen. Kerk en kerkvolk ten tijde van Maurits en Oldenbarnevelt* (Assen, 1974).

positions of adversity: a strong sense of providential destiny, an easy accommodation of trial and adversity. The reverse side of this was that it was by no means easy to make the psychological adjustment to positions of power and prosperity.

This problem of psychological adjustment might be labelled – as I have labelled it elsewhere – the problem of 'Coming to terms with Victory'.[54] The establishment of settled churches in the Netherlands was a sort of victory, but it also involved painful compromises, not least in recognizing a role for the lay authorities and an obligation to members of society who would not necessarily join the churches. For ministers and layfolk used to the comparative freedoms of exile, this brought new emotional, and ultimately theological, perplexities. For where were the elect to be found in a situation where all, or a high number, were able to attend the true Calvinist Church?

In this situation many Calvinists seem to have felt the need to recreate themselves as a minority. One sees something of this in Calvin himself: both his sermons and his correspondence are marked by a repeated tendency to see himself in an embattled minority, even when he was clearly the dominant voice in Geneva's councils. Perhaps it is in this framework that one should read his final deathbed address to his colleagues in Geneva, which can be seen either as a self-pitying lament, or an expression of this theological sense of the elect as a very small number.[55]

Perhaps this minority imperative is more common in sixteenth-century Protestantism than we recognize. The same phenomenon can certainly be observed for the religious writings of the reign of Edward VI, where Protestants found it extremely difficult to move from writings of an essentially destructive nature, excoriating the Mass, to church building, with its worrying responsibilities and inevitable compromises.[56] One can almost sense the relief with which some of

---

[54] 'Coming to terms with Victory: the upbuilding of a Calvinist church in Holland, 1572-1590', in Andrew Pettegree, Alastair Duke, and Gillian Lewis, eds, *Calvinism in Europe, 1540-1620* (Cambridge, 1994), pp. 160–80.

[55] Included with the *Letters of Calvin*, 4, pp. 373-7.

[56] Catharine Davies, ' "Poor persecuted little flock" or "Commonwealth of

the Protestant writers reverted to the language of the minority on the accession of Mary.

It seems to me that this sense of minority is particularly strong in Calvinism, which is what perhaps makes it potentially such a brooding, unrelenting psychology in places where Calvinist systems became entrenched. And perhaps this psychological need for minority has not been sufficiently recognized in modern use of these theological writings as sources. The sermon description of an unregenerate people resisting reform was a theological commonplace, not a historical analysis. This was certainly the spirit in which Calvin lambasted the citizens of Geneva. Take this extract, for instance, from his sermons on Micah:

> How sad it is nowadays there is among us more unbelief and impiety than has ever been seen before, and that this is so plain to be observed. In truth the Lord makes his Grace available to us in as much abundance as one could ask, but we trample it underfoot. . ... Everywhere around, there is nothing to be seen but blasphemies, scandals and ruin; the world is so disorderly that the impiety I can see in Geneva today is of such enormity that it is like seeing down a chasm into the very mouth of hell.[57]

Are we to take it that this was Calvin's considered view of a city he would soon come to dominate, intellectually and spiritually? Or is it more an indication of Calvin the preacher, whose perception of his own career, bearing the cross in obedience to God's will, demanded a continuing sense of adversity and oppression? Perhaps these are questions which those who use Calvin's letters and writings as sources for his ministry should ask more rigorously. Materials of this sort, where preachers lamented the hardness of their lot and the continuing unregenerate nature of the people to whom they preached are certainly

Christians": Edwardian Protestant concepts of the Church', in Lake and Dowling, *Protestantism and the National Church*, pp. 78–102.

[57] Duke, Lewis, and Pettegree, *Calvinism in Europe: Documents*, p. 33.

not, and should not be taken as, evidence of the 'failure' of the Reformation.[58]

If Calvinists thus sought continually to reinvent themselves as a minority, perhaps this was a reflection of the fact that this was how they had been at their most successful. And in this their sense of their own place in the scheme of sacred history played a crucial role. Members of the churches found much in Scripture of comfort to a church which was self-evidently a minority. Here it was significant that the New Testament provided in the Church of the apostles and early Church models of church practice and organization entirely appropriate for the small secret congregations struggling to develop a model of community life in a hostile, Catholic world. But the Old Testament was also not without helpful and encouraging lessons, for the Old Testament too is characterized by a progressive narrowing of the people of God, from the People of Israel, to Judah, to the remnant in exile.[59] Notwithstanding the common Protestant identification with the people of Israel, early Calvinists could identify equally with this exile experience, and take comfort from the repeated waves of Old Testament history, where every reverse was followed by a period of retrenchment and restoration.

But if sacred history provided the models of church organization, and a source of encouragement in adversity, one must look elsewhere, I think, for the theological inspiration behind the restless activism which is so characteristic of Calvinism in this first phase of its emergence as a dynamic international movement. This, I believe, derives from other elements in their culture. Some of this is fundamental to Protestantism generally, since the doctrine of justification by faith is, at one level, inevitably a sanctification of individual action based on an immediate relationship between God and the individual Christian. To the extent that

---

[58] Gerald Strauss, 'Success and failure in the German Reformation', *P&P*, 67 (May, 1975), pp. 30–63; idem, *Luther's House of Learning: Indoctrination of the Young in the German Reformation* (Baltimore, 1978); Christopher Haigh, 'Anticlericalism and the English Reformation', in his *The English Reformation Revised* (Cambridge, 1987), pp. 56–74.

[59] A point made to me in conversation by my colleague in St Andrews, Bruce Gordon.

this relationship introduced new obligations which could on occasion subvert and cut across normal social relationships and obligations, this was a doctrine of great potency; and it could be argued that the history of Luther's later years saw him desperately attempting to repair the breaches in the social fabric caused by his own initial theological bombshell.[60] Calvinism's potency as a historical force lay partly in the fact that it embraced once again a social context of individual theological action, allied to a sense of providential partisanship which made light of persecution and minority status. Therein lay the movement's revolutionary quality, and its potential for social disruption. 'To suffer persecution for righteousness' sake is a singular comfort', wrote Calvin, a message echoed in the dramatized, stylized narratives of the martyrologists. Calvinism's strength lay in the fact that so many ordinary men and women acted as if they believed this to be literally true; and that their sacrifice was perceived as a staging post to ultimate victory.

St Andrews Reformation Studies Institute

---

[60] For the conservatism of the 'later' Luther see particularly Mark Edwards, *Luther and the False Brethren* (Stanford, 1975); idem, *Luther's Last Battles, Politics and Polemics, 1531–46* (Leiden, 1983).

'BY THIS MARK YOU SHALL KNOW HIM': CLERICAL CELIBACY AND ANTICHRIST IN ENGLISH REFORMATION POLEMIC

by HELEN L. PARISH

'Antichrist', wrote William Tyndale in 1528, 'is not an outward thyng, that is to say a man that should sode[n]ly appear with wonders as our fathers talked of him. No, verely, for Antichrist is a spirituall thing. And this is as much to say as agaynst Christ, ye one that preacheth against Christ.'[1] Such a definition of Antichrist marked a departure from the traditional medieval legend, which was based upon the prophecy of a single future figure of evil.[2] This new image of Antichrist as a permanent and spiritual presence in the world is a central feature of English Protestant polemic, informing interpretations of both biblical prophecies, and the history of the Church. It was not history which engendered right understanding of Scripture, but Scripture that offered the means of interpreting the past. The Bible offered paradigms for the understanding of history because it was the embodiment of divine truth, which was irreproachable and immutable. In the words of John Bale, 'yet is the text a light to the chronicles, and not the chronicles to the text'.[3]

If Antichrist did not have to be equated with an individual yet to come, the term could be applied by Protestant polemicists to cover not only individuals, including the pope and Mohammed, but also their followers, the company of the reprobate, throughout history. The body of the Church, it

[1] William Tyndale, *Parable of the Wicked Mammon*, in John Foxe, ed., *Whole Works of W. Tyndale, John Frith, and Doctor Barnes* (London, 1573) [hereafter *WW*], p. 60.
[2] Bullinger suggested that the medieval legend actually concealed the working of Antichrist in the Church: Heinrich Bullinger, *Of the end of the world, and iudgement of our Lord Jesus Christ to come*, trans. T. Potter (London, *c.* 1580), fol. 4r; Richard Bauckham, *Tudor Apocalypse: Sixteenth Century Apocalypticism, Millennarianism, and the English Reformation from John Bale to John Foxe and Thomas Brightman*, Courtenay Library of Reformation Classics, 8 (Sutton Courtenay, 1978), p. 99.
[3] John Bale, *Image of Both Churches* (London, 1550), sig. Aii*.

was suggested, had been corrupted by the working of the so-called 'mystery of iniquity', leading to the introduction of false doctrine and reflected in moral degeneracy. The true faith had been preserved among a persecuted minority, an invisible Church which existed alongside the visible, false Church throughout time.[4] Church history was therefore perceived as a permanent, dualistic conflict between this group and those who adhered to the faith of Christ, and reformation, or separation from the visible Church, was justified by reference to the word of God in Scripture.

The ability to identify the followers of truth and falsehood throughout history was central to the arguments of Reformation polemicists, given the fact that the true Church was by nature an invisible institution. With the identification of Antichrist as spiritual, the defining characteristics of the two Churches were moral and doctrinal; membership of one Church or the other was not institutional, but ideological and historical. It was continuity of faith, not of the visible edifice, which revealed the origins of a Church. As Tyndale wrote in reply to Thomas More, 'not all they that are of Israell are Israelites, neither because they be Abraha[m]s sede, are they all Abrahams childre[n]: but onely that folow the faith of Abraham'.[5] Scripture was the constant which revealed both truth and falsehood, and history was exploited as a repository of moral examples to be used in the identification of manifestations of evil in the Church.

In attempting to relate this theory to the events of the past and circumstances of the present, Protestant polemicists turned in particular to one issue which could be shown to encompass aspects of both morality and doctrine associated with the false Church – the celibacy of the clergy. The identification of clerical celibacy as a mark of the false Church was executed at two levels. First, the issue could be related to the prophecies of Antichrist as the man of sin and the agent of doctrinal innovation, who would feign holiness in order to draw the faithful from Christ (II Timothy 3.1–9). Secondly,

---

[4] Ibid., sigs. Kiii[r], Kvii[r], Miii[v]; Tyndale, *Answer to More*, in *WW*, p. 412; Tyndale, *Wicked Mammon*, in *WW*, p. 60; George Joye, *Exposicion of Daniel the Prophete* (Geneva, 1545), sig. Qiii[r-v]; John Old, *A short description of Antichrist* (Emden, 1555), sig. Avii[r].
[5] Tyndale, *Answer to More*, in *WW*, p. 268.

the historical enforcement of celibacy on the priesthood offered reformers a chronological framework for the rise of Antichrist in the Roman Church and papacy. Both the forbidding of marriage to the clergy, and the moral degeneracy which was arguably the natural concomitant of such a prohibition, were employed in the consolidation of this image. At the most basic level, to deny marriage to the clergy was seen as an act of disobedience to the will of God. Marriage, Protestant writers argued, was a divinely instituted state, honoured by Christ's first miracle, and thus deserving of honour.[6] St Paul had warned against those who would forbid marriage and demand abstinence from meat, arguing such teaching to be the 'doctrine of devils'.[7] John Ponet, himself a married bishop, presented the reader with a stark choice on the basis of Paul's epistle:

The apostles taught one thyng: the byshop of Rome brought in another. Nowe iudge you whether it is beste for vs which professe to follow the Apostles of Christ, or the Romish Antichrist. The laws of God, whych wylleth bishopes and priests to mary: or the doctrine of the deuyll, as Paule calleth it, which forbyddeth theym marryge.[8]

If the members of the false Church were to be considered as those who condemned marriage, they were also to be marked by their hypocrisy in failing to adhere to the ideal of celibacy that they had established, and in using this feigned chastity to their own advantage. Again, the foundations of these assumptions were laid in Scripture. John Frith, referring specifically to the text of II Peter 2, alleged that the clergy of the false Church, mixing their traditions with the truth of the Gospel, would use their feigned holiness to spread evil.[9] The

---

[6] I Cor. 7. John Bale, *A Declaration of Edmund Bonner's Articles* (London, 1560), fols 6r, 16v; Heinrich Bullinger, *Golden Book of Christian Matrimony* (London, 1543), sig. Aii^v.

[7] I Tim. 4. Cf. Thomas Becon, *A Comfortable Epistle*, ed. J. Ayre, PS (Cambridge, 1844), p. 198; Bale, *Declaration*, fol. 11r.

[8] John Ponet, *A defence of the mariage of Preistes, by Scripture and Aunciente Wryters* (London, 1549), sig. Ci^r.

[9] John Frith, *A Pistle to the Christen Reader* (Antwerp, 1529), fol. 17r.

chastity of the clergy was a cloak behind which the corruption of the Church could be concealed. John Foxe warned that Antichrist would cultivate 'a sweete and amiable countenance of hypocritical holinesse, a counterfeit sincerite of unspotted life, yea outward resemblance of religion, therby to dazel more easily the eyes and heartes of the unlettered'. For John Bale, the extent of clerical hypocrisy was exemplified in the actions of Johannes Eck, whom he accused of fathering three children in the same year as he had condemned those clergy who would have allowed the breaking of vows of celibacy by marriage.[10]

Underlying the suggestion that clerical obedience to the rule of chastity was little more than a pretence, with the objective of appearing to be holy, was the argument that the clergy generally failed to keep to their vows, and the equation of such behaviour with that expected of members of the false Church. John Bale described the immorality of the kingdom of Antichrist, and traced the descent of such behaviour among the members of the false Church in a line which could be drawn from the devil through the Sodomites, Ishmael, Bel, Baal, and Judas. Moral and theological corruption were coterminous. Bale wrote of the Catholic clergy 'beastly are they in their doctrine and living',[11] and there appeared little doubt as to the symbiotic relationship between debauchery and the false Church. The daily incidences of clerical immorality, Frith argued, proved that Satan, embodied in the papacy, must be the author of the decree which had prohibited marriage to the clergy.[12]

Both the exaltation of the celibate ideal over the state of marriage, and the alleged failure of the clergy to keep to their vows of chastity were clearly central in the identification of the Roman Church as the false Church. By depicting the fruits of vows of celibacy as evidence of the devilish origins of the prohibition of marriage to the clergy, Protestant

[10] John Bale, *Yet a course at the Romish Fox* (Zurich, 1543), sig. Ivi'. For a similar argument, against Cardinal John of Cremona, see Ponet, *Defence*, sigs Cviii'-Di', Aiv'; Joye, *Daniel*, sigs Sviii'-Ti', citing Oecolampadius.

[11] Bale, *Romish Fox*, sig. M1; Bale, *Mystery of Iniquity* (Geneva, 1545), fols 2r, 10v.

[12] Frith, *Pistle*, fols 53v-4r, 67r, 71v.

writers were able to treat such behaviour as symptomatic of the rise of Satan within the Catholic Church and the papacy. The roots of the argument lay in the assertion that Scripture alone contained all that was necessary to salvation. Since, it was argued,[13] the clergy of the early Church had been free to marry, the denial of marriage to the clergy was a form of doctrinal innovation which could be used to measure the extent of corruption in the teaching of the Catholic Church. Protestant polemicists interpreted Church history in a manner which gave new meaning to both the past and the present.

Varying chronologies for the rise of Satan in the Church were put forward. Praising Jerome for what he regarded as a rebuke to those who claimed that men who had taken a second wife after baptism should not be admitted to the priesthood, Tyndale wrote that Jerome's protest had been of no avail, since 'The God of Rome would not hear him. For Sathan began then to worke his misteries of wickedenes.'[14] Calvin also located the rise of Satan in the early centuries of the Church. The fact that the Catholic Church had perverted the true worship of God, teaching the 'doctrine of devils', was, he argued, testimony to the extent to which 'Satan's darkness generally prevailed' first among the heretics – the Cathars, Tatianists, and Montanists – and later among the very people who had at first condemned them.[15] Successive popes were seen to promulgate teachings that their predecessors, and the apostles, had condemned.

Biblical prophecies were a fertile hunting ground for writers looking to relate clerical celibacy to the rise of Antichrist. Especially significant in this context are two commentaries on Revelation which circulated in English in the sixteenth century: Bale's *Image of Both Churches* (1550), and Bullinger's *A Hundred Sermons upon the Apocalypse* (1561). Images in the Book of Revelation were applied to general and

---

[13] Ponet, *Defence*, sigs Avi[v], Bv[r-v]: Martin Bucer, *Gratulation* (London, 1549), sigs Evii[r], Fiii[v].

[14] Tyndale, *Answer to More*, in *WW*, p. 310.

[15] John Calvin, *The Second Epistle of Paul the Apostle to the Corinthians, and the Epistles to Timothy, Titus, and Philemon*, ed. D. W. and T. F. Torrance (Edinburgh, 1964), p. 261; John Calvin, *The First Epistle of Paul to the Corinthians*, ed. W. D. Torrance (Edinburgh, 1960), p. 134.

specific aspects of Church history. Bale argued that the first horse symbolized the purity of the Church in the age of the apostles, and was ridden by Christ to defeat the forces of Antichrist.[16] The opening of the second seal revealed the state of the Church after the apostles, and the introduction of new laws and rituals which departed from the teaching of Christ. The issue of clerical celibacy was used to define this age, since during this period, Bale argued, 'some people forbade marriage as an vncleane thynge, to bring in all abhominacions and fylthynesse'.[17] In Bale's interpretation the dawning of the sixth age was revealed in monastic practice and ritual, while the sounding of the sixth trumpet offered release from the bondage inflicted upon the clergy 'yoked with vnaduised vowes'.[18] After the opening of the sixth seal, and the darkening of the sun, the people took to the mountains hiding in caves. Bullinger identified the caves as monasteries, from which the monks would flee when they realised that their celibate lives counted for nothing before God, and Bale argued that after this time the working of Antichrist would cease, with the result that the clergy would have to lay aside their vows of chastity.[19]

The appearance of the dragon (Revelation 12) offered Bale the opportunity to elaborate upon the theme of the persecution of the true Church, and the corruption of the false.[20] As the persecution of the dragon was marked by the forbidding of marriage, so the authority of the beast would be marked by moral degeneracy, as was evident among the clergy.[21] Part three of Bale's commentary covered the last chapters of Revelation, which described the fall of Babylon. Its immoral inhabitants were identified by Bale with the cardinals, bishops, priests, and religious of the Catholic

[16] Bale, *Image*, sig. Ji[r–v]; cf. Rev. 6.2.

[17] Ibid., sig. Kii[r–v]. The forbidding of marriage, along with the introduction of relics, fasts, and the doctrine of purgatory, was also used to identify the inception of the period of the black horse, epitomized for Bale in the pontificate of Boniface III: ibid., sigs Kviii[v]–Li[v].

[18] Bale, *Image*, sigs Rii[v], Rviii[r], Siii[r]; Bale, *Romish Fox*, sig. Civ[v]; Frith, *Pistle*, fol. 46v. Cf. Rev. 9.20–1.

[19] Heinrich Bullinger, *A Hundred Sermons upon the Apocalypse* (London, 1561), sig. Qii[r–v]; Bale, *Image*, sig. Niv[v]. Cf. Rev.7.

[20] Bale, *Image*, sigs Eiii[r]–Fvi[r].

[21] Ibid., sigs Fviii[v]–Giii[r].

Church, who would receive a due punishment for their misdemeanours. The faithful would follow the call to leave Babylon (identified with the Church of Rome), on the grounds that 'whilest the Church of rome hath prohibited lawful marriages and of God permitted to ecclesiastical persones, it hath opened the gates to fornicators, adulteries, whoredomes, and lusts abhominable'. 'There nede no words', Bullinger wrote of the same text, 'the thing it self speaketh.'[22]

Once the connection between clerical celibacy and key passages of Revelation had been established, these images were applied to the history of the Church. Individual popes and historical events, particularly the prohibition of clerical marriage, were seen as the fulfilment of the prophecies of Revelation. Among the popes, it was Silvester II and Gregory VII who were most commonly blamed for the enforcement of compulsory celibacy upon the clergy, and allowing Antichrist to occupy the papal throne and spread false doctrine. Philip Melanchthon, condemning the 'deuillish decrees' that had forbidden marriage to the clergy, attributed their spread to the labours of Gregory VII; and Rudolph Gualter referred to Gregory as 'the hellhounde hildebrande, called Gregorie the .7. the varlet of all wickednesse and mischief'.[23] Bullinger, commenting on Revelation 20.7-10, which dealt with the loosing of Satan, described the signs by which it would be known that this time had been reached. The Gospel, he claimed, would have a place in the world until the year 1073, the start of the pontificate of Gregory VII. The confirmation of the loosing of Satan at this time lay in the enforcement of celibacy upon the priesthood. Whereas it had once been honoured, Bullinger claimed, 'holy matrimony waxed vile after those thousande yeres, in so much that ministers of the Church were prohibited to marry. Then waxed whoredom rife, rape, and aduoutrie.'[24] Similar descriptions featured in the works of English writers. Denouncing

---

[22]   Bale, *Image*, sigs Av^r-Avi^v; Bullinger, *Sermons*, sig. Mmi^r. Cf. William Turner, *A New Book of Spiritual Physick* (Basle, 1555), sig. Lv^v.

[23]   Philip Melanchthon, *A Very Godly Defence. . . defending the marriage of preistes* (Antwerp, 1541), sig. Biv^v; Rudolph Gualter, *Antichrist: that is to saye A true reporte that Antichriste is come* (Southwark, 1556), sigs L2v-L3r.

[24]   Bullinger, *Sermons*, sig. Ssi^{r-v}.

Gregory VII's insistence on clerical celibacy, John Pilkington distorted the name Hildebrand to 'Hell-brand', as did Foxe, who also referred to him as 'the soldier of Satan', noting that the beast of Revelation had now appeared.[25] The association of celibacy with false holiness allowed Bale to attack Gregory VII on the same grounds. The devil, he claimed, had 'practised craftelye to ouerthrowe the name of Christ by this counterfaite monke, vnder the colour of religion'. Gregory, Bale stated, had held a synod in Rome with the Italian bishops, at which clerical marriage was prohibited, although Bale noted that this did not forbid the clergy from begetting children. By the work of 'this hellish Hildebrand', he argued, the clergy were elevated to the status of angels, although they were in fact 'the drose of the deuyll and poyson of all Christyanyte'.[26]

Bale's denunciation of Gregory VII included the allegation that he was guilty of necromancy, and that this could be associated with his actions against clerical marriage. 'For holy pope Hildebrande', Bale wrote in 1545 'which was a necromanser made this constitution / that non shuld be admitted to holye orders / vnlesse he foreoreware marriage for the terms of his lyfe'.[27] This association was far from accidental. Bale had drawn the same parallel between celibacy and witchcraft in *Romish Fox* and in *The Pageant of Popes*.[28] Tyndale had suggested in 1531 that the papacy, rather than sanction clerical marriage, gave the clergy licences to keep whores and practise necromancy.[29] The argument had even greater effect when applied to the pontificate of Silvester II, which spanned the year 1000 and coincided with the chronology of the loosing of Satan in the Book of Revelation. Silvester II had certainly been noted for his interest in magic during his lifetime, and Bale exploited this to great advantage. Silvester was credited both with the loosing of Satan, and with the prohibition of clerical marriage; and there was

---

[25] John Pilkington, *A Confutation of an Addicion*, PS (Cambridge, 1842), pp. 564–5; Foxe, *Acts and Monuments*, 2, p. 120.

[26] John Bale, *The Pageant of Popes* (London, 1574), sig. Lii[v]; John Bale, *The Actes of the Englysh Votaries*, pt II (London, 1561), fols 32v–4v.

[27] Bale, *Mystery*, fol. 17v.

[28] Bale, *Romish Fox*, sig. Kiii[r]; idem, *Pageant*, sig. Lii[r].

[29] Tyndale, *Answer to More*, in *WW*, p. 115.

no doubt in the mind of Bale that the two were related. Clerical marriage, he argued, had been accepted in the primitive Church, and had continued to be so, 'tyll Syulvester the .2. ded fatche the deuyll from hell by his necromancye (where he was a fore tyed vp for a thousande years)'.[30] The Book of Revelation offered the key to the interpretation of such events. By relating the events and dates of Silvester's pontificate with the schematic structure of Revelation, Bale was able to verify simultaneously both the assertion that it was Silvester who had conjured up the devil from the pit, and the correlation between clerical celibacy and the false teaching of Antichrist.[31] This argument had the additional advantage that it offered a point from which the start of the process of theological corruption in the Church could be dated.

The pace at which evil was seen to spread in the Church was not uniform. Indeed English Protestant polemicists, and Bale in particular, argued that the English Church had existed uncorrupted for centuries before the arrival of Catholicism with Augustine. From the perspective of the 1540s, English Church history acquired a new interpretation and significance, but one which was once again informed by scriptural prophecy. Bale's *The Actes of the Englysh Votaries* was composed with the aim of providing details of the historical deeds of the English clergy, almost entirely in relation to the origins and consequences of their vows of celibacy. Originally intended to run to four volumes, only the first two were completed; but these, despite diatribe and exaggeration, reflect the emergence of a new understanding of history, and of the history of England in particular. The work dealt with the perceived corruption of the English Church, at a late stage, by the introduction of Roman theology and practice under Augustine. England had received Christianity, Bale argued, from Joseph of Arimathea, a married man who had

---

30 Bale, *Romish Fox*, fol. 16v. Cf a similar allegation made against John XIII, Bale, *Pageant*, sigs Iii', Iviii', Lii', Liii', Zvi'; idem, *Image*, sigs Kviii'-Li'; idem, *Mystery*, fols 16v, 58r. Bale was the first English writer to emphasize the pontificate of Silvester II in providing a chronology for the working of the mystery of iniquity.

31 John Foxe followed Bale in accusing Silvester and Hildebrand of necromancy, although he did not overtly associate their insistence on clerical celibacy with such practices: *Acts and Monuments*, 2, pp. 94–5, 119–21, 125, 128.

arrived in the country in AD 63, long before the mission of Augustine.[32] With the arrival of Augustine, it was argued, the votaries had laboured 'to prepare Antichriste a seate here in England, agaynst the full tyme of his perfight age of .666.'[33] Bale identified this year with the consecration of Theodore of Tarsus, under whom the preparations for the reign of Antichrist were completed, although on this occasion he sacrificed accuracy to the overall scheme of his historical interpretation. In fact Theodore had not been consecrated until 668, but the polemical potential of the date 666, when equated with Revelation 13.18, the prophecy of the beast, was too great to miss.[34]

The doctrine and practice of the English Church had continued to deteriorate after that date, especially with the approach of the crucial year 1000. Bale's account of Silvester II's pontificate was paralleled by events in England, where the rise of Antichrist within the Church was evident in the actions of Dunstan. Bale alleged that when Dunstan had visited Rome, he 'there receyued therwith for a great summe of money, autoryte & power of the Beast [Revelation 13] vtterly to dyssolue prestes maryage, that hys monkes by that means myght possess the cathedrall churches of Englande'.[35] Thus in England, as in the papacy, the release of Satan, and his false doctrine, were revealed by the enforcement of clerical celibacy. Bale told how the introduction of clerical celibacy in England had been accompanied by stars falling from the heavens, a supernatural sign.[36] The falling stars of Revelation 6.13 had accompanied the breaking of the sixth seal, and were traditionally seen as the concomitants of the day of Yahweh (Amos 8.9). Basing his account on the images

---

[32] Bale, *Votaries*, I, sigs Av^v-vi^r, Biv^v, Cvii^v; Rainer Pineas, 'William Tyndale's influence on John Bale's polemical use of history', *ARG*, 53 (1962), p. 86.

[33] Bale, *Votaries*, I, sig. Dviii^r.

[34] Ibid., I, sig. Eii^v. Bale must have known that his chronology was mistaken, since Bede clearly dated Theodore's consecration to 668; L. P. Fairfield, *John Bale, Mythmaker for the English Reformation* (West Lafayette, Ind., 1976), p. 98, n.46. Foxe accepted the significance of the year 666, the time at which Theodore had brought Roman religion to England, but regarded Mohamet as the beast: *Acts and Monuments*, 1, p. 355.

[35] Bale, *Votaries*, I, sig. Hv^r; idem, *Mystery*, fol. 19r. Cf. Foxe, *Acts and Monuments*, 2, p. 68.

[36] Bale, *Votaries*, I, sig. Fii_v.

of Revelation, Bale claimed that Dunstan had expelled the married clerks from Worcester, and replaced them with the 'layse lean locustes which not longe afore had leaped out of the bottomless pytt',[37] the locusts referred to in Revelation 9.7. It was by no accident that Bale concluded the first part of the work, the 'rising' of the clergy, with the date 1000.

Despite the fact that the *Actes of the Englysh Votaries* was never completed, the theory which underpinned Bale's interpretation of history had important implications for the Protestant understanding of contemporary events. If the sixth seal had already been broken, unleashing the battle between the forces of good and evil, then the progress of the Reformation in England and Europe could be understood in relation to the same images of Revelation. Contemporary events revealed the extent of the influence of Antichrist in the Church but, more importantly, the prophecies of the Bible offered an explanation for these events and the means of identifying the chief protagonists as members of either the true Church or the false. Given the consistent assertion that the two Churches were to be separated by their teaching on marriage, it is not surprising that the issue of clerical celibacy, and its enforcement in the Act of Six Articles, attracted the attention of Protestant polemicists. Stephen Gardiner, seen as the driving force behind the Six Articles, was regarded by George Joye as the chief agent of Antichrist in England; while Bale compared him with Nemroth, and his supporters with the citizens of Gomorra.[38] Echoing the association between clerical celibacy and witchcraft, William Turner accused Stephen Gardiner of necromancy and equated his actions with the later deeds of Antichrist.

The application of such images to the king was more problematical. The early exiles appeared to pin their hopes upon opening the eyes of Henry VIII to the deeds of his prelates and ministers, but their works contain asides and references which reveal a deeper dissatisfaction. George Joye, in a discussion of clerical marriage in his *Exposicion of Daniel*, issued the warning that 'siche forbidders of wedlok shall

37 Ibid., fol. 67v.
38 Bale, *Image*, I, sig. Bi[r]; cf. idem, *Mystery*, fols 40v, 66v.

neuer haue good sucesse and fortune in their owne mary-ages'.[39] The warning could hardly have been directed towards the celibate priesthood; and placed in the context of the 1540s it is likely that Joye was alluding to Henry VIII's own marital difficulties. The marriage to Anne of Cleves had been annulled in 1540, and Katherine Howard was found guilty of adultery in 1541. Such was the judgement of God upon Henry's failure to effect a total break with the teachings of the Church of Antichrist. Bale, discussing clerical celibacy in 1543, filled his margins with references to Old Testament figures whom he regarded as members of the false Church. By enforcing the Six Articles, Henry VIII was seen to have allied himself with the false Church; and references to Deuteronomy 28 and II Samuel 12 made the comparison more explicit. The recent contempt shown for marriage in England, both in the prohibition of clerical marriage and by the King himself, Bale suggested, cast Henry in the role of Nathan, threatening the posterity of the house of David by his adultery with Bathsheba.[40] Scriptural types were employed both to assess the progress of reform, and to pass comment upon its failure.

Drawing upon the argument that the devil had always laboured to destroy marriage, William Turner claimed that Satan had been resisted by members of the early Church. He had therefore approached 'hys vicare in erth the bishop of rom', whom he persuaded to destroy matrimony and 'alow comon stewes', promising the pope great riches in return. Yet again, however, Satan was thwarted, this time by the 'Germans', who recognized compulsory clerical celibacy as the doctrine of devils and encouraged Henry VIII to reject the authority of the pope on these grounds. However, just as Henry moved to destroy the last remnants of papistry in the kingdom, he was persuaded by Satan to retain the prohibition on the marriage of priests.[41]

Greater force was added to the argument by drawing parallels between events in England and specific images in

[39]   Joye, *Daniel*, sig. eiii^r.
[40]   Bale, *Romish Fox*, sig. Kiii^{r-v}.
[41]   William Turner, *Rescuynge of the Romishe Fox* (Bonn, 1545), sigs Hviii^r–Hviii^v; idem, *Huntyng of the Romyshe Wolfe* (Emden, ?1555), sig. Evi^{r-v}.

Revelation. Where Turner had loosely identified the prohibition of clerical marriage with the influence of Antichrist, Bale
related the progress of reform in England to the text of
Revelation 13, the wounding of the beast. The evidence that
the progress of reformation in England was not yet complete
– that the beast had been wounded and not killed – lay in the
survival of papist practices, 'Jewyshe ceremonies, theyr
priestybulouse priesthode, their vowing to haue no wiues,
their Sodomiticall chastitye'.[42] While the Six Articles reflected
the extent to which the 'kingdom of the whore' survived in
England, the forces of opposition, the true preachers of the
Gospel, were equated with the ten horns on the head of the
beast of Revelation 17.16.[43] The influence of the pope in
England, and the doctrine and practice of those who adhered
to his faith, acted as a mirror which reflected prophecies of
the workings of Antichrist in the world, and placed
contemporary events in the overall historical scheme.

For early Protestant polemicists, clerical celibacy was the
ideal mark by which to separate the two Churches, and
cement the identification of the Catholic Church as the
Church of Antichrist. Arguments against doctrinal innovation, the elevation of tradition over Scripture, and clerical
hypocrisy or immorality could be grounded in reality by
reference to the compulsory celibacy of the clergy, both in its
acceptance and transgression. From the well-illustrated
premiss that the forbidding of marriage was the doctrine of
the devil, the working of Antichrist in the world was
chronicled in the creation of a celibate priesthood. In terms of
the identification of periods of human history with the divine
plan revealed to the prophets, the fact that the forbidding of
clerical marriage could be fixed chronologically was clearly
important. The identification of clerical celibacy as a mark of
the Antichrist was therefore instrumental in the development
of a specifically Protestant interpretation and understanding
of both the past and present, one which could be verified by

---

[42]   Bale, *Image*, sigs Gv^v–Gvi^v.
[43]   Ibid., sigs Svii^v–Sviii^r. Bale's identification of the horns which had already
been revealed appeared to reflect his pessimism regarding events in England, since
while the King of Denmark and the Duke of Saxony were included in the list, Henry
VIII was not.

Scripture. By reference to this one teaching, it could be demonstrated that the pope was indeed Antichrist, that, since the pontificate of Gregory VII at the latest, the Roman Church had fallen prey to the influence of Satan, and that the Reformation was justified according to the injunction of Revelation 18.4. The restoration of clerical marriage would be a sign of a complete Reformation, and from this, the purity of the Church in England in periods as diverse as the first century and the sixteenth could be gauged, and the influence of Antichrist measured. No wonder then, that the English martyr John Hooper wrote of compulsory clerical celibacy that it was 'the true mark to know Antichrist by'.[44]

Jesus College, Oxford

---

[44] Hooper, *A Brief and Clear Confession* in *The Later Writings of Bishop Hooper*, ed. C. Nevinson, *PS* (Cambridge, 1852), p. 56.

THE IMPORTANCE OF DYING EARNESTLY:
THE METAMORPHOSIS OF THE ACCOUNT OF
JAMES BAINHAM IN 'FOXE'S BOOK OF MARTYRS'*

by THOMAS S. FREEMAN

Readers of the second edition of John Foxe's *Acts and Monuments*, or any of the subsequent editions of that massive history of the persecutions inflicted on the Church, popularly known as 'Foxe's Book of Martyrs', would have found a coherent, lucid description, filled with circumstantial and often dramatic details, of the ordeals of James Bainham. According to this account, James Bainham, a member of the Middle Temple and the son of a Gloucestershire knight, was accused of heresy in 1531, arrested, and transported to Lord Chancellor More's house in Chelsea. There he was tied to a tree in More's garden and whipped; subsequently he was taken to the Tower and racked in More's presence. Eventually, after repeated interrogations and under the threat of burning, Bainham abjured and did penance at Paul's Cross. Yet Bainham's conscience tormented him and, a little over a month after his release, he prayed for God's forgiveness before an evangelical congregation, meeting secretly in a warehouse in Bow Lane. A week later, Bainham stood up on his pew in St Austin's church, clutching a vernacular New Testament and William Tyndale's *Obedience of a Christian Man* to his chest and tearfully declared that he had denied God. He prayed for the congregation's forgiveness and exhorted them to die rather than to submit as he had done. If this defiance was not sufficiently public, Bainham sent letters proclaiming his doctrinal convictions to the Bishop of London and others. Rearrested and re-examined, he was inevitably condemned to death as a relapsed heretic. While being burned, he cried out from the stake: 'O ye Papistes, beholde, ye looke for miracles, and here now ye

* I am grateful to Maurice D. Lee, William Connell, and Susan Wabuda for their valuable comments on earlier versions of the paper.

267

may see a miracle, for in this fire I feele no more payne then if I were in a bed of roses.'[1]

It is ironically appropriate that art historians have discovered that the famous Holbein portrait of Bainham's nemesis, Sir Thomas More, was retouched and repainted a number of times before the serene visage of the humanist and statesman was created. For if the narrative of Bainham's martyrdom in the second (1570) edition of the *Acts and Monuments* is compared with the narrative of the same event which had appeared in the first (1563) edition of Foxe's book, significant discrepancies and contradictions appear between them. If these differences, moreover, are thoroughly examined, it becomes clear that Foxe's portrait of Bainham, like Holbein's portrait of More, was repeatedly redrawn and retouched before the desired and superficially authoritative version was created. At the same time, detailed study of these accounts and of the sources for them casts considerable light on the *Acts and Monuments*, and on some of the particular problems involved in trying to recapture and depict the Church's past.

Foxe's first description of Bainham's martyrdom appeared in the *Rerum in ecclesia gestarum* of 1559, after he had fled England during Mary's reign. In this brief account, Foxe stated that George Baynam (sic), a lawyer, was burned at Bishop Stokesley's behest, in 1532, for denying the existence of purgatory and attacking the cult of St Thomas Becket. Foxe also provided a graphic and horrifying description of Bainham's fiery end, emphasizing the martyr's constancy and patience. A striking aspect of this description is Foxe's claim that Bainham died holding a book in his arms.[2]

This terse narrative was considerably enlarged in the first edition of the *Acts and Monuments*, published less than four years after the *Rerum* had appeared. After mentioning Bainham's background and describing his arrest by Thomas

---

1   John Foxe, *The Ecclesiastical History, contayning the Actes and Monuments of Thyngs passed in every kynges tyme in this realme especially in the Church of England...*, 2nd edn (London, 1570), pp. 1168–72. Hereafter each of the four editions of this work published in Foxe's lifetime will be designated by the year in which it was printed (i.e., Foxe, *1563*, Foxe, *1570*, Foxe, *1576*, and Foxe, *1583*). All of these editions were published by John Day in London.

2   John Foxe, *Rerum in ecclesia gestarum ... commentarii* (Basle, 1559), pp. 126–7.

More, Foxe related the stories of Bainham being whipped, and later racked, at the Lord Chancellor's command. All of this would be repeated in subsequent editions of the *Acts and Monuments*. What was unique to this edition, however, was a very brief account of Bainham's examinations, which concluded triumphantly that Stokesley and his officials 'were not able to resist him, he was both myghtie in the scriptures and argumentations, that he was able to confounde them with their owne argumentes and reasons'. Omitting any mention of Bainham's abjuration, Foxe went on to relate that Bainham was condemned to death, and presented a detailed account of his execution. This account, markedly different from that which would be published in subsequent editions, begins with an unsuccessful attempt by a Dr Simons, confronting Bainham in prison, to effect an eleventh-hour conversion of the heretic. Simons was directed by the sheriff to continue his efforts at the stake, but intimidated by the large crowd, he fled. Bainham prayed and embraced the stake. He then addressed the crowd, denouncing Thomas More for 'being both my accuser and judge'. The condemned man denied the existence of purgatory and the sanctity of Becket; he proclaimed that the Bishop of Rome was the Antichrist and the Scripture should be available in the vernacular. One 'Pave' (actually William Pavier, the Town Clerk of London) cried out that Bainham was a liar, and was trying to conceal the fact that he had also denied the sacrament of the altar. Bainham responded that he did not deny the sacrament as instituted by Christ and practised among the apostles, but he emphatically rejected transubstantiation. An enraged Pavier cried out for the fire to be lit under Bainham. As death and the flames approached, Bainham 'lifted up his eies and handes unto heaven, and said to Pave, God forgive thee and show thee more mercy than thou shewest to me, the Lorde forgeve sir Thomas More and pray for me al good people, and so praying til the fier took his bowels and his head, etc.' This narrative of Bainham's death was followed by a detailed account of William Pavier's suicide in the next year, which Foxe saw as divine retribution for the Town Clerk's conduct at Bainham's execution.[3]

---

[3] Foxe, *1563*, pp. 492–3.

With the most abrupt possible transition, in which Bainham's abjuration is mentioned for the first time (although it, and the circumstances in which it was made, are never described or explained), Foxe printed a list of articles (but not Bainham's answers) which were presented to Bainham when Stokesley examined him on 15 December 1531.

> All these articles aforesayde, he worthely defended and maintained before the said byshop, not only by sub-scribing his hand to the same, but also by sondrie notable quotations, sette downe with his own hande in the margent of the sayde byshoppes register, but alacke, the frayeltie of the flesh was suche, that through perswasion and feare the next day followyng, he did in a manner recant all the forsayde articles.

Foxe added that Bainham made a formal abjuration and did public penance. Foxe then printed documents which were part of the process against Bainham as a relapsed heretic – but did not, however, explain in this edition that Bainham had publicly renounced his abjuration. These documents included two interrogations of Bainham by Richard Foxford, the vicar-general of the diocese of London, as well as Foxford's condemnation of Bainham. With unusual precision, Foxe adds that Bainham was burned at 3 o'clock on the afternoon of 30 April 1532. In conclusion, Foxe asserted that Bainham was 'very cruelly handled' during his imprisonment, having been imprisoned in stocks in Stokesley's residence, chained to a post for two nights in More's house, and whipped in the Tower.[4]

This was not Foxe's last word on Bainham in this edition. Over 1,200 pages later, in 'The appendix or after notes belongyng to the volume of this history', Foxe first gave a varying account of Bainham's execution, in which the martyr declared that the spectators might behold a miracle, since he felt no more pain while being consumed by the flames than if he stood in a bed of roses.[5]

---

[4] Foxe, *1563*, pp. 493–5.
[5] Foxe, *1563*, p. 1703 [recte p. 1730].

Foxe made a number of major alterations to this material in the account of Bainham for the second edition of the *Acts and Monuments* seven years later in 1570. For one thing, all the material was placed in chronological order and shaped into a coherent, complete narrative. The brief account of Stokesley's examination of Bainham, which had emphasized Bainham's defiance and glossed over his abjuration, was replaced with a series of documents (transcripts of examinations of Bainham in December 1531 and the following February) which detailed Bainham's gradual retreat from his heretical positions and his reluctant submission.[6] Foxe also reprinted the questions put to Bainham on 15 December, but this time he added Bainham's answers.[7] An especially interesting addition to this new account was the description of Bainham's tortured conscience and his declarations of repentance before the congregations in Bow Lane and St Austin. This had been in the first edition of the *Acts and Monuments*, but there these actions had been attributed to John Tewkesbury, a London leatherseller who had also abjured, relapsed, and had been burned in 1531.[8] Another interesting change was the replacement of much of the original account of Bainham's death by that in the appendix of the first edition, with Bainham proclaiming that standing in the fire was like standing in a bed of roses.[9] Part of the original account of Bainham's execution, dealing with Pavier's angry exchange with him and his final prayer heaping burning coals on the heads of Pavier and More, was reprinted elsewhere in the *Acts and Monuments*, along with an account of Pavier's suicide taken from *Hall's Chronicle*.[10] The narrative of Bainham's martyrdom printed in the second edition was reprinted, essentially unchanged, in the two subsequent editions of the *Acts and Monuments* published during Foxe's lifetime.[11]

---

6 Foxe, *1570*, pp. 1169–70.
7 Foxe, *1570*, pp. 1168–9.
8 Foxe, *1570*, pp. 1170–1; also see Foxe, *1563*, p. 486.
9 Foxe, *1570*, p. 1172; compare Foxe, *1583*, pp. 492–3.
10 Foxe, *1570*, p. 1199. Also see Edward Hall, *The Union of the Two Noble and Illustre Famelies of Lancastre and Yorke*, ed. H. Ellis (London, 1809), p. 806.
11 Foxe, *1576*, pp. 999–1002, 1027; Foxe, *1583*, pp. 1027–30, 1055.

Having discussed how Foxe presented the information on Bainham which he had acquired, we have gained an understanding of when Foxe acquired it. Can this be extended into an understanding of Foxe's sources? It seems clear that John Bale was the source for the brief account of Bainham in the *Rerum*. First of all, Bale was not only Foxe's mentor, but during their exile in Basle, when the *Rerum* was written, he and Foxe lived in the same house.[12] Moreover, fifteen years before the *Rerum* was printed, Bale had anticipated Foxe's account by writing that Bainham was burned 'for [denying] purgatorye and for not allowinge Thomas Becket for a saynct'. Clinching the identification of Bale as Foxe's source is the fact that in repeated references to Bainham, he invariably calls him 'George' – the same error Foxe made in the *Rerum*.[13]

By 1563, Foxe had energetically added to the material Bale had given him but, in contrast to Foxe's usual practice, this new material was not incorporated into the text as a coherent narrative presented in chronological order. Instead, the account of Bainham in the first edition of the *Acts and Monuments* consists of four very imperfectly integrated sections. The obvious reason for this is that Foxe acquired some of his new information as that first edition was being printed, and inserted these items into the text as he discovered them. The first section is the narrative, beginning with a description of Bainham's background and character, which continues with a description of his mistreatment by More, and concludes with the first description of his execution, in which he prays for More and Pavier.

Foxe's source for most, if not all, of this material can be identified as Joan Bainham, the martyr's widow, who had married Bainham after the death of her previous husband, the anti-clerical polemicist Simon Fish. In the 1563 edition of the *Acts and Monuments*, Foxe introduced an account of Fish receiving the protection of Henry VIII. The King gave his

[12] See John Bale, *Scriptorum illustrium maioris Brytanniae . . . catalogus* (Basle, 1557), p. 763.

[13] John Bale, *The Epistel Exhortatorye of an Inglyshe Chrystian . . .* (Marburg, 1544), fol. 13v, and idem, *Select Works of John Bale*, ed. Henry Christmas, PS (Cambridge, 1849), pp. 394, 586.

signet ring to Fish and directed him to tell More to cease persecuting him. Fish informed More of the royal commands but the Chancellor, while acknowledging that Fish was under Henry's protection, argued that this protection did not extend to Fish's spouse, who was in trouble for refusing to permit Latin prayers in her house. More finally released Fish's wife, but only because her daughter had caught the plague and required her attention. Fish himself died of the plague within six months.[14] Reprinting this account of Fish in the 1570 edition of the *Acts and Monuments*, Foxe stated that his information came 'from the reliable reports and personal testimony of his own [i.e., Fish's] wife'.[15] There is every indication, moreover, that this statement was accurate.[16]

Although Foxe did not name a source for the narrative of Bainham's martyrdom which appeared in the 1563 edition of the *Acts and Monuments*, there can be little doubt that Joan Bainham was also that source. Apart from the fact that it would have been surprising indeed if the widow of Simon Fish and James Bainham had talked to Foxe about one husband and not discussed the other, the biographical detail supplied in both the accounts of Fish and Bainham, that the latter was the son of Sir Alexander Bainham of Gloucestershire, was accurate and could not have been widely known.[17] Moreover, there are a number of common features between the narratives concerning Fish and Bainham. In both accounts, a point was made of mentioning that Bainham married Fish's widow. In both accounts, Joan figures

---

[14] Foxe, *1563*, pp. 448–9.

[15] 'Ex certa religione, vivoque testimonio propriae ipsius coniugis' (Foxe, *1570*, p. 1153).

[16] See Thomas S. Freeman, 'Research, rumor and propaganda: Anne Boleyn in Foxe's *Book of Martyrs*', *HistJ* [forthcoming].

[17] James Bainham was the youngest son of Sir Alexander Bainham, the head of the most prominent family in the Forest of Dean. James's mother, Elizabeth, was the sister of William Tracy, whose distinctively Protestant will provoked the ecclesiastical authorities into exhuming his body in 1531 and burning it for heresy. The affair became a *cause célèbre*, particularly after Tracy's will was printed by William Tyndale and John Frith. James Bainham's cousin, Richard Tracy, assisted Hugh Latimer in destroying that celebrated object of veneration, the Blood of Hailes, in 1538, and became an ardent Protestant pamphleteer. See Caroline J. Litzenberger, 'Responses of the laity to changes in official religious policy in Gloucestershire (1541–1580)' (Cambridge University Ph.D. thesis, 1993), pp. 79, 81.

prominently in the narrative; in the account of Bainham's martyrdom she is described as being arrested, sent to the Fleet, and having her household goods confiscated because she refused to disclose where Bainham's heretical books were hidden. And in both accounts Thomas More is seen as the source of the persecution she and her husbands endured. (This, by the way, is in marked contrast to the account of Bainham in the *Rerum*, which did not mention More but castigated Stokesley for Bainham's death. Foxe did not begin, at least in this case, with a pre-conceived idea of More's responsibility but only arrived at it after investigating Bainham's martyrdom.)

The second distinct group of materials in the 1563 edition is the documents – the list of articles Stokesley presented to Bainham and the interrogations of Bainham in April 1532 – which Foxe reprints or closely paraphrases. Judging from his comments, Foxe had obtained access to the originals of these documents, which are from court books of Stokesley's which are now lost.[18] Why did Foxe clumsily print these records *en bloc*, rather than integrating them with the narrative of Bainham's life, as he would do in subsequent editions? Undoubtedly, because he only obtained this information as the 1563 edition was being printed and he did not have time to shape the material into a seamless, unified narrative. Foxe seems to have worked on the London diocesan records in reverse chronological order, beginning with the most recent records and then working backwards through time to the oldest surviving records. He had apparently reached records from the years 1527–32 by the time the first edition of the *Acts and Monuments* was being printed. There is confirmation for this theory in the fact that other documents from the London diocesan records, which date from this four-year period, also show signs of being very hastily and incompletely incorporated in the 1563 edition.[19] (This would also

[18] Foxe observed that marginal comments to the articles were written in Bainham's hand (Foxe, *1563*, p. 494).

[19] In the 1563 edition, Foxe printed a list of people who had abjured in a sweeping persecution of Lollards, and evangelicals in the diocese of London, which began in 1527 (Foxe, *1563*, pp. 418–20). But in the 1570 edition, he not only listed these individuals, he also printed the charges against them along with whatever background information (age, vocation, place of residence, etc.) the records provided

explain why Foxe printed only the articles charged against Bainham in the first edition and did not print Bainham's answers to there articles until the second edition.)

This point about access to information is of some importance when considering the next section of Foxe's 1563 account of Bainham. If Foxe only acquired details of the London records after he obtained the account of Joan Bainham, then the tale of Bainham's cruel treatment by Stokesley and More which follows after the London records was garnered not from Joan Bainham, but from another informant. This is also borne out by the contradictions between the two versions of the mistreatment of Bainham: Joan Bainham did not claim that her husband had been placed in the stocks, while the other informant did not claim that it was More who had Bainham whipped. Finally, the story of Bainham comparing the flames which engulfed him to roses came from yet another informant, and was the last piece of information about Bainham which Foxe obtained before the publication of the first edition.

Apart from an expanded use of the London diocesan records and the addition of the account of Pavier's suicide from Hall's *Chronicle*, the only new material added to the account of Bainham in the 1570 edition was the dramatic story of Bainham's public declarations of repentance for abjuring his beliefs. As we have seen, the penitent was identified as John Tewkesbury in the 1563 edition. Thus it is extremely doubtful that Joan Bainham was the source for this story, and it can only be assumed that it was related to Foxe by yet another informant.

(Foxe, *1570*, p. 1184). At the same time, the 1570 list contained a number of names apparently overlooked by Foxe in 1563. Finally, the 1563 list included the names of people who are described (correctly) as having been persecuted in the wake of the Act of Six Articles and who abjured in 1541 (Foxe, *1570*, pp. 1378–80). It is clear from all of this that the list of abjurations which Foxe printed in 1563 was cursorily compiled from the London records, and a lack of time between the unearthing of these records and the publication of the first edition is the most logical explanation. Similarly, Foxe first printed documents from Bishop Tunstall's records pertaining to Humphrey Monmouth (a London alderman who supported Tyndale and who was arrested for heresy in 1528) in the appendix to the 1563 edition, while in the next edition these documents were incorporated into the main text (Foxe, *1563*, pp. 1737–8; Foxe, *1570*, pp. 1133–4). Again, this suggests that documents in the London diocesan records from around 1528 were being discovered as the 1563 edition was being printed and were incorporated into it with difficulty.

Foxe faced a formidable challenge in writing about martyrs in the early years of the English Reformation. Dust for decades, with the ranks of those who remembered them growing thinner by the year, it was difficult to learn much about them; in fact in some cases it was impossible even to ascertain their names.[20] Even for such celebrated (or notorious) figures as Tyndale, Frith, Bilney, or Barnes, biographical information was often hard to come by; for the more obscure figures such as Bainham, who did not write books or figure in major theological or political controversies, it was that much more difficult to acquire. The account of Bainham provides an excellent example of how Foxe overcame these obstacles.

Thanks to Bale, Foxe had a reasonably accurate knowledge of Bainham and the circumstances of his martyrdom; it is even possible that Bale gave Foxe some leads on where he could obtain more information on the martyr.[21] Whatever the truth of this, Bale's knowledge of what had happened during the Henrician Reformation often enabled Foxe to acquire important information upon his return to England.[22] By 1563, Foxe had worked his way through much of the material in the London diocesan archives. And as the account

[20] If this seems to be hyperbole, compare the various names, occupations, and geographical origins given to the three people executed along with Anne Askew in John Bale, *The lattre examination of Anne Askew* (Wesel, 1548), fol. 67r; idem, *Illustrium maioris Brytanniae scriptorum . . . summarium* (Wesel, 1548), fol. 229v; idem, *Catalogus*, p. 6709; *The Grey Friars Chronicle of London*, ed. J. G. Nichols, Camden Society, 53 (London, 1852), p. 51; Charles Wriothesley, *A Chronicle of England during the Reigns of the Tudors*, ed. William Douglas Hamilton, 2 vols, Camden Society, ns 11 (London, 1875), 1, pp. 169–70.

[21] It is worth pointing out that despite some errors in the account of Bainham in the *Rerum* (such as Bainham's first name), it was quite accurate about the charges for which he was condemned. Even the erroneous statement that Bainham was burned holding a book may be a garbled version of Bainham's declaration of remorse at St Austin's.

[22] Another good example of this is Foxe's expansion in the 1563 edition of his account of the burning of a rood in a church at Dovercourt, Essex. In the *Rerum*, Foxe stated that three young men were hanged for having destroyed the Dovercourt Rood in 1532 and that a fourth participant, one Robert Gardiner, had fled (*Rerum*, p. 126). Once again, Bale, who had detailed knowledge of this incident (see *Epistel Exhortatorye*, fol. 13r), was almost certainly the source for the *Rerum* account. Once again, Foxe was able to add significantly to this account in 1563, this time with information derived from a letter Robert Gardiner had written describing the act of iconoclasm and its aftermath, which Foxe had obtained from a Londoner to whom it had been written (Foxe, *1563*, pp. 495–6).

of Bainham in the first edition shows, Foxe was continually gathering oral information even as the book was being printed. The result was a work which was not only marked by impressive detail, but was based on a range of sources – oral, archival, and printed – that very few historical works written in Europe during the sixteenth century could rival.

But how reliable were the sources Foxe depended on for his narrative of Bainham's martyrdom? Joan Bainham was obviously an informed source and her account of her second husband's arrest and her own imprisonment must be given credence. Similarly, the first account of Bainham's execution almost certainly came from her, and since there is every reason to believe that she was an eyewitness to it, this version of her husband's end might well have been considered authoritative. At the same time, the first account of Bainham's execution contains a wealth of circumstantial detail, some of which can be confirmed.[23] However, there is what appears to be one glaring inaccuracy in her account – the statement that More had her husband tied to a tree in his garden and whipped. More vehemently denied allegations that he had heretics scourged in his garden, and scholars have tended to give credence to his denials.[24] But it is easy to understand how Joan Bainham could have believed such a story. Remember that another source told Foxe that Bainham was whipped while imprisoned in the Tower. Whatever the truth of this report, it demonstrates that rumours that

[23] The first account of Bainham's execution states that Dr Simons, who was sent to convert Bainham to orthodoxy, fled from the stake, intimidated by the large crowd. The Venetian ambassador, in a letter written to the Signory four days after Bainham's execution, claimed that 'the greater part of the population was present at his death.' The ambassador also confirmed that Bainham was praying aloud while he burned, although he did not describe the content of the prayer (Rawdon Brown, ed., *Calendar of State Papers Venetian, 1527-33*, 33 vols [London, 1868-1947], 4, p. 334). The last words attributed to Bainham in this version, denouncing More for having been both his accuser and his judge, raised an apposite point, which would have occurred naturally to a lawyer. As Chancellor, More had the authority to investigate, arrest, and detain suspected heretics, but he did not have the authority to try or condemn people for heresy; the latter task was the responsibility of the ecclesiastical courts. The fact that several of Stokesley's examinations were conducted at More's house (even assuming that More did not participate in the examinations) blurred, at the least, the division between the two jurisdictions.

[24] Thomas More, *The Apology*, ed. J. B. Trapp in *The Complete Works of St Thomas More*, 15 vols (New Haven, 1963-90), 9, pp. 117-20.

Bainham was beaten after his arrest were circulating. At the same time, More's defence of himself indicates that charges that he beat accused heretics after their arrest were circulating within a year of Bainham's execution. It would have been natural, indeed almost inevitable, that the two reports would have been conflated, especially since Bainham had been detained at More's house. Certainly Joan Bainham, in prison when this beating was supposed to have taken place, would have readily believed the worst of More, who had persecuted both of her husbands and repeatedly sent her to prison.[25] J. B. Trapp has also maintained that Foxe excised the story of Bainham's praying at the stake for More's forgiveness from the second edition, and implied that he did so because he suspected it was false.[26] As we have seen, however, the story was not excised, but rather moved to another location in the text and reprinted in every edition.

Nevertheless, if Joan Bainham was a knowledgeable source she was also a very biased source, naturally anxious to present her late husbands in the best light. And while it appears that most of what she told Foxe was accurate, it also appears that she tried to hide one important fact from the martyrologist – the fact that her second husband had abjured. This would explain why the narrative she contributed misleadingly emphasized Bainham's skill in argument and omitted any mention of his submission. It also would explain why Foxe only mentioned Bainham's abjuration when introducing the London episcopal records which dealt with it; he only learned of it from these records.

The reliability of Foxe's other informants was even more problematical. The account of Bainham's public repentance

---

[25] Interestingly, Foxe was quite cautious elsewhere in raising this charge against More. In the second edition, Foxe introduced an account of Sygar Nicholson (whom More had expressly denied whipping) and guardedly wrote: 'The handlying of this man was too cruell, if the report was true, that he should be hanged by thoses [sic] partes, which nature wel suffreth not to be named' (Foxe, 1570, p. 1184). Why was Foxe willing to assert that More tied Bainham to a tree and whipped him, but relatively hesitant to say the same about Nicholson? Perhaps because the version of Nicholson's ordeal which Foxe heard included outlandish embellishments (Foxe's wording suggests that this might be the case) and because the account of Bainham's beating came from Joan Bainham, whom Foxe considered a reliable source, which may not have been the case with the Nicholson story.

[26] More, *Apology*, p. 348.

for abjuring was clearly the contribution of someone with a faulty memory, who had initially confused John Tewkesbury with James Bainham. Presumably the error was brought to Foxe's attention by readers of the first edition and then corrected for the second edition. Simple forgetfulness or confusion are not, of course, the only impairments to memory and subtler problems seem to have undermined the accuracy of another of Foxe's informants. For, if the account of her husband's execution which Joan Bainham supplied was accurate, then the story of Bainham crying out from the stake that the flames were as sweet to him as a bed of roses was almost certainly false. If Bainham had made such a striking remark, then surely his wife, anxious to burnish her husband's reputation for constancy, would have included it in her account of his martyrdom. Adding to the suspicion that the remark was apocryphal is the fact that very similar remarks were commonly attributed to martyrs in medieval hagiographies. In *The Golden Legend* (a work which had enjoyed enormous popularity in England in the early sixteenth century) the legend of St Sebastian relates that St Tiburtius, one of his converts, when forced to walk across burning coals, exclaimed that he felt as if he were treading on rose leaves.[27] In the same work, Saints Gorgonius and Dorotheus are said, while being roasted on iron grates, to have 'seemed to lie there as if on a bed of flowers'.[28] Protestant martyrs, or their martyrologists, also co-opted this imagery: one martyr, executed in Belgium in 1523, is supposed to have exclaimed that the faggots under his feet felt like roses.[29] Even a relatively unsympathetic observer like the Venetian ambassador conceded the Bainham 'died with the greatest fortitude' and it is easy to understand how someone sympathetic to Bainham would have wished to highlight his constancy and consciously or unconsciously would have drawn on the rich traditions of hagiography to do it.

[27] Jacobus da Voragine, *The Golden Legend*, trans. William Granger Ryan, 2 vols (Princeton, N.J., 1993), 1, p. 100.

[28] Ibid., 2, p. 164.

[29] Heinrich Pantaleon, *Martyrum historia* (Basle, 1563), p. 39. Foxe translated and reprinted this story (Foxe, *1563*, p. 421).

If Foxe's sources were tedentious, moreover, in reporting or concealing details of Bainham's martyrdom, so was Foxe himself. The most significant alteration Foxe made to the information he received was the suppression of much of Joan Bainham's description of her husband's execution and the transferring of the remainder to a different part of the *Acts and Monuments*. Clearly this suppression did not occur because Foxe doubted the accuracy of Joan Bainham's narrative, since he retained the parts of it concerning Pavier and it is hard to believe that Joan was better informed about Pavier's death than about James Bainham's. We do not know who contributed the story about Bainham's comparing the fire to roses or even if this informant was actually present at the martyr's demise. But if Foxe believed this story was credible, he could simply have melded the story with Joan Bainham's account, or even printed the two accounts together and left it for the reader to choose between them, a practice Foxe used elsewhere in the *Acts and Monuments*.[30] There is only one reason for Foxe to have eliminated so many of the details about James Bainham's execution which his wife had provided: Foxe did not want these details to distract his readers from the account of Bainham's triumph over the agony of being burned at the stake.

To Foxe and his contemporaries, influenced by a revival of Stoic ideas in Renaissance England, this conquest of pain, or *apathiae*, was an indispensable prerequisite of the true martyr of God.[31] Both the martyrs and those who witnessed their sufferings believed that there was an absolute correlation between the constancy of the martyrs and the veracity of their religious convictions. Robert Farrar, an Edwardine Bishop of St Davids, who was executed for heresy in Mary's reign, told a spectator that 'if he saw him once to styre in the paynes of his burning, he should then give no credite to his

---

[30] See for example Foxe, *1563*, fol. 69r-v, where Foxe presents differing versions of the death of King John.

[31] See Patrick Collinson, ' "A magazine of religious patterns": an Erasmian topic transposed in English Protestantism', in his *Godly People: Essays on English Protestantism and Puritanism* (London, 1983), pp. 510-25; Thomas S. Freeman, ' "Great searching out of bookes and autors": John Foxe as an ecclesiastical historian' (Rutgers University Ph.D. thesis, 1995), pp. 115-33.

doctrine'.[32] Nothing demonstrates both the importance of this issue and the value of the speech attributed to Bainham as a demonstration of it than the determined attack on Foxe's account of the latter by Nicholas Harpsfield, the most important contemporary Catholic critic of the *Acts and Monuments*. According to Harpsfield, one of the chief ways in which the Protestant 'pseudo-martyrs' deluded people into believing that they were martyrs of Christ was through their displays of fortitude. The outstanding example of this supposed constancy was Bainham's claim that he felt no pain while being burned alive. Harpsfield argued that if it was really a miracle of God, then he would have displayed his power by preventing the fire from consuming Bainham, rather than simply making him insensible to pain. Harpsfield posited two explanations for Bainham's speech: either sorcery had indeed made him impervious to pain or, desperate to win unmerited acclaim and adoration as a martyr, he concealed the agony he really felt.[33] At the beginning of the next century, Robert Parsons repeated and developed Harpsfield's arguments about Bainham's constancy, demonstrating the continuing importance of this example of *apathiae* in confessional controversy.[34]

But if Foxe suppressed Joan Bainham's account of her husband's execution at one point, why did he resurrect those parts of it concerning William Pavier at a later point in his book? The reason is that Pavier's animosity to one of God's martyrs, followed by his suicide, was a vivid example of divine retribution being visited upon a persecutor of one of God's saints. Foxe zealously included a virtually endless parade of divine judgements through the pages of the *Acts and Monuments*, but examples of God's retribution against those who had harassed or injured the martyrs held a special place in his heart and in his book. Aside from liberally sprinkling his text with such examples, Foxe also added a lengthy

---

[32] Foxe, *1570*, p. 1724. For a similar incident see Foxe, *1563*, p. 1162.

[33] Nicholas Harpsfield, *Dialogi sex contra summi pontificatus, monasticae vitae, sanctorum, sacrarum imaginum oppugnatores et pseudomartyres* (Antwerp, 1573), pp. 541, 696-7.

[34] Robert Parsons, *The Third Part of a Treatise intituled Of Three Conversions of England* (St Omer, 1604), pp. 419-20.

appendix devoted to anecdotes of the Lord's vengeance in each edition, under the title 'The severe punishment of Gods mighty hand upon Priestes and Prelates, with such other, as have been persecutors of his people and the members of the true Church.'[35] Although Foxe did not want details from Joan Bainham's account of her husband's execution to detract from the portrait of James Bainham's extraordinary *apathiae*, he also clearly did not want to omit a striking story of providence smiting a persecutor. By transferring the portions of Joan Bainham's account which described Pavier and his fate to another part of the *Acts and Monuments*, Foxe was able to have his cake and eat it too. But in all of this juggling and manipulation of the two accounts, their accuracy was clearly a secondary consideration with Foxe; what mattered most was their didactic and homiletic quality.

Foxe also appears to have twice suppressed material in the records of Bainham's examinations for polemical reasons. In both cases, this material mentioned the celebrated evangelical preacher, Dr Edward Crome. As Susan Wabuda has pointed out in a fascinating article, Foxe held a relatively generous view of Crome when he was writing the first edition of the *Acts and Monuments*; but as he became aware of Crome's history of multiple recantations during the reigns of Henry VIII and Mary, Foxe deleted favourable references to Crome from the second edition and now included some criticisms of Crome's submissions.[36] This pattern of alternating deletions is also at work in Foxe's account of Bainham. In the first edition, Foxe did not print Bainham's statements that Crome lied and spoke against his conscience during his first recantation when he denied the existence of purgatory, and that Crome's printed confession was 'a very folish thyng', although these remarks were printed in all subsequent editions of the *Acts and Monuments*.[37] Conversely, Bainham's statement that 'he knew no man to have preached the word of

---

[35] Foxe, *1563*, pp. 1703–7; Foxe, *1570*, pp. 2298–302 [recte 2318]; Foxe, *1576*, pp. 1990–2005; Foxe, *1583*, 2099–166. The title varies somewhat from edition to edition.

[36] Susan Wabuda, 'Equivocation and recantation during the English Reformation: the "subtle shadows" of Dr. Edward Crome', *JEH*, 44 (1993), pp. 238–9.

[37] Compare Foxe, *1563*, p. 493 with Foxe, *1570*, p. 1169.

God sincerely and purely after the vayne of Scripture, except M. Crome and M. Latymer', while included in the second and third editions of Foxe's work, was unceremoniously dumped from the fourth.[38] It is possible (although a little unlikely) that Bainham's disparagement of Crome was not included in the first edition simply because Foxe overlooked it, along with other diocesan records he only had time to examine cursorily. But there can be little doubt that Foxe deliberately deleted Bainham's praise of Crome from his book.

Furthermore, there is no doubt at all that Foxe suppressed another, and most interesting, piece of information. Extant among Foxe's papers, but never printed in any edition of *Acts and Monuments*, is a report of a conversation Hugh Latimer had with Bainham when he visited the condemned lawyer on the eve of his execution. After exchanging greetings, Latimer declared the purpose of his visit:

> Mr. Baynham we here saie that youe arr condempned for heresie to be brent and many men are in doubt wherfor ye shuld suffer and I for my parte am desirous to understand the cause of your death, assuryng you that I do not alowe that any man sholde consent to hys own death oneles he hadd a right case to die in. Lett not vayne glorie overcome you in a mather that men deserve not to die [for], for therein you shall neither please God, do good to yourself nor your neighbor and better yt were for you to submit yourself to the ordynaunces of men than so rashlie to fynyshe your lyf without good ground. And therefore we praie you to let us to understand ye Articles that you are condempned for.

Bainham then explained that he was condemned for declaring that Thomas Becket was a traitor but Latimer admonished him that this was not a sufficient cause to die for. Bainham then stated that he was also condemned for denying the existence of purgatory and this met with Latimer's approval.

---

[38] Compare Foxe, *1570*, p. 1169 and Foxe, *1576*, p. 1000 with Foxe, *1583*, p. 1029.

After further conversation, in which Latimer assured Bainham that God would provide for Joan Bainham after her husband's death, the future bishop departed, after having warned Bainham again to 'beware of vaynglorie for the devill wilbe redie nowe to infecte you therwith when you shall come unto the people'.[39]

Why did Foxe neglect to print this exchange? It was not from doubts about its reliability; Ralph Morrice, who sent Foxe the account of Latimer's visit (and who claimed to be an eye-witness to it) was a trusted informant whose contributions were frequently cited in the *Acts and Monuments*. Susan Wabuda has suggested that Latimer, in this interview, was trying to persuade Bainham to submit and that this was why Foxe did not print Morrice's account.[40] In my opinion, however, this misinterprets Latimer's intentions. Like virtually every other cleric in Christendom, Protestant or Catholic, Latimer was a firm believer in the patristic dictum that *non poena, sed causa martyrem facit*.[41] Latimer's questions seem to have been designed not to induce Bainham to recant, but to establish that Bainham's *poena* would be suffered for a legitimate and sufficient *causa*. I suspect that it was Latimer's repeated and forceful warnings to Bainham about the dangers of being infected with vainglory, and the way in which these warnings inadvertently appeared to confirm Harpsfield's assertions about the true causes of Bainham's imperviousness to pain, which caused Foxe to censor Morrice's story.

After all this, it should be remembered that there were limits to Foxe's tendentiousness. He did not invent any of the material which formed his account of Bainham; even the story of Bainham's comparison of being burned to standing in a bed of roses was, as is shown by its awkward insertion

39   BL, MS Harley 422, fol. 90r–v.

40   Wabuda, 'Equivocation', p. 240.

41   On the universal belief in this dictum see Leon-E. Halkin, 'Les Martyrologes et la critique: Contribution à l'étude du martyrologe protestant des Pays-Bas', in *Mélanges historiques offerts à Monsieur Jean Meyerhoffer* (Lausanne, 1952), p. 58. John Jewel can hardly be accused of exaggeration when he maintained that 'It is knowen to children, [that] it is not the death, but the cause of death that makes the martyrs' (J. Ayre, ed., *The Works of John Jewel*, 3, PS [Cambridge, 1845], p. 188). For Latimer's declaring that the Anabaptists were not true martyrs, despite their constancy, because they died in an unrighteous cause, see *The Seconde Sermon of Maister Hugh Latemer* (London, 1549), sigs L8v–M1r.

into the appendix of the 1563 edition, related to Foxe by someone else. And in tracing the course of his research on Bainham, it is readily apparent that Foxe's account of Bainham was built on solid foundations. But is also cannot be denied that the material Foxe so assiduously gathered was carefully shaped (or completely suppressed) to suit his purposes. Examples of Foxe suppressing evidence have been discussed before, although his reasons for doing so and his general accuracy are in need of more systematic discussion and analysis.[42]

Underappreciated, however, is the tendentiousness of Foxe's informants and the ways in which they shaped his history. The reasons which led Joan Bainham to whitewash her husband's abjuration were relatively straightforward, if compelling, and perhaps require little discussion. The attribution of a speech to Bainham which strikingly parallels speeches attributed to the martyrs of the early Church highlights a more subtle element of distortion in the *Acts and Monuments* which, however, should not be overlooked. Martyrdom is perhaps the most extreme form of mimesis; as Donald Kelley has put it, it is '*imitatio Christi* with a vengeance'.[43] All Christian martyrs must be seen to be in conformity with the acknowledged models of martyrdom – Christ and the martyrs of the early Church. This was particularly true in the Reformation where the martyrs of one confession would be denounced as fanatics, sorcerers, and unregenerate heretics by members of other confessions. Certainly, Foxe frequently and elaborately compared Protestant with patristic martyrs.[44] There are also grounds for believing that his informants, driven by the same concerns, falsely attributed remarks or actions to the persecuted Protestants which heightened the identification with the ancient martyrs. This seems to have happened in the case of

[42] By far the best discussion of this issue to date is Patrick Collinson, 'Truth and legend: the veracity of John Foxe's *Book of Martyrs*', in A. C. Duke and C. A. Tamse, eds, *Clio's Mirror: Historiography in Britain and the Netherlands* (Zutphen, 1985), pp. 31-54.

[43] Donald R. Kelley, 'Martyrs, myths and the massacre: the background to St Bartholomew', *AHR*, 77 (1972), p. 1328.

[44] See, for example, Foxe's comparison of John Hooper to Polycarp (Foxe, *1570*, p. 1683) or of Laurence Saunders to St Laurence (Foxe, *1563*, p. 1048).

Bainham and it also appears to have been true of the most famous remark made by a martyr in the *Acts and Monuments*: Latimer's injunction to his fellow martyr to 'Be of good comfort M. Ridley, and play the man: we shall this day lyght a candle by Gods grace in England, as (I trust) shall never be put out.'

The remark obviously echoes Eusebius' account of the martyrdom of Polycarp, which relates that 'when Polycarp entered the arena there came a voice from haven: "Be strong, Polycarp, and play the man." '[45] Latimer certainly knew of Eusebius' account, and it is hardly impossible that this supremely articulate individual would have made such a statement. But in the 1563 edition of the *Acts and Monuments*, Foxe had printed a very detailed narrative of the joint execution of Ridley and Latimer, based on the testimony of George Shipside, Ridley's brother-in-law, who was present at the grim event. Latimer's celebrated remark does not appear in this account and was, in fact, only added to the *Acts and Monuments* in 1570.[46] It is hard to believe that Shipside, who was a close observer of what happened, and who paid particular attention to the final words and actions of the two martyrs, would have failed to notice such a striking remark.

[45] Eusebius, *Ecclesiastical History*, LCL, IV, xv, 15, p. 347.
[46] Compare Foxe, *1563*, pp. 1376-9 with Foxe, *1570*, p. 1937. Latimer's companion, Augustine Bernher, also wrote a brief account of the executions of Ridley and Latimer as part of his dedication (to the dowager Duchess of Suffolk) of a collection of Latimer's sermons published in 1562. Two features of this account (Latimer's crying out 'Fidelis est Deus, qui non sinit nos tentari supra id quod pussumus', and Latimer's heart bursting open and bleeding profusely during his burning) are also in the account in the first edition of the *Acts and Monuments* (compare *Latimer's Sermons*, 1, pp. 322-3 with Foxe, *1563*, pp. 1376-9; I am very grateful to Professor Susan Wabuda for bringing Bernher's account to my attention). There is no way of knowing if these details were given to Foxe by Shipside, but it is very likely that Bernher had also described the executions to Foxe. For one thing, both Bernher and Foxe claim that the blood gushing forth from Latimer's heart was an answer to the martyr's prayer that he be allowed to shed his heart's blood for the Gospel. Admittedly, Foxe could have simply been repeating the observation from Bernher's already-published account. But Bernher made it clear in his dedication that he knew in advance what the contents of Foxe's account of Latimer would be in the forthcoming 1563 edition of *Acts and Monuments* (*Latimer's Sermons*, 1, p. 322). Thus it is almost certain that Foxe had consulted Bernher about his friend and mentor, and highly likely that they had discussed Latimer's martyrdom. But even if it is not true, the fact remains that two eye-witnesses, Shipside and Bernher, each devoted to the memory of Ridley and Latimer, do not mention Latimer making his famous remark about 'playing the man'.

It is far more likely that someone told Foxe that Latimer had made such a remark (just as someone told Foxe that Bainham had declared that he felt no pain while being burned) and that Foxe, believing what he wished to believe, accepted these reports uncritically and reprinted them with alacrity.

It is at once very appropriate and slightly ironic that Bainham's public abjuration should have been discussed in Stephen Greenblatt's seminal work, *Renaissance Self-Fashioning*.[47] For while Foxe's account of Bainham provides a spectacular example of self-fashioning, it also illustrates hidden complexities in its operation. Successful self-fashioning is, paradoxically but necessarily, a collaborative achievement. The impact of Bainham's actions lay not only in the conformity of those actions to accepted models of heroic behaviour, but also in the perception of this conformity by others. The involvement of other viewpoints in Bainham's fashioning of himself into first a penitent sinner and then a triumphant martyr inevitably introduced elements of contradiction, ambiguity, and even confusion into the process. These elements were intensified when Foxe drew on the memories of those involved, or who claimed to have been involved (if only as spectators) in Bainham's martyrdom and the events which led up to it, as retrospection, being a selective process, further widens the differences between viewpoints already created by varying circumstances, biases, and ideals.

In Bainham's case, matters were complicated still further by the different purposes retrospection served for Foxe's informants and Foxe himself. Joan Bainham wished to manipulate the past to remove any threats to her second husband's reputation as a martyr; while the informant who claimed that Bainham declared to the 'papists' that he felt no pain in the fire also sought to enhance Bainham's reputation, but did so in order to justify the cause for which the martyr died and to disparage its adversaries. Foxe's goals were more complex: while also anxious to secure the maximum polemical advantage from Bainham's martyrdom, he was at

---

[47] Stephen Greenblatt, *Renaissance Self-Fashioning: from More to Shakespeare* (Chicago, 1980), pp. 74–87.

the same time concerned that his readers draw the appropriate homiletic message from Bainham's history. These varying objectives repeatedly came into conflict. While Joan Bainham was anxious to suppress any mention of James Bainham's abjuration, Foxe described it and the martyr's tormented conscience in order to emphasize that God's grace and forgiveness were available to all repentant sinners, even those who had denied him. Conversely, Edward Crome's repeated recantations, which did not culminate in martyrdom, served no homiletic or pastoral purpose and were a polemical liability. As a result, Foxe excised Crome from the pages of his history. Occasionally Foxe's diverse purposes came into conflict with each other, as when he wished to suppress part of Joan Bainham's account of her husband's execution but went out of his way to retain that part of it which recounted the providential punishment of William Pavier.

Far from being the sole arbiter of the contents of the *Acts and Monuments*, as he is often portrayed, Foxe zealously worked to re-shape and re-arrange the data given to him by informants who had already shaped it to their own ends.

Rutgers University

CONCILIAR AUTHORITY IN REFORMATION SCOTLAND: THE EXAMPLE OF THE KENNEDY/DAVIDSON DEBATE, 1558-63*

by MARTIN HOLT DOTTERWEICH

'For to the most parte of men, lawfull and godlie appeareth whatsoever antiquitie hath received', complained John Knox in his 1558 *First Blast of the Trumpet against the Monstrous Regiment of Women*[1] – and indeed for Knox and his fellow Protestants, the question of historical pedigree was troublesome. Catholic polemicists frequently posed some form of the question, 'Where was your Church before Luther?', and contrasted this problem with their own historical continuity, unbroken since the apostle Peter.[2] Knox's homeland of Scotland saw comparatively little sixteenth-century theological debate, but as in Reformation disputes on the continent, in Scotland historical superiority was claimed by Catholic and Protestant alike. A useful means of legitimation for either side, as Knox had said, was to demonstrate greater similarity to the primitive Church than one's opponent. The appeal to superior historical precedent was particularly central to one Scottish debate, the printed theological exchange between Quintin Kennedy and John Davidson, and here it was slightly unusual in that these authors focused on the general council, rather than the papacy or episcopacy, as the means of historical legitimation.[3]

* I would like to thank my supervisors, Mr D. F. Wright and Dr Jane Dawson, for their helpful comments on this paper.

[1] John Knox, *The Works of John Knox*, ed. David Laing, 6 vols (Edinburgh, 1846–64), 4, p. 370 (also in *John Knox on Rebellion*, ed. Roger A. Mason [Cambridge, 1994], p. 7).

[2] For a general discussion of the argument from historical continuity, see Jaroslav Pelikan, *The Christian Tradition: A History of the Development of Doctrine*, 5 vols (Chicago, 1971–89), 4, pp. 303–6; comments on Luther and Calvin may be found in David Steinmetz, *Luther in Context* (Bloomington, Ind., 1986), pp. 85–97.

[3] An overview of sixteenth-century debates concerning the authority of Church councils may be found in G. R. Evans, *Problems of Authority in the Reformation Debates* (Cambridge, 1992), pp. 241–59. On Protestantism and the conciliar principle see J. T. McNeill, *Unitive Protestantism* (New York, 1930), pp. 89–129.

Councils were a logical point of debate in Scotland, given its Church's conciliarist heritage. A substantial number of Scottish clerics were involved with the Council of Basle (1431–49), and although the conciliar movement lost its momentum after this time, conciliar thought survived in Scotland (as elsewhere) well into the sixteenth century.[4] The primary exponent of this continued tradition in Scotland was John Mair, who taught at Glasgow and St Andrews, and found a number of Scottish students while teaching in Paris as well.[5] Moreover, Scottish libraries of the early to mid-sixteenth century contained the works of continental conciliarists including Jean Gerson, Pierre d'Ailly, Panormitanus, and William of Ockham.[6]

Some vestiges of this conciliarist influence may also be seen in two documents produced by the reforming Scottish provincial councils of 1549 and 1552.[7] The 1549 council produced a list of questions for inquisitors which encouraged action 'against those who deny that a General Council has any authority in defining dogmas and who reject its canonical decisions' – but it included no questions regarding the pope or apostolic succession.[8] The 1552 council commissioned a

---

[4] See especially three works by J. H. Burns, *Scottish Churchmen at the Council of Basle* (Glasgow, 1962); 'The conciliarist tradition in Scotland', *ScHR*, 42 (1963), pp. 89–104; 'Conciliarism, papalism, and power, 1511-18', in Diana Wood, ed., *The Church and Sovereignty c. 590–1918*, SCH.S, 9 (1991), pp. 409–28.

[5] Mair's arguments are analysed in James K. Cameron, 'The conciliarism of John Mair: a note on *A Disputation on the Authority of a Council*', in Wood, *The Church and Sovereignty*, pp. 429–35. Cameron has also translated the relevant portions of Mair's commentary on Matthew in Matthew Spinka, ed., *Advocates of Reform* (London, 1953), pp. 175–84.

[6] See John Durkan and Anthony Ross, *Early Scottish Libraries* (Glasgow, 1961), as indexed. See also Burns, 'The conciliarist tradition', pp. 99–100. No copy of Mair's commentary on Matthew, containing his fullest conciliarist argument, has been found in a Scottish library of the time.

[7] There was another council in 1559. For an account of the workings of these councils, see Thomas Winning, 'Church councils in sixteenth-century Scotland', in David McRoberts, ed., *Essays on the Scottish Reformation 1513–1625* (Glasgow, 1962), pp. 332–58. Winning's belief that these councils anticipated the Trent decrees seems improbable, but neither can they be called anti-papal: Michael Lynch, *Scotland: A New History*, rev. edn (London, 1992), p. 194.

[8] *Statutes of the Scottish Church 1225–1559*, ed. David Patrick, Scottish History Society, 54 (Edinburgh, 1907), pp. 126–7. Only two heresy trials took place after the 1549 provincial council had issued this list: those of Adam Wallace in 1550 and Walter Myln in 1558, for which Foxe records no accusations regarding either the papacy or the councils: *The Acts and Monuments of John Foxe*, ed. Stephen

lengthy vernacular catechism, commonly known as *Hamilton's Catechism*, which made no mention of the pope, though it maintained the authority of general councils.[9] Although these documents cannot strictly be called 'conciliarist', since they do not discuss the power of councils in comparison to the pope,[10] their silence regarding the papacy does seem to demonstrate the lasting heritage of Scottish conciliarism.

The effect of conciliarist influence on Scottish Reformation debate is clearly seen in the exchange in print between the Catholic apologist Quintin Kennedy (*c*.1520–64) and the Protestant John Davidson (*c*.1520–*c*.1572). Kennedy, the commendator abbot of Grossraguel in Ayrshire, had been present at the first provincial council of 1549.[11] His first treatise, *Ane compendius Tractiue conforme to the Scripturis of almychtie GOD, ressoun, and authoritie, declaring the nerrest, and onlie way, to establische the conscience of ane christiane man, in all materis (quhilks ar in debate) concernying faith and religioun*, was published in 1558, and he followed it with other polemical tracts primarily dealing with the Mass.[12] According to Kennedy's opponent, the *Compendius Tractive* was influential: 'thare hes bene mony movit to continew still in thare auld superstitione and idolatrie, throw the reasonis contenit in the same, quha had imbracit the sincere and trew Religione of Christe or thir dayis, and it had bene supprest in its infancie'.[13] The fact that a refutation was still considered

Reed Cattley, 8 vols (London, 1837–41), 5, pp. 636–41, 644–7. The only trial in which Foxe records an accusation of defiance of the authority of general councils is that of George Wishart in 1546: ibid., 5, p. 633.

[9]   *The Catechism of John Hamilton*, ed. Thomas Graves Law (Oxford, 1884) [hereafter *Ham. Cat.*].

[10]   This point is made by Maurice Taylor, 'The conflicting doctrines of the Scottish Reformation', in McRoberts, *Essays*, p. 263. Taylor attempts to demonstrate that in fact there was significant 'deference' to the pope in Scotland at this time, but most historians have maintained rather that the papacy found considerable disregard and indifference. See, e.g., Gordon Donaldson, *The Scottish Reformation* (Cambridge, 1960), pp. 35, 43–5; or Jenny Wormald, *Court, Kirk, and Community: Scotland 1470–1625* (Edinburgh, 1981), pp. 78–9, 120.

[11]   It would seem probable that he attended the other provincial councils as well, but no registers of attendance survive.

[12]   Ed. David Laing, in *The Miscellany of the Wodrow Society* (Edinburgh, 1844), pp. 95–175 [hereafter *Wod. Misc.*]. Two other tracts are found in *Quintin Kennedy (1520–1564): Two Eucharistic Tracts*, ed. Cornelis Henricus Kuipers (Nijmegen, 1964).

[13]   Ed. David Laing, in *Wod. Misc.*, pp. 181–258 (quotation at p. 186).

necessary five years later – and three years after the 'Reformation Parliament' of 1560 had abolished the authority of the pope, outlawed the Mass, and accepted the Scots Confession of Faith – is further testimony to its influence.[14]

The refutation was composed by John Davidson, who had been appointed Principal of Glasgow University in 1557. His conversion to Protestantism in 1559 had surprised many; Winzet referred to Davidson as 'our wind-fallin brether, laitlie snapperit in the cummerance of Calvin'.[15] Davidson stated that his work, *Ane Answer to the Tractiue, set furth in the zeir of God. 1558. be Maister Quintine Kennedy, Commendatar, Abbote of Crossraguell, for the establisching of ane Christiane mannis conscience (as he alledgis) the Forth and strenth of his Papistrie, and all vthers of his Sect, as appearis weil be his Epistle direct to the Protestantes, and Prentit in the last part of this Buik*, was requested by Alexander Cunningham, fifth Earl of Glencairn, and was composed in order that 'the people of God sould not be langer abusit with his captious sophisticationes'.[16] It is impossible to discern how much influence this refutation enjoyed.

This is not the place for an examination of the sources used by Kennedy and Davidson; however, an important precedent was set for Kennedy by *Hamilton's Catechism*. According to the catechism, the way to know what the Scriptures are and what they mean is to examine the 'consent and authorite of our mother the haly kirk ... specially quhen it is lawfully gadderit be the haly spirit in ane generall counsel'. Individuals should consider the determinations of the councils to be 'the trew word of God, and ... infallible'.[17] Those who oppose

---

[14] It is worth noting that the 'Reformation Parliament' did not end theological debate in Scotland; to the contrary, after the political disaster of 1560, Scottish Catholic apologists stepped up their efforts to offer theological challenges to the Protestant Church. Kennedy produced some tracts after 1560, and held a public debate with Knox at Maybole in 1562. A second Catholic apologist, Ninian Winzet, also began writing polemical tracts after 1560, including – significantly for the present theme – a translation of Vincent of Lérins' *Commonitorium* in 1563.

[15] For the conversion, see John Durkan, 'The cultural background in sixteenth-century Scotland', in McRoberts, *Essays*, p. 330. The Winzet quotation is cited by Laing, *Wod. Misc.*, p. 179. Further biographical details of both men can be found in Laing's introductions to their works; ibid., pp. 89–94, 177–80.

[16] Ibid., pp. 186–7.

[17] *Ham. Cat.*, pp. 40–1; cf. p. 47.

the teaching of the councils are heretics, for the councils are given by God 'to be ledar, techar, and direckar' of the Church, which is 'trewly representit' in them.[18] Kennedy maintains this position on conciliar authority throughout his historical argument in the *Compendius Tractive*.[19]

Kennedy begins his argument not with history, but by asking whether there is an order by which disputes in the Church can be settled in 'thir dayis, quhairinto all hereseis apperis to be assemblit, and gatherit togidder as ane arrayit hoiste, to invaid, oppres, and alluterlie dounthryng the congregatioun'.[20] The cause of such disputes is a wrong understanding of the Scriptures, but the Scriptures cannot themselves settle the issue, for they are called a witness in John 5.39, and cannot be both witness and judge simultaneously. Those who claim that Scripture itself is the judge wish by doing so to use it as a 'scheild and bucklare to thair lustes and heresiis'; were Scripture in fact the judge as well as witness, 'perpetuale debait and incertitude' would reign in the Church, for all would have their own opinions of its meaning.[21] Therefore, the Church is called to judge disputes, but not everyone is gifted to discern the true meaning of God's Word; hence, there is 'ane speciale member' whose decisions have 'the sam denominatioun, strenth, and effect; as geve all the rest of the membris had concurrit, and bene present thare with'.[22]

Kennedy now looks back to the primitive Church to bolster his position on conciliar authority. The 'special member' appointed to settle debates, since the days of the apostles, has always been the general council.[23] Kennedy poses the simple historical question to his opponents, whether there have been any heresies since the days of Christ. Assuming agreement on this point, he asks if there was any order given by which to suppress them other than the

[18] Ibid., pp. 45, 47.
[19] Kennedy's arguments also bear comparison to those of Jacopo Sadoleto in his letter to the Genevans: *A Reformation Debate: John Calvin and Jacopo Sadoleto*, trans. Henry Beveridge, ed. John C. Olin (Grand Rapids, Mich., 1976), pp. 29–48.
[20] *Wod. Misc.*, p. 100.
[21] Ibid., p. 101.
[22] Ibid., pp. 100-2.
[23] Ibid., p. 103.

councils, and assumes a negative reply.[24] He next offers a bit of narrative history. Due to rampant persecution and heresy, no councils were convened before the time of Constantine, but since then they alone have dealt with heresy on behalf of the Church. Kennedy briefly describes the first four councils, noting that the heretics they suppressed all claimed scriptural support, just like his opponents; and he claims that all subsequent general councils have the same authority as these four.[25]

But Kennedy knows that 'thair is sum swa religious and clene fyngerit, that thair wyl na thyng perswade thaim without testimony of Scripture', so he endeavours to offer biblical support for his position.[26] This statement clarifies Kennedy's audience: he means to convince readers who will not accept his initial argument, based as it is upon extra-biblical history. But the biblical support is itself a citation of historical precedent, with Deuteronomy 17.8–13 and Acts 15 the chief texts. Kennedy begins with Acts 15, the council of the early Church in Jerusalem. Citing the text at length, Kennedy draws three primary lessons from it. First, since Paul and Barnabas went to Jerusalem to settle the issue of the circumcision of gentiles, Kennedy concludes that no private number of persons, however godly and learned, may settle a religious dispute on their own. Second, although the apostles and elders were the only ones convened, their decision carried the same strength as if the whole Christian Church had gathered, and the same is true of later councils. Third, the combination of the apostle James's statement, 'I judge', and the authoritative phrase in the council's letter, 'It has pleased the Holy Spirit and us', shows that the determination of such matters pertains to the Church and not to Scripture.[27] Much of Kennedy's emphasis is on this passage, which offers both scriptural and historical precedent, and allows him to avoid the more difficult issue of later councils.[28]

---

24 Ibid., pp. 118-19.
25 Ibid., pp. 110-13.
26 Ibid., p. 119.
27 Ibid., pp. 105-6.
28 The later councils could, by this time, be easily referenced in either of two editions, that of Merlin (1525) or Peter Crabbe (1538, second edition 1551). The second edition of Crabbe, as well as Merlin's edition of the first four councils (1535),

But historical precedent may be found even earlier, argues Kennedy, in the Old Testament. He cites Deuteronomy 17.8–13, in which God gives authority to the Levites to judge disputed matters, rather than to the Scriptures.[29] Turning to Haggai 2.9, 'Gret salbe the glore of this latter hous, mair nor the first', Kennedy applies this principle to the Levite judges. If the Levites judged disputed matters, how much more do the councils of the New Law?[30] Thus those claiming that Scripture alone is the authority for judgement in disputes, and denying the authority of councils, are proved wrong by the historical record of the Bible itself.

A key historical challenge posed by Protestants to the authority of the councils concerned the sinfulness of the latter's members. Kennedy answers again from scriptural – and historical – precedent. He first rejects the notion that these men were corrupt; in fact, they were the 'maist godlie and best learnit men in the warld for the tyme'. But even had they not been godly, it would not derogate from their authority, for their authority comes from God, not their own merit. They are thus able to discern the correct interpretation of Scripture even if they are wicked. To support this contention, Kennedy offers three scriptural examples of correct judgement in spite of personal wickedness: the high priest Caiaphas' prophecy of Christ's death; the priests who told Herod where Christ would be born; and Judas' apostleship. And surely, says Kennedy, no ministers of the New Law are so wicked as these. The same pattern holds true for the dispensing of sacraments by wicked ministers: their sins do not take away their authority to fulfil their calling.[31]

Kennedy also endeavours to answer from historical precedent the charge that the councils disagree with Scripture

---

are known to have been in Scottish libraries of the time. See Durkan and Ross, *Early Scottish Libraries*, as indexed.

[29] Though one wonders what Scriptures Kennedy thought existed at this point!

[30] *Wod. Misc.*, pp. 107–8, 119–20.

[31] Ibid., pp. 135–7. It is perhaps surprising that Kennedy did not level a charge of Donatism – a popular accusation in Reformation debates – against those who denied conciliar authority on the basis of wicked ministers in attendance. See D. F. Wright, 'The Donatists in the sixteenth century', in the forthcoming papers of the Second Symposium on the Church Fathers in the Fifteenth and Sixteenth Centuries, Copenhagen, 1–5 April 1995.

and with one another. The question of inter-conciliar agreement was quite important in the continental debate concerning councils; Luther made the disagreement between councils a key point of attack on their authority in his *On the Councils and the Churches* (1539).[32] In answer, Kennedy distinguishes matters of religion and matters of faith. The former are such things as ceremonies, civil ordinances, and Church laws, which are changeable; concerning these, some councils have of course differed from their predecessors, if the matters of religion are no longer expedient to the time. But matters of faith are those things necessary to salvation, and there has been no change in the councils concerning these at any time. Some provincial councils, like Cyprian's African council, may have differed on a matter of faith, but these are always to be referred to a general council.[33] On the other hand, the Protestants disagree with one another over the most fundamental matters of the faith, a distinguishing mark of heresy.[34]

Finally, Kennedy addresses the important issue of the relationship of Scripture to the Church. He begins by making the point that the individual must 'lein to the jugement of the Kirk' because some things necessary for salvation, such as infant baptism, are not found explicitly in Scripture. Further, only the Church can validate which writings are genuine Scripture: the Gospel of John, for example, could not be proven authentic Scripture by other Scriptures, being written later, but only by the testimony of the Church. For these reasons, Augustine said 'that he walde nocht beleve the Evangell except the authoritie of the Kirk hade movit hym sua to do'.[35] But with this said, Kennedy assures the reader

---

[32] Martin Luther, *On the Councils and the Churches*, trans. and ed. Charles M. Jacobs, in *Works of Martin Luther*, 6 vols (Philadelphia, 1915–32), 5, pp. 125–263. See also Steinmetz, *Luther in Context*, p. 89.

[33] *Wod. Misc.*, pp. 146–7, 155–6.

[34] Ibid., pp. 157–60, 166.

[35] Ibid., pp. 168–70. The quotation from Augustine is mis-cited in the margin of Kennedy's work as *De praescriptione haereticorum*, which is in fact a work of Tertullian. The correct reference is to Augustine, *Contra epistolam quam vocant fundamenti*, 5, for which see *Sancti Aurelii Augustini De utilitate credendi; De duabus animabus; Contra Fortunatum; Contra Adimantum; Contra epistulam fundamenti; Contra Faustum*, ed. J. Zycha, Corpus scriptorum ecclesiasticorum latinorum, 25 (Prague, Vienna, and Leipzig, 1891), p. 197 (also in *PL*, 42, col. 176). This statement of Augustine's had

that he does not think that the Church 'extenuatis and obscuris the glore of Goddis worde'. He says, 'Sum superstitius men ascrives that to the Kirk quhilk is aganis all veritie, affirmand the Scripture to tak authoritie of the Kirk, quhilk but dout takis authoritie of the Haly Gaist onelie'. To the contrary, the Church in fact merely 'testifeis . . . and certifiis' which Scriptures are genuine, which does not mean that it gives authority to the Scripture, nor that it is adding to the Scripture in defiance of Revelation 22.18–19. The authority of the Church does extend beyond Scripture, however, for it existed long before the Scriptures were even written. Historical examples of this may be seen in Christ's giving authority to the apostles before the giving of Scripture (Matthew 16.18–19, John 20.21–3), and the Church's charge to Paul and Barnabas by the authority of the Holy Spirit alone. 'Nochtheles', says Kennedy, 'the Scripture and Kirk ar baith alyke trew, equale of strenth, power, and dignitie, governit evir with the samyn Spirite of God.'[36]

It is important to take note of what Kennedy has left out of his argument. Like *Hamilton's Catechism*, he has made no reference to the pope in his historical argument concerning the authority of the Church and the settling of religious controversy.[37] Neither does Kennedy discuss who has the authority to call councils,[38] and he does not mention the then-recessed Council of Trent (1545–63).[39] By grounding his argument in historical precedents from the Bible, Kennedy seems to have felt that the need to deal with later councils was obviated, and so discussion of even the first four councils is extremely limited. His argument from history was from biblical history, making a Protestant response more difficult.

been debated for some time; for examples from Luther, see *Luther's Works*, 55 vols (Philadelphia, 1955–86), 35, pp. 150–2; 36, pp. 107–8; cf. *Ham. Cat.*, p. 41.

[36] *Wod. Misc.*, pp. 171–2. Kennedy mis-cites the Matt. passage as Matt. 15.

[37] There is one passing reference to the pope, ibid., p. 125, but it has nothing to do with the argument itself: 'Hes nocht Christ bocht us als deir as older Bischop, Abbot, Prior, or Pape?'

[38] Although he does mention that Constantine assembled the Council of Nicaea, and praises the fact that he did not himself sit in judgement: ibid., p. 111.

[39] It is, however, possible that Kennedy had Trent in mind when discussing whether the laity should read Scripture; he may speculate on the issue 'because the Kirk as zit hes nocht diffynit thairupon': ibid., p. 132.

But Kennedy cannot have been aware of the special difficulty his argument would pose for a Protestant response in Scotland. From 1560, Scottish Protestants had organized their Church under the central authority of the General Assembly, which adjudicated in matters of doctrine and ecclesiastical discipline.[40] The importance of the Assembly to Scottish Protestants is illustrated by a statement of John Knox during the Assembly of December, 1561: 'tack from us the fredome of Assemblies, and tack from us the Evangell; for without Assemblies, how shall good ordour and unitie in doctrine be keapt?'[41] General Assemblies were based at least loosely on the conciliar principle – a connection made explicit in the *Second Book of Discipline* (1578), which grouped General Assemblies with general councils.[42] Thus Protestants could not attack the authority of councils without having to qualify the authority of the Assembly.

Prior to the convention of the first General Assembly, the Scots Confession of Faith had offered an official position on general councils. According to the Confession's eighteenth article, when controversies arise, 'we ought not sa meikle to luke what men before us have said or done, as unto that quhilk the halie Ghaist uniformelie speakes within the body of the Scriptures', which contain 'all thingis necessary to be beleeved for the salvation of mankinde'.[43] The interpretation of 'ony Doctor, Kirk, or Councell' which opposes the Word of God does not come from the Holy Spirit.[44] In its

[40] See Duncan Shaw, *The General Assemblies of the Church of Scotland 1560–1600* (Edinburgh, 1964), as well as the introduction to the *Second Book of Discipline*, ed. James Kirk (Edinburgh, 1980), pp. 101–2, 116–21. Strangely, the formation of General Assemblies had not been specifically prescribed in the 1560 *Book of Discipline* or Scots Confession of Faith, and these works mentioned Assemblies only incidentally. See the introduction to *The First Book of Discipline*, ed. James K. Cameron (Edinburgh, 1972), p. 69.

[41] Knox, *Works*, 2, p. 296 (also in *John Knox's History of the Reformation in Scotland*, ed. William Croft Dickinson, 2 vols [London and New York, 1949–50], 2, p. 26).

[42] *Second Book of Discipline*, pp. 205–6. A basic conciliar principle may also underpin the Exercise, a regular meeting of ministers and laypeople to discuss the Scriptures, prescribed in the *First Book of Discipline*, pp. 187–90.

[43] *Scots Confession, 1560 and Negative Confession, 1581*, ed. G. D. Henderson (Edinburgh, 1937), p. 77. The Confession was penned by a committee of six, including Knox.

[44] Ibid., p. 79. This standard Protestant position is also found in the *First Book of Discipline*, pp. 87–8. It was certainly nothing new; see, for example, Calvin's *Reply to Sadoleto*, in Olin, *A Reformation Debate*, p. 92; or Calvin's *Institutes*, IV, ix.

nineteenth article, the Confession leaves no question regarding the balance of authority between Scripture and Church: 'We affirme, therefore, that sik as allege the Scripture to have na uther authoritie bot that quhilk it hes received from the Kirk, to be blasphemous against God, and injurious to the trew Kirk.'[45] The twentieth article deals specifically with general councils.[46] The authors, perhaps attempting to find a middle course on councils, state that they do not 'rashlie damne' the determinations of councils; but on the other hand, they will examine these determinations in light of the fact that the men in the councils were fallible, and hence have erred. So long as the council agrees with the Word of God, it is acceptable; if it does not, then it teaches the 'doctrine of Devils'. Councils were convened not to make perpetual laws, nor new articles of faith, nor to give the Scriptures authority, 'meikle les to make that to be his Word, or zit the trew interpretation of the same, quhilk wes not before be his haly will expressed in his Word'; rather, they met 'partlie for confutation of heresies, and for giving publick confession of their faith to the posteritie following', and partly to keep good order in the Church.[47] These sections of the Confession may have been written to refute Kennedy's treatise,[48] and the Confession was undoubtedly known to John Davidson.

[45] Henderson, *Scots Confession*, p. 79. Kennedy had specifically denied holding this view.

[46] It is difficult to trace influences on this article, though it does bear similarities to article 21 of the English Church's 42 Articles of 1552. See Thomas Muir, 'The Scots Confession of 1560: its sources and distinctive characteristics' (Edinburgh University, Ph.D. thesis, 1926), p. 73. Interestingly, the draft of these articles, originally numbering 45, was sent to Edward VI's royal chaplains for approval – one of whom was Knox, who subscribed them: *Calendar of State Papers, Domestic Series of the reign of Edward VI, 1547–1552 preserved in the Public Record Office*, rev. edn, ed. C. S. Knighton (London, 1992), p. 268. Article 21 began with the phrase, 'Generalia Concilia sine jussu et voluntate Principum congregari non possunt'; Knox appears to have changed his mind on this by 1561: see n. 41 above. The manuscript version of the 45 Articles which Knox subscribed also included a significant phrase that was later excised, 'Possunt reges et pii magistratus non expectata conciliorum generalium sententia aut convocatione in republica sua juxta Dei verbum de rebus religionis constituere': cited in Charles Hardwick, *A History of the Articles of Religion*, 2nd edn (Cambridge, 1859), p. 302 n. 5.

[47] Henderson, *Scots Confession*, p. 81. This understanding was repeated in the *Second Book of Discipline*, pp. 197, 205–6.

[48] A brief statement of this view, together with a short discussion of conciliarism in the Scots Confession may be found in W. Ian P. Hazlett, 'The Scots Confession 1560: context, complexion, and critique', *ARG*, 78 (1987), pp. 305–6.

Davidson's task in responding to Kennedy would not be easy, for he had to refute arguments for the authority of general councils without diminishing the authority of the General Assembly in matters of interpretation and discipline. Also difficult was the fact that he could not simply point to inter-conciliar disagreement, as Luther had done, for Kennedy had based his argument on historical precedent from Scripture.

Davidson opens his *Answer* with a statement of purpose similar to Kennedy's: he wishes to explain how religious disputes are to be settled.[49] He makes the general Protestant claim that since humans are fallible, they can mistake the meaning of Scripture, even though they have been given the 'ordinarie meanis' to understand it, by which he means 'the sciences callit Liberal Artes, the knawledge of the thré principall Languages, conference of Scriptures with Scripturs, the preceptis of the maist ancient Doctors, and siclyke thingis that servis men to bring thaim to the knawledge of the Scriptures'.[50] Even in council, humans can make mistakes. It should be noted that Davidson subtly introduces an element of selectivity here not unlike Kennedy's justification for the 'speciale member': not everyone will be skilled in these 'ordinarie meanis', but rather the learned are best qualified to interpret Scripture.

In answer to Kennedy's contention that Scripture cannot be both witness and judge, Davidson notes that while this principle is true of fallible things, it does not hold for things 'everlasting and immortal' like the Word of God.[51] Further, if a special member of the Church is to be judge of the Scripture, Davidson asks, why is this vocation not found within the New Testament lists of ministries? Were judging the Scripture a genuine vocation, this would lead to perturbation in the Church, for everyone would want to seek

---

[49] *Wod. Misc.*, p. 183.

[50] Ibid., pp. 190–1. Davidson does not discuss the issue of the perspicuity of Scripture in the *Answer*; but for Luther and Calvin alike, this was the source of 'exegetical optimism' in their refutations of conciliar authority. See Steinmetz, *Luther in Context*, p. 96. The 1549 provincial council had complained of ignorance of the liberal arts, which Davidson mentions here. See Patrick, *Statutes*, p. 84.

[51] *Wod. Misc.*, p. 195.

such judges on every issue. The actual judges of religious disputes are the Word and Spirit of God alone.[52]

Davidson now offers an alternative account of the purpose of Church councils. Because Scripture is often difficult to understand, men well-versed in the ordinary means of understanding Scripture gather to seek out the judgement of the Word and Spirit of God. This use of the ordinary means is not a judgement, but rather human consent and approbation to the Holy Spirit. Like Kennedy, Davidson seeks an historical precedent in Acts 15. At the Council of Jerusalem, Paul and Barnabas gathered to use the ordinary means to discover the judgement of the Word and Spirit; the words 'it has pleased the Spirit and us' indicate that the Holy Spirit was 'judge, gyde, and president' at the council. The apostles and elders were also named with the Spirit, but only as they gave the assent which is required of the Church to the judgement of the Word and Spirit.[53]

But Davidson has not yet dealt with the full historical force of Kennedy's argument, so he now gives attention to the way in which heresy was suppressed in the early Church. It is Davidson's contention that no heresies have ever been suppressed by a council of itself, but only by the Word and Spirit of God.[54] This is seen in Acts 15, the first council, where Peter and James cited Scripture throughout their speeches. Although his opponents hold Scripture to be the dead instrument in such a case, Davidson cites Hebrews 4.12 in support of his point that Scripture is in fact the living agent at work in suppressing heresy, and those men through whom the Spirit speaks are the dead instruments. Furthermore, according to I Corinthians 2.14, the natural man cannot perceive the Holy Spirit; since those in the councils were so fleshly, how could they have perceived the

---

[52]   Ibid., pp. 193–5.

[53]   Ibid., pp. 184, 199-202. Davidson cites Exod. 14 to defend this position, which reflects his use of the Geneva Bible of 1560; Exod. 14 is found in the Geneva Bible's cross-references for Acts 15, and Davidson's statement 'thay belevit the doctryne that he teachit thaim in the name of the Lorde' is a direct quotation of the Geneva Bible's note on Exod. 14.31 (rendered into Scots); ibid., p. 202.

[54]   On this point, Davidson is stricter than the Scots Confession, which did attribute to councils the occasional refutation of heresy.

will of the Spirit? This has been the case especially since the time of Pope Silvester I, but even before him there were few godly councils.[55]

Davidson now turns to his own historical argument, using the issue of heresy in the early Church to attack Kennedy's position on conciliar authority. What, he asks, of the many heresies that occurred before the council of Nicaea? Did the Fathers who combated them labour in vain? And even after Nicaea, many heresies were refuted by the Fathers, especially Augustine, rather than in councils. Councils as judges would in fact be impracticable, since no pastors could settle the consciences of their flocks until a council decreed the answer – Davidson may have had the long-running Council of Trent in mind here.[56] He next offers a very brief attack on the early councils and their agreement: they were liable to err, and have indeed erred, so how can they be trusted to refute heresy? But the only examples of error Davidson offers are from early provincial councils.[57] By doing so, he rejects Kennedy's notion that general councils are substantially different from provincial councils with regard to the liability to err; and in any case, Davidson argues, the idea that there has been a genuinely universal council representing the whole Church since the days of the apostles is but 'ane dreame devoitly dreamit'.[58]

As for Augustine's remark about not believing the Gospel had the authority of the Church not moved him to do so, Davidson insists that the verb (*commoveret*) should be translated into Scots as 'commovit', which indicates that the Church cannot act apart from the Scripture in its evangelism.[59] The same is true of the Church's approval of the authenticity of Scripture. The Church did not judge the writings given it by the apostles, but merely received them

[55]   Ibid., pp. 211–15.
[56]   Ibid., pp. 216–18.
[57]   Ariminum, the 'Robber Synod' of Ephesus, and Cyprian's African council; he also mentions the seventeen followers of Arius at Nicaea.
[58]   Ibid., pp. 218–19.
[59]   This is an artificially forced translation of the compound verb *cum-movere* hence 'moved with', or 'co-moved'. Bucer discussed whether the verb was *commoveret* or *commoneret*: Martin Bucer, *Common Places of Martin Bucer*, ed. D. F. Wright, The Courtenay Library of Reformation Classics, 4 (Appleford, 1972), pp. 191, 217–18.

from authors it knew to be filled with the Holy Spirit and then bore witness to their validity. In the same way, the priests of Israel did not judge the Old Testament, but merely safeguarded it in the Temple. Davidson offers the illustration of a royal proclamation coming to a city: the leaders in the city may examine whether the message is forged, but if it is not forged or corrupted, they cannot alter it, but must obey it. In the same way, 'the Kirk of God nother admittit nor refusit the Scriptures be its awin autoritie', but accepts and keeps them.[60]

Toward the end of his *Answer*, Davidson contests Kennedy's use of Scripture for the historical precedent of conciliar authority. As for Deuteronomy 17.8–13, Kennedy has completely misread the passage. The Levites were not judging disputes about the interpretation of the Law, but rather the appropriate sentencing of those who transgressed it. A better translation of their role than 'judge' would be 'president'.[61] Thus, Kennedy's argument that the judgement of the Levites can be applied to Haggai 2.9 is of no value; but even if it were, the Levitical priesthood had been superseded by Christ's institution of the priesthood of Melchisedek.[62] Davidson then offers a counter-argument from Scripture, the convention of Jewish elders in Acts 4 which decided to prevent the preaching of the Gospel. This was a duly convened council which erred grievously, for it did not have the Holy Spirit to show the proper judgement. Likewise more recent councils, in spite of the fact that they have the New Testament and the ordinary means to understand the Scripture, err if they do not have the Holy Spirit.[63]

In response to Kennedy's claim from Acts 15 that Paul and Barnabas went to Jerusalem because they would not decide the issue of the circumcision of gentiles themselves,

---

[60] *Wod. Misc.*, pp. 224–7. On this point, Davidson does not substantially differ from Kennedy; it is the Church's establishment of extra-scriptural teaching that divides them. The illustration was nothing new; see, e.g., Bucer's use of it in *Common Places*, pp. 184, 198 n. 53.

[61] This point had also been made previously by Bucer: ibid., p. 214.

[62] The priesthood of Melchisedek had been an issue in Kennedy's 1562 debate with Knox at Maybole; reprinted in Knox, *Works*, 6, pp. 169–220.

[63] *Wod. Misc.*, pp. 231–5.

Davidson first points out that if this is true, then all the popes and Fathers who have declared upon religious controversies have been in the wrong. But in fact, Paul was never in doubt about his own teaching on the matter; he went merely to 'confer' on the issue, a verb interpreted by Jerome to mean the discussion of equals, in order that he might have the validation of the Spirit and the apostles for his position. Kennedy's second claim, that only the apostles and elders were gathered and thus represented the whole Church, is countered by Davidson with various phrases from the text suggesting a larger crowd: the 'whole multitude', 'all the Kirk', 'the brethren', 'the Holy Spirit and us'. Third, Kennedy had claimed that James's statement 'I judge' demonstrated the judging role of the Church. Davidson first claims that lexically the Greek κρίνω is closer to 'It is my opinion'. But this is not the only problem with Kennedy's third point, for it also 'savoris ... Of Papistrie' in giving James the ability to speak for all the apostles due to his title, and it 'savoris of ambitione' amongst the apostles. Both of these Davidson regards as unacceptable *prima facie*.[64] So, the apostles did not judge the Scriptures in this passage, but merely found out the Holy Spirit's judgement. Kennedy has therefore slighted the role of the Holy Spirit in Acts 15.[65]

In his *Answer*, Davidson attempted to undermine Kennedy's arguments from scriptural and historical precedents for conciliar authority. In spite of his frequent use of the term 'Papistes', it is clear that he saw the councils as his point of contention with his opponent. Moreover, he is at pains to show that he approves of 'godly' councils, provided they acknowledge the judging role of the Spirit and Word. But Davidson does not mention Trent, nor does he call for a general council as had the early continental Protestants, as well as Knox and the Scottish Protestant

[64]   Ibid., pp. 238–46. Kennedy had not mentioned the papacy in connection with the apostle James here, though earlier authors had argued that James's role in the council disproved Petrine primacy among the apostles, and demonstrated the authority of councils: Pelikan, *Christian Tradition*, 4, pp. 114–15. Davidson does not appear to have been familiar with Luther's lengthy exposition of Acts 15 in *On the Councils and the Churches*.

[65]   *Wod. Misc.*, p. 249.

nobility; perhaps this is because the Protestant Church had now been established in Scotland and did not need to appeal to a general council for legitimation and survival.[66]

The debate between Kennedy and Davidson provides an illustration of the use of history as an argumentative tool, with each trying to prove that past precedent supported his own position and undermined that of his opponent. The emphasis on general councils in this context, rather than on Petrine succession, seems to reflect the conciliarist influence in Scotland. For both authors, the burning question of authority was best addressed by pointing back to the nature of the primitive Church, particularly its first council as recorded in Acts 15. A reader convinced by such an historical account, so both authors hoped, would also opt for the corresponding means of settling his or her conscience with regard to contemporary religious disputes. By approaching the debate over authority in this way, Kennedy and Davidson combined elements of Christian humanism and scholasticism, joining an interest in antiquity with conciliar thought.

Ironically this debate over Church authority, centred on councils, ignored the general council which had been meeting since 1545. Their silence regarding Trent probably reflects the general dissatisfaction of many with this Council. But with neither reference to Trent nor calls for another council, the debate may have seemed somewhat irrelevant to contemporary readers aware that the cause of the conciliarist movement had long since failed. It is impossible to tell exactly how much impact this printed debate had in Scotland. No continuation of the debate could take place, as Kennedy died in the year following publication of Davidson's *Answer* to his treatise. Three years after his death, Mary Stewart would be forced to abdicate for her son James, and Scotland's Protestant Church attained much greater institutional security. But the process of convincing the people was anything but complete for the Protestant

---

[66] Knox's appeals may be found in Knox, *Works*, 4, pp. 431, 469 (also in Mason, *John Knox*, pp. 49, 74); those of the Scottish Protestant nobility in Knox, *Works*, 1, pp. 310, 367 (also in Dickinson, *John Knox's History*, 1, pp. 155, 195).

Church. Perhaps part of its gradual, overall success came from its continuity with the conciliar principle of Church government.

New College,
University of Edinburgh

IMPOLITIC PICTURES: PROVIDENCE, HISTORY, AND THE ICONOGRAPHY OF PROTESTANT NATIONHOOD IN EARLY STUART ENGLAND

by ALEXANDRA WALSHAM

This paper explores the religious politics of remembering and visually depicting the recent past in early modern England. In the first quarter of the seventeenth century, the commemoration of a series of critical moments in the reigns of the last Tudor monarch, Elizabeth, and her Stuart successor, King James I, became a powerful bulwark of both Church and State. The story of the nation's providential rescues from Catholic treachery and oppression, pre-eminently the defeat of the Spanish Armada and the discovery of the Gunpowder Plot, evolved into an enduring myth which fused Protestantism with patriotism – a myth which, moreover, engendered its own highly emotive iconography. By the 1630s, however, the celebration of these same anniversaries grew increasingly contentious: as the theological complexion of the episcopal hierarchy gradually shifted, such events became the victims of a species of ecclesiastical amnesia. Caroline clerics began to take deliberate steps to discourage retrospection, to control the memory of historical milestones which were now regarded as a source of embarrassment. Here I want to suggest tentatively that this trend can be traced into the realm of pictorial representation. In the process, we may learn something more about the relationship between the Calvinist strand of the Reformation and the graphic arts.

In the winter of 1621, a remarkable print engraved in Amsterdam began to cause ripples in England (Plate 1). 'Invented' by Samuel Ward, a popular puritan preacher employed by the corporation of Ipswich, this composite image portrayed God's 'double deliveraunce' of Great Britain from 'ye invincible Navie and ye unmatcheable powder Treason'. In the left-hand frame of this elaborate triptych, heaven-sent winds disperse a formidable arc-

Plate 1   Samuel Ward, *Deo tri-uniBritanniae Bis Ultorui in Memoriam Classis Invincibilis Subversae Submersae/Proditionis Nesandae Detectae Disiectae. To God, in memorye of his Double Deliveraunce from the Invincible Navie and the Unmatcheable Power Treason* (Amsterdam, 1621) (British Museum, Department of Prints and Drawings, satire series, no 41; by permission of the Trustees of the British Museum).

shaped fleet, making a mockery of the Spaniards' 'potent might' in that 'mirabilis Annus', 1588. In the middle a conspiratorial cabal of the pope, King Philip IV of Spain, the Jesuit Henry Garnet, and Satan himself 'strayne their witts' to contrive 'some rare stratagem' to overthrow the ruling regime and usher in a Catholic Counter-Reformation. On the right, the 'dire intendments of this damned crew' are frustrated by the Lord's 'never slumbring EYE': garbed in spurs, hat, and a voluminous cloak and lighted by a lantern, Guy 'Faux' is caught in the dastardly act of igniting the barrels and faggots beneath Parliament House on the eve of November the fifth. 'Video Rideo, I see and smile', proclaims the shaft of light descending from the mysterious hieroglyph

308

of the Hebrew tetragrammaton.[1] For Calvinists hot under the collar about the perils of idolatry, this abstract symbol was the only acceptable way of signifying the Almighty – traditional anthropomorphic depictions of the deity as a bearded patriarch enthroned in a bolster of clouds were categorically banned.[2]

Ward's print was a compelling embodiment of orthodox anti-Catholicism. It epitomized the prevalent belief in God's singular benevolence towards the people of England, his repeated interventions to protect the country from both her foreign enemies and foes and the dangerous fifth column lurking within. Yet in the context of the early 1620s it was little short of explosive. With the negotiations for a dynastic marriage between Prince Charles and the Habsburg Infanta Maria at a delicate stage, an engraving displaying her father consulting with the devil to destroy her intended husband's regal inheritance was bound to have international repercussions. Creating quite a stir among the politically articulate, it also provoked an indignant protest from the Spanish ambassador, Don Gondomar, which led directly to the Ipswich lecturer's arrest and subsequent imprisonment. Overt reference to these sparkling highlights in recent Protestant history amounted to a major diplomatic gaffe. As John Chamberlain remarked laconically to Sir Dudley Carleton in March of 1621, it was 'not goode rubbing on that sore'.[3] Like the succession of preachers censured during the following year for daring to inveigh against the projected wedding or the papists from prominent London pulpits, Ward's artistic endeavours could not be allowed to pass unreproved. According to Thomas Scott, author of the notorious *Vox Populi*, this was one of 'two facete and befitting

[1]   Samuel Ward, *Deo Trin-uniBritanniae Bis Ultori* (Amsterdam, 1621). See F. G. Stephens and M. D. George, *Catalogue of Prints and Drawings in the British Museum. Division I. Political and Personal Satires (1320–1832)*, 11 vols (London, 1870–1954) [hereafter BM *Satires*], no. 41, and A. M. Hind, *Engraving in England in the Sixteenth and Seventeenth Centuries*, 3 vols (Cambridge, 1952–64), 2, pp. 393–4.

[2]   See Margaret Aston, *England's Iconoclasts, I: Laws against Images* (Oxford, 1988), pp. 452–7.

[3]   *The Letters of John Chamberlain*, ed. Norman Egbert McClure, Memoirs of the American Philosophical Society, 12, 2 vols (Philadelphia, 1939), 2, p. 349. See also the letters of Joseph Mede, Fellow of Christ's College, Cambridge, to Sir Martin Stutevile: BL, MS Harley 389, fols 13r–v, 15v, 22v.

pictures' which the authorities took drastic steps to repress.[4]

In a petition to James I in April 1622, Ward claimed to have devised this 'embleme ... five yeeres since in imitacion of auntient rites gratefully preserving the memories of extraordinarie favours and deliverences ... without anie other sinister intencion, especiallie of meddling in any of your Majesties secrett affaires'. Far from seeking to interfere in *arcana imperii* he was simply 'coupling the two grand blessings' which divines 'daylie joyned' in anniversary sermons and intercessions without any molestation whatsoever.[5] His print was not a savage attack on royal policy but, as a bookseller's advertisement had described it several months before, a 'most Remarkable Monument ... Necessary to be had in the House of every good Christian, to shew Gods loving and wonderfull providence, over this Kingdome'.[6] Notwithstanding his protestations of innocence, the timing of Ward's decision to send this picture to the printers is very suspicious. It may well have been an ingenious attempt to sabotage the Spanish match. Although Ward was released after promising to be 'more cauteious for the future', the incident did cast a shadow over the rest of his clerical career.[7]

Commemoration of the nation's salvation from the malign forces of Rome and Spain was of course entirely conventional. Indeed, as David Cressy has shown, it had its origins in the high politics of Whitehall and Westminster. The English reformers substituted the medieval cycle of feast and saints' days with a new calendar which hinged upon miraculous moments in the immediate past – above all the

[4] Thomas Scott, *Boanerges* (Edinburgh [London], 1624), p. 25. See also idem, *The Second Part of Vox Populi* (Goricom [London], 1624), p. 17. For the censure of other preachers in 1622, see Thomas Cogswell, *The Blessed Revolution: English Politics and the Coming of War, 1621–1624* (Cambridge, 1989), pp. 27–34 and Godfrey Davies, 'English political sermons, 1603–1640', *Huntington Library Quarterly*, 3 (1939), pp. 9–13.

[5] London, Public Record Office, State Papers [hereafter PRO, SP] 15/42/76.

[6] Samuel Ward, *The Life of Faith*, 2nd edn (London, 1621), p. 117.

[7] PRO, SP 15/42/77. Ward was simultaneously prosecuted for nonconformity by Bishop Harsnet of Norwich. See Patrick Collinson, 'Lectures by combination: structures and characteristics of church life in 17th-century England', in his *Godly People: Essays on English Protestantism and Puritanism* (London, 1983), pp. 488–9.

accession of Queen Elizabeth, the failure of the Armada and the prevention of the Gunpowder Plot, which Parliament legislated to ensure was kept in 'perpetual Remembrance'.[8] This was an archetypally 'invented tradition'.[9] By the mid-Jacobean period, the memorialization of such 'icon events' had become a flourishing industry. Every year, preachers rehearsed these legendary tales of eleventh-hour escape to their congregations, ignoring human frailty, freak weather conditions, and clever detective work in rousing narratives which stressed the overpowering providence of God. In some parishes, like St Martin Orgar in London, lectures against the barbarous and 'bloud thirsty papistes' were specially endowed by zealous inhabitants.[10] Outside in the streets, ritual rejoicing in the form of bonfires and bells was sanctioned if not financed by the civic authorities.[11] Poets and annalists chronicled these mercies for the benefit of posterity in verse and prose; puppet plays, ballads, and chapbook-sized collections of ditties and songs helped to imprint this inspiring historiography on the consciousness of the semi-literate, adolescent, and poor.[12] Jingoism, xenophobia, and apocalyptic anti-popery were combined in a virulent mixture.

[8] David Cressy, *Bonfires and Bells: National Memory and the Protestant Calendar in Elizabethan and Stuart England* (London, 1989) and idem, 'The Fifth of November remembered', in Roy Porter, ed., *Myths of the English* (Cambridge, 1992), pp. 68–90. For the Acts of 1606, see *The Statutes of the Realm*, ed. T. E. Tomlins et al. (London, 1819), 3 Jac. I. c.1.

[9] See Eric Hobsbawm and Terence Ranger, eds, *The Invention of Tradition* (Cambridge, 1983).

[10] London, Guildhall Library, MS 959/1 (Vestry minutes and churchwardens' accounts, St Martin Orgar, 1471–1615), fol. 391v. For an entirely typical example of a set of anniversary sermons, see Daniel Dyke, *Certaine Comfortable Sermons upon the 124. Psalme: tending to stirre up to Thankefulnesse for our Deliverance from the Late Gunpowder-Treason* (London, 1616).

[11] See Cressy, *Bonfires and Bells*, ch. 5 and *passim*, and Ronald Hutton, *The Rise and Fall of Merry England: The Ritual Year 1400–1700* (Oxford, 1994), pp. 182–5.

[12] For example, Francis Herring, *Popish Pietie, or the First Part of the Historie of that Horrible and Barbarous Conspiracie, commonly called the Powder-Treason*, trans. A. P. (London, 1610); Samuel Garey, *Great Brittans Little Calendar: or, Triple Diarie. In Remembrance of Three Daies* (London, 1618); T. S., *A Song or Psalme of Thanksgiving, in Remembrance of our Great Deliverance from the Gun-powder Treason* (London, 1625); John Rhodes, *The Country Mans Comfort* (London, 1637) (an enlarged edition of a book of 'religious recreations' first printed in 1588, no copy of which now survives). For puppet plays, see Ben Jonson, *Bartholomew Fayre: a Comedie, acted in the Yeare, 1614*, repr. in *Three Comedies*, ed. Michael Jamieson (Harmondsworth, 1966), V.i.11–14.

The clergy recurrently unleashed their tongues against the pestiferous designs of the papal Antichrist and his confederates. They triumphed over the rout of the flotilla of ships sent by Philip II, 'that Senacherib of Spaine' who was so confident 'to have swallowed us up quicke at one morsell', and they emphatically denounced the foiled Catholic coup of 1605 as 'the Quintessence of all impiety, and the confection of all villany'.[13] These famous deliverances were seals and testaments of the Lord's holy covenant with his new Israel, England, signs of paternal interest in the spiritual fate of the entire Anglo-Saxon race. But the self-congratulation was always tinged with anxiety: if biblical history provided a parallel for Britain's blessings, it also offered a prophetic paradigm of the devastating judgements she too could expect if, like the Jews, she remained ungrateful and impenitent.

It was considered incumbent upon the generation which witnessed such wondrous works to engrave them with 'a Penne of Iron, with the Point of a Diamond, on the Tables of our hearts, on the Postes of Houses, on the Hornes of our Altars', in 'capitall Letters' and 'characters indeleble'. Men and women must metaphorically erect 'eternall Trophees' in their souls, insisted ministers like Daniel Dyke and Thomas Taylor, as well as 'an everlasting record' in books. To bury these 'monstrous birth[s] of the Romish harlot' in 'the dark pit of oblivion', declared another, was an unforgivable sin. Their memory should be preserved in 'a Monument of Marble' for all ages to come.[14]

At least some contemporaries took the preachers' imperatives quite literally. In encapsulating the mythology of Protestant nationhood in a picture, Samuel Ward was in fact building on an established iconographical tradition. He had done little more than refine and juxtapose three pre-existing and frequently recycled motifs. The crescent Armada scattered by a supernatural gust has a prototype in a silver

---

[13] Theodore Hering, *The Triumph of the Church over Fire and Water* (London, 1625), p. 26; Garey, *Great Brittans Little Calendar*, p. 184.

[14] See Hering, *Triumph*, 'To the Reader'; Dyke, *Certaine Comfortable Sermons*, p. 9; Thomas Taylor, *An Everlasting Record of the Utter Ruine of Romish Amaleck*, in *Two Sermons* (London, 1624), esp. p. 24; Herring, *Popish Pietie*, sig. A3r.

medal struck in Middelburg in 1588,[15] the evil conclave of machiavellian politicians was undoubtedly another 'visual cliché',[16] and Guy Fawkes stealthily approaching the cellar to effect his 'deed of darknes' can be found in two earlier engravings on the ever-popular theme of the 'papists powder treason'. Dating from the mid-1610s, these printed artefacts were two-dimensional memorials, triumphal arches and sacred shrines constructed of paper rather than stone.[17] Like its forerunners, Ward's monument was indebted to the emblem book and to the commemorative coins and pictures produced by the precociously advanced craftsmen of the Dutch Republic. Crowded with complex symbols and littered with Latin phrases and tags, these densely allegorical images were relatively expensive items, aimed at an emerging market of 'middling sort' buyers and largely beyond the means of regular consumers of the cheapest types of print.[18] It may be misleading to characterise them as political cartoons, 'engines of agitation' designed to swing and influence public opinion,[19] since their main function seems to have been mnemonic. These were images which pious householders might hang above the mantelpieces of their parlours to remind them of historical events with whose religious significance they were already deeply imbued.

Such providential 'monuments' lend weight to Tessa Watt's suggestion that the iconophobic bias of second-generation Protestantism has been exaggerated and overstated.[20] There can be no doubt that Swiss-style divinity was inherently hostile to traditional devotional imagery involving God the Father, Christ, Mary, and the saints, but it is wrong to infer

[15] London, National Maritime Museum, A2251, reproduced in M. J. Rodríguez-Salgado et al., *Armada 1588-1988* (London, 1988), fig. 16.12.

[16] The phrase is Roy Porter's in 'Seeing the past', *P&P*, 118 (Feb. 1988), p. 196.

[17] Richard Smith, *The Powder Treason* ([London, *c*. 1615]) (BM, *Satires*, no. 67); *The Papists Powder Treason* (London, [?1679] first publ. *c*. 1612]) [San Marino, California, Huntington Library, RB 28300 IV: 21]. See Hind, *Engraving in England*, 2, pp. 342, 394-5.

[18] See Tessa Watt, *Cheap Print and Popular Piety, 1550-1640* (Cambridge, 1991), pp. 141-2, 159. For a more detailed discussion of the 'monument' tradition, see my 'Aspects of Providentialism in Early Modern England' (Cambridge University Ph.D. thesis, 1994), pp. 210-24.

[19] Porter, 'Seeing the past', p. 191.

[20] Watt, *Cheap Print*, pt 2, esp. pp. 134-9.

that it effectively stifled all aesthetic impulses and left late-sixteenth- and early-seventeenth-century England in an 'artistic vacuum'.[21] Calvin and his disciples conceded that there was and 'ever hath been a lawfull and laudable civill use of Pictures . . . both for adornation of houses and convenient places, and for commemoration of persons and things'. Graphic representation for strictly political and utilitarian purposes was not prohibited.[22] Along with the 'godly tables' and narrative 'scripture stories for walls' which Dr Watt has explored, visual remembrancers like Ward's 'Double Deliveraunce' were compatible with the ideological priorities of the religion of the Word. At least some hard-line Protestants had no scruples about combatting the idolatrous papists with pictorial satire of a kind they themselves produced.[23] Writing to Lord Burghley in 1597 and enclosing 'two homely Emblems' of his own invention entitled *A paire of ridles againste the philistynes of Rome*, the radical Yorkshire preacher Giles Wigginton defended the legitimacy of 'counterpicturinge' as confessional propaganda. Surely, he asserted, it was permissible for 'anie man to beate a fole with his own bable (if not to kylle Goliath with his owne sworde)'?[24]

Samuel Ward's engraving, then, was a typical example of a developing genre of anti-Catholic prints. It attracted attention only because the circumstances of the Spanish match

[21] Karl Josef Höltgen, 'The reformation of images and some Jacobean writers on art', in Ulrich Broich et al., eds, *Functions of Literature: Essays Presented to Erwin Wolff on his Sixtieth Birthday* (Tübingen, 1984), p. 123. Also Patrick Collinson, *From Iconoclasm to Iconophobia: The Cultural Impact of the Second English Reformation*, The Stenton Lecture 1985 (Reading, 1986), pp. 22-6, restated in *The Birthpangs of Protestant England: Religious and Cultural Change in the Sixteenth and Seventeenth Centuries* (London, 1988), pp. 115-21. On the centrality of the campaign against idolatry, see Aston, *England's Iconoclasts, passim*, and Sergiusz Michalski, *The Reformation and the Visual Arts: The Protestant Image Question in Western and Eastern Europe* (London and New York, 1993), esp. ch. 2.

[22] Quotation from John Vicars, *The Sinfulness and Unlawfulness, of Having or Making the Picture of Christs Humanity* (London, 1641), sig. B1r. See also John Calvin, *Institutes of the Christian Religion*, trans. John Allen, 2 vols (Philadelphia, 1936), I, xi, 12; William Perkins, *A Warning against the Idolatry of the Last Times* in his *Workes*, 3 vols (Cambridge, 1608-9), 1, p. 670.

[23] See, for example, 'A showe of the Protestants petigrew', discussed and reproduced in Watt, *Cheap Print*, pp. 154-5.

[24] BL, MS Lansdowne 84, fol. 238r.

Plate 2   George Carleton, *A Thankfull Remembrance of Gods Mercy* (London, 1627 edn; first publ. 1624), frontispiece (Cambridge University Library, shelfmark SS.32.15; by permission of the Syndics of Cambridge University Library).

made its ebulliently patriotic themes profoundly embarrassing, as Thomas Middleton noted in his equally inflammatory comedy, *A Game at Chesse*, performed in 1624. The Black Knight, a thinly disguised caricature of Count Gondomar, boasts 'Who . . . Made pictures that were dumbe enough before, Poor sufferers in that politic restraint?'[25]

Belligerent Protestant images did, however, enjoy a brief respite in the wake of the collapse of the marriage talks in Madrid in October 1623 and the 'blessed revolution' in foreign policy the following February, which led to England's military intervention in the Thirty Years' War to assist her beleaguered Continental brethren.[26] Like other manifestations of exuberant anti-popery, 'monuments' to the Armada and Gunpowder Plot benefited from the disintegration of the Anglo-Spanish entente. One symptom of this general reprieve was Bishop George Carleton of Chichester's *A Thankfull Remembrance of Gods Mercy*, a survey of the nation's deliverances from papist conspiracies since 1558, prefaced by a 'comely frontispiece' dominated by the serenely maternal figure of 'Ecclesia Vera'. The banners unfurled behind her by Deborah and Solomon, Queen Elizabeth and King James, bear what by now were familiar motifs: crudely simplified versions of the salvation scenes juxtaposed by Ward three years before (Plate 2).[27] Similar miniatures featured on the title-page of Christopher Lever's *The History of the Defenders of the Catholique Faith*, published in 1627.[28] The same engraver also prepared nineteen copperplate illustrations for the third edition of Carleton's popular book (Plate 3), adapting the designs from a double folio sheet first printed in 1625. Sold separately or as a folding 'synopsis' of the text, this print was intended as a pedagogic device by which

---

[25] Thomas Middleton, *A Game at Chess*, ed. J. W. Harper (London, 1966), III. i. 102-3.

[26] See Cogswell, *The Blessed Revolution*, and Simon Adams, 'Foreign policy and the Parliaments of 1621 and 1624', in Kevin Sharpe, ed., *Faction and Parliament: Essays on Early Stuart History* (London and New York, 1978), pp. 139-71.

[27] George Carleton, *A Thankfull Remembrance of Gods Mercy. In an Historicall Collection of the Great and Mercifull Deliverances of the Church and State of England* (London, 1624). BM, *Satires*, no. 98; Hind, *Engraving in England*, 2, pp. 297-9.

[28] Christopher Lever, *The Historie of the Defendors of the Catholique Faith* (London, 1627). BM, *Satires*, no. 9: Hind, *Engraving in England*, 3, p. 214.

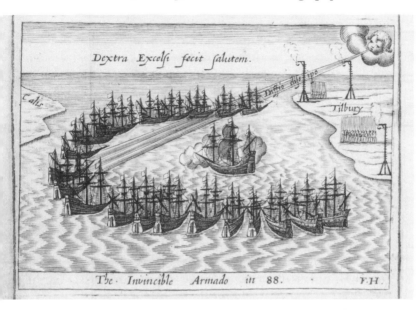

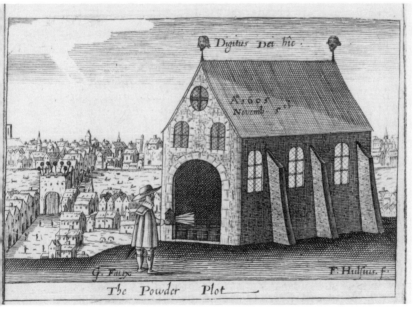

Plates 3a and 3b George Carleton, *A Thankfull Remembrance of Gods Mercy* (London, 1627 edn; first publ. 1624), pp. 144, 248 (Cambridge University Library, shelfmark SSS.32.15; by permission of the Syndics of Cambridge University Library).

parents could instruct their children in the central tenets of Protestant historiography. It showed an obelisk divided into sixteen blocks displaying Catholic conspiracies from the Northern Rising in 1569 to the machinations of 1605. Prince Charles's heroic homecoming in 1623 without a Habsburg bride filled the last box in the base of the commemorative pyramid.[29] Another 'monument' dating from this decade also had a dual existence as a broadside and a set of plates for *Crums of Comfort*, a bestselling anthology of prayers and meditations compiled by Michael Sparke, the puritan stationer later pilloried for publishing William Prynne's impudent *Histrio-mastix*. This was a memorandum of three national miracles: the defeat of the Spanish 'Armado', the discovery of the 'hellish and horible Pouder-Treason', and the end of the major outbreak of bubonic plague in 1625, 'with a zealous Prayer to turne from us the fourth Judgement, that is likely to fall upon us by the Sword'. The upper frames of the picture revealed Philip II's huge navy off the English coast, Guy Fawkes *en route* to St Stephen's Chapel, egged on by a demon dancing with glee, and the devastation wrought by disease and the skeleton of death. Below were joyous scenes of heartfelt thanks-giving.[30]

All these ephemeral engravings echo Ward's classic 'Double Deliveraunce', but it left an even more interesting legacy in silk, metal, and stone. Pasted in paper above the fire places of pious middle-class homes, the same patterns can be found on tapestry wall hangings and cushion covers embroidered by wealthy gentlewomen, one of whom couldn't resist inserting a mermaid, lamb, hare, and a lolloping lion (Plate

---

[29] Carleton, *A Thankfull Remembrance*, 3rd edn (London, 1627), see esp. pp. 144, 248. The print is entitled *A Thankfull Remembrance of Gods Mercie. By G. C.* (London, 1625) [Oxford, Ashmolean Museum, Sutherland Collection, Lar, vol. iii]. See also Hind, *Engraving in England*, 2, pp. 298–9.

[30] Michael Sparke, *To the Glory of God in Thankefull Remembrance of our Three Great Deliverances unto Etern[al] Memory* (London, 1627) [London, Society of Antiquaries, Lemon Collection, no. 266]; idem, *Thankfull Remembrances of Gods Wonderfull Deliverances of this Land. With other Speciall Prayers*, bound with *The Crums of Comfort* (London, 1628). See also Hind, *Engraving in England*, 3, p. 101. On Sparke, see Henry R. Plomer, *A Dictionary of the Booksellers and Printers who were at Work in England, Scotland and Ireland from 1641 to 1667* (London, 1907), p. 169.

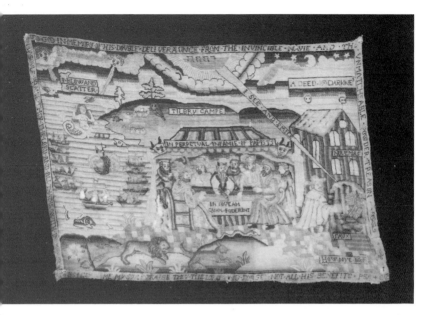

Plate 4 Cushion cover, dated after 1621 (Lady Lever Art Gallery, Port Sunlight, LL5292; by permission of the Board of Trustees of the National Museums and Galleries on Merseyside).

4).[31] Relatives of Dame Dorothy Selby, the 'Dorcas' whose nimble fingers stitched another surviving sampler, had the same image incised in slate on her funeral slab erected in Ightham parish church to mark her passing in 1641.[32] Monuments to the providential events of the recent past inside ecclesiastical buildings were by no means rare. Inscriptions placed in Preston St Mary near Lavenham directly recall Samuel Ward's influential print, and the Somerset family of Strode had part of it engraved on brass, adding a divine ear eavesdropping in the villains, which was labelled 'I heare and laugh.'[33] By the late 1620s many London

---

[31] Cushion cover, after 1621 (Liverpool, Lady Lever Art Gallery, LL5292), discussed in Xanthe Brooke, *The Lady Lever Art Gallery Catalogue of Embroideries* (Stroud, 1992), pp. 18–20, who refers to another piece of needlework based on this design described in the will of one James Carcase dated 1637 as a 'long pillow of tenteworke wherein is the Story of 88 and the Powther plott of the fiefte of November' (PRO, PROB 11/182/f5).

[32] Edward R. Harrison, *The History and Records of Ightham Church* (Oxford, 1932), pp. 16–18, and relevant plates.

[33] Robert Reyce, *Suffolk in the XVIIth Century: The Breviary of Suffolk*, ed. Francis Hervey (London, 1902), pp. 201–4; Philip Whittemore, 'A brass plate commemorating the defeat of the Gunpowder Plot' and John Blatchly, 'The "Gunpowder Plot"

319

churches contained tablets to Elizabeth I, 'Britaine's Blessing, Englands Splendor, Religions Nurse, The Faiths Defendor'. At St Mildred Bread Street a local worthy by the name of Captain Nicholas Crispe commissioned a stained glass window for the chancel with five 'artfull and curious' panels depicting the Armada, the Virgin Queen, the Powder Plot, the terrible epidemic, and finally the pious benefactor and his dependants.[34] Were they variations on the standard designs repeated elsewhere? We do not know: if the flames of the Great Fire did not engulf them, they were probably lost in the Blitz.

But by the time this memorial was installed in 1628 the ideological tide was once again starting to turn. Passionate anti-popery was tacitly devalued as Arminian and Laudian clerics began to occupy ever more rungs on the episcopal ladder. As Anthony Milton has demonstrated, the irenic posture these divines adopted transformed relations between Canterbury and Rome from an 'immortal fewde' to a cordial truce. The traditional identification of the pope as Antichrist foretold in Revelation was jettisoned, as was the precept that Catholicism was a false religion, the very 'mystery of iniquity'. Violent rhetorical attacks on an institution it was now fashionable to acknowledge as a true if erring Church were sharply discouraged and even actively censored. The polemical commonplaces that were an integral part of remembering 1588 and 1605 became a positive liability to a hierarchy seeking to draw closer to European superpowers which committed Calvinists still regarded as their confessional enemies.[35]

The rise of Laudianism involved a corresponding reorientation towards ecclesiastical history. Its scholars and apologists discarded the apocalyptic framework which

---

plate; a postscript', *Transactions of the Monumental Brass Society*, 13 (1985), pp. 549–57 and 14 (1986), pp. 68–9 respectively.

[34] John Stow, *A Survey of London* (London, 1633), pp. 859–60, and note the 'Queen Elizabeth Monuments' described in the 'Perambulation or Circuit-Walke foure miles about London'. I owe this reference to Dr Julia Merritt.

[35] Anthony Milton, *Catholic and Reformed: The Roman and Protestant Churches in English Protestant Thought 1600–1640* (Cambridge, 1995), pt 1. Michael Sparke was one publisher of anti-Catholic propaganda prosecuted in court: William Prynne, *Canterburies Doome* (London, 1646), p. 185.

underpinned John Foxe's famous *Acts and Monuments* and reframed their reply to the old Catholic taunt 'where was your Church before Luther?' Quietly setting aside the idea of an unbroken pedigree of proto-Protestant sects, an invisible succession of sincere believers submerged within an otherwise corrupt religious structure, they stressed instead the Church of England's complete jurisdictional continuity with her medieval predecessor, which they increasingly viewed not as the Scarlet Whore but as a Reverend Mother. The revisionist historiography of the 1630s thus entailed a reinterpretation of the Henrician Reformation as a reluctant political schism rather than a frenzied flight from Babylonish captivity.[36]

One aspect of this campaign to reshape the past in line with the ecumenical priorities of leading prelates was an attempt to muffle the memory of anti-papal landmarks like the never-to-be-forgotten Armada and Gunpowder Treason. Ritual celebration of these red-letter-days in the Protestant calendar was regarded with growing distaste and distrust. Rowdy festive practices were frowned upon as manifestations of extreme Calvinist intolerance.[37] Laudian anniversary sermons avoided the vindictive tone of their Elizabethan precursors, explaining the crime with reference to extenuating circumstances,[38] and when the liturgy for the fifth of November was reissued in 1635, its vituperative wording was subtly but significantly tempered – or so it seemed in the hypersensitive eyes of the puritans.[39] To William Prynne all this was witness to a despicable scheme to conciliate the papists and consign

---

36 Milton, *Catholic and Reformed*, ch. 6. See also Damian Nussbaum's essay in this volume, pp. 329-42.

37 Cressy, *Bonfires and Bells*, p. 153. See also Thomas Taylor, *Christs Victorie over the Dragon* (London, 1633), p. 491.

38 See, for example, Jeremy Taylor, *A Sermon Preached in Saint Maries Church in Oxford. Upon the Anniversarie of the Gunpowder-Treason* (Oxford, 1638) and BL, MS Harley 7019, fol. 78r, where complaint is made of one Mr Kempe, a fellow of Queens' College, Cambridge, who 'extenuated the fact of the powder traitors' on 5 Nov. 1637.

39 *Prayers and Thanksgiving to be used . . . for the Happy Deliverance . . . from the most Traiterous and Bloody Intended Massacre by Gun-powder, the fift of November, 1605* (London, 1635), sig. B4v (I am grateful to Mr Peter Glazebrook for allowing me to consult the copy of this rare liturgy in the Old Library of Jesus College, Cambridge). See also William Laud, *The Works of the Most Reverend Father in God, William Laud, DD.*, 7 vols (Oxford, 1847-60), 4, p. 406; 6, p. 52.

God's mercies to undeserving England to permanent oblivion.[40] David Cressy has already highlighted how they clung defensively to this threatened heritage and hijacked the Powder Plot holiday as a licensed occasion to berate and revile the religious innovations of the Caroline establishment.[41] For one such provocative homily Henry Burton, rector of St Matthew Friday Street, lost a portion of his ears; and in 1633 Samuel Ward himself was hauled before the High Commission for suggesting that the best way of demonstrating 'thanckfullnes' for this divine deliverance was 'a more stricte observacion of the Ten Commandements', including the fourth. Innocuous enough on the surface, in the context of the proclamation of that anti-sabbatarian document, the Declaration of Sports, this was construed as implicitly seditious. For this and other 'gross misdemeanours' he was later muzzled and suspended from his ministry.[42] And it may be more than a mere coincidence that Lady Eleanor Davies, semi-professional prophet and arch-adversary of William Laud, predicted that same year that he should 'very few days outlive' November the fifth.[43] Such statements can only have heightened the determination of the hierarchy to play down these patriotic anniversaries.

Was the iconography of English nationhood another casualty of this escalating trend? Were monuments to the two great watersheds in Britain's post-Reformation history one more target of the clampdown on rabid anti-Catholicism? Early modern censorship was never wholly effective and, in the absence of adequate evidence, it would be unwise to do more than conjecture and speculate. But one or two celebrated episodes are highly suggestive. When, in 1637, the London schoolmaster John Vicars sought a licence for the second edition of his translation of a Latin poem about the

[40] See [William Prynne], *A Quenche-Coale* ([Amsterdam], 1637), pp. 12–18; idem, *Canterburies Doome*, pp. 246–7; and Henry Burton, *For God, and the King. The Summe of Two Sermons Preached on the Fifth of November last in St Matthewes Friday-Streete. 1636* ([Amsterdam], 1636), pp. 130–8.
[41] Cressy, *Bonfires and Bells*, esp. pp. 152–5.
[42] Burton, *For God, and the King*; PRO, SP 16/335/69. On Ward, see PRO, SP 16/278/65, fol. 144r; Prynne, *Canterburies Doome*, p. 361; Laud, *Works*, 5, p. 334, and pp. 328, 340.
[43] Ibid., 3, p. 220.

S Ee, here, the Popiſh *Pouder-plots* fair thriving;
  Fauks and his *Father-Satan* fit contriving
  The *fatall-Inſtruments*, to puffe and blow
Hell out of *Earth*, a State to over-throw,
At *Once*, for *All* : But, here, behold likewiſe,
Heavens *All-ſeeing-Eye*, which *deepeſt-pits* eſpies :
This deſperate *Worke of Darkneſſe* ſees moſt clear,
And, *timely*, makes the miſchiefe *All* appeare:
To *Iſraels* bleſſed *Shepheards* endleſſe glory,
As is *full-ſhown* in *this* ſucceeding *Story*.

Plate 5 John Vicars, *November the 5. 1605. The Quintessence of Cruelty, or Master-peece of Treachery, the Popish Powder-Plot* (London, 1641), sig. A1r (British Library, Thomason Tracts, shelfmark E1100(1); by permission of the British Library).

Plate 6   *The Book of Common Prayer* (London, octavo edn, 1676)
(Cambridge University Library, shelfmark Adams 7.67.14; by permission
of the Syndics of Cambridge University Library).

'Master-peece of treachery' thwarted in 1605, he was flatly refused by Laud's chaplain, Samuel Baker. Baker allegedly said 'that we were not so angry with the Papists now, as we were about 20. yeares since, and that there was no need of any such Bookes as these to exasperate them, there being now an endeavour to winne them to us by fairnesse and mildnesse'. That the pamphlet, when eventually published in 1641, included illustrations adapted from the relevant portions of Michael Sparke's earlier engraving was surely not utterly irrelevant. Vulgar depictions of 'Heavens All-seeing-Eye' discovering the nefarious deeds of '*Fauks* and his *Father-Satan*' can hardly have been aesthetically pleasing to Charles I's ecclesiastical regime (Plate 5).[44] Even more striking are the instructions Laud gave William Kingsley, Archdeacon of Canterbury, in April 1636 regarding a tablet to the Armada and 'Gun-pouder Treason' in the city church of either St Gregory or St George. If this stood in the east end of the chancel it was to be immediately removed and erected elsewhere, so as not to profane the sacred space set aside for the altar. Once relocated, a painter was to be employed to 'put out of the Monument, all that concernes the Fleet in 88. because that belongs to a Forreigne Nation'. Inscribed with the motto 'In perpetuam Papistarum infamiam, &c' there can be little doubt that the memorial was yet another replica of Samuel Ward's 'Double Deliveraunce'. For Prynne, who recorded it in *Canterburies Doome* in 1644, the incident was further proof of a conspiracy to erase and obliterate the memory of the 'icon events' in England's epic struggle against Spain and the papacy.[45] Was there deliberate irony in the fact that the frontispiece of Prynne's book portrayed the Archbishop on trial in a House of Lords bedecked with tapestry 'Hangings of 88'?[46]

[44] John Vicars, *November the 5. 1605. The Quintessence of Cruelty, or Master-peece of Treachery, the Popish Powder-Plot* (London, 1641), sig. A1r; Prynne, *Canterburies Doome*, p. 184. In his *Englands Halle-jah* (London, 1631), sig. B3r, Vicars referred in the margin to 'Mr Wardes Disslo, Dissipo'.

[45] Prynne, *Canterburies Doome*, pp. 91–3. No churchwardens' accounts survive for this period for either of these parishes and the Royal Commission on the Historical Monuments of England has no record of the monument. St George's was badly damaged in bombing raids during the Second World War.

[46] Ibid. The same engraving can be found in Prynne's *The Breviate of the Life of William Laud Archbishop of Canterbury* (London, 1644).

To speak of Laudian iconoclasm of puritan pictures may seem strange in the light of Caroline ceremonialism and the programme to restore to ecclesiastical settings the 'beauty of holiness'. But image-breaking and making, no less than the creation and demolition of myths, are interrelated aspects of the perennial process of forging and cementing identity. While Protestants of one persuasion might embellish their private chapels and personal Bibles with pious representations of Christ and the saints and be condemned by their critics as stinking idolaters,[47] Protestants of another were decorating their parish churches and drawing rooms with providential engravings which some of their neighbours probably regarded as boorish and crude – if not a badge and talisman of adherence to a dissident creed.

After 1640, as the Long Parliament dismantled the policies of the Personal Rule, we find a resurgence of the stock pictorial motifs I have argued had become ideologically charged. Vicars's suppressed *Quintessence of Cruelty* with its impertinent plate appeared in time for the Gunpowder anniversary of 1641, part of a fresh wave of popular antipopery sweeping the country. In the less hostile climate of the Civil War, Cromwellian Protectorate, and Restoration, emblematic miniatures of 1588 and 1605 were once again able to flourish. They continued to reappear in pocket books of history like Samuel Clarke's *Englands Remembrancer* (1657). In a similar tract published in 1671 Clarke added a further 'popish plot' to the iconographical canon – the Great Fire of London of 1666.[48] New impressions of Jacobean prints were issued whenever collective anxiety about Catholicism grew acute, especially during the scares surrounding Titus Oates's slanders in 1678, the Exclusion Crisis, and the Glorious Revolution. The same images were also adjusted to suit the rather different format of the playing card, and could be

---

[47] See Peter Lake, 'The Laudian style: order, uniformity and the pursuit of the beauty of holiness in the 1630s', in Kenneth Fincham, ed., *The Early Stuart Church, 1603–1642* (Basingstoke, 1993), esp. pp. 161–85; George Henderson, 'Bible illustration in the age of Laud', *Transactions of the Cambridge Bibliographical Society*, 8 (1982), pp. 173–204.

[48] Samuel Clarke, *Englands Remembrancer* (London, 1657) and *A True and Full Narrative of those Two Never to be Forgotten Deliverances* (London, 1671).

purchased either in packs or 'in sheets fit to adorn studies and houses'.[49] Ward's 'Double Deliveraunce' was revamped by a 'Transmariner' in 1689; it rose again like a phoenix in 1740 against a backdrop of Jacobite activity, and eighteenth-century propagandists resurrected the detail to satirize the intrigues of the politician Henry Fox, the subject of a humorous sketch entitled 'Guy Vaux the 2d'.[50] This was unquestionably an image which entered into the visual imagination of the populace at large. Adapted for insertion in octavo editions of the Prayer Book and Bible during the reign of Charles II, it was one which generations of Protestant children must have surreptitiously inspected in their pews and perhaps copied, traced, and coloured-in in their nurseries and schoolrooms (Plate 6).[51] And was it not this stereotype which shaped that belated Victorian accretion to the popular culture of the Gunpowder Plot, the burning of his effigy on a bonfire and the begging of 'a penny for the guy'? Such stuffed figures were, in a very real sense, three-dimensional cartoons. Notwithstanding the efforts of William Laud and his colleagues, this powerful visual tradition had become an indelible part of Britain's cultural heritage.

So what can the swinging fortunes of these pictures tell us about 'The Church Retrospective'? They offer us, I think, some important insights into the ecclesiastical politics of history, memory, and iconography in the early seventeenth century. For stalwart Calvinists struggling to resist the Laudian regime, images recalling England's former victories over her papist enemies became a symbol of defiance and an ensign of dissent. For Caroline prelates

[49] Late seventeenth-century impressions survive of *The Papists Powder Treason* (see n. 17) and *A Thankfull Remembrance of Gods Mercie* (see n. 29), which was re-titled *Popish Plots and Treasons* (BM, *Satires*, no. 13). For the playing cards, see J. R. S. Whiting, *A Handful of History* (Totowa, N.J., 1978), esp. pp. 42, 45, 52, 55, quotation at p. 50.

[50] See BM, *Satires*, nos 42–44, 1223, 2456. For Henry Fox, see no. 3439. For other echoes, see nos 837, 1030, 6007. Dorothy George, *English Political Caricature to 1792* (Oxford, 1959), pp. 31, 51, 63–4, 105, 165 and Plate 29(a).

[51] See, for example, *The Book of Common Prayer*, 8° edn (London, 1676), CUL copy (classmark Adams 7.67.14), facing the 'Form of Prayer' for 5 Nov.; *The Holy Bible* (London, 1669), CUL, British and Foreign Bible Society copy, plate facing Pss 10–14.

striving to redefine their nation's religious identity, such prints were graphic reminders of a past it was better to forget.

University of Exeter

LAUDIAN FOXE-HUNTING? WILLIAM LAUD AND THE STATUS OF JOHN FOXE IN THE 1630s

by DAMIAN NUSSBAUM

Whe hen the prosecutors of William Laud were seeking damning evidence against the Archbishop, they seized upon the fate of John Foxe's *Acts and Monuments* in the 1630s. They produced a catalogue of abuses, occasions on which Laud had attacked, impugned, or banned the volumes. In his report of the trial, Prynne gave these cases of Foxe-hunting an important position, directly after the accusation that Laud had hindered the distribution of Bibles. The prominence given to Foxe, and the close association with the Bible, were typical of the ways the martyrologist was handled in the early seventeenth century, and tell us much about the regard in which he was held within the English Church. His *Book of Martyrs* had attained the status of a quasi-biblical text. His works, invoked with an almost scriptural reverence, were appealed to as an unquestionable authority on matters of ecclesiastical history and Protestant tradition.[1]

In at least two senses, Foxe symbolized the Church retrospective to English Protestants of the early seventeenth century. His *Acts and Monuments* presented the past – especially the pre-Reformation past – as it had been re-formed by Protestant historiography. Foxe became synonymous with that strain of English thought which traced the lineage of the Church back along a 'path of blood'. Adherents of the Foxeian tradition preferred to seek their spiritual forebears amongst the faithful remnant, scattered in every age and country, rather than looking to the alleged corruption and idolatry of the institutional Church.[2] By the 1630s,

---

[1] John Foxe, *Acts and Monuments*, ed. S. R. Cattley, 8 vols (London, 1837–41). For William Prynne's heavily partisan account of Laud's trial see *Canterburies Doome* (London, 1646). Alleged attacks on John Foxe are cited on pp. 87–8 and 183–4.
[2] Foxe's interpretation of history is outlined by Jane Facey, 'John Foxe and the defence of the Anglican Church', in Peter Lake and Maria Dowling, eds, *Protestantism*

however, Foxe not only presented this vision of Church history, he also represented it. Foxe had become a part of ecclesiastical history in his own right, as a symbol of orthodoxy to be referred to, cited, and quoted. His direct involvement with the Marian exile and the subsequent restoration of the reformed faith gilded his work with the perceived purity of early Elizabethan Protestantism. This sense of Foxe as being intimately bound up with the very identity of the English Church was encapsulated by William Prynne. Championing the martyrologist against a detractor, Prynne maintained that an attack against Foxe's calendar of martyrs in the *Acts and Monuments* was by definition 'against our own English martyres, the Professors of the Protestant Religion in all ages and so by consequence against our Religion it selfe.'[3]

At Laud's trial in 1644, the fate of John Foxe in the previous decade was exploited to the full. Little or no evidence survives to suggest what Laud's attitude to Foxe might have been in private. Here, as so often, Laud's personal preferences remain stubbornly elusive. But did Laud really attack the reputation of the martyrologist in public? If we are to believe William Prynne, who helped in the prosecution, then indeed he did. But Prynne's account of the proceedings, about which even his relatively sympathetic biographer is doubtful, commenting that it tells us more about Prynne than about Laud's trial, is hardly a source to inspire confidence.[4] Prynne was not alone, however, in depicting Laud as anti-Foxeian. Recently Anthony Milton has echoed Prynne's

---

and the National Church in sixteenth-century England (London, 1987), pp. 162–92. See also W. W. Wooden, *John Foxe* (Boston, 1983), pp. 24–40.

[3] The attack on Foxe came from the pen of John Pocklington, chaplain to Charles I, in his *Altare Christianum* (London 1637), p. 92. Prynne's defence appeared in *Canterburies Doome*, p. 193.

[4] William Lamont enters a double caveat against Prynne's report of the proceedings. Not only did the writer of *Canterburies Doome* enlarge his account with material amassed after the trial had ended, and which therefore went unanswered by Laud; he also focused on the secondary rather than the primary charge. The peers in the House of Lords had concentrated on Laud's constitutional misdemeanours, accusing the defendant of usurping powers which rightly belonged to the monarch, people, Parliament, and judiciary. Prynne was more exercised by the religious case against Laud, and his account centred almost exclusively on the charge that Laud had sought to undermine the Church of England in favour of popery. See William Lamont, *Marginal Prynne, 1600–1669* (London, 1968), pp. 119–48.

conclusion, arguing that the Laudians were quick to distance themselves from the martyrologist. In a telling comparison, he contrasts Laud's bid to repudiate the heritage of the moderate Elizabethan puritans with Archbishop Bancroft's attempts to appropriate their legacy. In Milton's view, 'Laudians made a point of denigrating and distancing themselves from the Elizabethan moderate puritan tradition of English Protestantism, represented by figures such as John Foxe, Laurence Humphrey, John Rainolds, William Whitaker, William Fulke, William Perkins and indeed Andrew Willet.' According to his interpretation, the symbols of puritan orthodoxy were happily jettisoned by the Laudians, and heading the list of casualties was John Foxe.[5]

If Anthony Milton, and for that matter Prynne, are right, then the 1630s marked a sharp decline in Foxe's fortunes: from Jacobean saint to Laudian sinner within a decade. As a case study through which to evaluate Milton's thesis, and explore its conclusions, I have chosen a trial from the year 1630. In fact the trial in question had the added advantage of constituting one of Prynne's own examples of Laud's misdemeanours. He reported the Gellibrand case at some length, as a significant proof of Laud's guilt. Here, if anywhere, we should find a clear and unambiguous rejection of Foxe, to bear out Milton's contention, and to prove Prynne, at least in this instance, to have been right.[6]

In late 1630 Henry Gellibrand, Professor of Astronomy at Gresham College, found himself in court. His offence arose from an almanac which he had compiled and had published under the name of his manservant, William Beale.[7] His accuser was the then Bishop of London, William Laud, who had taken umbrage at the changes to the traditional pattern of almanacs which Gellibrand had seen fit to make. The

---

[5] Anthony Milton, *Catholic and Reformed: the Roman and Protestant Churches in English Protestant Thought, 1600–1640* (Cambridge, 1995), pp. 539–40. Of the examples Milton cites to illustrate his case, over half relate to Foxe.

[6] To reconstruct the events of the Gellibrand case, I have drawn on the three surviving accounts of the proceedings, penned by William Prynne, William Laud, and John Browne, clerk to the House of Lords. See *Canterburies Doome*, pp. 182–3; William Laud, *Works*, 7 vols (Oxford, 1847–60), 4, p. 265; John Browne, in M. F. Bond, ed., *HMC, The Manuscripts of the House of Lords*, 11 (London, 1962), pp. 427–8.

[7] William Beale, *An Almanacke, for the yeere of our Lord God, 1631* (London, 1631).

problem was not a directly political one – Gellibrand's almanac did not contain the kind of politically sensitive material with which such works were filled during the Interregnum. In fact that section of the almanac convention-ally devoted to prognostication, where political comment could be cloaked in astrological prediction about the events of the next year, was omitted altogether. Gellibrand seems to have shared that mistrust of prognostications not uncommon amongst those of a more puritan frame of mind.[8]

For Laud, the objection to Gellibrand's almanac was not so much the political content as the religious implications of his editorial decisions. In conventional almanacs, saints' days and holy days were recorded much as they had been before the Reformation. A similar calendar also survived in the Book of Common Prayer, assigning feasts to significant saints and prescribing which were to be observed as holy days.[9] Gellibrand had excluded most of these saints, and he recruited Protestant martyrs and confessors to take their place. For Laud this constituted an abuse of the calendar, and he was galvanized into action, ordering that Gellibrand should be brought before the Court of High Commission to be punished for his presumption. There is even reason to suppose that Laud was prodded into action by Queen Henrietta Maria herself, who had taken offence at this implicitly anti-Catholic production.[10]

[8] For the deep-seated suspicion of almanacs held by puritans such as William Fulke and William Perkins, see Bernard Capp, *Astrology and the Popular Press: English Almanacs 1500–1800* (London, 1979), p. 32. One of Gellibrand's closest professional colleagues was the mathematician Henry Briggs, who had taught at Gresham College from 1595 to 1620. Briggs was a man renowned both for his strong puritan sympathies and his antipathies towards astrology. A contemporary described him as 'the most satirical man against it [astrology] that hath been known': William Lilly, *History of his Life and Times* (London, 1822), pp. 237–8. For Gellibrand himself, see Ian Adamson, 'The foundation and early history of Gresham College, London, 1569–1704' (Cambridge University Ph.D. thesis, 1975), pp. 86–7, 128–30, 143–5; John Ward, *The Lives of the Professors of Gresham College* (London, 1740), pp. 81–5.

[9] David Cressy, *Bonfires and Bells; National Memory and the Protestant Calendar in Elizabethan and Stuart England* (London, 1989), pp. 1–12. Cressy outlines some of the changes made in the calendar of the Prayer Book, but the full story still remains to be told.

[10] The evidence for Henrietta Maria's involvement rests solely on the uncorroborated testimony of John Gellibrand (the brother of Henry Gellibrand). Laud remained studiously non-committal on the subject, arguing that even if the Queen had sent a message to him, he could not have prevented her from doing so.

From Laud's point of view, the trial did not go quite as planned. Gellibrand produced powerful evidence which began to unravel the case against him. According to the astronomer, the almanac had not been a presumptuous innovation of his own invention, as Laud had alleged. His publication was based on the calendar contained in John Foxe's *Acts and Monuments*, a book printed by royal authority, and placed by order of Convocation in every cathedral church.[11] Unsurprisingly, the verdict went against Laud. Gellibrand was judged by the court to have acted legally, and, since his almanac was ostensibly based on Foxe, there was no question that it be banned and its author punished. Laud, however, was unwilling to let the matter drop, or at least loath to let Gellibrand go scot-free. He accused the astronomer of holding conventicles at Gresham College, and threatened him with a return appearance before the court. And there remained yet one last twist to the plot, when Laud threw in a final charge, blaming Gellibrand for stirring up intrigues and creating factions at court.

That accusation, hinting at far-reaching political reverberations, suggests just some of the many discourses which intertwined with the Gellibrand case. For the legal historian, the trial provides an additional source of evidence for Laud's power, or lack of it, in the Court of High Commission during the 1630s.[12] For the purposes of religious history it offers an insight into the Laudian reception of the 'moderate Elizabethan puritan' inheritance, and a chance to test the

---

He side-stepped the two pressing questions – did she send a request, and, if so, did he act on it? For Henrietta Maria's limited political role and lack of power during the early 1630s see Kevin Sharpe, *The Personal Rule of Charles I* (London and New Haven, Conn., 1992), p. 304.

[11] In 1571 Convocation ordered that *Acts and Monuments* be placed in every cathedral (but not in every parish church as is so often claimed): *A Booke of certaine Canons . . . of the Churche of England . . . 1571* (London, 1571), pp. 6, 9.

[12] The standard monograph on the High Commission is R. G. Usher, *The Rise and Fall of the High Commission* (Oxford, 1968). Usher's work should, however, be treated with some caution. It is best read in conjunction with Philip Tyler's newly added introduction which, in its concern to bring Usher's findings into line with modern research, comes close to undermining the original thesis altogether. On the High Commission in the 1630s, Kevin Sharpe echoes Usher's conclusions, arguing that the Laudian court was, by and large, impartial and just in its dealings. Sharpe, *Personal Rule*, pp. 374–83.

thesis that Laud denigrated Foxe, and ultimately rejected him. The Laudians, I will argue, adopted a range of responses to the *Acts and Monuments*. Their sporadic interventions aimed to level down Foxe's authority and to mute his voice in debate, but never attempted to exclude him completely. They may have disliked the central role he played in the English Church, but they never insisted that he be driven out of religious life altogether.

At the heart of the Gellibrand case stood a question fundamental to the identity of the Church of England: which version of ecclesiastical history should it espouse as its own? The choice lay between two competing visions of the Church retrospective. Both traced lines of descent linking early modern England back to the purity of first-century Palestine. Both advanced arguments showing the Church of England to be a 'true' Church, firmly anchored in the teachings of Christ. Both had profound implications for the nature of the contemporary Church. The different approaches were apparent during the Fisher debates, that series of formal disputations organized by the English authorities in the early 1620s to refute the case for Rome championed by Friar Fisher. In his encounter with the Roman apologist, Laud was pressed on the origins of the reformed English Church, but carefully avoided the standard Foxeian defence of its past. The widely-held idea, that in the Middle Ages the visible Church had fallen into error and become that Whore of Babylon prophesied in Revelation, found no place in Laud's scheme of things. While his colleagues on the Protestant side pushed the claims of the Waldensians, the Hussites, and the Lollards to be the fore-runners of the reformed English Church, Laud remained silent.[13] His version of the Church's history was quite different. For Laud the Reformation was not the moment at which the faithful, a scattered remnant hidden in isolated congregations, had been able to return from 'exile' to

---

[13] Daniel Featley, arguing the Church of England's case against Fisher, compared the institutional pedigree of the Church, favoured by Laud, with the Foxeian tradition. For Featley, origins traced through a succession of popes and bishops were a 'slipperie and dirty way', and thoroughly undesirable in comparison to the 'more excellent way' which could be found in *Acts and Monuments*: Daniel Featley, *The Romish Fisher caught and held in his owne net* (London, 1624), sig. K*3$^{\text{a-b}}$.

take their place at the heart of the established Church. In Laud's eyes the faithful were already *in* the institutional Church, and always had been there. Throughout the Middle Ages, there was no question in Laud's mind that the English Church had always remained a true and faithful member of the Church of Christ. At the Reformation, the English Church had exercised its right as a national Church to leave the corruption of Rome in order to purify itself, and such departures were a traditional – and legal – part of Church history. For the Archbishop, the Reformation has been less a theological watershed than an administrative reorganization.[14]

Laud's prosecution of Gellibrand's almanac sprang from his view of the Church's past. The saints and their traditional repository, the calendar, were a sign of continuity, a symbol shared by the English Church both before and after the Reformation. Gellibrand's almanac struck Laud as a puritan attack on this symbol of ecclesiastical unity. If the saints were replaced by Protestant martyrs, then a vital link with the Catholic past was severed. Honouring Lollards, Hussites, and Waldensians broke the link implicitly, for it discredited the institution which had banned and burnt them as heretics. Laud looked to this medieval Catholic Church as the forerunner of the reformed Church of England, and an almanac which replaced the traditional medieval saints with new Protestant martyrs assailed his vision of the past head-on. By implication it also challenged his view of the present, for the nature of the contemporary Church was in part defined by its history. Laud feared that a past celebrating groups which had separated themselves from the official Church set a dangerous precedent. Would it not encourage the obstinacy of those extremists who preferred the purity of their own religious practices to full participation in the life of the national Church? The charge of holding conventicles was dealt with severely by the High Commission, both under Laud's regime and before it. The court devoted a good deal of time and effort to suppressing what it regarded as 'nurseries of errors and heresies', which misled the innocent with their

---

14 Laud, *Works*, 2, pp. 170-8, 191-5, 213.

'errors and schismes'.[15] This horror of puritan separation was a common Laudian theme and haunted Laud during the Gellibrand case. When he was forced to back off from his accusations against the almanac, he retreated to a charge of holding a conventicle. This second accusation against Gellibrand was neither substantiated at the time, nor followed up by Laud later. It is significant, however, for revealing the context into which the almanac was presumed to fit. In Laud's mind there was a close connection between a Gellibrand who rejected the institutional version of ecclesiastical history embodied by the medieval saints, and a Gellibrand who withdrew from the contemporary Church. A common thread explained both events: the nonconformist wish for purity even at the cost of separation from the national Church, be it medieval or contemporary.

This brings us back to the issue of whether Laud's attack on Gellibrand's almanac was aimed only at an extreme separatist position, or formed part of a wider rejection of the symbols of Protestant orthodoxy. The alleged Laudian intolerance of the moderate puritan heritage was the crux of the argument a dozen years later, when the question became part of a renewed struggle over ecclesiastical history. On trial for his life in 1644, William Laud fought tenaciously with his opponents to define what had been the Laudian Church's attitude to the past, and to determine what kind of religious history it had sponsored. It was Prynne's contention that in the case of Foxe, Laud's opposition to the broad tradition of English Protestantism was undeniable. He had prevented production of the *Acts and Monuments*, advocated its exclusion from churches, and licensed books against it. Laud had a long criminal record of attacking the Elizabethan martyrologist, it was claimed. The most blatant instance occurred during the Gellibrand trial, when Laud used the astronomer's almanac as a flimsy cover to attack Foxe's book itself. Gellibrand's almanac and Foxe's calendar were 'verbatim the same'

---

[15] S. R. Gardiner, *Reports of Cases in Star Chamber and High Commission* (Westminster, 1886), p. 212. Other proceedings against those accused of holding conventicles are to be found in ibid., pp. 198–238 and 274 (the very full account of the case against M. Vicars in 1632), 284–5, 308–10, and in Usher, *High Commission*, p. 265.

according to Prynne, and any suggestions that they were different he brushed peremptorily aside. In Prynne's eyes, the Gellibrand case was Laud's earliest public attack on Foxe, and his most extreme. The Archbishop, of course, painted a very different picture. He did not deny the attack on Gellibrand's almanac, merely that the relationship between Foxe and Gellibrand was so close. To Laud, the name of Foxe was a distraction, invoked to lend respectability to a 'base business'. He did admit to some connection, acknowledging that the martyrs' names had been drawn from the *Book of Martyrs*, but he complained that the adaption had been a botched job, for Gellibrand had left out those solemn days which had originally been included in Foxe. In fact Gellibrand had removed 'all the Saints, Apostles and all'.[16]

Was Gellibrand's almanac identical to Foxe's, or was Laud correct to argue that the pretended link was merely a cover for Gellibrand's own presumption? This is at least one question which can be resolved, since both Foxe's calendar and Gellibrand's almanac survive, although no one consulted them at the trial to determine their composition. Close comparison reveals that the two differed slightly, undermining Prynne's claim that Gellibrand's almanac 'was Verbatim the same with Mr Foxe his authorized Kalendar'. But if Prynne was off the mark, Laud missed by even more when he portrayed the association with Foxe merely as a smoke-screen for Gellibrand's scandalous innovations. The almanac adapted Foxe's calendar, simplifying and recasting it in a new genre. In the process dozens of Foxeian martyrs were lost, simply because their spaces were needed for other purposes. When the beginnings and ends of law terms were recorded, out went those days' martyrs. When the moveable festivals were inserted, or the signs of the zodiac added, another swathe of martyrs was lost.[17] The printers themselves were

---

[16] Prynne, *Canterburies Doome*, p. 184; Laud, *Works*, 4, p. 165. The modern secondary literature is equally divided. Bernard Capp acknowledges the relationship, describing Gellibrand's almanac as 'drawn from Foxe': Capp, *Astrology and the Popular Press*, p. 47. Anthony Milton notes that the almanac cannot have been an extreme puritan production because it included bishops, but does not point out the Foxeian connection: Milton, *Catholic and Reformed*, p. 314.

[17] In the entries for the month of December, for instance, those Foxeian martyrs abandoned for want of space included Erasmus, Phagius, Bucer, and Hunne.

guilty of one or two slips.[18] The overwhelming impression, however, was of fidelity to Foxe's text, and an eagerness to reproduce the Foxeian calendar within the constraints imposed by the smaller dimensions of an almanac.

All this raises fundamental questions of what Laud was up to in the Gellibrand case: why was it that he targeted this Foxe lookalike? Was the Gellibrand case also an attempt by Laud to attack the reputation of John Foxe, albeit indirectly? In his own trial, Laud was quick to dissociate Foxe from Gellibrand, and insist that his onslaught had been solely directed against the almanac. But while holding a Foxe-friendly position was expedient in 1644, when Laud faced a hostile bench at his trial, it might not have been Laud's original attitude when he took Gellibrand to court in 1630.[19] Once the hidden identity of Gellibrand's almanac was revealed before High Commission, that it was in fact a reincarnation of Foxe's calendar, an obvious step would have been for Laud to condemn Foxe's original with equal venom. That is what we would expect, if we are to believe the thesis that the Archbishop denigrated and rejected the 'moderate Elizabethan puritan' inheritance. Laud had taken on the Foxeian tradition as it was embodied by Gellibrand, so why not attack its arch-exponent, John Foxe?

It was just this kind of head-on attack which Prynne was desperately hunting for as he amassed his catalogue of accusations to lay against Laud. He listed no fewer than five occasions on which he claimed that the Archbishop had attacked, disparaged, or derided the *Acts and Monuments*. Prynne's list was not wholly convincing, and like so much of his case against Laud, lacked that final piece of conclusive proof to convict the Archbishop. Part of Prynne's evidence concerned events at St Gregory's, a church situated in the

---

[18]   The most glaring printer's error concerned the Conversion of St Paul, which enjoyed two entries in the almanac on consecutive days. On the second occasion a precise date for the Damascene vision was mistakenly added, which rather unexpectedly reckoned the event as having taken place in the year '1557'.

[19]   That Parliament was keenly sensitive to any attack on Foxe was apparent from its earliest sessions. To mark its opening, two sermons were preached drawing extensively on Foxe. See William Haller, 'John Foxe and the Puritan Revolution', in Richard F. Jones, ed., *The Seventeenth Century: Studies in the History of English Thought and Literature from Bacon to Pope* (Stanford, Conn., 1951), pp. 209-24.

heart of London directly adjoining St Paul's. St Gregory's was catapulted into national prominence when a dispute over the proper location of the communion table was finally adjudicated before the court. Laud, arguing for an altar-wise placement of the table at the east end, became thoroughly exasperated by the arguments of the parishioners for a table-wise position. When both Foxe and Jewel were cited as authorities against, he could stand it no more, and furiously exploded that if his opponents so 'misused' the two Elizabethan divines, then he wished their works be removed from St Gregory's. Even though Laud's complaint was, strictly speaking, directed against a particular interpretation of their works rather than Foxe and Jewel themselves, Prynne exploited the outburst as yet more evidence of Laud's rejection of the Protestant heritage.[20] If even the hint of a similar outburst had occurred at the Gellibrand trial, Prynne would hardly have forgone the chance of seizing on such a damning piece of evidence and squeezing every last drop of propaganda out of it. Despite all his industry, his over-imaginative mind, and his abundance of witnesses, Prynne failed to come up with the evidence. Although Laud was quite ready to lambast Gellibrand's almanac for dishonouring the saints, once its true pedigree became known he chose not to extend his attack to Foxe, the almanac's source.

Laud may not have challenged Foxe directly, but neither did he champion him. Rather than outright rejection or acceptance, the Gellibrand case shows Laud adopting a more complex and subtle approach to the martyrologist. Though he carefully avoided direct criticism of Foxe, he hardly bent over backwards to promote him either. There was none of the heart-felt praise one might expect, no protestations of admiration for his work, or ringing endorsements of his authority. Given the status of Foxe in the early seventeenth

---

[20] For an account of the St Gregory's case, see Julian Davies, *The Caroline Captivity of the Church: Charles I and the Remoulding of Anglicanism, 1625–1641* (Oxford, 1992), pp. 205–50. Davies's interpretation is questioned by Nicholas Tyacke. He argues that Laud's role was more important than Davies allows, with the Archbishop instrumental both in launching the St Gregory's case itself, and in shaping altar policy during the 1630s: N. Tyacke, 'Anglican attitudes: some recent writings on English religious history, from the Reformation to the Civil War', *JBS*, 35 (1996), pp. 139–67, esp. 156–62.

century, the quasi-biblical reverence in which his work was held, Laud's omission was a reverberating silence. In his published works, Laud rarely alluded to Foxe or the *Acts and Monuments*. In fact the occasions when he positively chose to refer to the martyrologist are only two or three in number. Even if Foxe was familiar to Laud, he was clearly not one of his favourite writers, not a valued item of Laud's intellectual furniture. Effectively Laud minimized Foxe's importance by denying him the oxygen of publicity.[21]

Occasionally Laud ventured beyond his customary position of malign neglect, to make his views slightly more explicit. Referring to *Acts and Monuments*, and with it to Jewel's *Apology*, he complained that these books should not be treated as infallible authorities, and were not above making mistakes themselves. He argued that 'though these two were very worthy Men of their Time, yet every thing which they say is not by and by the *Doctrine of the Church of England*'. Even in this instance of disenchantment, however, Laud's aim was not to destroy Jewel's and Foxe's positions, but to transform them. He wished to reduce their status, so that in matters of history and doctrine their judgement would no longer be unquestionable, nor their authority irrefutable. He asserted his right, 'upon good reason', to 'depart from their Judgement in some Particulars, and yet not differ from *the Church of England*'.[22]

On the spectrum of Laudian attitudes to Foxe, Laud occupied the middle ground. In public at least, he never took the more confrontational route adopted by the royal chaplain, John Pocklington. In Pocklington's *Altare Christianum*, Foxe's calendar is vilified as a repository of rebels, heretics, murderers, and traitors. Since its first publication some seventy years before, the martyrologist's work had never suffered such a violent onslaught from any, except

---

[21] Laud's allusions to Foxe are sparing indeed, see for instance *Works*, 4, pp. 226, 265–6, 405, 497.

[22] Laud, *Works*, 4, p. 265. Laud's sentiments were echoed by John Pocklington in his *Altare Christianum*, pp. 89–90, though solely in connection with Jewel. Pocklington was quick to insist that Jewel was not to be regarded as gospel, as the Romanists treated their Masters of Sentences. Having circumscribed the extent of Jewel's authority, Pocklington was quite ready to use Jewel in support of his position and to urge that the former Bishop of Salisbury be properly respected.

Catholic opponents. At the same time, even Pocklington retained some caution in relation to Foxe: although there was no doubt as to the intended target of his outburst, the identity of the calendar in question was never actually named in his text.[23]

If Pocklington stood at one end of the Laudian spectrum in the 1630s, Peter Heylyn was at the other. In 1637, during the disputes over the right positioning of the altar, whether it was to be altar-wise or table-wise, Heylyn allowed himself to be drawn into a long historical exchange with William Prynne. Laud's chaplain did not initiate the use of Foxe as an authority. Once *Acts and Monuments* was brought into play, however, he was as eager as his opponent to appropriate Foxe for his own case, or at least to prevent him from being seized by the other side.[24]

What we witness in the Gellibrand case was not, then, part of a wholesale Laudian rejection of the 'Elizabethan puritan tradition'. The evidence points to an ad hoc array of responses, rather than a coherent policy. Laudians shared a reluctance to deploy 'moderate puritan' works, preferring to pass over other brands of Protestantism in silence, whilst noisily championing their own. When they did engage with the moderate puritan heritage, they usually did so prompted by their opponents. Their approach was characterized by a defensive determination not to cede to their adversaries the advantage of claiming the likes of Foxe and his fellows as their own. At the same time they intended to diminish the regard enjoyed by the Elizabethan puritan tradition, transforming its role from absolute authority to legitimate opinion. If Foxe was to play a part, then the Laudians were resolved that he be taken down from his pedestal,

---

[23] Pocklington, *Altare Christianum*, p. 92. Despite his attack on the calendar, Pocklington deployed Foxe elsewhere in the *Altare*, claiming legitimation for the Laudian position on altars through the authority of Foxe's martyrs. It was, however, polemical expediency rather than personal enthusiasm which governed Pocklington's use of *Acts and Monuments*: see, for instance, *Altare Christianum*, p. 110.

[24] Peter Heylyn, *Antidotum Lincolniense* (London, 1637), pp. 68-9, 87-99. Heylyn's use of Foxe had been prompted both by the original letter to the Vicar of Grantham and by William Prynne's later appropriation of the martyrologist in his *Quench-Coale* (London, 1637), pp. 41-64.

stripped of his privileged status, and side-lined, henceforth to be consulted merely as one amongst many historians of the Protestant past.

Queens' College,
Cambridge

TEXT BEFORE TROWEL: ANTONIO BOSIO'S
ROMA SOTTERRANEA REVISITED[1]

by SIMON DITCHFIELD

B efore returning home to his royal master, the ambassador of Poland went to say farewell to the reigning Pope, Pius V. They met in St Peter's Square, where the ambassador asked for a relic to take back with him to Poland. In reply, the pontiff bent down and took earth from the square with both his hands and placed it in a handkerchief, before handing it to the understandably bemused Pole with the reassurance that this was no ordinary earth but that mixed with the blood of Christian martyrs (*nobis notum omnino erat, Vaticanum pulverem Martyrum sanguine plenum esse*). The earth then proceeded to bleed, staining the handkerchief to the wonder and amazement of all present.

This miracle, referred to by five witnesses who testified at Pius's Roman remissorial trial of 1597,[2] takes us straight to the heart of the matter to be discussed in this paper: just what exactly was behind the Oratorian-inspired revival of interest in the early Church and, specifically, in that subterranean environment so redolent of early Christian suffering, the catacombs? This question is not a new one. Indeed, the story of St Philip Neri's role as godfather of Christian archaeology occupied the attentions of the saint's own contemporaries. However, it can be argued that the quality and range of the resultant scholarly output has led historians to confuse the means with the end. By casting scholars such as Baronio, Gallonio, and Bosio in the anachronistic roles of 'proto-

---

[1] The writing of this paper was greatly facilitated by the assistance of Dott. Giorgio Finocchiaro of the Biblioteca Vallicella, Rome. I am extremely grateful for his help in guiding me through the tangled erudition of *le carte bosiane*.

[2] This trial was to ascertain a candidate for canonization's sanctity *in specie*, and represented the second stage of the judicial process (after the *processus inquisitionis et informationis*). Reference to the miracle (witnessed by one person directly, and four indirectly) may be found in the report made to Urban VIII by the Auditors of the Rota in 1629, which is excerpted in *ActaSS. Maii I* (Antwerp, 1680), pp. 714–17 (at p. 715E).

scientific' pioneers in the disciplines of history, hagiography, and Christian iconography – Bosio enjoying the sobriquet 'Columbus of the catacombs' – historians risk losing sight of the fact that their over-riding concern was not with the material culture of paleo-Christian Rome *per se*, but rather with the spiritual reality it symbolized and mediated. In other words, though clearly on one level works of erudition, at a deeper level studies such as Baronio's revisions of the Roman Martyrology, Gallonio's comprehensive survey of the varieties of torture suffered by the early Christian martyrs, and Bosio's edition of the acts of St Cecilia, were works of devotion, facilitating a *lectio divina* of Rome's sacred landscape.[3]

The principal focus for this paper is a work which has traditionally occupied a pre-eminent place in the attentions of historians of sacred erudition in general and of Christian archaeology in particular: Antonio Bosio's *Roma sotterranea*, a prefatory papal brief to which allows us to date its posthumous publication to 1634, despite the date of 1632 on the work's frontispiece.[4] As printed, the 656-page *Roma sotterranea* consisted of four books. The first was divided into twenty chapters, and dealt with the death and burial of the Christian martyrs. After an opening chapter on the catacombs in general, the reader was offered a gruesome account of the ways in which the bodies of the martyrs were burned, thrown into rivers, hidden, cut up, and mixed together with other corpses (chapters II–VI). Then, after a

---

[3] *Martyrologium romanum ad novam kalendarii rationem et ecclesiasticae historiae veritatem restitutum . . . accesserunt notationes atque tractatio de martyrologio romano auctore C. Baronio . . . secunda editio ab ipso auctore . . . aucta* (Antwerp, 1589), cf. edns of 1586 and 1598; A. Gallonio, *Trattato de gli Istrumenti di Martire e delle varie maniere di martorirare usate da'Gentili contro Cristiani* (Rome, 1591); A. Bosio, *Historia B. Caeciliae virginis Valeriani, Tiburti et Maximi martyrum necnon Urbani et Lucii Pontificum et mart. vitae atque Paschales papae I literae de eorundem sanctorum corporum inventione et in urbem translatione* (Rome, 1600).

[4] The papal brief is dated 6 Oct. 1634. The only monograph wholly dedicated to Bosio is A. Valeri's dated but still useful *Cenni biografici di Antonio Bosio* (Rome, 1900), whose appendix contains, *inter alia*, an inventory of Bosio's library (pp. 84–110). I am indebted to Dott. Finocchiaro for making available to me a xerox of this rare work. Cf. N. Parise's article in *Dizionario biografico degli italiani*, 13 (Rome, 1971), pp. 257–9, and G. Ferretto, *Note storico-bibliografiche di archaeologia cristiana* (Rome, 1942), pp. 140–61.

ROMA SOTTERRANEA

In Roma appresso Guglielmo Facciotti MDCXXXII con licenza de Superiori e privilegio.

Plate 1   Antonio Bosio, title page to *Roma sotterranea* (Rome, 1632 [1634])
(photo: Warburg Institute).

single chapter (VII) on the working of Providence in having preserved so many of these bodies over and against the attempts of the pagans to disperse them as previously described, there were six chapters on the care taken by the early Christian community to recover and bury these holy relics. There next followed three chapters (XIV–XVI) on the blood and other relics preserved and of the vigils held in their honour, before the book closed with a final three chapters dedicated to an account of the way in which the bodies were washed and prepared for burial, and how they were then carried to the catacombs and entombed there (XVII–XX).

Books two and three (of twenty-two and sixty-six chapters respectively) were then given over entirely to a systematic topographical survey of the catacombs. This began with the Vatican area, and then proceeded anti-clockwise, taking each consular road out of the city and its adjacent burial complexes in turn, from the via Aurelia to the via Flaminia. Classical and patristic references to the roads and individual catacombs began Bosio's scholarly treatment, which then proceeded to draw on his exhaustive readings of the Church fathers, councils, and historical martyrologies to construct a history of each catacomb. *Roma sotterranea* closed with a final book of fifty chapters given over to explanations and illustrations of the images found in the catacombs. It is as well to note straightaway that the visual material for which the work has become so famous is largely restricted to this final book which, as we shall see, had not even been written up at the time of Bosio's death.

Near the beginning of this century, the Benedictine polymath Henri Leclercq went so far as to compare Bosio's work with Vesalius' *De humani corporis fabricae* and Mabillon's *De re diplomatica* as books which had placed emerging disciplines on new plateaux of scholarly competence.[5] Even if we today cannot share such a fulsome tribute to Bosio's achievement, we surely have to acknowledge that there can be few areas of scholarship where a single work has at a stroke created the field, largely determined its priorities, and dominated research in the area for over two centuries. When

[5]   H. Leclercq, *Manuel d'archéologie chrétienne depuis les origines jusqu'au VIII siècle*, 2 vols (Paris, 1907), 1, p. 3.

Giovanni Battista De Rossi (1822–94) came to publish the first volume of his classic study in 1864, not only did he borrow Bosio's title (with merely the suffix *cristiana* added), but also inherited the latter's recognition of the importance of textual sources for the interpretation of archaeological material combined with the desire for topographical comprehensiveness which doomed his project to incompleteness from the start. Thus, despite its title, *Roma sotterranea cristiana*, De Rossi's three-volume 1,600 page study (published 1864–77) actually got no further than the catacombs of Calixtus (which he correctly identified as a complex independent of the catacombs under S. Sebastiano with which they had been confused until then) and, in the continuing absence of an integrated general survey, seekers after information about the other Roman subterranean burial sites (of which there are more than forty) still have little choice but to leaf through the indexes of specialist journals, notably the *Rivista di archeologia cristiana* (1924ff).[6]

Before focusing on *Roma sotterranea*, however, something needs to be said of the context within which Bosio nurtured his subterranean interests. Discussion, naturally enough, begins with St Philip Neri's nocturnal catacomb vigils. The second chapter of Ponelle and Bordet's dated but still essential treatment of the saint and his milieu is advisedly entitled: 'The Hermit'. Gallonio, in his first testimony in favour of St Philip's canonization, talked of how the latter had scarcely arrived in Rome from Florence when 'he decided to lead the life of a hermit, eating poor food', adding that he had heard Philip say on several occasions, 'how he had been three whole days without any food and that he had the bare earth for his bed'.[7] This 'half-hermit' existence, 'wandering

---

[6] The most important figure in the history of Christian archaeology in Rome between Bosio and De Rossi (which was characterized for the most part by apathy and sloth) was the latter's teacher, the Jesuit Giuseppe Marchi (1795–1860), whose work shifted interest decisively towards the corridors and structure of the catacombs themselves and away from the use of the latter primarily as evidence for the life and liturgy of the early Christians. This was reflected in the title to volume one of his classic study which was focused on the catacombs of S. Agnese: *Monumenti delle arti cristiane primitive nella metropoli del cristianesimo: I – architettura della Roma sotterranea cristiana* (Rome, 1844).

[7] 'Si dette a far vite eremitica, nutrendosi di cose grosse. Et io li ho inteso dir più volte, dal padre, che era stato tre giorni intieri senza pigliar cibo alcuno, et che per

from church to church' in the words of St Philip's later secretary, Germanico Fedele,[8] appears to have lasted some ten years (1540–50) during which time, in the recollection of an early Dominican acquaintance, Francesco Cardoni, the saint had lived continuously in the catacombs of S. Sebastiano where he ate bread and vegetable roots.[9] Years later, Antonio Berti glossed Cardoni's recollection with the added detail that Philip had spent all his time 'doing much penance',[10] a fact which combined with the word originally chosen by Cardoni to describe the saint's adoptive home, '*grotte*', calls to the mind's eye the patristic image of a desert father such as Jerome doing penance in his cave.

Although St Philip's continuous residence at and around S. Sebastiano is gainsaid by evidence elsewhere, the implications of Cardoni's testimony are clear. For the first decade of the saint's time in Rome, the catacombs, together with major early Christian churches – all of which were situated on the periphery of the city's *abitato* where he would walk, eat, and sleep, recite the Offices (sometimes by the light of the moon),[11] and meditate on his sinfulness – functioned as a fundamental point of reference for him. So even before the great age of catacomb rediscovery began in 1578, Rome and its immediate hinterland already constituted for St Philip a sacred landscape saturated with numinous significance. Furthermore, in his devotional processions to the seven principal basilicas of early Christian Rome a practice which also predates the heroic period of Christian archaeology, those who attended were asked to meditate on scenes from Christ's passion between each church. In this way, the universal Christian message of redemption was grafted on to

---

suo letto era la terra nuda', G. Incisa della Rocchetta and N. Vian, eds, *Il primo processo per San Filippo Nero* (hereafter *Il primo processo*), 4 vols (Vatican City, 1957–63), 1, p. 173, testimony dated 7 Sept. 1595.

[8] 'Ho inteso dire, che, nel principio, che venne il beato Filippo a Roma . . . faceva una vita mezza eremitica, andando alle chiese . . .', *Il primo processo*, 3, p. 277, testimony dated 8 June 1610.

[9] '. . . che dieci anni era stato nelle grotte di S. Sebastiano, dove viveva di pane e di radiche d'herbe', *Il primo processo*, 1, p. 133, testimony dated 1 Sept. 1595.

[10] '. . . a fare molte penitenze', *Il primo processo*, 3, p. 178, testimony dated 7 May 1610.

[11] See *Il primo processo*, 1, p. 248.

the particular topography of Rome in a way that indicated what for St Philip was the ultimate reality.

It was therefore thoughts of the Christian martyrs who in their worship and suffering had born witness to the universal message of Christ's sacrifice, rather than the place itself, which inspired St Philip's nocturnal vigils in the catacombs of S. Sebastiano. S. Carlo Borromeo was similarly prompted when, according to a near contemporary tradition, he symbolized his visceral attachment to the early Christian martyrs in the most literal terms possible by collecting the bones he found there and placing them in terracotta caskets.[12] Central to Gregory Martin's experience of the city of Rome, where he had lived from 1576 to 1578, was the opportunity to visit 'the places where they [the martyrs] prayed, preached, fasted, were imprisoned, dyed'.[13] Unfortunately for Martin, he had already left Rome just before the so-called *Coemeterium Priscillae* (identified correctly today as *dei Giordani*) was discovered, but nevertheless made special reference to it in his devotional portrait of the spiritual capital of the Tridentine Church written in 1581:

> The greatest vault of al, was found of late . . . ful of dead bodies, with their monuments and superscriptions both Greke and Latin, almost a mile without the gate Pinciana . . . there are altars and the images of Christ and his Apostles, evident tokens of antiquitie, when the Christians in time of persecution assembled into these vaults or cryptes to divine service, and to burie their dead. 'Scarcely even have we heard report how full Rome is of buried saints, how richly her city's soil blossoms with holy tombs.'[14]

---

[12] See G. Severano, *Memorie sacre delle sette chiese di Roma* (Rome, 1630), pp. 453–4 of the Rome 1675 edn. Borromeo, who regarded the catacombs as *pietate stimulante*, also restored his titular basilica of S. Prassade which involved the rearranging of many of the relics of the 2,000 martyrs whom Pope Paschal I had brought to that church from the catacombs for safekeeping in the ninth century. In the absence of catacombs *per se* in Milan, Borromeo also used to keep nocturnal vigils in the crypt of the cathedral there. I am grateful to Anthony Wright for this last item of information.

[13] G. Martin, *Roma sancta (1581)*, ed. G. B. Parks (Rome, 1969), p. 7.

[14] Ibid., p. 44. The final quotation (given by Martin in the original Latin) is taken

As W. W. Meyer put it succinctly, for Martin 'the catacombs are not sources of historical evidence, illustrating the apostolicity of the Roman church. They were devotional stations, sites to be used by the pilgrims and penitent to enhance the practice of counter-reformation piety.'[15]

The degree to which St Philip's contemporaries identified with the age of early Christian martyrdoms could sometime reach what to modern eyes might seem bizarre lengths. The young Cesare Baronio, in a letter to his mother of 3 December 1563, asked her to pray to God for him so that he might become another martyr like Stephen or Lawrence:

> This is my desire: may the love that unites you to me be such that you may be able to act like those Christian women of the first ages who, with eager desire and joy, led their own sons to martyrdom; she indeed thought herself happy who was worthy to have a martyr son.[16]

Central to this renewed interest in the catacombs and the consequent efforts to rediscover their location – only those of S. Sebastiano on the via Appia had been visited more or less uninterruptedly since the early Middle Ages[17] – was the conviction that the subterranean corridors and cubicles had been the setting for the suffering and the liturgical life of the early Christians. In the words of Bosio's contemporary, Ottavio Panciroli, written in a work published to coincide with the Holy Year of 1600 (and reprinted for that of 1625), they

> not only provided a place of burial for the dead but also sheltered the living during the most cruel persecution

from Prudentius, *Peristephanon*, bk II, lines 541–44. The translation is that of the Loeb edition by H. J. Thompson (2, p. 141).

[15] W. W. Meyer, 'The Church and the Catacombs: British responses to the evidence of the Roman catacombs, 1578–1900' (Cambridge University Ph.D. thesis, 1985), p. 28. I am grateful to Dr Judith Champ for having drawn my attention to this useful study.

[16] Rome, Biblioteca Vallicelliana [hereafter BVR], *Cod. Q. 46*, fol. 34, reprinted in H. Lämmer, *De Caesaris Baronii literarum commercio diatriba* (Freibourg im Breisgau, 1903), p. 38. Cf. L. von Pastor, *History of the Popes*, 19 (London, 1952), p. 171.

[17] For an excellent survey of the *fortuna* of the Roman catacombs down to the fifteenth century see J. Osborne, 'The Roman catacombs in the Middle Ages', *Papers of the British School at Rome*, 53 (1985), pp. 278–328.

against the Christians, which lasted three hundred years. Lacking, above ground, any place where they could rest their afflicted bodies, they took refuge underground and there celebrated divine rites, including mass, heard the Word of the Lord and received the Blessed Sacraments. To this end they constructed chapels, decorating them with the images of saints as one can see today . . .[18]

Further down on the same page, Panciroli related how some Christians had been buried alive in the catacombs as a direct result of pagan persecution. As Giovanni Severano reminded readers of his guide to the seven principal basilicas of the city: 'walking to the church of S. Sebastiano, all the countryside you cross should be considered sacred, since there are many catacombs', details about which he then promised to give the reader, '. . . so that you may walk on it with due devotion'.[19]

Another writer of early Church history from this period, Pompeo Ugonio, who accompanied Bosio on the latter's first descent into the catacombs on 10 December 1593, exemplifies the degree to which under St Philip's impetus the topography of Rome had become saturated with the subterranean associations linked to this most heroic period of Christian suffering. In the introductory *discorso* to his *Historie delle stationi di Roma* of 1588, Ugonio canvassed a variety of possible origins for the Christian use of the word *station* before settling on the word's military associations in pagan Rome. In this context, *station* had signified units of local militia, which, led by their bishops, had retreated into the catacombs in order to shelter from the persecution of the pagan emperors.[20]

In the note to the reader which prefaced Bosio's *Roma sotterranea*, the catacombs were described as nothing less than

the very images and pictures that portray with immediacy [*al vivo*] the early Church. [They are] theatres and circuses where the true and holy gladiators of Christ trained and prepared themselves so as to gain victory

[18]   O. Panciroli, *Tesori nascosti dell'alma città di Roma* (Rome, 1600), p. 18 of Rome 1625 edn. Cf. A. Bosio, *Historia passionis B. Caeciliae virginis. . .*, pp. 65–6.

[19]   G. Severano, *Memorie sacre delle sette chiese di Roma* (Rome, 1630), p. 419.

[20]   P. Ugonio, *Historie delle stationi di Roma* (Rome, 1588), sig. tt 4r–v.

and the eternal crown. [They are] arsenals, where [the martyrs] armed themselves for combat against the heretics and particularly against the iconoclasts who impugn sacred images which abound in the catacombs.

Even when stripped bare of their precious bodies and bones, Bosio continues, 'the corridors themselves, adorned and sanctified with the blood of the martyrs and with the signs and tears of the faithful exude sanctity'.

Accordingly, like their muse St Philip, in their researches and writings Bosio, Panciroli, Ugonio, and others, regarded the catacombs above all as *vestigia* of that purest and most heroic period of Church history during the time of the imperial persecutions. *Vestigia* over which, importantly, Catholic Rome had an effective monopoly, to be displayed as title deeds to its unique status as successor to the apostolic Church over and against Protestant counter-claims. It is in this respect that works such as Bosio's might be considered as constituting a *lectio divina* on the sufferings of the martyrs; a meditation on a sacred landscape which Bosio and his fellow *eruditi sacri* people with praying, bleeding, and dying Christians whose martyrdoms were given almost tactile presence by the details of paleo-Christian material culture which were then being uncovered.

A counterpart to the symbolic role of the catacombs as a sign of a deeper spiritual reality was the primary authority of texts: liturgical, hagiographical, and historical – as opposed to the trowels of workmen and speculators – in their discovery and description. The Augustinian scholar Onofrio Panvinio (1529/30–68), whose premature death incidentally enabled subsequent Oratorian dominance in the field, listed no fewer than forty-three catacombs in his pioneering treatise on early Christian burial practice, *De ritu sepeliendi mortuos apud veteres christianos et eorundem coemeteriis liber* (Cologne, 1568). However, it appears that he knew the actual location of only three or four.[21]

---

[21] They were, apart from S. Sebastiano, those of Pope Julius I (near the church of S. Valentino) on the via Flaminia; of Balbina or S. Marco between the via Appia and Ardeatina; and that of Cyriaces, next to the basilica of S. Lorenzo fuori le mura. Fremiotti believes that these are not references to the catacombs Panvinio had visited

This is scarcely surprising when one considers the exclusively written nature of his sources. Panvinio cites the *Liber pontificalis*, a collection of popes' lives with lists of their gifts and foundations from St Peter down to AD 870, then thought to have been begun by Pope Damasus (366–84) and completed by the ninth-century librarian Anastasius; the so-called *Chronograph of 354* which was an almanac comprising, *inter alia*, lists of emperors, popes, and martyrs from the pontificate of Liberius; the *Liber censuum*, a register of the spiritual and secular institutions dependent on and owing dues to the Holy See compiled by Cencio Savelli (later Pope Honorius III) in 1192; and, finally, various martyrologies which listed the feast day of a saint and, where possible, the place where she or he died, in calendar format.

The fact that Panvinio's list of catacombs appeared in a treatise devoted to early Christian burial practice also shows how such knowledge was used to validate current Catholic devotional practice: in this case, the endowment of masses for the souls of the dead (chs IX–X). The three chapters listing the catacombs themselves (chs XI–XIII) must be set firmly within the context of Panvinio's over-riding concern to find evidence in the early Christian period for contemporary practice. Chapter one, for example, was given over to the indispensable part played by the sacraments of Confession, the Eucharist and Extreme Unction in committing a person's soul to God. The last chapter, meanwhile, was dedicated to early Christian expressions of a Catholic practice under particular attack from the Protestants: pilgrimage to the tombs of the saints.

This preoccupation with the devotional life of the early apostolic Church expressed liturgically and sacramentally as a way of justifying contemporary practice was also central to the section Bosio had clearly intended to constitute book one of *Roma sotterranea*, but which the Oratorian scholar Giovanni Severano, who had been entrusted with the task of preparing

but only to those which were then open to the public. See P. Fremiotti, *La Riforma cattolica del secolo decimosesto e gli studi di Archaeologia cristiana* (Rome, 1926), p. 34. For an extensive treatment of Panvinio's contribution to Christian archaeology see ibid., pp. 26–41.

the manuscript for publication, decided to omit.[22] Even a cursory look at the contents of this missing section reveals a direct affinity with that of Panvinio's pioneering treatise. There were separate chapters dedicated to the custom of visiting the sick or those awaiting martyrdom (ch. 1); to confession (ch. 3); to the *viaticum* (ch. 4); to the anointing of the sick (ch. 5); to the duties of those attending the ill and dying (ch. 6); and to the prayers and psalms appropriate to such vigils (ch. 8). The rest of this section (chs 9–13) which provided details concerning the collection, preparation, and burial of the bodies of the martyrs, corresponded more closely to the contents of the first book as finally published. This emphasis on what the catacombs could reveal about the devotions of the early Christians (as opposed to representations of their dead) is clear from the frontispiece of the book as published. The central scene is taken up *not* by the tombs themselves, nor by martyrs or the instruments of their martyrdom (which decorate the borders) but by an act of burial.

The reasons why Bosio wished to preface *Roma sotterranea* with such details about the liturgical and devotional life of the early Christians were outlined in the preface to this unpublished section.[23] Here he made it abundantly clear that his priority was to demonstrate that the rites and ceremonies he was describing were in conformity with current (Tridentine) practice even though the early Christians had been forced to tolerate and adapt heathen practices in the first centuries. In defence of the latter policy of pragmatic

[22] BVR, *Cod. G. 31*, fols 94–246. A list of the chapter titles to this section is given in L. Spigno, 'Della Roma sotterranea del Bosio e della sua biografia', *Rivista di archeologia cristiana*, 52 (1976), pp. 277–301 (at pp. 278–9). For the fullest available discussion of *G. 31* see this article and an earlier one by Spigno: 'Considerazioni sul manoscritto vallicelliano G. 31 e la Roma sotterranea di Antonio Bosio', ibid., 51 (1975), pp. 281–311. Cf. G. B. De Rossi, *Roma sotterranea cristiana*, 3 vols (Rome, 1864–77), 1, pp. 33–5; but see now G. Finocchiaro, 'La *Roma sotterranea* e la Congregazione dell'Oratorio. Inediti e lacune del manoscritto vallicelliano G. 31', in B. Tellini Santoni and A. Manodoro, eds, *Messer Filippo Neri, santo: l'apostolo di Roma*, a catalogue of the exhibition held at the Vallicelliana Library, 24 May–30 Sept. 1995 (Rome, 1995), pp. 189–93. I am indebted to Dott. Finocchiaro for having drawn my attention to Spigno's articles and for kindly sending me a copy of the catalogue.

[23] *G. 31*, fols. 94r–5r. Cf. the transcription given in Finocchiaro, 'La *Roma sotterranea* e la Congregazione dell'Oratorio', pp. 192–3.

accommodation, Bosio quoted with approval from Gregory the Great's famous letter to Mellitus where the Pope advised the latter gradually to supplant local customs with the Roman rite.[24] It was most likely this sophistication of Bosio's understanding of how the nascent Christian Church gradually evolved its rites and ceremonies in relation to pagan and even Jewish practices that decided Severano to exclude Bosio's original book one.[25]

The notion of liturgical development implicit in such a nuanced understanding would clearly have offered ammunition to Protestant polemicists in their efforts to undermine the legitimacy of Tridentine worship, despite the fact that Bosio made frequent reference to the relevant decree of Trent in his text.[26] Another area where his efforts to do justice to complex subjects fell foul of Severano's wish to present a more cut and dried account concerned the strategies adopted by the pagan persecutors to make it difficult for Christians to retrieve the bodies of the martyrs. Bosio tells of how, during the reign of Julian the Apostate, their bones were deliberately mixed with those of asses and camels.[27] Such a detail would have been used by Protestant polemicists to cast yet further doubt on the cult of relics, although, for Bosio, it provided an occasion to praise the very heroic lengths which early Christians had to go to in order to give their champions a decent burial.

Elsewhere Severano's editorial policy was rather more straightforward, being essentially motivated by the desire not to overlap with ground he had already covered in his own study of the seven principal basilicas of the city, concerning the burial areas of the churches of St Peter's and St Paul outside the Walls.[28] Here, in addition, Severano could argue

---

[24]   G. 31, fol. 94v. Cf. J. Richards, *Consul of God: the Life and Times of Gregory the Great* (London, 1980), pp. 244–5.

[25]   Bosio identified Jewish influence, for example, in several aspects of early Christian burial practice, including the practice of saying prayers for the dead (G. 36, fols 218v and 240r).

[26]   E.g. in relation to his account of the early history of the sacrament of confession, G. 31, fol. 101r–v.

[27]   G. 31, fols 195r-6r.

[28]   The relevant sections of G. 31 which were crossed out by Severano are fols 271r–385r (on St Peter's) and fols 541v–71r (on St Paul's).

that he enjoyed the authority of Bosio himself, as the latter had read the Oratorian's manuscript with considerable pleasure and indicated that he would be quite happy to remove what he has written on the topic from his own text.[29] However, it has to be said that even here, in his enthusiasm for the rich and complex nature of early Christian culture, Bosio had included details that Protestant polemicists would have seized upon with glee. One such was his account of the enormous wealth of St Peter's and St Paul's, derived from offerings at the apostles' tombs, which came to an annual total of over 30,400 gold florins.[30] Bosio further revealed that at one stage the right to this income at St Peter's was farmed out (*in appalto*) to people who then agreed to maintain the shrine and take care of the running expenses which even included payment of judges' wages.[31]

Altogether, around thirty per cent of the manuscript *Roma sotterranea* – most of it only indirectly concerned with the catacombs themselves – failed to find its way into the published version. If we add to this the fact that book four of the printed text, that is to say, the part devoted to explanations of the images found in the catacombs, is nowhere to be found in Bosio's original manuscript,[32] then one can begin to see that, notwithstanding his sobriquet as 'Columbus of the catacombs', *Roma sotterranea* directly follows on from Panvinio's tradition of textual scholarship which at the hands of Oratorian *eruditi sacri* such as Cesare Baronio and Antonio Gallonio had been supplemented by a veritable 'census of the sacred' for the early Christian period. This material was easily accessible to scholars such as Bosio in the Vallicelliana Library, and the frequent references in his text to 'ms. Vallic. 1, 2, 3,', etc., may with confidence be

---

[29] See in a letter from Bosio to Giacomo Crescenzi of 28 Feb. 1629 in *Cod. G. 20*, fol. 221r. Bosio's death on 7 Sept. the same year prevented him from carrying out his intention of removing the surplus material.

[30] *G. 31*, fol. 286r–v.

[31] 'Fu per alcun tempo usato di dare in appalto le oblazioni della confessione di S. Pietro e quello che le comprava si obligava et era tenuto di dare le sudette cose e fare le spesi soliti. ... da essa Sacra Confessione si pagavono fin gli stipendi de'ministri di giustitia'. Ibid., fols 283v–4r.

[32] This part of *Roma sotterranea* was put together by Severano using, for the most part, material which Bosio had collected (*Codd. G. 3* and *G. 4*).

identified with codices *H. 1–20* in that library, which contained overwhelmingly hagiographical and patristic material.[33] Bosio's own notes, also located at the Vallicelliana (codices *G. 3* and *G. 4*), logically reflect this emphasis and (except for a fifty-page iconographical index bound at the beginning of *G. 3*, out of a total of 2062 pages between the two volumes), notes about archaeological finds such as inscriptions and other material objects are conspicuous by their rarity.[34]

The very frequency with which Bosio cited Baronio's Church history (the *Annales ecclesiastici* of 1588–1607) and historical notes to successive revisions of the Roman Martyrology testify to the importance Bosio attached to textual sources in the interpretation of material evidence revealed with the aid of the trowel. Returning home from a subterranean visit to the catacombs of S. Priscilla where he had been puzzled by the image of a woman depicted there, Bosio suddenly remembered it was that saint's feast day; whence he derived the conclusion that the image must have been of Priscilla herself.[35] The precise contribution to the stimulation of the mind's eye of *eruditi sacri* such as Bosio by early martyrologies with their telegraphic reports of saintly suffering, often tantalizingly incomplete, has yet to be fully measured. In their basic form such martyrologies were simply an annotated calendar of martyred saints, consisting of the day of the anniversary, the place of veneration and the saint's name, which were read out daily at the Office of Prime. But guided by these 'hagiographic co-ordinates'

[33] For a summary list of the contents to *H. 1–20* see A. Poncelet, *Catalogus codicum hagiographicorum latinorum bibliothecarum romanarum praeter quam vaticanae* (Brussels, 1909), pp. 400–43. *H. 24* consists of an index to some of the additional hagiographical manuscripts Bosio consulted. They include nine from the Vatican; four from St Peter's; two from St John Lateran; two from S. Cecilia in Trastevere; one from S. Maria ad Martyres (the Pantheon) as well as twenty-one from the *Codd. H* series in the Vallicelliana.

[34] Bosio's notes are entitled, *Acta et vitae sanctorum, antiqua monumenta sacra et profana, itemque adversaria variae eruditionis pro illustrando opere de sacris coemeteriis* (BVR, Codd. G3 and G4). In *G. 4* there is a colour drawing of Pope Leo I's body and coffin taken from Giacomo Grimaldi's famous description of the excavations involved in building the new St Peter's (p. 1164) and the depiction of a ferocious-looking pair of forceps also found under the basilica (p. 1492).

[35] See Fremiotti, *La Riforma cattolica*, pp. 81–3.

Bosio and his contemporaries structured their subterranean experience, giving it form and providential purpose. This is well illustrated by one particularly striking example.

Two hours before sunrise on Sunday, 29 July 1618, Bosio, together with an artist and two labourers armed with spades and pickaxes, descended into a catacomb situated next to the via Portuense on land owned by the English College. They were searching for the tombs of the martyrs Abdon and Sennen. After three hours or so of fruitless searching they came across the tombs near the original entrance to the catacombs, which they had to clear of earth and debris. Bosio concluded his account with the words: 'We are grateful for the grace we received', adding somewhat disingenuously, 'because by chance [*impensamente*] we found the ancient tomb of the holy martyrs Abdon and Sennen, on the eve of their feast.'[36]

Carlo Cecchelli went as far as to say that but for the historical and martyrological foundations laid by Baronio it would be difficult to believe that Bosio could have written anything more than a few detailed and incomplete studies.[37] It might well be added that it is in passages from the pages of Baronio's magisterial statement of the Tridentine church's continuity with its apostolic predecessor – the *Annales* – that one perhaps gains the clearest sense of what the discoveries of this subterranean dimension to their Church's past meant to educated contemporaries.

It is with wonder [wrote Baronio] that we have seen and several times visited the cemetery of Priscilla, as soon as it was discovered and excavated. We can find no better words to describe its extent and its many corridors than to call it a subterranean city. All Rome was filled with wonder, for it had no idea that in its neighbourhood there was a hidden city, filled with tombs from the days of the persecutions of the Christians. *That which we knew before from written accounts and from a few cemeteries which*

[36] Bosio, *Roma sotterranea*, p. 127. Cf. Ferretto, *Note storico-bibliografiche di archaeologia cristiana*, p. 141.

[37] C. Cecchelli, *Il Cenacolo filippino e l'archeologia cristiana* (Spoleto, 1938), pp. 22–3.

*were only partially opened out, we can now realize fully, and,
filled with wonder, see with out own eyes the confirmation of the
accounts of Jerome and Prudentius.*[38]

In this last sentence Baronio eloquently expresses the way
in which trowel fulfilled text. Even where it did not, that
failure may, ironically, serve to emphasize the point even
further, because of the scale of the misinterpretation
involved.

Pictures of martyrdom were extremely rare in the
catacombs, but this did not prevent contemporaries moulding what they discovered to accord with their expectations. A
notorious example of this may be found in a collection of
drawings of subterranean images most probably owned by
that early foreign enthusiast of subterranean Rome, the
Netherlander Philip de Winghe.[39] Avowedly copied from the
catacombs of Domitilla, the image is of a naked woman who
appears to be unharmed by the flames which are being fed by
four figures bearing bundles of wood. The prototype for this
composition of female martyrdom has now been traced to an
unusual representation of the Adoration of four Magi in
those very catacombs. Similarly, Bosio interpreted an image
from the catacombs of S. Giulio papa which to us is clearly
the representation of adult baptism as that of a saint being
immersed in a tub of boiling water or oil.[40]

Such creative misinterpretation of visual evidence should
be set squarely in the context of a charged, almost febrile,
sense of optimism which the very existence of figurative
decoration in the catacombs had helped to create. For there
could surely be no more authoritative reply to the Protestant
iconoclasts. In the felicitous phrase of Francis Haskell, 'the
paintings of the catacombs may seem – to the reader of our

[38]   C. Baronio, *Annales ecclesiastici*, 12 vols (Antwerp, 1597–1609: 1st edn, Rome,
1588–1607), 2, ad an. 130, n. 2, p. 81 (emphasis added). Cf. ibid., 1, ad an. 57, n. 112,
and 2, ad an. 226, nn. 8 and 12. The catacomb referred to erroneously by Baronio as
Priscilla was in fact that of the Giordani.
[39]   BVR, *G. 6*, the relevant image may be found on fol. 9r. Cf. T. Buser, 'Jerome
Nadal and early Jesuit art in Rome', *Art Bulletin*, 58 (1976), pp. 431–2, where it is
discussed and illustrated.
[40]   A. Bosio, *Roma sotterranea*, p. 579.

day – to have been described before they had ever been seen.'[41]

By retrieving the spiritual context within which works like Bosio's *Roma sotterranea* came to be written, we can see not only how they were the products of devotion as much as of erudition, but also the methodological implications of such a standpoint. But one must be careful not to oppose devotion to erudition. Authors such as Pancinio and Bosio clearly believed that they were getting closer than their predecessors to the early Christian past. Indeed, the range of resources deployed in Baronio's comprehensive and painstaking restoration of the paleo-Christian basilica of SS Nereo ed Achilleo clearly shows that the Cardinal saw himself as doing something fundamentally new and different, even if we today regard it as archaeologically naive and misleading in several important respects.[42]

The main point is rather that the central mission of *eruditi sacra* such as Bosio, to create a liturgical/devotional continuum sustained by scholarship, implied and indeed derived from the priority of text which, in turn, informed trowel (and, of course, eye). In such circumstances, the Tridentine Church retrospective was firmly anchored in space – or rather, underground Rome – but outside time altogether: *semper eadem*. The polemical use to which the Magdeburg Centuriators had put the idea of history as development ensured this state of affairs until the persevering genius of Cardinal Newman in the nineteenth century.

University of York

---

[41] F. Haskell, *History and its Images: Art and the Interpretation of the Past* (New Haven and London, 1993), p. 123. For a fuller discussion of Baronio, Bosio, and the confessional interpretation of visual evidence from the catacombs, see also pp. 102–10.

[42] R. Krautheimer, 'A Christian triumph of 1597', in D. Fraser et al., *Essays in the History of Art Presented to Rudolf Wittkower* (London, 1967), pp. 174–8. For a much fuller account of the scholarship Baronio brought to bear on the project, see now A. Herz, 'Cardinal Cesare Baronio's restoration of Ss. Nereo ed Achilleo and S. Cesareo de'Appia', *Art Bulletin*, 70 (1988), pp. 590–620.

FONTEVRAULT LOOKS BACK TO HER FOUNDER: REFORM AND THE ATTEMPTS TO CANONIZE ROBERT OF ARBRISSEL*

by J. M. B. PORTER

The abbesses of Fontevrault recognized the work of their founder, Robert of Arbrissel, in a number of different ways.[1] It has been suggested by modern scholars that the first abbess of the Order, Petronilla of Chemillé, was dissatisfied with the *vita* written by Baudry of Dol and commissioned a new one from a Fontevrist canon who has long been thought to have been Robert's personal chaplain.[2] However this second *vita* may have been produced for other reasons, and it may not have been originally written to further the cause of his canonization. In the seventeenth century, Jeanne-Baptiste de Bourbon, the Abbess of Fontevrault and illegitimate daughter of King Henry IV, applied to Pope Innocent X in an attempt to canonize Robert

* A bursary from the Society for the Study of French History made it possible for me to visit a number of French archives; a bursary from the Ecclesiastical History Society made it possible for me to attend the conference at which this paper was given: it is a pleasure to acknowledge their financial support. I am indebted to Prof. Bernard Hamilton for his advice and encouragement, and to Inge Verstraeten, who provided a place to write the initial draft of this paper and saved me from making a number of mistranslations. I should also like to thank Berenice Kerr for sending me a copy of a paper she presented at Oxford in February 1995, and Simon Ditchfield, Colin Heywood, Elisabeth Stopp, and Anthony Wright for their many helpful suggestions and comments. Many ideas for this paper were first developed over croquet with the late Andrew Martindale at the Nottingham Conference of this Society in 1994.

[1] The most important studies of Robert of Arbrissel are by Jean-Marc Bienvenu, *L'Etonnant fondateur de Fontevraud* (Paris, 1981); Jacques Dalarun, *Robert d'Arbrissel, fondateur de Fontevraud* (Paris, 1986); and idem, *L'Impossible sainteté* (Paris, 1985), which has a comprehensive bibliography. Two shorter studies provide a good introduction to the life and works of Robert of Arbrissel in English: Jaqueline Smith, 'Robert of Arbrissel: *Procurator mulierum*', in Derek Baker, ed., *Medieval Women*, *SCH.S* 1 (Oxford, 1978), pp. 175–84; and Penny Schine Gold, *The Lady and the Virgin* (Chicago, 1985). For the medieval canonization process, see Eric W. Kemp, *Canonisation and Authority in the Western Church* (London, 1948), pp. 36–81.

[2] Baudry of Dol, *Vita B. Roberti de Arbrisello* [hereafter, *VP*], in *PL*, 162, cols 1043–58; Andrew of Fontevrault, *Vita Altera B. Roberti de Arbrisello* [hereafter *VA*], in *PL*, 162, cols 1057–78.

of Arbrissel, a cause which also had the support of (among others) King Louis XIV and Queen Henrietta Maria of England. Her attempt failed, in part because of the publication of letters critical of Robert's way of life written in the twelfth century by Geoffrey of Vendôme and Marbode of Rennes.[3] After Robert's relics were re-discovered in 1842, the nuns of the three Fontevrist houses founded after the French Revolution attempted once again to canonize the founder of their order, but clerical opposition to his cause and ambiguities about his relics meant that their petition was unsuccessful. This paper shows how the Order of Fontevrault and its abbesses looked back at their own history in their attempts to return to Robert's original ideal for Fontevrault and how, by having their founder created a saint, they hoped to enlist his support in their reform of the Order, thus preserving their unique way of life at Fontevrault.

* * *

The perception of the apostolic life held by the twelfth-century hermit-preacher Robert of Arbrissel led him to renounce the world whilst leading a mendicant life of active evangelism. He was born in Arbrissel, a village close to the Angevin frontier near Rennes, some time in the middle of the eleventh century.[4] His father, Damalioch, was a priest, as was his father before him; charter evidence seems to indicate that his mother, Orguende, was of the lesser aristocracy, perhaps the sister of the crusader Fulk de Mateflon, a lieutenant of Fulk de Réchin.[5] Other than what is recorded in the *vita* written by his contemporary Baudry of Dol (which at times lapses into the hagiographic convention of pious fiction), very little is known of Robert's life until his studies took him to Paris during the pontificate of Gregory VII.[6] It seems likely that he was ordained in Paris; although the precise date remains unknown, he must have been ordained by 1089,

[3] Geoffrey of Vendôme, *ep.* 6, in *PL* 171, cols 1480–92.

[4] His exact date of birth is a matter of some controversy: see Smith, '*Procurator mulierum*', p. 176.

[5] *Catalogue des Actes de Foulque Nerra, Geoffroi Martel, Geoffroi le Barbu, et Foulque le Réchin*, in Louis Halphen, *Le Comté d'Anjou au XIe siècle* (Paris, 1906), no. 293, p. 330.

[6] *VP*, 7: *PL*, 162, col. 1047.

when Robert returned to Brittany at the request of Sylvester de la Guerch, the reforming Bishop of Rennes, who summoned Robert to his diocese to become archpriest of the cathedral church. Robert spent four years there, 'making peace between quarrellers, liberating churches from slavery to the laity, separating the incestuous unions of priest and laity, opposing simony, and manfully opposing all sins'.[7] Robert's zeal in ridding the church of corruption and abuse earned him many enemies and he was forced to leave Rennes after Sylvester's sudden death in 1093. He spent two years in the cathedral school in Angers, where he became well known for both his ascetic way of life and for his skillful preaching. In 1096, he was granted the disused church later known as La Roë in the forest of Craon, in which he established a community of Augustinian canons with himself as abbot. The day before this grant he was granted permission by Pope Urban II to preach: according to his biographer Baudry of Dol, the Pope had appointed Robert as 'preacher second only to himself as a sower of the Word of God in men's hearts with orders to travel everywhere in the performance of his duty'.[8] It seems likely that, in order to circumvent opposition to the reform movement by the simoniacally elected and incompetent Bishop Geoffrey of Angers, Robert was licensed to preach in order to further the reform movement in a diocese hostile to reform and not (as commonly assumed by Crusade historians) to preach Crusade.[9] Fontevrault was founded less than four years later, in order to house the growing number of men and – worryingly for Church authorities – women whom he had converted to the apostolic life.

★ ★ ★

Robert died in 1117, and the first of his two *vitae* was commissioned by Petronilla of Chemillé, the Abbess of Fontevrault, sometime after 1120. Written by the celebrated

---

[7]   *VP*, 9: *PL*, 162, cols 1048–9.

[8]   *VP*, 14: *PL*, 162, cols 1050–1; cf. Acts 17, Matt. 13.3–8.

[9]   J. M. B. Porter, 'Preacher of the First Crusade? Robert of Arbrissel after the Council of Clermont', paper presented at the Second International Medieval Congress, Leeds, July 1995.

poet Archbishop Baudry of Dol, this first *vita* glorifies Robert's spectacular eremiticism in the forest of Craon; his wandering preaching and denunciation of the vices of the Church and the world; his enthusiastic evangelism and his welcoming of all, including prostitutes, without distinction; and his special ministry for the poor and leprous; and ends by putting him beside the apostles.[10] Speaking about Fontevrault, Baudry especially mentions the first idealistic beginning of an egalitarian and fraternal community where no group was of higher value than another. It is clear that Baudry believed Robert to be a saint, and his *vita* follows the standard hagiographical conventions of his day.[11] However, no mention is made of Petronilla, nor does he mention what is perhaps the distinctive feature of Fontevrist monasticism, the subordination of the community of men to that of women. Similarly, Baudry does not mention the statutes by which the men submitted themselves to the rule of the abbess.[12]

This was useless to Petronilla, if we assume that she was determined not to promote a *popular* (as opposed to a strictly internal) cult of her order's founder, and wanted an affirmation of her authority which appears to have been contested by several of the men in the community. Baudry's work glorified Robert but did not mention that he had placed his new community under the direction of women, at first Hersende of Montsoreau and after her death Petronilla of Chemillé. This omission may have provided Petronilla's opponents with arguments against her authority, and thus may have been the inspiration for the commissioning of a new *vita* from Robert's chaplain Andrew, who had witnessed Robert's death and had stayed loyal to his original vision of a male community subordinate to women for the good of their souls. However, it has

[10] *VP*, 26: *PL*, 162, col. 1058.

[11] For an examination of hagiography as a literary form, see Thomas Head, *Hagiography and the Cult of the Saints* (Cambridge, 1990), pp. 102–34. Among the miracles attributed to Robert was the ability to raise the dead: see *VP*, 23: *PL*, 162, col. 1055.

[12] Fragments of these statutes survive: see *PL*, 162, cols 1080–5. See also Gold, *The Lady and the Virgin*, pp. 98–101.

been argued that Andrew was not commissioned to write this *vita* by Petronilla, but instead had chosen to record what is, for a medieval hagiography, an impartial record of the final six months of Robert's life.[13] The absence of a dedication to Petronilla lends a great deal of credence to this theory, as one would expect such a dedication if she had indeed commissioned it.

The *vita altera* by Andrew of Fontevrault is usually seen as being little more than a sequel to the first *vita*, elaborating on Baudry's account of Robert's last days. Like Baudry, Andrew's *vita* also describes Robert as 'very saintly' (*sanctissimus*), but he also records Petronilla's election as abbess, the papal confirmation of her election, and the brothers' promise to obey and serve her.[14] If this *vita* was commissioned by Petronilla, the author's reluctance to praise Petronilla, he says to avoid being thought a flatterer, seems unusual.[15] On the other hand, one could read into the brief reference to the meeting between the dying Robert and Petronilla a conscious decision by the author to de-emphasize Robert's last recommendations to the abbess.[16] The *vita altera*, by making it understood that Robert's decisions had been accepted without difficulty or opposition from any part of the community, uses the long speeches attributed to Robert on the subordination of the men and the importance placed on Petronilla's role in the community to emphasize that Robert had intended from the beginning to create a religious institution in which the male community was under the authority of the abbess. Prior Andrew's *vita altera* gave Abbess Petronilla the opportunity to justify her authority over the entire community by quoting the words of her Order's founder in order to support her position.

Petronilla appears to have made no effort to foster the popular cult of Robert of Arbrissel as a saint. During her reign as abbess, no miracles were recorded at his tomb, nor was a popular cult promoted. However, there is strong

---

13 This argument is put forward by Gold, *The Lady and the Virgin*, p. 96.
14 *VA*, 4–6: *PL*, 162, vols 1059–60.
15 *VA*, 8: *PL*, 162, col. 1061.
16 Bienvenu, *L'Étonnant fondateur*, 164.

evidence which indicates that there was a desire within the Order to promote an internal cult of Robert of Arbrissel, which would spare the community the nuisance of dealing with the large numbers of pilgrims to his shrine, with the attendant disruption to the community that a large popular cult would entail. There are other incidences of monasteries discouraging large popular cults: miracles associated with Robert of Chaise Dieu attracted so many pilgrims to his shrine that the monks of that house begged him to stop; for the same reason, the abbot of Clairvaux held St Bernard to his vow of obedience and ordered him to cease performing miracles.[17] The monastic enclosure was not to be compromised: one of the Fontevrault statutes forbids seculars from keeping vigils in their churches.[18]

The French scholar Jean-Marc Bienvenu has argued that Petronilla and the nuns of Fontevrault conspired to consign Robert of Arbrissel to oblivion, and cites the absence of a *rouleau de mort* in support of this claim.[19] However, there are indications of an internal cult of Robert at Fontevrault, as his relics are mentioned in the formula for the profession of the nuns, and the grave difficulties Petronilla encountered and overcame in her fight against both civil and ecclesiastical authorities to secure Robert's body indicates the respect in which Fontevrault held her founder.[20] By burying his body in the nuns' church – instead of in the lepers' cemetery as Robert had requested[21] – Petronilla may have been seeking to limit access to his remains so as to restrict devotion to his cult within the community of nuns at Fontevrault, whilst protecting the mortal remains of her Order's founder from graverobbers.[22] By maintaining the cult of Robert of Arbrissel as a strictly internal devotion, Petronilla and her successors could maintain control of his relics and not be

---

[17] D.-A. Segal, *L'Homme et le miracle dans la France médiévale* (Paris, 1985), pp. 223–5.

[18] *Regulae Sanctimonialium*, 31: *PL*, 162, col. 1081.

[19] Bienvenu, *L'Étonnant fondateur*, pp. 161–9.

[20] *VA*, 33: *PL*, 162, cols 1073–4; Suzanne Tunc, 'Après la mort de Robert d'Arbrissel; le conflit entre l'abbesse et l'évêque', *Le Moyen Age*, 98 (1992), p. 382.

[21] *VA*, 33: *PL*, 162, cols 1073–4.

[22] Dalarun, *L'Impossible sainteté*, pp. 294–5; Patrick J. Geary, *Furta Sacra: Thefts of Relics in the Central Middle Ages* (Princeton, N.J., 1978).

pressured into sacrificing their way of life to the demands of pilgrims visiting his tomb.

⋆ ⋆ ⋆

Jeanne-Baptiste de Bourbon, the illegitimate daughter of Henry IV and Charlotte des Essarts, was the first Abbess of Fontevrault seriously to attempt to have the sanctity of Robert of Arbrissel externally recognized. During her thirty-three-year reign (1637–70), Abbess Jeanne-Baptiste continued and completed the reform of Fontevrault begun under Marie de Bretagne (1457–77); part of Jeanne-Baptiste's continuation of this reform programme was to gain official recognition of her Order's founder, thus invoking his name in her efforts to prevent the male element of the community from taking over Fontevrault or forming a separate observance independent of the abbess's authority.[23] Marie de Bretagne's extensive reforms included the creation of a definitive rule for the community based on the Rules of St Benedict and Augustine, supplemented by the original statutes of the Order. Her new rule, approved by Pope Sixtus IV in 1475, appears to have involved the conversion of the male element of the community from canons to monks.[24] However, the implementation of this change appears to have been delayed until 1641, when Jeanne-Baptiste secured royal confirmation of her reform.[25]

Although the reform of a number of religious houses was carried out with the support of King Henry IV, he did not appear to have a policy regarding the reform of entire Orders, despite the appearance of a reform movement supported by Pope Clement VIII which began to sweep through France in the 1590s.[26] Despite papal, and with the accession of Louis

---

[23] For the reform of the Order, which began in 1459, see Abbé F. Uzureau, 'La Réforme de l'ordre de Fontevrault, 1459–1641', *Revue Mabillon*, 13 (1923), pp. 141–6; for the reforms of the latter abbesses, see Patricia Lusseau, *L'Abbaye royale de Fontevraud aux XVII et XVIII siècles* (Paris, 1986).

[24] In charters and early statutes the men are described as *fratres*, not monks or canons: see the Fontevrault chartulary, BN, MS nouv. acq. lat. 2414, and the early statues for Fontevrist men, *Præcepta recte vivendi*: PL, 162, cols 1083–4.

[25] Raymund Webster, 'Fontevrault', in *Catholic Encyclopedia*, 6 (London, 1909), p. 130.

[26] J. A. Bergin, 'The crown, the papacy and the reform of the old orders in early seventeenth-century France', *JEH*, 33 (1982), pp. 239–41.

XIII in 1610 royal, support, these monastic reformers made slow progress and were unable to reform more than a few houses of an Order, which seems to have encouraged the creation of small observant congregations cut off from the rest of the body.[27] In 1606, Fr Joseph du Tremblay had proposed a mild reform for the Order of Fontevrault to Abbess Eleanor de Bourbon; this was accompanied by a more radical reform for those in the Order who had aligned themselves with Eleanor's coadjutrix and niece Antoinette d'Orléans, who desired to lead a strictly cloistered life of contemplation. The strict reform movement led by Antoinette d'Orléans led to the foundation of an observant congregation, the Congregation of Our Lady of Calvary, which was promoted to the status of an independent Order by a papal bull in 1617.[28] Fr Joseph's reforms for Fontevrault show that the Order was once again having difficulties with its male component; during Eleanor's reign and that of her successor, Louise de Bourbon de Lavedan (1612–37), there were a number of attempts by the abbesses to improve the men's status and to establish theological seminaries for them. Other aspects of Louise's reforms would later have unexpected consequences. In 1622 she had Robert's relics transferred to a plain lead reliquary which was placed in a new tomb erected in the choir of the mother house when it was completed in 1624.

Popular devotion to Robert began to grow in the late sixteenth and early seventeenth centuries in Brittany and Berry, especially at Arbrissel, his birthplace, and Orsan, the priory where he died and where his heart was kept as a relic in a stone pyramid. It was not until Jeanne-Baptiste de Bourbon's reign as abbess that the popular devotion to Robert of Arbrissel gained official encouragement from the Order he founded. Jeanne-Baptiste also commissioned Michel Cosiner, the curé of Fontevrault, to re-edit and

---

27 Ibid., p. 240.
28 See Aldous Huxley, *Grey Eminence: A Study in Religion and Politics* (London, 1941), pp. 88–93; and Henri Bremond, *Histoire littéraire du sentiment religieux en France*, 11 vols in 12 (2nd edn, Paris, 1967–8), 2, pp. 186–92. Fr Joseph, a Capuchin, was aided in his reform of Fontevrault by the young Bishop of Luçon, Armand Jean du Plessis de Richelieu.

publish the *vitae* by Baudry of Dol and Andrew of Fontevrault in the form which later became the accepted version of these works.[29] A number of other works appeared during her reign, written both by prominent members of the Order and by others under her influence – mainly Jesuits – and all with the same basic theme: Robert of Arbrissel lived a saintly life and should be canonized.[30] In 1645 she asked Pope Innocent X for a licence to celebrate the office of Robert; her request was supported by Louis XIV and a number of powerful laywomen, including Anne of Austria (the widow of her half-brother Louis XIII) and her half-sisters Queen Henrietta Maria of England, Queen Elizabeth of Spain, and Christine, Duchess of Savoy. She sent the Jesuit Honorat Nicquet, Robert's hagiographer and an apologist of Fontevrault, to Rome to further her cause; she sent Jean Lardier, the archivist of Fontevrault, to the priory of Orsan, where Robert had died, to attempt to recover the stone pyramid containing Robert's heart which was responsible for miracles in 1569 and 1633/4.[31] This relic was finally translated to the church of St John of the Habit – the men's house of the mother abbey at Fontevrault – in 1648.

That same year, Sébastien Ganot and Jean Chevalier published their account of Robert's life and miracles, *Les gloires ou les éminentes vertus de Robert d'Arbrissel*, in which they claimed that Robert's canonization was imminent.[32] As we

---

[29] Michel Cosiner, ed., *Fontis Ebraldi Exordium, complectens opuscula duo, cum notationibus de vita B. Roberti de Arbrissello. Fontebraldensis ordinis institutoris, et quaestionibus aliquot de potestate abbatissae* (La Flèche, 1641). According to Bienvenu, this edition, which was the basis for the versions published in the *Acta Sanctorum* (henceforth *ActaSS*) and *PL*, was censored, probably on the instructions of Abbess Jeanne-Baptiste, to remove any reference to the fact that Robert's father was a priest from a family of priests: Bienvenu, *L'Étonnant fondateur*, p. 17.

[30] These works include Honorat Nicquet, S.J., *Histoire de l'ordre de Font-Evraud contenant la vie et les merveilles de la sainteté de Robert d'Arbrissel et l'histoire chronologique des abbesses* (Paris, 1642); Jean Chevalier, S.J., and Sébastien Ganot, *La Vie du bienheureux Robert d'Arbrissel, fondateur de l'ordre de Fontevrault* (La Flèche, 1648); and Jean Lardier's manuscript, *La Saincte Famille de Font-Evraux*, vol. 3, which was written for the library of St John of the Habit of Fontevrault in 1650, and is now Château-Gontier, Bibliothèque municipale, MS 12.

[31] Bienvenu, *L'Étonnant fondateur*, pp. 170–1.

[32] Jean Chevalier, S.J., and Sébastien Ganot, *Les gloires ou les éminentes vertus de Robert d'Arbrissel, fondateur de l'order de Fontevrauld* (La Flèche, 1648). This prediction appears in the dedication by Ganot; the remainder of the text was written by Chevalier.

know, the opposite was the case, mainly because of the publication in 1610 of the collected letters of Geoffrey of Vendôme by the Jesuit priest Jacques Sirmond.[33] These included Geoffrey's letter to Robert denouncing his unusual penitential and ascetic practices, including sleeping with virgins in order to overcome the temptations of the flesh.[34]

Abbess Jeanne-Baptist's predecessor, Eleanor de Bourbon, had responded to the publication of Geoffrey of Vendôme's letter criticizing her Order's founder by sending two canons to the abbey library at Vendôme to destroy the manuscript letter from the twelfth-century copy of Geoffrey's letters kept there. They were only able to destroy one of the two folios containing this letter, but this action allowed two other Fontevrist canons to testify in 1652 before Dom Marsolle, the future head of the Maurists, that no such manuscript existed.[35] This elimination of the historical record shows how important the perception of the past was for the abbesses of Fontevrault in their veneration of Robert of Arbrissel.

The case to canonize Robert was still pending when Pope Innocent X died in 1655. The canonization process appears to have stalled during the reign of his successor Alexander VII (1655–67), although Jeanne-Baptiste did arrange for the publication of the two twelfth-century *vitae* in Bolland's *Acta Sanctorum*.[36] She also commissioned a new work on Robert by Balthazar Pavillon, and paid for its publication in 1666,[37] in order to present it as a part of her petition to Pope Clement IX (1667–9). 1668 also saw the publication of a new hagiography written by the Bishop of Poitiers, Chasteignier

[33] Jacques Sirmond, S.J., *Goffridi abbatis Vindocinensis S. Priscae, cardinalis, epistolae, opuscula, sermones* (Paris, 1610).

[34] For a discussion of this ascetic practice, known as syneisaktism, *virgines subintroductae*, or *mulierum consortia*, as practised in Brittany, see Roger E. Reynolds, '*Virgines subintroductae* in Celtic Christianity', *HThR*, 61 (1968), pp. 547–66; Louis Gougaud, '*Mulierum consortia*, étude sur le synéisaktisme chez les ascètes celtiques', *Eriu: Journal of the School of Irish Learning*, 9 (1921–3), pp. 147–56; and Dominique Iogna-Prat, 'La Femme dans la perspective pénitentielle des ermites du Bas-Maine (fin XIe–début XIIe siècle)', *Revue d'histoire de la spiritualité*, 53 (1977), pp. 47–64.

[35] Bienvenu, *L'Étonnant fondateur*, p. 172.

[36] *ActaSS*, Feb. III (25 Feb.) (Antwerp, 1658), cols 593–616.

[37] Balthazar Pavillon, *La Vie du bienheureux Robert d'Arbrissel, patriarche des solitaires de la France et instituteur de l'Ordre de Fontevrault, divisée en deux parties et justifiée par titres rares, tirés de divers monastères de France* (Paris and Saumur, 1666).

de la Roche-Posay.[38] Jeanne-Baptiste's petition to Clement IX was not particularly over-supplied with miracles, and she was hard pressed to explain why the cult of Robert had not spread much beyond the daughter-houses of an isolated abbey in the woods. Bienvenu has suggested that her petition to Clement IX failed because the idea of showing such favour to a religious order governed by the aunt of Louis XIV did not appeal to the Pope.[39]

Like Petronilla before her, Jeanne-Baptiste was confronted with the persistent indiscipline of the male community at Fontevrault. They sought to organize themselves as an independent body separate from the control of the abbess, a development that may have been related to the foundation of the Calvaristes in 1617.[40] Jeanne-Baptiste may well have been attempting to enlist the founder of her Order in an attempt to reinforce her authority over them, which is why she fought so vigorously to canonize Robert.[41] That desire to canonize her founder did not die with her, nor was his cause without support in high places. For example, during the reign of Jeanne-Baptiste's successor, Gabrielle de Rochechouart (1670–1704), Jeanne de la Mainferme published his *Clypeus nascentis fontebraldensis ordinis*, yet another account of Robert's saintly life;[42] and Cardinal Lambertini, later Pope Benedict XIV (1740–58), supported his cause before he became pope, yet did not take it up after his elevation to the chair of St Peter.[43]

★ ★ ★

[38] Chasteignier de la Roche-Posay, *Roberti Abrissellenis Ordinis Fontis Ebraldi conditoris vita, transitus, elogia et miracula ex variis scriptoribus et aliis quampluris inpenum collectis et evitis* (Rouen, 1668).

[39] Bienvenu, *L'Étonnant fondateur*, p. 173; see also Paul Sonnino, *Louis XIV's View of the Papacy (1661–1667)* (Berkeley and Los Angeles, 1966). For two accounts of the seventeenth-century canonization process see Simon Ditchfield, 'How not to be a Counter-Reformation saint: the attempted canonization of Pope Gregory X', *Papers of the British School at Rome*, 60 (1992), pp. 379–422; Elisabeth Stopp, *St Francis de Sales: A Testimony by St Chantal* (London, 1967).

[40] Huxley, *Grey Eminence*, pp. 88–93; Bremond, *Histoire littéraire*, 2, pp. 186–92; Webster, 'Fontevrault', p. 130.

[41] See Suzanne Tunc, 'L'Autorité d'une abbesse: Gabrielle de Rochechouart', *RHE*, 87 (1992), p. 81.

[42] Jean de la Mainferme, *Clypeus nascentis Fontebraldensis Ordinis contra priscos et novos calumniatores*, 3 vols (Paris and Saumur, 1684–92).

[43] Bienvenu, *L'Étonnant fondateur*, p. 175.

The reforms of Jeanne-Baptiste de Bourbon and her successors revived Fontevrault during the Counter-Reformation; although it had not suffered the serious decline both in numbers and morale that had afflicted male monasteries, its character changed considerably in the two centuries that followed.[44] During the reign of Gabrielle de Rochechouart de Montmart (1670–1704), the abbey school flourished and the nuns of Fontevrault were entrusted with the education of a number of aristocratic children, including the daughters of Louis XV. By the Revolution there were still 200 nuns at Fontevrault, but the few remaining monks were only to be found at the mother house.[45]

The French Revolution's ecclesiastical policies reflected the Enlightenment principles of utility and freedom, and although the National Assembly did not intend to be hostile to the parish clergy, monastic life was such an affront to these principles that it attracted the Assembly's full attention.[46] It was widely believed that many monks and nuns had been forced into the cloister and were being held there against their wills – contemporary accounts describe monasteries as tombs and their inmates as 'victims wrapped in chains'.[47] It was therefore not surprising that the taking of solemn vows and the admission of new members to both male and female monastic houses was at first suspended by the National Assembly on 28 October 1789; later, a decree of 13 February 1790 not only forbade the taking of solemn vows but also abolished religious orders with solemn vows and confiscated their property unless they were engaged in educational or medical work.[48] Those who had already taken solemn vows could stay together until death but they were granted a

[44] Joseph Peter and Charles Poulet, *Histoire religieuse du Département du Nord pendant la Révolution* (Lille, 1930), pp. 29–30.

[45] Webster, 'Fontevrault', p. 130.

[46] Ralph Gibson, *A Social History of French Catholicism 1789–1914* (London, 1989), p. 36. For the Enlightenment's views on the monastic life, see the entry for *religieuse* in Diderot's *Encyclopédie*, 14 (Neufchastel, 1765), pp. 77–8.

[47] Jean Desobry, 'Un Aspect peu connu de la Révolution française de 1789 à Amiens: le Monastère des Clarisses', *Mémoires de la Société des Antiquaires de Picardie*, 56 (1986), pp. 64–5.

[48] Alphonse Aulard, *La Révolution française et les congrégations* (Paris, 1903), p. 14; Elizabeth Rapley, ' "Pieuses contre-révolutionnaires": the experience of the Ursulines of Northern France, 1789–1792', *French History*, 2 (1988), pp. 453–5.

pension if they left the cloister. At Fontevrault, as elsewhere, most monks chose the latter course, whilst most nuns opted to stay on.[49] Although the National Assembly decreed in 1793 that those nuns who had not taken the Civic Oath of 1790 should be deprived of their pensions and driven out of their monasteries: 'exclues des places qu'elles occupaient, regardées comme suspectes et traitées come telles',[50] the nuns had by then already left Fontevrault; in January 1793 the people of the village of Fontevrault had ransacked the deserted abbey and many of the contents were sold. The house remained empty until October 1804, when the National Assembly issued a decree ordering the conversion of the once noble monastery of Fontevrault into a prison.[51]

The French Church made considerable efforts to rebuild religious Orders for women during the Empire and under the Restoration; these new religious Orders were not contemplative and the official encouragement was more to meet the demand for religious education for girls than for any spiritual reason.[52] The refoundation of Fontevrault was preceded and aided by a renewed interest in her founder. In 1802, Chateaubriand published a romantic account of Robert of Arbrissel which placed him on the same spiritual level as St Bernard of Clairvaux, whilst politely overlooking the scandals that prevented his canonization in the seventeenth century.[53] The re-birth of Fontevrault began the next year when a school at Chemillé was opened by Madame Rose,

[49] Bienvenu, *L'Étonnant fondateur*, p. 176; Gibson, *Social History*, p. 36. The declaration of the Ursulines of Lille, made on 13 Oct. 1790, is perhaps typical: the nuns desired 'conformément à leurs voeux, vivre et mourir dans la Maison'. Lille, Archives Départementales du Nord, 149H6, cited in Elizabeth Rapley, ' "Pieuses contre-révolutionnaires" ', p. 462.

[50] Lucien Misermont, *Les bienheureuses Filles de la Charité d'Arras* (Paris, 1920), p. 101.

[51] Bienvenu, *L'Étonnant fondateur*, p. 176.

[52] Roger Price, *A Social History of Nineteenth Century France* (London, 1987), p. 319; Guillaume de Bertier de Sauvigny, *The Bourbon Restoration* (Philadelphia, Penn., 1966), p. 301.

[53] F. R. de Chateaubriand, *Génie du Christianisme*, 4 vols (Paris, 1829), 4, pp. 155–6. It is certainly conceivable that Chateaubriand's romantic vision may have been encouraged by his mistress, the Comtesse de Beaumont, who was educated at Fontevrault before the Revolution: see Joan Evans, *Chateaubriand, a Biography* (London, 1939), p. 128.

who had been a nun at Fontevrault before the Revolution.[54] Three years later she was able to buy a house and begin living the communal life with the approval of the bishop of Angers, although at first only temporary vows were taken. The pre-revolutionary rule of Fontevrault was followed as closely as possible, although the many fasts mandated by Marie de Bretagne's rule were unsuitable for those involved in teaching and were eventually modified by a General Chapter of the Order held in 1849.[55]

The favourable account of Robert of Arbrissel in Jules Michelet's *Histoire de France* in 1833 certainly did not hurt the newly refounded Order, which had by then established daughter-houses at Boulaur, near Toulouse, and at Brioude, in the Haute-Loire. Michelet's description of Robert as a romantic hero who endeavoured to glorify women must have held a special attraction to these nuns struggling to rebuild their once great religious Order, but it was the rediscovery of Robert's tomb, heart, and staff during construction work at Fontevrault in 1842 which did the most to further the renewed cause to canonize Robert of Arbrissel.[56] It is likely that the nuns of the new Order, essentially little more than a minor teaching congregation under the authority of the local bishop, sought to canonize Robert in the hope of regaining some of the status and prestige that they had before the Revolution, when they were a large and influential contemplative Order.[57]

---

[54] For this and what follows, see Webster, 'Fontevrault', p. 130; for the rebirth of the female religious Orders after the Revolution in general, see Gibson, *Social History*, pp. 104–5, 117–27. I have not been able to consult Abbé G. Chalubert, *Un prieuré de Fontevrault au XIXème siècle: Sainte Marie de Chemillé* (Angers, 1897) or the history written by the nuns of Boulour after their exile to Spain: *Histoire de l'Ordre de Fontevraud, 1100–1908*, 3 vols (Auch, 1911–15).

[55] Webster, 'Fontevrault', p. 131.

[56] Jules Michelet, *Histoire de France*, 2 vols (Paris, 1835), 2, pp. 297–301; Smith, '*Procurator mulierum*', pp. 176–7; see also Reto R. Bezzola, *Les Origines et la formation de la littérature courtoise en Occident*, 5 vols in 3 (Paris, 1960), part 2, 2, pp. 275–92; Régine Pernoud, *La Femme au temps de cathédrals* (Paris, 1984), pp. 129–69.

[57] The status of pre-Revolutionary nuns has been examined by J. Michael Hayden, 'States, Estates and Orders: the *Qualité* of female clergy in early modern France', *French History*, 8 (1994), pp. 51–76. The teaching Orders of the nineteenth century are thoroughly explored in Calude Langlois, *Le Catholicisme au féminin: les congrégations françaises à supérieure générale au XIXeme siècle* (Paris, 1984).

In 1847 the nuns of the revived Order received permission from King Louis-Philippe to translate Robert's relics from the prison that had once been their mother house to Chemillé. The nuns of Chemillé, Boulaur, and Brioude managed to secure the support of a number of French bishops when they presented their petition to Pope Pius IX in 1853 in what would be the third and last attempt to canonize Robert of Arbrissel. Their application was denied by the secretary of the Congregation of Rites in 1855, who demanded a full canonization dossier containing more evidence of Robert's sanctity and miracles. With the support of Bishop Angebault of Angers and the arch-traditionalist Bishop Pie of Poitiers, the nuns of Fontevrault continued in their attempt to canonize their founder; in 1860 Abbé X. Barbier de Montault re-opened Robert's tomb and acknowledged that the relics were authentic. However, when he published his account of Robert's life in 1863, Barbier de Montault claimed that he had identified the remains of a second corpse, that of Bishop Peter II of Poitiers, in Robert's tomb. Robert had proclaimed Peter and his successors as the protectors of the Order of Fontevrault; Peter was buried in the choir of the mother house in 1115, which is indicative of the great respect the nuns of Fontevrault had for him. Barbier de Montault further alleged that the nuns of Fontevrault did not sufficiently revere their founder's remains, for they had combined them with those of another in 1622 and kept them in a simple lead reliquary instead of one made of more valuable materials. It is clear that Barbier de Montault did not support the nuns' cause, and his revelations prevented the canonization petition from succeeding. Because of Barbier de Montault, it was not possible for the nuns of Chemillé, Boulaur, and Brioude to put forward any evidence of miracles at Robert's tomb that occurred after 1622, for any miracles that occurred after then could no longer he definitely attributed to him.[58] Despite the official rejection of Robert's sanctity, the Bishop of Poitiers included his feast in the Poitiers calendar and gave him the title 'Bienheureux', indicative of both the local veneration of

[58] Bienvenu, *L'Étonnant fondateur*, pp. 178–9. I have been unable to consult X. Barbier de Montault, 'Étude hagiographique sur Robert d'Arbrissel, fondateur de l'Ordre de Fontevrault', *Répertoire archéologique de Maine et Loire* (1863).

Robert of Arbrissel and Bishop Pie's recognition of his role, as Bishop of Poitiers, as protector of the order.[59]

* * *

In the twelfth century, Petronilla of Chemillé, the Abbess of Fontevrault, had tried to gain some official recognition of the holiness of the founder of her Order whilst simultaneously stamping out any attempt to create a popular cult in his memory. It seems clear that Petronilla feared that if Robert was canonized, she and her successors would lose control of not just his relics but also of the Order itself. By only encouraging an internal cult of Robert of Arbrissel, Petronilla was able to control access to his relics, preserve the unique features of the religious institution he had founded, and retain the control of the Order in the hands of the abbess.

In the seventeenth century, Jeanne-Baptiste encouraged popular devotion of Robert's relics, and utilized his memory in her attempts to reform the Order. The males of the community objected to her reforms, but her attempts to canonize Robert had the beneficial side-effects of reminding the Fontevrist monks of Robert's original vision of Fontevrault, where the men were in the service of the women. Jeanne-Baptiste was able to invoke his memory to keep the men of St John of the Habit under the control of the abbess of Fontevrault, which, although her attempt to canonize Robert was unsuccessful, showed how she was able to use the Order's past to reinforce her ideal of reform.

When the Order was refounded after the French Revolution and Robert's relics re-discovered in 1842, the nuns of the new Order again attempted to have Robert of Arbrissel canonized, no doubt in the hopes that success would lead to increased support and prestige for the Order. The restrictions placed upon monastic life after the Revolution necessitated drastic changes in the Fontevrist way of life. They had been forced to become a teaching Order to survive, for it was impossible for them to return to the enclosed life of contemplatives. This last attempt to canonize Robert was

---

59 Although Robert has never been officially beatified, he is usually granted this title as a courtesy: see, for example, Donald Attwater and John Cumming, *A New Dictionary of Saints* (Tunbridge Wells, 1993), pp. 274–5.

probably more than just part of a broader movement of ecclesiastical renewal; arguably it also reflected the nuns' frustrations over their loss of status. They no longer had lay-sisters to perform domestic work and they no longer had a community of men attached to the Order to care for their spiritual needs. Perhaps they hoped that with Robert's canonization new attention would be paid to the unique form of religious life that had once existed at Fontevrault and that Robert's original vision of a community of men and women, living together as the 'poor of Christ', could be restored.

University of Nottingham

'TO LET THE MEMORY OF THESE MEN DYE IS INJURIOUS TO POSTERITY':[1] EDMUND CALAMY'S *ACCOUNT* OF THE EJECTED MINISTERS

by DAVID L. WYKES

Edmund Calamy is celebrated as the biographer of Restoration Nonconformity. His account of the sufferings of the ministers ejected from their livings following the Restoration religious settlement is well known to historians of Dissent. As a biographer he was responsible for rescuing many details and even the names of ejected ministers which would otherwise have been lost. His account remains therefore the pre-eminent source for the study of the early history of Nonconformity. In addition to the biographical details about individual ministers, he included much incidental information on the organization and structure of early Dissent. Nevertheless, the significance of his work went beyond the biographical accounts. Modern religious Dissent dates from the Restoration of Charles II and the passing of the 1662 Act of Uniformity, which saw about 2,000 ministers, preachers, and teachers suffer the loss of their livelihoods for their refusal to conform. The Great Ejection was, however, more than just an historical event. As A. G. Matthews, the compiler of the outstanding revision of Calamy's list of ejected ministers, wrote:

the event, as remembered by successive generations of Nonconformists, played a part in fashioning their distinctive denominational consciousness. For many years their authors, when they wrote of 'Black Bartholomew Day', had the words printed in outstanding capitals. In the Nonconformist mind it assumed similar proportions, living as the memory of a great wrong, which those of later generations had vicariously suffered

---

[1]   E. Calamy, *An Account of the Ministers . . . who were Ejected or Silenced after the Restoration in 1660* (London, 1713) [hereafter *Account*], p. iv.

in the persons of their forefathers, the martyrs and confessors of 1662. . . . Rightly or wrongly that was the way in which Nonconformists read their history, and that they did so was in large measure due to the influence of a book for long a standard work in their libraries, Edmund Calamy's *Abridgment of Mr. Baxter's History of his Life and Times.*[2]

Calamy's *Abridgment*, in offering both an interpretative framework and a source of evidence, has proved so dominant that even modern historians continue to see early Dissent very largely in terms of the sufferings of the ejected clergy. Lay support has received comparatively little attention, and where it has been studied the focus has been similar; historians have sought to record the penalties suffered under the penal laws for recusancy or for holding conventicles.[3] There have been few attempts to examine the evidence relating to the organization and activity of dissenters before the modern period. But Calamy's work, in addition to helping to mould the Nonconformist outlook and even to shape modern historiography, also contributed to the contemporary political debate between the High Church Tories and their opponents, the Whigs and their dissenting allies.[4] The publications of the *Abridgment* shortly after the accession of Queen Anne provoked a fierce reaction from High Churchmen, who were outraged at the portrayal of the Church of England as a persecuting Church with dissenters as the innocent sufferers, and at the attack on the Act of Uniformity. The most celebrated rejoinder was John Walker's *An Attempt towards recovering an Account of the Numbers and Sufferings of the Clergy of the Church of England*, eventually published in 1714. Both Calamy and Walker employed the past to support their interpretations of the

---

[2] A. G. Matthews, ed., *Calamy Revised: Being a Revision of Edmund Calamy's Account of the Ministers and Others Ejected and Silenced, 1660-2* (Oxford, 1934) [hereafter *Cal. Rev.*], p. xvi.

[3] M. Watts, *The Dissenters: I, From the Reformation to the French Revolution* (Oxford, 1978), ch. 3; B. White, *The English Baptists of the Seventeenth Century* (London, 1983), ch. 3.

[4] R. C. Richardson, *The Debate on the English Revolution* (London, 1977), pp. 35-7.

Church: Calamy to defend dissenters from the continuing embarrassment caused by the political legacy inherited from the Civil War and to justify their nonconformity; and Walker to dismiss Calamy's claims concerning the ejected ministers and to highlight the loyalty and sufferings of the Church of England clergy during the 1640s and 1650s.

Calamy's role as the historian and defender of Nonconformity grew out of his experience as Matthew Sylvester's assistant at Meeting-house Court, Blackfriars, and the latter's failings as an editor. Richard Baxter, the most celebrated late seventeenth-century puritan minister, had left his unpublished manuscripts, including an autobiographical narrative, to Sylvester. It is clear that Baxter's choice of Sylvester as his literary executor was seriously misguided, and that he allowed his judgement to be clouded by his affection for the younger minister.[5] Sylvester proved unequal to the task. He had neither the skill nor the resolve to arrange and edit the mass of personal papers for publication, and the result proved disastrous. Sylvester was aware of his own limitations, and he clearly found the responsibility a great burden. 'My Heart akes exceedingly at every remembrance of my incumbent Trusts: . . . I am deeply sensible of my inability for such Work; even to discouragement, and no small Consternation.'[6] According to Calamy, Sylvester's excessive reverence for Baxter's memory made him incapable of making the necessary changes to the text. He 'counted it a sort of a sacred thing, to have any hand in making alterations of any sort, in which I could not but apprehend he went too far'; indeed he 'was cramped by a sort of superstition'.[7] In 1696 Sylvester finally published the autobiographical account, though after little

---

[5] G. F. Nuttall, 'The MS of Reliquiae Baxterianae (1696)', *JEH*, 6 (1955), p. 76; N. H. Keeble, *Richard Baxter, Puritan Man of Letters* (Oxford, 1982), pp. 145-6. For evidence of Baxter's affection for Sylvester, see *Reliquiæ Baxterianæ: or Mr Richard Baxter's Narrative of the Most Memorable Passages of His Life and Times*, ed. M. Sylvester (London, 1696) [hereafter *Rel. Baxt.*], Part 3, p. 96, § 206: 'Mr Silvester . . . a Man of excellent meekness, temper, sound, and peaceable Principles, godly Life, and great ability in the ministerial work'.

[6] *Rel. Baxt.*, preface, § VIII.

[7] Edmund Calamy, *An Historical Account of My Own Life*, ed. J. T. Rutt, 2 vols (London, 1830), 1, p. 377.

effective editing. The weakness of the cumbersome 800-page folio volume is clear. It consists of 'a disjointed narrative with a confused chronology, overburdened with large blocks of documentation', in which 'Baxter's personal story, often of intense interest and value, was interrupted by arid wastes of those casuistic subtleties which were the great divine's disastrous foible'.[8]

Calamy was certainly very aware of the defects of *Reliquiæ Baxterianæ*. He had been allowed to read the manuscript before publication, and with only limited success had persuaded Sylvester to make a number of alterations.[9] He was, however, unable to induce Sylvester to make any larger changes to the organization and contents of the volume. The ill-digested and confused structure remained largely untouched. As Calamy diplomatically told the Leeds antiquarian, Ralph Thoresby, the work was 'a book of as great variety as the age has afforded'. Unfortunately, such an unmanageable volume was of little service to the dissenting cause. Calamy was therefore persuaded to undertake a new edition involving the abridgement and rearrangement of the original work to create a more manageable and coherent volume. As he informed Thoresby,

> Being solicited by many, I have undertaken to abridge it – cast it into another form – lopp off excrescencys – and putt it into something of a modern dress and make it more easy and pleasing [and] consequently more useful. Being thus engag'd . . . I have bin press'd to add a list of the ministers who were ejected after King Charles's Restauration, to make way for the new settlement, together with the most memorable passages of the lives, the characters, and works of the most considerable among them.[10]

[8] N. Keeble, preface to *The Autobiography of Richard Baxter*, ed. J. M. Lloyd Thomas (rev. edn, London, 1974), p. v; *Cal. Rev.*, p. xvii.

[9] Calamy, *Historical Account*, 1, pp. 377–8.

[10] Calamy to Ralph Thoresby, Leeds, 17 Jan. 1701/2, printed in W. T. Lancaster, ed., *Letters addressed to Ralph Thoresby*, Publications of the Thoresby Society, 21 (1912), p. 113.

Calamy's *Abridgment* was published in 1702. The first edition was 'soon sold off, and another desired, with amendments and farther improvements, with great earnestness'.[11]

Part of Calamy's objective, perhaps his original intention, was to make Baxter's personal account more accessible. In the preface he explained his method in preparing the *Abridgment*.

> I was willing to do what I could to make my Abridgement of general Use. . . . Personal Reflections, and little Privacys I have dropt, and things that were out of Date, I have pass'd over lightly; sometimes I have kept pretty much to his Language, and sometimes I have taken the freedom to use my own.[12]

As well as re-organizing the material and dividing the volume into chapters to create a more coherent and logical work, he recast Baxter's narrative in the third person to form a general history of Dissent. Although Calamy's account of the earlier history of Nonconformity was derived almost exclusively from Baxter's narrative, the interpretation given to the events recorded in the *Abridgment* was largely his own. A comparison between Sylvester's *Reliquiæ Baxterianæ* and Calamy's *Abridgment* of certain key events during the Civil War helps reveal the changes that Calamy made. Professor Lamont has argued that Calamy not only omitted a number of crucial phrases from the *Reliquiæ Baxterianæ*, thus altering the explanation for the causes of the Civil War, but that he gave much greater prominence in his work to the Antrim plot and to the implication of Charles I in the 1641 Irish Massacre. Sylvester, anxious to preserve Baxter's reputation, suppressed references to his millenarian ideas and anti-monarchism, emphasizing instead his belief in non-resistance and the sovereignty of the Christian magistrate. He also, Lamont argued, placed Baxter's controversial references to Charles I and the Antrim plot out of sequence in an attempt

---

11 Calamy, *Historical Account*, 1, p. 455.
12 E. Calamy, *An Abridgment of Mr Baxter's History of his Life and Times* (London, 1702) [hereafter *Abridgment*], preface, unnumbered first page.

to conceal their significance.[13] If Lamont is correct, because of losses in the original manuscript Sylvester's omissions may have had a greater impact on modern perceptions of Baxter's ideas. Nonetheless Calamy edited Baxter's narrative to provide his own account of the history of Nonconformity. The *Abridgment* was published at a crucial juncture in the history of Dissent. The whole work was intended as a popular statement and defence of Nonconformity against the High Church attack on Dissent and toleration.[14]

It was Calamy's own additions to the *Abridgment* which proved to be the most significant and controversial. He continued the narrative from 1684, where Baxter's own account ended, up to the time of the latter's death in 1691. Calamy was particularly concerned, however, to refute the calumnies of certain High Churchmen against the ejected ministers. 'Some angry Persons have taken much Pleasure in bespattering these worthy Men, whose Names rather deserv'd Embalming', and he cited in particular Anthony à Wood's *Athenae Oxonienses*. Other critics, such as Samuel Parker, had accused dissenters of exaggerating the number of ejected ministers, and by disparaging their claims had sought to diminish the significance of the Great Ejection. The largest section of the volume therefore was his 'List of the Silenc'd Ministers, with the Character of many of them'. It formed the ninth chapter of the book, totalling 315 pages, and accounted for over two-fifths of the volume. It was the part on which he expended the most effort, and 'this I can say, it hath cost me much Time' and 'gave me the most Trouble'. There is also little doubt that the account of the ejected ministers was the part of the work which offered Calamy the greatest satisfaction in preparation and writing. As he wrote

[13] W. M. Lamont, *Richard Baxter and the Millennium* (London, 1979), pp. 23–4, 79–82, 87–90, 92–3, 106, 112, 289–96. For other references to Calamy's editorial changes, see Nuttall, 'MS of Reliquiae Baxterianae', pp. 76–9; Keeble, *Richard Baxter*, p. 147.

[14] There is evidence of Calamy's anxiety to finish the volume before the rising of Parliament in May 1702: see Edmund Calamy, Hoxton, to Ralph Thoresby, 2 June 1702, in [J. Hunter], ed., *Letters of Eminent Men, addressed to Ralph Thoresby*, 2 vols (London, 1832), 1, pp. 417–18. The volume was clearly in preparation before William III's death: Calamy was collecting material on ejected ministers in December 1701; see J. H. Turner, ed., *The Rev. Oliver Heywood, B.A., 1630-1702; His Autobiography, Diaries . . .*, 4 vols (Bingley, 1885), 4, pp. 289, 290, 291.

in the preface to the volume, 'Lives and Characters are very entertaining.' He also told Ralph Thoresby privately that 'Biography is what hath bin always extremely pleasant & Delightful to me.'[15] When the *Abridgment* was republished in 1713, the narrative of Baxter's life was left largely unaltered, though two additional chapters took the history down to the passing of the Occasional Conformity Act in 1711, while the ninth chapter was expanded into a separate volume, the *Account*. A further two volumes containing corrections and additional information on the ejected ministers, the *Continuation of the Account*, were issued in 1727.[16] Although the later editions included substantial additional material and corrections, Calamy's interpretation remained unchanged. The discussion which follows is therefore concerned with the first edition of 1702.

Calamy intended that the biographies of the ejected ministers should form part of his account of the history of Nonconformity and the justification of their principles. Baxter in his autobiography had provided character sketches of those ministers he had known personally. Calamy incorporated these sketches into his ninth chapter, but his work was part of a much older tradition of Protestant hagiography popularized by John Foxe's *Acts and Monuments* and Samuel Clarke's *Lives*.[17] Calamy's account was not simply a record of the sufferings of the ejected ministers, but was intended to encourage the contemporary generation to maintain its Nonconformity. His work was also influenced by the current political conditions of Queen Anne's reign and the need to emphasize the loyalty of the ejected ministers. To Calamy, they were men of outstanding piety and learning

---

[15] Oxford, Bodleian Library, MS Eng. Hist. c. 237, fol. 64r, Calamy, Hoxton, to [Ralph Thoresby, Leeds], 29 Jan. 1701/2. The recipient of the letter is identified from internal evidence.

[16] See *Account*; E. Calamy, *A Continuation of the Account of the Ministers . . . who were Ejected and Silenced* (London, 1727). Calamy increased the size of the ninth chapter from just over 300 pages in the *Abridgment* to over 850 pages in the *Account*, including the index, with the addition of another 1000 pages in the *Continuation*.

[17] P. Collinson, ' "A magazine of religious patterns": an Erasmian topic transposed in English Protestantism', *SCH*, 14 (1977), pp. 223–49. I am grateful to the Revd Dr G. F. Nuttall for this point, and for his more general comments on the paper.

who had suffered because of their refusal to compromise their consciences.[18] High Churchmen were not impressed.

> As in the Story of Mr Baxter he gives his account as in Romances, the Knight always beats the Gyant. So 'tis in the characters of his Worthys, they had no faults, nothing could be charged upon them but Nonconformity: sober, peaceable, prudent, moderate, learned, calm, grave, sound in judgment, an excellent preacher; this agreed to most of them.[19]

Matthews has defended Calamy from the charge that he deliberately concealed damaging or unfavourable details about the ejected ministers, noting that he was willing to be candid as to ministerial inadequacies and personal failings. Calamy himself told his readers in the preface to his second edition,

> I am far from taking all the Two thousand who were ejected, to have been Men of like Piety, or strictness in their Morals. And yet think, Two thousand such Men to have been a great Blessing to the World and the Church, and the loss of their Labours to have been an unspeakable Damage.[20]

Nevertheless, a careful examination of the use that Calamy made of the brief biographies that Baxter had written on the ejected ministers he had known personally in Worcestershire and elsewhere reveals that, as with the narrative, Calamy made significant changes to Baxter's original text. Baxter described Simon Moor, preacher at Worcester cathedral, as 'an old Independent, who somewhat lost the People's Love, upon Reasons which I here omit'. In the *Abridgment* Calamy dropped Baxter's description and only listed Moor's name. In the *Continuation* he provided an account of Moor after St Bartholmew's Day, who 'was through the Fury and Rage of

---

[18] *Abridgment*, Preface, unnumbered fourth and fifth pages.
[19] Oxford, Bodleian Library, MS J. Walker, c. 2, fol. 211v, Joshua Reynolds, Christ Church, Oxford, to Walker, Exeter, 23 Jan. 1704/5.
[20] *Account*, p. xxvi.

the Justices and People, forc'd to leave Worcester: After which he retir'd to London', but he still did not include Baxter's unfavourable gloss.[21] Baxter's account of John Howe noted his learning and his ability as an author, but also that he was 'sometime Household-Preacher to Oliver Cromwell, and his Son Richard, till the Army pulled him down', though he was 'not one that medled in his Wars'. In the *Abridgment* Calamy ignored the fact that Howe had been Chaplain at Whitehall between 1656 and 1659, and merely recorded that he was 'well known by his Works'.[22] Baxter's reference to Edward Boucher's brother, James, 'a Husbandman, who can but write his name', was omitted by Calamy. In addition, he did not include Baxter's description of Thomas Baldwin's growing separatism, which so alienated him 'from Prelacy, and Conformity, and the People with him, that though afterwards they got a godly, Conformable Minister, I could not get them to Communicate with him, though I got them constantly to hear him'.[23] Matthews notes that as a Presbyterian Calamy disliked sectarianism, and that he generally avoided the term Independent with its association with the Interregnum sects; when he did mention that a minister was a Congregationalist or a Baptist he often added some apologetic qualification. Even in his account of the great Congregational minister John Owen and of the Baptist leader Henry Jessey he failed to record their denominational affiliations.[24]

Matthews accepted that Calamy's accounts of individual ministers were stylized character sketches rather than detailed biographies. He also acknowledged that the accounts, following the conventions of the period, too often did no more than attest to the 'general good character' of the ejected minister. 'Of more lifelike portraiture there is very little.'[25] The fact that the biographies followed a common form is evidence of the extent of Calamy's editorial mediation. The

[21] *Rel. Baxt.*, pt 3, p. 91, § 202; *Abridgment*, p. 342; *Account*, p. 769; *Cal. Rev.*, p. 354.
[22] *Rel. Baxt.*, pt 3, p. 97, § 208; *Abridgment*, p. 303; *Cal. Rev.*, pp. 279–80.
[23] *Rel. Baxt.*, pt 3, p. 92, § 202; *Abridgment*, p. 344; *Cal. Rev.*, pp. 26, 66.
[24] *Cal. Rev.*, p. xlii.
[25] *Cal. Rev.*, pp. xlviii–xlix. Cf. A. Gordon, 'Calamy as a biographer', *Transactions of the Congregational Historical Society*, 6 (1914), pp. 233–4.

addition of personal details was perhaps secondary, included only if they helped to establish the learning of the individual, the sufferings experienced under the penal laws or the firmness of the principles underlying the refusal to conform. Calamy was less concerned with the modern preoccupation of historical objectivity than with attesting to the reputation and learning of his ejected ministers. He intended his ninth chapter both to establish the reputation of the ejected ministers and to serve a polemic purpose, to strengthen succeeding generations in their Nonconformity. He concluded the chapter with a strong appeal to his fellow dissenters in which he identified them as the successors of the ejected ministers and exhorted them to maintain their principles.[26] In the following chapter he set out 'The Grounds of the Nonconformity of the Ministers who were Ejected. Their Vindication of themselves, and such as adher'd to them', where he summarized their writings on the reasons for separating from the Church. The chapter ended with a defence of occasional conformity. This alone was likely to prove highly controversial at a time when the High Church attack on Nonconformity and toleration was growing.

The *Abridgment* as a whole was intended to make a firm political statement justifying Nonconformity, and the work was dedicated to the leading Whig politician, the Marquess of Hartington, later the second Duke of Devonshire. Calamy admitted in his memoirs that even before publication the work 'seemed not unlikely to draw some consequences after it'.[27] It was not only the subject matter, but the way in which Calamy addressed the issues, which proved to be controversial. He attacked the Act of Uniformity as having destroyed the unity of the Church, and if the ejected ministers who refused to compromise their consciences by conforming were the heroes, the responsibility for the Act lay with the vindictive authors of the Restoration Settlement. Any reflection on the Act of Uniformity and the Restoration religious settlement was certain to antagonize High Churchmen bitter on the one hand at the breach in the Church of England's

---

26 *Abridgment*, p. 496.
27 Calamy, *Historical Account*, 1, p. 442.

monopoly following the passing of the Toleration Act and on the other at the fate of the non-jurors. The *Abridgment* provoked a fierce and bitter response from Churchmen. As Calamy himself wrote, 'for some Years there was scarce a Pamphlet came out on the Church side, in which I had not the Honour of being referr'd to in the invective Part of it'.[28]

High Churchmen condemned the *Abridgment* outright. For Isaac Sharpe it was 'an Infamous, Venemous, Falsifying piece of History, Publish'd with the greatest Effrontery against the Church and State, designed by Mr Calamy to bring an universal Odium upon both'. The ninth chapter, with its account of the ejected ministers and Calamy's criticism of the Act of Uniformity, provoked the most bitter condemnation. The anonymous author of *Seditious Preachers* was moved by 'honest Zeal and just Indignation, to find a Bold sectarian Preacher undertake to Canonize for Saints, and Confessors, those very Men . . . whose misguided Zeal had filled the former Age with Blood and Confusion'.[29] A Hampshire clergyman asked, 'is it come to [16]40 againe? are the saints to reigne in this century? why does not your London clergy Arraigne such a varlet, in parlament, if not for that List, yet for Laying so many & grivious imputations, upon the act of uniformity?' Walker himself prepared several lengthy defences of the Act in his 'Adversaria Calamistica', though they were never published.[30]

As one High Church critic expressed it, the *Abridgment* 'lays all the dismal Effects of the late and long Rebellion . . . at the Door of the Church and King Charles the Martyr'. Nothing caused more outrage than Calamy's revival of the

---

[28] *An Abridgement of Mr Baxter's History of his life and times*, 2nd edn (London, 1713), Preface; *Cal. Rev.*, pp. xviii–xix.

[29] Philalethes [Isaac Sharpe], *Animadversions on some Passages of Mr Edmund Calamy's Abridgment of Mr Richard Baxter's History* (London, 1704), p. 7, Preface sig. A2; *Seditious Preachers, Ungodly Teachers* (London, 1709), Preface, sig. A2.

[30] Oxford, Bodleian Library, MS J. Walker, c. 1, fol. 211v, Stamford Wallace, Chilcomb by Winchester, to Robert Clavel, Walker's London publisher and agent, 30 May 1705; MS J. Walker, e. 6, 'Adversaria Calamistica', notes and materials for Walker's proposed examination of Calamy's ninth chapter, fols 73v, 209-42; MS J. Walker, e.12, 'Materialls & Collections for the remaining parts of the work', fol. 58; A. G. Matthews, ed., *Walker Revised; Being a Revision of John Walker's Sufferings of the Clergy* (Oxford, 1948), p. ix. See also the MS J. Walker, c. 1, fol. 225r, Thomas Rowell, Rector of Great Cressingham, Norfolk, to Clavell, 24 April 1705.

libel that Charles I was responsible for the Irish Massacre in 1641. Charles Leslie, the non-juror, fulminated against Calamy's *Abridgment*, 'Wherein that Blessed Martyr is Represented as the most Unnatural and Bloody Monster, and most Harden'd Hypocrite that ever the Earth bore'.[31] A more balanced response to Calamy's work was provided by moderate churchmen who were drawn to defend the terms of their own conformity. One of the earliest answers of any churchman to the *Abridgment* came from the moderate conformist John Ollyffe, vicar of Denton in Oxfordshire, who in 1702 published *A Defence of Ministerial Conformity*, 'to free our selves from those Reflections, which Mr Calamy doth very often insinuate', and to answer his continual 'Misrepresentation of the Terms of Conformity, which we have comply'd with'. The most convincing reply to Calamy's justification of the ground for Nonconformity was advanced by Benjamin Hoadly, the future Bishop of Bangor, in his *Reasonableness of Conformity*, published in 1703.[32] John Walker's *Sufferings of the Clergy* was the most lasting response to Calamy's account of the ejected ministers. Although exhibiting all the violent language and anger typical of the High Church response, Walker did attempt to obtain evidence from the original sources and to establish the accuracy of his facts.[33]

The contemporary Nonconformist reaction is less easy to discern. According to Calamy's own testimony, the book rapidly sold out and there was a demand for a revised edition. The book clearly did sell well amongst dissenters, and indeed churchmen are also known to have purchased copies of the *Abridgment*.[34] In September 1705, the Exeter Assembly wrote

[31] [Charles Leslie], *A Case of Present Concern* [London, 1703], p. 2; the second edition published as *A Vindication of the Royal Martyr King Charles I* (London and Westminster, 1704). Cf. T. Long, *a Review of Mr Richard Baxter's Life* (London, 1697), p. 190; idem, *A Rebuke to Mr Edmund Calamy* (London, 1704), p. 7; [Mary Astell], *Moderation Truly Stated* (London, 1704), p. 64; T. Carte, *The Irish Massacre set in a Clear Light* (London, [1714], 2nd edn 1715), preface, sig. A2, pp. 4–5, 22.

[32] John Ollyffe, *A Defence of Ministerial Conformity* (London, 1702), sig. A3, pp. 43–5, 99; Benjamin Hoadly, *The Reasonableness of Conformity* (London, 1703).

[33] Matthews, *Walker Revised*, pp. x–xiii.

[34] Calamy, *Historical Account*, 1, p. 455; Oxford, Bodleian Library, MS J. Walker, c. 1, fol. 86r, John Wilson, Ely, to Dr Charles Goodall, 4 July 1704.

to Calamy 'to desire him to print his 2nd edition of Mr Baxter's Life so as that it may be no prejudice to such as have bought the first, by printing a sufficient number of distinct supplements'.[35] It is likely, however, that Calamy's *Defence of Moderate Non-Conformity*, written in response to Ollyffe and Hoadly's attack on the tenth chapter of the *Abridgment*, made a more significant contribution to contemporary opinion. The Presbyterian Fund Board, increasingly concerned at the number of students supported by the Fund who conformed on completing their studies, ordered in February 1700 'that the Tutors instruct the young Men in the grounds of Nonconformity as well as in other things'. William Bilby and the future Nonconformist tutor Thomas Dixon were among a number of young men 'in suspense between conformity and nonconformity' who were confirmed in their dissent by Calamy's *Defence* in 1704. Bilby, a voracious reader, also read Calamy's *Abridgment* sometime after he became minister at Hinckley in 1706.[36]

The publication of the later volumes, the *Account* and the *Continuation*, devoted entirely to the history of the ejected ministers, helped to circulate Calamy's interpretation of the Great Ejection. In August 1726, George Illidge obtained a copy of the *Continuation*, which his mother had already asked to borrow for her brother. The following year, Illidge wrote to a friend telling him that Calamy's new work was now out, and that 'I am in pane to see it.' The Derbyshire Nonconformist minister, James Clegg, after reading 'some lives and characters of the Ejected ministers in Dr Calamys account . . . was much affected with their piety, zeal and steadiness', but he asked 'where is that spirit now to be found?' Philip Doddridge in his academy at Northampton gave lectures on

[35] A. Brockett, ed., *The Exeter Assembly*, Devon and Cornwall Record Society, ns 6 (1963), p. 58.

[36] E. Calamy, *A Defence of Moderate Non-Conformity*, 3 vols (London, 1703–5); London, Dr Williams's Library, MS OD68, Presbyterian Fund Board minutes, vol. 2, 5 Feb. 1694/5 – 4 June 1722, p. 75 (5 Feb. 1699/1700), H. McLachlan, 'Thomas Dixon, M.A., M.D., and the Whitehaven-Bolton Academy, 1708–29', in H. McLachlan, *Essays and Addresses* (Manchester, 1950), p. 133; Calamy, *Historical Account*, 2, pp. 31–4; Nottingham, Nottingham Subscription Library, 'Some Remarkable Passages in my life' by William Bilby [Copy at Dr Williams's Library, MS 12.68], Cap. 13 and Appendix, 'Hist. Chronol. Geography', No.21.

civil law, ancient mythology, English history, and 'particularly the History of Nonconformity, and the Principles, on which a separation from the Church of England is founded'.[37] The enduring appeal and indeed influence of Calamy's account of the ejected ministers is evident. His interpretation of the Great Ejection as an historical event helped mould the outlook of successive generations of dissenters, and provided the interpretative framework by which they justified and maintained their continuing Nonconformity. Undoubtedly his account of the sacrifice and sufferings of the ejected ministers maintained its popularity amongst Nonconformist audiences, and by the end of the eighteenth century it had achieved the status of a Nonconformist classic, though largely as a result of Samuel Palmer's *Nonconformist Memorial* which condensed and brought order to the confused arrangement of biographical entries in Calamy's different editions.[38] Daniel Neal's *History of the Puritans*, published in four volumes between 1732 and 1738, was a far more convincing and comprehensive history, and came to replace Calamy's historical account, but it is Calamy's perspective of the consequences of the 1662 Act of Uniformity which has come to dominate interpretations of Restoration Dissent.[39]

University of Leicester

---

[37]   BL, Add MS 42849, Henry Papers, fol. 42r, George Illidge, Chearbruck, 17 Aug. 1726; V. S. Doe, ed., *The Diary of James Clegg*, Derbyshire Record Society, 2 (1978), p. 41 (8 Sept. 1728). See also J. Hunter, ed., *Diary of Ralph Thoresby*, 2 vols (London, 1832), 2, pp. 183, 190 (13 Feb., 16 May 1713); J. Orton, *Memoirs of . . . Philip Doddridge* (Shrewsbury, 1766), pp. 89–97.

[38]   Samuel Palmer, *The Nonconformist's Memorial* (London, 1775; 1777-8; 2nd edn 1802). Elizabeth Gaskell has Mr Hale in *North and South* quoting John Oldfield's personal testimony from Calamy to explain why he was giving up his Anglican ministry. Interestingly, her source was Theophilus Lindsey's *Apology . . . on resigning the vicarage of Catterick* (2nd edn, London, 1774), see A. Easson, 'Mr Hale's doubts in *North and South*', *Review of English Studies*, 31 (1980), pp. 33-5.

[39]   D. Neal, *The History of the Puritans*, 4 vols (London, 1732-8).

DUTCH PROTESTANTISM AND ITS PASTS

PETER VAN ROODEN

The Dutch Reformed Church acquired its modern past fairly recently, at the beginning of the nineteenth century, during the first years of the new Kingdom of the Netherlands. From 1819 to 1827 the four volumes of Ypeij and Dermout's *History of the Dutch Reformed Church* appeared, some two and a half thousand pages all together.[1] The work has not fared well. Its garrulous verbosity, weak composition, and old-fashioned liberalism have been rightly denounced. Only the four accompanying volume with notes, more than a thousand dense pages full of facts and quotations, have been admired for their scholarship. Protestant academic ecclesiastical history prefers to trace its origin to the founding in 1829 of its scholarly journal, the *Nederlands Archief voor Kerkgeschiedenis*, by the two first occupants of the newly founded chairs for Church history at the universities of Leiden and Utrecht.

Yet if we choose not to situate Ypeij and Dermout's work as a contribution to academic scholarship, but rather as an expression of the self-understanding of Dutch Protestantism, then their work is very important indeed. Their book was a startlingly new representation of the past of the Church. The public Church of the Dutch Republic had not used ecclesiastical histories to produce a past, but had linked itself to its origin by means of rituals, lists, and administrative routines. This paper will show how this change in the way in which the Church produced its past was intimately linked to a fundamental shift in the understanding of the place of religion in Dutch society. The argument develops in three steps. First, it focuses on the public Church of the Dutch Republic and its past. This will be followed by an analysis of Ypeij and Dermout's work. The last part will briefly sketch

---

[1] A. Ypeij and I. J. Dermout, *Geschiedenis der Nederlandsche Hervormde Kerk*, 4 vols (Breda, 1819–27).

393

the tremendous influence their work had on the way in which the Dutch ecclesiastical past has been conceptualized, even by those who rejected these authors' theological views.

★ ★ ★

Every three years, from 1641 to the end of the eighteenth century, representatives of all the provincial synods of the Dutch Reformed Church travelled to The Hague, the seat of the States-General of the Dutch Republic. There they inspected the chest which contained the acts of the national Synod of Dordrecht. At this Synod, held in 1618–19, the public Church had committed itself to a mitigated version of the doctrine of double predestination and had expelled the Arminians, who organized themselves as a dissenting church. The next day the delegates of the provincial synods travelled in two boats from The Hague to Leiden, where they were received by the mayors. In the town hall they were shown the chest which contained the manuscripts of the so-called States translation, the Dutch translation of the Bible on which the National Synod had decided, and which had been financed by the States-General. After satisfying themselves that worms and moths had not consumed the papers, the box was locked again, everybody had a sumptuous dinner, and the participants sailed back. The whole outing was highly ritualized and hierarchized, with prayers preceding and following the opening of the chests, and occasional bickerings about precedence and slights to status breaking out.[2]

This visitation was the most prominent way in which the Dutch public Church related itself to its past. It was certainly the only national occasion on which the ecclesiastical past was invoked. The Dutch Republic was more or less a federation of seven sovereign provinces. All provinces upheld the Reformed religion, as it had been defined at the national Synod of Dordrecht of 1618. This shared confession was one of the Republic's most important symbols of unity. On the other hand, as the principle of

---

[2] A. Fris, *Inventaris van de archieven behorende tot het 'Oud Synodaal Archief' van der Nederlandse Hervormde Kerk, 1566–1816* (The Hague and Hilversum, 1991), pp. xvi–xviii; J. W. Verburgt, 'De totstandkoming van den Staten-Bijbel en de bewaring zijner oorspronkelijke stukken', *Leids Jaarboekje*, 30 (1938), pp. 138–63.

subordination of ecclesiastical to political authority was well established and the provinces were jealous of their sovereignty, the Dutch public Church was organized on a provincial basis. The Synod of Dordrecht was the last national synod held during the Republic. Links between the various provincial synods were upheld by the practice of sending delegates to each other's meetings. It would be wrong to speak of provincial Churches, in so far as the consciousness of the clergy of subscribing to a common confession upheld by public authority was very strong. They knew they made up the public Church of the Republic. Yet all provinces had more or less their own church order and administrative particularities. Movement of clergy between provinces was comparatively rare. Nor did a national labour market for ministers exist.[3] No wonder then that the only literary ways in which the public Church of the Republic constructed its past reproduced this organizational fragmentation. In the eighteenth century, provincial collections of legal acts and decisions concerning religion since the Reformation were published.[4] In a similar way, books containing lists of ministers who had served the towns and rural parishes since the Reformation were organized on a provincial basis.[5]

---

[3] Peter van Rooden, 'Van geestelijke stand naar beroepsgroep; De profesionalisering van de Nederlandse predikant, 1625-1874', *Tijdschrift voor Sociale Geschiedenis*, 17 (1991), pp. 361-93.

[4] N. Wiltens, *Kerkelyk Plakaatboek*, 5 vols (The Hague, 1722-1807); J. Smetius, *Ordre of reglement voor de classis in Gelderland* (Nijmegen, 1698); J. Smetius, *Synodale ordonnantiën ende resolutiën* (Nijmegen, 1699); C. Nauta, *Compendium der kerkelijke wetten* (Leeuwarden, 1757); J. Lindeboom, 'Classicale wetboeken. Een bijdrage tot de kennis van het kerkelijke leven in de achttiende eeuw', *Nederlands Archief voor Kerkgeschiedenis*, 41 (1956), pp. 65-95.

[5] M. Soermans, *Kerkelijk Register* [Synod of South-Holland] (Dordrecht, 1695; 2nd edn Haarlem, 1702); M. Veeris, *Kerkelyk Tyd-registerz* [Synod of North Holland] (Amsterdam, 1697; 2nd edn Amsterdam, 1705); H. van Rhenen, *Lyst van ... de Predikanten* [Synod of Utrecht] (Utrecht 1705; 2nd edn Utrecht, 1724); A. Moonen, *Naamketen van Predikanten* [Synod of Overijssel] (Deventer, 1709); C. Adami, *Naamlyst der Predikanten* [Synod of Groningen] (Groningen, 1721; 2nd edn Groningen, 1730); H. de Jongh Azn, *Naam-lyst der Predikanten* [Synod of Gelderland] (Leiden, 1750). In Friesland, separate books were published for the six *classes* making up the provincial synod, by M. Laurman, J. Engelsma, W. Columba, H. Grevenstein, A. Greydanus, and H. Reinalda, all appearing in Leeuwarden in the years 1751-63. In Zeeland, where the Estates did not allow the meeting of a provincial synod, no lists of ministers were published.

This last invocation of the past took place locally as well. The custom of placing boards with the names of all ministers that had served the parish since the Reformation against the wall of the parish church stems from the seventeenth century.[6] Other local constructions of the past centred on the sacraments. In 1729, for instance, Bernard Smytegelt, a minister of Middelburg, casually remarked in a sermon that on the previous Sunday communion had been celebrated for the 845th time since the Reformation.[7]

Though brief, this is also an exhaustive overview of the various ways in which the public Church of the Republic related itself to its past. Clearly, this is not ecclesiastical history as we now know it. This was not for lack of historical consciousness or scholarship. At the Dutch universities during the seventeenth and eighteenth centuries, some general Church histories were produced. Most of these were meant for use in academic teaching. These Latin works followed the conventions of Protestant historiography. They documented the gradual decay of the Church from the times of the New Testament to the end of the Middle Ages and the brink of the Reformation, and defended the Reformation against the charge of being an innovation. Even when they bring the story up to their own days, this polemical interest remains paramount. These academic histories do not devote much attention to the Republic and its public Church.[8]

Some ministers of the public Church engaged in popular historical writing. They published in the vernacular.[9] Essentially, this popular historiography offered overviews of the history of the Dutch Republic, stressing its miraculous rise to Great Power status. The works are full of examples of God's direct intervention in battles and sieges. The explanation of God's particular care for the Republic is found in its upholding of true religion.

---

[6] C. A. van Swigchem, T. Brouwer, and W. van Os, *Een huis voor het Woord. Het protestantse kerkinterieur in Nederland tot 1900* (The Hague and Zeist, 1984), p. 283.

[7] Bernardus Smytegelt, *Keurstoffen of verzameling van vyftig uitmuntende predicatien* (Middelburg and The Hague, 1765), p. 429.

[8] The various works are reviewed by Christiaan Sepp, *Bibliotheek van Nederlandsche Kerkgeschiedschrijvers* (Leiden, 1886), pp. 27–36.

[9] J. C. Breen, 'Gereformeerde populaire historiografie in de zeventiende en achttiende eeuw', in *Christendom en Historie* (Amsterdam, 1925), pp. 213–42.

In short, during the Republic, academic, general Church histories, only marginally interested in the history of the Dutch Church, stand next to confessionally-inspired popular histories of the Dutch Republic, while the past of the public Church is created by means of rituals and lists. These peculiar relations of history, Church, and political community can only be understood if one takes into account the self-understanding of the public Church of the Republic. A good place to start is Jacob Fruytier's *Struggles of Sion, or historical dialogues about the various bitter tribulations of the Church of Christ*, published in 1715.[10] As the title indicates, Fruytier was more interested in the past of the Church than most other popular historical works. His book is divided in three parts. The first deals with the Reformation, the second with the Arminian troubles in the Dutch Church, the third with the attacks on the Church in his own days. The work assumes the form of a dialogue, in which the fictitious character Nathanael discusses the history and situation of the Dutch Church with his female interlocutors Truth and Piety. The latter explain to Nathanael that the crisis of the Church results from the public attacks undertaken by various philosophers and theologians upon the religious truth upheld by the Church. 'Public' is the central category of this analysis of the state of religion. The truth of religion is essentially a public truth. The first two parts of Fruytier's work concern the establishment of this truth as a public phenomenon. The Reformation and the Synod of Dordrecht are depicted as the founding moments of a public religious order, with the doctrine upheld at the Synod of Dordrecht as its most important element.[11] It defines the public Church of the Republic. Only this doctrine ought to be preached publicly.

10 Jacob Fruytier, *Sions worstelingen, of historische samenspraken over de verscheide en zeer bittere wederwaerdigheden van Christus' kerke, met openbare en verborgen vyanden. I. In de Reformatie II. Ten tijde van de Remonstranten. III. In dese onse dagen* (Rotterdam, 1715).

11 Only the Arminians published books about the Synod of Dordrecht and its previous history: J. Utenbogaert, *Kerckelicke Historie* (n.p., 1646) and the magisterial work of G. Brandt, *Historie der Reformatie*, 4 vols (Rotterdam, 1671–1704). Theologians of the public Church published refutations of these works. Attempts undertaken by the public Church in the direct aftermath of the Synod to publish an official history came to nought: J. G. R. Acquoy, 'Mislukte pogingen der Nederlandsche kerken om hare geschiedenis te doen beschrijven', in *Geschiedkundige opstellen aangeboden aan Robert Fruin* (The Hague, 1894), pp. 229–58.

Fruytier was not alone in locating religion in the visible, public order of society. Sermons preached at annual days of prayer commissioned by the States-General, the most important civic ritual of the Republic, almost invariably ended with an overview of the duties of the bearers of authority in society: magistrates, ministers, church councils, parents, and employers.[12] Although the theologians of the public Church of the Republic carefully distinguished between political and ecclesiastical authority and always upheld the theoretical independence of the latter, they conceived of society as a body informed by both kinds of authority. This conception tied in rather well with the extremely decentralized and differentiated nature of the body politic of the Republic. As the Republic was imagined as a whole of interlocking ordering elements, provincial and local differences in the details of the political and ecclesiastical order were not considered to be of great importance. The same held for the presence of dissenters and Catholics. Provided they did not encroach upon the visible and public religious order, their existence did not call into question the view of society upheld by the public Church. What was decried was their encroachments upon public space, in the form of church buildings or blatantly anti-Reformed polemics, not their presence or resistance to incorporation within the public Church.

This does not mean that the public Church of the Republic had no sense of the importance of individual commitment on the part of its adherents. On the contrary, it always upheld rather high standards for full membership.[13] Various pietistic movements, of different shapes and inspirations, were active within the Church, almost from the very beginning of the seventeenth century. The practice of distinguishing between truly converted and only formal members of the Church grew steadily, becoming an almost invariant feature of eighteenth-century sermons. Yet these widely shared pietistic ideas and endeavours did not influence or replace the conception that religion was pre-eminently present in the

[12] Peter van Rooden, *Religieuze regimes. Over godsdienst en maatschapij in Nederland, 1570-1970* (Amsterdam, 1996), ch. 3.
[13] A. Duke, 'The ambivalent face of Calvinism in the Netherlands', in idem, *Reformation and Revolt in the Low Countries* (London, 1990), pp. 269-94.

visible order of society. In Fruytier's dialogue, for instance, Truth repeatedly explains to Nathanael that Piety follows her, leaving if she leaves, staying when she stays.[14] Public truth precedes private belief. In a revealing passage, Fruytier states that external discipline and orderly behaviour are necessary for internal conviction.[15]

Its peculiar conception of its place as part of the order of Dutch society explains why the public Church of the Republic constructed its past as an origin, not as a history. The visit to The Hague and Leiden was a ritual inspection of the founding charters of the public Church. The lists of ministers attested to its presence as a public body since the Reformation. Only the Republic has a history, of which the explaining factor is its upholding of the religious order.

⋆ ⋆ ⋆

Ypeij and Dermout's work does not document an origin. It tells of the development and history of the Dutch Reformed Church. Its four volumes span the three centuries from the beginning of the sixteenth to the beginning of the nineteenth century. Slightly more than half of their work is devoted to the eighteenth century. They organize their material by periods, usually of about half a century. Most transitional years between periods are derived from important turning-points in the history of the Dutch Republic: 1625, 1648, 1700, 1748, 1795, 1815. Each period is treated in two chapters. First the history of the Church is told; then its internal and external state are reviewed. The histories mainly consist of overviews of internal dogmatic controversies. The reviews of the external state of the Church offer rough estimates of its success in converting Catholics and Menno-nites and its growth in numbers through immigration. The expansion of its organization is described as well, both in the Republic itself and in the areas administered by the East India Company. The attempts to evaluate the internal state of the Church are the result of a much more ambitious endeavour. In these reviews, Ypeij and Dermout evaluate for each period the piety of the members of the Church.

---

[14] Fruytier, *Sions worstelingen*, pp. 177, 583, 836.
[15] Ibid., pp. 814–15.

Clearly, this structure presupposes a new view of the place of religion in society. Religion is no longer located in the Church as part of the structural and symbolic order of society, but in the inner selves of believers. The leading interest in the descriptions of the history of the Dutch Church is its effectiveness as a means to educate believers and mould their moral characters. Ecclesiastical conflicts are denounced as obstacles to this fundamental task of the Church; theological positions are evaluated according to their effectiveness in morally informing the believers.

This location of religion in the inner selves of believers determines the way Ypeij and Dermout treat the Reformation. They make a clear distinction between the reformation of the Dutch Church and the founding of a Reformed Church in the Netherlands, dividing these events between different chapters.[16] Already, in the first half of the sixteenth century, enlightened preaching by the Dutch clergy had convinced all those inhabitants of the Netherlands not tied by worldly interests to Catholicism to adopt sentiments and opinions that are properly called Protestant.[17] The founding and organizing of a Protestant Church in the second half of the sixteenth century was more or less a secondary event, an external confirmation of an inner conviction already shared by the overwhelming majority of Dutch men and women. In their sketch of the founding of the public Church, Ypeij and Dermout stress its character as a societal event. They do not describe it as the result of measures by central political or ecclesiastical authorities. People found themselves in basic agreement and set up an ecclesiastical organization to suit themselves.[18]

This dialectic between internal religious conviction and its external social forms, the result of Ypeij and Dermout's location of religion in the inner selves of believers, determinestheir treatment of the history of the Dutch public Church. They are no radical pietists, rejecting every externalization of religion. Although they express high

---

[16] Ypeij and Dermout, *Geschiedenis* 1, pp. 47–160, 161–293.
[17] Ibid., 1, pp. 98–9.
[18] Ibid., 1, pp. 202–3.

regard for most of the pietistic endeavours within the Dutch Church, as serious attempts to educate and moralize the people,[19] they strongly condemn those revivalistic or mystic conceptions that tend to empower people in ways other than by education and civilized influence.[20] They do so for two closely related reasons. Inner piety must have a universal character, and Ypeij and Dermout conceive of the universality of true piety through its links, by means of education, to the world of scholarship. Esoteric or inspirational doctrines can therefore never result in true piety. In the second place, such doctrines tend to foster separation. All religion which involves organization as a separate group within society becomes an instance of particularity, because it dissolves the distinction between inner, personal conviction and its outer, social form.

It will come as no surprise that Ypeij and Dermout denounce the Synod of Dordrecht. They deplore its introduction of a rupture and an explicit formulation of particularity within Dutch Protestantism. Throughout their volumes, they describe the Arminians as part of the Dutch Church, and review their scholarship and piety in the overviews of the internal state of the Church.[21] According to Ypeij and Dermout, Arminian and Calvinist sentiments had been present within the Dutch Church since the Reformation. The conflict broke out because this theological difference was taken up within a political struggle. All involvement of religion with political strife is bad, because it ensures that piety will become partisan and lose its universal character.[22] The analysis of the Arminian troubles plays a paradigmatic role in the work of Ypeij and Dermout. All later theological quarrels are related to political struggles as well. It is not theological difference as such, but political partisanship that destroys the proper societal role of religion. They consider it a blessing upon the Dutch Church that it reached theological consensus at the end of the eighteenth century, just before the destruction

19   Ibid., 3, pp. 46–7.
20   Ibid., 3, p. 114; 4, pp. 28–9.
21   Ibid., 1, p. 474; 3, pp. 7, 49–50.
22   Ibid., 2, pp. 294–5.

401

of the old Republic started a whole new area of political struggle.[23]

In effect, Ypeij and Dermout define true religion as an inwardness which relates itself to the nation. It is the relation to the whole nation, conceived of as a moral community of individual citizens, that ensures the universality of piety. Political partisanship introduces particular moments in piety, destroying its religious character. This religious nationalism explains the favourable judgement which Ypeij and Dermout pass on the involvement of political authority with the public Church of the Republic. They welcome the support public authority offered to the education and disciplining of the people, and its subduing of quarrels among the theologians.[24] The State represents the nation as bearer of universality.

The location of religion in the inner selves of individual citizens of the nation has three consequences for Ypeij and Dermout's conceptualization of the way religion functions in society. In the first place, it introduces a very strong process of cultural class formation. All citizens are potentially equal, because they can be morally educated. Only a minority, however, is truly educated and civilized. This is the basis for a distinction between the civilized elite and the rude common people who need to be educated. Ypeij and Dermout locate pure religious sentiments mainly in the upper middle class (the *fatsoenlijken burgerstand*).[25] Consequently, they strongly support the way in which cultural and social dominance can be translated into moral influence.[26]

In the second place, they embrace the principle of the separation of Church and State, and do not wish one particular ecclesiastical body to be privileged over others. All churches should be supported by the State as they contribute to the formation of moral selves and therefore of virtuous citizens. Allowing the adherents of one particular church a monopoly on political office and on the advantages distributed by political patronage corrupts piety by confounding it with secular interests. In the third place, this new

---

[23] Ibid., 4, pp. 203–5.
[24] Ibid., 1, p. 378; 2, pp. 230–1.
[25] Ibid., 3, p. 50.
[26] Ibid., 1, p. 201; 3, p. 176.

location of religion immediately creates new exclusions. Ypeij and Dermout evidence strong anti-Catholic sentiments. They consider Roman Catholicism the symbol of tyranny in religion, of an impure mix of power and piety.[27] It is no longer, as it had been for the public Church of the Republic, a pollution of the public sphere: it is an obstacle to the proper religious and moral education of Dutch citizens.

The new vision of the place of religion in society which forms the basis of Ypeij and Dermout's work was widely shared. In the 1760s, a strong cultural nationalism developed within the Dutch Republic, stressing the duty of all citizens to be morally involved with the nation. In the 1780s, in the aftermath of a disastrous military defeat of the Republic at the hands of Great Britain, this nationalism became politicized and led to a revolution, which in 1787 was put down by Prussian regular troops.[28] In 1795, the French invaded and put the revolutionaries of the 1780s back into power. They completely overhauled the Dutch Republic, making it into a modern nation-state. One of their first acts was to separate Church and State. The new Kingdom of the Netherlands, established after the final defeat of Napoleon, inherited both the ideal of the nation and the effective central bureaucracy of its revolutionary predecessors, and continued their centralizing policies. Both the former public Church and Old Dissent, the Mennonites, Arminians, and Lutherans, received effective organizational structures from the central authorities. Henceforth, they would be dependent not on local elites, but on the central government, as mediated by strong ecclesiastical organizations, staffed by members of the clergy.

Ideological differences between Protestants were reduced. Apart from the most traditional Mennonites, all Protestant clergy were trained at institutes of higher learning along more or less the same lines. All of them considered the Netherlands a nation of citizens, and saw their own churches as means to further the welfare of this nation by morally educating its citizens. All of them received members of the other churches at communion. In fact, the former public

27   Ibid., 1, p. 24; 2, pp. 293–4; 3, p. 6.
28   Margaret C. Jacob and Wijnand W. Mijnhardt, eds, *The Dutch Republic in the Eighteenth Century: Decline, Enlightenment and Revolution* (Ithaca and London, 1992).

Church together with Old Dissent became an informal national establishment, which saw it as its task to further the identity of the Dutch nation by teaching and civilizing the common people. Dutch national identity was furnished with religious characteristics, such as a simple piety, strong moral sentiments, and the validation of common sense and tolerance.

★ ★ ★

Because Ypeij and Dermout's work offered a vision of the past that fitted in extremely well with the newly perceived location of religion in the inner selves of the members of the nation, their conceptualization of Dutch Church history was immediately convincing. Their work created a past that was not an origin legitimating a present order, but a story of the continuous attempt of the nation to shape itself as a moral community, an endeavour still going on in the present. All general Church histories of the nineteenth century share this conception of the Church as a means morally to inform the nation, even when they reject Ypeij and Dermout's theological liberalism. Such works are very much interested in the Church as a teaching organization, focusing on the universities and the ministers.[29] The former public Church itself understood its task in the nation as a continuation of older endeavours. It started to call itself the national (*vaderlandse*) Church. All theological currents were united in their unrelenting emphasis on the necessity of educating the people. The nineteenth and the better part of the twentieth century witnessed an unprecedented catechetical effort.

In academic Church history Ypeij and Dermout's vision of religion as an inner piety relating itself to the whole nation, essentially independent of formal ecclesiastical organization, translated itself into an interest in the Dutch medieval Church and the early Reformation and its precursors. Ypeij and

---

[29] B. Glasius, *Geschiedenis der Christelijke kerk en godsdienst in Nederland*, 3 vols (Amsterdam, 1842–4); B. ter Haar, et al., *Geschiedenis der Christelijke kerk in Nederland*, 2 vols (Amsterdam, 1864–9); G. J. Vos Azn, *Geschiedenis der vaderlandsche kerk*, 2nd edn (Dordrecht, 1888); Peter van Rooden, 'Het Nederlands protestantisme en zijn vaderland', in J. M. M. de Valk, ed., *Nationale identiteit in Europees perspectief* (Baarn, 1993), pp. 95–115.

Dermout had started their work with the disarming observation that it had not been sufficiently remarked that the
European Reformation was due to the Dutch invention of
printing, the Dutch Brethren of the Common Life, and the
Dutchman Erasmus. Such presumptuous claims were not
made by later Dutch Church historians, but such historians
were, until quite recently, interested in proving at least the
Dutch origin of the Dutch Reformation.[30]

Perhaps the best example of the strength of the new
conception of the past of the Church is its adaptation by
Abraham Kuyper and his adherents in the last quarter of the
nineteenth century. Kuyper introduced modern mass politics
in the Netherlands, mobilizing people both politically and
ecclesiastically. He forced through a secession from the
former public Church and organized his adherents as a
separate moral community within the nation, reinstating the
predestinarianism of the Synod of Dordrecht as a means to
divide Dutch Protestantism.[31]

Yet Kuyper still located religion within moral selves, and
his affirmation of particularity did not take the form of a wish
to reinstate Calvinism in the public sphere. He offered a
vision of the national past that holds that the Dutch nation
has always been divided between three different groups,
Calvinists, Erasmian liberals, and Catholics. The Calvinists
are to be found among the common people. He considered
them, in a stunning reversal of the cultural class formation
entailed by Ypeij and Dermout's vision of the homogenous
Protestant nation, not to be lacking in knowledge, but, on the
contrary, to be bearers of a truth that has been forgotten by
their social betters.

★ ★ ★

Dutch Protestant Church history reached its greatest flower-
ing during the two generations following Kuyper's secession.

[30] D. Nauta, 'De reformatie in Nederland in de historiografie', *Serta Historica*, 2
(1970), pp. 44–71; J. C. H. Blom and C. J. Misset, ' "Een onvervalschte
Nederlandsche geest": Enkele historiografische kantekeningen bij het concept van
een nationaal-gereformeerde richting', in E. K. Grootes and J. den Haan, eds,
Geschiedenis Godsdienst Letterkunde (Roden, 1989), pp. 221–32.

[31] Peter van Rooden, 'Contesting the Protestant nation: Calvinists and Catholics
in the Netherlands', *Etnofoor*, 8 (1995), pp. 15–30.

Bitter quarrels about the legitimacy of the various theological positions within contemporary Dutch Protestantism were fought out by means of research into the ecclesiastical history of the Dutch Republic. Quite high standards of historical craftsmanship concerning the use of sources were reached. Yet all scholars shared Ypeij and Dermout's novel conception of Dutch Church history as the unfolding story of the way in which the moral selves of the members of the national community were shaped. In a certain sense, the greatest achievement of Dutch academic ecclesiastical history has been its success in obscuring the fact that its own origin during the early years of the nineteenth century indicates that a fundamental shift in the way religion was understood had taken place.

Research Centre Religion and Society,
University of Amsterdam

'STANDING IN THE OLD WAYS': HISTORICAL LEGITIMATION OF CHURCH REFORM IN THE CHURCH OF ENGLAND, c.1825-65

by R. ARTHUR BURNS

During the early and mid-nineteenth century the Church of England underwent a wide-ranging series of institutional reforms. These were intended to meet the pastoral challenges of industrial society, acknowledge the changing relationship of Church and State, and answer the more pertinent criticisms of its radical and dissenting antagonists. Particularly during the 1830s, the constitutional adjustments of 1828–32, the accession of a Whig administration, and widening internal divisions appeared to place the Church in a newly perilous position. The reforms were consequently enacted in a highly charged and febrile atmosphere. Each measure was closely scrutinized by concerned and sometimes panic-stricken Anglicans,[1] seeking to establish whether it would strengthen the Church or was in fact a manifestation of threatening forces. In such circumstances, the legitimation of reform assumed crucial importance. As ever, the prospective reformer required a legitimation which would appeal to the widest possible constituency. Among allies, it could serve to embolden waverers, doubters, and often the reformer himself. If possible, it should engage the sympathies of potential opponents. It was also essential that the legitimation would not so constrain the reformer that the initiative's practical effectiveness was blunted.

In seeking legitimations which fulfil these requirements, clerical reformers often turn to the past, not least on account of the centrality of historicity to the identity of the Church. However, existing discussions of the institutional Church reforms of the second quarter of the nineteenth

---

[1] For a few examples of panic, see Owen Chadwick, *The Victorian Church*, 2 vols (London, 1971), 1, p. 47.

century stress instead the importance of a contrasting rhetoric. This was a discourse of *utility, pragmatism, rationality,* and *necessity,* openly embracing the disregard of ecclesiastical precedent and prescription. It found its most developed expression in the arguments of the driving-force of the Ecclesiastical Commission, Charles James Blomfield, Bishop of London, that 'priest in the temple of expediency'.[2] Blomfield envisaged sweeping away 'ornamental parts' that stood 'in the way of improvements calculated to enhance and give lustre to the true beauty of the church – the beauty of its holy usefulness'.[3] Contrasting the luxuries of St Paul's cathedral with the surrounding spiritual destitution, he challenged anyone to justify leaving St Paul's intact as 'an ancient corporation which must be maintained in its integrity . . . I would rather take my stand upon the stronger ground of necessity'.[4] This discourse was the common coin of a broad range of reforming initiatives of the 1830s: Blomfield also employed it in his other capacity as Poor Law Commissioner.[5] Historians have presented its deployment in Church reform debates and its triumph there over historical legitimation as a painful but necessary 'modernization' of clerical thinking, a coming-to-terms with the realities of the post-1832 world. As Geoffrey Best put it, these arguments 'could not be much improved on, by anyone who tried to see church and nation as a whole, not abstractly nor in the terms of conventional rhetoric, but in the modern way'.[6] In contrast, those pamphleteers employing historical legitimation who

[2] The Duke of Newcastle's coinage, cheerfully accepted by Blomfield: *Hansard,* ser. 3, 19, cols 914–18 (19 July 1833).
[3] C. J. Blomfield, *A Charge Delivered to the Clergy of the Diocese of London* (London, 1834), pp. 16–17.
[4] *Hansard,* ser. 3, 55, cols 1138, 1137 (30 July 1840).
[5] For the Poor Law, see ibid., 25, col. 598 (28 July 1834). Geoffrey Best characterizes this approach to Church reform as 'the manifestation, in the ecclesiastical sphere, of the general reforming spirit of the age, professional, pious, and (in no precise philosophical sense) utilitarian': G. F. A. Best, *Temporal Pillars: Queen Anne's Bounty, the Ecclesiastical Commissioners, and the Church of England* (Cambridge, 1964), pp. 399–400.
[6] Best, *Temporal Pillars,* p. 347. See also Olive J. Brose, *Church and Parliament: The Reshaping of the Church of England, 1828–1860* (Stanford, Calif., and London, 1959), p. 208; Kenneth A. Thompson, *Bureaucracy and Church Reform: The Organizational Response of the Church of England to Social Change, 1800–1965* (Oxford, 1970), pp. 14, 17.

responded to the crisis with alternative suggestions or who challenged the Commissioners' approach are convicted of arguing from 'sentimental grounds – grounds which, however, were frankly raised by many conservatives to the level of principle'. Their pamphlets 'do not ... make bright reading'; they adopted 'the "safe" men's way, spiritless, unimaginative'.[7] In deploying 'conventional rhetoric', they teetered on the brink of anachronism. This reflected the prominence among them of conservative pre-Tractarian Orthodox High Churchmen, with their 'sort of Religious Respect for whatever is old',[8] themselves now marginalized, having lost the influence over public policy formerly exercised through Lord Liverpool, and ceding leadership within High Churchmanship to the Tractarians. Their reform proposals were either unrealistic and thus stillborn, insignificant, or went unheeded. Indeed, if one is to look for concrete achievements in this period which *were* legitimated through reference to the ecclesiastical past, current historiography would suggest a need to turn from institutional reform and explore instead the very different projects of the Tractarians, Ritualists, and Ecclesiologists.

There is little cause to quarrel with the analysis of the legitimation for reform associated with the Ecclesiastical Commission outlined above – although even Blomfield at times resorted to historical precedent for the *assault* on ancient institutions[9] – or with the centrality of the Commission to Church reform in the early to mid-nineteenth century. None the less our understanding of the dynamics of this Church reform has been skewed by a historiography which focuses on legislative initiatives and the Commission, while neglecting other aspects which made a vital contribution to the institutional reinvigoration of the Church. Any assessment of the importance or otherwise of historical legitimation must take into account its significance in these other approaches.

This paper will consider the role of historical legitimation in perhaps the most significant such reform initiative in the

---

[7] Best, *Temporal Pillars*, pp. 340, 280, 275.

[8] Lord Liverpool to Bishop Tomline, 24 Jan. 1821, quoted ibid., p. 177.

[9] For example, justifying the redistribution of Church property: *Hansard*, ser. 3, 55, cols 1138–9 (30 July 1840).

early to mid-nineteenth-century Church of England, which I have elsewhere described as the 'Diocesan Revival'.[10] Originating in the 1790s and gathering pace into the 1820s, this involved the reform, revival, or development of all aspects of diocesan machinery, leading up to and providing an important stimulus for the widespread revival of diocesan assemblies in the 1860s and 1870s. It predated, was more universal in its impact across the Church of England, and was more wide-ranging than the reinvigoration of episcopacy sometimes attributed to Samuel Wilberforce at Oxford and Tractarian influence, or some isolated 'proto-Wilberforces' among the late Hanoverian episcopate. It was both an important series of reforms in its own right and a vital auxiliary to the work of the Commission without which the latter would have been much less effective. In contrast to the reforms associated with the Commission, much of the Diocesan Revival was accomplished without reference to Parliament, relying instead on initiatives originating within the dioceses from bishops, archdeacons, or the diocesan clergy. There was an equally striking contrast in the forms of legitimation employed by reformers. The Diocesan Revival was characterized by frequent and successful resort to the ecclesiastical past in order to legitimate reform.

To illustrate the full significance of historical legitimation throughout the wide range of reforms associated with the Diocesan Revival is not feasible here. Many of its characteristic features, however, can be observed in the case of its single most important initiative, the revival of the rural dean and ruridecanal chapters.[11] Although rural deans survived in a few dioceses in 1800, they had generally fallen into disuse since the sixteenth century. From the 1790s onwards, however, the office was gradually reinstituted or

---

[10] For the early stages of the Revival, see R. Arthur Burns, 'A Hanoverian legacy? Diocesan reform in the Church of England, c.1800–1833', in John Walsh, Colin Haydon, and Stephen Taylor, eds, *The Church of England, c.1689–c.1833: from Toleration to Tractarianism* (Cambridge, 1993), pp. 265–82; this supplies some corrections to the fuller account in idem, 'The Diocesan Revival in the Church of England, c.1825–1865' (Oxford University D.Phil. thesis, 1990).

[11] The revival of both rural deans and ruridecanal chapters is often misdated and misunderstood. For a full and more accurate account, see Burns, 'Diocesan Revival', ch. 4, with corrections in idem, 'Hanoverian legacy?', pp. 267–70.

reinvigorated across the Church of England; by 1865 rural deans were active in all dioceses. The Church was thus equipped with some 700 additional executive officers active in clergy discipline, school inspection, Church extension and repair, and as episcopal and archidiaconal advisors and dogsbodies: as one wag put it, if archdeacons were the *oculi episcopi*, the deans were 'the Bishop's spectacles'.[12] The revival of the deans was accompanied from 1839 by the reinstitution of ruridecanal chapters, initially promoted as a means of increasing clerical solidarity and counteracting the polarizing growth of Church party. In this the chapters were judged a considerable success, as well as yielding 'the hard cash of definite results' in improving pastoral practice and support for diocesan societies.[13] They soon developed into an important means of consultation between bishop and clergy, and, with annual diocesan meetings of rural deans, were of central importance in the subsequent development of diocesan conferences. In some places the chapters also provided a context for the incorporation of church-going laity into ecclesiastical structures. Rural deans and their chapters both played a crucial role in many important reform initiatives, not least, despite their title, in the urban context, where the rural deanery assisted the co-ordination of pastoral efforts across archaic parish boundaries.

This was a highly successful, practical reform initiative, with concrete results which could be quantified in empirical and pragmatic terms. Yet the rhetoric adopted by the champions of this reform contrasts strikingly with Bishop Blomfield's utilitarianism. It received its most concise formulation when Francis Lear, the Orthodox High Church Archdeacon of Salisbury responsible for the first revival of ruridecanal chapters in 1839, justified this initiative:

in proportion as we search out the practices of our forefathers . . ., as we stand in the old ways marked out for our guidance, and submit to those ecclesiastical rules

---

[12] *Ecclesiastic and Theologian*, 7 (1849), p. 39.

[13] See, for example, J. C. Hare, *Privileges Imply Duties: A Charge to the Clergy of the Archdeaconry of Lewes* (London, 1842), pp. 43–54; J. Sinclair, *On Divisions in the Church* (London, 1846), p. 56.

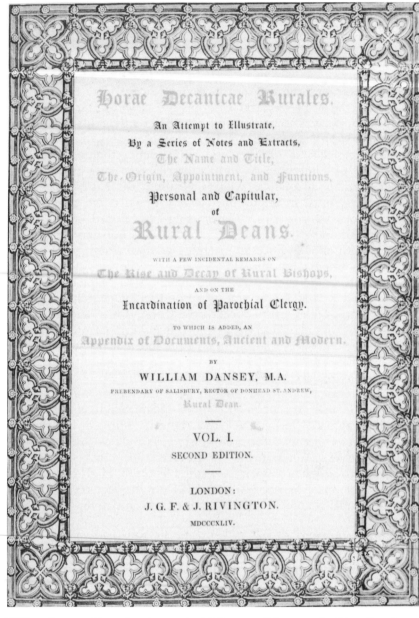

Horae Decanicae Rurales.

An Attempt to Illustrate,
By a Series of Notes and Extracts,
The Name and Title,
The Origin, Appointment, and Functions,
Personal and Capitular,
of
Rural Deans.

WITH A FEW INCIDENTAL REMARKS ON
The Rise and Decay of Rural Bishops,
AND ON THE
Incardination of Parochial Clergy.

TO WHICH IS ADDED, AN
Appendix of Documents, Ancient and Modern.

BY
WILLIAM DANSEY, M.A.
PREBENDARY OF SALISBURY, RECTOR OF DONHEAD ST. ANDREW,
Rural Dean.

VOL. I.
SECOND EDITION.

LONDON:
J. G. F. & J. RIVINGTON.
MDCCCXLIV.

William Dansey, *Horae decanicae rurales*. Title page of the second edition (London, 1844) and [opposite] the first page of the preface from the first edition (London, 1835) (Source: Author's collection).

꤮reface.

NON abs re mihi vifum eft fore, fi quæpiam afferrem, ut facilius ad memoriam revocarentur fanctiffima priorum inftituta, quibus obfervatis, noftra CHRISTIANA RESPUBLICA et aucta eft femper et confervata. *JOH. FRANC. PICI, MIRANDULÆ DOMINI*, De Reformandis *Moribus Oratio.* *FASCICULUS RERUM*, p. 417.

HE *object of the following pages is fufficiently explained by the title prefixed to them. The circumftances, to which their commencement, pro-grefs, and completion are owing—though of little importance—may be thus briefly ftated.*

Having been requefted by my venerable diocefan, foon after his acceffion to the fee of Sarum (A.D. MDCCCXXV.), to accept the appoint-ment of rural ꤮ean—*then recently revived in the diocefe—I was naturally defirous of obtaining what information I could on the hiftory and conftitution of the office.*

413

of government from which our reformers never meant we should depart, we shall find ourselves, under God, compact and strengthened.[14]

Contemporaries requiring further evidence of these 'old ways' could find them exhaustively explored in the more voluminous expression of the same ethos produced by Lear's close associate and fellow Orthodox High Churchman, William Dansey. Dansey had an undistinguished clerical career, serving as rector of Donhead St Andrew, Wiltshire, from the year after his ordination in 1819 until his death in 1856, his only further preferment being a prebendal stall at Salisbury in 1841. In 1835, however, Dansey published *Horae decanicae rurales: Being an Attempt to Illustrate, by a Series of Notes and Extracts, the Name and Title, the Origin, Appointment, and Functions, Personal and Capitular, of Rural Deans. With a Few Incidental Remarks on the Rise and Decay of Rural Bishops, and on the Incardination of the Parochial Clergy. To which is Added, an Appendix of Documents, Ancient and Modern.*[15] This two-volume work of over 900 pages at first sight could not appear less calculated to contribute to reform: Dansey himself confessed its arrangement to be 'perplexed and unsatisfactory'. It is the work of an antiquarian, the outcome of a decade of researches inspired by Bishop Thomas Burgess of Salisbury's decision to appoint Dansey a rural dean in 1825. Reading up on his new office Dansey found standard works uninformative, and had therefore determined to 'explore the archives of ecclesiastical antiquity'. His 'antiquarian ardour' was increased by the discovery in his own deanery of a manuscript on the office dating from 1667, which Dansey published in 1832.[16] As finally presented to the public, *Horae decanicae rurales* fully lived up to its subtitle. The main text charted the history, various duties, development, and subsequent decline of the office and its antecedents both in England

---

[14] Quoted in William Dansey, *A Letter to the Archdeacon of Sarum, on Ruri-Decanal Chapters* (London, 1840), p. 44.

[15] William Dansey, *Horae decanicae rurales*, 2 vols (London, 1835).

[16] John Priaulx, *A Brief Account of the Nature, Use and End of the Office of Dean Rural, Addressed to the Clergy of the Deanery of Chalke, AD 1666–7*, ed. W. Dansey (London, 1832).

and in the wider Church from the earliest times, drawing on a wide range of printed sources. Then, in almost 300 pages of appendices, Dansey assembled both extracts and whole documents arranged by diocese from all ages and all parts of the Church: from Ireland, France, the Netherlands, Germany, Switzerland, Italy, and both the Orthodox and Lutheran Churches of Russia; from medieval English records via the *Valor ecclesiasticus* and *Reformatio legum ecclesiasticarum* and a speech by Francis Atterbury to the recent commission issued by the Evangelical Bishop Charles Sumner of Winchester, supplied by his equally Evangelical archdeacon, Charles Hoare. As Dansey observed, 'Nothing appertaining to the office of dean rural in any historical, canonical or conciliar collection, within the compiler's knowledge, is omitted.'[17] Not only was the content of the book antiquarian: so was its physical appearance, with a consciously archaic gothic type and the long 'S', florid capitals, miniature illustrations, and – in the second edition of 1844 – an elaborate title page. Charles le Bas, writing in the *British Critic*, thought it 'redolent of good old times': 'We are firm believers in the physiognomy of books . . . the author has the organ of veneration brought out into ample development.'[18] (See Plates).

In the past *Horae decanicae rurales* has sometimes been incorrectly credited with inspiring the revival of the rural dean;[19] in fact deans were already operational in seventeen dioceses by 1835. However, it rapidly established itself as the main point of reference for other pamphleteers and dignitaries; indeed Bishop Burgess issued the volume as a manual to the Salisbury deans.[20] Dansey himself and others drew on it in their attempt to expedite the revival of the chapters. If the

[17] Quotations from preface to Dansey, *Horae decanicae rurales*, 1, pp. v–xxi.
[18] *British Critic*, 19 (1836), p. 274.
[19] For example, D. L. Edwards, *Christian England: From the Eighteenth Century to the First World War* (London, 1984), p. 201; A. J. Russell, *The Clerical Profession* (London, 1980), p. 44.
[20] *Gentleman's Magazine*, ns 5 (1836), p. 171. For examples of others employing Dansey, see Charles Goddard, *A Charge Delivered to the Clergy of the Archdeaconries of Lincoln and Stow* (London, 1836), p. iv, praising its 'solid ecclesiastical and antiquarian views'; J. C. Hare, *The Better Prospects of the Church*, 2nd edn (London, 1840), pp. 80–2; W. B. Stonehouse, *The Office of Deans Rural* (London, 1841).

author's original preface suggested an extravagant exercise in vanity publishing, the work achieved a sufficient circulation to justify a second and expanded edition in 1844. Moreover, *Horae decanicae rurales* was unique in its learning and ambition, but was only one among many contemporary publications employing historical legitimation in discussing the rural dean.[21] It was to such legitimation that bishops and archdeacons turned when announcing revivals of deans and chapters, or the expansion of their activities, even when such expansions could have had no direct parallel in the past: for example, the integration of rural deans into the diocesan societies, or their employment as school inspectors. Indeed, it is striking that while reference to the past was ubiquitous, it was never slavish, and was exploited more for its potential in legitimating innovations than prohibiting them.

As suggested above, historical legitimation was fundamental to the success not only of the revival of the rural dean but to the whole series of reforms which can together be understood as constituting the Diocesan Revival. It was equally prominent in calls for the reinvigoration of the episcopate and the archidiaconate, the creation of diocesan assemblies, the improvement of clergy discipline, and the better integration of the cathedral into the life of the diocese through, for example, the creation of theological colleges. Many of these themes were often addressed simultaneously in the treatment of the diocese itself as an institution whose effective operation was vital to the success of Church reform, and through such discussions historical legitimation could be extended to aspects of diocesan machinery for which there was no historical precedent, as in the case of diocesan societies in support of Church extension and education. Such discussions figured prominently in the Church reform pamphleteering of the 1830s dismissed by Best. The concrete results of the Diocesan Revival suggest that his verdict needs to be at the very least qualified.

---

[21] For example, J. Storer, *A Plan of Reformation for the Church of England* (London, 1833), p. 24; H. Robinson, *Church Reform on Christian Principles* (London, 1833); W. D. Willis, *Suggestions for the Regulation of Church Patronage, Preferment, &c. &c., in a Letter to his Grace the Archbishop of Canterbury* (London, 1835).

A number of explanations can be offered for the prevalence of reference to the ecclesiastical past in the Diocesan Revival. One of the most important is the leading role assumed by Orthodox High Churchmen both among the pamphleteers advocating the reforms and the dignitaries enacting them. If the Orthodox had been displaced from their former prominence as ecclesiastical advisors to government, they remained entrenched in both the episcopate and archidiaconate long after 1830, and constituted a sizeable proportion of parochial clergy. The historical legitimation of the Diocesan Revival directly reflected the distinctive theological and ecclesiological tradition of the Orthodox which, despite later Tractarian claims to the contrary, was far from exhausted by 1833.[22] As Peter Nockles has recently demonstrated, among its most striking features were a respect for the heritage of the Church of England on both sides of the Reformation and for the Reformers themselves; a discriminating interest in the early Church; a belief in the value of the establishment which did not imply Erastianism; and a more entrenched sense of the iniquity of Rome than was to be characteristic of their Tractarian successors.

The marked differences between the Orthodox attitude to Church history and that of the Oxford Movement helps explain why, although many Tractarians actively supported the Diocesan Revival, the prevailing character of its historical legitimation can be distinguished from that characteristic not only of the Tractarians, but also of the Ecclesiologists of the Camden Society and of the Ritualists. Firstly, many of the appeals to the ecclesiastical past of the Diocesan Revival were far more inclusive than those of the other movements. Dansey's portmanteau approach contrasts with the Ecclesiologists' preference for particular decades of the fourteenth century; recent scholarship has equally demonstrated the highly selective approach to Church history typical of the Oxford Movement.[23] Secondly, the prominence

[22] See Peter B. Nockles, *The Oxford Movement in Context: Anglican High Churchmanship, 1760-1857* (Cambridge, 1994), *passim*.

[23] For two important treatments of the relationship of the Tractarians to the ecclesiastical past, see Stephen Thomas, *Newman and Heresy: The Anglican Years* (Cambridge, 1992), and in particular Nockles, *Oxford Movement in Context*, esp. ch. 2.

of the *Reformatio legum ecclesiasticarum* in the footnotes of many of the advocates of diocesan reform is one indication of a fundamentally more positive attitude to the Reformation. Nor was appeal to the early Church necessarily to demonstrate the superiority of its polity before it became enmeshed with the state: one Orthodox pamphleteer, John Storer, pointed out that he looked instead to 'the ancient Church . . . not in its embryo state, but when it had assumed a national form but was yet in its purest and best days'.[24] Thirdly, a contrast can be suggested in the way in which the reformers related to their historical precedents. As we have seen in the case of the rural dean, the reliance on historical legitimation did not tie the hands of the reformers to the extent that they were unable to respond creatively to the contemporary situation. As a result, although many prominent Tractarians were sympathetic to the Diocesan Revival and supported many of its initiatives, they frequently regarded its treatment of ecclesiastical institutions as cavalier. This was nowhere more evident than over the question of diocesan assemblies, where the willingness of many diocesan reformers to adapt formerly clerical synods to involve church-going laity appalled extreme High Churchmen. Even Henry Phillpotts, whose links with the leading Tractarians were closer than those of many others involved in the Diocesan Revival, dismayed Pusey with his willingness even to contemplate the involvement of the laity in the diocesan synod he summoned in the course of the Gorham controversy in 1851.[25]

Finally, particularly in the context of the secessions to Rome and the Papal Aggression in the early 1850s, there was a notable shift to a more nationalist and anti-Catholic antiquarian rhetoric, no doubt in a conscious attempt to avert accusations of Romanizing clericalism. As George Trevor put it, calling for the inauguration of diocesan assemblies,

As *Protestants*, shall we not prefer the genuine Episcopacy of the Scriptures and the Primitive Church, which was carefully restored in the *Reformatio Legum* of

---

24 Storer, *Plan of Reformation*, p. 22.
25 See Burns, 'Diocesan Revival', p. 264, and more generally, ch. 9.

our own Reformers, to an Ecclesiastical *Autocracy* the offspring of the Middle Ages, and designed to be controlled by the Supremacy of the Papal See?[26]

It was the same context which produced perhaps the most remarkable variety of historical legitimation associated with the Revival. Several campaigners for diocesan assemblies presented them as part of an ideal Anglo-Saxon Church polity destroyed by a combination of state interference under the Conqueror and papal usurpation, in effect an adaptation of the radical rhetoric of the Norman Yoke. For example, William Pound argued that 'By synodical action within the diocese, in mixed assemblies of clergy and laity, the old Saxon independent action of the Church will be obtained.'[27]

Despite its origins in the Orthodox High Churchman's attitude to Church history, however, crucial to the success of the historical legitimation of the Diocesan Revival was its appeal to those outside its core constituency. As already suggested, it was at times able to mobilize the support of the younger, Tractarian, and Oxford–influenced High Churchmen. But among those who paid tribute to Dansey's labours was the Liberal Anglican Archdeacon of Lewes, Julius Hare; and as we have seen, those whose assistance was acknowledged in *Horae decanicae rurales* included, alongside many leading Orthodox High Churchmen, Charles Hoare, the Evangelical Archdeacon of Winchester. His diocesan, Charles Sumner, was a prominent diocesan reformer; while among the antiquarian pamphleteers of the 1830s was John Kempthorne, chaplain to the Evangelical Bishop Ryder of

---

[26] George Trevor, *Diocesan Synods* (London, 1851), p. vi.

[27] William Pound, *The Papal Aggression upon the Church of England to be Met and Successfully Repelled by the Revival of Diocesan Synods* (London, 1852), p. 8. The classic discussion of the 'Norman Yoke' is Christopher Hill, 'The Norman yoke', in John Saville, ed., *Democracy and the Labour Movement: Essays for Dona Torr* (London, 1954), pp. 11–66. However, historians are increasingly acknowledging its persistence long into the nineteenth century: see Eugenio F. Biagini, *Liberty, Retrenchment and Reform: Popular Liberalism in the Age of Gladstone, 1860–1880* (Cambridge, 1992), p. 56. In contrast, such references to the ancient constitution destroyed by the Norman Conquest seem to have disappeared from high political discourse, making their appearance in this context, and in the mouths of Tory Churchmen, all the more striking. See J. W. Burrow, *A Liberal Descent: Victorian Historians and the English Past* (Cambridge, 1981), p. 102.

Gloucester.[28] This indicates in part the blurring of party divisions in the pre-Tractarian Church,[29] and especially the respect for the historic institutions of the visible Church and commitment to the establishment which characterized Claphamite evangelicalism. But it also reflected the peculiar appropriateness of the variety of historical legitimation characteristic of the Revival to one of its chief objectives: preserving the unity of the Church of England in the face of internal party polarization. By avoiding the polemical theological aspect of the historical rhetoric of the Tractarians, and instead embracing the Reformation in an appeal to the continuous past history of the Church as a community of believers in both the diocesan and increasingly the national context, it could speak to all who valued the establishment and the ideal of a comprehensive national Church agreed on fundamentals: as William Emery, one of the chief architects of the introduction of diocesan conferences described it, the 'grand old National Church of England', 'the most tolerant church in the world'.[30] Its appeal was further widened by the absence of the polar opposition which existed between the more theological legitimation often employed by Tractarians and the utilitarian rhetoric of the Commission and legislative reforms.[31] Away from the parliamentary environment in which historical and utilitarian rhetorics were employed by opposing speakers in debates on the Commission, the two approaches to legitimation could comfortably be deployed side-by-side to provide mutual reinforcement.[32] Diocesan reformers were happy to justify their efforts in utilitarian terms alongside their historical arguments, while, in his own

---

[28] Hare, *Better Prospects*, pp. 80–2; J. Kempthorne, *The Church's Self-Regulating Privilege, a National Safeguard in Respect of Real Church Reform* (London, 1835).

[29] See Peter B. Nockles, 'Church parties in the pre-Tractarian Church of England, 1750–1833: the "Orthodox" – some problems of definition and identity', in Walsh et al., eds, *Church of England*, pp. 334–59.

[30] *The Official Report of the Church Congress, held at Portsmouth, . . . 1885* (London, 1885), p. 479; W. Emery, *Church Union and Progress* (Cambridge, 1867), p. 14.

[31] See Thompson, *Bureaucracy and Church Reform*, pp. 48–9; Burns, 'Hanoverian legacy?', pp. 281–2.

[32] As the climate for parliamentary Church reform became less hostile, historical legitimation similarly came to play a larger part in the justification of Commission reforms, which also increasingly took account of the effects of the Diocesan Revival.

diocese, Blomfield referred his clergy to Dansey's work when he revived the London rural deans in 1834.[33]

This last point underlines one significant reason for the contrast between Blomfield's parliamentary rhetoric and that employed in the Diocesan Revival: the contrasting audience to which such legitimation was primarily addressed. Utilitarian pragmatism was the rhetoric best suited to the parliamentary and public context of the debate on the Commission and legislation. Both parliamentary and public audiences contained many unsympathetic to the Church, and reformers had to answer directly both those who primarily sought a more effective national establishment and the radical critique which placed the Church at the heart of the nexus of 'Old Corruption'.[34] In contrast, while clerical support was desirable, once life-interests expired the statutory authority of the parliamentary reforms rendered that support ultimately unnecessary. For the diocesan reformer, however, securing consent from the clergy was of paramount importance. The debate over these reforms was largely conducted away from the gaze of the wider public at visitation assemblies, clerical meetings, and in publications explicitly directed *ad clerum*, so that less account needed to be taken of the sensibilities of the Church's critics. Moreover the reforms would, if enacted, lack the statutory backing which might permit them to be enforced on a recalcitrant clergy. With so many of the diocesan reforms, not least the revival of the rural dean, calculated to increase the authority of the bishop and so impinge on the independence of the incumbent, individual reformers needed to convince their clergy that their innovations were not simply a manifestation of their own budding episcopal tyranny. In such circumstances reference to historic precedent removed one possible platform for clerical resistance.

In conclusion, it must be re-emphasized that it is no part of the intention of this paper to deny the centrality of the legislative reforms legitimated through a rhetoric of utility

---

[33] Blomfield, *Charge*, pp. 64–5.

[34] See the prominence of the Church in John Wade, *The Extraordinary Black Book* (London, 1832; repr. Shannon, 1971). For a reassessment with implications for the study of Church reform, see Philip Harling, 'Rethinking "Old Corruption" ', *P&P*, 147 (May 1995), pp. 127–58.

and necessity to the history of the Victorian Church. Nor is it intended to deny that those calling for diocesan reform offered many impractical and fanciful proposals, not least in advocating schemes for a massive increase in the episcopate. However, these should not blind us to the fact that the same appeals to the past which underpinned such proposals in the Diocesan Revival contributed to an extremely effective institutional reform initiative which made an important and distinctive contribution to the reinvigoration of the Victorian Church. The use of historical legitimation enabled these reforms to mobilize in their support loyalties and deep-seated convictions which aggressively utilitarian Church reformers were more likely to encounter as inspiring opposition to their initiatives. The particular nature of the historical appeal employed also proved surprisingly successful in neutralizing one of the most significant obstacles to effective reform at the local level, the contemporaneous polarization of Church parties. In consequence it was ideally suited to a reform initiative which made the promotion of unity in the Church one of its key objectives.

More generally, this discussion underlines the importance of the context in which reforming rhetoric operated in determining both its nature and its effectiveness. Historians are only now beginning to chart the variety and interconnections of reforming rhetorics deployed in the full range of early to mid-nineteenth-century reform initiatives in both Church and State. This reflects not least the fact that it was the utilitarian and pragmatic discourse of reform so extensively deployed in the 1830s that established our own 'common-sense' expectations of what constitutes 'reform'. In the past, too many judgements on the potential of reform proposals dependent on historical legitimation seem to have been unduly influenced by the fact that their consciously antiquarian tone was less recognizable as a reforming rhetoric to modern historians than the pragmatic discourse of the utilitarian approach. In the context of the clerical communities of the dioceses of the early Victorian Church, however, this could be a positive advantage.

King's College London

BENJAMIN WEBB (1819-85) AND
VICTORIAN ECCLESIOLOGY

by J. MORDAUNT CROOK

We begin in Trinity College, Cambridge, in May 1839. It is 10 o'clock at night and three undergraduates named Neale, Webb, and Boyce are trying to persuade one of their dons, Archdeacon Thorp, to become senior member of a new society. They refuse to leave until he agrees. The Cambridge Camden Society is born. J. M. Neale becomes President, Benjamin Webb Secretary, and E. J. Boyce Treasurer. Within a year they are joined by another Trinity man with influence in a much wider sphere, Beresford Hope. By 1843 the membership list includes two archbishops, sixteen bishops, thirty-one peers and M.P.s, seven deans or chancellors of dioceses, twenty-one archdeacons or rural deans, sixteen architects, and seven hundred ordinary members.[1] In 1845 the society goes national, moves to London, and becomes the Ecclesiological Society.[2]

The Oxford Movement set out to revive the theological basis of the authority of the Church of England; the Cambridge Movement aimed to restore its architectural and liturgical expression. The Camden Society's programme of restoration – that is the revival of medieval forms in ecclesiastical worship and architecture – began notoriously with the Round Church, Cambridge, then spread like a fever. By 1854 a quarter of all Anglican parish churches had been 'restored' according to Camdenian rules, by 1873 one third. By 1852 Webb could boast that advice had been sent to 'the Canadas, Bombay, Ceylon, Sierra Leone, the Mauritius, the Himalaya, Tasmania, Guinea, Australia and New Zealand,

---

[1]   E. Towle, *Life of J. M. Neale* (London, 1906), p. 15.
[2]   This echoes the name of a similar society, founded at Trinity by Neale and Webb early in 1839, and dissolved a year later: Oxford, Bodleian Library, SC 44750 (e 406), B. Webb, 'Diary', 1839, *passim*.

Newfoundland and Hong Kong'.[3] By 1857 he could report that 'good principles, theological as well as aesthetical' were even finding 'an audience among our American brethren'.[4] When the society's journal, the *Ecclesiologist*, ceased publication in 1868, Webb was able to declare that victory was complete: 'our object all along', he wrote, 'has . . . been propagandism . . . and . . . we have the satisfaction of retiring from the field victors.'[5] During Webb's own lifetime, the work of his favourite architect, William Butterfield, even reached the Antipodes, in the substantial form of the cathedral of St Paul in Melbourne (1880 onwards).

Benjamin Webb's career followed the crest of this ecclesiological wave. His father, a prosperous London wheelwright, sent him to St Paul's School, and thence to Trinity College, Cambridge.[6] His first post was that of curate to his old tutor Archdeacon Thorp at Kemerton in Gloucestershire; he later arranged for Thorp's memorial to be installed there, along with an altar frontal by Butterfield.[7] Then he moved to London, as curate of Christ Church, Albany Street, where the Rossetti family were neighbours; years later there was to be a Rossetti–Morris window there.[8] Then he was briefly curate at Brasted, Kent; he had already married the daughter of the Rector, a Tractarian polymath named Dr W. H. Mill, Regius Professor of Hebrew at Cambridge. In the rectory at Brasted – designed by R. C. Carpenter, and described by the *Ecclesiologist* as 'of more pretension, but not less successful' than Butterfield's Coalpit Heath – young Webb was still very much at the heart of the

[3] *Eccl.*, 13, ns 10 (1852), p. 276. 'I am asked to give an idea of the number of churches improved under the auspices of the C.C.S. It would be as difficult almost as to count the stars on a clear frosty night': M. S. Lawson, ed., *Letters of J. M. Neale* (London, 1910), p. 17.

[4] B. Webb, review [App. no. 32], *Eccl.*, 18, ns 14 (1857), p. 368.

[5] *Eccl.*, 29, ns 26 (1868), pp. 315–16.

[6] F. Boase, *Modern English Biography*, 3 (London, 1901), cols 1242–3.

[7] J. Mordaunt Crook, *William Burges and the High Victorian Dream* (London, 1981), p. 388.

[8] Window (1870) in memory of Margaret Polidori and the Rossetti family, who lived at 45 Upper Albany St (later 166 Albany St, demolished 1959). Canon W. Burrows, second vicar of Christ Church, was a family friend of the Rossettis. Webb – living at 3 Park Cottages, Park Village – was curate to the Revd William Dodsworth, formerly of Margaret [Street] Chapel, who became a Roman Catholic in 1851.

Camdenian circle. Neale was a regular visitor, as were Thomas and Frederick Helmore, editors with Webb and Neale of the *Hymnal Noted* (1852).[9] Then came a change. Off went Webb, at Beresford Hope's bidding, to the borders of Staffordshire and Derbyshire, to the wild moorland parish of Sheen. His eleven-year curacy there from 1851 to 1862 must have seemed indeed perpetual. But he still had links with High Church politics: Beresford Hope in London, J. M. Neale in Sussex. He kept up a stream of journalism and correspondence. His parish church became a modest centre for progressive liturgy. And his vicarage was designed by Butterfield: the style, muscular Gothic.

At last, in 1862, came the appointment he had been waiting for, and for which Beresford Hope clearly lobbied: Vicar of St Andrew's, Wells Street.[10] This London church, near Oxford Circus - removed stone by stone in the 1930s to Kingsbury in Hertfordshire - became the focus of Webb's liturgical ambitions for the rest of his life.[11] In 1882 Hope also managed to secure him a prebendary's stall - and thereby much ecclesiological controversy - at St Paul's Cathedral. But it was St Andrew's which made his name. It had been founded in rather a poor district, a parish of about 5,000 souls, halfway between Harley Street and Tottenham Court Road. Outside it looked a dull building, designed by Hamilton and Daukes in 1845-7. Inside it became a treasure house: stained glass by Pugin and Hardman, Lavers and Barraud, and Clayton and Bell; altar frontals by Seddon; a font cover by Pearson; a reredos designed by Street and carved by Redfern (a self-taught sculptor discovered by Webb in Staffordshire); a lectern designed by Butterfield; a font, pulpit, and chancel screen designed by Street (the font replacing one by Pugin); and a litany desk, tomb, window, and full set of altar plate, all designed by Burges. Twice daily the psalms were sung. Each Sunday the choir sang masses by

9   *Eccl.*, 4 (1845), p. 189.
10 Hope credited Sir William Hayter with persuading Lord Palmerston to this appointment. See [A. Beresford Hope], Obituary of the Revd B. Webb, *Church Quarterly Review*, 21 (1885-6), p. 462.
11 Details in *Transactions of the St Paul's Ecclesiological Society*, 1 (1881-5), pp. xx-xxi.

Beethoven, Cherubini, Schubert, Haydn, Mozart, or Hummel. In the early 1870s Charles Gounod was a frequent attender, and his Passiontide motets were adapted from the Latin by Benjamin Webb.[12]

Ritual at St Andrew's was not, in fact, very High: there were candles but no fancy vestments, although Webb always kept to 'the eastward position' at the altar.[13] Even so, there was opposition. To Protestant eyes, the beauty of holiness was still papistical nonsense. And *Punch*, for instance, was merciless in its satire of the Ecclesiologists – or 'ecclesiolators' – and all their works. Webb had to face a good deal of this, while at the same time proving himself an exemplary parish priest. He even established, for example, the first day nursery or crèche in London.[14]

★ ★ ★

So much for the outline of his career. By the end of his life Webb's celebrity as a metropolitan liturgist had rather eclipsed his fame as a young Cantabrian ecclesiologist. But it was the Ecclesiological Society which gave him his place in history. Of course he was not alone: from Cambridge – besides Neale and Hope – there were Harvey Goodwin, later Bishop of Carlisle, Philip Freeman, F. A. Paley, and Edmond Venables; from Oxford there were William Scott, E. A. Freeman, and Sir Stephen Glynne. Still, it is Webb, Neale,

---

[12] For examples of original hymns by Webb, see J. Julian, *Dictionary of Hymnology* (London, 1892). On the whole Webb believed 'the age of hymns has passed'; 'the translation into English reduced everything to common sense – the curse . . . of our present ritual' (Towle, *Neale*, p. 208).

[13] [Hope], *Church Quarterly Review*, 21 (1885–6), p. 463. He refrained from the adoption of the eucharistic vestments, not from any objection in principle but on grounds of 'Christian charity, expediency and prudence' (evidence to Royal Commission of 1867, cited in *DNB*).

[14] *DNB*. Did the children, perhaps, sing J. M. Neale's hymns for children?
   I'm a little Catholic
   And Christian is my name,
   And I believe in Holy Church
   In every age the same,
   And I believe the English Church
   To be a part of her,
   The Holy Church throughout the world,
   Which cannot fail or err.
(Quoted in M. Chandler, *Life and Work of J. M. Neale* [London, 1995], pp. 186–7.)

and Hope who will always be remembered. Of these three men – the makers of the Ecclesiological Society, the Trinity trinity – Webb is the one who tends to be overlooked. Neale was a romantic sacramentalist, Hope was a romantic Tory. Webb was a Tory too,[15] but above all he was a romantic ritualist: like the others, his ideal was the beauty of holiness; but his temperament was less dogmatic than Neale's, less combative than Hope's. He could afford to stay on the sidelines. He was always comfortably off: richer than Neale, though not as rich as Hope; he left over £20,000 – twice as much as Ruskin.[16] As a Cambridge undergraduate he seems to have been more than a little precious: 'his dress was very peculiar', wrote one contemporary, 'and intended to designate ultra-highchurchmanship', – so much so that he was known as the 'Blessed Benjamin'.[17] But there was clearly a more practical side to him. It takes a rather extraordinary freshman to set up an international society. First as Secretary, then as Editor, he handled the bulk of the Society's day-to-day organization, eventually operating from his London house at 3 Chandos Street, Cavendish Square. Webb was supremely efficient. And thanks to his diary[18] – kept on a daily basis in a form of dog-Latin code – it is possible to trace the progress of his thinking through hundreds of articles and reviews which would otherwise be anonymous. Articles written, in particular, on the minutiae of ornament and liturgy – he was after all an F.S.A.[19] – and more generally on the problem of style. Through these writings – listed here for the first time (see Appendix) – we can begin to grasp one key facet of the Victorian mind: its capacity to express its aesthetic sense, its spirituality – indeed its very identity – through the art and architecture of the Middle Ages. By

[15] E.g. Government defeated: 'Hurrah! . . . Lord Derby sent for' (Diary, 20 Feb. 1858).

[16] He left £21,529. His effects, including a portrait by E. V. Eddis and his diaries, descended via his widow Maria (d. 1904) and his son Clement (1865–1954) to Westminster School and the Bodleian Library, Oxford (Probate records, Somerset House). Clement Webb became Professor of the Philosophy of the Christian Religion at Oxford.

[17] *Romilly's Cambridge diary, 1842–47*, ed. M. E. Bury and J. D. Pickles, Cambridge Record Society, 10 (1994), pp. 208–9.

[18] Oxford, Bodleian Library, SC 44750–88.

[19] *Proceedings, Society of Antiquaries*, 11 (1886), p. 145: obituary.

means of this process, the imagery of mid-nineteenth-century Anglicanism became increasingly medieval in form.

On the vexed question of liturgy, Webb might be described as cautiously High. When in 1858 the Revd John Purchas of Brighton dared to publish 'a Manual of Directions for the Right Celebration of the Holy Communion, for the saying of Matins and Evensong, and for the Decent and Orderly performance of all other Rites, Functions, Offices and Ceremonies of the Church, according to ancient Usages of the Church of England', Webb suggested that it might have been wiser to keep such things in the decent obscurity of Latin. Publishing so many details of vestment and rubric was surely offering hostages to fortune; no doubt the precedents were sound, 'but there is such a thing as proving too much'. 'We are bidden', he adds, 'to be "wise as serpents", and are warned against throwing pearls before swine.'[20] When in 1877 the Revd Arthur Tooth of St James's Church, Hatcham, was hauled before the civil courts for acts of ritualism – thus calling into question the whole balance between Church and State – Webb decided that the *via media* was ultimately defensible only in terms of tolerance and discretion. 'Rubrics were made for the Church', he decided, 'and not the Church for the rubrics.' The theory of Royal Supremacy – as exercised through the Judicial Committee of the Privy Council – was better left untested. 'Our ecclesiastical polity is the despair of technical canonists and *doctrinaires*', he concluded. 'But it has held things together fairly well for three centuries . . . "Let sleeping dogs lie." . . . Let what is doubtful remain doubtful. *In dubiis libertas.*'[21]

Webb's intellectual and spiritual journey is not untypical of his generation. Having pushed the Church of England as far as it could go in the direction of apostolicity, he discovered

---

[20] B. Webb, review [App. no. 72], *Eccl.*, 20, ns 18 (1859), pp. 31–4. Neale managed to veto a moderate article in the *Ecclesiologist* (probably by Webb) relating to ritualism at St George's in the East, London. 'Your article', Neale protested, 'comes simply to this: let us give the people as much Ecclesiology as they will bear without howling. Had we said that twenty years ago, there would have been none in England now.' (Lawson, *Letters of Neale*, p. 310.)

[21] [Webb], 'Further aspects of the Hatcham Case', *SatR*, 43 (1877), pp. 66–7. Webb's obituary in the *Guardian* (26 Oct. 1887) emphasized his *individual* position in ritual controversy.

that however Catholic it became, Anglicanism was still enmeshed by the constraints of Establishment.

As an undergraduate, Webb had been accused of 'Romanizing'.[22] When Newman's Tract XC appeared in 1841, he read it 'with approbation'.[23] After all, as Newman pointed out, the word 'Protestant' never appeared in the Prayer Book or Thirty-Nine Articles.[24] It was the next step which presented difficulties. When Webb actually visited Rome in 1844, what he saw of the foreign Church confirmed him in his Anglicanism: 'I am sadly disappointed' – and not just by the architecture – 'I *could* not join Rome.'[25] During 1845, as news of Newman's conversion filtered through to his former colleagues, Webb's diary becomes increasingly gloomy: 'bad news thickens';[26] and again, 'even music could not stop my sadness'.[27] In February 1846, a remarkably frank letter from Webb to Neale exposes the dilemma of this ecclesiological generation. Were they to follow Newman or Pusey

> You begin perhaps to feel the logical untenableness of the Anglican position. I dare not ask myself whether I do. There is, however, all the difference in the world between the time when we wrote up roodscreens [in Cambridge] and now. *Now* the whole heart is sick.[28]

By 1850, the Gorham Judgement had revealed once and for all the constitutional weakness of the Established Church. Webb noted the decision in his diary, cautiously (in Latin), and with foreboding: 'Judicium in re Gorham . . ., adversus Episc.[opum] Oxoniense datum fuit!! Deus nos protegat.'[29]

To his old friend Neale, he confides that he can 'scarcely hope to outlive this hurricane' as an Anglican. Yet outlive it he did, though only two years later he admits:

22 Diary, 19 Oct. 1839: Oxford, Bodleian Library, SC 44750 (e406).
23 Ibid., 21 March 1841.
24 H. Chadwick, *Tradition and Exploration: Collected Papers on Theology and the Church* (London, 1994), p. 167.
25 Diary, MS letters: Oxford, Bodleian Library, SC 44753 (f.97).
26 Diary, 3 Nov. 1845: Oxford, Bodleian Library, SC 44752 (e.408).
27 Ibid., 31 Oct. 1845.
28 Ibid., MS letters: Bodleian Library, SC 44752 (e.403).
29 Ibid., 9 March 1850: Oxford, Bodleian Library, SC 44754 (e.409).

we must accept the lay interference or shut up shop. In theory I am for the Roman line; and if anything ever drives me to Rome it will be, I suspect, the triumph of the lay element *chez nous* – even though by joining Rome I should become *of* the laity [i.e. without Holy Orders].[30]

It is hard to resist the conclusion that – as he admitted to Neale – what prevented Webb from 'going over' was in the end a mixture of 'pride, timidity and love of ease'.[31]

★ ★ ★

Unlike the Oxford Movement, the Cambridge Movement concentrated on aesthetics rather than theology, and thus managed to stay within the Anglican fold. Webb's generation believed they were calling in the Middle Ages to redress the philistinism and indifference of the Georgian Establishment. Georgian churches, he complains,

or rather sermon-houses, for they are not fit for prayer, remind one rather of auction or assembly rooms: the inside being full of comfortable boxes, and the outside having a fine portico [where] . . . carriages roll up with pride. . . . [And] most of the mischief comes from pues . . . pues half-roofed like country villas, and sometimes even *embattled* . . . [sometimes actually] fitted up like a drawing-room, with fireplace and chimney, and a separate entrance.[32]

'Sometimes', he laments, 'there isn't even a font': in one archiepiscopal city he actually saw an ancient font 'put out of the church to catch the rain from a water-spout. This is too painful . . . to dwell upon.'[33] Oh, for the full splendour of

---

[30] Ibid., Diary, MS letters. See similarly [B. Webb], 'The Report on the Commission of Ritual', *SatR*, 24 (1867), pp. 281–2.

[31] Lawson, *Letters of Neale*, p. 87: Webb to Neale, 10 Nov. 1844. For an illuminating discussion of the roots of Tractarian theology, see P. B. Nockles, *The Oxford Movement in Context: Anglican High Churchmanship, 1760–1857* (Cambridge, 1994).

[32] [B. Webb], *A Few Words to Churchwardens II, suited to Town and Manufacturing Parishes* (7th edn, London, 1851), p. 5.

[33] Ibid., p. 8.

sacramental symbolism! Such dreaming, Webb explains, is not just wallowing in a 'morbid excess of ceremonial'; it is a true awakening – symbolized in sign, in art, in hallowed practice – a 'waking up from the torpor and indifference of the Georgian era';[34] a revolution of the spirit. And the instrument of this revolution was to be the new science of Ecclesiology – seen, for example, at full blast in the new parish church of St Peter's, Leeds (R. D. Chantrell, 1839–41).[35]

Now ecclesiology means the science of church design, though to theologians it can also mean the study of 'the Church' as a mystical entity. But the late Canon Clarke put it better when he explained that ecclesiology is to church building as astrology is to astronomy.[36] In other words it was not so much the science as the mystique of church design. In practical terms, its implications were polymathic. 'Ecclesiology', Webb tells us,

> is . . . different. . . from mere Church architecture. . . . [It includes both Church architecture] and all its collateral branches of information. . . . First [the ecclesiologist] must be well versed in history, especially Church history: antiquities are, of course, a part of his study: of masonry and carpentry he should have some idea: music, so far as Ecclesiastical compositions are concerned, comes within what he requires: he must be able to draw: mechanics are also necessary: something of geology he should know . . .; the glazier's art is by no means below him: with embroidery, tapestry, and the like, he has much to do: of the goldsmith's craft he should know something . . .: of the potter's [enough] for encaustic tiles: some knowledge of the value of

[34] [B. Webb], review [App., no. 246], *SatR*, 38 (1874), pp. 803–4, 830–2.

[35] St Peter's was built for Dean Hook; the nearby church of St Saviour's (J. M. Derick, 1842–5) was built for Dr Pusey, with Webb's advice. See H. P. Liddon, *Life of Pusey*, 2 (London, 1893), pp. 476–80. For the context of ecclesiology, see N. Yates, *Buildings, Faith and Worship: the Liturgical Arrangement of Anglican Churches, 1600–1900* (Oxford, 1991) and G. Rowell, *The Vision Glorious: Themes and Personalities of the Catholic Revival in Anglicanism* (Oxford, 1983).

[36] B. F. L. Clarke, *Church Builders of the 19th century* (London, 1938; revised 1969), p. 78.

labour and the price of materials [would be useful] . . .:
some acquaintance with sculpture . . . and [enough] . . .
mathematics . . . for the computation of the calendar.[37]

In all this the Editor of the *Ecclesiologist* was expected to
share. Certainly, when it came to such arcane matters as 'low
side windows' or lychnoscopes, nobody was more learned
than the Revd Benjamin Webb.[38] When the occasion
warranted it, he could be a devastating reviewer.[39]

★ ★ ★

But first we must conjure up the excitement which fired this
generation of Anglicans, the ecstasy of ecclesiology. Neale
puts imaginary words into the mouth of his young companion, Benjamin Webb:

you cannot imagine the sublimity of a procession [at]
Amiens. . ... The stupendous height of the vaulted roof, –
the rich foliage of the piers – the tall lancet arches
throwing themselves upwards, – the interlacings of the
decorated window-tracery – the richness of the stained
glass, – the glow of the sunlight on the southern chapels,
– the knotted intricacies of the vaulting ribs, – the
flowers, and wreaths, and holy symbols that hang self-
poised over the head, – the graceful shafts of the
triforium, – the carved angels that with outstretched
wings keep guard over the sacred building, – the low,
yet delicately carved choir-stalls, – the gorgeous altar
faintly seen beyond them, – the sublime apse, with its
inimitably slim lancets, carrying the eye up, higher and
higher, through the dark cloister-gallery, through the
blaze of the crimson clerestory, to the marble grandeur
of the fretted roof, – lights, and carvings, and jewels,
and gold, and the sunny brightness of the nave, and the
solemn greyness of the choir. . ... The sweet music floats

[37] J. M. Neale, *Hierologus; or the Church Tourists* (London, 1843), p. 189. Neale put
Webb's words into the mouth of 'Paleologus'.
[38] E.g. 'E.E.' [B. Webb], 'On anker-windows or lychnoscopes', *Eccl.*, 19, ns 16
(1858), pp. 86–8.
[39] E.g. [B. Webb], review [App. no. 57], *Eccl.*, 19, ns 16 (1858), pp. 103–5.

along from the choir – the Amen bursts from the congregation. Now the organ . . . takes up the strain, sweetly and solemnly, like the music of far-off angels. . . . White-robed boys strew the way with rose leaves; there is the gleaming and the perfume of silver censers; there are the rich silver crosses and the pastoral staff; there is the sumptuous pall that covers the Host; there is an endless train of priests, with copes and vestments, bright as the hues of a summer sunset, gemmed with the jewels of many lands, lustrous with gold, and chased with flowers and wreaths and devices of pearl . . . all bearing, one symbol, the Cross . . . every knee is bent, every head bowed . . . fainter and fainter [comes] the holy hymn as they recede eastward . . . [until] with faint and mellowed sweetness, it steals [even] from the distant shrine of Our Lady . . .[40]

For Webb, a medieval church – however fragmented – was not just an antiquarian's laboratory; it was the sacramental system in stone. Restoration was 'an end, and a noble end too . . . but it is also the means to a higher and a nobler: it is to lead, by visible loveliness, to invisible beauty . . . a journey from Sion . . . to Jerusalem'.[41] By contrast, puritanism – with all its destruction of images – was *'the abomination that maketh desolate'*.[42] 'How glorious', he exclaims, 'would be the re-edification of [our ruined monasteries], *as a work of religion.'*[43]

Well, perhaps. But in what style?

★ ★ ★

As a young Camdenian, Webb thought English Decorated – as in the drama of Lincoln's west front – the acme of Gothic art.[44] 'In York you feel that you are gazing on a magnificent cathedral; in Lincoln you are lost to all considerations of time and place, and worship the Invisible alone . . .. [Still] nothing

---

[40] Neale, *Hierologus*, pp. 253–5. Neale assured Webb that 'Montalembert has read "Hierologus" and is delighted with it, and more particularly with the parts relating to Abbeys' (Lawson, *Letters of Neale*, p. 70; 11 Jan. 1844).

[41] Neale, *Hierologus*, p. 292.

[42] Ibid., p. 17.

[43] Ibid., p. 18.

[44] Ibid., p. 36.

short of [divine] inspiration could have produced either.'[45] By comparison, French Flamboyant – as at Notre Dame de l'Épine – seemed to him decoratively adjectival: 'a string of epithets without a substantive'.[46] Similarly, 'the besetting sin of Perpendicular work' was its 'want of unity of ideas';[47] in other words it suffered from grandeur of conception frittered away by ancillary form. So he preferred East Anglia to the West of England; equally fine were Lincolnshire and North-amptonshire: 'the queens of Ecclesiological splendour'. His favourite churches were perhaps Heckington, Lincolnshire, and Hawton, Nottinghamshire: 'the fairest parish churches in the kingdom'.[48] And, top of the list, Snettisham in Norfolk – its west window, incidentally, Pugin reputedly said he would willingly die for. Like most of this generation of Goths, Webb was hugely impressed by Pugin.[49] He remembered him as 'one of the most remarkable men of his generation . . . impetuous, prejudiced, but honest and sincere', with all the eccentricity of 'real genius'.[50] He admired his writings, he respected his buildings, and he delighted in his company. But, like Neale and Hope, he could never quite bring himself to follow Pugin, or Newman, to Rome.

During the early 1840s, the criticism of the ecclesiologists was mainly destructive: damning newly built churches as incorrect in style and plan. Of Barry's St Peter's Brighton (1824–8), for instance, Webb notes, 'That church was one of the first fruits of the [revival]', and though 'imposing' as a whole,

---

45   Ibid., p. 236.
46   Ibid., p. 38.
47   Ibid., p. 37.
48   Ibid., p. 236.
49   In 1841–4 Webb saw Pugin frequently in Cambridge and London. E.g. 'Lionised Pugin about [Cambridge] and saw him off on the Lynn coach. Delighted with his geniality and vigour': B. Webb, 'Diary', 29 Nov. 1842, Oxford, Bodleian Library, SC 44750 (e.406).
50   [B. Webb], reviews [App. nos. 135, 156], Eccl., 22, ns 19 (1861), pp. 305–10, 367–9 (reply). While advising Pusey as to the design of St Saviour's Leeds, he was himself acting as intermediary for stained glass designs by Pugin (Liddon, Life of Pusey, 2, pp. 476–80). In the early days of ecclesiology, Webb had praised Pugin – albeit anonymously – as a 'most eminent and profound architect and antiquary': [B. Webb], review [App. no. 5], Eccl., 1 (1842), p. 98. For this he was attacked (The Record, July 1842), and in later years he was more cautious.

there is not a detail in it which will bear examination. There is no pretence to a regular style; the outside is loaded with pierced battlements and other frippery. The tower, when examined closely, is perfectly ludicrous: it looks as if the upper part of one, and the lower part of another, had been stuck together, and would not fit.[51]

For Webb, in the mid 1840s, the model Camdenian church was R. C. Carpenter's St Mary Magdalen, Munster Square (1849–52). This north London church echoed fourteenth-century English prototypes fairly closely; though it was becoming increasingly obvious that medieval *country* shrines were hardly sensible models for nineteenth-century *town* churches.

Gradually, in pursuit of urban prototypes, the ecclesiologists began to look elsewhere, to Europe, and especially to Italy. They pinned their hopes on a new architect, William Butterfield, and a new type of town church. All Saints, Margaret Street (1849; 1850–9) became the new ecclesiological ideal: an urban church, Continental in inspiration, liturgically planned and symbolically decorated, but using modern materials and techniques, and adapting those new materials and techniques to traditional liturgical and sacramental ends. In this changing aesthetic – particularly the changing attitude to polychromy – Benjamin Webb played a key role. At its root lay a change of perception, and this in turn stemmed from a broadening of aesthetic horizons.

During the later 1840s, English attitudes to medieval Italian Gothic changed from curiosity to reverence. In 1835 Professor Robert Willis of Cambridge – perhaps England's greatest architectural historian: the man who first explained the Gothic vault – began the process of rescuing Italian medieval architecture from 'contempt' and 'undeserved neglect'.[52] But English Gothic revivalists only began to show a serious interest in Italy from 1845 onwards. That was the year in which Benjamin Webb returned from north Italy,

51 Neale, *Hierologus*, p. 39.
52 R. Willis, *Remarks on the Architecture of the Middle Ages, especially of Italy*, 1 (London, 1835), p. iii.

singing the praises of Italian Gothic; its colour, its massiveness of form, its simplicity of detail. First in a lecture of 1845 on the adaptation of Gothic to tropical climates;[53] then in a definitive publication – *Sketches of Continental Ecclesiology* (1848) – he set out the argument for a swing away from fourteenth-century English Decorated. Siena turned out to be a revelation. When he visited Verona, he found it 'dreamlike'.[54] When he visited Venice it was again 'the realisation of a dream'.[55] The Frari, for instance, he thought 'one of the most beautiful [churches] in Italy'. 'It is of the most severe simplicity, and of amazing grandeur of proportion, and is built of brick.' He especially enjoyed the first vespers of the Assumption sung there with 'an orchestra . . . and innumerable tapers. The service contrasted much with the extreme simplicity and sternness of the church.'[56] At Pavia, he found St Pantaleone (Sta Maria del Carmine) 'a magnificent brick church'; its west front 'very fine and richly moulded', in 'a hard glazed . . . brick', with 'very beautiful reliefs . . . in terra cotta'.[57] And at Cremona, the Torazzo or campanile seemed 'really very handsome', and the Baptistry 'very impressive' from the 'great simplicity' of its brickwork.[58]

Webb's report on such things to the Ecclesiological Society was quickly followed by the Revd Thomas James's pamphlet on *The Use of Brick in Ecclesiastical Architecture* (1847). James had travelled in north Italy towards the end of 1846. What he saw convinced him that the time was ripe for a brick revival: practical, ornamental, 'a real and economical style for modern churches', 'a material fully capable of being turned by a master-hand to the purposes of a high style of Ecclesiastical Architecture'.[59] Camdenian Gothic – fourteenth-century English Decorated – was about to give way to a new ecclesiology based on continental prototypes.

[53] B. Webb, 'On Pointed Architecture as adapted to tropical climates', *Transactions of the Ecclesiological Society* (1845), pp. 199–218.

[54] B. Webb, *Sketches of Continental Ecclesiology* (London, 1848), p. 242.

[55] Ibid., p. 299

[56] Ibid., pp. 277–81.

[57] Ibid., p. 226.

[58] Ibid., pp. 233–4.

[59] T. James, 'On the use of brick in ecclesiastical architecture', *Fourth Report of the Architectural Society of the Archdeaconry of Northampton* (1847), pp. 25–37.

In the previous decade English publications on medieval Italy – by Thomas Hope, Robert Willis, or Gally Knight – had been concerned with history, typology, and structure. Now the accent was on materials, on decoration, on colour, and all the old stereotypes of taste were overturned. Willis had drawn the line at Siena Cathedral: he thought zebra stripes were utterly 'destructive of architectural grandeur'.[60] Gally Knight thought it merely 'peculiar'.[61] But when Webb entered he felt as if he were in Westminster Abbey.[62] Knight found St Zeno at Verona in parts 'ludicrous', in general 'curious'.[63] But for Webb it was a building 'of prodigious merit'.[64] The most that Knight could say for St Mark's Venice, was that it seemed 'venerable and picturesque'.[65] For Webb its style was 'unique', and its 'gorgeousness of construction quite beyond description'.[66]

It was Benjamin Webb, therefore, not John Ruskin, who introduced Italian Gothic to the ecclesiologists. And, thanks to Webb's diary, we know that it was indeed he who wrote the famous review of *The Seven Lamps* in *The Ecclesiologist* for 1850.[67] Ruskin might be 'an enthusiast', he explained; he might be a 'transcendentalist', but his 'marvellous intelligence' had produced something far more important than a mere 'architect's *vade mecum*'. Here was an ethical justification for a new aesthetic.

★ ★ ★

How did this change of aesthetic affect the progress of the Gothic Revival in England?

Looking back, in the late 1850s, to the early days of the movement, Webb recalled that its original justification lay in the evils of the Picturesque and Neo-Classicism: 'when

---

60 Willis, *Remarks*, p. 12.

61 H. Gally Knight, *Ecclesiastical Architecture of Italy from the Time of Constantine to the 15th century*, 2 vols (London, 1842–4), i, p. xxiv.

62 Webb, *Sketches*, p. 381.

63 Knight, *Ecclesiastical Architecture*, pp. xi–xii.

64 Webb, *Sketches*, p. 251.

65 Knight, *Ecclesiastical Architecture*, p. xxxi.

66 Webb, *Sketches*, pp. 268–9.

67 [B. Webb], review [App. no. 12], *Eccl.*, 10, ns 7 (1850), pp. 111–20. Webb's only serious criticism related to Ruskin's 'unnecessary abuse of the un-reformed [Catholic] Church', a 'blemish' Ruskin himself removed in later editions.

things had come to their worst ... the first step towards
amendment was of necessity a step backwards'.[68] That had
been the message of Pugin's *Contrasts*: an escape from the false
Picturesque of the Regency – St Mary, Eversholt Street,
Euston (Inwood; 1824–7), for example – to the 'true
Picturesque' of Puginian Gothic, as at Cotton College,
Staffordshire (A. W. Pugin; 1840–8). Architects had first to
become literate in Gothic. As E. A. Freeman put it, this 'first
phase of ecclesiology was simple antiquarianism'.[69] Then,
once the old Gothic alphabet had been re-learned, it was
possible – in the post-Puginian generation – to build up a
new architectural language. Even Pugin's best work – St
Augustine's Ramsgate (1843–52), for instance – came to seem
just 'a happy reproduction', not 'a vigorous original design'.[70]
'The earliest stage of the revival was past', Webb noted, 'and
the eclectic period began.'[71] The turning-point, he believed,
was Butterfield's All Saints, Margaret Street.

Thanks to Benjamin's Webb's diary, it is now possible to
state that it was he who wrote one of the most famous pieces
in the whole of nineteenth-century architectural criticism, the
Ecclesiologist's commentary of 1859 on Butterfield's celebrated
church.[72] His was the comparison between Butterfield and
Millais; his the reference to 'deliberate ... ugliness'; his the
notion – developed from Coventry Patmore – of 'Pre-
Raphaelitism' in architecture, 'its coarse but honest originality', its 'same dread of beauty'. At All Saints, Webb
spotted from the start the relevance – the 'reality' – of
brickwork in an urban context; the infinite potential of brick
and tile and marble for polychrome pattern; the 'sublime'
abstraction of reductive forms. Some of the colouring – the
green voussoirs for instance – seemed to him over-strident;
the patterning above the chancel arch 'fragmentary and
crude', the clerestory glass mere 'gaudy bits of colour' – and
yet, this was indeed a memorable church: '*the* original work

68 [B. Webb], 'The prospects of art in England', *Bentley's Quarterly Review*, 1 (1859), pp. 143–82.
69 E. A. Freeman, *History of Architecture* (London, 1849), p. 4.
70 [B. Webb], review [App. no. 156], *Eccl.*, 22, ns 19 (1861), pp. 305–10, 367–9.
71 [Webb], 'Prospects of art', pp. 143–82.
72 [B. Webb], 'All Saints, Margaret Street', *Eccl.*, 20, ns 17 (1859), pp. 184–9.

of modern English art . . . a tentative solution of the problem [of] what the architecture of the future was to be'.[73]

But if that future style was ever to emerge, it would have to emerge in secular form. Hence the importance of the Foreign Office competition of 1858–9, especially Scott's Gothic design. 'This', Webb recalled, 'was the climacteric period of the revival. It trembled in the balance.'[74] Up to that point, the movement had made 'a steady and rapid march . . . [towards] triumphant success'.[75] The modern Gothic seemed to possess just that 'vitality of artistic power and the earnest moral conviction' needed to create a New Style based on the principles of 'progressive eclecticism'.[76] From this 'judicious eclecticism' would emerge 'a distinctive new style', as a kind of 'off-shoot of the Pointed revival'.[77] Scott's mixed Gothic – later realized at St Pancras Hotel (1865–74) – seemed to represent 'a genuine instalment of [that] improved and developed Pointed [mode which] may well be thought the characteristic style of our age'.[78] Here, or so it seemed, was 'the revived national style – a style so characteristic of our age that it is beginning to be called . . . Victorian'.[79] In 1859 'English architecture [seemed] . . . full of promise and overflowing with vigour. We stand', Webb claimed, 'on the threshold . . . of a great future.' There was only one cloud on the horizon: 'the mill and the factory have still be to rescued from a mere negation of style and clothed in a becoming architectural dress'. For 'no one', he admits, 'can ever conceive of a mere "architecture of construction" without [the] decorative [or] distinguishing characteristics of what we call style.'[80] Conversely, the *reductio ad absurdum* of the Ruskinian approach – architecture reduced to decoration – never appealed to him. 'We denounce the idea', he wrote, apropos the 1862 Exhibition, 'that a great building is but the

73 [Webb], 'Prospects of art', pp. 143–82.
74 Ibid.
75 [B. Webb], review [App. no. 45], *SatR*, 5 (1858), pp. 447–9.
76 Ibid.
77 [B. Webb], review [App. no. 54], *Eccl.*, 19, ns 16 (1858), p. 23.
78 [Webb], 'Prospects of art', pp. 143–82.
79 [Webb], 'The question of style for the new public offices', *SatR*, 6 (1858), pp. 303–5.
80 [Webb], 'Prospects of art', pp. 143–82.

lay figure on which the terra cotta moulder and the mosaicist and the sculptor are to hang their tags'; that way lies 'chaos . . . not cosmos'.[81]

There in a nutshell was the Victorian conundrum; and architects were already grappling with it, and would occasionally do so successfully: as at Ponton and Gough's corn warehouse on the Welsh Back, Bristol (1869–70), for instance. Webb, however, remained curiously detached from this developing industrial eclecticism.

Still, by 1860, his confidence was becoming quite infectious. In the ecclesiastical field, he announced, 'the battle of the styles has been fought and won'. In the secular field – Scott's Kelham Hall, Nottinghamshire (1858–62) is a good example – 'the war is still waging . . . though . . . with every prospect of a right conclusion. . . . The tide has turned in favour of the national Pointed style, and it is not yet high water'. Even Lord Palmerston's interference over the Foreign Office was no more than a temporary setback:

> We may be fated to have an Italianate Foreign Office, but . . . the prevailing style of the next age [will] be an offshoot and descendant of the Gothic . . . in another ten years the partisans of debased Italian will be an insignificant minority. . . . The pointed style, suitably developed, and enriched from the spoils of other times and other lands, will adapt itself with marvellous plasticity to every want of our modern civilisation – the palace and the cottage, the public office and school and institute, the bridge and railway station, the shop, the warehouse, the factory, and the mill.[82]

And two years after that, in 1862, he was just as optimistic. 'We see', he wrote, 'no reason to think that the progress of the Gothic Revival has reached its limit.'[83]

---

[81] [B. Webb], 'The new exhibition building', *SatR*, 12 (1861), p. 351.

[82] [B. Webb], 'Domestic architecture', *Bentley's Quarterly Review*, 2 (1860), pp. 474–517.

[83] [B. Webb], 'British architecture in the International Exhibition', *SatR*, 14 (1862), pp. 509–10. The aim was still a real 'nineteenth-century Gothic' ([B. Webb], review [App. no. 193], *SatR*, 15 [1863], p. 668); emerging from 'the eclectic style of

Ten years later, however, he was not so sure. 'Who can tell', he admitted in 1872, 'whether the Gothic Revival has culminated [no doubt he was thinking of Street's Law Courts, 1868–82], or has begun to wane again, in the perpetual flux and reflux of thought and sentiment.'[84] And the year after that, in 1873, he wondered whether the prospects not only for architecture, but for any real revival of the decorative arts, were at all promising. 'We are not so hopeful', he confessed, 'on this point as we once were.'[85]

The problem was that the movement's principles of development had never been established. Did you start developing where Gothic culminated, in the fourteenth century; or where it stopped, in the sixteenth? Or did you go back to where it all began, in the twelfth and thirteenth centuries? All three methods had been tried: Perpendicular, as in Pugin and Barry's Houses of Parliament (1840 onwards); Decorated, as in Carpenter's St Paul, Brighton (1846–8); early French, as in Burges's Cork Cathedral (1863 onwards). But the Victorian Style, that elusive vernacular, stubbornly refused to emerge. Or else it appeared in forms which seemed aesthetically indefensible: Ruskin's Frankenstein Monsters, caricatures of their medieval prototypes. It was Webb who spotted this link between the Gothic Revival and the Pre-Raphaelites, between Butterfield and Millais. Both art and architecture had come to share the same characteristics; both were products of 'a self-conscious, revivalist and eclectic age'. So too with music: Wagner's *Lohengrin*, he believed, fell into the same trap, sacrificing composition to detail, mistaking episodic reality for conceptual truth.[86]

Anyway, architects had once again begun to look elsewhere. As the 1870s progressed, the supremacy of Gothic was first threatened and then eclipsed by that congeries of revivals known as Old English and Queen Anne. The signs had been there in the mid-1860s for those with eyes to see.

Pointed architecture which is now making such hopeful progress' ([B. Webb], review [App. no. 202], *SatR*, 16 [-1863], p. 532).

84 [B. Webb], review [App. no. 242], *SatR*, 35 (1873), pp. 315–16.

85 [B. Webb], review [App. no. 241], *SatR*, 35 (1873), pp. 255–6.

86 [B. Webb], review [App. no. 200], *SatR*, 35 (1873), pp. 333–4.

Just as Whig versus Tory had given way to the subtleties of Conservative Liberal versus Liberal Conservative, so the old polarities of Gothic versus Classic had dissolved in the complexity of a new eclecticism.[87] The mid-Victorian dream – Benjamin Webb's dream – the dream of universal Gothic, was abandoned. In its place came a grudging acceptance of the pluralist ethos: not one style but many. Senior ecclesiologists were horrified. As Beresford Hope put it, this Aesthetic tendency – this separation of art and authority; this division of art and morality – seemed not only 'nonsense', but actually 'immoral nonsense'.[88]

How did the Gothic pundits react? Benjamin Webb simply lapsed into silence. Burges, Street, and Butterfield were all too set in their respective ways to change their styles in the 1870s. Butterfield went on producing weaker variations of his own formula: Webb thought Keble College, Oxford (1868–78), represented a distinct decline after the promise of All Saints, Margaret Street.[89] But other Goths were more flexible: they abandoned muscularity and settled for sensibility; they rediscovered the flexibility of late Gothic; they went back to the fifteenth and sixteenth centuries.[90]

This shift back to Perpendicular certainly shocked some of the older ecclesiologists. In the 1840s the ecclesiologists had regarded Perpendicular as symbolizing 'worldly pomp instead of the Catholic Faith'. 'It is a style', they announced, 'which we trust will never be revived, and which it is much to be wished had never been invented.'[91] To Gilbert Scott it represented 'corruption and decay'.[92] To Ruskin it was simply 'the despicable Perpendicular'.[93] Now, in 1872–3,

---

[87]   [B. Webb], 'Architecture in 1864', *SatR*, 17 (1864), p. 783. Even an anti-Goth like Robert Kerr was aiming 'his classic bow with many an arrow drawn from the Gothic quiver' ([B. Webb] reviewing R. Kerr, *The Gentleman's House* [1865], *SatR*, 19 [1865], p. 707).

[88]   [Hope], 'Art and morality', *SatR*, 35 (1873), pp. 273–4.

[89]   [B. Webb] review [App. no. 242], *SatR*, 33 (1872), pp. 382–3.

[90]   E.g. J. D. Sedding, *Building News*, 30 (1876), p. 267.

[91]   J. F. White, *The Cambridge Movement* (Cambridge, 1962), pp. 87, 91; K. Clark, *Gothic Revival*, 3rd edn, ed. J. Mordaunt Crook (London, 1995), p. 154.

[92]   G. G. Scott, *A Plea for the Faithful Restoration of our Ancient Churches* (London, 1850), p. 93.

[93]   J. Ruskin, *Seven Lamps* (London, 1849), p. 55.

G. G. Scott jnr proclaimed it the climax of Gothic art.[94] At Cattistock in Dorset, for example, in 1874, young Scott quite eclipsed his father's second pointed church with a Perpendicular tower modelled on nearby Charminster. And during the next two decades, young Scott, G. F. Bodley, J. P. Seddon, J. D. Sedding, T. G. Jackson, and W. D. Caröe proceeded to demonstrate the apparently infinite flexibility of late Gothic forms. In no more than forty years, the Victorian Gothic revival had indeed come full circle: from the Gothic of A. W. Pugin right round – via Anglo-Italian, Early French, and Eclectic – to the Gothic of G. F. Bodley.

★ ★ ★

So how should we sum up the achievements of Benjamin Webb? He was a principal agent in a double revolution: Anglican Ecclesiology and High Victorian Gothic; one of the very few artistic revolutions which began in this country and eventually swept the world. Its formulation involved 'a new science . . . [ecclesiology], combining architecture, art and ritual';[95] and a new style, a Victorian Style. Of the three men who engineered that revolution – Neale, Webb, and Hope – Neale was an enthusiast with no head for tactics; Hope was a grandee with influence and an obsession with aesthetics; Webb all his life was in love with ritual, but at the same time he was a steadying hand, a moderator, the man in the engine room of ecclesiology. As Hope put it, Webb 'never wasted himself by the superfluous indulgence of creating otiose change';[96] adding, in a later comment, 'Neale, with all his genius, was not judicious.'[97]

---

[94] G. G. Scott, Jnr, *Modern Village Churches* (London, 1873); *Church Architecture* (London, 1872); 'Modern Town Churches', *Building World*, 4 (1880), pp. 422–4, 5 (1880), pp. 11–14, 52–4.

[95] [A. Beresford Hope], *SatR*, 60 (1885), p. 772; obituary.

[96] [A. Beresford Hope], *The Guardian*, 2 Dec. 1885; reprinted in *Church Quarterly Review*, 21 (1885–6), 461–4.

[97] [A. Beresford Hope], *SatR*, 60 (1885), p. 772. See J. M. Neale, *Extreme Men: a Letter to A. J. B. Beresford Hope* (London, 1865). In 1846, Neale warned Webb: 'I cannot consent to have an element of compromise introduced into the *Ecclesiologist*' (Towle, *Neale*, p. 135). Similarly, he considered Hope to be 'infected with the miserable compromising spirit of the day' (Lawson, *Letters of Neale*, p. 93). Hope excluded Neale from the *Saturday Review* because he would 'upset the coach with ultraism' (H. W. and T. Law, *The Book of the Beresford Hopes* [London, 1925], p. 215).

Of course there were other factors at work, hugely affecting taste and religious attitudes in the mid-Victorian period: Oxford theology, Birmingham technology, Westminster politics; besides – no doubt – the operation of the *Zeitgeist* (which Webb would have translated as the Holy Spirit). But without the Revd Benjamin Webb the Church of England, in both a physical and a spiritual sense, would certainly have been very different. He was, as *The Times*' obituary put it – with dry understatement – 'a somewhat distinguished clergyman'.[98]

Royal Holloway and Bedford New College,
University of London

APPENDIX

Books, articles, reviews, letters, etc. by the Revd Benjamin Webb
(Material printed anonymously is indicated with an asterisk)

Note: No list of anonymous writings is ever likely to be complete. This bibliography of Benjamin Webb's literary works is based principally on the direct evidence of his diary; if the criteria for selection were extended to include indirect evidence, the list would be very much longer.

1 Editor, Annual Reports, Ecclesiological Society, 1840–66, re-published in *The Ecclesiologist*, ed. B. Webb, 1–29 (ns 1–3, 4–26) (Cambridge, 1841–5, London, 1846–68).
2 *An Argument for the Greek Origin of the Monogram IHS etc.* (Cambridge Camden Society, 1841).
3 [Joint ed.], R. Montague, Bishop of Norwich, *Articles of Enquiry and Direction for the Diocese of Norwich* [1638] (1841).
4★ [with J. M. Neale], *A Few Words to Churchwardens II, suited to Town and Manufacturing Parishes* (Cambridge Camden Society, 1841; 7th edn, 1851).
5★ Review: J. L. Petit, *Remarks on Church Architecture* (1841), *Eccl.*, 1 (1842), pp. 91–105.

There was no obituary of Neale in the *SatR*; but Hope himself wrote that devoted to Webb's career: 'How much the worship movement owes to Webb's wise, tolerant judgement cannot be overstated' ([Hope], *SatR*, 60 [1885], p. 772).
[98] *The Times*, 1 Dec. 1885, p. 8.

6 [with J. M. Neale], translation and introduction: G. Durandus, *The Symbolism of Churches and Church Ornaments: a translation of the first book of the Rationale Divinorum Officiorum* (Leeds, 1843). Re-issued 1893.

7★ [with J. M. Neale], *A Few Words to Church Builders* (Cambridge Camden Society, 3rd edn, 1844).

8 'On Pointed Architecture as adapted to tropical climates', *Transactions of the Ecclesiological Society*, pt 3 (1845), pp. 199–218.

9 *Sketches of Continental Ecclesiology; or Church Notes in Belgium, Germany and Italy* (1848).

10 [with J. Fuller Russel] Editor: *Hierurgia Anglicana, or Documents and Extracts Illustrative of the Ritual of the Church of England after the Reformation* (Ecclesiological Society, 1848; ed. V. Staley, 2 vols, 1902).

11 [with W. H. Mill] Editor, M. Frank, *Sermons*, Library of Anglo-Catholic Theology (Oxford, 1849).

12★ Review: J. Ruskin, *The Seven Lamps of Architecture* (1849), *Eccl.*, 10, ns 7 (1850), pp. 111–20.

13 Review: A. W. Pugin, *An Earnest Appeal on the Establishment of the Hierarchy* (1851), *Morning Chronicle*, 4 March 1851, p. 6.

14★ 'Great Exhibition: history and construction of the building'; 'Fine Arts of the Exhibition', *Morning Chronicle*, 12 May 1851, pp. 2, 2–3.

15 [with J. M. Neale] Editor, *The Hymnal Noted*, 2 parts (1851–2; 1856).

16 'Archaeological Itinerary of Paris', *SatR*, 1 (1855), p. 36.

17★ Review: J. Labarte, *Arts of the Middle Ages* (1855), *SatR*, 1 (1855), p. 304.

18 'The Lille Cathedral Job', *SatR*, 2 (1856), p. 152.

19★ 'The "Soulages" Collection', *SatR*, 2 (1856), pp. 726–7.

20 Editor, W. H. Mill, *Lectures on the Catechism* (Cambridge, 1856).

21★ Review: A. F. Rio, *De l'art chrétien* (Paris, 1856), *SatR*, 3 (1857), pp. 109–10.

22 Review: E. Young, *Pre-Raffaelitism* (1857), *SatR*, 3 (1857), pp. 332–4.

23 Review: J. A. Crowe and G. B. Gavalcaselle, *Early Flemish Painters* (1857), *SatR*, 3 (1857), pp. 380–1.

24★ Review: 'Exhibition of Art Treasures', *SatR*, 3 (1857), pp. 426–7.

25★ Review: 'The Water-Colours Gallery at Manchester', *SatR*, 4 (1857), pp. 155–6.

26★ Review: 'The Gallery of Original Sketches at Manchester', *SatR*, 4 (1857), pp. 179–80.

27 Review: 'The Galleries of Line and Mezzotint Engravings at Manchester', *SatR*, 4 (1857), pp. 201–2.

28★ Review: 'The Museum of Enamels and Goldsmiths' Work at Manchester', *SatR*, 4 (1857), pp. 263–4.

29★ Review: J. S. Harford, *Life of Michelangelo* (1857), *SatR*, 4 (1857), pp. 265–6.

30★ 'Competition for the Memorial Church at Constantinople', *Eccl.*, 18, ns 14 (1857), pp. 98–116.

31★ 'The Manchester Exhibition of Art Treasures', *Eccl.*, 18, ns 14 (1857), pp. 295–304.

32★ Review: J. Coleman Hart, *Designs for Parish Churches, in the Three Styles of English Church Architecture* (New York, 1857), *Eccl.* 18, ns 14 (1857), pp. 367–9.

33★ Review: 'The Success and Results of the Exhibition of Art Treasures at Manchester', *SatR*, 4 (1857), pp. 370–1.

34★ Review: J. Ruskin, *Elements of Drawing* (1857), *SatR*, 4 (1857), pp. 374–5.

35★ Review: 'Topographical archaeology', *SatR*, 4 (1857), pp. 426–7.

36★ Review: W. Cotton, *Sir Joshua Reynolds* (1856), *SatR*, 4 (1857), pp. 446–8.

37★ Review: K. Kottenkamp, *History of Chivalry and Ancient Armour*, trans. A. Löwy (1857), *SatR*, 4 (1857), pp. 586–7.

38★ Review: 'Recent literature of art', *Christian Remembrancer*, 34 (1857), pp. 267–99.

39★ 'The Mahometan architecture of Southern India', *SatR*, 5 (1858), pp. 60–1.

40★ Review: 'The new pictures at the National Gallery', *SatR*, 5 (1858), pp. 12–13.

41★ Review: J. Ruskin, *The Political Economy of Art* (1857), *SatR*, 5 (1858), pp. 90–1.

42★ Review: G. F. Waagen, *Galleries and Cabinets of Art in Great Britain* (1857), *SatR*, 5 (1858), pp. 195–6.

43★ Review: 'Proposed memorial of the Great Exhibition of 1851', *SatR*, 5 (1858), pp. 238–9.

44★ 'The Photographic Exhibition, 1858', *SatR*, 5 (1858), pp. 344–5.

45★ Review: G. G. Scott, *Secular and Domestic Architecture* (1858), *SatR*, 5 (1858), pp. 447–9.

46★ Review: 'The Water Colour Exhibitions', *SatR*, 5 (1858), pp. 531–2.

47★ Review: Mrs Anna Jameson, *Memoirs of the Early Italian Painters* (1858), SatR, 5 (1858), pp. 593–4.

48★ Review: J. Marryat, *A History of Pottery and Porcelain, Medieval and Modern* (1857), SatR, 5 (1858), p. 641.

49★ Review: [J. P. Sedden], *Memoir and Letters of the Late Thomas Seddon* (1858), SatR, 6 (1858), pp. 167–8.

50★ Review: 'The first exhibition of modern art manufactures at South Kensington', SatR, 6 (1858), pp. 279–80.

51★ 'The questions of style for the new public offices', SatR, 6 (1858), pp. 303–5.

52★ Review: J. Tanswell, *The History and Antiquities of Lambeth* (1858), SatR, 6 (1858), pp. 380–2.

53★ Review: E. and S. T. Polehampton, eds, *A Memoir, Letters, and Diary of Rev. H. S. Polehampton, Chaplain of Lucknow* (1858), SatR, 6 (1858), pp. 507–8.

54★ Review: G. G. Scott, *Remarks on Secular and Domestic Architecture, Present and Future* (1857), Eccl., 19, ns 16 (1858), pp. 16–23.

55★ 'Blenheim Palace Chapel', Eccl., 19, ns 16 (1858), pp. 71–3.

56 [as 'E. E.'], 'On anker-windows or lychnoscopes', Eccl., 19, ns 16 (1858), pp. 86–8.

57★ '*The Atlantis* on the structural characteristics of the basilicas', Eccl., 19, ns 16 (1858), pp. 103–5.

58★ Review: A. J. Beresford Hope, *The Common Sense of Art* (1858), SatR, 7 (1859), pp. 96–7.

59★ Review: Mrs Unwins, *A Memoir of Thomas Unwins*, 2 vols (1858), SatR, 7 (1859), pp. 217–18.

60★ 'The Sion College report on the city churches', SatR, 7 (1859), pp. 682–3.

61★ Review: M. E. Chevreul, *The Laws of Contrast of Colour* (1859), SatR, 7 (1859), pp. 756–7.

62★ Review: J. Ruskin, *The Two Paths* (1859), SatR, 8 (1859), pp. 260–1.

63★ Review: Black's *Guide to Scotland* (1859), SatR, 8 (1859), pp. 343–4.

64★ Review: J. Raine, ed., *The Fabric Rolls of York Minster* (Surtees Society, 35 [1858]), SatR, 8 (1859), pp. 427–8.

65★ Review: *Facsimile of the Sketchbook of Wilars d'Honecort*, A. Darcell, J. R. B. Lassus, J. Quicherat, and R. Willis, eds, SatR, (1859), pp. 518–20.

66★ Review: T. Hudson Turner, *Domestic Architecture in England from the Conquest to the end of the 13th century* (1851); J. H. Parker, *Domestic Architecture in England from Edward I to Richard*

II (1853); J. H. Parker, *Domestic Architecture in England from Richard II to Henry VIII* (1859), SatR, 8 (1859), pp. 647–8.

67★ Review: *Catalogue of Antiquities, Works of Art and Historical Scottish Relics* (Archaeological Institute, Edinburgh, 1859), SatR, 8 (1859), pp. 679–80.

68★ 'The prospects of art in England', *Bentley's Quarterly Review*, 1 (1859), pp. 143–82.

69★ 'The art exhibitions of 1859', *Bentley's Quarterly Review*, 1 (1859), pp. 582–628.

70 *Notes illustrative of the Parish of Sheen* (1859) [supplement to the *Lichfield Diocesan Church Calendar*, 1859].

71★ 'All Saints, Margaret Street', *Eccl.*, 20, ns 17 (1859), pp. 184–9.

72★ Review: *Directorium Anglicanum*, ed. J. Purchas (1858), *Eccl.*, 20, ns 18 (1859), pp. 31–4.

73★ Review: J. B. Waring, *The Arts connected with Architecture, illustrated by Examples, in Central Italy, from the 13th to the 15th Century* (1858), *Eccl.*, 20, ns 18 (1859), pp. 412–14.

74 'Dr. Mill and the Sanskrit Professorship at Oxford', *The Times*, 2 Nov. 1860, p. 10.

75★ Review: J. M. Neale, *A Commentary on the Psalms*, i (1860), *Christian Remembrancer*, 39 (1860), pp. 264–82.

76★ 'Domestic Architecture', *Bentley's Quarterly Review*, 2 (1860), pp. 474–517.

77★ Review: G. E. Freeman and F. H. Salvin, *Falconry* (1859), SatR, 9 (1860), pp. 20–1.

78★ Review: 'Two Parish Histories', SatR, 9 (1860), pp. 53–5.

79★ Review: F. Field, ed., *Vetus Testamentum Graece iuxta LXX Interpres* (1859), SatR, 9 (1860), pp. 118–19.

80★ Review: 'Stanford's Library Maps', SatR, 9 (1860), pp. 154–5.

81★ Review: M. Walcott, *The Cathedrals of the United Kingdom* (1860), and *The Minsters and Abbey Ruins of the United Kingdom* (1860), SatR, 9 (1860), pp. 250–1.

82★ Review: [Mrs. Burns], *Undercurrents Overlooked* (1860), SatR, 9 (1860), pp. 310–12.

83★ Review: T. L. Donaldson, *Architectura Numismatica* (1859), SatR, 9 (1860), pp. 376–7.

84★ Review: C. F. Secretan, *Life and Times of the Pious Robert Nelson* (1860), SatR, 9 (1860), pp. 408–9.

85★ Review: *The Publications of the Arundel Society, 1858* (1860), SatR, 9 (1860), pp. 438–9.

86★ 'Thirteenth Report of the Commissioners in Lunacy', SatR

(1860), pp. 464–6.

87* Review: I. Taylor, *Ultimate Civilisation* (1860), *SatR*, 9 (1860), pp. 533–4.

88* Review: J. P. Berjeau, ed., *Canticum Canticarum* (1860); N. H. J. Westlake, *Illustrated Old Testament History* (1860), *SatR*, 9 (1860), pp. 614–15.

89* Review: G. W. P. Custis and B. J. Lossing, eds, *Recollections and Private Memoirs of Washington* (1860), *SatR*, 9 (1860), pp. 649–50.

90* Review: 'Exhibited architecture', *SatR*, 9 (1860), pp. 743–4.

91* Review: H. Newland, *The Life and Contemporaneous Church History of Antonio de Dominus, Archbishop of Spolatro* (1859), *SatR*, 9 (1860), pp. 749–50.

92* Review: E. P. Ellet, *Women Artists* (1859), *SatR*, 10 (1860), pp. 54–6.

93* Review: M. A. Shee, *The Life of Sir Martin Archer Shee*, 2 vols (1860), *SatR*, 10 (1860), pp. 84–5.

94* Review: the Revd J. Wolff, *Travels and Adventures*, 1 (1860), *SatR*, 10 (1860), pp. 112–14.

95* Review: T. Taylor, ed., *Autobiographical Recollections by the late C. R. Leslie*, 2 vols (1860), *SatR*, 10 (1860), pp. 179–80.

96 Review: E. Venables, *Guide to the Isle of Wight* (1860), *SatR*, 10 (1860), pp. 213–15.

97* Review: A. H. Layard, *Giovanni Sanzio and his Frescoes at Cagli* (Arundel Society, 1860), *SatR*, 10 (1860), pp. 248–9.

98* Review: J. Ruskin, *Modern Painters*, 5 (1860), *SatR*, 10 (1860), pp. 273–5, 310–12.

99* Review: F. C. Husenbeth, *Life of Rt. Rev. Monsignor Weedall* (1860), *SatR*, 10 (1860), pp. 277–8.

100* Review: 'Additions to South Kensington Museum', *SatR*, 10 (1860), pp. 304–5.

101* Review: F. Kilvert, *Memoirs of the Life and Writings of the Rt. Rev. Richard Hurd, D.D., Lord Bishop of Worcester* (1860), *SatR*, 10 (1860), pp. 334–5.

102* Review: O. Delepiere, *A Sketch of the History of Flemish Literature* (1860), *SatR*, 10 (1860), pp. 394–6.

103* Review: J. Hewitt, *Ancient Armour and Weapons in Europe*, 3 vols (1855–60), *SatR*, 10 (1860), pp. 430–1.

104* Review: G. E. Waagen, ed., Kügler's *Handbook of Painting* (1860), *SatR*, 10 (1860), pp. 457–9.

105* 'Iron-Cased Frigates', *SatR*, 10 (1860), pp. 475–6.

106* Review: W. S. Okely, *Development of Christian Architecture in Italy* (1860), *SatR*, 10 (1860), pp. 528–9.

107★ Review: R. Pecock, *The Repressor of Over-much Blaming of the Clergy*, ed. C. Babington, 2 vols (1860), *SatR*, 10 (1860), pp. 596-7.

108★ Review: P. Delamotte, *Art of Illumination* (1860); J. W. Bradley, *Manual of Illumination* (1860), *SatR*, 10 (1860), pp. 628-9.

109★ Review: 'The iron-clad *Warrior*', *SatR*, 10 (1860), pp. 622-3.

110★ Review: A. Dressel, *Prudentius* (1860), *SatR*, 10 (1860), pp. 700-1.

111★ Review: P. Lorimer, *The Scottish Reformation* (1860), *SatR*, 10 (1860), pp. 843-4.

112★ Review: J. Hewitt, *Ancient Armour and Weapons in Europe*, vols 2 and 3 (1860), *Eccl.*, 21, ns 18 (1860), pp. 217-18.

113★ 'Protestant ecclesiology in Germany', *Eccl.*, 21, ns 18 (1860), pp. 283-5.

114 [Joint ed., with] F. H. Dickinson, *Missale ad usum insignie et praeclarae ecclesiae Sarum* [Sarum Missal] (Burntisland, 1861-83).

115★ Review: the Revd J. Wolff, *Travels and Adventures*, 2 (1861), *SatR*, 11 (1861), pp. 73-4.

116★ Review: C. W. King, *Antique Gems* (1860), *SatR*, 11 (1861), pp. 103-4.

117★ Review: 'New atlases', *SatR*, 11 (1861), pp. 174-5.

118★ Review: S. Lysons, *The Model Merchant of the Middle Ages, exemplified in the Story of Whittington and his Cat* (1861), *SatR*, 11 (1861), pp. 198-200.

119★ Review: C. H. Cooper, *Athenae Cantabrigienses*, 2 vols (1858, 1861), *SatR*, 11 (1861), pp. 225-6.

120★ Review: N. Davis, *Carthage and her Remains* (1861), *SatR*, 11 (1861), pp. 249-50.

121★ Review: W. Thornbury, *British Artists from Hogarth to Turner* (1861), *SatR*, 11 (1861), pp. 273-4.

122★ Review: J. Jackson Jarves, *Art Studies: the Old Masters of Italy – Painting*, 2 vols (New York, 1861), *SatR*, 11 (1861), pp. 321-3.

123★ Review: E. E. Viollet-le-Duc, *Military Architecture of the Middle Ages*, trans. M. Macdermott (1860), *SatR*, 11 (1861), pp. 345-6.

124★ Review: M. D. Wyatt, *The Art of Illuminating* (1860), *SatR*, 11 (1861), pp. 371-2.

125★ Review: *An M.P. in Search of a Creed* (1861), by the author of *Squires and Parsons* (1860), *SatR*, 11 (1861), pp. 399-400.

126★ Review: F. W. Fairholt, *Costume in England* (1860), *SatR*, 11

(1861), pp. 425–6.

127★ Review: J. Foulkes Jones, *Egypt in its Biblical Relations and Moral Aspect* (1860), *SatR*, 11 (1861), pp. 431–2.

128★ Review: 'The Watercolour Exhibitions', *SatR*, 11 (1861), pp. 475–6.

129★ Review: T. Somerville, *My Own Life and Times, 1741–1814* (1861), *SatR*, 11 (1861), pp. 485–6.

130★ Review: 'Ironmonger's Hall Exhibition', *SatR*, 11 (1861), p. 503.

131★ Review: T. Wright, *Essays on Archaeological Subjects*, 2 vols (1861), *SatR*, 11 (1861), pp. 618–19.

132★ Review: A. J. Beresford Hope, *The English Cathedral of the 19th Century* (1861), *SatR*, 11 (1861), pp. 643–4.

133★ Review: 'Exhibited sculpture and architecture in 1861', *SatR*, 12 (1861), pp. 15–16.

134★ Review: 'Botfield's Prefaces to the *Editiones Principes*', *SatR*, 12 (1861), pp. 73–5.

135★ Review: B. Ferrey, *Recollections of A. W. Pugin and his father Augustus Pugin* (1861), *SatR*, 12 (1861), pp. 121–3.

136★ Review: 'Publications of the Arundel Society for 1860', *SatR*, 12 (1861), pp. 148–9.

137★ Review: T. Bateman, *Ten Years' Diggings in Celtic and Saxon Gravehills* (1861), *SatR*, 12 (1861), pp. 252–4.

138★ Review: E. Churton, *Memoirs of Joshua Watson*, 2 vols (1861), *SatR*, 12 (1861), pp. 280–1.

139★ Review: T. Knight, *The English Cyclopaedia*, 22 vols (1861), *SatR*, 12 (1861), pp. 331–2.

140★ 'The new exhibition building', *SatR*, 12 (1861), p. 351.

141★ Review: J. Harland, *Mamecestra: being Chapters from the early recorded History of Manchester* (1861), *SatR*, 12 (1861), pp. 384–6.

142★ Review: J. H. and J. Parker, *Our English Home* (1861), *SatR*, 12 (1861), pp. 413–14.

143★ Review: J. A. Wade, *History of St Mary's Abbey, Melrose* (Edinburgh, 1861), *SatR*, 12 (1861), pp. 440–1.

144★ Review: W. Cureton, *History of the Martyrs in Palestine, by Eusebius* (1861), *SatR*, 12 (1861), pp. 464–5.

145★ Review: W. Muir, *The Life of Mahomet*, 4 vols (1858–61), *SatR*, 12 (1861), pp. 482–4.

146★ Review: L. Jewitt, ed., *The Reliquary*, *SatR*, 12 (1861), pp. 490–2.

147★ Review: J. T. Smith, *A Book for a Rainy Day; or Recollections of the Events of the Years 1766–1833* (revised 1861), *SatR*, 12

(1861), pp. 517–18.

148★ Review: W. Thornbury, *The Life of J. M. W. Turner*, 2 vols (1861), *SatR*, 12 (1861), pp. 542–4.

149★ Review: G. G. Scott, ed., *Gleanings from Westminster Abbey* (1861), *SatR*, 12 (1861), pp. 567–8.

150★ Review: T. Lewin, *Jerusalem* (1861), *SatR*, 12 (1861), pp. 643–4.

151 Editor, W. H. Mill, *Observations on the Attempted Application of Pantheistic Principles to the Theory and Historic Criticism of the Gospel* (Cambridge, 1861).

152★ Review: J. Okeley, *Development of Christian Architecture in Italy* (1860), *Eccl.*, 22, ns 19 (1861), pp. 5–8.

153★ Review: J. Murray, *Handbook to the Cathedrals of England. Southern Division*, 2 vols (1861), *Eccl.*, 22, ns 19 (1861), pp. 79–85.

154★ Poem: 'The Lay of Lincoln', *Eccl.*, 22, ns 19 (1861), pp. 224–6.

155★ Review: J. M. Neale, *Notes Ecclesiological and Picturesque on Dalmatia, Croatia, Istria, Syria, with a visit to Montenegro* (1861), *Eccl.*, 22, ns 19 (1861), pp. 289–96.

156★ Review: B. Ferrey, *Recollections of A. W. Pugin and his Father Augustin Pugin* (1861), *Eccl.*, 22, ns 19 (1861), pp. 289–96.

157★ Review: T. Wright, *A History of Domestic Manners and Sentiments in England during the Middle Ages* (1862), *SatR*, 13 (1862), pp. 77–8, 192–3.

158★ Review: J. Earle, *Legends of S. Swithun and S. Maria Aegyptiaca* (1861), *SatR*, 13 (1862), pp. 106–7.

159★ Review: H. L. Long, *A Survey of the Early Geography of Western Europe* (1861), *SatR*, 13 (1862), pp. 164–5.

160★ Review: J. W. Burgon, *Letters from Rome* (1862), *SatR*, 13 (1862), pp. 222–3.

161★ Review: *Scritti Vari del P. Vincenzo Marchese, Domenicano* (Florence, 1862), *SatR*, 13 (1862), pp. 251–2.

162★ Review: C. T. Newton, *Discoveries at Harlicarnassus* (1862), *SatR*, 13 (1862), pp. 303–4.

163★ Review: *Records of the Ministry of the Rev. E. T. March Phillips, M.A.* (1862) By the author of *My Life and What Shall I do with it?* (1860) ['An Old Maid', *sc.* Miss L. F. March Phillipps], *SatR*, 13 (1862), pp. 391–2.

164★ Review: R. H. Patterson, *Essays in History and Art* (Edinburgh, 1862), *SatR*, 13 (1862), pp. 422–3.

165★ 'Pugin Redivivus', *SatR*, 13 (1862), pp. 441–2.

166★ Review: R. H. Story, *Memoir of the Life of the Rev. R. Story*, *late Minister of Roseneath, Dumbartonshire* (Cambridge, 1862), *SatR*, 13 (1862), pp. 479–81.

167★ Review: G. E. Street, *Some Account of the Church of St. Mary, Stone, nr Dartford* (1862), *SatR*, 13 (1862), pp. 507–8.

168★ Review: 'The Arundel Society's publications for 1861', *SatR*, 13 (1862), pp. 540–1.

169★ Review: L. Jenyns, *Memoir of Rev. J. S. Henslow* (1862), *SatR*, 14 (1862), pp. 58–9.

170★ 'Ceramic Art and Glass in the International Exhibition', *SatR*, 14 (1862), pp. 137–8.

171★ Review: M. Hopkins, *Hawaii: the Past, Present and Future of its Island Kingdom* (1862), *SatR*, 14 (1862), pp. 202–3.

172★ Review: J. S. Burn, *The History of the Parish Registers in England* (1862), *SatR*, 14 (1862), pp. 261–2.

173★ 'Metalwork in the International Exhibition', *SatR*, 14 (1862), pp. 280–1.

174★ Review: C. Dresser, *The Art of Decorative Design* (1862), *SatR*, 14 (1862), pp. 318–19.

175★ 'Furniture and decorative carving in the International Exhibition', *SatR*, 14 (1862), pp. 344–5.

176★ Review: *Memorials of John Bowen, LL.D., late Bishop of Sierra Leone, compiled from his Letters and Journals by his Sister* (1862), *SatR*, 143 (1862), pp. 387–8.

177★ 'Textile art in the International Exhibition', *SatR*, 14 (1862), pp. 409–11.

178★ Review: 'Painted glass in the International Exhibition', *SatR*, 14 (1862), pp. 476–7.

179★ 'British architecture in the International Exhibition', *SatR*, 14 (1862), pp. 509–10.

180 'Foreign architecture in the International Exhibition', *SatR*, 14 (1862), pp. 538–9.

181★ Review: 'Works of the Philobiblon and Camden Societies', *SatR*, 14 (1862), pp. 604–5.

182★ Review: 'J. C. Robinson's catalogue of the Loan Exhibition at South Kensington', *SatR*, 14 (1862), pp. 720–1.

183★ Review: B. Burke, *Vicissitudes of Families* (1863), *SatR*, 15 (1863), pp. 57–9.

184★ Review: *The Sculptures of the West Front of Wells Cathedral* (Messrs Cundall and Downes, for the Architectural Photographical Association, 1862), *SatR*, 15 (1863), pp. 479–80.

185★ Review: J. M. W. Turner, *Liber Studiorum* (1862), *SatR*, 15 (1863), pp. 157–8.

186★ Review: 'Publications of the Arundel Society for 1862'

(1863), *SatR*, 15 (1863), pp. 219–20.

187★ Review: J. Murray, *Handbook to the Cathedrals of England: Eastern Division* (1862), *SatR*, 15 (1863), pp. 250–1.

188★ Review: *Black's General Atlas* (1862), *SatR*, 15 (1863), pp. 287–8.

189★ Review: 'The British Institution (modern artists)', *SatR*, 15 (1863), pp. 307–8.

190★ Review: J. S. Watson, *The Life of Bishop Warburton* (1863), *SatR*, 15 (1863), pp. 316–17.

191★ Review: G. R. Emerson, *London: How the Great City Grew* (1862), *SatR*, 15 (1863), pp. 387–8.

192★ Review: 'The French and Flemish Gallery', *SatR*, 15 (1863), pp. 567–8.

193★ Review: J. Fergusson, *History of the Modern Styles of Architecture* (1862), *SatR*, 15 (1863), pp. 667–9.

194★ Review: J. C. Robinson, *The Art Wealth of England: Works of Art on Loan to the Special Exhibition at the South Kensington Museum, 1862*, photographs by C. Thurstan Thompson (1863), *SatR*, 15 (1863), pp. 733–8.

195★ Review: J. B. de Rossi, *Inscriptiones Christianae Urbis Romae, septimo saeculo antiquiores*, 1 (1861), *SatR*, 15 (1863), pp. 771–2.

196★ Review: L. Frölick, *Etchings* (1863), *SatR*, 16 (1863), pp. 100–1.

197★ Review: W. Blakes, *The Life and Topography of William Caxton*, 2 (1863), *SatR*, (16 (1863), pp. 128–9.

198★ Review: W. Chaffers, *Marks and Monographs on Pottery and Porcelain* (1863), *SatR*, 16 (1863), pp. 198–9.

199★ Review: H. T. Ridley, ed., *Chronicles of the Mayors and Sheriffs of London* (1863), *SatR*, 16 (1863), pp. 298–9.

200★ Review: 'Musical publications: the Pre-Raphaelite School' [Lohengrin], *SatR*, 16 (1863), pp. 298–9.

201★ Review: E. Chesnau, *Le Peinture française au XIXe siècle* (Paris, 1863), *SatR*, 16 (1863), pp. 440–1.

202★ Review: S. Huggins, *The Course and Current of Architecture* (1863), *SatR*, 16 (1863), pp. 532–3.

203★ 'Church restoration in France', *SatR*, 16 (1863), pp. 582–3.

204★ Review: 'Mr. Longman's illustrated edition of the New Testament', *SatR*, 17 (1864), pp. 26–7.

205★ Review: Cardinal Wiseman, *The Religious and Social Position of Catholics in England* (Dublin, 1863), *SatR*, 17 (1864), pp. 295–6.

206★ Review: 'Architecture in 1864', *SatR*, 17 (1864), pp. 782–4.

207★ Review: *Photographs from Churches and other Ecclesiastical*

Buildings in France (Architectural Photographic Association, 1863), *SatR*, 18 (1864), pp. 31-2.

208★ 'Church architecture spoilt and mimicked', *SatR*, 18 (1864), pp. 270-1.

209★ 'Church restoration and destruction', *SatR*, 18 (1864), pp. 326-8.

210★ Review: 'P. C. Berjeau, *The Horses of Antiquity, Middle Ages, and Renaissance* (1864), *SatR*, 18 (1864), pp. 463-4.

211★ Review: R. J. Johnson, *Specimens of Early French Architecture, selected chiefly from the Churches of the Ile de France, and illustrated in Geometrical Drawings and Perspective Views* (Newcastle-upon-Tyne, 1864), *SatR*, 18 (1864), pp. 732-3.

212★ Review: C. Texier and R. Popplewell Pullan, *Byzantine Architecture*, *SatR*, 19 (1865), pp. 181-2.

213★ Review: G. E. Street, *Some Account of Gothic Architecture in Spain* (1865), *SatR*, 19 (1865), pp. 353-4.

214★ Review: W. Hepworth Dixon, *The Holy Land*, 2 vols (1865), *SatR*, 19 (1865), pp. 645-6.

215★ Review: R. Kerr, *The Gentleman's House* (1865), *SatR*, 19 (1865), pp. 706-7.

216★ Review: G. B. De Rossi, ed., *La Roma Sotteranea Christiana*, 1 (Rome, 1864), *SatR*, 19 (1865), pp. 776-7.

217★ Review: L. Jewitt, *The Wedgwoods* (1865), *SatR*, 20 (1865), p. 121.

218★ Review: 'The publications of the Arundel Society for 1865', *SatR*, 20 (1865), pp. 185-6.

219★ Review: *The Illustrations of Old Testament History in Queen Mary's Psalter. By an English artist of the Fourteenth Century.* Reproduced by N. H. J. Westlake and W. Purdue (1865), *SatR*, 20 (1865), pp. 280-1.

220★ Review: C. W. King, *The Natural History, Ancient and Modern, of Precious Stones and Gems, and of the Precious Metals* (1865), *SatR*, 20 (1865), pp. 371-2.

221★ Review: C. Babington, *An Introductory Lecture on Archaeology* (Cambridge, 1865), *SatR*, 29 (1865), p. 402-3.

222★ Review: J. Timbs, *The Romance of London*, 3 vols (1865), *SatR*, 20 (1865), pp. 493-4.

223★ Review: C. Texier and R. Popplewell Pullan, *The Principal Ruins of Asia Minor* (1865), *SatR*, 20 (1865), pp. 524-5.

224★ Review: A. W. Pugin, *Photographs from Sketches*, ed. S. Ayling (1865), *SatR*, 20 (1865), pp. 589-90.

225★ Review: J. Ruskin, *The Ethics of the Dust* (1865), *SatR*, 20 (1865), pp. 819-20.

226 Letter: St Andrew's Wells Street, *The Times*, 16 Oct. 1865, p. 9.

227* Review: C. Winston, *Memoirs Illustrative of the Art of Glass Painting* (1865), *SatR*, 21 (1866), pp. 365–6.

228* Obituary: J. M. Neale, *Eccl.*, 28 (1866), p. 265.

229* Review: J. C. Buckler, *The Restoration of Lincoln Cathedral* (1866), *SatR*, 22 (1866), pp. 281–2.

230* Review: Stanford's *Library Map of Africa* (1866), *SatR*, 22 (1866), pp. 404–5.

231* Review: E. Meteyard, *Life of Josiah Wedgwood*, 2 vols (1865–6), *SatR*, (1866), pp. 466–7.

232* Review: J. Fergusson, *History of Architecture*, 3 vols (1866), *SatR*, 23 (1867), p. 415.

233 'The Report on the Commission of Ritual', *SatR*, 24 (1867), pp. 281–2.

234 Letters: Music at the Crystal Palace, *Pall Mall Gazette*, 11 April 1868, pp. 11–12; 3 Dec. 1868, p. 5.

235* Review: W. D. Sweeting, *Parish Churches in and around Peterborough* (1863), *SatR*, 26 (1868), pp. 502–3.

236* Editorial, *Eccl.*, 29, ns 26 (1868), pp. 315–16.

237 *Instructions and Prayers for Candidates for Confirmation* (1870); 3rd edn (1882).

238 [with W. Cooke] Editor, *The Hymnary: a book of Church Song* (1872).

239* Review: the Revd H. R. Haweis, *Thoughts for the Times* (1872), *SatR*, 34 (1872), pp. 478–9.

240 Editor, W. H. Mill, *Five Sermons on the Temptation of Christ* (Cambridge, 1873).

241* Review: C. L. Eastlake, *Hints on Household Taste* (1872 edn), *SatR*, 35 (1873), pp. 255–6.

242* Review: C. L. Eastlake, *A History of the Gothic Revival* (1872), *SatR*, 35 (1873), pp. 315–16, 382–3.

243* Review: S. Birch, *History of Ancient Pottery; Egyptian, Assyrian, Greek, Etruscan and Roman* (1873), *SatR*, 36 (1873), pp. 354–5.

244* Review: F. C. Cook, ed., *The Holy Bible, according to the Authorised Version (1611) [Speaker's Commentary], New Testament*, 2, (1873), *SatR*, 36 (1873), pp. 483–4.

245* Review: C. Drury and E. Fortnum, *A Descriptive Catalogue of the Majolica, etc. in the South Kensington Museum* (Science and Art Dept, 1873), *SatR*, 36 (1873), pp. 674–5.

246* Review: A. J. Beresford Hope, *Worship in the Church of England* (1874), *SatR*, 38 (1874), pp. 803–4, 830–2.

247* 'St. Paul's School', *SatR*, 39 (1875), pp. 342–3.

248* Review: E. Meteyard, *Handbook of Wedgwood Ware* (1875), *SatR*, 39 (1875), pp. 799–800.

249* 'The Hatcham Case', *SatR*, 43 (1877), pp. 39–41, 66–7.

250* Review: 'Cardinal Pitra's *Analecta*', *SatR*, 44 (1877), pp. 557–8; 68 (1884), pp. 354–5.

251* Review: G. B. de Rossi, *La Roma Sotteranea Cristiana*, 3 (1877), *SatR*, 46 (1878), pp. 281–3, 314–15.

252* Review: J. Spencer Northcote and W. R. Brownlow, eds, *Roma Sotteranea; compiled from the Works of Commendatore De Rossi*, 2 (1879), *SatR*, 50 (1880), pp. 272–4.

253* Leader: 'The Year', *SatR*, 50 (1880), pp. 793–7.

254* Review: 'The Catacombs of Rome', *Church Quarterly Review*, 11 (1880–1), pp. 1–24.

255* Review: *The New Testament of the Lord and Saviour Jesus Christ, Translated out of the Greek* (1611, revised 1881), *SatR*, 51 (1881), pp. 657–8.

256* Review: F. C. Cook, ed., *The Holy Bible according to the Authorised Version (1611) [Speaker's Commentary], New Testament*, 3 (1881), *SatR*, 52 (1881), pp. 457–8.

257* 'The Trimolet Collection at Dijon', *SatR*, 52 (1881), pp. 663–4.

258* Lady Mildred Hope, obituary, *The Guardian*, 30 March 1881, p. 449.

259 [Editor], *Church Quarterly Review*, 10–22 (1880–5).

260 [with C. Knight Watson], *Sermons preached in the Church of St. Andrew's, Wells Street after the death and funeral of Emma Jane Knight Watson* [privately printed, 1881].

VICTORIAN NONCONFORMITY AND THE MEMORY OF THE EJECTED MINISTERS: THE IMPACT OF THE BICENTENNIAL COMMEMORATIONS OF 1862

by TIMOTHY LARSEN

In the providence of God, St Bartholomew's Day, 1862, fell on a Sunday, just as it had two hundred years before. On that earlier Sabbath, some 2,000 ministers were ejected from their livings because they could not conscientiously swear their 'unfeigned assent and consent to all and everything contained and prescribed' in the new Prayer Book, or meet some of the other requirements of the new Act of Uniformity. Rejected by the Established Church, many of these men continued to fulfil their callings outside her pale and thereby gave a major, new impetus to Dissent. As the bicentenary of 'Black Bartholomew's Day' approached, Victorian Nonconformists resolved to make the most of 'the opportunity which God's providence has brought round to them'.[1] In this retrospective year, historical claims became powerful weapons in the struggle between Church and Dissent; and the past became contested territory which both sides sought to appropriate in order to add legitimacy to their present positions.

During the years just prior to the bicentenary, some Churchmen had begun to make concerted efforts to thwart the plans of militant Nonconformists and their political organization, the Liberation Society, which had as an objective the disestablishment of the Church of England. Although it had existed since 1844 (originally as the 'Anti-State Church Association'), Churchmen had begun only recently to pay it serious attention. In 1859, the Church Institution, a national organization for Church defence, was founded.[2] In 1861, a bill to abolish church rates, a major

---

[1] *Objects and Plans of the Central United St. Bartholomew Committee of Evangelical Nonconformists* (London, 1862), p. 5.
[2] M. J. D. Roberts, 'Pressure-group politics and the Church of England: the Church Defence Institution, 1859–1896', *JEH*, 35 (1984), pp. 560–82.

legislative goal of Dissenters, was defeated in the Commons for the first time since 1854.[3] The days when Churchmen would disdainfully ignore the activities of militant Dissenters had come to an end.

Throughout the early decades of Victoria's reign, there was an underlying divide in Dissent between militants, who wanted defiantly to advance a radical political agenda, and moderates, who were uneasy with such extremism. Moderates wanted to maintain cordial relations with their fellow Christians in the Established Church. The Church defence movement initially succeeded in tempting some moderates to distance themselves from the actions of their more extreme co-religionists. For example, the wealthy Baptist railway contractor, Sir Morton Peto M.P., quietly severed his connection with the Liberation Society in April 1860.[4] A year later, he went out of his way to assert his moderate credentials, telling the Commons 'he had never been an enemy to the Church of England, and had never taken part in any agitation against her' and that 'no one deplored more than he did the existence of such societies as the Liberation Society'.[5] At the start of the 1860s, the activities of militant Nonconformists were under intense scrutiny and moderate Dissenters did not wish to be held responsible for their excesses.

The Liberation Society was stung by the sudden change of climate. Its minutes for September 1861 include an introspective special report which acknowledged that the Society had lost much ground because of this counter-attack by Churchmen. It recommended that the Society should revitalize itself from the grass-roots through a campaign to spread its principles among its natural constituencies. Included in the report's list of specific proposals was the observation that the bicentenary 'will afford an opportunity for the inculcation of the Society's principles'. Because it was officially non-sectarian, the Society could not take the lead in

[3] J. P. Ellens, *Religious Routes to Gladstonian Liberalism* (University Park, Penn., 1994), pp. 167–203.

[4] London, Greater London Record Office, Liberation Society, Minutes of the Executive Committee, A/LIB/2, 13 April 1860, minute 1058.

[5] *Hansard*, 3rd Series, CLXII, 1024 (24 April 1861).

this, but nevertheless, the report recommended that members of its committee should take an active part in the commemorations which, it hoped, explicitly Dissenting bodies would initiate.[6]

Dissenters did not require any prompting to feel a need to commemorate this great event. The Congregationalists were already making preparations. The eminent layman, Joshua Wilson, prepared a paper for the Congregational Union meeting in October 1861 in which he suggested various ways the denomination could mark the forthcoming occasion. These included an energetic programme of chapel-building, the promotion of publications and lectures related to the themes of the bicentenary, and the establishment of a denominational hall in London.[7] These suggestions were accepted, and to them was added memorial fund-raising for every conceivable good work done in the name of the denomination. Congregationalism, at least, planned to fare well out of the memory of the ejected ministers.

Some Baptists and other Dissenters had hoped for a unified committee, but the Congregationalists would not abandon their independent scheme. Nevertheless, the 'Central United St Bartholomew Committee of Evangelical Nonconformists' was formed as well. It was not exactly a rival: there were four men on it who also served on one of the two Congregational Union committees which shared 1862. No fewer than seven members of the Bartholomew Committee were also on the Liberation Society committee, including its most prominent personality, Edward Miall, and the two employees who kept it running, J. C. Williams and H. S. Skeats. These various committees were all physically connected through the presence of the ubiquitous Samuel Morley, a wealthy textile manufacturer. The Bartholomew Committee included some prominent Baptists, notably William Brock, J. H. Hinton and Sir Morton Peto. The word 'united' in the committee's full title was given added credibility by the presence of a few men from other denominations, such as William Cooke from the

---

[6]   London, Greater London Record Office, Liberation Society Minutes, A/LIB/2, 27 Sept. 1861, minute 1206.

[7]   Joshua Wilson, *The Second Centenary of the Ejectment of the Nonconformist Ministers from the Established Church* (London, nd).

Methodist New Connexion and Robert Eckett from the
United Methodist Free Churches; and the qualifying word
'Evangelical' reminded Unitarians that unity had its limits.[8]
Although Edward Miall was himself a Congregationalist, he
realized that the Bartholomew Committee was the one which
was more likely to enlist the memory of the ejected ministers
in the cause of militant Dissent.[9]

Almost as soon as Nonconformists had expressed their
intention to commemorate, some Churchmen began to
protest. Central to their criticism was the allegation that
Dissenters were misusing history. On one level, they offered
a straightforward, tit-for-tat of historical facts, concentrating
on the persecutions which the puritans themselves had
inflicted. A fine example of this response was the much-
circulated tract by George Venables, *How Did They Get There?
or, the Non-Conforming Ministers of 1662. A Question for those
who would celebrate the Bi-Centenary of St. Bartholomew's Day,
1662.* This strident piece brought a blitzkrieg of counter-
history to bear; its blanket coverage of all possible target
areas extended even to the treatment of native Americans by
the Pilgrim Fathers.[10] A variation on this theme was attempts
to restore or refute specific historical details, such as whether
or not 2,000 was an accurate estimate of the number of
ejected ministers, and whether their number was larger or
smaller than the victims of the puritans.[11] Such points were a
continuation (and sometimes a mere repetition) of the work
done by the Nonconformist historian, Edmund Calamy, and
the response made to it by the Churchman John Walker, in
the early part of the eighteenth century.[12]

Many Church defenders saw the whole commemoration as
a ploy for advancing the political agenda of militant Dissent.
One of their number, J. B. Clifford, published an address
entitled *The Bicentenary, The Liberation Society; And To What Do
Its Principles Tend?* The crux of his argument was that 'the

[8] *Objects and Plans; The Congregational Yearbook* (London) for 1862, p. [x], and for
1863, p. [x]; Supplement to the *Liberator*, June 1862, p. 111.
[9] Arthur Miall, *Life of Edward Miall* (London, 1884), pp. 240–1.
[10] George Venables, *How Did They Get There?* (London, 1862).
[11] T. Lathbury, *Facts and Fictions of the Bicentenary* (Bristol, 1861).
[12] *DNB*, Edmund Calamy, D.D. (1671–1732); John Walker (1647–1747).

Bicentenary is being observed for Liberation purposes', but Nonconformists should have 'read history a little more closely' before they attempted this stunt.[13] The *Quarterly Review* likewise asserted that the bicentenary was 'not to be simply a Dissenting Saints' Day', but rather 'a great political agitation'.[14] Generally, the point was made that the ejected ministers were not militant Dissenters; they had no objection to church establishments *per se*. For example, Canon John Miller, a prominent Evangelical clergyman, helpfully reminded his audience that the word 'ejectment' implied 'the removing of a person who does not want to go'.[15] Moreover, the Two Thousand were mainly Presbyterians, so they could not be justly co-opted into the cause of Congregationalism; and what possible historical claim on these men could be made by such groups as the United Methodist Free Churches? In short, Church defenders argued that Victorian Nonconformists were so different from the ejected ministers that it was almost dishonest of them to evoke their memory. The Congregational minister, R. W. Dale, summed it up well when he said: 'We are charged with a kind of historical felony.'[16]

Because the battle had been initially joined through these pre-emptive strikes, by the time Dissenters actually started publishing and lecturing they were well aware of the case which they needed to answer. A few Nonconformists opted for direct defiance. The Congregational minister J. G. Rogers, in his bicentenary lecture, cited many of the charges before he reiterated his conviction that 'the principle I think best worth teaching in connection with this celebration is that of the Liberation Society'.[17] Some sought to show that the ejectment 'strikingly illustrates the evils of the State-Church principle', whether or not the ejected recognized it.[18] Others

[13] J. B. Clifford, *The Bicentenary* (Bristol, nd), pp. 32, 15. I am grateful to the Principal and Chapter, Pusey House, Oxford, for access to this source.

[14] *Quarterly Review*, 112 (1862), pp. 236–70.

[15] John Miller, *Churchmen and Dissenters*, 2nd edn (Birmingham, 1862), p. 11.

[16] Central United Bartholomew Committee, *The Willis's Rooms Lectures* (London, [1862]), p. 69.

[17] J. G. Rogers, *Puritans, Nonconformists, and Dissenters* (Manchester, [1862]), p. 31.

[18] *United Methodist Free Churches' Magazine* (May, 1862), p. 276.

appealed to the idea of historical development. The Dissenting journal, the *British Quarterly Review*, argued by analogy that Englishmen could look back with gratitude to 'those sturdy barons who wrung the provisions of the Great Charter from the hands of King John' even though these men may not have approved of the House of Commons.[19] A Dissenting minister in Macclesfield appealed to biblical imagery in order to show that Victorian Nonconformists were the 'valid successors' of the ejected men. He argued that 'The spiritual sons of spiritual fathers are the sons who do the works of those fathers.' Moreover, Nonconformists would never join the Church of England because they would not 'put their necks beneath a yoke which neither they nor their fathers would be able to bear'.[20]

Generally, however, Dissenters took note of the arguments against them and tailored their remarks accordingly. The Congregational committee published a volume of addresses and stated that it desired its 'aims and objects in the Bicentenary Commemoration may be judged of by what is found in these pages, and not by the mistakes or misrepresentations of others'. In the volume, one of the writers explained on their behalf that they wished to honour the ejected ministers because of their 'manliness', 'love of truth', 'fortitude' and 'faith'. He admitted that some might say that he had 'proved too much' by listing characteristics common to 'all good men' but, expounding on 'faith', he claimed that the desire to 'obey God rather than men' was 'the root principle of all Dissent'.[21] Even that qualification, however, hardly explained why they did not just commemorate St Bartholomew himself. Even the Bartholomew Committee followed suit:

No identity of ecclesiastical or theological faith between the willing Nonconformists of 1862 and the forced Nonconformists of 1662, is required to give a meaning

---

[19] *British Quarterly Review*, 37 (1863), p. 241.
[20] G. B. Kidd, *Are Nonconformists of the Present Day the Valid Successors of the Ejected of 1662?* (London, 1862), pp. 4–6.
[21] Robert Vaughan, et al., *St James's Hall Addresses* (London, 1862), preface and pp. 35–7.

to such a commemoration. It is not to the opinions, but to the conduct of the ejected that the present is a fitting occasion to do honour. Their heroic spirit, not their convictions – their fidelity to conscience, not their articles of belief – their unswerving loyalty to their spiritual King, not their ideas on questions of Church relations and Church government, commend them to attention, to sympathy, to imitation, in these times.[22]

If the desirability of disestablishment was a lesson too tenuously connected to the text at hand, these sweeping generalities were too common to innumerable texts – whether Protestant or Catholic, Christian or pagan. A lesson between these extremes needed to be identified; one which was historically sensitive, but nevertheless useful to the cause of Dissent. The evils surrounding clerical subscription, as laid down in the Act of Uniformity, matched this requirement well. The *Baptist Magazine* confidently announced: '*This* is the great lesson which Bartholomew's-day should recal [sic] to mind – that HONEST MEN CANNOT USE FORMULARIES WHICH THEY THINK TO BE UNTRUE, OR CONTRARY TO THE WORD OF GOD.'[23] The Bartholomew Committee dedicated an entire tract to this point.[24]

This piece of ground was chosen; and a bitter battle ensued. In January 1862, Canon Miller had moved the principal resolution at a meeting which was called for the purpose of founding a Church defence association in Birmingham. In support of it, he drew attention to the Dissenters' bicentenary plans, and warned that their behaviour was becoming so hostile that, despite a tradition of working together in non-denominational societies, 'it became a serious question as to how far that co-operation was possible in the future'.[25] In the following month he delivered a lecture for the newly-formed 'Birmingham Church of England Defence Association' entitled *Churchmen and Dissenters: their Relations as Affected by*

---

22 *Objects and Plans*, p. 4.
23 *Baptist Magazine*, ns 6 (1862), p. 79.
24 Central United Bartholomew Committee, *On Clerical Subscription* (London, [1862]).
25 *Record*, 27 Jan. 1862, p. 4.

the Proposed Bicentenary Commemoration of St Bartholomew's Day, 1662. In it, he prophesied correctly that this 'Commemoration seems likely to affect the relation in which Churchmen and Dissenters will stand in this country, for some time to come'.[26] In response, R. W. Dale gave a lecture under the same title in the Birmingham Town Hall. He aimed squarely at the Church of England in his own day, claiming that almost every party in it was uncomfortable with some part of the Prayer Book. He targeted the Evangelical clergy in particular, citing passages which seem to teach baptismal regeneration as incompatible with their true convictions. Dale concluded:

> The truest, fittest, sublimest celebration of the Bicentenary, would be for eight or ten thousand of the Evangelical Clergy who object to these services in the prayer-book, but who obtained their ministerial office and their ministerial income by avowing their 'unfeigned assent and consent' to all the book contains – to come out and to declare to the English people that they can no longer retain a position which they acquired by professing to approve what now at least they reject; that they can no longer use in the house of God and at the most touching and solemn crises of human history, words which their hearts condemn.[27]

Some Churchmen read this as a personal attack on their honest integrity; and it was not an isolated incident. The Evangelical Anglican newspaper, the *Record*, drew attention to a bicentenary tract circulating in Ipswich which claimed 'the Act of Uniformity shuts men up to this alternative – perjury or secession.' The *Record* warned: 'If moderate Dissenters do not wish to have a complete and final rupture with Churchmen, they must speak out.'[28] Dissenters often implied that Churchmen were resorting to the Jesuitical ploy of accepting the wording in its 'non-natural' sense or with 'mental reservations'.

26 Miller, *Churchmen and Dissenters*, p. 3.
27 R. W. Dale, *Churchmen and Dissenters* (Birmingham, 1862), pp. 19–20.
28 Supplement to the *Record*, 26 March 1862, p. [1].

Dale's appeal did not inspire Canon Miller to resign his living. Instead, he resigned his presidency of the Central Association of the Birmingham Auxiliary of the British and Foreign Bible Society.[29] Sir Culling Eardley, the animating spirit of the Evangelical Alliance, tried to mediate between the two Birmingham men, but without success. Even more tellingly, he was unsuccessful in his attempt to dissuade Sir Morton Peto from taking the chair at a bicentenary meeting where Dale was scheduled to speak, despite Peto's desire during the two preceding years to distance himself from the activities of militant Nonconformists. The best he could do was obtain a letter in which Peto said that if clergymen claimed to be satisfied that their convictions were reconcilable with their subscription then he would not 'sit in judgment upon them', even though he did not fail to add, 'I cannot see myself how they can be.' This was enough to please the irenic Eardley, but others were less impressed.[30] The appeals of Churchmen to moderate Dissenters had gone unheeded. The bicentenary commemorations and their attacks on subscription, far from driving a wedge between militants and moderates, were unifying influences within Dissent. The wedge was being driven between Nonconformists and Churchmen.

The truth was that some Churchmen were themselves uneasy about subscription. A High Church clergyman published a letter to Dale in which he praised his lecture and agreed with him that the Evangelical clergy did not hold to the teachings of the Church. He smugly claimed that what he and Dale had in common was 'English honesty'.[31] Lord Ebury introduced into the Lords his 'Act of Uniformity Amendment Bill'.[32] The clergymen who supported the Liturgical Revision Society were *ipso facto* admitting that change was desirable. One of their number wrote his own bicentenary tract in which he declared, 'Never had the Church of England such an opportunity as that which this

29 *Record*, 11 April 1862, p. 2.
30 *Watchman*, 14 May 1862, p. 157.
31 A Priest of the Church of England, *A Letter to the Rev. R. W. Dale* (Birmingham, 1862), p. 5.
32 *Hansard*, 3rd series, CLXVII, 2–29 (27 May 1862).

year presents of expressing regret for the past, by repealing or *amending the objectionable clauses* in the *Act of Uniformity*.'[33] Even the protest of Churchmen that Dissenters could not judge their consciences had its own internal taunt, for just a year earlier virtually every bishop in the land had signed a letter concerning the controversial *Essays and Reviews* in which they remarked, 'We cannot understand how these opinions can be held consistently with an honest subscription to the formularies of the Church.'[34] One clergyman, Christopher Nevile, actually did resign his livings, citing as his reason the need for a revision of the Prayer Book.[35] He took his place as a hero of Dissent, coming forward to speak at the Liberation Society conference 'amid loud cheers'.[36] Nevile and Miller, however, were both mavericks in their own ways; 1862 produced no mass exodus to match the Two Thousand, either from the Establishment or the Bible Society.

The irony of this story is that Church defenders, by labelling the bicentenary a political plot, actually achieved the worst of both worlds. Dissenters who took this accusation to heart stumbled into an attack on the Church itself, rather than just its established position. The Liberation Society had always avoided criticizing the Establishment as a Church; and this policy had had some influence on the behaviour of Dissenters in general. Any tendency toward this type of quietism was now seriously undermined. On the other hand, the perception that the Liberation Society was deeply connected with the bicentenary, which was established chiefly through the propaganda of militant Churchmen, if anything increased the love Dissenters had for that society.

Churchmen seemed unaware of the extent to which the ejected ministers had been revered by Dissenting communities for generations. It was surely a grave tactical error for some of them to try to slur their reputations, as George Venables did.[37] Robert Vaughan, who was known as one of

---

[33] Charles Girdlestone, *How Shall We Commemorate on August 24, 1862, the Bi-Centenary of the Act of Uniformity?* (London, [1862]), p. 7.
[34] R. G. Wilberforce, *Life of Samuel Wilberforce*, 3 vols (London, 1882), 3, pp. 4–5.
[35] *Nonconformist*, 30 July 1862, pp. 648–9.
[36] Supplement to the *Liberator*, June 1862, p. 111.
[37] Venables, *How Did They Get There?*, pp. 7–8, 17–19.

the more moderate and cultured Dissenters, wrote a reply.[38] It is interesting to note that Vaughan publicly recanted his opposition to the policy of militant Dissenters on state education – a position which he had fought for in print for over fifteen years – at the very same conference at which Joshua Wilson's paper on commemorating the bicentenary was read.[39] Vaughan was subsequently asked to implement one of these bicentenary plans by writing the official volume on the Ejectment.[40] The *British Quarterly Review*, which he edited, remarked in an article attacking the Act of Uniformity:

> It seems to have been discovered by some persons that this journal has taken new ground on questions of this nature. But there are times when it may be well to say little, or even to say nothing; and there are times when it is a right thing to speak, and to speak unmistakeably.[41]

It was not completely disingenuous of the journal to go on to claim it had not changed. The people behind it had always felt deeply about the ejected ministers. If standing with them meant being lumped together with Edward Miall, so be it. An ailing Joshua Wilson, another Dissenter who was more moderate than extreme, painstakingly prepared for publication a defence of the ejected ministers against the attacks of the *Quarterly Review*.[42] Even the *Record* was embarrassed by the curate in Paddington who took as his text on St Bartholomew's Day I John 2.19: 'They went out from us because they were not of us.'[43] All such attacks were counter-productive if quarantining militant Dissent was the goal.

It is also worth noting that 1862 was the year in which the admirers of Edward Miall honoured him with a testimonial. A partial list of those involved included not only a vast array of Dissenting radicals, from John Bright on down, but also more moderate and scholarly men such as the Revd Drs

38 Robert Vaughan, *I'll Tell You* (London, 1862).
39 *Nonconformist*, 16 Oct. 1861, pp. 827–9.
40 Robert Vaughan, *English Nonconformity* (London, 1862), pp. iii–iv.
41 *British Quarterly Review*, 35, 70 (April, 1862), p. 323.
42 Joshua Wilson, *Calumnies Confuted* (London, 1863).
43 *Record*, 25 Aug. 1862, p. 2.

Angus, Halley, and Waddington.[44] Dissenters across the land
wanted to commemorate the bicentenary, and this sense of
common cause served their more radical elements well.

The fuel which the bicentenary gave to political Dissent is
also illustrated by the attitude of the Unitarians. Evangelical
Dissenters had a habit of ostracising them, which tempted
them to think they had more in common with Broad
Churchmen than with other Nonconformists. The Unitarian
newspaper, the *Inquirer*, had declared its disdain for militant
Dissent in 1857. It attacked the name of the Liberation
Society and went on to say:

> we are reminded by the Orthodox Dissenters of our
> common Nonconformity, and our common sub-
> servience to a dominant Church. To this we would
> reply that we approve the principle of a National
> Church, and, as English Presbyterians, have more love
> for the Church of England than for the Independents or
> Baptists.[45]

Nevertheless, Unitarians possessed a good portion of those
congregations which descended from the ejected ministers
and the passions of the bicentenary were enough to push the
Inquirer in the direction of militant Dissent:

> Our readers are well aware that on the Church and State
> Question we have clung hitherto, through constant
> opposition, to the old Presbyterian idea of com-
> prehension. The discussions and controversies of the Bi-
> centenary year, the strong ecclesiastical reaction in the
> Church itself ... and the false position of Broad
> Churchmen themselves, have contributed materially to
> alter our views. ... we feel bound now to give our
> hearty support to many of the practical propositions of
> the Liberation Society ...[46]

Wesleyan Methodism, as a body, had always supported the
Established Church and seen itself as different from the rest

[44] Supplement to the *Nonconformist*, 14 May 1862, pp. 437–40.
[45] *Inquirer*, 7 Feb. 1857, p. 81.
[46] *Inquirer*, 29 Nov. 1862, p. 834.

of Dissent. It survived the bicentenary with this balancing act intact. The *Wesleyan Methodist Magazine* explained the line which its denomination had taken:

> The Methodist people had not seen fit, as a Connexion, to rouse themselves to any special effort, or to take any prominent part in the Bicentenary commemoration. This is not because they hold the two thousand in light esteem, or think them unworthy of any wreath which Christian love can lay on their tombs. It is, rather, because they fear to depart at all from that traditional policy which has made them 'friends of all, the enemies of none.' It is because they fear lest they should be forced unwittingly into a position which they would regret to occupy.

This comment illustrates both the widespread desire to honour the ejected men (further remarks conceded that some Wesleyans wished to do more), and the way in which the commemorations had taken on a political hue. Moreover, the magazine was willing to join in the attack on subscription remarking, among other jibes, that it would like to give clergymen the benefit of the doubt, but 'charity is very hard work sometimes'.[47]

The practical work which the Congregationalists undertook must also take its place as part of the enduring impact of the bicentenary. Because funds were given to existing projects which would have received some funding anyway and people were allowed to spread their contributions over several years, not to mention the numerous purely local efforts, it is difficult to tabulate the results. In April 1863, a regional organization for erecting memorial chapels in Lancashire and Cheshire had received subscriptions amounting to £17,567, despite the economic distress caused by the Cotton Famine. At the same date, the national fund had reached the sum of £195,749.[48] Memorial Hall, the proposed

---

[47] *Wesleyan Methodist Magazine*, Aug. 1862, pp. 732–6.
[48] *Fund to Aid the Erection of Memorial Chapels in Lancashire and Cheshire: First Annual Report of the Committee* (Manchester, 1863).

denominational headquarters, was eventually built as well. When it was opened in 1875, it was said to have cost £70,000, and the memorial fund had reportedly raised £250,000.[49] Welsh Nonconformists joined in the commemorations as well. They resolved to found a Memorial College at Brecon. It cost £10,000 to build and was opened in 1869.[50]

Nonconformists would perhaps have found other excuses for doing many of these good works. The more significant impact of the bicentenary is the deepening of the divide between Church and Dissent which it engendered, and the impetus which it gave to strident Dissent, both in its theological and political forms. All of the principal parties within the Church were affected. High Churchmen were leading the new work of Church defence and the bicentenary marked one of their first experiences of hand-to-hand combat at a unit. The Broad Churchmen suffered a weakening of their ties with their erstwhile friends, the Unitarians, as the latter rediscovered their identity as Nonconformists. Moreover, the focus on honesty in subscription caused others to glance suspiciously in their direction. The Evangelicals had endured some painful personal blows and the bicentenary left them feeling defiant and bitter.

Only one prominent Nonconformist publicly signalled his disapproval of the commemorations: the idiosyncratic C. H. Spurgeon. He complained, 'I fear lest it should be made an opportunity for strife among brethren.'[51] Some Churchmen made the most of this, but it proved to be cold comfort, for in two years' time he launched his own equally bitter war against the Church, beginning with his confrontational sermon on 'Baptismal Regeneration'.[52] In the years which followed the commemorations, the divide, if anything, continued to deepen. Although it would be inaccurate to give the impression that R. W. Dale was confined to the narrow world of militant Dissenters, it is not insignificant that he

[49] Edwin Hodder, *Life of Samuel Morley*, 3rd edn (London, 1887), p. 366; Albert Peel, *These Hundred Years* (London, 1931), pp. 239–41.

[50] Charles Miall, *Henry Richard, M.P.* (London, 1889), p. 166.

[51] Supplement to the *Record*, 26 Feb. 1862, p. [2]; *Watchman*, 7 May 1862, p. 147.

[52] Susannah Spurgeon, *C. H. Spurgeon, Autobiography*, rev. edn, 2 vols (Edinburgh, 1973), 2, pp. 55–7.

gained his favourable national reputation among Nonconformists through the part he played in the bicentenary. His
son wrote, recalling his bicentenary address, 'Dale found
himself suddenly lifted to a new position. The lecture – as he
said, looking back on his early years – "fairly launched" him
on his career of public service.'[53] The vast number of
publications which the bicentenary generated are one indication of the amount of passion which it unleashed. The editor
of the 'Congregational Literary Register' noted at the end of
1862 that his table was piled with over sixty bicentenary
volumes, just counting those written by Congregational
ministers and published during that year, and he was aware
that much of the provincial literature had 'not been heard of
in the metropolis'.[54] Indeed, one could probably find in many
parts of the country tracts with titles similar in kind to *The
Bicentenary Question. A Third Letter in Reply to the Second Letter
of "A Churchman," Which Appeared in the "Shepton Mallet
Journal," September 19, 1862.*[55] The Liberation Society could
look back on the bicentenary with some satisfaction;
Dissenters, moderates, and militants united together, had
been reminded why they were Dissenters and they were
ready to fight for it – to attempt to follow, in a way which
they felt was appropriate to their own era, the heroic example
of the ejected ministers.

Covenant College, Coventry

---

53 A. W. W. Dale, *Life of R. W. Dale* (London, 1898), p. 175.
54 *Congregational Yearbook* for 1863, p. 392.
55 James Allen, *The Bicentenary Question* (Shepton Mallet, [1862]).

CHRISTIAN CIVILIZATION AND ITALIC CIVILIZATION: ITALIAN CATHOLIC THESES FROM GIOBERTI TO PIUS XII

by OLIVER LOGAN

'Civilization' was a major keyword in the Italian Catholic discourse of the nineteenth century and the first half of the twentieth. Indeed Catholic Christian civilization was seen as synonymous with true civilization itself insofar as the post-classical era was concerned. The concept of 'Christian civilization' was closely allied to that of *cristianità*, as distinct from *cristianesimo* (Christianity). The terms *cristianità* and *chrétienté*, like English 'Christendom', had originally had primarily geographical connotations, but in post-Revolutionary Catholic thought they acquired connotations of a Christian order of society under the leadership of the Church, the evils of the modern world being presented as consequences of its breakdown. The allied discourse on 'Christian civilization' itself in the Italian Catholic world, as in the French one, was in large measure reactionary in character, associated with Counter-Revolutionary ideology and with opposition to liberalism. It asserted that a return of society to the Church was a precondition of social order.[1] Thus the myth of a lost universal order offered a paradigm for the future.

A major thesis was that the Catholic Church had inherited and extended both the Roman Empire's universal role of bringing a multitude of peoples into one community and its civilizing mission. She had preserved, purified, and sublimated what was best in classical civilization and she had

---

[1] Jacques Gadille, 'Le concept de civilisation chrétienne dans la pensée romantique', in Jean-René Derré et al., *Civilisation chrétienne. Approche historique d'une idéologie xviie–xxi siècle* (Paris, 1975), pp. 183–210; Giovanni Miccoli, 'Chiesa e società in Italia tra Ottocento e Novecento: il mito della "cristianità" ', in Giuseppe Alberigo et al., *Chiese nella società. Verso un superamento della cristianità* (Turin, 1980), pp. 151–245; Daniele Menozzi, 'La Chiesa e la storia. Una dimensione della cristianità da Leone XIII al Vaticano II', *Cristianesimo nella storia*, 5 (1984), pp. 69–106; idem, 'Intorno alle origini del mito della cristianità', ibid., pp. 523–62.

civilized the barbarians; here a particularly important role was often ascribed to Benedictine monasticism. One key issue, then, was Catholic Christianity's relationship to ancient Graeco-Roman civilization, which was seen as a mixture of good and evil elements. The High Middle Ages was generally, although not invariably, seen as the apogee of Christian civilization. One thesis asserted the organic unity of medieval thought and culture. Those with Christian Social preoccupations were likely to look here for a model of the just society. For Italy, the high point was liable to be seen as coming in the late communal period after the rise of the friars. Italians were deeply conscious of their Middle Ages as a period of conflict, and some Catholic writers saw the early communal period as one of rampant egoism, lust for lucre, and social conflict, somewhat similar to their own distraught age. The later communal period, however, might be cited by those of a Catholic Social orientation as one of social harmony and of respect for the principle of *bonum commune* under the guidance of the Church. The Reformation, representing the principle of hubristic individualism and of personal judgement, had, it was monotonously asserted, dealt a grave blow to Christian civilization, the French Revolution and the rise of liberalism and socialism being its ultimate consequences. The Renaissance, like ancient civilization, was seen in ambivalent terms. Catholic writers tended to contrast a Christian and Church-sponsored Renaissance with a pagan or excessively rationalist one which had paved the way for the Reformation.[2]

---

[2] In addition to other material mentioned in subsequent notes, the main sources used here are: anon. [but G. Busnelli, S.J.], 'L'Italia e la civiltà', *La Civiltà Cattolica* [hereafter *CC*], 1602 (17 March 1917), pp. 41–62; anon., 'Anniversari di guerra', *CC*, 1636 (17 Aug. 1918), p. 298; anon., 'Ragioni sociali dei centenari religiosi. S. Francesco d'Assisi', *CC*, 1815 (6 Feb. 1926), pp. 198–9; anon., 'Il centenario benedettino e le benemerenze sociali del monachesimo', *CC*, 1892 (20 April 1929), pp. 97–109; A. Brucculeri, S.J., 'Verso l'ordine nuovo', *CC*, 2166 (21 Sept. 1940), pp. 401–13; G. E. Williwoll, S.J., 'La missione di Roma negli scritti di Leone Magno' (2 pts), *CC*, 2209 (4 July 1942), pp. 33–9, and 2211 (1 Aug. 1942), pp. 152–9; Giovanni Semeria, Barbabite, 'La romanità di S. Agostino', *Vita e pensiero* [hereafter *VP*], 21 (1930), pp. 471–82; Cardinal Ildefonso Schuster, 'Lettera pastorale. Il xv centenario della morte di S. Agostino', *Rivista diocesana milanese*, 20 (April, 1929), pp. 208–22; idem, 'Lettera pastorale. Il xvi centenario della morte di S. Ambrogio', ibid., 29 (Sept., 1939), pp. 411–37; Igino Giordani, 'Italia madre', *Frontespizio*, 6/12 (Dec., 1934), pp. 7–8; Cardinal Eugenio Pacelli, inaugural address to the Congresso

The nineteenth-century Italian Catholic discourse on Christian civilization had much in common with the French Catholic discourse on the same theme; indeed De Maistre and Bonald, who ascribed a breakdown of political and social order to the undermining of the Catholic religion, were important influences on our Italian writers. The focus on the part of many of these on the medieval communes was, of course, a specific national feature. Furthermore, the stress on the *Roman* character of Catholicism, which was also strong among French reactionary writers, was here linked to the theme of Italy's special universal mission by virtue of the papacy, one inherited from the Roman Empire. Through this theme were asserted Catholic notions of Italy's true identity and of the rightful place of the Church in a united Italy.

What was meant by 'civilization'? The concept had a core of ethical connotations, or notions of right order; the degree to which it had cultural connotations was variable. Right order was often defined in contraposition to unrestrained individualism and to excessive state power, which were liable to be posited as two sides of the same coin. The concept of civilization was generally intensely Eurocentric.

Up until World War I there was quite a rich variety in theses about Christian civilization, although thereafter they tended to take the form of conventional truisms. There were throughout, however, differences in the polemical objectives of clericalist writers on the theme. Even the stock assertions could be manipulated and deployed in a variety of propagandistic contexts. Here, having described some of the more common features of the discourse on Christian civilization, we will now concentrate on varieties of approach and on polemical objectives, examining both liberal and diehard-Ultramontane exponents of the Catholic viewpoint.

Vincenzo Gioberti's *Del primato morale e civile degli Italiani* (1843) contained many of the key themes: the Roman Catholic Church as the inheritor of Rome's universal role and civilizing mission; her preservation and sublimation of what was best in antique culture, not least Roman law; the

giuridico internazionale (1934), in *Discorsi e panegirici* [hereafter *DP*], 2nd edn (Vatican City, 1956), pp. 333–44.

Church's and in particular the monks' role in civilizing the barbarians;[3] the organic unity of medieval thought.[4] Gioberti was concerned to assert that the historic merits of the Church and the papacy's unique role in Italian and European history qualified the Supreme Pontiff to preside over a united Italy, albeit a laicized society, while also emphasizing the value to society of the clergy and, more particularly, of the embattled religious orders. Gioberti presented a clericalist version of the theme of Italy's universal civilizing mission to rival Mazzini's secularist one; this mission Gioberti posited by virtue of her joint Roman imperial and Catholic Christian heritage. Italians were the 'Levites of Christianity'.[5] Rome was the immutable Eternal City, the soul of the human spiritual community.[6]

An exceptionally rich formulation of theses on Christian civilization, in some respects typical, in others idiosyncratic, is to be found in the *Prologomeni alla storia universale della Chiesa* (1861) of Luigi Tosti (1811–97), Abbot of Montecassino, a Catholic liberal who in the years after 1860 worked for reconciliation between Church and State. Tosti had indeed a theological philosophy of history (he maintained that the Catholic priest had two books, the Bible and history),[7] and 'civilization' was for him a theological concept. Christ's mission had been not only to redeem sinners but also to repair the consequences of Adam's sin for social life. History was the story of the unification of humanity in love and of its movement towards God. Christian civilization was the work of Christ in history.[8] For Tosti, history exemplified the principle that Grace does not annul nature but perfects it. Implicitly, in Tosti's thought, ancient civilization and the barbarian invaders, with their diverse virtues capable of further development, represented nature; the action of the Church represented Grace. What Tosti particularly valued in

[3] Vincenzo Gioberti, *Del primato morale e civile degli Italiani* (1843), ed. Gustavo Balsamo-Crivelli, 3 vols (Milan, 1946) 1, pp. 65–6, 69, 74, 90–2; 2, pp. 42–5, 49–52, 56–9, 63–71, 150–8; 3, pp. 134–43.
[4] Ibid., 1, pp. 131; 2, pp. 135–9, 149–50.
[5] Ibid., 1, pp. 54, 102, 117.
[6] Ibid., 1, p. 115; 3, pp. 199–204.
[7] Luigi Tosti, *Prologomeni alla storia universale della Chiesa* (1861), in his *Opere complete*, 12 (Rome, 1888), p. xiii.
[8] Ibid., pp. 19–20, 64–9, 245–6.

ancient civilization was the concept of *patria* which entailed an abnegation of the individual in favour of an embryonic universal principle which would become truly and fully manifested in the Roman Church.[9] Tosti's thought provides a significant exception to the picture of the discourse on Christian civilization in an Italian context as being generally reactionary in character. Tosti believed in progress in history; history was indeed guided by Christ and therefore its process could not fail.[10] One objective of the *Prologomeni* was to urge the Church to come to terms with the modern State and to accept the principle of responsible government. Tosti had asserted that the Church's relations with society had changed in the course of history, and he urged his fellow clergy to have faith in the Church's 'fecundity'.[11] The metaphor of maturation is central to his view of history. What reactionary thinkers saw as a breakdown of the Christian order he viewed, rather, as the outcome of a necessary process of development that had in some cases gone awry. The defeat of Boniface VIII, for Tosti a critical event in history, marked the end of a 'theocratic dictatorship' that had once been necessary; this defeat opened the way for an expansion of the ecclesial principle in the hearts and minds of the faithful. It was a question of the emancipation of a now mature adult from parental control.[12] One central theme of Tosti's teaching was the need for a balance between reason, which was a gift of God, and faith; this balance being above all exemplified by the Benedictine St Anselm.[13] The Renaissance marked a further stage of emancipation of a now mature Christian society from the Church's tutelage, but an over-impulsive embracing of ancient civilization had led to contamination by paganism.[14] Again, Luther's heresy represented a desire for

---

[9] Ibid., pp. 32–6; cf. idem, 'Roma eterna' (date uncertain), in *Scritti vari*, 1, *Opere*, 4 (Rome, 1886), pp. 3–46, at pp. 17–29.

[10] Idem, *Prologomeni*, pp. 432–3.

[11] Ibid., pp. 435–56.

[12] Ibid., p. 278. Gioberti had made a broadly similar point about the emancipation of society from a once necessary 'dictatorship' of the Church: *Primato*, 2, pp. 248–61.

[13] Tosti, *Prologomeni*, pp. 283–4.

[14] Ibid., pp. 298–307.

emancipation from authority carried to extremes.[15] Tosti saw the convulsions that threatened the Church in terms not of radical evil but of a straying from the golden mean.

Tosti provided an intellectually powerful articulation of the assumption, dominant in the Italian Catholic mind throughout the period examined, that civilization was a central value of Christianity, although his conception of historical process and of the role of Christ in the unfolding of history seems to have been without influence in the Italian Catholic world. Where Tosti was probably most influential was as an exponent of the thesis of the key role of the Benedictines in the passage from antiquity to the Middle Ages. In the *Prologomeni*, and in his last work, the *Life of St Benedict*, he considerably developed the Giobertian thesis that the religious orders provided Europe with 'an apprenticeship in the life of civilization', while giving this thesis an overwhelmingly Benedictine focus. Tosti portrays the commencement of the working out in history of Christ's mission for society as having been undertaken by the Roman St Benedict and his followers. Benedict's aim, he asserts, was not only to sanctify individual monks but also to create a society. He established in the institution of the abbey a society in miniature that would teach those peoples who lacked any society to create a larger one of their own. The Benedictines guided the barbarians into becoming a settled, disciplined, and industrious population by their own example of order and discipline and by teaching them the arts of husbandry. Thus Tosti's conception of the monks' civilizing mission embraced, as did Gioberti's, the notion of social utility, as well as the concept of a cultural role.[16] Both writers can be seen as responding to the campaign against the contemplative orders, stigmatized as performing no work of social utility, that had begun with the reform programmes of Enlightened Absolutism.

Tosti's serene vision was not in accord with the dominant climate in the Italian Church during the pontificates of Leo

---

[15] Ibid., pp. 307–11.
[16] Ibid., pp. 249–58; idem, *Della vita di S. Benedetto* (1892), *Opere*, 18 (Montecassino and Rome, 1892), pp. 1–14.

XIII (1878–1903) and Pius X (1903–14). While Tosti had seen the weakening of theocracy as the manifestation of a process of maturation of society, albeit a painful and partially aberrant one, the intransigentist and integrist writers who came after him saw only a lamentable breakdown of an ideal order. By 'intransigentism' is meant opposition to any compromise with liberalism and with the Italian state that had deprived the papacy of its temporal dominion. By 'integrism' is meant opposition to any *aggiornamento* in Catholic theology or in terms of the Church's relations with the modern world, together with a rejection of the ideologically pluralist society. Intransigentist and integrist clerical historians held up the model of *cristianità* in order to inspire the mobilized Catholic laity to fight for the resolution of the Roman Question on terms favourable to the papacy, and to increase the influence of the Church in society. Their vision of the past had perhaps something of the character of an 'animating myth'.

Monsignor Pietro Balan (1840–93) was the intransigentist historian par excellence.[17] His ideology was intensely theocratic. With him, the assertion that the Roman Catholic Church had subsumed ancient Rome's universalist role of uniting peoples supported his contention that the papacy was at the centre of world history, a position that in turn underpinned his defence of the pope's temporal dominion.[18] He saw the defeat of Boniface VIII, for whom he had nothing but praise, as the crisis of *la cristianità*; the subsequent partial withdrawal of the papacy from the leadership of society had left the way open for disorder and tyranny.[19]

Giuseppe Toniolo (1845–1918),[20] conventionally hailed as the father of Italian Catholic social thought, was a key

[17] Angelo Gambasin, 'Pietro Balan storiografo apologista del Papato (1840–1893)', *Archivum Historiae Pontificiae*, 4 (1966), pp. 349–54.

[18] Pietro Balan, *Storia d'Italia* (1875–90), 2nd edn, 11 vols (Modena, 1893–8), 1, pp. xii–xxiii, 616–17.

[19] Ibid., 3, pp. 198–200.

[20] Amleto Spicciani, *Giuseppe Toniolo tra economia e storia* (Naples, 1990); on Toniolo's historiography see ch. 13. Citations below are from G. Toniolo, *Opera omnia*, ser. 1 *Scritti storici*, 4 vols (Vatican City, 1947–52) [henceforth OOSS]. A condensed statement of his historical mythology can be found in *Le buoni tradizioni della storia d'Italia* (1891), in OOSS, 1, pp. 372–90.

elaborator of the myth of the medieval Italian communes as shining exemplifications of the Christian Middle Ages. Primarily an economic theorist, his constant concern was the influence of ethical factors on the economy and here religious factors were seldom far from his mind.[21] Furthermore, he imposed Social Catholicism's organicist–corporatist vision upon the Christian Middle Ages: the Church had fostered the system of intermediary bodies – estates and guilds for example – mediating between the individual and the larger collectivity.[22] Ultimately there is a certain ahistoricity in Toniolo's vision of history as the scene of a struggle between the powers of light and darkness that betrays his integrist viewpoint. In *Il socialismo nella storia della civiltà* (1899–1902), socialism is portrayed as an ever-present force of anarchy in the world from classical times onwards, held in check by the Church exercising her 'prophylactic action'. The threat was effectively contained during the Middle Ages when the Church exercised her social function to the full, but with growing rejection of her *magisterium* from the Renaissance onwards, socialism was increasingly able to rear its ugly head.[23] In *Problemi ed ammaestramenti sociali dell'età costantiniana* (*Social Problems and Lessons of the Age of Constantine*), published in 1913, Toniolo asserted that Christianity had countered the tendencies towards both individualism and 'state pantheism' within the Roman Empire;[24] his intransigentist Catholic readers would have recognized in these evils the marks of the liberal Great Beast.

A similarly ahistorical Manichean vision, which so markedly contrasts with Tosti's vision of process in Christian history, is very evident in the work of Monsignor Umberto Benigni (1862–1934), the arch-integrist and central figure of the secret anti-Modernist network, the Sodality of St Pius V. Enjoying some claim to the support of Pius X, he became an

---

[21] See esp. Toniolo, *Dei remoti fattori della potenza economica di Firenze* (1882), in *OOSS*, 4, pp. 221-9.

[22] Idem, 'La genesi storica dell'odierna crisi sociale economica' (1893), in *OOSS*, 1, pp. 103-97, at pp. 118-20; idem, *Problemi ed ammaestramenti sociali dell' età costantiniana* (1913), in *OOSS*, 1, pp. 1-102 at pp. 20-1.

[23] Idem, *Il socialismo nella storia della civiltà* (1899-1902), in *OOSS*, 1, pp. 267-446, *passim*.

[24] Idem, *Problemi ed ammaestramenti*, pp. 10-20.

increasingly isolated extremist figure in the Italian Church after that Pope's death in 1914.[25] Benigni's proclamation of the values of *cristianità* has a strongly theocratic tone: he asserted the necessity of the restoration of the Church's *imperium* over society in its totality,[26] albeit, writing in 1933, he deemed Boniface VIII's conception of the relationship between Church and State to be extremist.[27] While Benigni maintained that the Church had been the 'mother, wet-nurse and governess of European civilization',[28] inheriting ancient Rome's unificatory role, her history, in his account, was one in which she had been locked in continual struggle to contain the forces of evil. Benigni saw history as an ongoing conflict, one that lay at the roots of the contemporary crisis, between the Christian principle which stood for altruism, charity, and social justice, and the pagan principle, one of total egoism, as manifested both in the individual and in the omnipotent state.[29] Clearly Benigni's account of history was intended to inspire the Catholic forces for the battle with liberalism.

In the inter-war years, the liberal enemy long since eclipsed by the socialist one, the discourse on Christian civilization was bound up with a mental complex combining a deep sense of crisis with aspirations towards and expectations of a recatholicization of Italian society, the latter being given focus in Pius XI's pontificate by the official watchword of 'the social reign of Christ'.

A powerful exponent of this ideology was the Franciscan Agostino Gemelli (1878–1959), a central figure in the foundation of the Catholic University of Milan, and its first rector.[30] Gemelli was an enthusiast for Scholasticism while seeking to give Catholics the best scientific education

[25] Pietro Scoppola, 'Benigni, Umberto', in *Dizionario biografico degli Italiani*, 8 (Rome, 1966), pp. 506–8; Emile Poulat, *Catholicisme, démocratie et socialisme. Le mouvement catholique et Mgr. Benigni de la naissance du socialisme à la victoire du fascisme* (Tournai, 1977); on Benigni's historiography see pp. 334–41.

[26] Umberto Benigni, *Storia sociale della Chiesa*, 5 vols in 7 (Milan, 1906–33), 1, p. xviii.

[27] Ibid., 5, pp. 590–2.

[28] Ibid., 1, p. xiv.

[29] Ibid., 1, pp. xiii–xiv, 218–23; 2/1, pp. 24–30; 5, pp. 329–31, 338.

[30] Gustavo Bontadini, 'Gemelli, Agostino', in Francesco Traniello and Giorgio Campanini, eds, *Dizionario storico del movimento cattolico in Italia 1860–1980*, 3 vols in 5 (Casale Monferrato, 1981–4), 2, pp. 225–30.

available, and to create a Catholic technocratic elite imbued with a totalistic view of life which was truly Catholic.[31] Gemelli lamented the 'mechanical' (that is, fragmented and inorganic) character of modern thought, and aspired to the development of an organic culture that would synthesize the whole of human knowledge. He saw the key in a return to the spirit of Scholasticism, the 'perennial philosophy' which, however, he did not see in static terms. 'Medievalism', he wrote, 'gave me a sense of the universal.' The unity of medieval thought corresponded to the sense of collectivity in medieval society.[32]

The true nature of *romanità* (Romanness) was an issue of polemical debate between Catholic spokesmen and Fascists from the late 1920s. In the forefront on the Catholic side was the Jesuit team running the journal *La Civiltà Cattolica*; this team had a strong commitment not only to Scholasticism but also to the traditional education in the classics and, moreover, to Christian archaeology. Again, the Catholic position had a prestigious oratorical exponent in Eugenio Pacelli as Vatican Secretary of State. *Romanità* was a major Fascist keyword, with connotations of state authority, empire, and military and colonizing virtue.[33] Catholic spokesmen insisted that true *romanità* was represented by the Roman Catholic Church, of which Republican and Imperial Rome was a mere precursor. Here the conventional tropes were often accompanied by the assertion that true Roman virtue was represented by the early Christian martyrs, an assertion that linked up with the programme of promoting visits to the Colosseum by pilgrims. One major issue of polemic was whether it was Rome that had made Christianity into an organized world religion, or whether it was the Catholic Church that had truly made Rome the Eternal City; here Catholic spokesmen

[31] See, for example, Agostino Gemelli, O.F.M., *L'Università Cattolica del Sacro Cuore* (Milan, 1921).

[32] A. Gemelli, 'Medioevalismo', *VP*, 1 (1914), pp. 1–2; idem, 'Cultura e religione', *VP*, 9 (1919), pp. 217–26; idem, *Il mio contributo alla filosofia neoscolastica*, 2nd edn (Milan, 1932), pp. 15, 19–20, 89, 91, 97, 98, citations here from pp. 89, 97.

[33] Romke Visser, 'Fascist doctrine and the cult of the *Romanità*', *Journal of Contemporary History*, 27 (1992), pp. 5–52. We basically disagree with Prof. Visser's suggestion that 'the fascist cult of the *romanità* was essential for the propaganda in favour of the "coalition" between right-wing (Catholic) intellectuals and Fascism'.

were obliged to insist on Christianity's Hebraic roots.[34] What was ultimately at issue in this debate was in part the indispensability or otherwise of the Church in any new order, in part the human ideals that the contending parties were seeking to promote.

In the pronouncements of Pacelli as Pope Pius XII (1939–58) can be seen a certain emancipation from the conventional myths about Christian civilization, all the more remarkable in this quintessentially Roman cleric who had been a polished rhetorical exponent of a highly Romanist vision of Catholicism.[35] Pius XII asserted that the Church could not be identified with any given culture and hence that the Middle Ages, while representing *a* Christian culture, in which religion and life formed an indissoluble whole, did not constitute *the* Christian culture *per se*.[36]

The discourse on Christian civilization among the writers examined here had been in significant measure a polemical mode for discussing the issues of the present: for asserting the indispensability of the Catholic religion to political and social order, for claiming a privileged, even hegemonic, position for the Church and for the papacy in Italy. Here it must be remembered how central the concept of right order was to that of civilization, culture being something of an optional extra. The idea of Christian civilization and the allied myth and ideal of *cristianità* were bound up with a style of Catholicism which was focused on this life and on the collectivity, seeing religion in terms of order rather than of individual spiritual development and redemption, and thinking of the Church primarily as an institution. Inevitably, however, the growing emphasis in twentieth-century

---

34 Anon., 'La romanità di Madeleine Sofie Barat', *CC*, 1888 (16 Feb. 1929), pp. 329–36; A. Ferrua, S.J., 'La mostra augustea della romanità', *CC*, 2100 (18 Dec. 1937), pp. 481–91; M. Barbera, S.J., 'Romanità genuina nell'Istituto di Studi Romani', *CC*, 2110 (21 May 1938), pp. 292–303; A. Ferrua, S.J., 'La difesa della romanità', *CC*, 2165 (7 Sept. 1940), pp. 321–30; E. Pacelli, address to Pontificio Istituto d'Archaeologia Cristiana (1932), *DP*, pp. 91–8; idem, address to Catholic Youth, ibid., pp. 125–8; idem, 'Il sacro destino di Roma', address to the Istituto di Studi Romani (1936), ibid., pp. 507–14.

35 Cf. his address cited in nn. 2 and 34.

36 Pius XII, encomium on St Nicholas of Flüe (1947), in *Acta Apostolicae Sedis*, 39 (1947), p. 369; address to the Tenth International Congress of Historical Sciences (1955), ibid., 77 (1955), pp. 680–1.

Catholic theology on the Church as the mystical body of the faithful opened up alternative angles of vision, looking away from that ideal of the Church as a hegemonic institution in society that has so strongly animated the discourse on Christian civilization.[37]

University of East Anglia

[37] On the Christian Democrat intelligentsia emerging at the end of the Fascist period see Renato Moro, *Formazione della classe dirigiente cattolica (1929-1937)* (Bologna, 1979), ch. 11; Menozzi, 'La Chiesa e la storia', pp. 91-3.

RECONSTRUCTING THE REFORMATION:
F. D. MAURICE, LUTHER, AND JUSTIFICATION*

by JEREMY MORRIS

I know well the double danger of giving a mere dry summary of events, or of going into endless disquisitions. . . . But I do think both may be avoided if we seriously believe that our business is to study our records earnestly and devoutly; because they have a meaning in them which we may be helped to draw out; not because we must put a meaning into them.[1]

The Victorian Anglican F. D. Maurice, perhaps best known for his denial of the reality of eternal punishment and for his contribution to Christian Socialism, ranged in a huge published corpus over a wide field of contemporary theology. He is usually described as a Broad Churchman, and his influence on liberal churchmanship and Anglican apologetics has been enormous. And yet his description of the aim and study of history neatly encapsulates the ambiguity many historians and theologians have detected in his own work. Few theologians have been so emphatic in their claim merely to present the 'facts' of history and to let them speak for themselves, and yet few so determined to align those facts with a theological structure at times remote from the particularities of history. The range and depth of his influence mean that Maurice's retrospective view of the Church of England's history, and of its place in the history of the Christian Church as a whole, has exercised a powerful attraction for Anglicans seeking to understand the distinctive ecclesial standing of the Church of England. Yet Maurice's ability to assert time and again arguments which

* I would like to record my thanks to Mr B. L. Horne of King's College, London, for his comments on a draft of this paper.

[1] F. D. Maurice, *Queen's College, London: Its Objects and Method; a Lecture delivered in the Hanover Square Rooms* (London, 1848), p. 25.

seemed to owe little to historical context, despite his apparent readiness to advert to historical 'fact', has left an air of uncertainty hanging over subsequent retrospective interpretations of his own work. The real place of history in Maurice's work remains uncertain. As a consequence, the interpretation of Maurice has oscillated between two poles. On the one hand, there is a view, summed up recently by David Young, that Maurice possessed a 'profound historical sense', informed by his unusual background and education (born as a Unitarian, and received into the Church of England in his late twenties), and that this gave him an exceptionally clear insight into the theological controversies of his day.[2] On the other hand stands the view of Torben Christensen and others that Maurice 'completely accepted the Platonic idea of reality', forcing him into a highly idiosyncratic reading of the history and theology of the Christian Church.[3]

Maurice's treatment of Luther and the doctrine of justification by faith may be a useful test-bed for these differing views. Maurice had a high regard for Luther, verging on the reverence his brother-in-law Julius Hare felt for the German reformer, and Luther played a pivotal role in Maurice's interpretation of the Reformation, and of the whole sweep of Christian history. For long it was claimed, by Michael Ramsey amongst others, that Maurice represented 'one of the few exceptions to the almost constant failure of Anglican theologians to understand Luther'.[4] This view then faded into the background with a more critical reading of the effect of Maurice's Platonism on his understanding of history. But recently it has been restated forcefully by Paul Avis in his book *Anglicanism and the Christian Church*, which seeks to recover, for an authentic Anglican ecclesiology, continuities in the Anglican appropriation of Reformation doctrines of the Church. Avis claims that Maurice 'possessed a rare insight into the central concerns of Luther's thought', and that he

---

[2] David Young, *F. D. Maurice and Unitarianism* (Oxford, 1992), p. 11.

[3] Torben Christensen, *The Divine Order: A Study in F. D. Maurice's Theology* (Leiden, 1973), p. 296.

[4] A. M. Ramsey, *F. D. Maurice and the Conflicts of Modern Theology* (Cambridge, 1951), p. 28.

'probably did more than anyone to bring about the recovery of Reformation principles within Anglicanism'.[5]

Anyone alert both to Maurice's eclecticism in using theological resources and to his consistency in blending them into a quite distinctive theological framework might be inclined to cast some doubt on Avis's claim. Rather, as a historian, one might wonder whether it is far likelier that Maurice's use of Luther is thoroughly of his age, a reconstruction of the Lutheran Reformation in terms which directly served to buttress Maurice's Anglican apologetic and which was driven, at least in part, by nineteenth-century assumptions. Thus, there are three parts to this inquiry. First, how did Maurice interpret justification by faith, and to what extent, if any, did his reading of it differ from Luther's? Second, what role did this interpretation play in Maurice's assessment of the Reformation? And third, what role in turn did it play in his understanding of the Church of England?

Maurice's treatment of Luther in *The Kingdom of Christ* operates within a dialectical reading of each of the main strands of the Christian Church, by which he states first their positive principles, and then their corruption to the neglect of other principles. He describes three insights as central to Luther's theology: justification by faith, divine election, and the exclusive authority of Scripture.[6] Luther's great merit, in Maurice's eyes, is that he effected a reconnection of Christian belief to the reality of the living God, and that was achieved principally in the doctrine of justification by faith, for through it Luther came to perceive that his daily struggles to reconcile the promises conveyed in the Gospel with his intense awareness of his own sin could never be resolved by any effort on his own part. Luther, says Maurice, 'made mere dogmatism about morals look contemptible' as he showed how the 'justice or righteousness of God . . . was proclaimed as the deliverance from the bitter curse of the divine law'.[7]

---

[5] Paul Avis, *Anglicanism and the Christian Church. Theological Resources in Historical Perspective* (Edinburgh, 1989), p. 260.

[6] F. D. Maurice, *The Kingdom of Christ, or Hints to a Quaker respecting the Principles, Constitution, and Ordinances of the Catholic Church*, 2 vols (4th edn, London, 1891), 1, pp. 65–8.

[7] F. D. Maurice, *Moral and Metaphysical Philosophy*, 4 vols (London, 1850–62), 4, p. 122.

Put like that this sounds, by modern standards, a thoroughly conventional reading of Lutheran theology. Maurice came to it, in all probability, through Coleridge, whose own high estimation of Luther has frequently been noted.[8] For Coleridge, developing the Kantian distinction between Reason and Understanding, Reason provided a divinely-implanted mode of perceiving ultimate truth, antecedent to sense impression; Reason, then, was the divine logos in human beings, a non-human means by which 'a knowledge of spiritual truths . . . is rendered possible'.[9] Faith was the instrument, in effect, by which Reason was able to connect itself with God through the Spirit, in other words by which human beings could know God, not just formally, as Mansel was later to argue, but really and personally.[10] Maurice in large measure followed Coleridge's account. He saw faith, through Luther, as the act of going outside of oneself, 'the act of entering into union with another from whom all our graces are to be derived'.[11] But the justification received in faith owed nothing to human effort; it was nothing less than God speaking to the believer.[12]

Nevertheless, in Maurice's formulation, there were significant differences from Coleridge. The use of the term 'Reason' largely dropped out of Maurice's account, and instead its place was supplied by the conscience: it was the conscience to which God spoke.[13] This already marked an unconscious departure from the spirit of Luther; Maurice's use of the term 'conscious' - as when he speaks of the Bible as a book 'speaking directly to the conscience of man' - approaches what Gerhard Ebeling has called 'the usual but questionable interpretation of the conscience as the essence of

---

[8] L. O. Frappell, 'Coleridge and the "Coleridgeans" on Luther', *Journal of Religious History*, 7 (1972-3), pp. 307-23.

[9] S. T. Coleridge, *Aids to Reflection* (1884 edn), p. 67.

[10] H. L. Mansel, *The Limits of Religious Thought Examined* (Oxford, 1858). In *What is Revelation?* (London, 1859), Maurice attacked Mansel's treatment of revelation; there is an adequate account of the ensuring controversy in B. M. G. Reardon, *Religious Thought in the Victorian Age* (London, 1980), pp. 237-42.

[11] Maurice, *Kingdom of Christ*, 1, p. 90.

[12] F. D. Maurice, *Theological Essays* (London, 1853), p. 137.

[13] Ibid., p. 137: 'Of a light speaking to his conscience . . . Luther knew as much as any Quaker could have told him'; idem, *Kingdom of Christ*, 1, p. 63.

the normative contents of the consciousness'.[14] Another difference from Coleridge was that a logos theology was at best no more than implicit in Maurice. It is most strikingly absent, for example, from Maurice's commentary on John's Gospel, though in this Luther would have concurred with him.[15] Above all, however, in Maurice's hands, the direct relation which justification established between God and the believer began to take on a much more abstract form. Maurice, preoccupied as ever with the eternal verities behind human particularity, couched his interpretation in terms which seemed to generalize the God–human relation, to the point where the justification of the individual believer almost amounted to incorporation into a relation which existed in a timeless universe. Luther, said Maurice, disclosed the innermost law of human being, that 'union with another is his law; separation from him, his transgression'.[16] It is possible to see this as a simple linguistic quirk, concealing a doctrine which essentially conformed to the Lutheran perspective. But Maurice gave it a further twist, which has a resonance across the whole range of his theology. He saw the relation established in justification as already present, *in potentia*, as it were (although he never speaks directly of it as such). Accordingly, the emphasis in justification in his terms is not on the rescue of a sinner by an alien righteousness, but on the declaration of a state which is the deepest inner reality of the human condition. Just how un-Lutheran, and ambiguous, the resulting fusion of Platonism and Lutheranism could sound is evident from his description of the justified believer's faith: 'The Lutheran habitually contemplates a Divine Person, having a real distinct life; rejoices that He entered into ordinary human relations and circumstances; realises his own connexion with Him through those relations and circumstances.'[17] In the chapter on 'Justification by Faith' in his *Theological Essays*, Maurice denies that it is possible humanly

[14]   Ibid., 1, p. 69; Gerhard Ebeling, *Luther: An Introduction to his Thought* (London, 1970), p. 261.

[15]   F. D. Maurice, *The Gospel of St. John. A Series of Discourses* (London, 1857); see especially ch. 2, 'The Word the Light of Men'.

[16]   Maurice, *Kingdom of Christ*, 1, p. 88.

[17]   Ibid., 1, p. 76.

to draw a sharp line between the righteous and the wicked, asserting that 'God has ... Himself established eternal distinctions, which become clear to us when ... we are content to be the heralds of His free and universal love.'[18]

The parallel between Maurice's account of justification by faith and Luther's own account was partial at best. Maurice rightly perceived that faith, to Luther, was not the subjective, human feeling his opponents had alleged, but an encounter initiated and sustained by God himself. However he had come to this insight, whether through Coleridge or, as David Young implies, through Unitarian sources (both influences drawing in part on the Cambridge Platonists), it seems to have appealed to Maurice because it fitted so well his theology of revelation, according to which God discloses himself as Father of the race of humankind, and human beings are bound up with him in a filial union in which they know God as he is in himself.[19] This reflects an absolutely transcendental, 'top-down' view of revelation, which has led some to claim that Maurice was a forerunner of Barth, anticipating the Barthian critique of natural theology.[20] But there is another strand in Maurice, which struggled against this, and that is immanentist, seeing God's order as permanently present, merely, in a sense, needing to be declared. Put in this context, his view of justification departs substantially from Luther. It rejects the language of alien righteousness, tending to play down the reality of sin and putting faith once more back into a passive mode, against the active view which scholars now attribute to Luther.[21]

---

[18] Maurice, *Theological Essays*, p. 198.

[19] According to Young, it was Maurice's Christocentricity which drew him away from Unitarian theology, and not the idea of the filial relation of humankind to God, which he shared with Unitarians and which asserted that 'God is with and for man, not apart from and against him.' Young, *F. D. Maurice and Unitarianism*, p. 232.

[20] Ellen Flesseman-Van Leer, *Grace Abounding: a Comparison of F. D. Maurice and Karl Barth* (London, 1968).

[21] 'Unless a man has faith, he will never understand the true meaning of the cross, and its mystery will remain forever hidden from him. Equally, *unless he has faith, the perceived significance of the cross cannot be appropriated, and translated into the real and redeeming presence of Christ within the believer*': A. E. McGrath, *Luther's Theology of the Cross* (Oxford, 1985), pp. 174–5 [my emphasis].

This highly compressed and selective account of Maurice's treatment of Luther and justification leads on to the question of the role it played in Maurice's account of the Reformation. If, as Maurice asserted, Luther perceived that, through faith, we are declared righteous, and thereby the original (and underlying) union of God and human being is re-established, the preliminary question must be, How does this happen? For Maurice, shying away from the *theologia crucis*, it was through faith in the incarnation, because Christ is the head of the human race, ontologically as well as representatively: all human being, in other words, meets in Christ and through him is in union with the Father: 'Christ's resurrection declared Him to be the Son of man, the Head of man, and therefore that His justification was the justification of each man.'[22] From this, Maurice made a surprising ecclesiological deduction. The Lutheran theology of justification enabled faith to be reconnected with the real head of the Church, Christ himself. It replaced nothing less than a false head, a physical, temporal head, namely the pope: for Luther, 'ultimately all priests, doctors, Popes, mediators of any kind, must be pushed out of the way because they stand between him and the Mediator in whom he can see God and God can see him.'[23] Roman Catholic theology, Maurice claimed, implies that Christ is absent from his Church, and so there must be a visible, vicarious head of it.[24] Justification by faith frees the individual believer from his or her slavery to the religious despotism of this 'kingly' conception of the pope; the Reformation amounted to a proper reassertion of the religious rights of the individual.[25] Douglas Powell once argued that there was no logical connection between the Lutheran doctrine of justification by faith, and Lutheran political theory.[26] The link is explicit in Maurice, however: in his or her justification, the believer could say 'I do not belong merely to a great Christendom, I have a distinct individual

---

22 Maurice, *Theological Essays*, p. 200.
23 Idem, *Moral and Metaphysical Philosophy*, 4, p. 117.
24 Idem, *Kingdom of Christ*, 2, p. 175.
25 Idem, *Moral and Metaphysical Philosophy*, 4, p. 118.
26 Douglas Powell, unpublished paper on 'Reformation and Deviation in the Sixteenth Century', p. 17.

position', and this feeling, Maurice says, was connected to that 'of belonging to a particular soil, and speaking a particular language'.[27]

Now it is important to put this in the context of Maurice's understanding of history as a whole, a subject which has not received the attention it deserved.[28] It followed from Maurice's fusion of Platonistic ontology with a theology of revelation that God was working in and through history, and that the 'hidden history' of humankind, the story of its relationship with God, was being made manifest in the events of history. 'It is the great struggle of every time', he wrote to an admirer, 'to realise the union of the spiritual and eternal with the manifestations of it in time.'[29] Though an admirer of the spirit of scientific history, in practice Maurice was led to see history as an interaction of competing theological and philosophical ideas. In that sense, he was a 'dialectical idealist'. This is evident both in the seemingly synthetic way he treated different churches in *The Kingdom of Christ*, and in his method, in the *Moral and Metaphysical Philosophy*, of attempting to draw out the ideas for which particular thinkers were witnesses. He read the history of medieval Christendom as a history of rival ideas, which could be encapsulated in different aspirations for unity: the papacy represented one such, the conciliar movement another. But through Occam, and subsequently through the Florentine Academy, the perception of a real, divinely-ordained, and existing unity struggled to make headway against the false unity created by the papacy.[30] The real basis of unity, union with the real head of the Church, eventually burst forth in the

27 Maurice, *Kingdom of Christ*, 1, p. 71.

28 None of the accounts of Maurice's theology published in the last half-century or so give more than passing attention to his views on history. This is surely related to the almost complete neglect today of his *Moral and Metaphysical Philosophy*, an enormous and far from readable survey of Western philosophy and theology from ancient Greece to the nineteenth century, which attempted to expound the leading ideas of each period and to draw them together into a synthetic unity.

29 F. Maurice, *The Life of Frederick Denison Maurice*, 2 vols (London, 1884), 2, p. 264.

30 F. D. Maurice, *Moral and Metaphysical Philosophy*, 4, chs 1–3; see, for example, ibid., p. 31: 'May not each nation come at last to understand its own calling, to recognize it as a calling?'

Reformation, disclosing the spiritual constitution latent in certain forms of social organization – namely the family and, above all (for our purposes), the nation.

We might pause to consider briefly the implications of all this for Maurice's view of Luther himself, before passing on to the broader question of the character and identity of the Church of England. Maurice saw Luther in heroic terms, 'tilting at propositions' vehemently and asserting 'the right and duty to believe in God who justifies' as 'the deadly blow, to those who make faith consist in assent to propositions'.[31] He shared this view with Julius Hare, who praised Luther in almost apocalyptic terms in his *Vindication of Luther*.[32] He also shared it with Coleridge, and of course with Thomas Carlyle.[33] In all of these writers Luther was seen as a prophet of religious freedom, and thereby as an architect or forerunner of modern political freedom and the nation-state. This was a view which stood in contrast both to the then more cautious, mainstream Anglican reading of Luther as a necessary but blunt instrument of religious reform, and to the Tractarian reading of him as the progenitor of subjective theories of faith and hence of modern rationalism.[34]

However, this view of Luther cannot be cut out of its nineteenth-century context, as though it reaches back unquestionably to the 'real' Luther without retaining traces of its own era. This becomes very apparent when we look more closely at the role of Maurice's understanding of the Reformation in his Anglican ecclesiology and apologetic. Stephen Sykes has rightly accused Maurice of holding a 'romantic-idealist'

---

[31] F. Maurice, *Life*, 2, p. 615; 'the character of the Reformation is interpreted by those [mental conflicts] which tormented the Monk of Wittenberg': F. D. Maurice, *Kingdom of Christ*, 1, p. 62.

[32] J. C. Hare, *Vindication of Luther against his Recent English Assailants* (Cambridge, 1855), p. 293.

[33] Appreciative references to the 'lion-hearted Luther' (S. T. Coleridge, *On the Constitution of the Church and State* [London, 1972], p. 117) are scattered throughout Coleridge's writings; see especially Frappell, 'Coleridge and the "Coleridgeans" on Luther'. For Carlyle's view, see his *On Heroes, Hero-Worship, and the Heroic in History* (London, 1908), ch. 4, 'The Hero as Priest', pp. 346–88.

[34] See the evaluation of J. H. Newman's *Lectures on Justification* (London, 1837) by A. E. McGrath, *Iustitia Dei: A History of the Christian Doctrine of Justification*, 2 vols (Cambridge, 1986), 2, pp. 121–30.

view of national character and destiny.[35] His writing is shot through with references to the 'honest', 'practical', and 'manly' character of the English people.[36] He accused the Tractarians of throwing aside Anglican and national feelings.[37] The Reformation was a 'blessed step' in God's purpose, producing in the various Protestant national Churches the apprehension of the reality of the object of faith, by its dethroning of the papacy's pretence to embody the universal, spiritual society of the Church.[38] Once again, in all this Maurice demonstrated his debt to a variety of English sources, particularly to Coleridge and to Burke, whom he called 'the index to all modern thoughts and speculations on political subjects'.[39] From these writers he drew the conclusion that no sharp line could be set between the Church and the secular State; both Church and State were different aspects of the same underlying spiritual reality, the universal order God had established in human society. There was no opposition at all between the Kingdom of Christ and national society, though the two did not coincide absolutely; rather, the Kingdom of Christ was the 'quickening spirit' of national society, establishing itself through and alongside national forms.[40]

Despite Maurice's highly influential discussion of what he took to be the 'signs' of the Catholic Church, or spiritual society (baptism, the creeds, fixed liturgies, the Eucharist, the three-fold order of ministry, and the scriptures), and despite his asseverations that these are the definitive, constitutive marks of the Christian Church as a distinct body in the world, it is hard to escape the conclusion that side by side with this is a quite separate insight into the Church of England as constituted ontologically, and not just historically, as an expression of English national identity. He did

---

[35] Stephen Sykes, *The Integrity of Anglicanism* (Oxford, 1978), p. 16.

[36] See especially Maurice, *Kingdom of Christ*, 2, pp. 389–97, section entitled 'What is the Form of Character which belongs especially to Englishmen? To what kind of Depravation is it liable?'

[37] F. D. Maurice, *Three Letters to the Rev. William Palmer*, 2nd edn (London, 1842), p. 24.

[38] Idem, *Thoughts on the Rule of Conscientious Subscription, on the Thirty-Nine Articles, and on the Present Perils from the Romish System* (Oxford, 1845), pp. 47–8.

[39] Maurice, *Life*, 1, p. 217.

[40] Maurice, *Kingdom of Christ*, 2, p. 240–5.

not have an uncritical view of the Church of England: on the contrary, he was scathing about the existence within it of different 'parties' seeking to import into it 'systems' of opinion essentially foreign to it.[41] But he did appear to see it as a natural and structurally pure embodiment, in a national context, of the universal Church. 'What Englishmen chiefly want', he declared, 'is a clear recognition that the spiritual is also the practical. . . . This the Reformers provided.'[42]

Thus a series of strands can be drawn together. In the Lutheran doctrine of justification by faith, Maurice saw the re-emergence historically of the perception that in faith the individual man or woman is brought into union with God. Since this union already exists for all human beings through the sacrifice and justification of Christ, that which is real, that which eternally is, becomes manifest in the particularity of the life of the believer. The incarnate Christ, who is the head of the human race, was visibly enthroned once more as really and absolutely that head in the Churches of the Reformation. The dethronement of the kingly papacy, the pretence at a visible head of the Church, meant that through faith Christians spiritually become in a sense most fully what they already are, children of their divine Father. Their existence as individuals is restored to them. But, just as their own relation with God is uncovered, so is the divine order manifested in forms of human organization, above all that of the nation. In England, the Church of England's retention of the signs of the Catholic Church, its Lutheran insight into justification, as well as a common national culture, meant that it was the material embodiment of the universal spiritual society. On this view, it is not going too far to say that Maurice had reconstructed the Reformation according to a thoroughly nineteenth-century understanding of national identity.

In conclusion, three linked sets of observations may be put forward, suggesting how the Church of England has itself related in retrospect to Maurice and his theology. The first

[41] See especially F. D. Maurice, *Reasons for not Joining a Party in the Church* (London, 1841).
[42] Idem, *The Prayer-Book Considered Especially in Reference to the Romish System*, 3rd edn (London, 1880), p. 12.

concerns the question of Maurice's uniqueness or distinctiveness in modern Anglican theology. There has been a tendency recently, from a variety of perspectives, to isolate Maurice from his contemporaries, and to see him as a remote, prophetic, and undoubtedly obscure figure who remains, in Aidan Nichols's phrase, 'somewhat unplaceable'.[43] Whether he is seem primarily as a Platonist, according to Torben Christensen, and David Thompson, or as someone who never quite left Unitarianism behind, according to David Young, still he is contrasted with the main theological trends of his time.[44] That emphasis is surely misplaced, fuelled as it may be by Maurice's own rather exaggerated sense of persecution, and by his son's concern in the *Life* to vindicate him as a widely misunderstood figure. Not only is it possible to delineate a wide range of influences on Maurice, to construct a long list of Victorian clergymen and laity who held him in high regard and who to varying degrees echoed his views, to see him as the fountain-head of a distinct stream of social criticism within Anglicanism, and to trace his influence across a wide spectrum of modern theologians, embracing both Catholics and Protestants, it is also possible, as attempted here, to demonstrate how rooted his theology was in the assumptions and beliefs of his age.[45]

The second set of observations concerns the placing of Maurice within Anglican ecclesiological reflection, a tradition both Paul Avis and Stephen Sykes have recently begun to reinvigorate. Sykes and Avis reach assessments of Maurice which are almost opposed, Sykes dismissive of the arguments for Anglican 'comprehensiveness' allegedly derived from Maurice, Avis complimentary about Maurice's concern to

[43] Aidan Nichols, *The Panther and the Hind. A Theological History of Anglicanism* (Edinburgh, 1993), p. 176.

[44] Christensen, *The Divine Order*; D. M. Thompson, 'F. D. Maurice: rebel conservative', in S. P. Mews, ed., *Modern Religious Rebels* (London, 1993), pp. 123–43; Young, *F. D. Maurice and Unitarianism*.

[45] Kenneth Cracknell has recently demonstrated another series of connections, previously unexplored, in Maurice's influence on the study of comparative religion and on the theological formation of missionaries in the late nineteenth and early twentieth centuries: see his *Justice, Courtesy and Love: Theologians and Missionaries Encountering World Religions, 1846–1914* (London, 1995), ch. 2, 'Five Theologians and World Religions'.

emphasize the Church of England's Reformation heritage.[46] It is impossible fully to do justice to their respective cases here, but it ought to be clear that, while I have some scepticism about Avis's case, it seems to me that Sykes has appropriately identified one of the weaknesses of Maurice's ecclesiology, namely his reliance on one particular interpretation of national culture. Again, however, there is nothing unique about this aspect of his work. It can be found in a wide range of nineteenth-century Anglican apologists; in (to cite just a few examples) Robert Southey's controversy with the Catholic historians Charles Butler and John Milner; J. R. Seeley's contribution to *Essays in Church Policy* (1868) and in his other writings; and W. H. Fremantle's Bampton Lectures of 1883 on *The World as the Subject of Redemption* (1885).[47] Although it has virtually disappeared from modern Anglican theology, there has been a firm tradition of rooting the Church of England's justification for its own distinct ecclesial existence in an argument which owed much to a historical concept of national identity, and Maurice's ecclesiology certainly falls within that tradition.

Finally, there is the question of the influence of historical context on the reformulation of Christian doctrine. Maurice thought he had penetrated to the heart of Lutheran theology and uncovered the 'real Luther', and in the process had disclosed the inner meaning of the Reformation. In fact what he had effected was simply a reconstruction of the Reformation in nineteenth-century terms. Despite his own awareness of the dangers of prejudicial history, he was unable to disentangle his systematic theology from his historical analysis. As a result, his account of the Reformation, shared in outline by many of his contemporaries, bears considerable resemblance to the Whig caricature demolished by Butterfield so many years ago. Had he had the chance, he

---

[46] Sykes, *Integrity of Anglicanism, passim*; Avis, *Anglicanism and the Christian Church*, ch. 16, 'F. D. Maurice and the Shaking of the Seven Hills'.

[47] S. Gilley, 'Nationality and liberty, Protestant and Catholic: Robert Southey's Book of the Church', *SCH*, 18 (1982), pp. 409–32; R. T. Shannon, 'John Robert Seeley and the idea of a national Church', in R. Robson, ed., *Ideas and Institutions of Victorian Britain* (London, 1967), pp. 236–52; P. T. Phillips, 'The concept of a national Church in late nineteenth-century England and America', *Journal of Religious History*, 14 (1986), pp. 26–37.

might well have assented to Butterfield's warning that 'History is subtle lore and it may lock us in the longest argument in a circle that one can imagine.'[48] But I suspect he would not have been perturbed by that. For his primary assumption of a God working through human history is one it is extremely difficult to prise apart altogether from the working methods and discipline of the historian, if one believes as a Christian that God has revealed himself in time. If they are to be prised apart, either one must simply capitulate to a thoroughly providential understanding of history and abandon critical methods altogether, or one must presuppose some inner material dynamic or foundation to history which excludes any form of divine action. Neither seems an attractive option, either for church historians or for systematic theologians. Our perception that there was rather more 'reading into' than 'reading off' going on in Maurice's interpretation of the Reformation merely reminds us of continuing dilemmas in the attempt to study the history of the Christian Church.

Westcott House, Cambridge

---

48 H. Butterfield, *The Whig Interpretation of History* (London, 1931; 1973 edn), p. 27.

THE OXFORD MOVEMENT IN LATE-
NINETEENTH-CENTURY RETROSPECT:
R. W. CHURCH, J. H. RIGG, AND WALTER WALSH

by MARTIN WELLINGS

Although over 160 years have passed since John Keble's Assize sermon on National Apostasy, the study of the Oxford Movement continues to absorb the attention of historians. Within the last decade, for example, two major biographies of Newman have appeared, together with a careful examination of the relationship between Tractarianism and the Anglican High Church tradition.[1] In an essay on 'The Oxford Movement and its reminiscencers', Owen Chadwick commented concerning the historiography of Tractarianism that 'too many have made it an industry': the industry, however, still seems to be productive.[2]

The present paper examines the Oxford Movement from the perspective of the 1890s. This was the period of Tractarian reminiscence and biography, as the leading figures of the Oxford Movement reached the end of their lives.[3] Pusey died in 1882, and H. P. Liddon spent the next eight years working on his monumental four-volume *Life of Edward Bouverie Pusey*, published posthumously from 1893. Newman's brother-in-law, Tom Mozley, brought out his *Reminiscences chiefly of Oriel College and the Oxford Movement* in 1882, and three years later, Mark Pattison's *Memoirs* were published. Wilfrid Ward's *W. G. Ward and the Oxford Movement* appeared in 1889. Books, review articles, reminiscences, and conversation were therefore turning to the events of the 1830s as the key figures of the movement wrote memoirs or called forth biographies.

[1] Ian Ker, *John Henry Newman. A Biography* (Oxford, 1988); Sheridan Gilley, *Newman and his Age* (London, 1990); P. B. Nockles, *The Oxford Movement in Context: Anglican High Churchmanship, 1760-1857* (Cambridge, 1994).
[2] Owen Chadwick, 'The Oxford Movement and its reminiscencers', in *The Spirit of the Oxford Movement. Tractarian Essays* (Cambridge, 1990), p. 152.
[3] Chadwick, 'Oxford Movement', pp. 136-45.

The Oxford Movement in 1890 was far from being merely a topic for historical analysis. It was still both influential and controversial in English ecclesiastical life, as contemporary histories made plain. First, Tractarian theology and emphases had been widely assimilated in the Church of England (although by no means universally accepted), underscoring the position of Anglicanism as a *via media* between Rome and Geneva, setting store by the historic episcopate, the apostolic succession, and the liturgy of the Prayer Book, and emphasizing the calling of the Church to be a visible divine society marked by its sacramental life and pursuit of holiness.[4] Second, Tractarianism, especially in the eucharistic theology of its second generation and in the practical outworking of its principles in urban slums, was one stream feeding the development of ritualism, which had become a powerful force in the Church of England by the end of the nineteenth century. The Anglo-Catholic party of the 1890s was growing in strength and confidence, and whilst the flamboyant and provocative style of some of its members was far removed from the Tractarian ideal of 'reserve', it claimed continuity with the pioneers of the 1830s.[5] Third, opposition to Anglo-Catholic doctrine and ritualist practice continued to make the legacy of the Oxford Movement controversial. The pro-Tractarian English Church Union was matched by the staunchly Protestant Church Association. Ritualism was challenged by legislation and prosecution, so that in 1890 two celebrated cases were still before the courts, the defendants being a Liverpool incumbent, the Revd James Bell Cox, and the Bishop of Lincoln, Edward King, both facing charges of using illegal ritual.[6] The charge of Romanizing,

---

[4]   J. M. Turner, *Conflict and Reconciliation* (London, 1985), pp. 153–67; G. Rowell, *The Vision Glorious: Themes and Personalities of the Catholic Revival in Anglicanism* (Oxford, 1983).

[5]   Ibid., chs 5 and 6; O. Chadwick, *The Victorian Church*, 2 vols, 2nd edn (London, 1972), 2, pp. 308–19; *Report of the Royal Commission on Ecclesiastical Discipline*, 4 vols (London, 1906), 1, p. 296; 2, pp. 341–73.

[6]   On Protestant opposition to ritualism, M. Wellings, 'Some aspects of late nineteenth century Anglican Evangelicalism' (Oxford University D.Phil. thesis, 1989), chs 2 and 3; on ritual prosecutions, James Bentley, *Ritualism and Politics in Victorian Britain. The Attempt to Legislate for Belief* (Oxford, 1978), chs 3 and 5. Ian Farley, 'J. C. Ryle – episcopal evangelist. A study in late Victorian Evangelicalism'

frequently levelled against the Tractarians and their successors, received apparent reinforcement during the 1890s with the publication of details of Lord Halifax's negotiations with the Abbé Portal on reunion with Rome.[7]

The legacy of Tractarianism was widely disseminated by 1890 – more widely, perhaps, than critics were willing to recognize. The movement had done much to shape English Church life, and it had inevitably affected relations between the Church of England and the Free Churches.[8] The histories of the 1890s, therefore, were written against a background of acknowledgement, grudging or enthusiastic, of Tractarian influence, of confident Anglo-Catholicism, and of continuing militancy from Evangelicals and Free Churchmen. The following examination of three particular histories seeks to demonstrate the relationship between context and contents in the Church's reflection on its past, using three accounts published during that decade by authors whose knowledge, experience, and opinion of Tractarianism differed widely. One, R. W. Church, saw the movement from the inside and remained loyal to Tractarian principles throughout his long career in the Church of England. Another, J. H. Rigg, approached the movement from the standpoint of Wesleyan Methodism, and wrote one of the first primarily critical histories by a non-Anglican. The third historian, Walter Walsh, produced an influential piece of Protestant polemic which both arose from and interacted with the context of the 1890s, the era of 'the last Victorian anti-ritualist campaign'.[9] Together their works show how a concern for the past produced different perspectives, from differing viewpoints, which had reverberations in contemporary thought and attitudes.

(Durham University Ph.D. thesis, 1988), ch. 6, presents a different view of the Bell Cox case. Rowell, *Vision Glorious*, pp. 153–7, describes the Lincoln case.

[7] J. G. Lockhart, *Charles Lindley, Viscount Halifax*, 2 vols (London, 1936), 2, pp. 41–91.

[8] Turner, *Conflict and Reconciliation*, pp. 159–64; Wellings, 'Some aspects', pp. 87–95. One example of Wesleyan sensitivity was opposition to the use of Gace's *Catechism* in Church schools: *The Times* (London), 28 Nov. 1895, p. 9, and subsequent correspondence.

[9] G. I. T. Machin, 'The last Victorian anti-ritualist campaign, 1895–1906', *Victorian Studies*, 25 (1982), pp. 277–302.

The first author to be considered, Richard William Church, was born in 1815, the son of a mercantile family.[10] Much of his early life was spent in Italy, but the death of his father in 1828 brought the family back to England, where, unable to afford the school fees for Winchester, Mrs Church sent her son to 'a humdrum school of Evangelical character' near Bristol.[11] Church went on from there to Wadham College, Oxford, in 1833. Despite his Evangelical antecedents, or perhaps because of them, Church 'shrank from the very pronounced Evangelical men' at Oxford.[12] A family connection with George Moberly, Fellow and Tutor of Balliol, and a friendship with Charles Marriott brought Church into contact with the Tractarians, and while he was reading for a fellowship at Oriel (1836–8) he became a regular attender at St Mary's and a disciple of Newman.[13] From 1836 onwards Church was intimately involved in the development of the Oxford Movement, contributing to the *Library of the Fathers*, writing for the *British Critic*, and resigning his tutorship at Oriel over the Provost's opposition to *Tract 90*.[14] When the attempt was made to censure the *Tract* in Convocation in February 1845, it was Church as Junior Proctor who played the key role in persuading his senior colleague, H. P. Guillemard, to veto the resolution.[15]

Newman's secession was a devastating experience for Church, one 'so intensely painful' that he seldom referred to it.[16] He remained at Oxford until 1853, when he moved to Somerset as Rector of Whatley, spending eighteen years as a rural incumbent with leisure to produce a stream of books, articles, and reviews. In 1871 Church was persuaded to

[10] For biographical information on Dean Church, see Mary C. Church, ed., *Life and Letters of Dean Church* (London, 1895); D. C. Lathbury, *Dean Church* (London, 1905); A. B. Donaldson, *Richard William Church* (London, 1905); *DNB Supplement* (Oxford, 1901), pp. 431–4.

[11] Geoffrey Best, 'R. W. Church and the Oxford Movement', in his edition of *The Oxford Movement. Twelve Years. 1833–45* (Chicago, 1970), p. xi.

[12] Church, *Life and Letters*, p. 13.

[13] Ibid., p. 14.

[14] Oxford, Pusey House, Church MSS, misc. letters, Church to E. Hawkins, 23 March 1841, and Hawkins to Church, 29 March and 2 June 1841.

[15] Ibid., Church to Greenhill, ? Feb. 1845; *Record* (London), 13 March 1891, p. 248.

[16] Church, *Life and Letters*, pp. 59, 321–2.

accept Gladstone's offer of the Deanery of St Paul's, and he died in office in December 1890. First as Rector and then as Dean, Church exemplified the Tractarian ideal of pastoral ministry.

Church's working papers show that he was preparing a study of the Oxford Movement from the autumn of 1884 onwards.[17] Pusey had urged him to undertake such a project, and the appearance of Tom Mozley's *Reminiscences* in 1882, and of an expanded version of William Palmer's *A Narrative of Events connected with the Publication of the Tracts for the Times* a year later, made an accurate and sympathetic portrayal highly desirable to the friends of the movement.[18] Although Church had his first draft completed by May 1886, *The Oxford Movement. Twelve Years, 1833–45* was published only posthumously in 1891. Owen Chadwick has suggested that a combination of Tractarian reserve and the enduring pain of 1845 prevented Church from going to press before Newman's death in August 1890, by which time Church himself had less than four months to live.[19]

In a letter to Lord Acton, Church disclaimed any wish to 'write a history of the movement, or to account for it or adequately to judge it and put it in its due place in relation to the religious and philosophical history of the time'. His purpose, rather, was 'simply to preserve a contemporary memorial of what seems to me to have been a true and noble effort which passed before my eyes'.[20] He approached his task through a blend of biography and chronological narrative, offering essays on leading figures of the movement (Keble, Froude, Williams, Marriott, Ward) and on key events (the *Tracts for the Times*, the Hampden controversy, *Tract 90*, Ward's *Ideal*, Newman's secession). The figure of Newman dominated the narrative, from the preface, which hailed him as 'a man of genius, whose name is among the illustrious names of his age', to the concluding chapter, whose title, 'The

---

[17] Oxford, Pusey House, Church MSS, working papers for *The Oxford Movement*, dated between Sept. 1884 and May 1886.

[18] Chadwick, 'Oxford Movement', pp. 139–44; Best, 'R. W. Church', p. xix.

[19] Chadwick, 'Oxford Movement', pp. 143–5.

[20] R. W. Church, *The Oxford Movement. Twelve Years. 1833–45*, p. vi. This, and all subsequent quotations from *The Oxford Movement*, are taken from the 1900 reprint of the 3rd edn (London, 1892).

Catastrophe', summed up Church's view of the secession. Newman's career as a Tractarian set the bounds of the study, and Church strained every nerve to present a sympathetic account of his hero's theological pilgrimage.[21]

Space precludes a full critique of *The Oxford Movement*,[22] but a number of points may be made briefly. An experienced essayist, writing with a wealth of personal knowledge of the protagonists, Church produced a lucid and compelling account of the movement which has had an enduring historiographical significance. A contemporary Evangelical reviewer described Church's work as 'the calmest, the most judicial, as well as the most interesting account of the movement attempted on the side of its sympathisers'.[23] The same review, however, also drew attention to weaknesses in the book, and later historians have echoed contemporary criticisms. The undue concentration on Newman has already been noted, and Church's loyalty to his old friend led to a failure to take seriously the exasperation of those Tractarians who deplored the Romeward drift in the early 1840s. The portrayal of opponents and critics, notably R. D. Hampden and the Heads of Houses at Oxford, was uncharacteristically savage: 'In their apathy, in their self-satisfied ignorance, in their dulness of apprehension and forethought, the authorities of the University let pass the great opportunity of their time.'[24] The tone of the scene-setting chapter on 'The Church in the Reform Days' and the chronological boundaries of the book underplayed the continuity between Anglican High Churchmanship and Tractarianism, ignored the complex relationship between the Tractarians and a far from moribund Evangelical school, and exaggerated the significance for many outside Oxford of the 1845 secessions.[25] These

---

21 Ibid., pp. ix, 32, 130–2; Best, 'R. W. Church', pp. xv–vi and xix–xxi.

22 For such a critique, see ibid., pp. xvi–xxxi; Chadwick, 'Oxford Movement', pp. 145–53; Nockles, *Oxford Movement in Context*, pp. 6–7.

23 *Record*, 13 March 1891, p. 248.

24 Church, *Oxford Movement*, p. 247. Compare pp. 162 and 320–4 on Hampden. Chapter 9 consistently suggests that Hampden was theologically out of his depth.

25 Ibid., pp. 9–12 and 12–16. Contrast Nockles on the High Church school, and Best, 'R. W. Church', pp. xxviii–ix on the Evangelicals. The complex relationship between Evangelical and Tractarian influences on individuals has been studied by David Newsome in *The Parting of Friends* (London, 1966).

emphases revealed Church's own personal context: his background combined ignorance of the High Church tradition with antipathy to the Evangelicalism of home and school; his experience as one of Newman's closest friends left him needing to exorcize the ghosts of 1845; while his participation in the Tractarian and ritual controversies encouraged him to present the Oxford Movement as the first stage in 'the Church revival of this century'. Church wrote as an apologist: for Newman, in the light of Mozley's *Reminiscences* and Palmer's *Narrative*, for the High Church party in the face of the Public Worship Regulation Act, ritual prosecutions, and the Lincoln Case, and for himself, as one who came through the ordeal of 1845 believing in 'the Catholic foundations of the English Church'.[26] The qualifications of its author as protagonist, witness, and master of English prose, however, ensured an enduring place for Church's book in the historiography of the Oxford Movement.[27]

One writer who was not greatly impressed by *The Oxford Movement* was the Wesleyan Methodist James Harrison Rigg, whose *Oxford High Anglicanism and its Chief Leaders* appeared in October 1895. Rigg gave Church credit for 'fulness of knowledge' and 'mastery of details', but found the work incomplete, and far too charitable in its assessment of Froude and Newman. In Rigg's opinion, moreover, Church's position as 'a High Anglo-Catholic' was intellectually untenable, since it rested on a defective ecclesiology which offered no convincing defence against Roman claims.[28] It may be seen, therefore, that *Oxford High Anglicanism* took a markedly different stance from Church's sympathetic study.

Rigg, born in January 1821, was a well-known figure in the Wesleyan Connexion. Brought up in comparatively

[26] Church, *Life and Letters*, pp. 244ff., 321–2; Church, *Oxford Movement*, pp. ix, 397; Oxford, Pusey House, Church MSS, misc. letters, Church to J. B. Lightfoot, 4 May 1881 (on S. F. Green) and Church to E. W. Benson, 26 May 1887 (on Bell Cox).

[27] Chadwick, 'Oxford Movement', p. 153. The Chicago edition of 1970 placed *The Oxford Movement* in a series of 'Classics of British Historical Literature', justifying the inclusion on pp. vii–ix.

[28] J. H. Rigg, *Oxford High Anglicanism and its Chief Leaders* (London, 1895), pp. 87, 91 93–4, 101–2, 104–8.

straitened circumstances and educated at Kingswood School, he entered the Wesleyan ministry in 1845, rising to be Principal of Westminster College (1868–1903) and twice President of the Conference (1878 and 1892).[29]

Rigg was a self-taught scholar, without Dean Church's intimate personal knowledge of Tractarian Oxford.[30] He was also a prolific writer and a vigorous controversialist, as he demonstrated in his reply to criticisms of his book in *The Times*.[31] In his early years in the ministry he defended the Connexional leadership during the Fly-Sheet controversy and his first book, *Principles of Wesleyan Methodism*, published in 1850, was a justification of Wesleyan ecclesiology. Later works argued for a Connexional system of Church government against congregationalism on the one hand or episcopacy on the other. Rigg played an active part in denominational politics, defining his position as 'conservative-liberal'. He exercised considerable influence on Wesleyan education policy, and, through his editorship of the *London Quarterly Review* (1868–98), he had ready access to a platform for his trenchant opinions.

As one critic noted, *Oxford High Anglicanism* was not an entirely new book.[32] It drew together essays on various aspect of the Oxford Movement which had previously appeared in the *London Quarterly Review* and also used material from an earlier study of *The Character and Life-Work of Dr Pusey*, published in 1883. In the preface, Rigg wrote that he was taking the opportunity afforded by the appearance of biographies of Ward and Pusey, as well as that of Church's book, to write a history of the Oxford Movement from a Nonconformist point of view.[33] Several aspects of his study may be noted. First, the timescale of Rigg's book was very

[29] The fullest biography of Rigg is J. Telford, *The Life of James Harrison Rigg, D.D., 1821–1909* (London, 1909). There is also an entry in *DNB Supplement*, pp. 199–200, and a recent pamphlet by David Carter, *James H. Rigg* (Peterborough, 1994).
[30] *Church Quarterly Review*, 41 (1896), pp. 361–4, drew mocking attention to Rigg's lack of first-hand knowledge of Oxford ways and terminology.
[31] *The Times*, 28 Oct. 1895, p. 10; 29 Oct. 1895, p. 4; 2 Nov. 1895, p. 11; 5 Nov. 1895, p. 11; 7 Nov. 1895, p. 14; 11 Nov. 1895, p. 14; 13 Nov. 1895, p. 7; 15 Nov. 1895, p. 3.
[32] *Guardian* (London), 11 March 1895, p. 395.
[33] Rigg, *Oxford High Anglicanism*, pp. v–vii.

different from Church's. The Dean drew his account to a close with the 'catastrophe' of Newman's secession, whereas Rigg devoted a substantial portion of *Oxford High Anglicanism* to developments after 1845. Pusey's thought and work therefore received far more space than Newman's, although the chapter on Newman was still somewhat incongruously entitled 'The Master Spirit of the Movement'. The difference in scope perhaps reflected a difference in purpose: Church sought to explain the events of the 1830s and 1840s, Rigg to demonstrate the origins and tendencies of 'Puseyism'.

Second, Rigg's work adopted the highly critical view of the Tractarians and their successors which had marked the Wesleyan Methodist response to the movement at least since the early 1840s.[34] This response was deeply suspicious of the movement and profoundly unhappy with its central theological tenets. In *Oxford High Anglicanism* Rigg launched a vigorous attack on Tractarian theology, particularly on 'the two plague-spots of Puseyism . . . its sacramental perversions, whereby the holy seals of the Christian faith and profession are turned into superstitions; and its dehumanising doctrine of the confessional'. Scathing reference was made to 'Pusey's portentous misinterpretations of baptismal texts', while apostolic succession – 'the assumption . . . that the Catholic Church character descends of necessity and exclusively by the line of apostolico-episcopal succession' – was also given short shrift.[35]

Behind this theological antipathy was the conviction that 'Puseyism . . . is essentially Popery'. For Rigg, 'He who has accepted the main roots of the whole system of error in the sacramental and confessional doctrines, need not stumble even at the doctrine of the Immaculate Conception of the Virgin.'[36] At least in its theological tendency, Puseyism, in Rigg's opinion, paved the way for the restoration of popery.

[34] Turner, *Conflict and Reconciliation*, pp. 159–65; Gordon S. Wakefield, ' "A mystical substitute for the glorious gospel"? A Methodist critique of Tractarianism', in G. Rowell, ed., *Tradition Renewed: the Oxford Movement Conference Papers* (London, 1986), pp. 192–6; M. Selen, *The Oxford Movement and Wesleyan Methodism in England 1833–82: a Study in Religious Conflict* (Lund, 1992).

[35] Rigg, *Oxford High Anglicanism*, pp. 90, 94, 100, 298.

[36] Ibid., pp. 298–9.

Given their conviction that Puseyism was a temporary halting-place on the road to Rome, the phenomenon of Anglo-Catholicism was an uncomfortable one for nineteenth-century Protestants. In their attempt to account for the continuing presence of a large Anglo-Catholic party in the Church of England, Protestants appealed to two broad explanations: theological naivety and moral dishonesty. *Oxford High Anglicanism* contained elements of both explanations. Rigg's strictures on Dean Church's ecclesiology have already been noted. His study also included a far from complimentary assessment of the intellectual abilities of the Tractarian leaders. Keble, he wrote, was intellectually inferior to men like Copleston and Whately; Froude was characterized by 'immodesty, . . . intolerance, and . . . puerile asceticism'; Ward 'throughout life remained phenomenally ignorant' of history; Pusey 'without doubt . . . was intellectually below the Oriel standard', being 'singularly defective in logic and logical methods of thought and teaching'; Newman 'was greatly wanting in synthetic power' as a thinker.[37]

There was more to this appraisal of character than a simple repudiation of Tractarian hagiography. Rigg wished to demonstrate that Anglo-Catholic theology was intellectually confused. He also wished, moreover, to level a moral charge against the Tractarians. More scrupulous than some Protestant polemicists, Rigg steered clear of enlarging on the perceived moral iniquities of the confessional, and he left his readers to draw their own conclusions from his persistent attribution of the epithet 'feminine' to the Tractarian leaders. His moral case focused on the dishonesty of propagating Roman teaching within the Church of England. Pusey, wrote Rigg, 'spent more than forty years in carrying out . . . the same work of preparing the Church of England for amalgamation with the Romish Church which Newman began but found himself unable to carry through with the consent and co-working of his reason and his conscience'.[38] The suggestion that Anglo-Catholicism challenged reason

---

[37] Ibid., pp. 7, 9, 57–8, 62, 207.
[38] Ibid., pp. 31–2, 299. On the less scrupulous Protestants, see M. Wellings, 'The first Protestant martyr of the twentieth century: the life and significance of John Kensit (1853–1902)', *SCH*, 30 (1993), p. 355.

and conscience placed Rigg in the mainstream of late nineteenth-century Protestant polemic.

It was a short step from accusations of moral dishonesty to the suggestion that the Oxford Movement was an elaborate conspiracy to Romanize the Church of England. This was the burden of the third volume to be considered in this paper, Walter Walsh's *The Secret History of the Oxford Movement*, published in 1897.

In an address to Oxford undergraduates in 1878 Walsh claimed that his family background was Roman Catholic.[39] These antecedents notwithstanding, his adult life and career were dominated by the cause of polemical Protestantism. He spent two years with the Irish Church Missions in Dublin and five as lecturer for the Protestant Reformation Society in Oxford, where he played a key role in establishing a local branch of the Church Association. He was for a time employed by C. N. Newdegate, M.P., who waged a Parliamentary crusade against convents in the 1860s and 1870s. From 1884 he worked as assistant editor of *The English Churchman and St James's Chronicle*, the most militant of the Evangelical newspapers, combining this with the editorship of *The Protestant Observer* from 1888. In 1896 Walsh founded the Imperial Protestant Federation, which sought to coordinate the work of Protestant societies throughout the British Empire. As lecturer, journalist and agitator, therefore, Walsh was the epitome of what Hensley Henson described as 'the Protestant underworld'.[40]

In the words of Walsh's obituary in *The English Churchman*, 'The great success of Mr Welsh's [sic] career, that which brought him so prominently before the public, and gave him a remarkable reputation in the Protestant world, was his authorship of *The Secret History of the Oxford Movement*.'[41]

---

[39] *'Is Ritualism loyal to the Church of England?' Report of a Lecture and Discussion before Members of the University of Oxford* (Oxford, 1879), p. 23.

[40] Surveys of Walsh's career may be found in *The English Churchman and St James's Chronicle* (London), 29 Feb. 1912, p. 139; *The Protestant Observer* (London), April 1912, pp. 57–62; *Who was Who 1897–1915* (London, 1920), pp. 543–4. W. L. Arnstein, *Protestant versus Catholic in Mid-Victorian England. Mr Newdegate and the Nuns* (Columbia, Mo., 1982), makes no mention of Walsh. Henson's reference to the 'Protestant underworld' may be found in his *Retrospect of an Unimportant Life*, 2 vols (London, 1943), 2, p. 147.

[41] *English Churchman*, 29 Feb. 1912, p. 139.

Contrary to the expectations of friend and foe alike, the book, published in the late autumn of 1897, was a bestseller, reaching a fifth edition within sixteen months. Walsh became a Fellow of the Royal Historical Society on the strength of *The Secret History*, the only one of the three authors studied here to be so honoured. Before turning to consider the impact and success of *The Secret History*, its main points may be summarized.

According to Walsh, 'The great object of the Ritualistic Movement from its very birth, in 1833, was that of *Corporate* reunion with the Church of Rome.'[42] This aim, he asserted, was carefully concealed in the early years of the movement, and the Tractarian leaders masked their intentions by going so far as to make anti-Roman pronouncements in public. In reality, however, their scheme was the gradual Romanizing of the Church of England in doctrine, ritual, and practice. Walsh sought to trace a line of development through *Tract 90*, Ward's *Ideal*, the work of the Association for the Promotion of the Unity of Christendom, and the 'levelling up policy'[43] of Anglo-Catholic societies like the English Church Union and the Society of the Holy Cross, working to remove the barriers between Anglicanism and Rome. It may be seen that Walsh's interpretation of the Oxford Movement, despite wide reading and laborious research, forced sixty years of complex historical evolution into a polemical straitjacket.

For Walsh, the whole Anglo-Catholic enterprise was characterized by deception. The Tractarians set the tone with their teaching on 'reserve' and on the *disciplina arcani* of the early Church, seen by the Protestant polemicist as Jesuitism in English dress.[44] The true aims and beliefs of the movement only emerged gradually, often through the exposure of the work of ritualist 'secret societies'. This concealment was necessary, it was alleged, because the aims, methods, and characteristics of Romanism were offensive and repugnant to English people.

---

[42] W. Walsh, *The Secret History of the Oxford Movement*, p. 182 and chs 9 and 10. This, and all subsequent references, are taken from the popular edition of 1899 (London).

[43] Ibid., p. 237.

[44] Ibid., pp. 1–6.

The argument of *The Secret History* was by no means new in 1897. The conspiracy theory of the Oxford Movement was advocated by other pamphleteers in the 1890s,[45] and Walsh himself had published a lecture on *The Secret Work of the Ritualists* in 1894. The Church Association, which sponsored the publication of *The Secret History*, was not expecting the book to capture the public imagination as it did,[46] so it may be asked why this particular volume achieved such remarkable success.

The impact of *The Secret History* may be attributed to two causes: its contents and its context. Walsh wrote with passion, supporting his case with copious documentation from printed sources and from the 'secret' papers of the ritualist societies. The conspiracy theory, which vitiated the book as a work of historical analysis, gave pace and shape to the narrative. The story told, moreover, echoed traditional Protestant polemic, reinforcing stereotypes of scheming priests and concealed Jesuits. Even the title, as *The Church Times* acknowledged, served to promote interest, being 'redolent of intrigue, of backstairs influence, of cipher letters and disguised emissaries'.[47]

More significant than the content of the book, however, was the timing of its publication. The ecclesiastical press carried only brief reviews of *The Secret History* in early December 1897.[48] A month later, however, John Kensit launched his campaign against ritualism at St Ethelburga's, Bishopsgate. The spring of 1898 saw Kensitite protests in a series of London churches, while the controversy was given a fresh stimulus after Easter with the intervention of the Liberal leader Sir William Harcourt in his speech on the Benefices Bill and in a stream of letters to *The Times*.[49] *The Secret History*

---

[45] Compare T. Berney, *An Address presented to ... Parliament* (London, 1895); J. M. Sangar, *England's Privilege and Curse* (London, 1897).

[46] Lambeth Palace Library, Church Society MSS, Church Association Council minutes, 11, p. 66 (17 June 1897).

[47] *Church Times* (London), 9 Sept. 1898, p. 256.

[48] Ibid., 3 Dec. 1897, p. 663; *Guardian* (London), 1 Dec. 1897, p. 1920.

[49] Wellings, 'The first Protestant martyr', pp. 351–2; Alan T. L. Wilson, 'The authority of church and party among London Anglo-Catholics, 1880–1914, with special reference to the Church crisis of 1898–1904' (Oxford University D.Phil. thesis, 1988), pp. 42–71; A. G. Gardiner, *The Life of Sir William Harcourt*, 2 vols (London, 1923), 2, pp. 482–7.

played a role in this agitation, for as Henson wrote to Lord Halifax, 'it does succeed in fastening on the High Church clergy the hateful accusation of religious duplicity, and so raising against them the ignorant but essentially righteous manliness of average Englishmen'.[50] That the so-called 'crisis in the Church' also assisted sales of *The Secret History* may be seen from the rapidity with which new editions of the book appeared. It is significant that *The Church Times*, which had dismissed Walsh's work as 'a monumental collection of mares' nests' in December 1897, devoted three articles to detailed refutation nine months later,[51] while the second edition of Rigg's *Oxford High Anglicanism*, published in 1899, not only included a new preface and a supplementary chapter on the period 1895–9, but also modified the text of the original work to slant the interpretation more in the direction of Walsh's conspiracy theory.[52] Walsh, therefore, both caught and contributed to the rising tide of concern about ritualism in the Church of England which marked the later 1890s.

Peter Nockles's recent study of *The Oxford Movement in Context* has drawn attention to the selectivity and misconceptions of Tractarian historiography.[53] The present paper has sought to demonstrate how the movement itself fell victim to selective interpretation or substantial misrepresentation during the 1890s. The origins, composition, standpoint, and reception of the three studies surveyed here illustrated the needs and context of their authors. Dean Church wrote as the disciple of Newman deserted by his master in 1845, producing the *apologia pro vita sua* of a loyal Anglican. J. H. Rigg reflected the outlook of conservative Wesleyans,

---

[50] H. H. Henson, *Cui Bono? An Open Letter to Lord Halifax on the Present Crisis in the Church of England* (London, 1898), p. 32. Compare use of the *Secret History* by Harcourt and Samuel Smith: *Speeches of Samuel Smith, Esq., M.P., and the Rt. Hon. Sir William Harcourt, M.P., in the House of Commons . . . and an Address by Samuel Smith . . . on Ritualism and Elementary Education* (London, 1898), pp. 10, 40; Sir William Harcourt, *The Crisis in the Church*, 3rd edn (London, 1899), pp. 17, 66.

[51] *Church Times*, 9 Sept. 1898, p. 256; 16 Sept. 1898, pp. 284–5; 23 Sept. 1898, p. 330. The articles were reprinted in pamphlet form under the title *A Protestant Mare's Nest*.

[52] Rigg, *Oxford High Anglicanism*, 2nd edn (London, 1899), pp. vii–xii, 371–404. Stronger conspiracy references may be found, for instance, on pp. 43, 113, 133, 201, and 329.

[53] Nockles, *Oxford Movement in Context*, pp. 3–6.

deploring the perceived tendencies of 'Puseyism' as experienced in strained relations between Methodists and the Established Church. For Walter Walsh, the Oxford Movement was conspiracy from start to finish, and history a weapon in England's fight against the papacy.[54] 'It is a bad outlook for the Church of England', wrote Walter Lock, 'if Mr Walsh and not Dean Church is to be taken as the interpreter of the Oxford Movement.'[55] Lock's fears were not realized, and *The Secret History* has long outlived its popularity; but these three contrasting accounts of the controversies of the 1830s shed light not only on the equally fierce debates of the 1890s, but also on the deploying of historical retrospect as a weapon in contemporary battles.

[54] Walsh's last book, published posthumously in 1912, was *England's Fight with the Papacy.*
[55] *Church Times*, 16 Sept. 1898, p. 285.

THE STUDY OF THE CATHOLIC TRADITION OF THE KIRK: SCOTO-CATHOLICS AND THE WORSHIP OF THE REFORMERS

by DOUGLAS M. MURRAY

James Cooper, Professor of Ecclesiastical History at Glasgow University and a prominent High Churchman, once remarked that one of the main reasons for the Catholic revival in the Church of Scotland in the late nineteenth century was the renewed study of the history of the Scottish Church.[1] The Catholic revival, or Scoto-Catholic movement, found expression in the formation of the Scottish Church Society in 1892. The High Churchmen who formed the Society considered that a Catholic position was no novelty in the Kirk. According to Henry J. Wotherspoon, one of the leading theologians of the movement, the Presbyterian was from the first 'the High Catholic of Puritanism', and it followed that the material for a catholic revival lay at hand in the traditions of the Church. In its classic form and confessional position, he said, Presbyterianism

discerned the Kingship of Christ; it asserted the Church as a Divine imperium, 'visible, universal, and divinely ordered', independent and autonomous; it maintained Episcopate, none the less that it was Episcopate put into commission; it asserted for the Presbyterate Apostolic Succession; it held a very distinct sacramental system, cumbered only by the endeavour to combine it with a doctrine of election; it exercised a vigorous discipline; it adhered to the oecumenical creeds in every term of their definitions and on that ground claimed to be acknowledged as Catholic.[2]

---

[1] James Cooper, *The Revival of Church Principles in the Church of Scotland* (Oxford, 1895), p. 15.
[2] H. J. Wotherspoon, *James Cooper: A Memoir* (London, 1926), pp. 113–14.

A study of the history of the Church of Scotland during the Reformation and post–Reformation periods would show that such was indeed the Catholic tradition of the Kirk. In the view of the liturgical scholar George W. Sprott, such a study would ensure that Catholic views were given a fair hearing in Scotland. 'If Scottish people, as a rule, have little respect for the authority of the Church from the days of the Apostles till the time of John Knox', he said, 'they at least pay great deference to the opinions of the Reformers, and of the Westminster Divines'.[3] Sprott would be one of those most responsible for carrying out this historical research and he was joined in this task by Thomas Leishman. They were said to be the original 'foster fathers' of the High Church movement and they each occupied the chair of the Scottish Church Society in immediate succession following the death of William Milligan, the first president.[4] They were known as the 'Great Twin Brethren'.[5]

Before returning to a Scottish parish in 1866, Sprott had served as a minister in Canada and Ceylon. Along with other Presbyterian ministers who worked overseas, and who were thus exposed to the liturgical practices of other traditions, Sprott felt impelled to re-examine the basis of Reformed worship.[6] He thought that Presbyterians were often attracted to Anglican worship when the services of their own Church were unavailable, and he wished to resist the temptation simply to imitate Episcopal forms.[7] The Church of England loomed large, but in liturgical matters he felt that Presbyterians should look first to their own history and to the practices of other Reformed Churches.[8] Sprott, however, did not wish to separate worship from theological considerations. Reformed usages were to be followed because they were

---

[3] G. W. Sprott, *The Worship and Offices of the Church of Scotland* (Edinburgh and London, 1882), p. viii.

[4] James F. Leishman, *Linton Leaves* (Edinburgh, 1937), p. 146.

[5] Wotherspoon, *James Cooper*, p. 114.

[6] Douglas M. Murray, 'Disruption to Union', in Duncan B. Forrester and Douglas M. Murray, eds, *Studies in the History of Worship in Scotland* (Edinburgh, 1984), p. 81.

[7] G. W. Sprott, *The Worship, Rites and Ceremonies of the Church of Scotland* (Edinburgh, 1863), p. 49.

[8] Ibid., p. 2.

based upon the Bible and the early Church and were animated by the Spirit of God.[9] Thomas Leishman agreed with Sprott in considering the doctrinal revival to be of greater importance than the liturgical.[10] The son of Matthew Leishman of Govan, the leader of the Middle Party at the time of the Disruption, Leishman had been brought up in the tradition of Scottish churchmanship which emphasized the unity and catholicity of the Church.

Much of the scholarly work of High Churchmen consisted in editing some of the important liturgical texts of the Kirk's history. Sprott and Leishman began the process in 1868 with their edition of Knox's *Book of Common Order* and of the *Westminster Directory*.[11] Three years later Sprott brought out an edition of the liturgies which had been drafted in Scotland during the reign of James VI.[12] Later editions of these three works were published separately by the Church Service Society as part of a series of *Liturgies and Orders of Service used or prepared for use in the Church of Scotland since the Reformation*.[13] Later additions to this series were James Cooper's edition of the ill-fated *Laud's Liturgy* of 1637,[14] and Sprott and Wotherspoon's edition of the *Second Prayer Book of Edward VI* and of the *Liturgy of Compromise*, the service book used by Knox when in exile on the continent.[15] High Churchmen also contributed to the series of Lee Lectures, which had been founded in memory of Robert Lee, the pioneer of liturgical reform in Scotland. Sprott's lecture in 1893, *The Worship of the Church of Scotland during the Covenanting Period, 1638–61*, is still

---

[9] Ibid., p. 3.

[10] Leishman, *Linton Leaves*, p. 136.

[11] G. W. Sprott and Thomas Leishman, eds, *The Book of Common Order of the Church of Scotland, commonly known as John Knox's Liturgy, and The Directory for the Public Worship of God agreed upon by the Assembly of Divines at Westminster* (Edinburgh and London, 1868).

[12] G. W. Sprott, ed., *Scottish Liturgies of the Reign of James VI, The Booke of Common Prayer and Administration of the Sacraments* (Edinburgh, 1871).

[13] Edinburgh and London, 1901.

[14] James Cooper, ed., *The Book of Common Prayer and Administration of the Sacraments and other parts of Divine Service, for the use of the Church of Scotland, commonly known as Laud's Liturgy (1637)* (Edinburgh and London, 1904).

[15] G. W. Sprott and H. J. Wotherspoon, eds, *The Second Prayer Book of King Edward the Sixth (1552); The Liturgy of Compromise used in the English Congregation at Frankfurt* (Edinburgh and London, 1905).

the authoritative account of that subject.[16] Leishman gave the lecture in 1897, entitled *The Moulding of the Scottish Reformation*,[17] and he contributed an authoritative historical account of worship to a collection of essays about the Church of Scotland edited by R. H. Story.[18]

The influence of Sprott and Leishman upon the Scoto-Catholic movement was considerable. Thus Wotherspoon could state that

> The revival of Church principles among us may be dated more or less definitely from 1868, when with a common purpose Dr Leishman's annotated edition of the *Westminster Directory* and Dr Sprott's of the *Book of Common Order* were published. Dr John Macleod was accustomed to say that 'but for Leishman and Sprott there would have been no movement', and that it was they who opened the quarry and supplied the material – 'we younger men were but hod-men'.[19]

It was said at one annual meeting of the Scottish Church Society that Leishman and Sprott had stood out for the truths which were embodied in the programme of the Society 'in days that were darker ... and when friends were fewer'.[20] It was to these early days that Wotherspoon referred when he spoke of those who would later form the Society as arriving at their opinions separately and discovering each other with surprise.[21] At the annual meeting of the Society in 1902 he spoke of the time when he was a probationer minister and when there were few to whom one could turn for guidance and leadership; there was no Scottish Church Society, and Milligan, Macleod, and Cooper were just beginning their work. Twenty years before that, however, Sprott and

16   Edinburgh, 1893. Cf. A. C. Cheyne, 'Worship in the Kirk: Knox, Westminster, and the 1940 Book', in Duncan Shaw, ed., *Reformation and Revolution* (Edinburgh, 1967), p. 76.

17   Edinburgh, 1897.

18   Thomas Leishman, 'The ritual of the Church', in R. H. Story, ed., *The Church of Scotland Past and Present*, 5 vols (London, 1890), 5, pp. 307–426.

19   Wotherspoon, *James Cooper*, p. 114, n. 2.

20   Scottish Church Society, *Annual Report 1896–7* (Edinburgh, 1897), p. 13.

21   Wotherspoon, *James Cooper*, pp. 116–17.

Leishman stood as they stood now.[22] With the formation of the Scottish Church Society, the two liturgical scholars could see the fruit of their labours. At the same meeting, Sprott stated that when he had returned to Scotland from serving abroad the only churchman whom he knew was Leishman. Now, he said, he was pleased to see 'that there are an increasing number of young men who are getting hold of the proper conception of the Christian Church, and that the leaven is working in many directions'.[23]

In their study of the history of the Church of Scotland, members of the Scottish Church Society sought to identify what they termed the 'Catholic' tradition of doctrine and churchmanship. They wished to justify their position by a retrospective examination of the tradition of the Kirk in which they stood and which they hoped to develop in their own day. James Cooper said that there was soil in the Church of Scotland for the nourishment of a Catholic movement;

> Indeed we have a *catena* of divines all through who might justly be described as High Churchmen. There has always been a root of Catholic feeling, as well as of Catholic doctrine, among us; and if it is now springing up with considerable vigour it is because it was there before.[24]

The material for a Catholic revival, said Wotherspoon, existed within the Reformed standards of the Kirk.[25] J. Hepburn Millar, the first lay president of the Scottish Church Society, spoke of the tradition in which the Society sought to stand as the 'orthodox moderate' tradition which had begun, in his view, with John Craig of St Giles's in Edinburgh in the sixteenth century.[26] He was no doubt referring to the fact that Craig, who later became chaplain to James VI, was not so decided in his opposition to bishops as

[22] Scottish Church Society, *Annual Report 1901-2* (Edinburgh, 1902), p. 19.
[23] Ibid., pp. 16-17.
[24] Cooper, *Revival of Church Principles*, p. 15.
[25] Wotherspoon, *James Cooper*, p. 113.
[26] Scottish Church Society, *Annual Report 1916-17* (Edinburgh, 1917), pp. 13-14.

521

were Presbyterians such as Andrew Melville, and that he pursued a middle course with regard to the 'Black Acts' of 1584 which had asserted the spiritual authority of the king.[27] James Montgomery Campbell spoke of his father, George Campbell of Eastwood, and his friends as 'good old-fashioned churchmen of the Scottish type, holding to the best traditions of Presbytery, and yet inspired by a wide and sympathetic outlook upon the world of Catholicism'.[28] George Campbell had been one of the three founders of the Church Service Society in 1865 along with R. H. Story and J. Cameron Lees.[29]

The period which Scoto-Catholics thought of as the 'golden age' of the Kirk was from the Reformation in 1560 to the National Covenant in 1638, before the conflicts of the Civil War and before what they termed the 'baneful influence' of the English 'sectaries' was felt.[30] In order to promote the renewal of liturgy along Catholic lines, they wished to show that worship in this period was different from that which followed and which had remained the dominant tradition until the late nineteenth century. The way of worship which the Kirk had inherited thus did not always represent the liturgical practice of the Reformers. For example in the seventeenth century there had been a reaction against set forms such as the reading of prayers from a book. Yet the *Second Prayer Book of Edward VI* had been in use in Scotland prior to the Reformation and continued to be used thereafter.[31] The Reformers, in preparing and authorizing a book of 'Common Order', had sought to provide a normative pattern of worship. It was not a fixed liturgy, yet neither was it merely a book of suggestions.[32] In addition High Churchmen were able to show that practices such as the

---

[27] T. A. Kerr, 'John Craig, minister of Aberdeen, and King's Chaplain', in Shaw, *Reformation and Revolution*, pp. 104, 114–15, 120.

[28] Scottish Church Society, *Annual Report 1908–9* (Edinburgh, 1909), p. 14.

[29] Murray, 'Disruption to Union', p. 85.

[30] Leishman, *Linton Leaves*, p. 180.

[31] Wotherspoon, *Second Prayer Book*, p. 41. Cf. William McMillan, *The Worship of the Scottish Reformed Church, 1550–1638* (London, 1931), p. 41; Gordon Donaldson, 'Reformation to Covenant', in Forrester and Murray, *Studies*, pp. 35–6, 41.

[32] Sprott and Leishman, *Book of Common Order*, p. xxxiii; Leishman, *Moulding of the Scottish Reformation*, pp. 22–3. Cf. McMillan, *Worship*, pp. 65–6; Donaldson, 'Reformation to Covenant', p. 36.

saying of the Creed and of the Lord's Prayer, and the singing of the *Gloria Patri*, were features of the worship of the Kirk in this period.[33] Other characteristics of worship which they noted were kneeling at prayer, the use of instrumental music, and the singing of scriptural hymns and canticles as well as the Psalms.[34]

Of the greatest importance for Scoto-Catholics was the place of the sacrament of the Lord's Supper. Certainly preaching occupied a prominent position in the worship of the Kirk following the Reformation, due in part to the continued infrequency of communion.[35] Yet the pattern of worship was based on the celebration of the Lord's Supper as the norm. In the *Book of Common Order* the saying of the Creed, the prayers of intercession, and the Lord's Prayer all came after the sermon. Leishman stated that this structure was

> in accordance with the usage of the first Christian ages, when the instruction arose out of the Scripture of the day, and the prayers for the body of the faithful, with the Creed and the Lord's Prayer, were part of the Communion Service with which the worship of every Lord's Day closed.[36]

The ordinary service was thus kept in harmony with that of a Communion Sunday and was 'a testimony, as Calvin meant it to be, for the Lord's Supper as part of the complete service of the House of God'.[37] Calvin's words in favour of a weekly celebration of the Sacrament were frequently quoted by High Churchmen[38] and, although there was no similar statement

[33] Sprott and Leishman, *Book of Common Order*, pp. xxxiii-xxxiv. Cf. McMillan, *Worship*, pp. 89, 130-1, 132; Donaldson, 'Reformation to Covenant', p. 36.

[34] Sprott and Leishman, *Book of Common Order*, pp. lviii, lx, xxxv. Cf. McMillan, *Worship*, pp. 111, 115; Donaldson, 'Reformation to Covenant', p. 36.

[35] Leishman, 'Ritual', pp. 362-3. Cf. Donaldson, 'Reformation to Covenant', p. 37.

[36] Leishman, 'Ritual', p. 335. Cf. McMillan, *Worship*, p. 118.

[37] Sprott, *Worship and Offices*, p. 15. Cf. McMillan, *Worship*, p. 117; Donaldson, 'Reformation to Covenant', pp. 36-7.

[38] E.g. H. J. Wotherspoon and J. M. Kirkpatrick, *A Manual of Church Doctrine* (London, [1918]), p. 86, n. 1; John Calvin, *Institutes of the Christian Religion*, ed. John T. McNeill, trans. Ford Lewis Battles (Philadelphia, 1960), IV.17.4.

by the Scots Reformers, it was assumed that their ideal would have been the same. However, the monthly celebration favoured in the *Book of Common Order* was not realized in practice.[39]

On the other hand there were elements in the worship of this period which High Churchmen did not favour. The communion prayer in the *Book of Common Order* was somewhat meagre, and in particular lacked a prayer of invocation upon the elements or *epiclesis*.[40] Sprott considered that this defect was probably remedied in practice, a view which is shared by more recent scholarship.[41] Sprott and Wotherspoon regretted the fact that Knox had opposed the use of responsive prayer while ministering to the English exiles at Frankfurt.[42] Knox's troubles at Frankfurt meant that responsive prayer was out of the question in the Kirk, and the people's part in the service was thus restricted to the singing of the Psalms.[43]

A major difficulty faced by High Churchmen was the outright rejection by the Scots Reformers of the observance of the main festivals of the Christian year. Thomas Leishman tried to argue that the opposition to the celebration of Christmas and Easter, for example, was not to the festivals as such but because they became occasions for superstition and because the habit developed of communicating then and only then. The abolition of the Christian year was part of the Reformers' desire to increase the frequency of participation in the Lord's Supper. In 1570 the General Assembly authorized Easter Communion to be celebrated 'where superstition is removed'.[44] This marked a retreat, in Leishman's view, from the Assembly's objection in 1566 to the section in the *Second Helvetic Confession* which favoured the observance of the main festivals of the Christian year.[45] In practice, however, the

[39] Leishman, 'Ritual', p. 343.
[40] Ibid., p. 339.
[41] Sprott, *Worship and Offices*, p. 120. Cf. McMillan, *Worship*, p. 170.
[42] Sprott and Wotherspoon, *Liturgy of Compromise*, p. 223.
[43] Leishman, 'Ritual', p. 327.
[44] Thomas Leishman, *May the Kirk keep Pasche and Yule?* (Edinburgh and London, 1875), p. 15; Leishman, 'Ritual', p. 356. Cf. McMillan, *Worship*, p. 300.
[45] Leishman, 'Ritual', p. 356. *Second Helvetic Confession*, in Arthur C. Cochrane, ed., *Reformed Confessions of the Sixteenth Century* (London, 1966), XXIV, pp. 291-2.

festivals never did gain a foothold in the Kirk, although their abolition was in many ways unpopular. There certainly was some ambiguity in the Reformers' position since the Calendar of the *Book of Common Order* contained several feast days, some of which would still be required for the dating of fairs and markets in burghs and the terms of the law courts. But as Gordon Donaldson has pointed out, this Calendar includes, almost incredibly, 'The Assumption of Mary'![46]

Of primary importance for High Churchmen were the doctrinal principles of Scots Reformers. Communion was to be an integral part of worship, not just because Knox and his colleagues favoured a frequent celebration, but because of the theology of the sacraments which they held. The popular view in the Kirk, as James Cooper found out when his views were challenged during his ministry at the East Church in Aberdeen, was that the sacraments were merely commemorative in character and were not means of grace.[47] The Reformers, however, had rejected the view that the sacraments were 'bare signs'. It was with some feeling that Cooper, at an annual meeting of the Scottish Church Society, stated:

It is not we who in this matter have drifted away from what one gentleman calls 'the grand old simplicity of the Presbyterian system.' It is these who have abandoned the sacramental teaching of Calvin, of Knox, of our *First Confession* and of the *Westminster Confession*, and who have adopted what our reformers called 'the vanity of those who affirm sacraments to be nothing other than naked or bare signs' – it is they who have drifted already far from the true Presbyterian position.[48]

High Churchmen were right to draw attention to the 'high' doctrine of the sacraments found in the *Scots Confession* of

[46] Donaldson, 'Reformation to Covenant', p. 40.

[47] Douglas M. Murray, 'James Cooper and the East Church case at Aberdeen 1882-3: the high church movement vindicated', *Records of the Scottish Church History Society*, 19 (1977), pp. 227-8, 231-2.

[48] James Cooper, in Scottish Church Society, *Annual Report 1894-5* (Edinburgh, 1895), pp. 18-19. Cf. G. W. Sprott, *The Church Principles of the Reformation* (Edinburgh and London, 1877), pp. 13-14.

1560 and the later *Westminster Confession*. According to these statements the sacraments are the means by which the benefits of Christ are applied to believers.[49]

What is the means of Christ's presence in the sacraments? To answer this question, High Churchmen identified a doctrine of union with Christ which they held to be at the centre of Calvin's theology, and to be the basis of the position of the Scots Reformers. Sprott stated it in this way:

> The missing link in much that is called evangelical religion is the link of vital union with the Second Adam, including that bodily 'nexus' with his glorified Humanity, as signified and sealed in the sacraments, which Calvin held as dear as life, and which has been so emphatically asserted in every standard of our Church since the Reformation.[50]

Calvin's influence could be seen in the *Scots Confession* and in the recommendation of the *First Book of Discipline* that his Catechism should be used for the education of the young.[51] Members of the Scottish Church Society saw the theology of Calvin as crucial to the recovery of the Catholic tradition, even although they found it difficult to disentangle his doctrine of election from the rest of his thinking. In his address to the second conference of the Society in 1895, Leishman said:

> Some may think that Calvin, in his devotion to his favourite branch of Christian philosophy, worked it with needless elaboration of detail into his theology. But it would ill become a Society which desires to stand on the old paths of their fathers to disown the broad principles of that theology.[52]

[49] *The Scots Confession of 1560*, trans. James Bulloch (Edinburgh, 1991), XXI–XXII, pp. 18–21; *Westminster Confession of Faith* (Edinburgh, 1880), XXVII–IX, pp. 89–95.

[50] G. W. Sprott, *The Aims of the Scottish Church Society* (Edinburgh, 1896), p. 7.

[51] Thomas Leishman, 'Opening Address', in Scottish Church Society, *The Divine Life in the Church*, Conferences, 2nd ser., 2 vols (Edinburgh, 1895), 1, p. 7. James K. Cameron, ed., *The First Book of Discipline* (Edinburgh, 1972), p. 182.

[52] Leishman, 'Opening Address', p. 6.

Another member argued that the doctrine of predestination was not the central dogma of Calvin's *Institutes*.[53] High Churchmen thus felt able to emphasize Calvin's doctrine of union with Christ without also adopting his views of election. Wotherspoon could write of Christ as having united himself with humanity by his incarnation, and through his resurrection and ascension as still living to make intercession for his people. The Church is thus united with Christ in the sacraments, not by Christ coming down from heaven, but by the Holy Spirit who unites things separated by space and so also unites her with her ascended Lord.[54]

How successful were High Churchmen in identifying a 'Catholic' tradition in the Kirk? Were they guilty of interpreting history to suit their own concerns? Their study of worship in the Reformation and post-Reformation periods in Scotland has largely been confirmed by later scholarship. They can be criticized, however, for not always recognizing the extent to which the Church in this period was varied in its doctrine and practice. They did not advocate a complete return to the Church of the sixteenth century as there were elements in that period of which they did not approve and which did not fit into their outlook. They did not always give full weight to these elements and concentrated rather on those features which supported their position. Their retrospective examination was successful, however, in identifying a Catholic tradition in the Kirk, even if it was not the only one which could be discerned from a study of the past.

The University of Glasgow

---

[53] The Secretary of the Scottish Church Society, Paisley Abbey, Scottish Church Society Papers, 'To what extent is the Scottish Church committed to Calvinism?', p. 1.

[54] H. J. Wotherspoon, 'The Pentecostal gift in relation to the sacraments', in Scottish Church Society, *The Pentecostal Gift*, Conferences, 3rd ser. (Glasgow, 1903), pp. 145-7.

A PRE-MODERN INTERPRETATION OF THE MODERN: THE ENGLISH CATHOLIC CHURCH AND THE 'SOCIAL QUESTION' IN THE EARLY TWENTIETH CENTURY

by BARBARA WRAITH

Towards the close of the first decade of the twentieth century there emerged an organized movement within the English Catholic Church which can be distinguished as Social Catholicism. The Catholic Social Guild (CSG), which was founded at the Catholic Truth Society Conference in September 1909, largely represented Social Catholicism in England and, as such, constitutes the focal point of this paper. This small body comprised laypeople, secular priests, and members of religious orders. Of the lay component a significant number of middle-class converts to Catholicism were prominent; whilst at parish level working men and women were recruited largely through schemes of social study. Social Catholicism represented a novel phenomenon not only because of its essential focus upon addressing some of the more intractable social problems of the day but also because it embodied an inherently different social rationale from that of more mainstream Catholic endeavour in this field. Looking back to the Church of medieval times, Social Catholicism perceived an ideal Church which, through its social precepts and actions, had exerted an exemplary socio-economic influence. Moreover such an historical precedent might embody *the* answer to the 'social question' – a multiform modern problematic – provided the Catholic Church could transform its past experience of a pre-modern social engagement into initiatives of theoretical and practical relevance to the modern situation.

By the later nineteenth century pioneering surveys of social conditions in London had been instrumental in both revealing to the public the awful plight of the labouring poor and contributing towards a major shift in opinion away from the long-standing notion that individual failing was the root cause of modern pauperism to an increasing awareness of the role of wider economic and environmental causal factors. For the churches it was not merely the impoverishment beleaguering the vast majority of the working classes which was at issue but their state of utter degradation. Degraded poverty was not the poverty of Christ. In the great towns tens of thousands existed in appalling material circumstances, suffering exploitation at the hands of unscrupulous landlords and employers. Insanitary and overcrowded dwellings were subject to exorbitant rents. Chronic unemployment existed alongside large-scale use of 'sweated' labour which involved toil during long hours in wretched conditions in return for 'starvation' wages. The widespread problem of drunkenness remained despite temperance initiatives. Empirical investigations of the early twentieth century uncovered alarmingly high infant mortality rates, and much controversy ensued as to the causes. Taken together, social problems of such magnitude and such moral implication had become a pressing question for resolution. To social commentators hostile to its determining principles, the bulk of blame lay with the unrestrained forces of economic individualism which were perceived to have wrought a trail of social havoc leaving only deprivation, misery, and a burgeoning sense of resentment in their wake. From the beginning, Social Catholicism saw the crucial need for an approach which incorporated a Catholic critique of the socio-economic system.

Along with the Revd Charles Plater, S.J., the layman Leslie Toke had been instrumental in the establishment of the CSG.[1] From his address at the inaugural meeting it is possible to detect the genesis of a conceptual strategy which represented a departure from earlier Catholic interventions in the 'social question'. The socially conservative Cardinal Vaughan largely aimed at stemming the 'leakage' from the faith through provision of more Catholic charitable institutions and assistance to missionary priests striving with insufficient

---

[1] Oxford, Plater College archive, L. Toke, 'The Catholic Social Guild' (undated). [This archive is uncatalogued, and the material is therefore cited by author, title, and where possible date. Some of the material attributable to Toke appears under the *nom de plume*, F. Goldwell.]

resources to maintain the faith of the poor. The precedent set by his predecessor, Cardinal Manning, was admirable in terms of practical initiative, and Social Catholicism fully intended to proffer pragmatic solutions to contemporary problems. Manning had considered it to be 'a dereliction of duty and unlawful' to fail to enter the 'active service of the commonwealth',[2] and had demonstrated such conviction in his famous intervention in the London dock strike of 1889. But such worthy action had stemmed from a belief in 'a divine obligation binding the Church to enter into the most intimate relations with the natural society'[3] rather than any desire to adopt a theoretical standpoint in opposition to the dominant socio-economic ideology of the day. As such, his action can be characterized essentially as an outstanding Christian contribution to the widespread conservative social doctrine of paternalism. By contrast with such approaches Toke declared that

> Until and unless the ecclesiastical and lay leaders of Catholics in England recognize more fully and study more deeply than they have yet done the connection between the economic and social tyrannies of modern England and the terrible 'leakage' which they deplore so much and so fruitlessly, there is little hope of any return of the English populace to Catholicism.[4]

As a prominent contributor to Social Catholicism his statement can be seen to exemplify the movement's emphasis upon the socio-economic structure as a significant causal factor in regard to loss of faith and, more implicitly, to place the focus of concern specifically upon the broader social implications of this state of affairs rather than the implications for the Church alone.

In formulating a Catholic critique of the structure of modern society, whilst at the same time facing on-going ideological threat from various alternative secular Socialist critiques, Social Catholicism underpinned its theoretical

---

2 H. E. Manning, *The Catholic Church and Modern Society* (London, 1880), p. 18.
3 Ibid., p. 10.
4 L. Toke, *The Rationalist Propaganda* (London, 1909), p. 9.

rationale by embracing the neo-Thomism of the papal encyclical *Rerum novarum* (1891). The revival of Thomism itself represented a pre-modern philosophical engagement with the modern world, for the social doctrines of Aquinas were propounded as remedies to contemporary ills. In societies riven by class conflict the Church's call for a return to organic unity had strong appeal to those committed to a return to a Christian social order. Where industrialization, ruthless competition, and aggressive self-interest had brought the proletariat to the point of dehumanization, the Church's teaching against usury and in support of social justice was apposite in challenging a modern scandal. But Social Catholicism's commitment to a rationale which was both aligned to the national context and capable of facilitating practical resolution determined that it also incorporated significant influences specific to the English context.

From a relatively obscure quarter there came an input which was later to bear fruit in this connection. Edward Gilpin Bagshawe, Bishop of Nottingham from 1874 to 1901, was hardly known outside his own diocese, which was one of the poorest in England. No less concerned about the wretched plight of the poor than Manning, his approach to the 'social question' was by contrast largely theoretical. Bagshawe was influenced by the work of the Catholic economist, Charles Stanton Devas, whose recently published *Groundwork of Economics* (1883) had informed his social Pastorals of 1883-4. These Pastorals formed the substance of Bagshawe's publication *Mercy and Justice to the Poor the True Political Economy* (1885) which represented a critique of the existing socio-economic system on the basis of a social philosophy which drew largely upon the medieval Church's theories of 'general' and 'particular' justice.

Bagshawe himself, and subsequently those prominently involved in Social Catholicism, saw *Mercy and Justice* as anticipating the doctrines expounded later in *Rerum novarum*.[5]

---

[5] E. G. Bagshawe, *Pastoral on The Papal Encyclical* (Nottingham, 1891), p. 4; 'The social doctrine of Bishop Bagshawe', *Christian Democrat*, 15, no. 11 (Nov. 1935), pp. 163-5. [The monthly magazine, *Christian Democrat*, was the principal organ of the CSG from 1921 onwards, and much of its commentary appeared anonymously, but represented editorial initiative and viewpoint.]

Of the two, the former is arguably the more 'radical' attack upon the tenets of laissez-faire as it had developed in England. For example, Bagshawe held that the State had an obligation to enforce 'general justice' and that from this moral imperative derived the 'superior right' of the State to intervene. His repeated calls for positive 'public action' and his utter condemnation of private monopolies, such as the water companies, might imply that he had State ownership in mind.[6] He vehemently criticized the disingenuous dual standard which prevailed in regard to private ownership in declaring that 'It is only when the interests of the poor and helpless are in question ... that the State begins to be scrupulous and the wealthier among its subjects begin to say:– "You must respect private property; let each one do the best he can for himself." '[7]

On the basis of an admixture of the moral theology of neo-Thomism and a critique of present-day economics produced by Charles Devas, Bagshawe had begun to formulate a theoretical basis for positing an alternative socio-economic order. This was the harbinger of a synthesis between pre-modern and modern social thought which was to become manifest in Social Catholicism. Devas's major treatise, *Political Economy* (1892), represented in large part *the* English Catholic response to laissez-faire economics during this period. As a principal text employed by the CSG, it is possible to determine from its theoretical sources and dialectic a substantive framework of Social Catholicism's economic perspective. The formative influences upon Devas's thinking serve to illuminate certain characteristics to be displayed by this movement. As an undergraduate at Balliol in the late 1860s, Devas could hardly have failed to be aware of the teachings of the political philosopher, T. H. Green. For in this period Green was holding sway over the hearts and minds of so many of those who were to become prominent Christian Socialists, notably Charles Gore and Henry Scott Holland who became luminaries within the

---

[6] Nottingham, Nottingham Diocesan archive, G. D. Sweeney, 'A history of the diocese of Nottingham in the episcopate of Bishop Bagshawe' (1961), p. 42.

[7] E. G. Bagshawe, *Mercy and Justice to the Poor the True Political Economy* (London, 1885), p. 15.

Christian Social Union.[8] Another of those directly influenced by Green was Arnold Toynbee,[9] whose work influenced Devas's economic thinking. Although mediated, this sympathetic connection between Toynbee and Devas can be seen to pull English Catholic economic thinking into the orbit of Green's ideas. Green's intense hostility to Roman Catholicism would certainly have precluded a more direct input to the work of a convert.[10]

In referring to personal determining influences other than Catholic ecclesiastical authorities, Devas acknowledged his debt to a range of non-Catholic sources, perceiving the mid-nineteenth-century Christian Socialists, Thomas Carlyle and John Ruskin as particularly significant as proponents of what he termed the Religious or Ethical School (of economics). The first Christian Socialists under the leadership of F. D. Maurice had championed co-operation in the form of Working Men's Associations as a means of protecting the small producer from the ravages of unrestricted competition. This economic perspective exerted a degree of influence upon Catholic economics in England since Devas similarly endorsed workers' co-operatives and, in this respect, he can be seen to be drawing close to the associationist thinking of Maurice. But his standpoint also owes much to the model of the medieval trade guilds, since 'Co-operation is to a great extent the modern substitute for the guild property and the multiform rights of common formerly enjoyed by the poorer classes and taken from them by the legislation of economic liberalism.'[11]

Devas's keen admiration for aspects of the economic thought of both Carlyle and Ruskin exemplifies the influence of Romanticism upon him. For Ruskin, whom Devas deemed 'a torchbearer in an age of mental darkness',[12] the medieval period represented a Golden Age to be revered and reproduced. Other middle-class lay converts prominently

---

[8]   M. Richter, *The Politics of Conscience: T. H. Green and his Age* (London, 1964), p. 377 n. 4.
[9]   Ibid.
[10]   Ibid., p. 30.
[11]   C. S. Devas, *Political Economy* (London, 1911), p. 122.
[12]   Ibid., p. 657.

positioned within Social Catholicism held Romantic medieval visions in high esteem. Leslie Toke, for example, applauded William Morris's 'fervent admiration for the Middle Ages and his equally fervent desire to reproduce, under modern conditions, the greater and nobler lines of their social structures'.[13] The CSG executive adopted an English medieval saint as patron of the Guild in 1910. St Gilbert of Sempringham (*c*.1083–1189) had founded the Gilbertine Order during a period of great spiritual renaissance in the mid twelfth century.[14] It was not until Romanticism's interest in the Middle Ages that extracts from early thirteenth-century manuscripts of Gilbert's *Vita* appeared in the *Monasticon Anglicanum* (1830).[15] Here Gilbert was portrayed as devising 'a new type of religious life',[16] in foundations intended initially for the female religious and lay sisters but which soon included lay brothers and subsequently priests as canons, forming two communities within double monasteries, the Gilbertines modelled their lives upon the life of Christ, holding all things in common, and working tirelessly for the welfare of the poor by distributing alms and establishing hospitals. Such a worthy example no doubt reinforced the perception of the medieval Church's broad contribution towards remedying poverty and strife through the 'sumptuous provision made by the monasteries, convents, hospitals and guilds', all of which disappeared at the Reformation.[17] When the Catholic Workers' College was formed by the CSG in 1921 it was modelled on Ruskin College not only because of a shared ideal to educate working-class adults – an ideal which forges links back to F. D. Maurice's Working Men's College where Ruskin himself had taught – but also in the sense of training future champions of labour. While Romanticism had drawn upon an idealized version of the Middle Ages in its search for the earthly paradise, a closer approach to an understanding of the

---

13   F. Goldwell, *Guild Socialism* (Oxford, 1918), p. 6.
14   D. Knowles, *The Monastic Order in England*, 2nd edn (Cambridge, 1963), pp. 296–7.
15   R. Foreville and G. Keir, *The Book of St Gilbert* (Oxford, 1987), p. cx.
16   Ibid., p. 57.
17   H. Parkinson, *A Primer of Social Science* (London, 1913), p. 227.

significance of Romantic sentiment within Social Catholicism lies in its appropriation of the history of the Catholic Church to specific contemporary causes.

The attempted application of Catholic social theory can be critically examined from the perspective of Social Catholicism's engagement in two ideological battlegrounds where conflict ensured over social policy during the first two decades of this century. The first arena is that relating to the controversial findings of the Royal Commission on the Poor Laws which in 1909 produced Majority and Minority Reports. The former was largely the work of the Charity Organization Society, a conservative body which adopted the position that the State should provide a basic minimum, with voluntary agencies providing better standards for the more deserving. The latter was a Fabian Socialist document which essentially took the line that poverty was not due to individual failing but was rather a product of a socio-economic system informed by tenets of laissez-faire individualism. When the Fabian-backed National Committee for the Prevention of Destitution was formed in 1909 to promote implementation of the Minority Report, prominent contributors to Social Catholicism supported its endeavours as a means of replacing a despised Poor Law with an enlightened alternative. Monsignor Henry Parkinson, who became the first president of the CSG, was directly involved with the work of the Committee, producing on its behalf a pamphlet entitled *The Problem of Poor Law Reform* (1911).

Although other clerics like Father Plater were more publicly visible, Parkinson's was the greater contribution at this period to resolving the philosophical dilemma of how to apply Catholic principles to contemporary social problems. His stance appealed to the past for its precedents since 'after the break-up of the medieval order' the institution of the Poor Law system brought in its wake 'widespread social corruption',[18] but he concentrated upon exposition of a proposed modern-day solution. As Rector of Oscott College, Parkinson's concern to involve the Church in economic and social affairs led him to introduce lectures on the social

---

[18] Idem, *The Problem of Poor Law Reform* (London, 1911), p. 3.

sciences into his philosophy courses. A seminarian of the period 1903–10 recalled that the Fabians were a great influence upon him, particularly in their 'unemotional accumulation of facts in the service of social justice'.[19] Justice was the key to unlocking the door of want, and an approach which would facilitate this outcome could be fully endorsed. The appeal of the Fabian position was the central idea of 'prevention of destitution' as opposed to merely tackling its effects.

To support prevention was to reject the notion that poverty was due to personal failing and to assert that the fault lay with the economic system itself. Such an alignment was compatible with Social Catholicism's medievalist thinking since the social order of the Middle Ages, underpinned by the social teaching of the Church, was perceived to be inherently protectionist towards the individual. By contrast laissez-faire capitalism was responsible for the creation of a dispossessed proletariat. Former seizure of ecclesiastical lands, for example, marked the demise of landlords who had presided with largesse over the munificent manorial system. This was the sentiment behind Parkinson's statement that 'In the manorial days from the Conquest to the fifteenth century . . . the villeins and cottiers were provided for by the conditions of their service and tenure of land. . . . Extremes of wealth and poverty were not known, and the grinding, hopeless wretchedness of the slum was impossible.'[20]

Parkinson's decidedly romantic appeal to the distant past in the service of social justice stood in contrast to Beatrice Webb's consideration of the relatively recent past in formulating her position as a member of the Royal Commission on the Poor Laws. In a confidential memorandum of October 1907 she wrote:

The whole trend of English local government during the last half century points to expediency, for the sake of

---

[19] Oxford, Plater College archive, Drinkwater, 'On Mgr. Henry Parkinson' (*c.* 1959), Canon Drinkwater was a pupil of Parkinson's and became a writer on spiritual and social issues.
[20] H. Parkinson, 'A brief record of social conditions in England', in Mrs P. Gibbs, ed., *First Notions on Social Service* (London, 1913), p. 24.

economy as well as for the sake of efficiency, of concentrating the whole of the public provision for each service in any locality in the hands of its own specialized Local Authority.[21]

Fabian argument fell into line with such a trend in supporting the idea of placing specialized services under Committees of County or Borough Councils. During the early months of 1911 Sidney Webb's lectures emphasized the 'waste' caused by 'preventable disease' and 'preventable unemployment' as well as the 'squandering out of rates and taxes annually Seventy Millions sterling on the maintenance, schooling and medical treatment of the poor'.[22] Such argument was intended to discredit, on the grounds of cost, the notion of mere relief of destitution. But concepts of 'economy' and 'efficiency', so easily detached from ethical imperatives, were notably ancillary to Parkinson's argument. Expediency tended far too much towards what was politic as opposed to what was just. At the same time the idea at the core – prevention – remained valid in a modern industrialized context where the problem of destitution had become so widespread and intractable.

In attempting to address problems of modern society guided by pre-Reformation precedent and Catholic principle, certain proponents of Social Catholicism were drawn into a close affinity with Hilaire Belloc's thinking in his treatise *The Service State* (1912). Here he posited the thesis that contemporary industrial society tended towards the reinstatement of slavery and, as an antidote to such iniquity, proposed a socio-economic system based upon small proprietorship. Such a social model had earlier been advocated by Charles Devas in *Political Economy*. Belloc asserted that emancipation of the peasant had been fostered above all by the medieval guilds which had safeguarded the division of

[21] London, British Library of Political and Economic Science, Webb Local Gvmt Collection, vol. 286c, B. Webb, 'Some historical considerations bearing on poor law reconstruction', Oct. 1907.

[22] London, British Library of Political and Economic Science, Passfield Papers, Section IV Item 4/2, S. Webb, 'Unemployment and sickness insurance', 27 Feb. 1911; 'The financial waste of the present poor law', 13 March 1911.

property such that 'no proletariat [was] formed and no monopolizing Capitalist'.[23] As a personal friend of Belloc, Leslie Toke canvassed his opinion concerning the stance of Guild Socialists in respect of property ownership, and received the reply that they were 'wrong, like everybody else of the Socialist lot, on the very simple point of private property'.[24] Guild Socialism in certain of its aspects can be seen to have attracted Social Catholicism, for it incorporated within its complex of ideas strands of Distributist and Romantic medievalist thought. Both such strands found the history of the Middle Ages malleable to their causes. But caution was essential in avoiding the charge that the CSG carried the 'taint' of Socialism. Even before the founding of the CSG, and in a context in which scholarly Modernism had been quashed in 1907, Toke had urged: 'We must at all times . . . be careful about the outward and visible form of the society' in order that 'attempts at deeper and broader solidarities with extra-Catholic social and civic movements should be internally worked at and silently realized'.[25] The CSG textbook *Guild Socialism* was written under a pseudonym by Toke in 1918 and endorsed local guilds on the medieval model, which were perceived to have flourished under the influence of the Church and brought great social prosperity, as well as property ownership by individuals as opposed to ownership by the State. The opening remarks of that work had articulated a perspective which castigated 'the progressive oppression of the poor in England from the time [of] the Great Pillage of the 16th century . . . until our own days of fast-returning slavery'.[26] This viewpoint can be seen to exemplify the interpretation of both past and present at the close of the Great War even though the pre-war Liberal government had pursued an interventionist policy.

Commencing in 1906, and until the outbreak of war, the Liberal government had introduced a series of welfare reforms which effectively outflanked the recommendations

[23] H. Belloc, *The Servile State* (London, 1912), p. 49.
[24] Oxford, Plater College archive, Letter from H. Belloc to L. Toke, 19 Nov. 1917.
[25] Oxford, Plater College archive, L. Toke, 'In tempore opportuno' (*c*. 1908/9).
[26] Goldwell, *Guild Socialism*, p. 3.

of both the Majority and Minority Reports. This essentially New Liberal initiative, and particularly the minimum wage legislation incorporated in the Trade Boards Act of 1909, has been seen as significant principally because of its 'crucial break' with non–interventionist economic individualism.[27] The ideological watershed which this legislation represents shapes the context for the second arena of engagement by Social Catholicism in social policy formulation.

A living wage, as opposed to a minimum subsistence wage, was the ideal, and this was legitimized on the grounds of medieval precedent. In his *Primer of Social Science* (1913) Parkinson called for the provision of fair wages to be the primary stipulation made upon modern industry. It could be sanctioned on the basis of Social Catholicism's pre–modern model which called for an organic society underpinned by religious imperatives in which small proprietorship was the dominant economic model and where trade and craft guilds protected the living standards of their membership by fixing prices and wages. Such intervention in the economy was informed by the medieval Church's economic teaching. Whilst the Church did not enunciate a formulated economic theory, its teachings on the 'just price' and usury drew it directly into this realm. The concept of the 'just price' as conceived by the canonists belonged to the later Middle Ages (the twelfth century onwards) and can be viewed as 'simply the current price fixed in the free market or by the State',[28] with the qualifying *sine qua non* of Christian ethics which dictated that moral considerations held sway over com-mercial practice. Determining principles of price were social utility and particular need, as in time of famine for example, as opposed to cost of production. A price was deemed unjust if advantage was taken of a particular necessity or weakness on the part of the purchaser or if artificially manipulated by such malpractice as monopoly. But theoretical precept and actual practice tended to be difficult to reconcile. By the later

[27] S. Blackburn, 'Ideology and social policy: the origins of the Trade Boards Act', *HistJ*, 34 (1991), p. 45.

[28] J. Gilchrist, *The Church and Economic Activity in the Middle Ages* (London, 1969), p. 59.

Middle Ages canonistic teaching on monopolies and 'just price' had little practical effect at all.

Catholic perceptions of the medieval guilds, and indeed the medieval period in general, fell largely into line with widely held contemporary views of the Middle Ages. Certainly various strands of secular Socialism tended to see the period in a glowing light. For example, H. M. Hyndman of the Social Democratic Federation wrote that 'It may be doubted whether any European community every enjoyed such rough plenty as English yeomen, craftsmen and labourers. . . . Merry England it was then in spite of all drawbacks.'[29]

The medieval concept of the 'just price', with its integral bearing on the 'just wage', was enlisted by neo-Thomism in the ideological battle against economic individualism. In *Rerum novarum* Leo XIII had declared that there was 'a dictate of natural justice more imperious and ancient than any bargain between man and man, namely, that remuneration ought to be sufficient to support a frugal and well-behaved wage-earner'.[30] Only through receipt of a wage in return for labour could the modern industrial worker procure a livelihood and therefore that wage, as an absolute necessity, must ensure the natural right to a life of reasonable comfort. Such right to a degree of material well-being befitted the dignity of the worker who was not to be regarded as a mere wage-slave. This teaching stood in stark contrast to the social reality of sweated labour which was one of the most intractable problems of the day. Payment below subsistence level proliferated in such industries as tailoring, lace-making and chain-making. Following pressure from the National Anti-Sweating League, which as a non-political body drew wide support including that of all the religious bodies,[31] legislation incorporated in the Trade Boards Act fixed minimum wage rates in certain low-paid industries. Social Catholicism supported this Act as the latest move towards

[29]   H. M. Hyndman, *The Historical Basis of Socialism in England* (London, 1883), p. 1.
[30]   Pope Leo XIII, *Rerum novarum* [trans. *The Condition of the Working Classes* (London, 1913)], p. 40.
[31]   S. Blackburn, 'Sweated labour and the minimum wage' (University of London Ph.D. thesis, 1983), p. 94.

achievement of social justice through abatement of the intolerable sweating system, but considered that: 'It falls far short of satisfying even the demand for a living wage.'[32]

It has been noted that the CSG employed the arguments of both the New Liberal thinker, J. A. Hobson, and the Webbs to add weight to their anti-sweating stance.[33] To a degree Social Catholicism did engage with certain current ideological standpoints, which was necessary to facilitate the possible achievement of its goals and avoid consignment of Catholic social rationale to the realms of reactionary escapism. But whilst adopting the terminology of the National Anti-Sweating League, for example, in referring to 'parasitism', 'public waste', and 'loss of efficiency' in explaining the sweating system and its consequences,[34] Catholic principle was nevertheless upheld. Not only did 'considerations of human worth and dignity outweigh any considerations of . . . industrial advantage'[35] but the problem with 'Collectivists' was that

> the argument against sweating too often turns upon a question of national loss. The economic unit is the State; the importance of the individual falls into a lower plane. They advocate . . . the enforcement of a minimum below which no employer of labour may descend. . . . Every individual, however, has a right to a decent livelihood.[36]

Moreover, Social Catholicism not only claimed the right to a living wage for the individual but also one sufficient to support a family. In Catholic teaching the family, not the State, forms the social and economic unit. *Rerum novarum* had declared the family to be 'a society limited indeed in numbers, but no less a true society, anterior to any kind of State or

---

[32] T. Wright, ed., *Sweated Labour and the Trade Boards Act*, 2nd edn (London, 1913), p. 61.

[33] Blackburn, 'Sweated labour and minimum wage', p. 119.

[34] National Anti-Sweating League, 'Report of conference on the minimum wage – 1906', cited in Wright, *Sweated Labour*, p. 44.

[35] Wright, *Sweated Labour*, p. 44.

[36] Ibid., p. 54.

nation'.[37] The concept of the 'family living wage' was more controversial than that of a personal living wage. Leslie Toke pointed out that beyond admitting the claim of a worker to receive a wage sufficient to support a family, Christian opinion had reached no consensus upon its sanction.[38] He drew upon the work of Devas and the more recent work of the Revd John A. Ryan, S.T.D., a prominent contributor to this field within the American Catholic social justice movement, in determining the sanction that 'the labourer's right to a family living wage is one of commutative justice' as opposed to legal justice or charity.[39] But State action in respect of regulation of wages might incur the danger of State compulsion to labour and therefore Social Catholicism advocated protection of workers' remuneration 'by the transformation of trade unions or labour organizations into State-recognized, but autonomous, guilds regulating the various occupations'.[40]

Although this conclusion was based on a selective view of the past, it did not undermine the integrity of the intention to apply a Catholic solution to contemporary social problems. Much Christian Socialist argument was focused around historical precept, and in the early twentieth century Christian alignment with Guild Socialism can be seen as one manifestation of this stance. At a theoretical level the closest alignment of Social Catholicism with political thought prior to the Great War was arguably with the two strands of Guild Socialism which opposed State Socialism. In 1912 the journal *The New Age* produced a critique of both State Capitalism and State Socialism which were viewed as similarly exploitative of labour,[41] and Parkinson was moved to remark upon its significant contribution towards 'making the whole subject of Guilds so important just now'.[42] However, Social Catholicism's convergence with the Fabians in support of the

---

[37] *Condition of the Working Classes*, p. 17.
[38] In 1907 the Convocation of Canterbury adopted the doctrine of the living wage: see J. Oliver, *The Church and the Social Order* (London, 1968), p. 7.
[39] L. Toke, 'The living wage', in Wright, *Sweated Labour*, pp. 34–7.
[40] J. A. Ryan, *The Living Wage* (London, 1914), p. 16 n. 1.
[41] G. Foote, *The Labour Party's Political Thought* (London, 1985), p. 105.
[42] Oxford, Plater College archive, Letter from H. Parkinson to V. M. Crawford, 11 Oct. 1914. Crawford was Hon. Secretary of the CSG.

Minority Report was not altogether a strange alliance. As an intellectual coterie to the right of the mainstream at this period the Fabians were atypical Socialists.[43] The Fabian Society's staunch opposition to laissez-faire economics and support for non-revolutionary gradual change to the socio-economic system appealed to an essentially intellectual Social Catholicism. But the latter movement's commitment to a pre-modern theoretical model and Christian democracy was clearly out of step with Fabian affiliations to big business and advocacy of a Collectivist bureaucracy. Prior to the Great War when the Liberal policy of social reform embraced non-laissez-faire ideology by enacting the Trade Boards legislation, Social Catholicism rallied in support of a practical measure. This then was the nature of the engagement at a pragmatic level. In the same way certain Labour Party initiatives subsequently came to be seen as a practical means of promoting a just society.

Social Catholicism's pre-modern interpretation as a formulated response to the modern social problem might be dismissed as irrelevant except that it seemed to be capturing the quintessential spirit of the times and not simply reflecting the mood of fellow Catholics. In October 1908, writing in a non-Catholic journal, Charles Plater made a plea for a greater breadth of vision in order for all to see that the 'fundamental needs of our time' were to be 'educed from within' as opposed to applied from without. He advocated spiritual retreats for working people as the essential ingredient in achieving such social regeneration and contrasted this approach with the short-sighted alternative which produced only narrow practical initiatives. His call for a return to a society which was implicitly Christian clearly struck the right chord at the right moment for it created considerable interest from a wide spectrum of educated opinion.[44] Leslie Toke picked up this argument in 1917 when he perceived that a move towards Guild Socialism by the workers

<hr />

[43] E. J. Hobsbawm, 'The Fabians reconsidered', in *Labouring Men* (London, 1979), pp. 250–71.

[44] C. Plater, 'A great social experiment', *The Hibbert Journal*, 7 (Oct. 1908), pp. 49–62; idem, 'Retreats and reconstruction', *The Hibbert Journal*, 18 (July 1920), pp. 787–97.

indicated a predisposition towards a more religious society. He claimed that 'In dealing with the younger, non-Catholic working men today . . . the Guild Socialism of *The New Age* is now rapidly becoming the favourite doctrine among the keener [ones]. That is, so far, a gain for it is much nearer the traditional Christian view than the 19th century doctrines.'[45]

As an explicitly non-political religious organization, Social Catholicism applied itself to resolution of what was arguably the most formidable question of the early twentieth century. In so doing it not only drew upon the teachings of the medieval church and neo-Thomism but was also significantly influenced by mid-nineteenth-century Christian Socialist thinking and the idealized medievalist thought associated with the cultural phenomenon of Romanticism. Yet unlike that leading exponent of the latter, John Ruskin, its appropriation of the past did not anticipate a utopian realm. It was no plea for a simplistic return to the Middle Ages. It was rather a testimony to the desire of a minority of progressive Catholics to see a greater commitment from the English Catholic Church towards resolving the structural ills of contemporary society by looking to the Church's former social and economic roles as a source of inspiration. Retrospection fortified the voice of such Catholics in their resolve to interrogate the 'social question', to formulate from the past relevant terms for a contemporary dialogue and to articulate a response which posited a greater role for Christian ideals in the workings of modern society. Effectively it generated the potential for the formation of a cornerstone in the construction of an English Catholic social platform.

De Montfort University, Bedford

---

[45] Oxford, Plater College archive, confidential letter from F. Goldwell to C. Plater, 'The social unrest', 27 Oct. 1917, p. 2.

ST CLARE OF ASSISI AND THE POOR CLARES:
A NEW SPRING

by PAUL M. GERRARD

The Second Vatican Council (1962–5) called for religious orders to renew themselves in a two-fold return to the sources of their Christian life, jointly to the Gospels and to the inspiration of each institute's founder, a process to be combined with a movement to bring the religious life into line with the 'tenor of the times'.[1]

Thirty years after the issuing on 28 October 1965 of *Perfectae Caritatis*, the conciliar decree on the religious life, it seems particularly relevant to look at how far this renewal has been enacted since the Council. Furthermore, given the theme of this volume it seems especially apt to examine the role which that call for the rediscovery of the founder's spirit has played in one such renewal.

This paper examines the way in which one major female religious Order, the Poor Clares, has returned to its foundress, St Clare of Assisi (1193–1253), and the influence she has had in the renewal of two areas of the Orders' life; namely, the practice of poverty, and the mechanisms of authority within each community. These areas have been chosen because they reflect the different factors that have affected the renewal of the Order: the figure of Clare of Assisi herself and, concurrently, the teaching of Vatican II combined with the lessons on inculturation. The material from which these conclusions are drawn is a series of interviews and written questionnaires which have been carried out with Poor Clares from England, Wales, France, Italy, Kenya, Guatemala, and El Salvador.[2] In order to examine both the

---

[1] *Perfectae Caritatis* (28 October 1965) in *Vatican Council II – the Conciliar and Post Conciliar Documents*, ed. A. Flannery, O.P. (Dublin, 1992) [hereafter Flannery], pp. 611–22.

[2] All quotations from Poor Clare sisters are taken from a series of interviews and written questionnaires carried out by the author. Personal interviews were undertaken with some sisters and then, in the light of these interviews, a questionnaire was drawn up which was sent out to those sisters who preferred to

post-conciliar and the pre-conciliar past of the order the interviewees have been drawn from a wide age range, the eldest sisters having entered the Order in the early 1930s, and the youngest in 1992. The sources are the sisters' memories of their lives and of the changes which a greater appreciation of the past brought about. These interviews provide an oral history of how a medieval figure has affected a twentieth-century group of women.

Perfectae Caritatis made it clear that the position of each founder's ideals and spirit was to be vital in any successful renewal. It stressed that 'loyal recognition should be accorded to the spirit of the founders',[3] and this is reiterated in *Evangelico Testificatio*, the apostolic exhortation of June 1971, which re-affirms that each institute's renewal must be 'faithful to the spirit of their founders'.[4]

Clare was born into the nobility of Assisi in 1193/4 and joined Francis of Assisi and his followers when she fled her parental home in 1212.[5] She settled in the church of San Damiano and was soon joined by other young noble women who became the second, contemplative branch of the Franciscan Order. Two days before Clare died on 11 August 1253, she had become the first woman to have a rule she had written for her community approved by the papacy.[6] Clare was canonized on 15 August 1255 by Alexander IV (1254–61) who had previously been the Cardinal-Protector of the Order.[7] During her lifetime Clare not only wrote her own Rule but also four letters to Agnes of Bohemia[8] (who had founded a house along the lines of San Damiano in Prague),

---

answer by post. The different medium of each quotation, either interview or written questionnaire, is indicated in the relevant note, as is the date of the interview or the month in which the written questionnaire was received by the author.

[3] *Perfectae Caritatis*, 2b, Flannery, p. 612.

[4] *Evangelico Testificatio* (29 June 1971), 11, in Flannery, pp. 680–706.

[5] Modern work on Clare includes: Marco Bartoli, *Clare of Assisi*, trans. Sister Frances Teresa, O.S.C. (London, 1993); Margaret Carney, O.S.F., *The First Franciscan Woman: Clare of Assisi and Her Form of Life* (Quincy, 1993), and Brenda M. Bolton and Paul M. Gerrard, 'Clare in her time', in *The Way Supplement, Contemporary Reflections on the Spirituality of Saint Clare* (London, 1994), pp. 42–50.

[6] 'The Rule of St Clare (1253)', in *Clare of Assisi: Early Documents*, ed. Regis Armstrong, O.F.M.Cap. (New York, 1988) [hereafter Armstrong], pp. 60–77.

[7] 'Bull of Canonisation (1255)', in Armstrong, pp. 176–83.

[8] '1st, 2nd, 3rd and 4th Letters to Blessed Agnes of Prague', ibid., pp. 33–50.

another to Ermentrude of Bruges,[9] as well as a death-bed Testament[10] and Blessing.[11]

However, for the Poor Clares to renew themselves in his historical reality of their foundress in the period immediately after the Second Vatican Council was neither straightforward nor simple. For most sisters Clare was a shadowy figure about whom little apart from sparse biographical details was known. She appeared as a distant figure, and very few sisters felt they could relate to their foundress as a person: rather, she was a plaster-cast saint on a pedestal. A sister from Lynton succinctly confirmed a common attitude, 'it was not helpful – they all seemed to be saints always, from birth upwards and onwards'.[12]

Two reasons explain why Clare remained relatively unknown to the Poor Clares. Firstly, there was the position and role of St Francis of Assisi (1182–1226). So popular and well-loved was he, particularly from the late nineteenth century on, that he seemed far more accessible than Clare and therefore became the dominant historical figure for the Poor Clares themselves. Closely linked to this was the problem of the sources for Clare's life. Not only are such sources relatively few, comprising eight written pieces[13] and two biographical records,[14] but until comparatively recently they were inaccessible to most sisters. The Latin text of Clare's letters to Agnes of Bohemia was only published in 1924;[15] while English-speaking sisters had to wait until 1982 for a critical translation with the publication of *Francis and Clare: the Complete Works* by Regis Armstrong and Ignatius Brady.[16] Furthermore, the enormously important Process of Canonization of Clare, which consists of sworn testimonies from Clare's own sisters at San Damiano following her death in

---

9   'Letter to Ermentrude of Bruges', ibid., pp. 51–3.
10   'The Testament of St Clare (1247–1253)', ibid., pp. 54–9.
11   'Blessing of St Clare', ibid., pp. 78–9.
12   Written questionnaire, sister 5–03, Lynton convent, March 1994.
13   See notes 6, 8, 9, 10, and 11.
14   They are 'The Legend of St Clare', in Armstrong, pp. 184–240, and 'The Acts of the Process of Canonisation (1253)', ibid., pp. 125–75.
15   'The Letters from Saint Clare to Blessed Agnes of Bohemia', ed. Walter Seton, in *Archivum Franciscanum Historicum*, 17 (1924), pp. 509–19.
16   *Francis and Clare: the Complete Works*, Regis Armstrong, O.F.M. Cap., and Ignatius Brady, O.F.M., eds (New York, 1982).

1253, only became available to English-speaking sisters in 1988.[17] Therefore not only was Clare overshadowed by Francis, but any study of Clare was either difficult or nigh impossible because of the inaccessibility of the sources to ordinary sisters.

For the spirit of Clare to play a vital part in the renewal of the Order she needed to be studied, and her ideals discerned for modern religious life. The first step has been the critical investigation of the sources themselves; the last twenty-five years have seen huge progress in this field. Omachevarria in Spanish,[18] Armstrong in English and Godet, Matura, and Becker in French[19] have all produced invaluable work on the writings and sources for Clare.

The position of Clare within the Order she founded has been transformed. She is now an important figure in her own right: 'the return to the sources has let us see her as a great saint and foundress on her own account, not just as a follower of Francis.'[20] Clare's own personality, ideals, and character-istics are now discernible. In the words of a sister from Arundel, with this new scholarly work at hand the Poor Clares can now see Clare as a person, as 'real and human'.[21]

Naturally, with a foundress now so accessible and real, the Poor Clares have begun to look at Clare from a vastly different perspective. It is the role she has played in the renewal of Poor Clare life and how far it needs to be qualified by the influence of other factors that requires examination.

Poverty for Clare of Assisi was, according to R. C. Dhont, the single most important element of her religious life; it was the 'real essence of her charism and not a single virtue'.[22] The foundation-stone of Clare's life of poverty was the so-called Privilege of Poverty granted to her in 1216 by Pope Innocent III.[23] This document demonstrates Clare's life of insecurity,

---

[17] See note 14.

[18] *Escritos de Santa Clara y documentos contemporaneos*, I. Omachevarria, O.F.M., ed. (Madrid, 1970).

[19] *Claire d'Assise: Écrits*, Marie-France Becker, Jean-François Godet, and Thaddée Matura, eds (Paris, 1985).

[20] Written questionnaire, sister 10-02, Woodchester convent, March 1994.

[21] Interview, sister 1-11, Arundel convent, 7 Feb. 1994.

[22] Rene-Charles Dhont, O.F.M., *Clare among her Sisters* (New York, 1987).

[23] 'The Privilege of Poverty (1216)', in Armstrong, pp. 82-4.

setting out her proposal 'not to have any possessions, whatsoever'; trusting that 'He who feeds the birds of the heavens and clothes the lilies of the fields' would not fail her 'in either food or clothing'.[24] This refusal to accept possessions and therefore regular income is also evident from a document of 1238 when Clare and her San Damiano community transferred land which they had been given to the cathedral of San Rufino in Assisi.[25] For a group of stable, enclosed women to renounce all possessions and to rely on the fluctuations of divine providence for survival was unheard of in religious life. This insecurity was the real centre of Clare's conception of poverty, and the one thing on which she would not compromise.

That Poor Clares have always been poor is confirmed by an Arundel sister who commented that 'it has always been a point of examination, struggle, conflict and argument'.[26] *A Right to be Merry*, written by Sister Mary Francis of Roswell and first published in 1950,[27] gives an illuminating insight into Poor Clare life before the Second Vatican Council. She wrote that 'the apex, the depth and the core of a Poor Clare's life is most high poverty'.[28] The material dimension of poverty took a number of expressions, including a very harsh personal poverty. An Arundel sister remembers that when she first became a Poor Clare her community 'were very often short but we just got by'.[29] In many ways the Poor Clares emphasized the more obvious material nature of their poverty, a point confirmed by a sister from Lynton who says that 'material poverty was, in some of the more overt ways, greater in the past'.[30] The word 'overt' reveals a further dimension of Poor Clare poverty, its institutional flavour. There was a lack of reality in some of the sisters' customs regarding poverty, as they now recognize. For example, the same Lynton sister remembers that 'in the past one would have a rule that one could only use something for the single

24 Ibid., p. 84.
25 'The Mandate (1238)', ibid., pp. 107–8.
26 Interview, sister 1-09, Arundel convent, 14 July 1994.
27 Sister Mary Francis, P.C.C., *A Right to be Merry* (London, 1950).
28 Ibid., p. 60.
29 Interview, sister 1-01, Arundel convent, 14 July 1994.
30 Written questionnaire, sister 5-01, Lynton convent, Aug. 1994.

thing for which it was intended'.[31] Although the Poor Clares were, without doubt, poor in a material sense, they did sometimes lack an understanding of what being poor really meant, and a change in their appreciation of this fact has been one of the major upheavals within the order in the past thirty years.

Poor Clares lived a life of very harsh poverty, but with a different understanding of what poverty may have meant on the other side of the enclosure. As an Arundel sister commented, 'I think in the past Poor Clares lived very, very poorly and frugally, but were cut off at least externally from the poor.'[32] In the wake of Vatican II there has grown up within the Order a recognition of the need to relate the reality of Poor Clare poverty to the reality of poverty in society at large. One Lynton sister noted, 'I think we should always bear in mind the question: how do the poor live – in this country, time, wherever we may be, and somehow try to use that for our own yardstick.'[33]

Poor Clares now try to ground their poverty in the reality of society, and to live in the conditions of the poor. Certainly this feeling is expressed in the new constitutions of the Order which were approved in Rome in 1988.[34] In article 151.2 these identify the sisters with 'other poor people';[35] while article 117.2 says that the sisters should be 'happy to have such clothing as befits poor people'.[36]

This attempt to measure their poverty against that of the secular poor has produced great upheaval as the sisters try to discern what Franciscan poverty should be in the twentieth century, 'now there are no hard and fast rules'.[37] The Poor Clares are still poor, and the fact that their *per capita* income in England still falls well below the line where prescriptions and dental charges are levied proves this fact. However, for many Poor Clares there is a feeling, and a reality, that they are not

---

[31] Ibid.

[32] Interview, sister 1–01, Arundel convent, 14 July 1994.

[33] Written questionnaire, sister 5–04, Lynton convent, Aug. 1994.

[34] *The Rule and General Constitutions of the Order of Poor Sisters of St Clare* (Rome, 1988).

[35] Ibid., p. 62.

[36] Ibid., p. 49.

[37] Written questionnaire, sister 5–01, Lynton convent, Aug. 1994.

as materially poor as they were; in some cases their 'simple poverty' has been 'further eroded'.[38] At the same time, and in relation to the rest of society, they are still poor. This is well expressed by an Arundel sister who notes that she now has a radio to listen to in the morning. It is now 'unusual to find someone who doesn't have something to hear and you will probably find most of us have got a cheap radio in our room. But it is nothing like the systems others have.'[39]

There has also been a growing awareness of what poverty is for the poor outside, particularly in their living conditions. Therefore the sisters now no longer get friends to drive them to medical appointments, but use public transport as the poor would. Whereas in the past the sisters had little idea of the value of money, in today's life they are all aware of the need to budget: 'nowadays everyone is aware of the money we haven't got, and is expected to cut their cloth accordingly'.[40] The poverty of the Poor Clares is now real, so that, as other poor people cannot refuse meat, if the sisters 'are given something, for example meat, which we don't normally eat, then we eat it'.[41]

Poverty is seen as being far more than just material possessions and although the Poor Clares have always been aware of this it is perhaps more emphasized now. One El Salvadorean sister gives a clear example of this from her own unique experience which needs no gloss: 'we live in the poor areas, with the same dangers. I, we, were always in danger . . . we harboured members who were in danger – that for me was poverty, not that I owned three habits instead of two or ate three meals a day instead of fasting. I ate when offered food, knowing more often than not I would be sick after it from internal parasites or water that was not boiled.'[42]

Undoubtedly this new understanding of poverty as all-embracing has come from a greater understanding of Clare's spirituality, as expressed in her own writings. Furthermore, the fact that Clare herself chose to be identified with the poor

---

[38] Written questionnaire, sister 5-01, Lynton convent, Aug. 1994.
[39] Interview, sister 1-13, Arundel convent, Aug. 1994.
[40] Written questionnaire, sister 5-01, Lynton convent, Aug. 1994.
[41] Ibid.
[42] Written questionnaire, sister 7-01, San Salvador convent, Sept. 1994.

when she entered the Monastery of San Paolo as a servant, or *vilis*,[43] and insisted on manual labour, the lot of the thirteenth-century poor,[44] has also played a role in helping modern Poor Clares to identify with the experience of the poor of today.

However, at the same time other factors are at work which have been equally influential, and might even have directed the sisters to see these elements in Clare through a form of predetermined retrospection. Vatican II, and its insistence that the world was not intrinsically evil and therefore should not be fled from, had made it possible for the sisters to look at the world as their model for poverty. Similarly, the idea of 'a Church with the Poor' not just for the poor, the basis of liberation theology,[45] has naturally played a huge role in the sisters' expression of poverty. In addition the idea of inculturation, the process by which the Church's structures are conditioned by local cultures, so stressed in *Ad Gentes*,[46] has played a vital role in making Poor Clare poverty a real value in the twentieth century. The rediscovery of Clare's grounding of poverty in the experience of contemporary society echoes the broader and deeper call of Vatican II for the Church as a whole to share that experience. In that sense the charism of Clare and Francis was not only rediscovered by the Poor Clares alone.

These two influences, looking back to Clare the foundress and forward in accordance with the teaching of Vatican II, have combined to produce a new synthesis of poverty. The interdependence of the two is shown also in the renewal of the mechanisms of authority within the Order, but in different proportions.

In order to understand how Poor Clares functioned in the period up to 1970, there must be a clear appreciation of the way the vow of obedience was viewed and followed. For Poor Clares, and perhaps for most religious, obedience meant doing as they were instructed to, without question. A sister

---

[43] Sister Frances Teresa, O.S.C., *This Living Mirror: Reflections on Clare of Assisi* (London, 1995), pp. 33–5.

[44] 'The Rule of St Clare (1253)', VII, Armstrong, p. 70.

[45] Philip Berryman, *Liberation Theology: the Essential Facts about the Revolutionary Movement in Latin America* (London, 1987), p. 42.

[46] *Ad Gentes* (7 Dec. 1965), 26, in Flannery, pp. 813–62.

from Lynton remembers how 'previously one obeyed simply because one was told to'.[47] Furthermore, this obedience was not merely passive, being told what to do, it was also active, in that sisters needed the permission of the superior to do even the most trivial of things. One sister from Woodchester felt that there 'was a tendency, in the past, where Mother Abbess had to be consulted about everything'.[48] Obedience covered even the minutiae of everyday life; there were many 'permissions to ask in small ways',[49] recalled a Woodchester sister who entered in the 1930s.

One of the reasons why obedience was conceived as meaning following the will of the superior without question was that by doing so the sisters could not sin. One sister at Arundel remembered how even though an action may be wrong, 'the very fact that you were doing what you were told made it right'.[50] This is confirmed in *A Right to be Merry*, when it notes that 'an obedient religious simply cannot blunder while she obeys. The superior may be wrong in commanding, but the subject is still right in obeying.'[51]

The results of dependence by the sisters on the abbess for most of the decisions concerning their lives were, firstly, that the sisters lost any real sense of responsibility and, secondly, that the abbess needed to adopt a role of great power. Since the sisters had no responsibility for their actions, many were, in some senses, like children who wanted 'the abbess to make all the decisions, they don't want to have to say yes or no, just to do what they are told'.[52] This idea expressed itself most patently in the way that the abbess became 'Mother' and the sisters were daughters. As one Arundel sister remembered, the abbesses 'ran the convent like a father ran the house'.[53]

The abbess had to assume enormous responsibilities, in that she was in charge of the sisters' entire life. The experience of one Lynton sister was that 'the responsibility for running the

---

47 Written questionnaire, sister 5–03, Lynton convent, Feb. 1995.
48 Written questionnaire, sister 10–02, Woodchester convent, Feb. 1995.
49 Written questionnaire, sister 10–01, Woodchester convent, Feb. 1995.
50 Interview, sister 1–01, Arundel convent, 19 Jan. 1995.
51 Mary Francis, *A Right to be Merry*, p. 99.
52 Interview, sister 1–05, Arundel convent, 19 Jan. 1995.
53 Interview, sister 1–09, Arundel convent, 19 Jan. 1995.

community . . . fell entirely on Mother'.[54] A sister from Arundel elaborates on this point: 'I think in the old days the abbess did it all, but then it is very easy under that scenario for the abbess to become quite autocratic, and I think some of them did.'[55] It would certainly be true that it was the abbess alone, or with her Council,[56] who made the decisions that affected the way the community lived. The community itself played no role in how the house might change or develop; the instrument of government was the abbess, possibly with her Council.

A sister at Arundel, who has had experience of several communities, recalls that a decision would be made by 'the abbess, vicaress and the discreets' and then 'it would have come down to the community being told this is what we are doing'.[57] This is confirmed by one Lynton sister who felt that abbesses were 'perhaps . . . a little more autocratic in the past, there was no discussion or dialogue, or very little'.[58]

The abbess was on a very different level from the other sisters in term of executive powers and, perhaps naturally, she became separated from the sisters in many other ways as well. Her role focused all the sisters' attention on her, and she became the centre of everything. One Arundel sister remembers how when she first entered, recreation took the following form: the sisters 'sat in a circle . . . and had to address what they had to say to the abbess'.[59] The preeminent position of the abbess was also similar in the experience at Woodchester, where the abbess had 'a number of privileges . . . a tendress to do jobs for her, also bowing and kneeling to them on occasions'.[60] Further illumination is provided by an Arundel sister who recalls witnessing her first abbatial election. She says 'the immediate thing was that all

---

[54] Written questionnaire, sister 5–03, Lynton convent, Feb. 1995.
[55] Interview, sister 1–09, Arundel convent, 19 Jan. 1995.
[56] A Poor Clare Council consists of the abbess, the vicaress, and a number of sisters known as 'discreets', who are proportionate in number to the size of the community. Often the discreets are the other officers of the house, for example the novice mistress. See 'The Rule of St Clare (1253)', IV, Armstrong, pp. 66–7.
[57] Interview, sister 1–05, Arundel convent, 19 Jan. 1995.
[58] Written questionnaire, sister 5–03, Lynton convent, Feb. 1995.
[59] Interview, sister 1–12, Arundel convent, 19 Jan. 1995.
[60] Written questionnaire, sister 10–02, Woodchester convent, Feb. 1995.

the jobs she had been doing were parcelled down to other people instantly, so that she was immediately free from work. So that she actually had no job other than being abbess.'[61] Clearly the position of the abbess was one of a true 'superior'.

However, the mode of government which is now the norm is quite different, and the basis of this is a different application of the concept of obedience. In the past the sisters would expect the abbess to make all their decisions for them; now they have to think through the problem themselves. This has meant not only more problems, but also more responsibility, so that 'there is a lot more consultation where people are having to think about decisions where before they just waited for a decree . . . their lives are probably more bothered with decisions and consultations than they used to be'.[62] A sister from Lynton talked about a 'responsible obedience';[63] this is the key to the way Poor Clares live out their vow of obedience now. They have responsibility for their decisions through their discussions with their abbess.

This added personal responsibility has been reflected in the way that decisions are made that affect the community. Now all major decisions are made in the conventual chapter, that is the entire body of sisters gathered together. The Constitutions of 1988 lay down which decisions are reserved for the community and which can be decided by the abbess alone. For example, article 250 defines the times when the abbess should consult the conventual chapter, when the chapter should decide matters, and when it has to give its consent.[64] Significantly all major decisions and issues require the chapter to decide, or at least to give its consent to the policy adopted by the abbess. The government model which is now the norm is that of the abbess and the conventual chapter working together.[65]

61 Interview, sister 1-12, Arundel convent, 19 Jan. 1995.
62 Interview, sister 1-09, Arundel convent, 19 Jan. 1995.
63 Written questionnaire, sister 4-02, Lynton convent, Feb. 1995.
64 *Rule and General Constitutions of the Order of Poor Sisters of St Clare* (Rome, 1988), pp. 108-10.
65 Sister Frances Teresa, O.S.C., 'The fall and rise of the conventual chapter: from chapter 4 of the Rule to the General Constitutions', *Communion and Communication* (Rome, 1991), pp. 17-25.

Within this context the position of the abbess has changed quite dramatically. Firstly, her position in relation to each sister is one of dialogue and not instruction, thus placing the abbess on the same level as the sisters. What is quite clear is that the sisters now relate to the abbess on the level of a sister who has been given special responsibility. The abbess seems to be a 'sister and a friend' to most sisters,[66] which reflects the movement of the abbess back to a real sisterhood with her community. By no means the only example of this process, but perhaps the clearest, is the way in which one newly-elected abbess removed the abbatial chair from the choir in order to be a sister among sisters.[67]

Part of this movement, and perhaps also a response to it, has been the emphasis placed on the role of the abbess as a servant of the sisters. Not only is the abbess to be there as a servant for their spiritual needs, she now performs this role in a very real way. The abbess is a servant in a 'directly practical sense as well as in a spiritualized sense of "I'm always available for those who need me." '[68] The practical reality of this new emphasis and its novelty is well illustrated by the description of a sister from Arundel of her own abbess as 'the first abbess I have known who took a turn as cook and took a turn in serving in refectory'.[69]

We can see then that the mechanisms of authority have changed within Poor Clare life; the abbess is a sister-servant who works with the sisters through real dialogue and communication. She still retains substantial power, although as one Lynton sister noted, 'albeit somewhat less explicit than it used to be',[70] but the base of power is the conventual chapter and the abbess working together. The root of this has been the greater dialogue which has been invested in the vow of obedience, thus equipping the sisters to be capable of responsible decision-making concerning the life of the convent. The pattern of government has changed from an abbess at the top of the pyramid to that of the abbess in the circle.

66 Written questionnaire, sister 5-04, Lynton convent, Feb. 1995.
67 Interview, sister 1-06, Arundel convent, 19 Jan. 1995.
68 Written questionnaire, sister 5-01, Lynton convent, Feb. 1995.
69 Interview, sister 1-09, Arundel convent, 19 Jan. 1995.
70 Written questionnaire, sister 5-04, Lynton convent, Feb. 1995.

Once again the question is, what lay behind these changes? Here can be seen even more clearly the relationship of many different factors which combine with each other to produce the driving force of the Poor Clares' renewal. The whole revival of scriptural studies had led to the increased profile of the image of Christ as the servant. Added to this is the idea of collegiality, so stressed in the conciliar decree *Lumen Gentium* of 21 November 1964,[71] where responsibility is entrusted to the body with the head as the leader listening to the Spirit's call from the body. Furthermore, there is the effect of culture which in itself has shaped the aspirations of the novices who have since become the bedrock of the Order. One sister from Lynton commented that it was the personalities of abbesses, shaped by their experiences, that has changed the role of the superior.[72]

In addition there has been the influence of the figure of Clare herself which in this area has been enormous. It is the new appreciation of Clare's ideals, combined with the teaching of Vatican II, that has motivated the Poor Clares to produce a new synthesis of authority. By looking at what Clare actually wrote in her Rule it is clear that it is her ideas that have directed the Poor Clares in their renewal.

Clare's Rule clearly states that it is the sisters who should exercise the responsibility and power within the community through the chapter, which was to meet 'at least once a week'[73] to discuss all matters regarding the 'welfare and good of the monastery'.[74] When discussing the election of the abbess or officers, and the reception of novices, the 'common consent of the sisters' is required.[75] The fact that it is the sisters as a community who hold the executive force in Clare's scheme is also illustrated elsewhere. When Clare warns the sisters against allowing others to use the convent as a safe-house for belongings, she warns the 'abbess and her sisters'.[76] Furthermore, Clare sees the sisters as particularly

[71] *Lumen Gentium* (21 November 1964), III, in Flannery, pp. 350–426.
[72] Written questionnaire, sister 5–10, Lynton convent, Feb. 1995.
[73] 'The Rule of St Clare (1253)', IV, 15, in Armstrong, p. 67.
[74] 'The Rule of St Clare (1253)', IV, 17, ibid., p. 67.
[75] 'The Rule of St Clare (1253)', IV, 7, ibid., p. 66.
[76] 'The Rule of St Clare (1253)', IV, 20, ibid., p. 67.

responsible for their life in that once an election has taken place there is no need for this to be confirmed by any other authority; the sisters are competent enough for this task.[77] Clare sees the sisters, as a body, as responsible for their own life both in terms of their house's internal mechanisms and its relationship with outside superiors.

In addition to this the role of the abbess is quite clearly as a sister among sisters. Clare stresses that the abbess and the vicaress are to 'preserve common life in everything'.[78] This is a theme reiterated elsewhere in the Rule. Clare says that when the abbess has called together the chapter, 'both she and her sisters should humbly confess their common and public offences and negligences'.[79] The fact that Clare expects the abbess to confess her faults together with the sisters puts her with them in an explicit way. In her Testament Clare does not speak of an abbess but of the sister 'who is in office', which gives further evidence of the position of the abbess with her sisters.[80]

Clare's ideal of authority, which was the fruit of her forty years in San Damiano and legislated for in the Rule, is one in which sisters make their decisions with the abbess as being in 'office'. In the recent renewal of the mechanisms of authority the return to Clare as founder seems to have played the most important role, with other factors working to support her ideals.

Using the two examples of the practice of poverty and authority we can see how the renewal of the Poor Clares has been influenced by several factors. Undoubtedly their past, in particular the newly-discovered figured of Clare, has been influential; and in the changing role of the abbess in relation to her sisters the foundress has played a dramatically large part. At the same time it is important to note that the figure of Clare has been rediscovered as a result of the call of Vatican II for religious orders to return to their sources, a retrospection which was emphatically forward-looking in its intention. Meanwhile, other elements have also been at work, particularly

---

[77] 'The Rule of St Clare (1253)', IV, 6–8, ibid., p. 66.
[78] 'The Rule of St Clare (1253)', IV, 13, ibid., pp. 66–7.
[79] 'The Rule of St Clare (1253)', IV, 16, ibid., p. 67.
[80] 'The Testament of St Clare (1247–53)', 53, 61, ibid., p. 58.

the idea of inculturation which, with the rise of foundations abroad, has been very real to many communities.

When Alexander IV canonized Clare of Assisi he called her a 'clear spring' who 'has furnished a new fountain of living water for the refreshment of souls'.[81] As the Poor Clares continue to renew themselves, they do so with her ideals in the forefront. After centuries of being hidden, Clare is once again emerging to be a 'clear spring' for her spiritual daughters of the twentieth century as they equip themselves for the next stage of their history.

King's College,
University of London

---

[81] 'The Bull of Canonization (1255)', 9, ibid., p. 180.

INDEX

Abdias, Bishop of Babylon 120
Abelard, Peter 135 n.1, 179 n.7
  and Cistercian-Cluniac debate
    94, 111
Act of the Six Articles 263–5,
    274 n.19
Act of Uniformity (1662) 379,
    380, 388–9, 392, 459, 465–9
Acta episcoporum Rothomagensium
    121
Ad Gentes 554
Adaloald, son of Queen
    Theodolinda 199
Adamnan, *De Locis Sanctis* 52
Adelbertus Gallus 238
Adhémar of Chabannes 120
Ælfric, *Lives of saints* 65, 70, 73
aesthetics, and Victorian
    ecclesiology 423–44
Ætheldreda of Ely, St 64
Æthelfleda 71
Æthelgar, Abbot 73
Æthelgifu, Queen 71
Æthelthryth, Queen 71
Æthelwold, and monastic reform
    64–5, 73
Æthelwyn 67
Aetius, and neo-Arianism 82
    n.15
affectivity, spiritual 78, 80, 82,
    85
Agilulf, second husband of
    Theodolinda 196, 199–200,
    212, 218, 221
Agnes of Bohemia 548, 549
Agricola, Bolognese martyr 39
Ailly, Pierre d' 290
Alan of Lille, *Contra haereticos*
    138–9
Alberti, Leon Battista 57
Alberzoni, M. P. 149, 150 n.6,
    153, 154–5

Alcuin 67
Aldfrith, King 72
Alexander IV, Pope 548, 561
Alexander VII, Pope 370
All Saints, Margaret Street 435,
    438–9, 442
allegory 15, 313
almanacs *see* calendars
Ambrose of Milan, and
    Bolognese martyrs 39
Anabaptism 237, 284 n.41
Anacletus, St, and Petrine
    primacy 171, 172–3
Anastasius IV, Pope, and
    Bologna 51 n.29
Anatolius of Constantinople,
    and Chalcedonian Formula
    21, 26
ancestors
  and classical culture 9–11,
    14–15
  and early Christian past 6,
    11–17
  in Judaism 6, 12–13
Andrew of Fontevrault 361,
    364–5, 369
Angilbert, Abbot 52
Anglo-Catholicism *see* Church of
    England, High
    Churchmanship
Anglo-Norman Anonymous, *De
    officio regis* 182
Anselm of Alessandria 146
Anselm of Canterbury 179 n.7,
    182–4, 479
Anselm of Havelberg 107 n.73,
    110 n.83
Anselm of Laon 121
anti-clericalism 125
Antichrist
  and clerical celibacy 253–66,
    320

and papacy 238, 255, 259–62,
265, 269, 312
in Revelation 257–63, 265–6
as spiritual 253–4
Antiochene theology 21, 23, 26
antiquity, and tradition 8–9, 289
Antoinette d'Orléans 368
Antony of Egypt, St 84–5, 99–
100, 107, 114
apathiae, and martyrdom 280–2,
287
apocrypha, in Orderic Vitalis
119–20, 124
apologists, and early Church's
past 6, 9–11, 12–17
Aquinas, St Thomas, and church
government 166, 178
archaeology of catacombs
343–60
architecture, and Victorian
ecclesiology 427, 431, 433–43
Arfaxat 137, 138, 140–3
Arianism 136
Aristeides 16
aristocracy
and clergy 66–70, 177
and monastic lands 63–4
and origins of the Humiliati
157, 160
Aristotle
Physics 178, 185 n.28
Politics 166–9, 185 n.28
and time 178, 179 n.7, 180
Armada, in English iconography
307–8, *308*, 311, 312–13,
316–18, *317*, 320–1, 325
Arminianism
England 320
Netherlands 394, 397, 401, 403
Armstrong, R. 549, 550
Arnold of Brescia 238
Arnolfo 157–8
Arnulf of Metz, and secularity
and sanctity 69
Arsenius 84–5
asceticism
and Robert of Arbrissel 362–3,
370

and secularity 66–72, 74
and Symeon the New
Theologian 80–4
Assembly, General 298, 300,
524
Aston, M. 188–9
Athanasius, and Nicene Creed
20, 21
atheism, charge against early
Church 10
Athenagoras 13
Atterbury, Francis 415
Augustine of Canterbury, and
English Reformation 261–2
Augustine of Hippo
and authority of the Church
296, 302
and classical culture 15
De Baptismo 111 n.87
De Civitate Dei 108
De consensu evangelistarum 119
and Manicheans 145, 148
and time 129, 179 n.8, 180
Authari, first husband of
Theodolinda 196, 199, 200,
202, 203, 204
authenticity, and personal
experience 78, 85, 87–8
authority, conciliar 289–306
Avis, P. 488–9, 498–9

Bagshawe, Edward Gilpin,
Bishop of Nottingham 532–3
Bainham, James
abjuration 267, 269, 270–1,
275, 278–9, 282, 285, 287,
288
martyrdom 267–88
torture 267, 269, 270, 272,
275, 278
Bainham, Joan 272–5, 277–82,
284, 285, 287–8
Baker, Samuel 325
Balan, Pietro 481
Bale, John
Actes of the Englysh Votaries
261–3
and the Bible 253, 263

and clerical celibacy 256, 260–1, 264–5
Image of Both Churches 253, 257–9, 263, 265
and James Bainham 272, 276
The lattre examination of Anne Askew 276 n.20
Romish Fox 264
Balzarinus, and the Humiliati 155
Bancroft, Richard 331
Baptists, and Great Ejection 387, 461, 465
Barbier de Montault, X. 375
Baronio, Cesare 343–4, 350, 356–60
Barth, Karl 492
Bartholomew Committee 461–2, 464–5
Basil the Great, and desert fathers 100
Basle, Council (1431-49) 290
Baudry of Bourgueil, *Historia Ierosolimitana* 126
Baudry of Dol 361, 362, 363–5, 369
Bauer, W. 135
Baxter, Richard 381–7, 391
Beale, William 331
Becker, M.-F. 550
Bede
  Historia Ecclesiastica 62–5, 109, 117, 118, 121, 123, 129
  and Holy Places 52
  Letter to Egbert 62–3, 67
  Life of St Cuthbert 65
  and tenth-century monasticism 62–3, 65, 72–4
Bell Cox, James 502
Belloc, Hilaire 538–9
Belvederi, G. 43 nn.13,14, 47–8, 51 n.31
Benedict of Alignan, *Tractatus fidei* 142
Benedict, P. 230–1, 247
Benedict XIV, Pope 371
Benedictine Order
  and Bernard of Clairvaux 93–4, 98–100, 103

and civilization 122, 476, 478, 480
and the Humiliati 155–6
and monastic reform 61, 64, 73, 95–7, 113–14
and Orderic Vitalis 122, 123, 134
and Peter the Venerable 110
and Rupert of Deutz 104–7
and women 111
Benigni, Umberto 482–3
Berengar of Tours 125
Bernard of Clairvaux 92–3, 366, 373
  Apology 93, 94–5, 98–100, 102–3, 108, 110
  and heresy 135 n.4
  and the Humiliati 153–5, 156
  and monastic reform 101 n.42
  and the past 98–100, 110, 111, 114
  and Peter the Venerable 93–5
Bernard of Tiron 122
Bernher, Augustine 286 n.46
Berti, Antonio 348
Best, G. F. A. 408–9, 416, 506 n.25
Bible
  and Calvinism 251
  and the Church 292–304
  and clerical celibacy 255–6, 257–9
  and history 63, 116, 119, 239–41, 253–4, 257–9, 263–6, 294–6, 300, 303–5
  and liturgy 80, 116
  and tradition 265
  vernacular 269
  and William of Ockham 163–7, 168–71, 174–5
  and Wyclif 177
  see also Old Testament
Bienvenu, J.-M. 366, 369 n.29, 371
Bilby, William 391
Bindley, T. H. 19 n.1, 20 n.4, 23

bishops
and authority 170, 182–90
and *Essays and Reviews* 468
and reform in Church of
England 410, 416–17, 421–2,
502
Blomfield, Charles James 408,
409, 411, 421
Bobbio, and Theodolinda 210
Bodley, G. F. 443
Boethius, Anicius Manlius
Torquatus Severinus, and
wheel of Fortune 179 n.6
Bolland, John van, *Acta
Sanctorum* 370
Bologna *see* S. Stefano
Bolton, B. 149
Bonald, L. G. A. 477
Boniface III, Pope 258 n.17
Boniface VIII, Pope 479, 481,
483
Boniface IX, Pope, and the
Humiliati 160–1
Bonincontro de Morigia, and
Monza cathedral 206–12,
213–16, 221–2
Bonne-âme, William 121
Bononius, S. 51, 54
Book of Common Order 519, 520,
523–5
Book of Common Prayer 6, *324*,
327, 332, 429, 466, 468, 502
Bordet, 347
Borromeo, Federico 156 n.43
Borromeo, St Charles 349
Bosio, Antonio, *Roma sotteranea*
343–7, *345*, 350–2, 353–60
Boyce, E. J. 423
Bradwardine, Thomas, and time
179 n.7
Brady, I. 549
Brevis summula 142
Briggs, Henry 332 n.8
Brock, William 461
Bruno, St 112
Bruno of Cologne, St 68–9
Bucer, Martin 302 n.59, 303
nn.60,61

Bullinger, Heinrich 253 n.2, 257,
258–9
Bullough, Donald 67, 199
Burges, William 425, 441, 442
Burgess, Thomas, Bishop of
Salisbury 414, 415
Burke, Edmund 496
Butler, Charles 499
Butterfield, H. 499–500
Butterfield, William 424, 425,
435, 438–9, 441–2
Byrthferth of Ramsey 63, 65, 67
n.28
Byrton, Henry 322

Calamy, Edmund
Abridgment 380, 383–92
Continuation of the Account 385,
386–7, 391
*Defence of Moderate Non-
Conformity* 391
Historical Account 381–3, 388,
462
calendars
Protestant 310–11, 321, 330–3,
335–41
Roman 353, 357–8
Calixtus, Pope 125
Calvin, John
and exile 231–3, 244–5, 252
and iconography 314, 320
and individual action 247
Institutes 231–3, 237 n.22, 527
and minority imperative
249–50
and the sacraments 523, 526
and Satan and the Church 257
Calvinism, European 227–52
activism 229–31, 245–7, 248–9,
251–2
culture 231–52
and iconography 307–9, 320–1,
327
and individual and community
228, 245–7, 251–2
and martyrdom 231
and martyrology 234–44, 252
and minority imperative 248–52

and Providence 233, 241-2, 244-5, 247-9, 252
and setbacks to early Reformation 227-30
see also Dutch Reformed Church
Camden Society 417, 423-5
Campbell, George 522
Canterbury cathedral, and monastic reform 73
Capp, B. 337 n.16
Cardini, F. 54
Cardoni, Francesco 348
Carleton, George, *A Thankfull Remembrance. . . 315*, 316-18, *317*
Carlyle, Thomas 495, 534
Caröe, W. D. 443
Carolingians, and liturgy 52, 58
Carpenter, R. C. 424, 435, 441
Casale, Antonio 57
Cassian, John 99, 100, 102
catacombs, revival of interest in 343-60
Catharism
  and genealogies of heresy 136, 138, 141, 142-7
  and the true Church 144-6, 257
Catholic Social Guild (CSG) 529-45
celibacy, clerical, in Reformation polemic 253-66
Celsus, and early Church's past 9-10
Cerinthians, in polemical treatises 136, 143
Chadwick, Owen 501, 505
Chalcedon, Council (451), Formula 19-29
Chamberlain, John 309
change
  and doctrine 22-3, 28-9, 87-8, 254, 257-9, 265
  and tradition 6, 105, 108, 109, 227-8, 355
Charity Organization Society 536

Charles I of England
  and Antrim Massacre 383-4, 390
  proposed marriage to Infanta Maria 309, 310, 314-16, 318
Charles V, Emperor 228
Chateaubriand, F. R. de 373
Chevalier, Jean 369
Chibnall, M. 111 n.88
Childebert, Frankish King 199
Christensen, T. 488, 498
Christian Socialism 476, 487, 533-4, 543, 545
Christology
  and Chalcedonian Formula 19-29
  and heresy 143
  and Maurice 493, 497
Christou, Prof. 76 n.3
Church
  and anti-Cathar polemics 144-8
  and clerical celibacy 254-66
  early
    and general councils 293-4, 301-2, 305
    and monastic practice 6, 100, 110, 113
    and Protestant martyrologies 236-9, 241, 251
    and reform 61-74, 96-9, 227-8, 334, 417-18
    revival of interest in catacombs 343-60
    and tradition 5-6, 289
    and William of Ockham 163-75
  English, unity 64
  in Orderic Vitalis 118-19, 124-5, 126-7, 129, 133-4
  and Scriptures 292-304
  true/false 144-5, 238, 253-9, 263-5, 320, 334
  and Wyclif 177-9, 182-3, 187-93
  see also Church of England; conciliarism; Dutch Reformed Church; Nonconformity;

reform; Reformation; Roman Catholicism
Church Association 502, 511, 513
Church of England
 and continuity 321, 334-6
 and Diocesan Revival 410-22
 and Great Ejection 262, 379-92, 462-73
 High Churchmanship
  and appeal to early Church 5
  and Great Ejection 380, 384, 386, 388-90
  and reform 409, 411-14, 417-19
  and Tractarianism 501-3, 506-7, 509-10
  and Victorian ecclesiology 425, 427-8
  and Victorian Nonconformity 467, 472
  see also Oxford Movement; Tractarianism
 and legitimation of reform 407-22
 and Maurice 487-9, 495-9
 as true Church 334
 see also Camden Society; Ecclesiological Society; Evangelicalism
Church of England Defence Association 465-6
Church Institution 459
Church, R. W. 503, 504-7, 508-10, 514
Church of Scotland, and Catholic revival 517-27
Church Service Society 522
Church and State
 Britain 407, 420-2, 428-9, 463, 470, 496
 Italy 478-83
 Netherlands 394-9, 401-3
Cicero, Marcus Tullius, and time 178
Cistercian Order
 and Bernard of Clairvaux 92-3, 98-9, 102-3, 110

 and clothing 105-6, 108
 and desert fathers 99-100, 106, 107, 110, 111-12
 and Humiliati 154
 and manual work 106-7, 108-9
 and Orderic Vitalis 111-12
 and Peter the Venerable 108, 110, 113-14
 and Rupert of Deutz 104-7
 and William of Malmesbury 101, 112
 see also Exordium Magnum; Exordium Parvum
Cîteaux see Cistercian Order
civilization, Christian, and Italian Catholicism 475-86
Clare of Assisi, St
 and authority 559-60
 life 547-50, 559, 561
 and poverty 550-2, 554, 560
Clarke, B. F. L. 431
Clarke, Samuel 326, 385
Classen, Peter 115-17
Clegg, James 391
I Clement 12
Clement I, Pope 121
Clement VI, Pope 216
Clement VIII, Pope, and monastic reform 367
Clement IX, Pope 370-1
Clement of Alexandria, and past of early Church 9, 14
Clement of Rome 14
Clementine Recognitions 120
clergy
 and anti-clericalism 125
 celibacy 254-66
 and diocesan revival 421
 and Great Ejection 379-92, 459-73
 in Humiliati 150
 and lay patrons 91, 124, 190-1
 and monastic reform 62, 63-6, 107-8
 and Protestant iconography 312
 and secularity 66-7

in Wyclif 184–7, 189–90, 192
see also bishops; rural deans
Clermont, Council (1095) 113, 125
Clifford, J. B. 462–3
Clofesho, Council (747) 67
Cluny
and Clairvaux 98–100, 102, 112–13
and Orderic Vitalis 128
and Peter the Venerable 93–5, 108–9, 113
and prayers for the dead 133
Coleman, J. 171 n.42
Coleridge, S. T. 490–1, 492, 495, 496
Collamarini, E. 47
Columbanus 109, 122, 123
conciliarism, in Scottish Reformation 289–306
confession 132–3, 191, 353–4, 355 n.26, 509, 510
Congregationalism, and Great Ejection 387, 461–4, 471–2, 473
Conrad, Bishop, and Holy Sepulchre 52, 54
Conrad of Eberbach 113
consent, and tradition 8–9
Constable, G. 94–5
Constans, Emperor 204–6, 211
Constantine
and Council of Nicaea 297 n.38
and Holy Sepulchre, Jerusalem 31, 47–8, 49
and Sessorian basilica 50–1
Constantinople
primacy 21
and Rome 91
Constantinople, Council (381)
Creed 20, 21–8, *24–5*
and Petronius 36
continuity, and tradition 6–8, 12, 28–9, 90, 145, 241, 254, 289, 358
Cooke, William 461–2

Cooper, James 517, 519, 520–1, 525
Corbinian, and secularity and sanctity 69
Corti, M. 38
Cosiner, Michel 368–9
Courtenay, William, and papal supremacy 177
Cracknell, K. 498 n.45
Craig, John 521–2
Cranmer, Thomas 6
Crespin, Jean 234, 237–8, 239
Cressy, D. 310, 322, 332 n.9
Crocefissi, Simone de' 154
Crome, Edward 282–3, 288
Crusades
and Council of Clermont 113, 125
and Orderic Vitalis 125–7
and Robert of Arbrissel 363
and western imitations of Jerusalem 56, 58
culture, classical, and early Christian past 14–15
Cunningham, Alexander 292
Cuthbert, St 211
Cyprian, St
and early Christian past 15, 296
and Petrine primacy 171
Cyril of Alexandria, and Chalcedonian Formula 20, 21, 22–3, 28

Dale, R. W. 463, 466–7, 472–3
Dansey, William, *Horae decanicae rurales 412–13*, 414–17, 419, 421
Dante Allighieri 163
Davidson, John 289, 291, 299–300
Ane Answer to the Tractiue 292, 300–5
Davies, Lady Eleanor 322
Davies, Julian 339 n.20
Davis, N. 230
Day, John 268 n.1
De la Mainferme, Jeanne 371

De la Rivière, Jean 246
De la Roche-Posay, Chasteignier 370-1
De Maistre, Joseph 477
De Rossi, G. B. 347
decretalists, and canon law 168, 182
Denis, St 121-2
Dermout, I. J. 393, 399-406
desert fathers
  in monastic debate 99-100, 110, 111-13
  and St Philip Neri 348
  and Symeon the New Theologian 84-5
Devas, Charles Stanton 532-4, 538, 543
Dhont, R. C. 550
Diogenes of Cyzicus 27
Dioscorus, deposition 20
doctrine, and change 22-3, 28-9, 87-8, 254, 257, 265
Doddridge, Philip 391-2
Dolnikowski, E. W. 179 n.7
Dominican Order 151, 152
Donaldson, G. 525
Donation of Constantine 181, 187-8, 190 n.55
Donatism 138, 143, 295 n.31
Dordrecht Synod 394-5, 397, 401, 405
dualism
  philosophical 137, 139, 141-3, 145, 147
  political 177, 182, 187, 190
Dunstan
  and Antichrist 262-3
  and monastic reform 65-74
Durand of Huesca
  Contra Manichaeos 138, 139
  Liber antiheresis 136-44, 146
Durand of Troarn 128
Dutch Reformed Church
  and the past 393-9
  in Ypeij and Dermout 399-404
Dyke, Daniel 312

Eadmund, King, and Dunstan 66

Eadred, King, and Dunstan 66, 67-8, 70-1
Eadwig, King 68, 71-2
Eardley, Sir Culling 467
Ebeling, G. 490-1
Ebionites, in polemical treatises 136, 143
Ebrard of Béthune, Liber antiheresis 139
Ecclesiastical Commission, Britain 408-10, 420-1
Ecclesiological Society 423, 426-7, 436
Ecclesiologist 424, 428 n.20, 432, 437-8
ecclesiology
  and Church reform 417, 430-3
  and critical attitude 163-75
  and Maurice 488-9, 493-7, 498-9
  mystical 88-9
  and Oxford Movement 507, 510
  and Webb 423-44
Eckbert of Schönau, Sermones contra Catharos 141, 145-6
Eckett, Robert 462
Edgar, King 62, 72
Edward VI of England 229, 233-4, 249, 299 n.46
Egfrith, King 71
Eleanor de Bourbon 368, 370
elect see predestination
Eligius of Noyon, and secularity and sanctity 69
Elizabeth I of England 307, 311, 320
Emery, William 420
England
  Nonconformity 379-92, 459-73
  Protestantism 229, 249-50, 253-66, 307-28, 329-42
  see also Church of England
English Church Union 502, 512
Ephesus, Council (431), and Nicene Creed 20, 21
Ermentrude of Bruges 549

error, genealogy 136–48
Eucharist
  in Calvinism 242–3, 523
  and denial of transubstantiation
    269
  and laity 191
  in medieval debate 91, 125
  in Scoto-Catholic movement
    523–5
  in Wyclif 181, 182, 191
Eucherius of Lyons 39 n.7
Eugenius IV, Pope, and the
  Humiliati 155, 161
Eunomius, and neo-Arianism 82
  n.15
Eusebius
  Ecclesiastical History 7, 115, 117,
    118–20, 122, 124–5, 129
  and Jerusalem 49
  and persecution 10, 286
Eusebius, Bishop, and Bolognese
  martyrs 39
Euthymius 85
Eutyches, and Christology 19,
  20, 22, 27
Evangelicalism
  and Oxford Movement 506–7,
    511–15
  and Victorian Nonconformity
    466–7, 470, 472
Evangelico Testificatio 548
Evans, A. P. 135 n.1, 139, 141
Evans, G. R. 179 n.7
Evroult, St, Life 123–4
exegesis
  in William of Ockham 163–5
  see also allegory
exile, and Reformation 229–30,
  231–4, 243, 244–5, 247, 249,
  251, 272, 330
Exordium Magnum 95, 113
Exordium Parvum 95–7, 99, 109,
  110
experience, priority 77–8, 79–86,
  87–9

Fabian Socialism, and Catholic
  Socialism 536–8, 543–4

Faccioli, Raffaele 45
Farrar, Robert 280–1
Fascism, and Catholic social
  thought 484
father, spiritual 77–8, 79, 81, 85,
  87
feasting, and monasticism 67–8,
  71–2, 74, 103
Featley, D. 334 n.13
Fedele, Germanico 348
festivals, in Church of Scotland
  524–5
Fiamma, Galvani, and history of
  the Humiliati 153–5
Firenze, Tommaso da 58
First Book of Discipline 298
  nn.40,42,44, 526
Fish, Simon 272–4
Fisher, John, and Laud 334
Fitzralph, Richard 178, 185 n.31,
  186
Florence, and copy of Holy
  Sepulchre 57
Fontevrault
  decline and revival 372–5, 376
  and men 364–5, 367–9, 371,
    376–7
  and reform 367–8, 372, 376
  and Robert of Arbrissel 361–4,
    366, 375–6
  and women 363, 364–8
'Formula of Union' 23
Fortune, wheel of 179, 190,
  192–3
Fox, Henry 327
Foxe, John
  Acts and Monuments 234, 236,
    239, 260, 261 n.31, 262 n.34,
    267–88, 290 n.8, 320, 329–
    30, 333–4, 336–41, 385
  and Antichrist 256, 260, 262
    n.34
  and James Bainham 267–88
  and necromancy 261 n.31
  Rerum in ecclesia gestarum 268,
    272, 274, 276 nn.21,22
  status 329–42
Foxford, Richard 270

Fraenkel, P. 235
France
  and Catholicism 477
  Histoire écclesiastique 246
  and Reformation 229, 230,
    244–8
Francis of Assisi, St 548, 549–
  50, 554
Francis II of France 247–8
Franciscans 151, 152
  Spirituals 163
  and Waldensians 147
Franzio de Gluxiamo 208
Frederick Barbarossa 38
Frederick of Cologne 104
Freeman, E. A. 426, 438
Freeman, Philip 426
Fremantle, W. H. 499
Fremiotti, P. 352 n.21
French Revolution 372–4, 476
Frith, John
  and clerical celibacy 255, 256
  sources 276
  and Tracy 273 n.17
Frithegod, *Life of St Wilfrid* 70
Froude, R. H. 505, 507, 510
Fruytier, Jacob, *Struggles of Sion*
  397–9
Fulda, chapel of St Michael 55
  n.35

Gabrielle de Rochechouart 371,
  372
Galerius, Edict of Toleration
  10–11
Gallonio, Antonio 343–4, 356
Ganot, Sébastien 369
Gardiner, Robert 276 n.22
Gardiner, Stephen 263
Gaul, in Orderic Vitalis 120–2,
  123
Gellibrand, Henry 331–9, 341
Gellibrand, John 332 n.10
Gemelli, Agostino 483–4
Geneva, and Calvinism 230,
  232–3, 249–50
Gennadius 39 n.7
Geoffrey of Angers 363

Geoffrey of Orleans 117
Geoffrey of Vendôme 362, 370
Gerard of Monza 206
Gerson, Jean 290
Gervase of Canterbury 73
Gilbert of Sempringham, St 535
Gioberti, Vincenzo 477–8, 479
  n.12, 480
Glynne, Sir Stephen 426
Gnosticism 119–20, 125, 137,
  138
Goddu, André 164
Godet, J.-F. 550
'Golden Chain', Church as 88
The Golden Legend 279
Goodwin, Harvey 426
Gore, Charles 533
Gorham Judgement 418, 429
Gospel of Nicodemus 119
Gothic revival 44, 434–43
government
  apostolic 164–75, 177–8
  episcopal role 182–9
Gozzadini, Giovanni 45, 47, 49
  n.22
grace, and personal experience
  77–8, 79–89
Gratian, and definition of heretic
  145 n.28
Great Ejection 379–92
  Victorian commemorations
  459–73
Great Fire of London (1666) 326
Green, F. W. 19 n.1, 20 n.4, 23
Green, T. H. 533–4
Greenblatt, S. 287
Gregory I (the Great), Pope 111,
  355
  and Clairvaux-Cluny debate
  102, 105–7, 109, 111
  Dialogues 96–7, 200
  and mission to England 62, 63
  and Queen Theodolinda 200,
  201, 203, 206, 208, 210–11,
  221
  Responsiones 62
Gregory VII, Pope
  and Bologna 51 n.29

and clerical celibacy 259–60,
 261 n.31, 266
and Robert of Arbrissel 362
Gregory IX, Pope, and Wyclif
 182 n.17
Gregory Nazianzen, and primacy
 of experience 80, 81–2, 86
Gregory of Nyssa, and classical
 culture 15
Grisar, Hartmann 50
Grosseteste, Robert 178
Grundmann, H. 149
Gualter, Rudolph 259
Guild Socialism 538–9, 543–5
Guillemard, H. P. 504
Gunpowder Plot, in English
 iconography 307–8, *308*, 311,
 313, 316–18, *317*, 318, 320–
 2, *323*, 325–7
Guy of Porta Orientale, and
 Humiliati 151, 153, 154–5

Haemstede, Adriaan van 234–5,
 237–44
Hall, Edward, *Chronicle* 271, 275
Hall, S. G. 111 n.87
Hamilton's Catechism 291, 292–3,
 297
Hampden, R. D. 505, 506
Harcourt, Sir William 513
Harding, Stephen 101, 112
Hare, J. C. 419, 488, 495
Harpsfield, Nicholas 281, 284
Harsnet, Samuel 310 n.7
Haskell, F. 359–60
Hatto of Troyes 112–13
Hausherr, I. 76 n.3, 80 n.10, 81
 n.14
Hefele, C. J. 20 n.4
Hegesippus, and heresy 146
Heitz, Carol 52
Heller, H. 230
Helmore, Thomas & Frederick
 425
Heloise, and Cistercian-Cluniac
 debate 94, 111
Henrietta Maria, Queen 332,
 362, 369

Henry I of England 102, 117, 184
Henry II of Germany, Emperor
 157, 212
Henry IV of France 361, 367
Henry VIII of England 282
and clerical celibacy 263–4
and Simon Fish 272–3
Henson, H. H. 511, 514
heresy
and the Church 146–8, 257,
 293–4, 299, 301–2
genealogy 135–48
and Humiliati 149–50, 151,
 152–3, 156–7, 160, 161
innovation as 19, 22
and Orderic Vitalis 119, 125
popular 135 n.1
Hering, Theodore, *Triumph of the
 Church. . .* 312
Hermas, *The Shepherd* 15
hermeneutics, in William of
 Ockham 163–5, 168–71,
 174–5
Hersende of Montsoreau 364
Heylyn, Peter, and Foxe 341
Hilary, Pope, and the Holy
 Cross 50
Hinton, J. H. 461
Hippolytus, and heresy 146
history
Anglo-Saxon 61–74
and anti-heretical treatises
 135–48
and Bede 62–5, 109, 117, 118,
 121, 123, 129
and Bible 63, 116, 119, 239–
 41, 253–4, 257–9, 263–6,
 294–6, 300, 303–5
and Christian civilization
 478–83
and Clairvaux-Cluny debate
 92, 97–106, 108, 109–14
and Dutch Reformed Church
 394–9, 404–5
and early Christian origins
 6–15
and Eusebius 7, 115, 117, 118–
 20, 122, 124–5, 129

and the Humiliati 150–5,
156–61
and Maurice 487–9, 494, 497,
499–500
of monastic Orders 151–2
and Nonconformity 380–1,
462–3
and Orderic Vitalis 115–34
of Oxford Movement 501–15
and personal experience 85–90
as propaganda 62, 477
and Protestant martyrologies
234–41, 251, 284–5, 329–30
and reform 61–74, 96–9, 227–
8, 234–5, 289, 321, 334–6,
396, 407–22
and Revelation 258–63, 265–6
and revision 268–88, 307, 309–
10, 320–8, 329–42
Roman Empire 11–14
and selectivity 76, 284–5, 287–
8, 300, 417, 543
and the early Church 6–7,
14–15, 16–17
and history of Theodolinda
206–7, 221
and Wyclif 177–9, 187–8, 190,
192–3
see also tradition
Hoadly, Benjamin 390, 391
Hoare, Charles 415, 419
Hobson, J. A. 542
Holdsworth, C. 95 n.17
Holl, C. 80
Holland, Henry Scott 533
Holy Sepulchre, and S. Stefano,
Bologna 31–59
Holy Spirit
in Church of Scotland 527
in Constantinople creed 22, 23,
26, 27–8
in St Symeon the New
Theologian 75
Honorius III, Pope 182 n.17,
353
Hooper, John 266, 285 n.44
Hope, Beresford 423, 425–7,
434, 442, 443

Hugh of Amiens 102–3, 110,
112–13
Hugh of Cluny 100, 113
Hugh of St Victor 190 n.55
Humiliati 149–61
Constitutions 152
eviction from Gessate house
155–6
First order 150, 151, 154, 155,
157, 158
histories 153–61
and lay spirituality 149–50
and Master General 159, 160–1
origins 149, 150–3, 156–8
Second order 150, 151, 154,
155
and study 151–2
Third order 150, 151, 153–4,
155, 157
and wool trade 157–8
Hussites, and reform 334, 335
Hymenaeus, in polemical
treatises 137, 143
Hyndman, H. M. 541

iconography
opposition to 313–14, 320–7
and Protestant nationhood
307–28
identity
ancestral 11–17
early Christian 6–19
Idung of Prüfening, Dialogue 105
n.62, 110 n.83, 111 n.87
Ignatius, and Judaism 13
Illidge, George 391
inculturation 547, 554, 561
individual
in Calvinism 228, 245–7,
251–2
and Christian civilization 476,
479, 482
in Maurice 493–4, 497
Innocent III, Pope
and Clare of Assisi 550
and Humiliati 150, 151–2,
153–5, 159–60
and Wyclif 182

Innocent X, Pope, and Robert of
Arbrissel 361, 369, 370
innovation
opposition to 19, 22, 97, 254,
257-9, 265
and reform 227, 396, 416, 421
integrism 481-3
intransigentism 481-2
Investiture Contest 183
Irenaeus, and apostolic tradition
8, 19
Iron Crown of Lombardy 197,
221-2
Isidore of Seville, and heresy 146
Italy, and Christian civilization
475-86
Iurminburg, Queen 71

Jackson, T. G. 443
Jacques de Viotry, *Historia
Occidentalis* 152
James, Bruno Scott 99 n.31
James I, and Protestant
iconography 307, 310
James, Thomas 436
James of Viterbo 170
Jeanne-Baptiste de Bourbon
361-2, 367, 368-72, 376
Jelsma, A. J. 238 n.29
Jerome, St 115, 129, 169, 257,
304
Jerusalem
Anastasis 34, 43 n.12
Holy Sepulchre Church 34, 36,
39-40, *41*, *42*, 43, 49, 54-5
Martyrium church 47-8, 49-50
western reproductions 31-59
Jessey, Henry 387
Jewel, John 284 n.41, 339, 340
Joachim of Fiore, and history of
the Church 187
John the Baptist, and Monza
cathedral 200, 204-6, 210-11,
213, 216, 218, 220-1
John of Brera
Chronicon ordinis humiliatorum
155 n.36, 156
Excerptum 156, 158 n.52

John the Deacon, *Life* 109
John of Marliano 156 n.42
John of Meda, and the Humiliati
158-9, 161
John of Reims, and history 116
John of Salisbury, and Wyclif
182
John XXII, Pope 216
Jotsaldus, *De vita et virtutibus
Sancti Obonis* 133 n.71
Joye, George, *Exposicion of Daniel*
263-4
Judaism, and early Christian
origins 7, 8, 12-13
justification by faith
and individualism 251-2
in Maurice 488-94, 497
Justin Martyr 14

Keble, John 505, 510
Kelley, D. R. 285
Kempthorne, John 419-20
Kennedy, Quintin, *Compendius
Tractive* 289, 291-2, 293-300,
301-2, 303-5
Kensit, John 513
Kerr, Robert 442 n.87
King, Edward, Bishop of
Lincoln 502, 507
Kingdon, R. M. 230
Kingsley, William 325
Knight, H. Gally 437
knowledge, in Ockham 171-3
Knowles, David 73, 92-3, 94-5
Knox, John
First Blast. . . 289
and General Assembly 298,
299 n.46, 304
and liturgy 524, 525
see also Book of Common Order
Kolb, Robert 235 n.19
Koninck, Carolus de 245
Kunigunda, Queen 212
Kuyper, Abraham 405

Lactantius 10
laity
and the Bible 297 n.39

and Calvinism 231, 245, 249
and Church of England 411,
  418–19, 430
and English Social Catholicism
  529, 534–5
and Great Ejection 380
in Wyclif 191–2
see also Humiliati; patronage;
  spirituality, lay
Lambertini, R. 166–7
Lamont, W. M. 330 n.4, 383–4
Lanzoni, Francesco 39 n.8, 40,
  43, 47–8, 49–50, 54–6
Lardier, Jean 369
Latimer, Hugh
  and Bainham 273 n.17, 283–4
  martyrdom 286–7
Laud, William
  and Fisher 334
  and Foxe 329–42
  and Gellibrand trial 331–9, 341
  and iconography 322, 325, 327
  trial 329, 330, 336–9
Laudianism, and iconography
  320–8
Laurence of Canterbury 73
Le Bas, Charles 415
Lear, Francis 411–14
Lebon, J. 27
Leclerq, H. 20 n.4, 346
Leclerq, J. 93
Lee, Robert 519
Lees, J. Cameron 522
Leff, Gordon 163
Leishman, Thomas 518, 519–21,
  523–4, 526
Leo I, Pope, *Tome to Flavian* 20,
  22–3, 28
Leo X, Pope 34, 58
Leo XIII, Pope 480–1, 532, 541,
  542–3
Leslie, Charles 390
Letter to Diognetus 13
Lever, Christopher, *History of the
  Defenders of the Catholique Faith*
  316
Libelli de Lite 91
Libellus de diversis. . . 110

liberalism
  and Catholicism 475–6, 481,
    483
  and Maurice 487
Liberation Society 459–61, 463,
  468, 470, 473
Liddon, H. P. 501
Life of Maur 109
Life of Petronius 36–40, 47–8, 49,
  50, 54–8
Life of St Dunstan 65–74
Life of St Oswald 63, 65
literacy, and the Humiliati 151–2
liturgy
  in Church of Scotland 518–27
  early Church 351–5, 360
  and Ecclesiological Society 423,
    425, 426, 428, 435
  and history 116, 121
  Jerusalem 43 n.13, 51–2, 58
  and knowledge of the Bible 80,
    116
  and saints' days 116, 121
  stational 52, 54, 55–6, 348–51
Lives of the fathers 99
Lock, Walter 515
Lollardy 193, 274 n.19, 334, 335
Lombardy, Iron Crown 197,
  221–2
London agreement (1107) 183
Louis the Pious, and
  monasticism 105
Louis XIV of France, and Robert
  of Arbrissel 362, 369, 371
Louise de Bourbon de Lavedan
  368
loyalty, and early Church 10,
  12, 13–14, 16
Lubac, Henri de 164 n.7
Lucius II, Pope, and Bologna 51
  n.29
Lucius III, Pope, and Humiliati
  149
Lumen Gentium 559
Luther, Martin
  and Church history 235–7,
    479–80
  and conservatism 227, 252

and Maurice 488–93, 495, 497, 499
On the Councils and the Churches 296, 300, 304 n.64
and Reformation setbacks 245
Lutheranism, early setbacks 228–30

Macarius of Egypt, St 100, 107
McCann, Justin 103 n.50
Maccarrone, M. 149
McGrath, A. E. 492 n.21
McKitterick, Rosamund 105 n.62
Macleod, John 520
Mair, John 290
Mani/Manicheans 136, 137, 138, 139, 141–7
Manning, Henry Edward 531, 532
Mansel, H. L. 490
Map, Walter, *De nugis curialium* 132
Marbode of Rennes 362
Marcellus, and Petrine primacy 171
Marchi, Giuseppe 347 n.6
Marcian, Emperor, and Chalcedon 19–20
Marcionites, in polemical treatises 136, 143, 146
Marcus Aurelius 12, 13
Marie de Bretagne 367, 374
Marinus Scotus 118
Mark the Hermit 77, 82–3
marriage, clerical 63, 65, 255, 256–61, 263–6
Marriott, Charles 504, 505
Marsilius of Padua 163, 164, 169–70, 173–4, 177
Martial, St 120–1
Martin, Gregory 349–50
Martin of Tours, St 108
Martindale, Andrew 1–3, 31, 92, 195n., 223
martyrdom
and Calvinism 231, 234
and conquest of pain 268, 270, 279–82, 284, 287

early Church 234–5, 285–6, 344–5, 348–59, 484
and Great Ejection 380
of James Bainham 267–87
and rightness of cause 283–5, 287
martyrology
as pedagogy 234–5, 241–4, 288
Reformation 234–44, 252
Roman 344, 353, 357
and tradition 6–7, 8, 15–16, 17, 279
see also Foxe, John, *Acts and Monuments*
Mary Francis, Sr 551, 555
Mary Tudor 2–4, 229, 250, 268, 282, 330
Matthew of Albano 102, 110
Matthews, A. G. 379–80, 386–7
Matura, Thaddée 550
Maur, St, and Benedict 106, 107, 108–9, 114, 123
Maurice, F. D.
and Christian Socialism 534
and Luther 487–500
Medici, Giovanni de' (later Leo X) 34
Meinwerk, Bishop of Paderborn 55 n.35
Melanchthon, Philip 235, 259
Melito of Sardis 14
Melville, Andrew 522
memory, in medieval culture 61, 64, 73
Menabuoi, Giusto de' 154
Mennonites, Netherlands 399, 403
Mercati, G. 156 n.42
Methodism
and commemoration of Great Ejection 461–3, 470–1
and Oxford Movement 503, 507–11, 514–15
Meyer, W. W. 350
Miall, Edward 461–2, 469
Michelet, Jules 374
Middle Ages
and Christian civilization 476–8, 480, 482, 484–5

and Social Catholicism 529,
534–5, 537, 538–41, 545
and Victorian ecclesiology 427–
8, 435–43
Middleton, Thomas, *A Game at
Chesse* 316
Milano, Ilarino da 149
Millar, J. Hepburn 521
Miller, John 463, 465–8
Milligan, William 518, 520
Milner, John 499
Milton, A. 320, 330–1, 337 n.16
Minucius Felix 9
Mitchell, John 195n.
Moberly, George 504
Modernism, Catholic 482, 539
Modestus, Patriarch, and Holy
Sepulchre, Jerusalem 43
Mominot, Gilbert 132
monarchy
and episcopacy 182–90
and papacy 177
monasticism
and Anglo-Saxon past 61–74
and Byzantine spirituality
75–90
and Cistercian-Cluniac debate
91–114
and clergy 62, 63–6, 107–8
and clothing 105–6, 108
and the early Church 6, 100,
110, 113
and French Revolution 372–4
and length of novitiate 109
and manual work 106–7, 108–
9, 151, 554, 557–8
and medieval debate 91–2
and Orderic Vitalis 122–3,
129–30
and property-ownership 96,
100, 107–9, 123, 190
and reform 61–74, 96–9, 367–
8, 372, 376
and Reformation critique
258
and Second Vatican Council
547–9, 552, 554, 559–60
and Social Catholicism 535

see also Benedictine Order;
Bernard of Clairvaux;
Cistercian Order; Cluny;
Columbanus; desert fathers;
Humiliati; patronage; Peter
the Venerable; Poor Clares;
women
Moneta of Cremona, *Adversus
Catharos et Valdenses* 140,
142–4
Monophysites, and Chalcedonian
Formula 26, 27
Montanism, and true Church
257
Montesquieu, C. de Secondat
177
Montorsi, W. 39, 47, 48, 54
n.33
Monza cathedral
ampullae 209, 210
façade 196, *197*
foundation legends 200–6, *205*,
220–1
frescoes 195, 197–206, *201*,
210–11, 218, 220–2
ground plan *198*
history 207–10
and holy oil 208–11, *209*, 213,
221
Queen Theodolinda's chapel
195–223, *201*
rebuilding 208–11
treasure 207–10, 213–18, *214*,
215, *217*, 220–2
tympanum 218–20, *219*, 221
Moore, R. I. 125 n.47
More, Thomas
and James Bainham 267, 274–
5, 277–8
and Simon Fish 273–4
Morley, Samuel 461
Morrice, Ralph 284
Morris, William 535
Mozley, Thomas 501, 505, 507
Muratori, L. 221–2
Myln, Walter 290 n.8
mysticism, of Symeon the New
Theologian 75, 77–83, 88

Neal, Daniel, *History of the Puritans* 392

Neale, J. M. 423, 425, 426–7, 428 n.20, 431–4, 443

necessity, and church government 164, 167–9, 190

necromancy, and celibacy 260–1, 263

Neo-Arianism 82

Neri, St Philip, and catacombs 343, 347–52

Nestorius, and Christology 19, 21, 22–3

Netherlands
and Dutch Revolt 245
and Reformation 229, 230, 231, 234–45, 247–9
see also Dutch Reformed Church

Nevile, Christopher 468

Newdegate, C. N. 511

Newman, J. H.
and doctrinal development 28, 87–8, 360
and histories of Oxford Movement 501, 504–7, 509–10, 514
and Victorian ecclesiology 429, 434

Nicaea, Council (325)
Creed 20, 21–8, *24–5*
and tradition and change 22, 109, 297 n.38

Nicetas Stethatos, and Symeon the New Theologian 76

Nichols, A. 498

Nicholson, Sygar 278 n.25

Nicodemism, and Calvin 232

Nicolaitans, in polemical treatises 137, 143

Nicquet, Honorat 369

Nockles, P. B. 417, 506 n.25, 514

Nonconformity
and the early Church 5
and Great Ejection 379–92, 459–73
and the Oxford Movement 507–11

Notger, Bishop 73

Oberman, Heiko 229

Occasional Conformity Act (1711) 385

Ockham *see* William of Ockham

Oda of Canterbury 70, 73

Odilo of Cluny 100, 133

Odo of Cluny 100, 113, 114

Odo of Glanfeuil, *Vita Sancti Mauri* 123

Offler, H. S. 165 n.8

Old English account of King Edgar's establishment of monasteries 63

Old Testament
and early Christian past 12–13, 15
and monastic practice 110
and Protestant Reformation 235, 238, 240–1, 251, 264, 295
and Wyclif 177, 186 n.40, 187

Oldegar of Barcelona 128

Ollyffe, John 390, 391

Omachevarria, I. 550

Orderic Vitalis
and Church reform 124–5
and the Crusades 125–7
Ecclesiastical History 115–34
and history of Gaul 120–2, 123
and lives of the saints 121–2, 123–4, 127–8
and monasticism 111–12, 122–3
and speculative debate 128–9
use of legend 124, 128
use of sources 119–24, 126–8
and vision of Walchelin 128, 130–3

Origen
and Celsus 9–10
and classical culture 15

Oswald, St, and monastic reform 63, 64–5

Otto III, Emperor, and Monza 196

Ousterhout, Robert 43 n.12

Owen, John 387

Oxford Movement 423, 429–30
and nineteenth-century
retrospect 501–15
see also Tractarianism

Pacelli, Eugenio 484, 485
pain, and martyrdom 268, 270,
279–82, 284, 287
Paley, F. A. 426
Palmer, Samuel, *Nonconformist
Memorial* 392
Palmer, William 505, 507
Palud, Peter de la 170
Panciroli, Ottavio 350–1, 352,
360
Panormitanus (Nicolò de'
Tudeschi) 290
Pantaleon, Heinrich, *Martyrum
historia* 279 n.29
Panvinio, Onofrio 352–3, 354,
356
papacy
and Antichrist 238, 255,
259–62, 265–6, 269, 312,
320
and authority 124, 164–9, 297,
304, 477–8, 481, 485
and clerical celibacy 256–7,
259–60, 264–5
and general council 290–1
and Maurice 493, 494, 496–7
and necromancy 260–1
and Petrine primacy 164,
169–75, 177, 183, 184, 188,
305
and *plenitudo potestatis* 164–8
and reform 227
and Reformation 236, 238
Paradosis (Tradition) 76, 85–6,
87–8
Parker, Samuel 384
Parkinson, Henry 536–8, 540,
543
Parsons, Robert 281
Paschal I, Pope 349 n.12
Paschal II, Pope
and Bologna 51 n.29
and episcopacy 183–4

past *see* ancestors; history;
tradition
Patricelli, Francesco 57
patriotism, and English
Protestantism 307, 316, 322
patronage, lay 63–4, 91, 124,
187, 190–1, 363
Pattison, Mark 501
Paul the Deacon, *Historia
Langobardorum* 196, 199–200,
204–7, 211–12, 221, 222–3
Paul, St, and history of the
Church 187
Pavier, William 269, 271, 272,
275, 280, 281–2, 288
Pavillon, Balthazar 370
Penthos, doctrine of 78
Perfectae Caritatis 547–8
Perpetua, martyrology 8, 15–16
persecution
and early Church 'atheism' 10,
12, 16
and Reformation 228–9, 231–4,
237–43, 252, 254, 258
and sanctity 70–1
see also Foxe, John, *Acts and
Monuments*; Great Ejection;
martyrdom; martyrology
Peter, St, primacy 164, 169–75,
177, 183, 184, 188, 305
Peter of Blois 132
Peter of Bruys 125
Peter II of Poitiers 375
Peter of St John 112–13
Peter the Venerable
and Bernard of Clairvaux 93,
94–5, 108–9, 112–13
De miraculis 133
Letter 28 94–5, 108–9
and Saracens 125
Peter Damian 100 n.37, 133
n.71
Peter Martyr, St, *Summa contra
haereticos* 139–40, 141
Peterborough Chronicle 132
Peto, Sir Morton 460, 461, 467
Petronilla of Chemillé 361, 363–
7, 371, 376

Petronius, St, and Holy Sepulchre of S. Stefano 34, 36–40, 43, 49, 50–2, 54–6
Pettegree, A. 230
Philetus, in polemical treatises 137, 143
Philip II of Spain 312, 318
Philip IV of Spain 308–9
Phillpotts, Henry 418
Photius, and Mark the Hermit 82
pietism, Netherlands 398–9, 400–1
pilgrimage
 and imitations of Jerusalem 52, 57–8
 to tombs of saints 124, 350, 353, 366–7
Pilkington, John 260
Pipino, Francesco, *Chronicle* 153 n.22
Pius V, Pope 343
Pius IX, Pope, and Robert of Arbrissel 375
Pius X, Pope 481, 482–3
Pius XI, Pope 483
Pius XII, Pope (Eugene Pacelli) 484, 485
Plater, Charles 530, 536, 544
Plato, and time 179 n.5
plenitudo potestatis, and papacy 164–9
Pocklington, John 330 n.3, 340–1
Polycarp, martyrdom 16, 285 n.44, 286
Ponelle, 347
Ponet, John 255
Poor Clares
 and authority 547, 554–60
 and poverty 550–4, 560
 Rule and General Constitutions 552, 557, 559–60
 and St Clare 547–50, 559–60, 561
Porter, R. 313
potestas ordinis/iurisdictionis 183, 185, 190, 192

Pound, William 419
poverty
 apostolic 167–8, 177, 187, 189, 192
 and Humiliati 151
 and Poor Clares 547, 550–4, 560
 and Social Catholicism 529–33, 535–9
Powell, D. 493
power
 episcopal 182–90, 192–3
 and the papacy 164–9, 183, 184
 and the past 61–2, 73
prayer for the dead 133, 355 n.25
predestination 180, 249, 527
 and Dutch Reformed Church 394, 405
 and genealogy of heresy 139–40
Presbyterianism
 and Great Ejection 391, 463, 470, 487
 see also Church of Scotland
progress, and history 479
propaganda 62, 314, 327, 477
property, and monasticism 96, 100, 107–9, 123, 190
Protestantism *see* Calvinism; Dutch Reformed Church; England; iconography; martyrology; Puritanism; Reformation; Scotland
Providence
 and Protestant iconography 307–28
 in Reformation thought 233, 237, 241–2, 244–5, 247–9, 252, 282
Prynne, William
 and anti-papalism 318, 320 n.35, 321–2, 325
 and Laud 329–31, 336–9, 341
Pseudo-Aurelius, *Life* of St Martial 120
Pseudo-Marcellus, *Passio SS Petri et Pauli* 120

Pugin, A. W. N. 425, 434, 438, 441, 443
Pulcheria, Empress 23, 26
Purchas, John 428
purgatory 133, 268–9, 272, 282, 283
Puritanism
  and Great Ejection 262
  and Laudianism 325–6, 329–42
Pusey, E. B. 418, 429, 431 n.35, 434 n.50
  and histories of Oxford Movement 501, 505, 508, 509–10
Pythagoreanism 136, 138, 139, 142

Quasten, J. 83 n.19

Rabus, 237
Ramsey, A. M. 488
reform
  and appeal to the past 5, 61–74, 96–9, 227–8, 396
  in Church of England 407–22, 430–3
  and Cistercian-Cluniac debate 91–114
  and Orderic Vitalis 124–5, 126
  and Robert of Arbrissel 363
  and Symeon the New Theologian 75–6, 78, 79–86
  and Wyclif 177, 188–93
  see also monasticism
Reformation
  and clerical celibacy 254–66
  and conciliar authority 289–306
  and the early Church 5
  and Maurice 488–9, 493–7, 499–500
  mid-century collapse 228–30, 245
  and the true Church 253–4, 334–5
  and Wyclif 189–91, 193
  see also Calvinism; Dutch Reformed Church; martyrology

Reformation Parliament (1560) 292
Regularis Concordia 62, 64, 67
Reims, Council (1119) 117, 128
relativism, historical 79, 87
relics
  of the Cross 31, 39, 50–1
  of saints 38, 64–5, 70, 75, 124, 211, 213, 355, 366, 368–9, 374–6
Renaissance, and the Church 5, 476
Reply to Bernard's Apology 102–3
Rerum novarum 532, 541, 542–3
Revelation, and Antichrist 257–63, 265–6, 320
Ridley, Nicholas 286
Rigg, J. H. 503, 507–11, 514–15
Ripon, and Wilfrid 63, 64, 70, 71–2
Ritualism, and Church of England 417, 427–8, 443, 502, 507, 512–14
Robert of Arbrissel
  cult 362, 365–7, 368–71, 375–7
  and Fontevrault 361–77
  life 362–3
  Lives 361, 363–5, 368–9, 371, 373–4
Robert of Chaise Dieu 366
Roger du Sap 117
Rogers, J. G. 463
Roman Catholicism
  and catacombs 352–5
  and Christian civilization 475–86
  and Church of England 418–19, 429–30, 434, 503, 507, 509–12, 515
  and doctrinal change 28–9, 254, 257–9
  and Dutch Reformed Church 399, 403, 405
  and early Church practice 351–5
  and Laudian clerics 320–3
  and Maurice 493

and Protestant iconography
307–20, 322, 326–7
seen as false Church 255–9,
264–6
and Social Catholicism 529–45
Roman Empire
and ancestral tradition 11–15
and the Church 10, 13–14
and Council of Chalcedon 19–
21, 23–4, 28
Romanticism, and Social
Catholicism 534–6, 539, 545
Rome
and Christian civilization 477–
8, 481, 484–5
and Constantinople 91
and devotion to Holy Cross
50–1
Sessorian basilica 50–1
Rosenberg, D. 230
Rouen, Council
1072 124
1097 124
Royal Commission on the Poor
Laws 536, 537–40, 544
Rudolph, C. 95 n.14
Rule of St Benedict
and Cistercian-Cluniac debate
94, 95–7, 99, 103–5, 110
and Fontevrault 367
and Peter the Venerable 109
and Rupert of Deutz 104–7
and St Maur 106, 107, 108–9,
123
and tenth-century reform 62,
64
and William of Malmesbury
101, 112
and women 111
Ruotger, *Life of Bruno* 68–9
Rupert of Deutz, *On certain
chapters of the Rule of St
Benedict* 94, 103–8, 109
rural deans, and diocesan revival
410–11, 414–16, 418, 421
Ruskin, John 437, 439, 441, 442,
534, 535, 545
Ryan, John A. 543

S. Stefano, Bologna 31–59, *33, 44*
Basilica of the Cross 32, 40,
47–8, 49
and *catino di Pilato* 34, *37*, 50
n.24
and *cortile di Pilato* 34, 39, 47, 49
edicule of the Holy Sepulchre
34, *35, 46*
monastery 32, 47, 54
and Mount of Olives 38, 52,
55–6
and Petronius 34, 36–40
restoration 43–9, 58–9
S. Sepolcro church 32–4, *36*,
39–43, 45–7, 49, 55–6
SS. Vitale e Agricola church
32, 47, 48
Trinità church 32, 47–8
Sabas, St 85
sacraments
in Church of Scotland 524–7
see also Eucharist
Sadducees, and genealogy of
error 137, 140, 142–3
Sadoleto, Jacopo 293 n.19
St Andrew's, Wells Street, and
Webb 425–6
St Bartholomew's Day massacre
248
St Evroul monastery, and
writing of history 116–17
St Mammas monastery, and
Symeon the New Theologian
78–9, 81
saints
cult 38, 64–5, 364, 365–71,
375–7
and Protestant martyrs 334–9
sanctity
and *praxis* 83
and secularity 65–72, 74
and Theodolinda 212–13
Sanctus, martyr 16
Schlageter, Johannes 164 n.7
Scholasticism
and Catholic social thought
483–4
see also Thomism

Schüssler, Hermann 164 n.7
Schwartz, E. 20 n.4, 23–7,
  24–5
Scotland
  and Catholic tradition in the
    Kirk 517–27
  and conciliar authority
    289–306
Scots Confession of Faith 298–
  9, 301 n.54, 525–6
Scott, G. G. Jr 443
Scott, Sir George Gilbert 439,
  440, 442
Scott, Thomas 309–10
Scott, William 426
Scottish Church Society 517–
  18, 520–1, 525–6
Second Book of Discipline 298,
  299 n.47
Second Coming, and Wyclif
  178, 193
Second Prayer Book of Edward VI
  519, 522
Second Vatican Council 547–9,
  552, 554, 559–60
sects, and heresy 136, 145–8
secularity, and monasticism 62,
  63–72, 74
Sedding, J. D. 443
Seddon, J. P. 425, 443
Seeley, J. R. 499
Selby, Dame Dorothy 319
Sellers, R. V. 20 n.4
Serchia, L. 43 n.12, 48–9
Severano, Giovanni 351, 353–6
Sharpe, Isaac 389
Shipside, George 286
Sigebert of Gembloux 118
Silvester I, Pope 302
Silvester II, Pope 259, 260–2
Simon of Gitta 119–20
Simon Magus 119–20, 127, 139
Simons, Dr 269, 277 n.23
simony 119, 125, 363
Sirmond, Jacques 370
Sixtus IV, Pope, and
  Fontevrault 367
Skeats, H. S. 461

Social Catholicism 482, 529–45
socialism
  and Catholicism 476, 482–3,
    531–41
  and Maurice 487
Sorabji, R. 129 n.61
Southern, R. W. 97, 182
Southey, Robert 499
Sparke, Michael, Crums of
  Comfort 318, 320 n.35, 325
spirituality
  lay 144, 148
    see also Humiliati
  of Poor Clares 553
  of Symeon the New Theologian
    75, 77–9, 80, 82–6, 87
  and Victorian ecclesiology
    427–8
Sprott, George W. 518–21, 524,
  526
Spurgeon, C. H. 472
Stefano, A. de 149, 159, 161
Stephanus, Vita Wilfridi 70–4
Stephen of Nicomedia 78
Stevenson, J. 23
Stokesley, John, Bishop of
  London 268–9, 270, 271,
  274–5, 277 n.23
Storer, John 418
Story, R. H. 520, 522
Street, George Edmond 425, 442
Studium monastery, and Symeon
  the New Theologian 77, 78,
  85
succession, apostolic 173–4, 290,
  352, 358, 502, 509, 517
Sulpicius Severus, Second Dialogue
  108
Sumner, Charles 415, 419
Suyskens, C. 158
Swithun, St 64–5
Sykes, Stephen 495–6, 498–9
Sylvester, Matthew 381–4
Symeon Eulabes 77, 80–2, 85,
  86, 87–8
Symeon the New Theologian
  and Byzantine spiritual renewal
    75–90

Catechetical Discourses 80, 83, 85
as Higumen of St Mammas
    monastery 78–9, 81
Hymns of Divine Love 75
Letter to the Synkellos Stephen 81
life 76–9
trial for heterodoxy 75, 78, 79,
    86
visions 77–8, 80, 84
Symmachus, Pope, and the Holy
    Cross 50
syneisaktism 370

Tatianists, in polemical treatises
    137, 143, 257
Taylor, Jeremy, *A Sermon. . .* 321
Taylor, M. 291 n.10
Taylor, Thomas 312
tears, necessity for 78, 80, 82
Tertullian
    and early Christian past 10, 13,
        15
    and innovation 19
    and tradition and truth 111
        n.87, 296 n.35
Tewkesbury, John 271, 275, 279
Theobald of Étampes 110 n.83
Theodolinda, Queen
    life 199–200, *202*, 203–4, *203*
    and Monza chapel 195–223,
        205
    religious qualities 212–13,
        220–1
    sources 199–200, 206–10, 221
Theodore of Mopsuestia 141
    n.20
Theodore of Tarsus, St 262
Theodoric, 'King of the Goths'
    196
Theodosius II, Emperor 36
theotokos, denial 22
Thirty Years' War 316
Thomism
    and church government 166
    revival 532–3, 541, 545
    see also Scholasticism
Thompson, D. M. 498
Thoresby, Ralph 382, 385

Thucydides, and historiography
    115
Thurstan of York 110 n.83
Tiberius of Parma 152
Tierney, Brian 164, 168 n.26
time, in Wyclif 177–82, 188, 190
    n.55, 193
Tiraboschoi, Girolamo 154, 155
    n.35
Toke, Leslie 530, 531, 535, 539,
    543, 544–5
Toniolo, Giuseppe 481–2
Tooth, Arthur 428
Tosti, Luigi, *Prolegomeni* 478–81,
    482
Toynbee, Arnold 534
Tractarianism
    and diocesan revival 409, 410,
        417, 418–20
    and High Church tradition
        501–3, 506–7, 509–10
    and Maurice 495–6
    see also Oxford Movement
Tracy, Richard 273 n.17
Tracy, William 273 n.17
Trade Boards Act (1909) 540,
    541–2, 544
tradition
    ancestral 7, 11–17
    and the Bible 265
    and classical culture 14–15
    and credibility 7–8, 11–12
    development and change 28–9,
        87–8, 109, 227, 360, 479
    and the early Church's past
        6–17
    invented 11, 311
    oral 126–8
    and priority of experience 78,
        79, 81–6, 87–90
    reception and transmission
        87–90
    and reform 75–6, 289
transubstantiation 269
Trapp, J. B. 278
Tremblay, Joseph de 368
Trent, Council 297, 302, 304,
    305, 355

Trevor, George 418–19
truth
  and apostolic tradition 8–9, 19–20, 144–6
  two-source theory 170, 174
  in William of Ockham 171–2
Tunstall, Cuthbert 274 n.19
Turner, William 263, 264–5
Tyacke, N. 339 n.20
Tyler, P. 333 n.12
Tyndale, William
  and Antichrist 253
  Obedience of a Christian Man 267
  and papacy 260
  sources 276
  and Tracy 273 n.17
  and true Church 254, 257

Ugonio, Pompeo 351, 352
Ultramontanism 477
Unitarianism
  and Great Ejection 462, 470, 472
  and Maurice 488, 492, 498
universality, and tradition 8–9
Urban II
  and Crusades 113, 124
  and Robert of Arbrissel 363
Usher, R. G. 333 n.12

Vacandard, 94
Val d'Elsa, and copy of Holy Sepulchre 58
Valentinians, in polemical treatises 143
Valeri, A. 344 n.4
Van Engen, J. H. 104 n.58
Vaughan, Herbert 530–1
Vaughan, Robert 468–9
Venables, Edmond 426
Venables, George 262, 468
Verdickt, Gilles 237–8, 242–4
Vicars, John
  Quintessence of Cruelty 322–5, *323*, 326
  Sinfulness and Unlawfulness 314 n.22

Vincent of Lérins, and tradition 8–9
vine, as metaphor of the Church 118–19, 129
Visconti, Andrea 160–1
Visconti, Galeazzo 207, 211
Visconti, Giovanni 216
Visconti, Matteo 213
visions
  of Symeon the New Theologian 75, 77–8, 80, 84
  of Walchelin 128, 130–3
Visser, R. 484 n.33
vita apostolica, and heresy 147–8
Vita Petronii 36–40, 47–8, 49, 50, 54–8
Vita of St Evroul 123–4
Vita of Symeon the New Theologian 75–9
Vitalis, Bolognese martyr 39
Vitalis of Savigny 122
Voragine, Jacobus de, *The Golden Legend* 279

Wabuda, S. 282, 284, 286 n.46
Wakefield, W. L. 135 n.1, 136, 139, 141
Walchelin, vision 128, 130–3
Waldensians
  and the Church 163, 334, 335
  and genealogies of heresy 147
Waldman, Thomas 102
Walker, John 262, 380–1, 389–90
Wallace, Adam 290 n.8
Walsh, Walter 503, 511–15
Ward, B. 111–12
Ward, Samuel, *Double Deliveraunce* 307–10, *308*, 312–14, 316, 318–19, 322, 325, 327
Ward, W. G. 501, 505, 508, 510, 512
Warin des Essarts 117
Watt, T. 313–14
Webb, Beatrice 537–8, 542
Webb, Benjamin, and ecclesiology 423–57

Webb, Sidney 538, 542
Westminster Confession 525–6
Westminster Directory 519, 520
wheel of Fortune 179, 190,
  192–3
Wiggington, Giles 314
Wilberforce, Samuel 410
Wilde, Oscar, *The Importance of
  Being Earnest* 5
Wilfrid, St 63, 64, 70–2, 74
William, Abbot of Saint-Thierry
  98–9, 110 n.83, 112
William of Corbeil 110 n.83
William of Gellone, St 127
William of Jumièges, *Gesta
  Normannorum ducum* 117, 118
William of Malmesbury 73
  Gesta Regum Anglorum 101, 112
William of Ockham 290, 494
  and Petrine primacy 164, 169–
  75, 177
  and the primitive Church 163–
  75, 178
  theory of knowledge 171–3
  and use of the Bible 163–7,
  168–71, 174–5
William of Wykeham, and
  authority 177, 184, 189
Williams, J. C. 461
Willis, Robert 435, 437
Wilmart, André 93, 102
Wilson, Joshua 461, 469
Winchester, and monastic reform
  73
Winghe, Philip de 359
Winning, T. 290 n.7
Wino, Abbot of Helmershausen
  55 n.35

Winzet, Ninian 292
Wishart, George 290 n.8
women
  and monasticism 96, 111, 158,
  160, 363–8, 371–4, 376–7,
  548
  see also Poor Clares
à Woods, Anthony 384
Wormald, Patrick 66
Worms, Concordat (1122) 183
Wotherspoon, Henry J. 517,
  519–21, 524, 527
Wulfstan of Winchester, *Life of
  St Æthelwold* 65
Wyclif, John
  and the church 163, 177–9,
  182–3, 187–93, 237
  and clergy 184–7, 192
  and laity 190–2
  and papacy 177, 181–2, 183,
  184, 188
  Summa theologiae 178
  and time 177–82, 190 n.55,
  193

Young, D. 488, 492, 498
Ypeij, A. 393, 399–406

Zanoni, L. 149, 154, 156 n.43
Zarohen 137, 138, 140–3
Zavattari brothers, and Queen
  Theodolinda's chapel 195,
  199–200, *201*, 206, 218,
  220–2
Zeno 140, 141
Zoroaster 141
Zurvan 141

Compiled by Meg Davies (Registered Indexer, Society of Indexers)